AS
FAR
AS
THE
EYE
CAN
SEE

AS
FAR
AS
THE
EYE
CAN
SEE

Reflections of an
Appalachian Trail Hiker

David
Brill

RUTLEDGE HILL PRESS
Nashville, Tennessee

Published in Nashville, Tennessee, by Rutledge Hill Press, 513 Third Avenue South, Nashville, Tennessee 37210

Typography by Bailey Typography, Inc., Nashville, Tennessee

Library of Congress Cataloging-in-Publication Data

Brill, David, 1955-
  As far as the eye can see : reflections of an Appalachian Trail hiker / David Brill.
    p.   cm.
  ISBN 1-55853-073-8
  1. Backpacking—Appalachian Trail. 2. Hiking—Appalachian Trail.
  3. Appalachian Trail—Description and travel. 4. Brill, David,
  1955- . I. Title.
  GV199.42.A68B75   1990   90-45387
  796.5'1'0974—dc20   CIP

Printed in the United States of America
1 2 3 4 5 6 7 8 — 96 95 94 93 92 91 90

I went to the woods because I wished to live deliberately, to front only the essential facts of life, and see if I could not learn what it had to teach, and not, when I came to die, discover that I had not lived.

Henry David Thoreau, *Walden*

Contents

Preface

On September 27, 1979, I ascended the mile-high summit of Mount Katahdin, a broad-shouldered peak rising from the Lake Country of central Maine. The fall frost had tinged the sugar maples bright red, the birches shone like burnished gold, and their color stretched away endlessly from the base of the mountain to the horizon.

Mount Katahdin ranks as one of the most majestic peaks east of the Mississippi, but for me it held special significance. It marked the northern terminus of the 2,100-mile Appalachian Trail, and it signaled the completion of a five-month wilderness journey that traced some five million steps through the eastern wilderness over hundreds of other peaks, through fourteen states, and dozens of small mountain towns.

When I began planning for my trek, friends and relatives seemed puzzled by my interest in forsaking the conveniences of modern society for a months-long sojourn in the wilderness. "Why are you doing this?" they asked, finding my commitment to the trail a bit extreme. All I could tell them was that hiking the Appalachian Trail was something I wanted and needed to do.

Today, eleven years later, I realize that my decision to hike the Appalachian Trail wasn't as capricious as it might have seemed at the time. My pilgrimage toward the trail began years earlier, in fact, with my first exposure to the natural world as a child and at the hand of my grandmother.

Our family made weekly trips to her house, which sat on a quiet side street two blocks from a large, forested hill.

9

Each Sunday, after we had finished our early afternoon dinner, Grandma asked my brother and me if we wanted "to go up on the hill." Then, clad in her floral print dress and walking shoes, she ushered our small hiking party out the front door and toward the woods.

Through the eyes of a child, the hill loomed as large as the Appalachian peaks I would ascend years later. Though it was nothing more than a glorified nob, one of many punctuating the hilly geography of southwestern Ohio, for me it was a magical place that exposed me to countless discoveries.

Each week, as we walked along the well-worn trail, wending higher and higher up the hill, Grandma shared her knowledge of the woods. Though she hadn't completed high school, she knew so much. She could identify scads of wildflowers—Dutchman's breeches, jack-in-the-pulpit, violets—and she knew the names of almost all the birds.

She showed us how to nip off the ends of honeysuckle blossoms, slowly draw out the pistils, and taste the sweet drop of nectar that clung to the tip. She held grasshoppers by their wings, saying, "Spit tobacco," and on command they would deposit a small drop of brown juice from their mouths onto her index finger. She could join small twigs into crosses or squares by peeling back some of the flexible green bark and using it as twine. She knotted clover blossoms into necklaces and draped them around our necks or tied them around our wrists.

When we passed the small brook that cascaded down the hill, she pointed to tadpoles wriggling across dark pools. She overturned rocks, revealing crayfish or slithering, spotted salamanders. Then she provided us with nature's play dough. Scooping soft gray clay from under the falls, we molded it into figures of people or animals and set them out to harden in the sun.

But Grandmother taught me much more. A serene, shy woman, who seemed to prefer the company of trees over that of people, Grandma often retreated to the woods, alone, to struggle with problems or just to think. She lived in communion with nature and seemed thoroughly at ease ambling along a wooded trail. By watching the ease that accompanied her into the woods, I learned to trust the wilderness while embracing its gifts.

We sometimes sat on rocks or downed logs for long minutes and looked down on the orderly rows of houses and streets in the distance. Or we just sat, listening to the cacophony of woodland sounds until sunlight waned and it was time to return to the house. My brother and I often made our descent by rolling down a long, gently sloping hillside covered with grass, and we arrived at the bottom giggling and dizzy, giddy from sheer joy.

I balk when I try to explain how it felt to be in the woods with my grandmother. It's like trying to explain the color purple to a blind person. The feeling was so sublime, so serene, so personal. In the woods I found hope, peace, healing; no matter how sour my mood, the woods seemed always to soothe me, to resurrect sagging spirits. In the woods there was a sense of being at home, of being where I ought to have been all along.

Like my grandmother, I've often walked to the woods to think, to reflect, to sort things out. Even as an adolescent, when I encountered difficult times, I sought the peace I knew I would find there. In high school, when my grandmother died, I instinctively followed my grief to the hill where I sat for an hour or more, looking, listening for an answer. And I believe I found it at the brook that, to this day, traces the clay banks down the hill, just as it did on my first visit some thirty years ago.

Years would pass before I learned about the Appalachian Trail in 1977, during summer break before my senior year in college. At the time, I was working on a landscaping crew, and one day during our lunch break I sat in the cab of the truck with Jim Koegel, a quiet, intense man, four years my senior. A radio news program came on, and the announcer made some reference to the Appalachian Trail. Between bites of his sandwich, Jim mentioned that he had hiked it.

I had no idea what the trail was or where it went, so I probed him for information. He explained that the trail extended 2,100 miles from Maine to Georgia and that he had hiked it from end to end the summer before, starting in Georgia. At first I was incredulous: could a person really walk that far in one summer? Then I pressed Jim for details, asking the same questions I would face dozens of times while on my hike: Was the way marked? What did he eat? Where did he sleep? Did he hike alone? Did he encounter wild animals? What did he do when it rained?

As the summer passed, I drew more and more information from Jim, not so much the information that pertained to logistics or miles but more about the experiential value of his summer in the wilderness, how the trail had changed him, and what lessons it had taught. And I became ever more captivated by his varied experiences.

At the time, I was primed for a challenge. The years of my adolescence had been difficult ones, not just for me but for most of the men and women of my generation. To some extent, we had been shaped by the Vietnam War and all the events it had precipitated. During those years the country was rife with conflict and chaos.

Evenings, we watched the nightly news with our parents and saw mangled corpses being dumped into body bags. We watched reports of the 1968 Democratic National Convention in Chicago, where Mayor Daley's police thrashed panic-stricken protestors. We heard our hard-line elders denigrate the unpatriotic hippies and peaceniks who protested the war. Meanwhile, race riots ripped the inner-cities and in ways reached our snug, middle-class suburbs. I was surprised to learn from a friend that his father slept with a loaded shotgun under his bed.

Amid all the chaos there was excitement, and it reached into every living room, every institution, every life. Everyone was full of passionate intensity, regardless of beliefs or convictions. So much was at stake. Men of draft age who had exhausted the deferment process faced war, prison, or escape to Canada. Blacks and other minorities faced continued oppression. And the establishment—middle-class Americans—feared an end to traditional values.

For those of us yet to come of age, there was a sense of an impending showdown. How would we respond when we received our draft notices? Would we go to war and earn the respect of our elders? Would we flee to Canada and face being disowned by our families? Would we be secure enough in our opposition to the war to accept a prison term by refusing to do either? Like most young men my age, I deferred the decision until I was forced to choose.

When I graduated from high school in 1974, I was eighteen and ready for the passage into adulthood, but by that time the matter had been rendered moot. The war was, in effect, over, and the government had begun pulling troops out of combat. The protests had ended. The commotion died. The era drew to a close. And everyone seemed badly in need of rest.

As the fury died, I was left feeling like a man who had spent years preparing—mentally, emotionally—for a test, only to arrive a day late to a darkened classroom and to realize that I would never know how well I might have done.

In the years following World War I, there emerged a generation of young Americans termed by Gertrude Stein *la generation perde*, the lost generation. It was a generation of restless young men and women, including Hemingway, Fitzgerald, Ezra Pound, T. S. Eliot, and others, who had fled America out of disgust or boredom for the excitement of the Parisian Left Bank. Once there, the expatriates pursued a life of abandon—living, drinking, loving to excess—while trying to make sense of their world and times.

Then, after World War II, novelist Jack Kerouac chronicled the attitudes of a similar generation, the "beat generation," in his book *On the Road*.

It seems that there follows in the wake of war a pestering complacency that sends youthful seekers out in search of excitement and meaning. Those of us affected by Vietnam were no exception.

I won't go so far as to say that I envied my peers who had been born five years earlier, but at least they had been forced to examine their beliefs, to make decisions, and, once made, to put them to the test. I envied them the personal growth they had derived from being in the core of the revolution or in the heart of the battle.

But for me there was no war, no showdown. Instead, there was only college and a continuation of my comfortable life. Once in school, and without having made the slightest sacrifice, I savored all the privileges won by the young people who had preceded me and had waged the social revolution.

During my first year in college, the resident radicals who had orchestrated the college protests during the war years still appealed to the students to support one cause or another, but by that time they had begun to resemble caricatures of themselves. By the time I graduated in 1978, benign indifference had supplanted the zeal of the late sixties. Oxford-cloth shirts and khaki pants had replaced jeans and T-shirts, and the emphasis had shifted from pursuing spiritual, sensual, and political goals to securing high-paying jobs. The whole scene left me flat.

I graduated, fulfilling an obligation to my parents who had helped pay my way through college and expected me to finish. The rest of my life was my own, but I had no idea what I wanted to do with it. I only knew that I craved experience outside of the cozy environs that had sheltered me for the first twenty-three years of my life. I wanted to be challenged. I wanted to confront something new and different. I wanted to find out what I was made of.

Thanks to Jim Koegel, I knew just where to find such challenge. After hearing his tales of adventure in the eastern wilderness, I made the Appalachian Trail my quest. I had heard so many people lament lost dreams, things they had longed to do but never found the time for. I was determined to see that that didn't happen to me. The trail would pose a wonderful setting where I could live, as Thoreau expressed in *Walden*, simply and deliberately, with room to grow, to breathe, to change, to discover what really mattered to me.

In the end, the Appalachian Trail provided all those things and more. Like every one of the other two thousand or so end-to-enders who have hiked the trail since its completion in 1937, I emerged from the Maine woods transformed.

This book is a collection of experiences and encounters, stories of fear and courage, of risk, of friendship and intimacy, of the power and beauty of nature. It contains one hiker's reflections and is one of several volumes that chronicle the Appalachian Trail experience, each different in its focus and impressions, yet each predicated on the same essential truths that have always beckoned man away from civilization and back into the wilderness.

For more than fifty years, the Appalachian Trail has offered footloose seekers a wooded path to spiritual and physical growth, to communion with the natural world, and to discovery of self. May it continue to do so.

The Author

Acknowledgments

I would like to thank the following people for their support while I hiked the Appalachian Trail and, later, while I wrote about it.

Dan, Paul, and Nick, and all the other backcountry travelers whose companionship has enriched my life.

The Appalachian Trail Conference and all the trail volunteers for their devotion to the trail, its maintenance, and its preservation.

Jean Cashin, for her boundless enthusiasm for the trail and its people.

Benton MacKaye, who in 1921 conceived the outlandish notion of an Appalachian Trail.

My wife, Susan, most of all, who loves me despite the chaos that often attends a writer's life.

AS
FAR
AS
THE
EYE
CAN
SEE

To Dad,
    who believed in my quest—and in me—long be-
    fore he understood either
    and who taught me that compassion is at the
    heart of all worthwhile journeys

CHAPTER · ONE

Fear

I'm lying under a wind-and-rain-buf-
feted tarp in a mountain gap in Georgia. I can hear wind
gusts begin miles away, then gather intensity and plow
through the gap, and with each gust the tarp sounds as if it's
about to rip from its tethers. The trees creak, and I can hear
limbs crack. I am terrified and awed by the power and vio-
lence of nature, and I realize that there's nowhere I can go to
escape it. I never appreciated how vulnerable I'd feel away
from the shelter of a roof and four sound walls.
—April 24, 1979, Tesnatee Gap, Georgia

Just before a spring thunderstorm ham-
mers the mountains, the animals disappear. The songbirds
stop singing. The chipmunks stop scurrying. The spring
peepers stop peeping. The crickets stop grinding. And an
eerie quiet settles over the woods.

When twisters accompany those storms and rip their own
random trails across the landscape, you nestle down in the
deepest part of your sleeping bag and hope that your luck
holds.

You also swear that you will never, ever, camp in a mountain gap again. Tornados, like the pioneers of centuries past,
often follow the gaps across mountain ranges. I know that

now, but on April 24, 1979, as I lay under a nylon tarp in Tesnate Gap, Georgia, I didn't.

There was, however, one thing that I knew for certain that night. I was frightened.

I had watched the storm approach from the west in the late hours of the afternoon. Columns of cumulo-nimbus clouds lumbered into view above the faraway hills, erasing the sun. The air smelled and felt pregnant with moisture, and, as the first winds began to buffet my camp, the atmosphere took on a sick, green cast.

By 6:00 P.M., it was dark, and I lay ensconced under my rain fly, waiting, as the first peals of thunder rumbled a few miles away. I had learned that by counting the seconds that lagged between each lightning flash and peal of thunder, I could estimate my distance from the heart of the storm. A one-second lag meant the storm was roughly one mile away. At 6:30 P.M., the storm was four miles away and approaching fast.

By 7:00 P.M., the counting game ended when the storm enveloped my camp. The ground rumbled beneath me, and the wind and rain raged above. I had experienced storms in the lowlands, secure inside four walls, but never in the mountains. At three thousand feet, I was wrapped in the low-slung clouds and, thus, inside the storm, and the thunder seemed to surround me before rolling away to the valleys.

Lightning bolts cast stark silhouettes of tree branches against the nylon of the tarp. First the flash, then immediately after, the resounding crack of thunder, like the slow splintering of huge bones. Then there was the rain, which fell so heavily at times that the tarp sagged under its assault and brushed against my face, and I could hear torrents of water channeling downhill, carving away earth and stone.

The wind howled and churned like an errant locomotive, and its force all but deadened the sound of the thunder and falling rain. I could hear walls of wind originate miles away in the valleys, then thrash toward me gathering intensity as they approached. They plowed through the gap, bowing the trees, scattering leaves, and snapping limbs. As each passed, the rain fly popped and bucked and surged, and I feared that it would tear from its tethers and disappear into the darkness, leaving me exposed and even more vulnerable.

I cowered under the fly, feeling utterly helpless, like a prairie dog trapped under the hooves of stampeding cattle, and I prayed for the storm to deliver me unharmed. Through the night I felt like a victim, as if all the storm's violent energy had been directed at me and as if raw vengeance bolstered the wind and powered the rain. Though I wouldn't realize it until the next morning, a twister had already cut a swath through another gap a few miles to the north. I had been spared.

When day broke, I surveyed the damage wrought through the night. Tree trunks had been splintered, severed branches lay scattered about, and uprooted trees criss-crossed the trail with gray clay and stone still clinging to their dying roots.

At that point, I was four days and thirty-seven miles into the Appalachian Trail. I had begun my hike at Springer Mountain, the trail's southern terminus some sixty miles northeast of Atlanta, and I was determined to trek all the way to Mount Katahdin, the trail's northernmost point, in central Maine.

A month earlier I had resigned my job as manager of a Washington, D.C., tennis shop and had committed myself and my meager $1,500 in savings to completing the trail. I wanted to become one of several hundred "thru-hikers" who had navigated the route from end to end in one summer, but other reasons, too, had drawn me toward the trail. Among them was the desire to confront and overcome my fears, but in the wake of the storm, I realized that I had only begun to identify them. Moreover, I acknowledged that I couldn't hope to banish my fears until I had pushed deeper into the eastern wilderness and probed much further into myself.

Though fear is a solitary condition, at least I had not had to endure the storm alone. I had shared my camp with Dan Howe, a twenty-three-year-old former architectural planner for a large oil corporation who had swapped his business suit and fast-track career for a pair of lug-soled boots, a backpack, and 2,100 miles of adventure. When we had set out on the trail, we had known each other just over a month and had met face to face only a half-dozen times.

Dan and I had first met during a program on the Appalachian Trail at a Washington-area backpacking shop. The program featured Ed Garvey, a well-known thru-hiker and author who had hiked the trail in the early 1970s. I had arrived for Garvey's talk fully reconciled to the notion that I would begin and finish the trail by myself, despite the fact that my previous backpacking experience had been limited to four or five overnighters; the longest duration had been three days. Over the previous months, I had telephoned every friend I had, and even a few casual acquaintances, in hopes of cajoling one or more of them into taking up the trail with me.

Most of them, like me, were in their first year out of college but, unlike me, had devoted their energies to charting career paths rather than ambling along wilderness trails. While they regarded the Appalachian Trail as a romantic pursuit, they also recognized its potential for stalling a career climb, and one by one they declined my invitation. So I had attended Garvey's presentation with the dim hope of finding a partner there.

As Garvey concluded his presentation, he asked if anyone among the thirty people in the audience intended to attempt the trail that summer. Tentatively, I raised my hand and then quickly scanned the room. One other hand waved in the air, and it belonged to a sandy-haired, bearded man who appeared to be about my age. After the meeting disbanded, I approached him and introduced myself, trying not to seem too eager or needy and realizing that to ask him abruptly if he would commit to spending the next five months with me was tantamount to proposing marriage on a first date.

Within a half-hour, Dan and I sat at a nearby tavern drinking beer and discussing our hopes, dreams, and expectations for our months on the trail. As we talked, I discovered that we had planned to begin the trail at about the same time—late April—and that we shared many common attitudes. Both of us had lived through the turbulent years of the late 1960s and early 1970s, and we both had emerged with a sense that if society failed to provide the peace and stability we sought, we might find it in nature.

While I had begun the trail seeking nature's healing powers, over the first four days I had found only disappointment, discovering that nature was capable of more violence than I had ever experienced in civilization. I found disappointment, too, in discovering the fear that dwelt within me.

In the throes of the storm, I had lain awake, my heart thumping like that of a snared rabbit, while Dan slumbered peacefully beside me. Through the long night, my head churned a maelstrom of doubt and anxiety, and I began to suspect that I possessed neither the courage nor the stamina to reach Mount Katahdin more than two thousand miles to the north. I also suspected that I had invested my hopes in a folly that would break me the way the wind had cracked away the branches of the surrounding trees and that I would limp back home wounded by failure. Those feelings may have been amplified by the storm, but they had just as surely accompanied my first tentative steps on the trail four days earlier.

Early on the morning of April 21, my parents had driven Dan and me up a ten-mile stretch of gravel road to Nimblewill Gap, which reaches within three miles of Springer Mountain and represents the nearest road access to the southern terminus of the Appalachian Trail.

An alternate route to the top follows an approach trail, which begins at Amicacola Falls State Park and ascends nine miles to Springer. We had heard stories about the stiff vertical ascent from the park to the trailhead, reputed to be among the trail's most difficult sections. This was especially the case for neophyte hikers who lacked the fitness and stamina that hundreds of miles on the trail would later provide. Among the dozens of hopeful thru-hikers who abandon the trail each year, in fact, many stumble back down the mountain—defeated—before ever reaching the summit of Springer. We didn't want to be among them, and by starting our hike at Nimblewill, we reasoned, we would at least make it as far as the official starting point.

We arrived at the gap in my parents' new sedan, and Dan and I climbed from the car smelling of soap and shampoo, fresh from our last hot shower for many days. Once out of the car, Dan, a seasoned woodsman who had logged countless miles on backcountry trails, hefted his pack from the trunk and slid effortlessly into its straps. The process wasn't quite as easy for me.

First, there was the actual heft of my pack. I realize now that there is no more reliable method for gauging a hiker's confidence than studying the contents of his pack. The least experienced hikers labor under a yoke of fear and worry, cluttering their packs with devices they hope will duplicate the security of more familiar environments. Veteran hikers, whose packs are characteristically Spartan, have discovered that a well chosen poem or quotation, which weighs nothing once committed to memory, can provide more solace in the face of fear than a welter of gadgets and trinkets.

Since I was a novice, my backpack burgeoned with expendable items that catered either to my fears or to my vanity but which served no purpose other than to occupy space with their bulk and stress my knees with their weight. While Dan's pack weighed a respectable thirty-five to forty pounds, mine surpassed fifty-five. I had read and reread backpacking how-to books, which sang the praises of lightweight packs bearing only the essentials. In the months before the outset of my hike, I had loaded the pack dozens of times, and each time I tried to assess honestly the merit of each item I slipped into the pockets. Gradually, I had pared the pack down to forty pounds. As the day of departure approached, however, my doubts and fears reversed the trend, and I found myself sneaking small items back into the pack until the scales again topped fifty-five.

On the eve of the hike, I had down-loaded the pack one last time, and I resolved to leave it just as it was. To assuage my fears, though, I had stashed the discarded items in the trunk of the car. As I wrestled the pack onto the ground in Nimblewill Gap and glimpsed them for the last time, each suddenly seemed essential, and I realized that once the trunk was closed, I would be forced to live without them.

Wouldn't the two-pound pair of binoculars in their leather case bring me closer to wildlife and help me identify the denizens of my new environment? Wouldn't the plastic egg-carrier and fifty feet of braided marine rope prove indispensable? What about the extra cook pot, aluminum plate, and oven mitt? Would one pair of long trousers be enough, and did I need a third pair of wool socks? Would the sheath knife, with its six-inch blade, protect me from wild beasts, or would my Swiss Army knife be sufficient? Would the package of firecrackers and can of dog repellent chase marauding bears from our camps? Would the metal pocket mirror, which doubled as a signal mirror, become an invaluable grooming aid or even save my life if I became lost? Wouldn't the one-pound hammock help make my leisure hours more comfortable? Would my health fail without the three-month supply of vitamins and the bulky first-aid manual?

As I deliberated, Dan shifted impatiently, and I resolved finally that the egg-carrier, binoculars, oven mitt, sheath knife, and marine rope would stay behind. The mirror, the first-aid guide, the firecrackers, the hammock, the extra pair of socks and trousers, the supplemental pot and plate, the vitamins, and dog repellent, I reasoned, would justify their weight.

At the time, my pack, as heavy as it was, seemed far less burdensome than the emotional and physical challenge that awaited me, and as I glimpsed the trailhead, I first registered the full impact of what I was about to do. I had been raised by conservative and protective parents, who tended not to venture far from the cloister of their snug middle-class environment. From the time I was young, my life had been predicated on safe decisions. Now I was about to embark on a five-month journey through the unknown where I would face risks more real than any I had known before.

Fueling my fears was the knowledge that once I entered the backcountry I would leave behind the familiar trappings of the civilized world—electric lights to chase away the darkness, television sets and radios to help fill the idle hours, modern appliances to ease the chores of daily life—and the comfort they provided. I had fully enjoyed the morning's hot shower and the meal at the hotel restaurant. I felt no shame in ascending into the mountains inside the climate-controlled environment of the car, and I wasn't at all sure I could endure life without those and other amenities.

In some ways, the act of climbing from the car was tantamount to exiting the womb: I faced a strange and forbidding new world. At least in the first instance I had been blessed with conscientious parents who shepherded me clear of major pitfalls. Once I entered the woods, I knew that there would be nothing to shield me from hardship and danger except my own resources, which I had never really tested.

When the time to leave came, I embraced my parents and hoped they would offer some advice or guidance, yet I realized that I was about to enter a realm they knew little about.

"Be careful," said my mother, with tears welling in her eyes.

"Yes, and have fun," Dad advised, as I took the first of the five million steps that would lead me to Mount Katahdin. After a few hundred feet, I turned one last time to see the white sedan disappear in a cloud of dust as it descended the gravel road. For the first time in my life, I was truly on my own.

Within an hour and a half, we reached Springer, a rounded mountain cloaked in hardwood trees, their branches tipped with opening buds, and we discovered a sign-in book wedged into a mailbox planted on the summit. We took the register to a grassy clearing and basked for a few minutes in the eighty-two-degree sunshine as we read the entries logged by other hikers who had begun the hike in previous days and weeks. Dan and I noted that eight hikers, all bound for Maine, had signed in over the weekend, and we were two of the nearly five hundred who would set out on the northward pilgrimage that summer. At that point, none of us knew who would be among the one hundred or so who would reach our goal.

I penned a brief message about my dream of reaching Katahdin and then signed my name. Under it I drafted the thru-hiker symbol: a capital *T* nestled under and joined with the crossbar of a capital *A*. Beside it I printed the letters *GA*, the designation for Georgia, with an arrow pointing to the letters *ME*, the abbreviation for Maine, and added the year: 1979. In so doing I became an official Appalachian Trail thru-hiker.

Before continuing north, Dan and I posed for pictures beside a forest service sign. It listed Springer Mountain and its elevation of 3,782 feet along with the distance to a few major mileposts ahead. The last entry was Mount Katahdin, mileage two thousand miles (since the sign had been erected, trail relocations had added about one hundred miles). From the perspective of the wooded hills of Georgia at the base of the Appalachian spine, the northern terminus wouldn't have seemed more remote if it had been located on the surface of the moon.

For the next several days we traversed the three thousand-foot peaks of the Chattahoochee National Forest. I count those days among the most difficult I have endured. I spent most of them absorbed in the rigors of survival in an environment that seemed foreign and hostile. In short, I was consumed by apprehension and fear.

I was afraid of my own ineptitude. I fumbled with my new stove, lost track of items stored in my pack, and listened at night as mice gnawed through my foodbag before I learned to hang it out of their reach. I had no idea how to bushwhack down a mountainside to locate a water source, what to do to protect myself on an exposed ridge in a thunderstorm, how to patch myself back together after I had sliced myself with my pocketknife, how long to boil lentils and rice, how much stove fuel to carry for the days and nights between supply stops, and how much and what type of food I would need to keep from starving.

I was afraid of my own weakness. My lungs burned, my thighs were seared, and my feet throbbed as my boots rubbed my tender heels to blisters on the first few steep ascents, and I wondered if I had the fortitude to keep pushing on through the pain. When late April storms drenched the woods, I dreaded leaving the dry warmth of my shelter to set out for fifteen miles through the downpour. I was afraid, too, of facing my friends back home if I failed to meet those challenges and had to pack it in.

I was afraid of being alone. Dan's woods-sense far exceeded my own, and I stuck by him like moss on a log, worried that if I let him out of my sight, I would never catch up to him and would be left to earn my proficiency through hardship and failure. As it turned out, Dan taught me much, and we remained a team to the very pinnacle of Mount Katahdin. During our five months on the trail, we propped each other up when our spirits flagged, fought like badgers when our egos pulled in different directions, and shared our food, our shelter, and our thoughts. When the trip ended, we had spent more than 150 days and nights together and had forged a friendship that will endure no matter how much time and distance separate us.

I was afraid of the vast mystery of nature. The chilling echo of hoot owls, the distant drumming of male ruffed grouse beating the air with their wings, the constant rustling in the brush around our camps after we'd extinguished our evening campfires were all unfamiliar sounds that fueled my fear.

And I was afraid when, under a tarp in Tesnatee Gap, I first experienced the raw power of nature.

The fear inspired by that first spring storm—and all the fears that accompanied me along my first miles on the trail—soon fused into a pervading sense of dread. As I watched Dan confront the trail's challenges with courage and confidence, I began to resign myself to the belief that I wasn't quite suited for an extended stay in the woods. One evening, while I sat on a log downcast and preparing to tell him that I had decided to leave the trail, a toy collie strayed into camp. Though I didn't realize it at the time, I was about to learn the first, and perhaps the most enduring, lesson about life on the trail. Put simply, if one is receptive and open to change, the trail—and in a larger sense, nature itself—seems always to answer one's questions and meet one's needs. It sounds mystical, and I wouldn't believe it if I hadn't experienced it so many times along my journey.

Just behind the dog, a woman in her late fifties labored up the trail, the huge pack she carried dwarfing her slight frame. Her legs appeared much too frail to support her own weight, much less the weight of the pack, and her face, framed by silver shoulder-length hair, registered the pain of every step.

She paused for a few minutes, leaning on her walking stick, and told us that her name was Elizabeth and that she was hiking alone. Her destination, like ours, was Mount Katahdin. She told us that her husband had died the previous year and that she had taken up the trail to ease her grief and to chart a new direction for her life. She said she covered twelve to fifteen miles per day, beginning at dawn and continuing until dark.

She declined our invitation to join us in our camp, saying that she hoped to cover a few more miles before it became too dark to navigate the boulder-strewn trail. Soon she called to her dog and resumed her slow, deliberate pace.

Later, as Dan and I sat beside the fire plotting our mileage for the next several days and as I struggled with the decision to continue on or abandon the trail, I couldn't shake the memory of Elizabeth. It had taken me five hours to cover the twelve miles to camp that day; she had been plodding along for nearly twice that long. At the end of each day, my twenty-three-year-old thighs and feet ached. How, then, must hers have felt? I had shuddered as the storm blew through our camp, and I had flinched in the darkness when the trees creaked and wild animals crept unseen through the underbrush. Yet I had the comfort of a companion. How did she contend with such fears during her solitary days and nights on the trail? How had she become so brave?

Frankly, in spite of her apparent courage, I had dismissed Elizabeth's goal of completing the trail as foolhardy. Yet one evening some five months later, while Dan and I camped in the woods of central Maine, a toy collie entered camp. As soon as we saw it, we looked at one another and smiled. Then we turned and looked up the trail. A slender figure soon emerged from the trees. It was Elizabeth.

Although the previous five months had wrought physical changes in all of us, the rigors of trail life had completely transformed Elizabeth. Her face was wan and haggard, and dark circles had formed under her eyes. Her legs seemed to have lost what little muscle tone they had had, and her silver hair had billowed into a tangled mass. Her gait seemed even more painful and unsteady than when I had first seen her.

Once she joined us in camp, she explained that she had made it as far as New England before realizing that at her pace, she could not hope to reach Katahdin before the end of October, when Baxter State Park officials bar access to the mountain because of unpredictable weather. She had decided to "flop," as do many of the slower-moving hikers, and travel to Katahdin, then hike south to where she had left off. I later learned that she reached her goal.

When I refer back to my journal entry on the night we first met Elizabeth in Georgia, I find a message of hope. There I termed her "Our Lady of the Trail" and wrote that "she seems weak and distant and unaware of the difficulty of the task that awaits her. We have heard about other hikers who have already gotten discouraged and gone home. But after these few days, she is still here, still moving north. How, I don't know. She will always be an inspiration to me."

Thereafter, Elizabeth became my guiding spirit, like a figurehead on an old wooden ship leading frightened sailors through uncharted seas. When my confidence began to fail, I would think of her and her frail body, facing the wilderness alone with no one to ease her fears or share her discoveries.

From then on I resolved that although I could not conquer my fears outright, I could at least confront them squarely. As I did, they seemed to lose their power over me.

As the weeks passed, my blisters began to heal, and my thighs grew hard and strong. My camp routine became well enough ingrained that I could fetch water, fire the stove, cook and eat dinner, and hang my food without a wasted motion. My pack and its contents became more familiar to me than my dresser drawers at home, and I eventually discarded the spare socks, extra cook pot and plate, vitamins, firecrackers, dog repellent, and several other pounds of extraneous gear. I gave the extra trousers to a fellow hiker who had ripped the seat out of his own, and soon my pack dipped to a manageable thirty-five pounds.

From then on I carried only the essentials. As the load in my pack decreased, my initial fear of the wilderness mellowed, and I began walking my fifteen to twenty miles each day alone, fascinated with the process of spring awakening around me. I even began to regard thunderstorms, which weeks earlier had pitched me into panic, as among nature's most formidable and entertaining displays, more potent and grand than anything I had witnessed in civilization. Many evenings, as storms approached, I scrambled to an open perch on a ridge-line from which to watch them, as their charcoal-gray sentries floated across dusky skies stretching to the horizon. I sat captivated as their silver talons raked nearby mountain peaks and their thunder shook the earth. As I watched, I began to realize that my transformation from visitor to resident of the wilderness had begun and that there was much yet to learn about my new home.

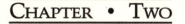

CHAPTER · TWO

Learning to Walk, Learning to See

This lifestyle certainly allows plenty of time for introspection. Most days I spend six or seven hours alone, walking, out of sight and sound of any other human being. Some days my thoughts turn inward, and I pass the miles exploring memories of people and events that have shaped my past. Other days my mind nestles into meditative daze, and I sense myself connected to the birds, the plants, the flowers, the trees, like a man floating on the breeze through a boundless garden.
—May 29, 1979, Iron Mountain Shelter, Tennessee

We often define ourselves by our primary occupations. A person who busies himself painting houses, for instance, is a painter. A person who devotes his energies to growing crops is a farmer. In that sense, during my months on the Appalachian Trail, I was a hiker, and the simple act of hiking—lifting each boot, planting it squarely, and biting off another three-foot section of trail—came to define who I was.

Though simple in terms of mechanics, hiking proved to

be a complex process that evolved over time into an almost meditative act that touched me daily in physical and spiritual ways. But before I could savor the more sublime virtues of hiking, I had to submit to an often demanding apprenticeship, one that I undertook at the heels of my companion, Dan.

There was a grace inherent in Dan's gait, and I detected it the first time we hiked together. On our first shakedown hike, a two-day trip to the Shenandoah National Park, we covered fifteen miles under a constant downpour. During the first day I watched in awe as Dan approached a rain-swollen stream, leapt from the ground onto a downed tree spanning the creek, and crossed without breaking stride. The tree was maybe six inches in diameter and had been stripped of its bark, making it as slick as a greased iron post. The murky stream had spilled over its banks and roared beneath. Adding to the challenge were the hard-rubber soles of our hiking boots, which provided precarious footing at best on a wet surface. Nonetheless, Dan ambled across the log as surely as if he were traversing a flat dirt path wearing baseball spikes, and once on the other side he stopped to watch me make my pass.

I eased onto the log, feeling my muscles tighten, and after taking two unsteady steps, with my arms and legs tracing hula hoops in the air, I plunged waist-deep into the stream. Dragging myself up the far bank, I unleashed a string of expletives as Dan, laughing, disappeared up the trail. That night, while I slumbered restlessly in the tent, I had a dream that fashioned my frustration into a metaphor.

In the dream I awoke in the darkness and found myself clinging to a life raft that was being dragged through rough seas at high speed. As the foam spattered my face, I spied through the darkness a long rope tethered to the raft and leading a few hundred yards forward to the stern of a huge cruise ship. The ship was kicking up a fearful wake, and I could see Dan standing aboard ship and peering at me from the deck.

I didn't require an analyst to interpret the dream. I obviously was worried that I would never match Dan's speed or agility, and I saw myself forever in the wash, slogging along the trail in wet boots and sodden clothes, careening into every stream and tumbling over every obstacle. What I failed to realize at the time was that the problems I encountered did not lie in any inborn lack of balance or coordination. Rather they lay in my inexperience, which made me regard the pack as an accessory, rather than an extension of my physical self.

Once on the trail in April, I underwent a period of adjustment during which I gradually learned to accommodate the load on my back through subtle shifts in muscles and balance. Actually the change took place unconsciously, much the way a mail carrier might gradually lean in one direction to offset the weight of the mailbag. It would be weeks, however, before I had accomplished the necessary changes and could stride surely across such obstacles as fallen logs. Eventually the pack became a part of me, and I soon felt only partially clothed without it.

Once I had adapted to the pack, I began to experience the opposite problem and discovered that my balance wavered when I took it off at the end of a long day. I wasn't alone in that regard. I recall watching many of my fellow hikers arrive in camp and, once relieved of their loads, stumble like drunken men.

Balance was one component of hiking; strength and endurance were others. During our first days on the trail, the twelve- and thirteen-mile days seemed interminable, and as each day passed, I grimaced as I glanced up the trail and beheld yet another ascent lurking ahead. The trail seemed to be a never-ending continuum of ascents that taxed my thighs and descents that stressed my knees, with hardly a flat quarter-mile stretch to ease the twitching in my fatigued muscles.

At the same time, I suffered a pestering preoccupation with distance, how much mileage I had covered through each day and how much remained ahead until I would reach camp. I even wore a pedometer attached to my belt to measure my progress by the length of my stride. It worked, in a sense, but by wearing it I became like the motorist who fixes on the odometer while excluding the scenery rolling past. Like such a motorist, I never seemed to draw much closer to my destination.

Beyond my daily mileage, there was the larger perspective—the distance to the northern terminus of the trail—and I found myself constantly subtracting the miles I had covered from the total to Mount Katahdin. Even at the time that struck me as ludicrous, like counting every chisel stroke invested in carving the presidents' heads into Mount Rushmore, and it imparted little sense of motion. Such a means of gauging my progress—focusing on the remaining miles to the trail's end rather than taking each day in turn—reminded me of a line from T. S. Eliot's poem, "The Love Song of J. Alfred Prufrock," about a man who ponders his misspent life and concludes, sadly, that he's measured out his life "with coffee spoons." Prufrock had his coffee spoon; I had my pedometer.

Thru-hiking was not, after all, a race, though some hikers seemed inclined to view it as one. Over the summer, each of the dozens of thru-hikers I met seemed to fall into one of two categories. First were those intent on savoring the trail experience, while still viewing Katahdin as the ultimate goal. They tended to measure the miles in terms of quality—of events and experience—rather than quantity. These were the hikers who, I believe, learned and grew the most while on the trail. Most of my colleagues fell into this camp. Shortly after discarding my pedometer, I joined their ranks.

There were others—the peak-baggers—who viewed completing the Appalachian Trail as a Spartan feat that would enhance their sense of machismo without reconfiguring their attitudes or values. To many of them, the trail became an ultraendurance footrace that, once completed, would provide another certificate to hang on their walls and another patch to sew onto their backpacks. Covering the 2,100 miles with their hearts and minds fixed on the final peak, they missed the important peaks that led to it.

Among us were men and women who embodied the extremes of each philosophy. There were, for instance, hikers who dallied too long in trail towns or who sacrificed too many days by refusing to walk in the rain. In the end, completion of the trail eluded them. I recall a pair of hikers from New Jersey who hiked when they felt like it and lounged around in camp or hitchhiked into town when they didn't. Most of the time they didn't, and, as far as I know, they never reached Katahdin.

There were others who dallied not at all and dashed up the trail as if pursued by demons. Late one evening in a shelter near Erwin, Tennessee, for instance, a hiker arrived in the dark, at 9:30 P.M. After a hasty greeting, he munched a few handfuls of dry trail mix, unrolled his bag, slept until 5:30 A.M., munched a few more handfuls of Good Old Raisins and Peanuts (GORP), and hit the trail by 5:45. As he ate, I propped myself on one elbow, disinclined to leave the warmth of my sleeping bag, and asked him a few questions.

I discovered that he had less than three months to finish the trail before he had to return to school, and he covered twenty-five to thirty miles each day. What's more, he had not taken a day off since he had left Springer and was fully reconciled to the fact that his entire summer might pass without a single idle day to laze around town or wallow in a mountain lake. As I listened, he outlined his schedule for the next several weeks: Harpers Ferry by this date, the White Mountains by another, and Katahdin by another, leaving him less than a week to digest the trail experience, return home, gather his books, and return to school. The schedule could not have been more oppressive if it had belonged to an overworked corporate executive.

Another such hiker, George, a Massachusetts native known as Pigpen because of his stolid refusal to bathe, had secured a four-month leave of absence from his accounting firm in Boston. The leave left him just enough time to finish the trail, baring any unexpected problems. I hiked with George for several days in Georgia and North Carolina before he blasted ahead under the strain of his deadline.

I learned later that once George reached New England, the trail had worked its magic and his priorities had shifted. The threat of losing his job and his single-minded determination to reach Mount Katahdin, which had propelled him ahead at his furious pace, suddenly seemed to contradict the essence of the trail experience, that it's the journey itself, not the journey's end, that offers the greatest reward. George finally called his boss, asked for and received an extension, finished the trail, and eventually returned to the office. The last I heard, he was considering chucking both his navy-blue suits and his job to take up long-distance cycling.

By late May, the trail had begun to affect me too, and I began to view my daily mileage as a wholesome addiction. I had reached a level of physical stamina that I had not known before and have never achieved since, and each day's end found me feeling energized, cleansed, and relaxed, with endorphins (the body's natural opiates released by exercise) coursing through my system. I soon settled into a constant three-mile-an-hour pace, no faster or slower than that of my fellow hikers, Dan included. The pace seldom varied, whether I was climbing or descending, unless of course I decided to throttle back to take in a view or study the flowers lining the trail.

I had come to relish hiking and the feeling of physical prowess that accompanied it, but it wasn't until the day in late May when we ascended Roan Mountain, a hulking six-thousand-footer in northeastern Tennessee, that I first experienced the sheer bliss of foot travel. The ascent to the top led up two thousand vertical feet, which would have destroyed me a month earlier. A freak snowstorm had blown in the previous day, layering the entire wilderness in a crystal glaze, and I remember the climb as a continuum of fairytale scenes and vistas: the surrounding snow-clad peaks, pink rhododendron and delicate mountain laurel blossoms frozen in full flower, and ice-laden spruce boughs shimmering in the sun. Along the steep ascent, utter fascination supplanted any concern I might have had over distance or altitude. As I reached the open, sun-drenched alpine meadows at the top, I realized that I would gladly have scaled four thousand more feet just for the opportunity to see it.

After the ascent, I realized how effortless climbing could be if one simply let the muscles and lungs work while savoring the beauty of each mile in its turn. Hiking soon evolved into a meditative act. There was euphony in the measured, purposeful sound of motion: the rhythmic rise and fall of breath, the thump of the heart, the cadence of boots crunching soil and rock, the steady tap of the walking stick, the bending of knees and the flexing and relaxing of thigh muscles, calf muscles, hip muscles.

There were days when I focused on the scenery, and I ambled along the trail feeling connected to the birds, plants, flowers, and trees, like a man floating on the breeze through a boundless garden. There were other days when the trees melded into two green labyrinthine walls that contained and guided me, and my mind traced other trails, scattered with people and events drawn from my past.

Memories I had lost or forgotten seemed to surface of their own accord, bringing with them vivid images, sensations, emotions, and voices, and I spent hours in their company. I relived my first date—with a shy brunette—in eighth grade; I embraced my high-school lover in the back seat of my old blue Impala; I circled the bases as a Little Leaguer after hitting my first and only grand slam home run; I sparred with a high school rival at a Friday-night dance over the affections of a young woman; I relived the long summer afternoons as a child with my grandmother, exploring the woods and identifying wild flowers; and I relived the night my father entered my bedroom and, crying, told me she was dead.

And so—lost in thought—I passed the miles, and often by day's end I was jarred from my reverie by the sound of companions ahead in camp. I would then realize that I had traveled six or ten or twelve miles without recalling a single step.

I began to notice, too, how changes in the weather conjured up different moods. When gentle rains came, the woods swirled with mist, the leaves drooped, the ground became sodden brown, and the air hung rich with the smells of damp humus and musky ferns. On rain days, I cinched my parka hood around my face and drew within, enshrouded in the same clouds that swallowed the treetops and muted vibrant colors to hues of brown and gray.

Rain days were quiet days, with the *hisss* of a million drops plinking the palms of leaves and drowning the sounds of birds and wind and even the cadence of my boots. Often during such days, I delved into the repertoire of poems I had memorized since grade school—poems by Frost, Coleridge, Yeats, Kipling—and recited them aloud as I hiked, confident that no one could hear.

Or I bellowed lyrics of favorite songs into the indifferent face of the rain and fog. One of them, "Taxi," a Harry Chapin song, always seemed to fit the mood of the rain: "It was raining hard in Frisco; I needed one more fare to make my night. . . ." The song, about a taxi driver who encounters his former lover on a dismal night, seemed doubly tragic in the rain, and I always enjoyed the pang of sadness it aroused.

On the other hand, sunny days were expansive days, especially when the trail snaked across bald-topped mountains or over exposed rock ledges where one's perspective was as broad as the horizon. Spence Field, in the southern section of the Great Smoky Mountains National Park, offered such a view, and we lazed for an hour or more in the grassy meadows there, tracing the mountains to where they yielded to the foothills and beyond to where the hills gave way to the plains and further still to where long-fingered TVA lakes probed into hidden coves.

If my experiences during my first weeks on the trail taught me a new way to walk, they also provided me with a new way to see. Much as a novice audiophile might fail to appreciate the subtle qualities— tempo, pitch, melody, harmony—hidden in a musical composition, I, too, failed to notice many of the woods' subtle offerings before I had developed a sensitivity to the sounds and rhythms of the wilderness. There were bald-faced hornets' nests hanging in branches; songbirds and woodpeckers flitting among the leaves; lizards and snakes slithering across sunbaked rocks; groundhogs burrowing among fallen leaves; hawks and buzzards circling on thermals; bears nestling in treetops. And there was spring in the Appalachians. Each day, as the frail-green phalanx of opening buds crept up the mountains, the trail revealed new secrets.

CHAPTER THREE

Seasons

The colors of the leaves are incredible! In just the past few days they have broken into full fall color. Reds and oranges predominate in the lowlands, and dark evergreens contrast with yellow birches on the mountain tops. The foliage should be at its peak when we climb Katahdin within a week, and we're all grateful for the perfect timing. The arrival of fall marks the fourth season we've walked through, completing the cycle. When we began in April, winter clung to the upper elevations as spring began its slow ascent. Then, summer overtook spring. Fall, like winter, takes the opposite route, beginning at the mountain tops and working its way down the slopes, sparking summer green to fire as it advances.

There is no describing the hiker's eye-view of the changing seasons and living the continuous transition day by day, hour by hour.

—September 22, 1979, Cooper Brook Falls Lean-to, Maine

Even today—more than ten years after I completed the trail—I suffer pangs of nostalgia with the onset of spring. When those first spring days arrive and the whole world seems charged with passion and energy, I sit at a traffic light, bound for work in some climate-controlled office, and roll down my windows to savor the spring air, fragrant with the aroma of a million blossoms. I eye the landscaper, the carpenter, the maintenance worker seated in the truck beside me. I see him clad in work clothes, with the first ruddy traces of sun coloring his cheeks, and I envy him for his days spent outside and his intimacy with the seasons.

I realize that I, with my desk job, will witness the spring in scattered glimpses, while paused at traffic lights, at lunch hours spent on park benches, on weekends spent tilling my garden. And I realize, sadly, that one day the spring will have passed and it will be summer, and I will remind myself, as I always do, to pay closer attention next year. But I seem never to succeed at it; too many things distract me. At such times, I fondly remember my journey through the Appalachians where, in my memory, it is always spring.

The trail forever changed my perspective on the seasons. On the trail I *lived* the seasons. I *experienced* them moment to moment, sensing one season's gradual surrender to the next. There was no urgency, just the perennial cycle of death and life played out in slow, fluid motion, every morning providing new evidence of change.

First there was winter, gripping the higher elevations where barren limbs rattled in icy winds and where everything was dormant brown except the green conifers, the clusters of shiny galax, and the scatterings of aromatic wintergreen. Meanwhile, at the lower elevations spring's most resilient sprigs probed through layers of decaying foliage and buds burst open on deciduous trees. A phalanx of frail green marked the place where the two seasons met.

I remember the first time I saw it. I had ascended Albert Mountain, a boulder-strewn nob topped with a fire tower in North Carolina one hundred miles north of Springer Mountain. It was April 29, and as I looked out across the surrounding ridges and valleys, first I saw the deep green swatches of fir trees. Then I noted the barren mountain crests. Far below were lowlands tinged in green. Between, an asymmetric line of the faintest green traced the boundary between death and life, between winter and spring. If someone were to have asked me at that moment where and when spring arrived, I could have provided an answer. Pointing to that line I would have said, "There, this very minute, along that faint green line, spring is overtaking winter." And if we had paused long enough and were patient enough, we could have watched it move. Naturalists claim that the line ascends at a rate of six feet per day, three inches every hour.

As we traced the line of the ridges and dipped into saddles and sags on our way north, we crossed that boundary countless times. As the days passed, the last vestiges of winter retreated higher and higher up the mountains until finally, by June, spring had surmounted even the six-thousand-foot peaks. Meanwhile, deep in the valleys summer awakened and began its own slow ascent.

There was so much to see in the spring; every parcel of trail presented a colorful floral display. Dan carried a wildflower identification book in his pack, and evenings in camp, he reported his latest findings. Together we learned to call each flower by its rightful name.

There were delicate bluets, their four lavender lobes emerging from a golden, star-burst center and their needle-thin stems rising out of trailside grass. Wild irises, their rigid spiked leaves deep green and their blossoms curled like lips into a rich purple kiss. Jack-in-the-pulpits, with their green mottled leaves curled around and over a phallic spadix, a legion of upright preachers ministering to the emerging vegetation of the season's fertile rite. Lady's slippers, with their soft pink labia transmitting a similar, though more delicate, message. Trilliums—pink ones, yellow ones, purple ones, striped ones—with their tri-lobed heads and leaves nourished beside rotting logs.

Bloodroot, with its variegated leaves, shaped as if by elfin scissors, sheltering a shy white flower. Buttercups, with tiny, waxen gold pedals. Yellow and purple violets. Mayapples, with tight-wrapped leaves slowly swirling open like green picnic umbrellas, shading a round, white flower. Flame azalea trees, burning like fire with bright orange blossoms visible from hundreds of yards away. Fiddlehead ferns, uncoiling like cobras along the trail. Dutchman's breeches, with white blossoms dangling from a pale bowed spike, like tiny trousers hung on a line to dry. Showy orchis, a two-tone blending of violet and pure white. And the dogwoods decked in white and pink.

As the forest floor began to teem with flowers, the birds also awakened. Scarlet tanagers lit in dogwood trees, lending their red plumage to the bouquet of white blossoms. The brown wood thrush, with its auburn head, brown wings, and brown-spotted belly, trilled its lyrical flute-like song, of which Thoreau wrote, "Whenever a man hears it he is young, and nature is in its spring." Pileated woodpeckers, with their oversized, tufted red heads and narrow necks, screeched through the woods like winged banshees. Indigo buntings glowed iridescent purple in the sunlight. Chickadees, tufted titmice, and rufous-sided towhees seemed to inhabit every tree and bush. Hoot owls' eerie four-syllable calls echoed through the trees around our camps, and we joked that they were really saying, "Whooo cooks for yooooo?"

And then there were the whip-poor-wills that irked us through many nights with their frenetic calls, beginning their arias about the time we climbed into our bags and often continuing until dawn. We frequently lobbed rocks in their direction but never scored a direct hit. More often than not, our mortars seemed only to intensify their maddening songs.

By late June, the spring buds had given way to the first of summer's flowering plants. Softball-sized rhododendron blossoms, ranging from rose-red to pink-white, exploded in such profusion that they washed entire mountainsides with their color. Mountain laurel, with its white, star-shaped blossoms punctuated with ten rosy dots, offered itself to us from bushes that draped over the trail. Pink musk thistle, white daisies, and golden black-eyed Susans bowed to summer breezes in open fields and along country roads. Turk's-cap lilies, their knifelike petals curled into spotted orange turbans, grew as tall as seven feet and peered down on us as we traversed ridge-line trails through Virginia. Firepink and

Indian paintbrush advertised their presence along the trailside with neon-red, dime-sized blossoms.

The bounty of edible plants and berries enhanced the
beauty of the forest in bloom. Ramps, wild leeks with
drooping green rabbit-ear leaves, thrived along the trail in
Georgia, North Carolina, and Tennessee. The Indians used
the plant's essence to treat insect bites; hikers use the bulbs
and leaves to add garlic tang to soups and stews.

We had been searching for ramps for days after encountering a mountain woman, clad in a gingham dress and carrying a woven basket, who scoured the trail for ramps, wild
mushrooms, and edible snails brought out by spring rains.
She had shown us a ramp and slit open the bulb with her
thumbnail, inviting us to sniff. The aroma brought tears,
and we reasoned that anything with such a potent smell
would pose an easy quarry. We were mistaken, and after
plucking from the loam dozens of trout lilies, which also
boast drooping green leaves but no tang, we were ready to
abandon hope. Then, as we passed through Beech Gap three
miles north of the summit of Standing Indian Mountain, I
spotted a trio of green leaves and determined to make one
last try. I tugged on the leaves, which snapped off in my
hands, and realized I had found our illusive ramp as the odor
of garlic filled my nostrils.

That night, camped at the Carter Gap Shelter, we had a
rampfest, slicing, dicing, and chopping the leaves and bulbs
and dropping handfuls into our evening stews. One of our
more daring colleagues, who experimented by eating an entire bulb raw, soon sat weeping over his cook pot, a beatific
grin spreading across his tear-stained face.

Unfortunately, while the mountain woman had cited the
culinary virtues of ramps, she had said nothing about their
disastrous side effects. The morning after our ramp orgy, the
shelter reeked in spite of its open face. Well into the next
day, acrid ramp burps curled my tongue, and I would have
parted with my sleeping bag and pack for a single roll of
antacid tablets. As my stomach churned, I swore off ramps,
vowing to starve before I ever sampled another bulb. Unfortunately, my hiking buddies were not so inclined, and they

continued to spice their evening meals with ramps until the leaves toughened later in the season, and the plant sprouted a cluster of white flowers.

I soon learned that although eating ramps is pure bliss for the strong of stomach, for the abstainer, living alongside anyone who has eaten them is pure hell. The pungent aroma not only stays on the breath but is exuded through the skin, taints the sweat, and lingers on clothing for days afterward.

Fortunately, most of nature's bounty was more sweet than acid. The same woman who had helped us identify ramps also showed us lemon balm, a member of the mint family with a square stalk, reddish-green variegated leaves, and a tart lemony smell. We steeped the leaves in boiling water, added honey, and drank lemon-balm tea.

Near Hot Springs, North Carolina, thirty-five miles north of the Smokies, a toothless wanderer who shared our camp disappeared at dusk and returned with an armload of poke, a green edible weed with poison roots and dark red-blue berries later in the season. He boiled the leaves, dumped the water, and boiled them again. Once done, he smothered the leaves in butter from a squeeze tube and offered them around. The poke "salit" was rich and slightly bitter but good, and it provided us with the fresh greens that our standard menus of noodles, rice, and lentils lacked.

Into southern Virginia the blossoms yielded to fruit on flowering trees. As we descended through a grassy meadow into Newport, I felt something crawling along my calf, and when I glanced down I spotted a legion of wood ticks creeping up my socks. After brushing them off, I spied hundreds of red berries nestled beneath green variegated leaves. Wild strawberries! Soon Jeff, a blond hiker from Kansas, and Mark, a long-haired eighteen-year-old thru-hiker from Maryland, joined me, and together we filled a gallon-sized Ziploc bag before continuing into town. We made our first stop the general store, and soon each of us sat under the store's awning savoring dollops of vanilla ice cream smothered in fresh berries.

Through Virginia the trail frequently followed abandoned

wagon and carriage roads past remains of eighteenth- and nineteenth-century settlements. We often walked along rusted barbed-wire fences past decaying homesteads. One day we encountered a fresh-water spring near where the hand-hewn timbers of a cabin had rotted away from an erect, field-stone chimney. As we sat in the shade envying the former inhabitants their idyllic setting and simple life, I looked up and noticed that we were surrounded by cherry trees, their branches hanging heavy with ripe red fruit. We soon emptied our quart water bottles and filled them with sweet cherries. We sat for an hour munching fruit and spewing pits into the brush. But the cherries, too, posed uncomfortable side effects, and for the next several days toilet paper was at a premium.

Further north, we plucked blackberries and raspberries from tangled thickets of briars. But even fresh native fruits and berries could not mitigate the less desirable effects of summer—oppressive heat, humidity, and biting insects. The summer months, which ushered us through the trail's central states—Maryland, Pennsylvania, New Jersey, and New York—posed the most difficult miles of the trail for most of us. Not because of the difficulty of the terrain. On the contrary, passage through the central states brought with it a pestering boredom. The elevation of the mountains dipped below three thousand feet; there were few stunning vistas; and miles of trail coursed along roads and through congested urban areas. So frequent were the road crossings and encounters with developed areas that we had little sense of being in the woods at all. In the 161 miles through New Jersey and New York, the trail is crossed by 64 roads, an average of one in every two-and-a-half miles. The most auspicious road crossing is the Interstate-80 overpass, where the trail crosses the busy four-lane freeway via a fenced-in cement walkway. A green highway sign posted on the walkway alerts motorists that they're passing under the Appalachian Trail. In my travels between Washington, D.C., (where I lived the year prior to my hike), and my parents' home in Cincinnati, I passed under the bridge a half-dozen times, and with each pass I wondered how a hiker would feel to exit the woods onto a platform above four lanes of thundering semis and speeding automobiles.

During the summer, we constantly sought relief from the heat and boredom by wallowing in mountain streams and lakes. Evenings we wrestled with the decision to bake in our sleeping bags and thus avoid the swarms of mosquitoes and gnats, or to sleep—cooler—on top and awake to find our arms, legs, and faces swollen and itching from insect bites. I carried a bottle of jungle juice, a potent insect repellent developed for use by U.S. troops in Vietnam, which kept the bugs away but at a cost. It burned, and we joked, only half in jest, that it removed the top layer of skin. A few of us carried black-fly hoods—head-coverings sewn from mosquito netting—and evenings we resembled a corps of mournful beekeepers. Jimmy, a young man who hiked with us for several days and who had a knack for spinning macabre trail tales, used the hood as a theme for a fireside story about the Black-Fly Hood Murderer, who allegedly prowled the New Jersey woods, stalking unwary hikers and arriving in their camps after dark to hack them to bits with his hatchet.

Through the summer our clothes stayed drenched in sweat, and our fluid intake escalated as the water levels of backcountry streams and springs dwindled. Gone were the cold, free-flowing springs of the South whose water we quaffed without a thought as to its purity; we were forced to take water from stagnant bogs and slow-moving creeks. We expended precious stove fuel boiling the water, or we doctored it with iodine tablets that left behind a rancid chemical taste. This routine also tended to turn our dinners an unappetizing shade of blue when the iodine reacted with the starch in our pasta. Increasingly, we left the trail to ask for tap water at nearby houses.

On the day we crossed Bear Mountain Bridge, which spans the Hudson River in New York, the temperature soared into the hundreds. As we climbed into shallow caves along the route, we spent blissful rest breaks in their constant fifty-degree temperatures.

Through the midsummer months, we longed for the arrival of fall and a return to the larger mountains we knew we would find in New England. It turned out that we encountered both on the same day. We had just exited New York and were covering the forty miles of trail through Connecticut. On August 6, as we began our hike, the heat, as usual, bore down on us, but as the day progressed, a stiff wind blew in from the west and slowly began to sap the humidity from the air. When we ascended to the summit of Bear Mountain, a 2,316-foot peak near the Massachusetts border topped with a crumbling stone edifice built in 1885, the summer, with all its attendant misery, was gone. Crisp blue skies replaced the haze; billowy tufts of cumulus clouds floated by on the wind; and the air temperature plunged into the seventies, holding the promise of fall.

In Connecticut we reentered the wilderness and began to scale larger mountains, mountains with views. The springs and streams, which had dwindled to murky, mosquito-infested puddles, again gave forth clean, cold water. When we descended Bear Mountain, crossed into Massachusetts, and descended into Sages Ravine, with its series of falls and deep pools, the air was too cool for swimming.

Once we arrived in New England, the trail still held a vestige of the wild fruit we had enjoyed in the South. On the day I crossed the open rock ledges leading to Bear Mountain, I suddenly noticed I had lost my companion, Paul, a long-legged strider, who normally blazed by me. Dillon, a New Englander, had recognized the scrub berry bushes, while I, absorbed in the views, had passed them by. He had slowed his pace, raking the bushes for fruit. Hours later, when he finally arrived in camp, his purple grin and red-stained fingers brought laughter from the rest of us who had wondered what was taking him so long. For days afterward, the berries became a morning staple, finding their way into our pancakes, granola, and hot oatmeal.

By the time we crossed into New Hampshire on August 22, we had had our cold-weather woolens sent back to us. Crisp mornings found us layered in sweaters and windbreakers, and our evening fires provided warmth and smoke screens to drive away biting insects.

Then, in Maine, a state rich with birches, sugar maples, and oaks, the fall colors arrived on the heels of Hurricane David, which blasted the northern woods with wind and cold rain in early September. By the time we had reached Monson, the last major town for the trail's final 116 miles, the frost had tinged the maples blaze-red, the birches mottled entire hillsides in gold, and the oaks dappled the mountains in bursts of orange and yellow.

Our ascent of Mount Katahdin brought with it a taste of winter. Ice layered Thoreau Spring, situated a mile below the summit, and the wind pierced our layers of nylon and wool. But if it was a day of ice, it was also a day of fire. Sprawling away from the base of the mountain, fall flames fringed the cool blue ponds of the Lake Country.

Over the course of five months, we had traced the cycle of the seasons, from the wintry peaks of the southern Appalachians in April, through the months of spring and summer, to the fall and the brink of another winter in central Maine. Though I have lost the intimacy with the seasons since my hike, I retain the sense of perfect order, of graceful succession and surrender, and of the bold brilliance of fall leaves as they yield to death.

CHAPTER FOUR

Our Gang

I proceed for all who are or have been young men,
To tell the secret of my nights and days,
To celebrate the need of comrades.
        Walt Whitman, "In Paths Untrodden"

By the time Dan and I entered Virginia June 1, we had become a trio. Nick Gelesko, known on the trail as the Michigan granddad, a fifty-seven-year-old retired engineer from Dawagiac, Michigan, had joined us. By the time we reached New Jersey, we were a foursome, having adopted Paul Dillon, a twenty-year-old, long-legged former competitive skier from Peterboro, New Hampshire. From then on, we were virtually inseparable.

Of all the trail's gifts, none was more precious to me than that of friendship. We were a corps of men and women united by our common love of nature, by our shared needs and experiences, and our affection for one another was as real and enduring as the love of brothers and sisters. We lived side by side, and we shared of ourselves—our thoughts, our fears, our hopes, our experiences past and present—as freely as we shared our food and shelter.

I remember a series of nights in the company of trail friends, some spent around campfires, others in open, star-lit fields, some under rain-pummeled tin roofs, many beside churning brooks, and I remember talking, sometimes for hours, about love, death, God, spirit, nature. Or about more earthy concerns: blisters, bent tent poles, wet boots. Perhaps more significant than the ease with which we discussed our feelings were the remarkably unself-conscious stretches of silence when we were content just to have close friends nearby.

Evenings, each of us followed his own interests. At dusk Dan often retired with his penny whistle to a stream, where his notes mingled with the melodic tumble of water. Paul, our trailside Lord Byron, frequently scribbled odes about love or nature in his journal, which he shared with us around evening fires. Each night after dinner, Nick, squatting on his haunches, meticulously measured, mixed, and stirred his beloved chocolate pudding, as his baritone voice hummed some forgotten ballad from the 1950s. The rest of us always knew that when he finished, we would find a dollop of dessert left in his cook pot for each of us. While my colleagues pursued their evening diversions, I pursued my own, reclining against a tree and recording the whole wonderful scene in my journal.

These are the things I remember about my trail family.

Dan

Dan, a former architectural planner for a major oil corporation, had left a promising fast-track career to walk in the woods. He may have left the job, but he retained his gift for organizing, leading, orchestrating, planning. Dan was our field marshal who, perhaps more than the rest of us, kept his eye on our daily progress, constantly measuring the months against the miles and making sure we reached Katahdin before winter snows closed the mountain down in October. In spite of his drive to cover the miles, he was just as attuned to natural wonders as the rest of us—perhaps even more so—and he frequently called our attention to plants, animals, or birds that had escaped our notice.

Unlike Dan, I had become oblivious to accumulated mileage and more inclined to amble and roost when I found a snug nest along the way. Had it not been for Dan and his intense desire to drive north, I suspect I might have whiled away the summer lazing in mountain lakes or stooped over fresh-scented flowers and might have missed my date with Katahdin altogether. On most occasions, we yielded to Dan's scheduling and advanced at his pace, but not always happily.

In mid-Pennsylvania, after Nick had slowed his pace to hike with his wife, Gwen, who had joined us for a couple of weeks, and before Paul had joined our group, Dan and I were again a twosome. We decided to do an easy day out of Duncannon to a campsite sixteen miles away. Once we were out of town and over the broad bridge spanning the Susquehanna River, Dan blasted ahead, while I throttled back, taking extended rest stops and rummaging through my food bag for the candy and other sweet treats that always attended my departure from town. At 5:30 P.M., I arrived at our scheduled stop, ready to relax. Instead of finding Dan scribing in his journal, I discovered a hand-written note. He had arrived in camp early, become restless, and decided to push on an additional eleven miles, making for a twenty-seven-mile day.

Hiking, like most other endurance activities, is a mental as well as physical pursuit. That is particularly true when you face high-mileage days. Even hikers in prime condition suffer aches, pains, and fatigue after long miles. Most often, when we confronted twenty-plus-mile days, they were planned, allowing us time to psych ourselves up for the long stretches. In the days prior to a long-mile hump, we ate more, rested more. Consider that a hiker who maintains a three-mile-an-hour pace, which is about as fast as one can travel mountainous terrain on foot with a loaded pack, will walk continuously for a full nine hours to cover twenty-seven miles. That includes no time for eating, drinking, resting, or smelling the flowers. Discovering at 5:30 P.M. that I faced an additional eleven miles did not make me a happy camper.

I would have stayed the night where I was, but there were a few complicating factors: Dan carried the guidebook, half of the tent, and half the stove. Without a guidebook, I had no means for gauging my progress over the remaining eleven miles other than by multiplying my average speed (three miles per hour) by the elapsed time and stopping when my watch indicated that I had covered the distance. I also was left without means for protecting myself from the elements, and I was not about to hack down perfectly healthy trees to make a den. At the time, I saw one option: to bust ass and catch Dan.

If I hustled, allowing no food or water breaks, I surmised I would reach the shelter by about 9:10 P.M., a half-hour past dusk. That is, provided I could find the blue-blazed side trail to the shelter in the darkness. Never mind the hundreds of fist-sized rocks—Pennsylvania is famous for them—that tottered with each step and gouged the soles, and never mind the thriving population of rattlesnakes inhabiting the area—Pennsylvania's second most notable distinction. I wolfed down two high-energy breakfast bars, gulped down a liter of water, and set out.

At about 7:00 P.M., still seven-and-a-half-miles from my destination, I passed a group of day-hikers on the trail. Had they seen Dan, the low-life son of a bitch who had abandoned me a few miles back? Yes, a high-school-aged girl answered.

"He figured you might be a little upset," she said.

"And be careful up ahead," she called after me. "There was a big rattlesnake coiled in the middle of the trail!"

I never saw the rattlesnake, but then I didn't look for it. Anger, it seemed, has a wonderful way of dampening one's fear.

By 9:15 and now moving through dusk, I slowed, looking for the blue-blazed trail to the shelter. Blue blazes are difficult enough to spot in the daylight, let alone after dark. Besides, during July, such side trails are frequently overgrown and barely discernible. By 9:20, now following the beam of my mini-flashlight and with my thighs twitching and the soles of my feet feeling as if I had trodden across hot glass shards, I still hadn't spotted the blaze. As I was about to roll out my bag in the weeds and eat a cold dinner, I finally spied it. Soon I was wheeling along toward the shelter. When I reached it, Dan greeted me tentatively. Until my temper calmed, I said nothing at all.

What followed had all the makings of a backwoods lovers' spat. I explained that I could appreciate his yen to cover more miles but didn't appreciate being left with no stove, shelter, or guidebook. Dan sympathized but went on to explain that this was his trip and that he was going to do it his way. That hurt. It reawakened the feelings I had confronted in Georgia, the fear that I couldn't keep pace with him, that I was bogging him down.

I suggested that perhaps it would be best if we split up, dividing the gear, he taking the stove and I taking the shelter and both of us making arrangements to acquire the additional equipment we needed. I'm thankful that it didn't come to that. We both seemed to realize that after investing so much time and energy in the relationship, it would have been a shame to dissolve it. I know I would have missed his company, and I suspect he would have missed mine. Besides, what would our backcountry neighbors have said when they learned that Dan and Dave, one of the more stable trail marriages, had separated? The next morning we continued north, our union intact after surviving our first quarrel.

The next time Dan's drive for miles provoked a rift, we were four—Nick and Paul had joined us—and this time our voting bloc prevailed. It happened in Vermont on August 12, the day we hiked through the spruce-clad northern Berkshires to the 3,491-foot summit of Mount Greylock, the highest peak in Massachusetts. That day we confronted some of the worst weather the Appalachians can muster: the temperature hovered just above freezing. Wind and cold rain stung our faces and hands, and we frequently stepped ankle-deep into mucky spruce bogs as we picked our way to the top. By early afternoon we arrived at Bascom Lodge, an ample rough-hewn summit house built in 1937. Once over the threshold, I was convinced we had perished on the trail and had passed into hiker heaven. A fire blazed in each of two three-foot-square fireplaces, one in each of the two thirty-by-twenty-five-foot great rooms. There were hot coffee, hamburgers, junk food. Old furniture—great comfortable couches and easy chairs—sat in the warmth of the fires.

After peeling off our wet clothes, we sat by the fire sipping hot coffee. When Dan suggested that we take it easy for an hour or so then push back out into the rain for a few more miles, we were incredulous. We held fast and finally reached a compromise: We would stay the night at the lodge and make up the lost mileage over the next few days. The four of us helped wax the scarred wooden floors in exchange for the night's lodging. I spent most of the evening perched at a wooden table, facing a bank of large picture windows. Through the glass I glimpsed the wind-buffeted spruce trees and the swirling fog and rain—the very misery we had escaped—and I slept that night thoroughly content with our decision to stay. I suspect Dan did too.

Maybe Dan was driven, but he was also endowed with other attributes that allow people to thrive in the wilderness. Though slight in stature, at five-feet-ten-inches tall and 145 pounds, and with straight, sandy-blond hair and brown eyes, Dan was rock steady, courageous, and tough. Over the five months we spent together, I never saw his courage falter. He was crazy, too. Crazy to expand his margins and experience new things. More than once, in the midst of a cold spring rain, I watched him strip off his clothes and step under a frigid waterfall or plunge into an icy pool just to savor the rush it would bring.

He demonstrated those hard-edged qualities again and again over our months together, but never more convincingly than on the trail that led us out of Hanover, New Hampshire, in late August.

We had just left the road and had begun our ascent back into the mountains. I led and soon pulled away from my three companions. About a half-mile up the trail, I encountered a hand-written note attached to some evergreen boughs that had been arranged across the trail. The note warned of a bees' nest ahead and advised us to skirt around it. I looked ahead and saw a hole two feet in diameter seething with yellow jackets, and I called back to the others a couple hundred yards behind to be careful. Nick, ahead of Dan and Paul, nodded, though in retrospect it is clear he hadn't understood my warning. I veered into the brush, passed around the nest, and continued up the trail.

In seconds I heard Nick shout, and I turned just in time to see him break into a run. He had overlooked the sign and had continued right over the nest. Though he had escaped being stung, he had pitched the bees into a protective frenzy. Then I watched and listened—helplessly—as Dan began flailing and emitting a horrible series of screams, each marking a sting. I wanted to run and help him, but I realized that there was nothing any of us could do; we would just have become targets ourselves. The attack—and the screaming—lasted for nearly a minute before Dan reached a safe distance from the nest and the swarm retreated. Once it was over, I reeled from spent adrenaline. All of us did.

Anyone who has ever been the victim of a yellow jacket knows the instant, throbbing acid burn of a single sting. In all, Dan had suffered twenty-six stings. The bees had pierced his bare face, arms, and legs and had swarmed inside his shorts and shirt. He was a mass of red, acid-oozing welts, and I realized that if he were allergic to the venom, as many people are, he would die quickly. His breathing tube would swell shut, and he would asphyxiate.

Within minutes Dan had completely regained his calm. He sat quietly on a rock, focusing, pulling himself back together, as Nick, Paul, and I buzzed frantically around him offering to help, though I'm not sure how we could have eased his discomfort. He declined our offers and continued to sit. Within five minutes of the attack, he rose and, unbelievably, started walking back toward the hive.

"I dropped my walking stick," he said.

Dan had found the stick, a twisted, gnarly branch, on Springer Mountain, and he had grown attached to it. I would learn later that he aimed to deposit it, in a private ceremony, on Mount Katahdin, making it a 2,100-mile stick. He crept cautiously to within three feet of the hive, picked up his staff, returned to where we stood, climbed into his pack, and continued up the trail. Meanwhile, the rest of us—stunned—fumbled into our pack straps and followed.

Some days later, I too became a yellow-jacket casualty. Though stung only four times, I cursed and shrieked, wheeled and spun, flailing at unseen adversaries. Afterward, as I stood panting and shaking, I wanted to sit in self-pity and lick my wounds, but, remembering Dan's example, I glanced ahead to the next white blaze and kept on walking.

Nick

We met Nick Gelasko over a vegetarian dinner at the Inn in Hot Springs, North Carolina. The Inn, a restored nineteenth-century resort hotel, had once served an upscale clientele that sought the healing powers of the hot mineral springs located a few blocks away. Though the springs had passed from vogue years earlier, by 1979 the Inn—which featured bountiful vegetarian meals, new age music, and hundreds of books—reigned as a mecca for hungry hikers.

Seated at the round wooden table, Nick wore a khaki shirt bearing an Appalachian Trail patch and a matching pair of khaki pants. He was Sean Connery handsome, with a tanned face, sharp features, bright brown eyes, and, like Connery, a bald pate. Dressed as he was in his khaki uniform and surrounded by an air of confidence and authority, I initially mistook him for a park ranger. Through the meal

Nick assumed the role of table host, drawing out some of the more reluctant hikers and sharing bits of his own stories. I soon detected in him irrepressible charm and charisma.

Over the ensuing summer, those attributes made Nick an endearing sidekick. They also became a secret weapon, one we employed countless times in asking for—and receiving—favored treatment from townsfolk along the way.

Because of his age, at first Nick posed a fatherly threat to some of us younger men who were out on the trail to exert our independence, to find our own way and shed the tethers of adult authority. He had fought in the South Pacific during World War II—our fathers' war—he had raised his children to adulthood, and his attitudes were decidedly conservative. At many of our fireside chats early on, he represented the establishment point of view while we argued in behalf of the new order.

But the trail, along with the social healing brought on by the 1970s, had softened many of Nick's attitudes about the younger generation, just as it had altered our attitudes regarding his. One night near the end of the trail Nick discussed his relationship with his son who had fled to Canada during the Vietnam War rather than face the draft. As a veteran, Nick had initially responded by severing ties with his son and his family, but eventually his love for his son and his increasing sympathy for the young men who had become entangled in the complexities of the conflict changed his thinking, and he and his wife, Gwen, had made a trip to Canada.

As our relationship developed and we became more closely bound by our shared experiences, Nick and the rest of us found common ground on many issues. Soon our age differences were as insignificant as the regions of the country we hailed from.

Nick ultimately became one of my closest friends and companions, a man whom I still admire as much as anyone I've ever known. Whatever courage it took for me—a twenty-three-year-old man—to face the wild, his was greater. Though the body of a fifty-seven-year-old man can't cover the miles at the same clip as men less than half his age, he kept pace with us, never complaining about his ailing knees and feet while many of the rest of us vented our physical woes almost nightly.

As for our secret weapon: Nick was charming, so charming, in fact, that I'm convinced that, given time, he might have persuaded Donald Trump to turn over his casinos, all of his rental properties, all his worldly possessions, all of his lands, and that once the deal was struck, somehow Nick would have left him feeling that he—not Nick—had profited in the transaction. What's more, Nick was confident enough to ask for anything from anybody, and his older, more mature countenance stood him in good stead with local folks, many of whom were distrustful of us younger guys. The combined effect of his charm, chutzpah, and maturity became our ticket to a bounty of special privileges.

The first time I saw Nick work his magic, I ascribed it to luck. Dan and I had arrived at the road crossing where a little-traveled Virginia highway cut the trail, and we had arranged to meet Nick, who was some distance behind, in town. While Dan and I baked in the sun, our thumbs eagerly thrust in the air, car after car inhabited by sour-faced people zoomed by. Some of the drivers were so leery of us that they swerved into the oncoming traffic lane to be sure we didn't leap through the open window and commandeer their vehicles. After we had spent nearly an hour of smiling, waving, and looking as harmless as possible, a huge Buick slowed, swung onto the berm, and stopped. I immediately recognized Nick's tan porkpie hat and grinning face through the windshield of the passenger seat.

"You fellas need a lift?" he asked.

After we loaded our packs into the trunk, Nick introduced us to the driver, a middle-aged man whom he addressed with the familiarity of an old friend. Thoroughly charmed, the man had agreed to drive us into town, to wait while we bought our groceries and washed our clothes at the local laundromat, and then to shuttle us back to the trailhead to resume our hike.

The next time it happened, I began to suspect that there

was more to Nick's good fortune than simple dumb luck. On a similarly isolated stretch of highway a few days farther north, we repeated the same scenario, with Dan and me— thumbs in the air—ruefully watching an armada of cars and trucks roll past. Then a battered flatbed swung off the road and stopped, and a familiar, grinning face topped with a porkpie hat poked from the passenger's window.

"Come on over," Nick called through the window. "I'd like for you guys to meet my friend, Martin, who's been kind enough to give us a lift into town."

From then on, in a slightly skewed version of the old hitchhiker's ruse in which the alluring blonde flags down a lift while her male friend hides in the bushes, Nick acted as our front man. He stood prominently on the highway while Dan and I lingered just out of sight until Nick called us over to meet our chauffeur. Once we got to town, we loaded our packs at the local store, and Dan and I sat on the store stoop while our envoy roved through the store lot, scanning the parked cars for those that offered ample room for three hikers and their packs. Then he waited. When the owners arrived, he launched into his routine, which went some-thing like this:

"Good afternoon (morning, evening), ma'am (sir, young man, young lady), my name is Nick, and I'm out hiking the Appalachian Trail. I just want you to know that my buddies and I sure are enjoying the scenery around (town name here). In fact, it's some of the most beautiful country we've seen so far, and the people sure are friendly. Hey, by the way, we're trying to find a way back up (highway name and number here) to the trail junction so we can continue our hike. Would you know of anyone around here who might be willing, say, to earn a few extra bucks by giving us a lift?"

More often than not, the first contact would assent, but if not the first, always the second. Soon Nick would motion us over to meet his new friend. Often, en route, the drivers handed us a couple of cold beers, a bag of chicken legs, or a ham sandwich, and in spite of Nick's offer to pay for the lift, few of them accepted our money. They were just happy to help us out.

After weeks of practice Nick became thoroughly proficient at procuring food, drink, and transportation from strangers, yet we exhausted our vocabularies in searching for a word to describe what he did. It really wasn't "scamming." Sure, Nick sometimes exaggerated the direness of our circumstances by insisting that we were "bone weary" or by claiming that our hunger or misery was so abject that we might perish if we didn't get to town soon. But he never knowingly deceived anyone, and he never attempted to force anyone to help us. In some ways I think the donors benefited from their contact with us, particularly the drivers, who often seemed hungry for company and welcomed our companionship. And everyone enjoyed our trail stories. But still, what to call Nick's magical process? Finally, after weeks of searching we fixed on a term for Nick's natural aptitude: *Geleskoing*, derived from his last name.

Gelesko-ing: the use of tact and persuasion by Appalachian Trail hikers to influence local townsfolk to provide goods and services free of charge.

We applied the word in the following ways:

"Where did you get that sandwich?"

"I *Geleskoed* it from some picnickers a few miles back on the trail."

"How did you get into town?"

"I *Geleskoed* a ride from a nice couple returning from church."

"Where did you stay last night?"

"I *Geleskoed* a family into letting me stay in their guest bedroom."

Among Nick's most notable coups, I count the following: We were staying the night in a ski lodge on Sugarloaf Mountain in central Maine. The lodge, a circular structure with a massive central fireplace and walls of windows looking out on the surrounding peaks, was abandoned but had been left open as a refuge to hikers. We laid our bags out on the wooden benches surrounding the fireplace and stoked the flames from the ample pile of firewood provided by the caretaker.

Midafternoon, I heard a clang, then the clattering of

gears, and ran to one of the windows. I turned to the lift cables, which had sat idle since we had arrived in the early afternoon, just in time to see Nick's hat through the rear window of a gondola descending toward the mountain's base. Where was he going? He had left without giving us a clue. It turned out that the caretaker, who just happened to be in the lodge, had been Geleskoed into operating the lift in spite of dangerous winds. Before we could probe him for information regarding Nick's mission, he had left the lodge and begun hiking down the mountain.

Several hours passed, and the winds increased. At one point, the wind howled so fiercely that when I stepped outside to dump a pot of dishwater, the wind ripped the pot from my hand and threw the water back in my face with such force that it stung.

More time passed. Still no sign of Nick. Just before dusk, I heard the gears grind into motion, and far down the mountain I could see a red gondola ascending the cable. The car bucked and swayed like a carnival ride run amok, and when it neared each of the towers that supported the lines, it stopped. Inside, I could see Nick, swinging back and forth, captive in the round red pendulum. He would swing left, toward the tower, then as he swung right, away from the obstacle, the motor would again engage, and the car would advance, each time barely missing the tower on its backswing. The process was repeated at each of the half-dozen towers, and the lift operator at the base of the mountain would gauge the rhythm of the swinging car as he rocked it past the tower. At last the car entered the gondola shed, the engine stopped, and Nick emerged carrying two grocery bags.

One of the bags contained three half-gallons of ice cream. The other contained several bags of cookies and a bottle of wine. It turned out that Nick had made his tempest-tossed voyage in search of sweets, and as we all attacked the bounty of confections, he explained his adventure.

Struck by an irrepressible craving for sugar, Nick had consulted his map. Noting that the road at the base of the mountain led into Stratton, he had approached the caretaker (who also served as the lift operator) for a ride to the bottom. When the caretaker refused, explaining that the wind conditions made it unsafe to operate the lift, Nick persisted. Finally, the caretaker agreed to send Nick down the mountain. Once at the base, Nick had persuaded—Geleskoed, rather—some kindly local folks into giving him a lift to the grocery store. After cleaning out the ice-cream freezer at the store, he had persuaded another kindly local to give him a lift back to the gondola. Then, after waiting futilely for a full hour for the winds to calm, he had cajoled the lift operator, who by now had returned to the base, into giving him a ride back to the top. As a result of his expedition, Nick may well rank as the only Appalachian Trail hiker ever to risk death for a few half-gallons of Breyer's vanilla ice cream.

Then there was the night in Rangeley, Maine.

We arrived in Rangeley on September 6, driven from the woods by the tail end of Hurricane David, which whipped the surface of Lake Rangely into a froth of rolling white caps. Rangeley is a quiet New England resort town set on the shores of the lake and cluttered with quaint shops and restaurants competing for the tourist trade.

In several towns along the trail, local churches had opened their doors to hikers, providing them a place to sleep for the night. According to the scuttlebutt on the trail, a Protestant church in Rangeley was one such place. We had made our requisite stop at the local grocery store and, after scampering along rain-drenched streets, found our way to the church just after dark.

Once inside, we made ourselves at home in the recreation room, which featured a full kitchen and a number of banquet tables. We soon commenced the ritualistic food binge that accompanied our arrivals in town by preparing heaping root beer floats. Nick had wandered into the sanctuary and had found a Bible, and as we sat slurping our floats, he began flipping through it, looking for familiar passages. Soon we were engaged in a discussion of Christian ethics and the role of Christ as teacher and provider, which inspired us to give thanks for having such a snug refuge from the storm.

Though we frequently discussed religious philosophy, we didn't often discuss the specific tenets of Christianity. But this night the topic was Christ: His resurrection, the redemption He offered the world's sinners. Christian love, we determined, whether the doctrine behind it was or was not the only way to salvation, was a beautiful force at work in the world. After all, we agreed, though the congregation of this church did not know us, they had opened their doors to us.

At 8:00 P.M., our discussion of Christian love was brought to an abrupt halt when the church caretaker arrived and, explaining that hikers were no longer welcome to stay in the church, threw us out into the bleak, cold night.

We made our way from the sanctuary into the gutter, arriving some minutes later at Doc Grant's, a local watering hole perhaps best known for its alleged location precisely halfway between the equator and the North Pole. The placemats at the bar depict a map bisected by a line. In the upper half is a sketch of an Eskimo clad in mukluks and a fur coat. In the lower half is a rendering of a hula girl in grass skirt.

We sidled up to the bar, ordered a round of cold beers, and watched reruns of the "Andy Griffith Show." Meanwhile, we had no notion of where we might be sleeping that night. The hotels in town were decidedly upscale and priced beyond our budgets, and the hurricane had made conditions outdoors insufferable. Our tents would have been ripped to tatters by the wind and rain. We had asked—begged really—a place to stay from every patron at the bar but received no firm offers. On our march from the church to the bar, we had noticed a theater marquee sheltered by a large overhang and decided that, if worse came to worst, we could always sleep there. For the first time on our trek, we were plum out of tricks. Or so we thought. That's when Nick went to work.

While the rest of us sat at the bar, Nick got a few dollars' worth of quarters and a phone book and walked over to the pay phone. First he called the local hotels. It was prime tourist season, and there were no available rooms. Then he called all the local churches. Still no luck. After learning the names of the town's elected officials from the barkeep, he called the mayor. Even he balked. Then Nick called the chief of police and finally struck pay dirt. Smiling, he rejoined us at the bar.

"Our ride will be here in five minutes," he said, returning to his beer. And so it was. In a few minutes the chief of police, clad in a rain slicker, entered the bar, asked for Nick, introduced himself, and ushered us out of the bar into a waiting cruiser. We soon arrived at the police station, our home for the night. It was the first and only night I've spent in jail, and I couldn't have been happier.

Only once did I see Gelesko's charm fail. We had arrived at Farmers Mills Shelter, set two hundred feet off a back road near Stormville, New York. The shelter, our scheduled destination for the night, turned out to be a fetid, cinder-block hovel surrounded by heaps of trash and a mosquito-infested swamp. Gelesko took one look at it and decreed that he wasn't about to sleep there. Soon he moved on up the country road to make other arrangements. With the rest of us in tow, he approached a nearby house that boasted a large garage and knocked at the door. When a middle-aged woman cracked open the door, he began his pitch.

"Good afternoon, ma'am. My name is Nick Gelesko, and a few buddies and I are hiking the Appalachian Trail."

"Yes?" she asked suspiciously.

"Well, it's been so darned hot the past few days, and that shelter up the road is really a mess, you know, with trash and mosquitoes, and I was wondering if you know of anyone around here who might have, well, say, a *garage* where we might roll out our bags and sleep the night."

At that point, Nick, having emphasized the word *garage*, turned and casually glanced at its counterpart around the corner of the house.

"Sure don't," the woman answered without hesitating.

Undaunted, Nick continued. "You know, a *garage* or some place we could lay out our bags? We sure would be grateful."

"No, I'm sorry."

"You know, if someone were to have a *garage*, we'd be more than happy to do a little cleaning up to help pay for the kindness . . ."

The three of us stood within ear shot, and, frankly, we couldn't believe what we were hearing. Was it actually possible for someone—anyone—to resist being Geleskoed by Gelesko himself? Gradually the woman began to soften.

"Well, I can't let you stay in my garage because my husband's out of town, and he wouldn't approve. But there's a young guy up the road who lives in a barn, and he might take you in."

On her advice, we pushed up the road until we arrived at a red barn that had been converted to a suitable, though drafty, residence. Nick knocked at the door, and a young man answered. In less than a minute, Nick waved us all toward the door. His magic was back. He introduced us to our host for the night, and soon we were upstairs, sipping cold beers and flipping through the man's record supply, blissed out on rock 'n' roll music.

Paul

When we encountered twenty-year-old New Hampshire native Paul Dillon in Pennsylvania, he was making his third attempt on the Appalachian Trail. Paul had begun the trail at Springer Mountain in 1976, reaching as far north as the Cumberland Gap in Pennsylvania. He set out on the trail again in 1978 and reached as far as the Blue Ridge Parkway in Virginia. He returned to the trail in 1979, starting his hike where he had left off in Pennsylvania, and Dan and I met him just north of Port Clinton. As it turned out, the encounter would benefit all of us.

Dan and I had suffered our first major battle of wills a few days earlier over the planned sixteen-mile day that evolved into a twenty-seven-mile marathon, and though we were speaking to one another, our relationship lacked any semblance of brotherly affection. Paul's inclusion in the group immediately eased the tension between us. At the same time we offered Paul the two things he seemed to need most. First was companionship. He had mistimed his first and second ventures on the trail and had missed the mass of northbound thru-hikers. After spending days and nights alone, he had decided to leave the trail. The second thing we offered Paul was Dan's knack for organization and goal setting, which would impose a schedule on Paul and the rest of us and would guarantee to lead us to the summit of Katahdin by summer's end.

Despite his thwarted attempts on the trail, Paul possessed an aptitude for wilderness travel. While Dan and Nick tended at times to muscle their way along, confronting obstacles with will and determination, Paul seemed inclined to abide by whatever nature threw his way and to try to make the best of it. As far as Paul was concerned, whatever we encountered along the trail was okay, as long as he was able to glean some significance from it. For Paul, miles did not measure linear distance so much as they traced units of experience. Paul sought the sadness, the happiness, the beauty, the wisdom lurking in the wilderness, and he translated those things into the verses and songs he composed along the way. While the rest of us orally recounted the highlights of our days as we sat around campfires, Paul was often inclined to apply his thoughts to paper and, once finished, to share them in the group.

Paul had carried his penchant for poetry so far as to have had a friend embroider a verse onto the front flap of his green nylon framepack. The verse, taken from *On the Loose,* Jerry and Renny Russell's book on adventure and the environment, reads:

> So why do we do it?
> What good is it?
> Does it teach you anything?
> Like determination?
> Invention?
> Improvisation?
> Foresight?
> Hindsight?

Love?
Art?
Music?
Religion?
Strength or patience or accuracy or quickness or tolerance
or which wood will burn and how long is a day and how far is
a mile and how delicious is water and smoky green pea
soup?
And how to rely on yourself?

The verse embraced the essence of the trail quest, but
more than that, it captured the grace and rhythm that
seemed to govern everything Paul did, whether writing a
poem or traversing a ridge.

I will forever picture Paul ambling along the trail, smiling
and shirtless, his lanky, six-foot-one-inch frame clad only in
blue corduroy Ocean Pacific shorts, knee-high gaiters,
socks, and boots, and with his shoulder-length brown hair
bound by a red bandana tied pirate-style.

A former competitive downhill skier and college tennis
player, Paul had been an accomplished athlete long before
taking up the trail. Though he was lean, his strength and
endurance powered him past most other thru-hikers on
long ascents, and his physical poise and skier's balance allowed him to dance effortlessly down steep, rock-strewn descents where most hikers crept cautiously along.

I didn't fully appreciate just how graceful Paul was on his
feet until we reached the White Mountains in New
Hampshire, where the open, treeless ridges allowed us to
glimpse other hikers from miles away. On the afternoon
that Dan and I arrived at Lakes of the Clouds Hut, nestled
below the summit of Mount Washington, we dumped our
packs and climbed to the top of Mount Monroe, a secondary
peak a few hundred yards from the hut.

From our perch a couple of hundred feet above the trail,
we watched hikers wend their way along the rocky path
heading north. As practitioners of the art of walking, we
had developed a habit of evaluating the style of other foot
travelers. Among those we scrutinized that day, some
cullumphed along like human jackhammers, assaulting the

trail with their heavy footfalls. Others surged ahead like jack rabbits, stopping to rest at two hundred-yard intervals before surging ahead again. A few labored painfully along like arthritic octogenarians, pausing after each step to peer ahead, hoping to glimpse the hut and the termination of their misery. After watching them pass, Dan and I fixed on a lone hiker who, unlike the others, eased effortlessly across the open ridge.

"Look at that guy move," Dan said, pointing.

"God, he's graceful," I said. And he was. Every step, every aspect of his stride, from the bend of his knees to the pivot of his torso to the plant of his walking stick, was as fluid as a brook coursing its way between and over the boulders of a streambed.

It wasn't until he neared the base of the mountain that we recognized the familiar green backpack and red bandana as belonging to our own poet laureate, Paul.

CHAPTER • FIVE

Linear Community

> *Whatever concerns I had about this trail lacking human companionship were resolved this evening. There are nineteen hikers and two dogs wedged into the shelter. Further cramping our space are hikers' packs and foodbags, which hang like ripe fruit from the rafters—to keep them from the mice, rats, and skunks who also call this place home. There are hikers here from Indiana, Illinois, Ohio, Tennessee, North Carolina, Massachusetts, Virginia, and Georgia, and though we all have different backgrounds and come from different parts of the country, we are unified by our shared love for the wilderness. Here are nineteen strangers existing so peaceably, sharing food, thoughts, equipment, and trail tips under conditions that would pitch most city dwellers into panic. What is it about our society that inhibits such wonderful—and spontaneous—acceptance and sense of community?*
> *—May 6, 1979, Russell Field Shelter, Great Smoky Mountains National Park*

Many people envision the Appalachian Trail as a remote, isolated wilderness path where hikers pass days—even weeks—in utter solitude and with no access to roads or towns for supplies and companionship.

Even some novice trail hikers maintain such a skewed vision of the trail. A pair of would-be thru-hikers I met near Springer Mountain in 1987, for instance, believed that once a person had set out on the trail, there was no means of egress and that the hiker was committed to traveling at least as far as Harpers Ferry, nearly one thousand miles north, before he could bail out or acquire fresh supplies. As a result, the two wretched souls carried nearly one hundred pounds of gear each, including extra boots and a two-month supply of food.

I'll acknowledge that the image of a hiker confronting the eastern wilds alone is romantic. Perhaps the trail's pioneers, including Earl Shafer, who logged the first end-to-end hike in 1948, did experience such isolation. By 1979 the trail attracted dozens of hopeful thru-hikers and thousands of "weekenders" or "short-timers" who visited the trail for one- or two-day hikes. According to Appalachian Trail Conference statistics, as many as four million people visit the trail each year.

No, the Appalachian Trail was not a lonely place. On the contrary, Dan and I passed few days without encountering at least one other person on the trail. In the more popular sections—through national parks—we often met and talked with dozens of people. For those who sought isolation, the trail's human population may have been a disappointment, but for others—most hikers, really—the thriving backcountry society only enhanced the experience. Any hiker who has spent weeks along the route knows that the real story of the Appalachian Trail is found among the people who walk it.

The social quality of the trail inspired Nancy Sills, wife of Normal Sills, a Connecticut native who thru-hiked the trail in 1985, to dub the trail a linear community, and of all the descriptions applied to the trail, I find hers most fitting. My experience is that if the trail was a community, it was a community predicated on trust, fellowship, and sharing— values that too often seem lacking in the more "civilized" society we had left behind.

During our days of hiking through the Smokies—the

most heavily used national park in the country—we met dozens of other hikers. Many, like us, were thru-hikers bound for Maine, but there were also many day-hikers and weekend backpackers. On the night we slept in Russell Field Shelter, tucked in a hardwood grove seventeen miles south of Clingman's Dome, the highest point on the trail, as daylight waned, hikers continued to arrive at the shelter until nineteen people and two dogs occupied a space designed to accommodate twelve. Among them was a woman who lived in a tepee in Massachusetts; another woman and her bearded boyfriend, both from North Carolina, who had packed in a glass bottle of tequila; two college students from Dayton, Ohio; and others who hailed from Indiana, Georgia, Virginia, and Illinois.

Because of the cramped conditions, late-comers, and the two dogs, slept on the floor. Once all of us and our gear were ensconced inside, the nineteen packs and accompanying foodbags—of orange, blue, red, maroon, turquoise, and brown nylon—hung like ripe fruit from the shelter's rafters.

That night chatter filled the shelter as hikers swapped backpacking tips, compared equipment, and talked of faraway home towns. For me it marked the first time I had experienced the communion shared among hikers in the backcountry. It did not matter who you were, where you were from, or how much you were worth. If you were a backpacker, you were okay.

The rigors of life on the trail tended to screen out most undesirables, while those same rigors tended to unify those of us who were tough and committed enough to forge on. We climbed the same mountains; we plodded through the same rainstorms; we suffered the same aches and pains as our bodies adapted to the physical challenge of fifteen- to twenty-mile days. We drank from the same springs; we stopped at the same towns to resupply; we experienced the same insatiable hunger—which I termed "hiker's disease"—as our bodies metabolized as many as six thousand calories a day. We carried the same equipment; we swatted the same mosquitoes; and we slept in the same three-sided, rough-hewn shelters. We shared the same quest.

We learned to depend on one another. If a hiker failed to arrive in camp by nightfall, we mounted a search party and set out with our flashlights. The night we camped at Ice Water Springs, four miles north of Newfound Gap, the midway point of the Smokies, a hiker in the shelter expressed concern that his companion had not yet arrived in camp a half-hour after dark. Though beautiful by day, the Smokies posed certain hazards by night, among them bears and the roving bands of three-hundred-pound wild boars that use their formidable tusks to scavenge for food after dark. We organized a search party, left the security of the fence-enclosed shelter, and followed our flashlight beams into the darkness. As I pushed up the trail past the darkened groves of hardwoods, a line from Robert Frost's poem "Stopping by Woods" kept tumbling through my mind: "The woods are lovely, dark and deep . . . ." And they were. Every sound and shadow teased my imagination. Rocks wore faces, tree trunks sheltered gnomes, branches shivered and squeaked.

Within a half mile, I detected a beam of light sweeping the trail ahead and realized that we had found our lost hiker. He had taken a wrong turn at a trail junction a few tenths of a mile back and had followed it a couple of miles before realizing his mistake. He was relieved to see us, and his gratitude was our reward. I knew, without really knowing much about him except that he was a backpacker, that he would have done the same for me.

In a similar way, if someone ran short of food, we delved into our food bags and shared what surplus we had. Within minutes the famished hiker would find himself stationed before a mountain of Ziploc bags of rice and noodles. And if someone turned an ankle and twisted a knee, we carried some of the weight from his pack until his injury healed. Victor, an upbeat man in his early twenties from North Hampton, Massachusetts, who had linked up with Dan and me in Georgia, pulled a calf muscle the day we entered the Smokies. As we moved north and Victor's limp became more and more conspicuous, we volunteered to carry some of his weight. When he refused, we insisted. Unfortunately, it was not enough, and Victor then wrestled with the decision to abandon the trail.

When Victor seemed to have reached his limit, we encouraged him to plod on, and, in spite of his injury, he continued on to Hot Springs, North Carolina, thirty-five miles north of the Smokies. Realizing that if he continued, he would just slow us down, he bought a bus ticket home. When he departed the trail, we embraced him and wished him well, and for days afterward we felt that an important part of our family was absent. The separation proved to be only temporary, however. Months later when we entered New England, Victor rejoined us for weekends and joined us for the final 120 miles of the trail.

Though most hikers shared the same experiences, we were all different in terms of ages, backgrounds, and regions of the country. On one night at Muskrat Creek Shelter three miles beyond the North Carolina–Georgia line, I shared the shelter with a sixty-five-year-old mathematics professor from Ottawa, who had navigated a mountain bike loaded with bulging panniers to the shelter; a seventy-two-year-old retired army sergeant and veteran of World War II and Korea; two tattooed heavy-metal mavens in their early twenties from northern Kentucky; and a clean-cut twenty-six-year-old butcher from Washington, D.C. It occurred to me that if we had met under any other circumstances, we probably would not have had much to talk about. We had all arrived at the A-frame shelter after walking through a driving thunderstorm, and, although we were virtual strangers, we spent the evening packed under a ten-by-twelve-foot roof, discussing religion, philosophy, and our personal reasons for being on the trail, while swapping samples from our cook pots. At bedtime we slithered into our sleeping bags in the dank shelter illuminated by a single candle, and as the rain peppered the roof, someone told a joke, then another, and another. For more than an hour we lay awake listening and laughing together. The barriers of age, education, and social status couldn't have mattered less.

A couple of hundred miles farther north, at Cherry Gap

Shelter, a day's hike south of Roan Mountain in the north-eastern corner of Tennessee, we had a similar experience. It was May 24. We had been on the trail for just over a month, and the continuing warming of spring had inspired Dan and me to ship our woolens, gloves, and heavy sweaters home from Erwin, believing that we had suffered winter's last blast. We were mistaken.

Dan and I began shivering soon after we arrived in camp that afternoon. The temperatures during the day had lingered in the sixties and seventies—too warm to induce shivering—and so we ascribed our chills to the flu-like effects of bad water. By dusk, however, we realized that the air temperature had dropped more than thirty degrees. The next morning we awoke to two inches of snow. It blanketed the ground and bowed the trees, now in full summer foliage. As we prepared to leave the shelter, a combination of snow and sleet began to fall, and we abandoned our travel plans for the day. We spent the morning hours drinking herbal tea and reading, and by noon the first of our benumbed colleagues began to arrive. Some of them had slept under ponchos through the night's storm. By midafternoon eleven hikers were wedged into a shelter designed to sleep six, and only by alternating head to foot could we squeeze everyone in.

Nestled in our sleeping bags, we read our books, wrote in our journals, munched surplus food, or stared out into the icy woods. Someone passed around a plastic bottle filled with Jack Daniel's, and by dusk we were one very happy family. Through the evening hours we sang verses of a blues song, creating new verses as we progressed, and joking about the wicked weather, the flatulence that resulted from our heavy dietary regimen of legumes, our ailing feet, or the wild stench that rose from eleven filthy, pressure-packed bodies. What had the makings for a bad scene still endures among my most cherished memories of the trail. It was a prime example of making do with what nature throws your way and finding contentment in companionship and simple pleasures.

If there was any sense of isolation from being on the trail

for months at a time, it was isolation from world and national news. We spent from three to ten days at a stretch between resupply trips to town. We didn't carry radios, and during our stopovers we rarely picked up newspapers. Frankly, there wasn't much going on in the world that interested us. The big news during the summer of 1979, for instance, was the gas shortage and the fuel rationing programs in effect in major cities. We heard stories about escalating gas prices, long lines at the pump, and the occasional shooting that resulted when someone edged his way into line. To us, the gas crunch meant only one thing: by the end of the summer it cost us eight, rather than six, cents to fill our fuel bottles.

Much more important to us was the latest trail news. We gleaned most of this news from the spiral notebooks left in many of the trail shelters. On these pages hikers signed in, mentioned the highlights or low points of their days, described the weather, listed the other hikers in their parties, drew caricatures of themselves, and sometimes waxed philosophical about the vicissitudes of life on the trail.

Through the summer, we followed the exploits of other thru-hikers: Otel (who, according to rumor, sometimes hiked in the buff) and his dog A.T.; Al and Moonie, a couple of good-natured cutups from New Jersey; the Phillips brothers, Paul and Robin, two siblings from Florida, who packed heavy photographic equipment; Woodstock and Nancy and Phil and Cindy, two of the trail's few man–woman teams; Byron and Jimmy—Byron, who had a ready joke for every occasion and who eventually lost his pack to a trailside thief, and Jimmy, who, we heard, recorded humorous and bawdy trail tales in the registers. On later trips to the trail I followed Sunshine and Daydream, a newlywed couple from Connecticut; Captain Kangaroo, an Australian hiker who became a friend; Pigpen, an accountant from Boston who refused to bathe; the Bluegrass Boys, a trio of hikers from northern Kentucky.

Through register entries, we came to know each of the hikers who plodded along anywhere from a few hours to days and weeks ahead of us before we even met them. We learned of their likes and dislikes, the types of food that filled their bellies, their struggles, their triumphs, the professions they had left to hike the trail, and even what they looked like, the styles of packs they carried, and what they wore. When we caught up with them, we could call them by name before they had a chance to introduce themselves, just as the hikers behind us would often come into camp and without hesitation announce, "You must be Dan and Dave. I've been on your heels for two weeks."

We often used the registers to communicate messages to those behind us, urging them to hustle to catch us for a beer bash or a megafeed at a town stop or telling them, sadly, when someone in our party had reached his limit and had gone home. At times the efficiency of our primitive communications network amazed us. Near the end of June, for instance, Dan and I approached Harpers Ferry, West Virginia, headquarters for the Appalachian Trail Conference and the unofficial halfway point. As we progressed north, we left a series of entries inviting other thru-hikers to hitchhike the fifty miles from Harpers Ferry into Washington, D.C., for the Fourth of July celebration on the Mall. We planned to meet at noon at the Jefferson Memorial.

By noon on the fourth, nearly a dozen hikers—many of whom we had never met—straggled to the memorial. We spent the afternoon swapping trail stories and enjoying the bounty of junk food available from sidewalk vendors.

Southbounders on the trail—those who had begun their hike in Maine rather than Georgia—became another source of trail news. When we encountered them, we often slipped from our packs and shared a bag of trail mix while we exchanged data. Our news was as vital to them as theirs was to us; each could provide the other with information about what lay ahead: the friendliest towns, the cheapest hotels and restaurants, the most taxing ascents and descents, the locations of reliable water sources.

Through the summer we leapfrogged with dozens of other northbounders who had left Springer about the same time we had. Among them were the Phillips brothers, Jeff Hammons from Kansas, Tennessee native Gary Owens, and

Mark Gornick from Maryland. We would link up with them for several days, or even weeks, losing them after we or they had stopped for an extended stay in one place. Two or three months later, we would catch them at a shelter farther north and spend hours around the campfire detailing the important events of our lives and discussing how we had changed.

In terms of our appearance, the changes were obvious. One night in Maine I rejoined Al, a solitary hiker from New York, whom we had last seen in Hot Springs, North Carolina. Al had adopted a mongrel dog he had found near Wayah Bald in North Carolina and had named the animal Wayah. Wayah had contracted a bad case of mange, and as Dan and I left Hot Springs, Wayah—completely bereft of fur—lay wheezing in the grass. Both Dan and I wrote her off as a lost cause.

Yet some four months later, Al and Wayah, the latter sporting a luxurious new coat of fur, entered camp. We laughed at Wayah's changed appearance, and Al laughed at ours. Al, who had started the hike with a billowy beard, really hadn't changed much, but we had. I had started the trail with a haircut, a clean-shaven face, ten pounds of unwanted fat, and a crisp new hiking outfit. I had long ago surrendered my threadbare khakis and now wore a pair of tattered fatigue trousers with holes in the knees and seat. My beard had grown to three inches, and I had hardened, having lost ten pounds.

Although the trail provided an ample measure of male companionship, during my five months in the wilderness, I suffered a pestering hunger for the physical affection of a woman. Along the trail, when virtually all of one's sensibilities became attuned to sensual cues and when one spent his days surrounded by beauty, peace, and harmony, it seemed natural to hunger for touch and to surrender, like all of nature's creatures, to the attraction of members of the opposite sex. The problem was that the pickings were slim.

Though the ratio of men to women is becoming more balanced each year, in 1979 we met fewer than ten women who aspired to complete the trail. If we did want to meet women, it seemed, we would have to create them in our own imaginations, which we often did. One night over a few ounces of bourbon by a campfire, Dan and I created mythological Venuses we dubbed the "Scandinavian hiking queens." In our minds they were beautiful, lithesome women who would love us, share our experiences, and provide feminine companionship. They became the object of our hormone-inspired quest, although neither one of us ever imagined we actually would encounter them in the flesh. Against the odds, in the White Mountains of New Hampshire I met a woman who more than matched my fantasy.

The White Mountains, for all their stark, alpine beauty, also tend to attract throngs of hiking enthusiasts, which for us created nightly contests for shelter space. On August 29 we had left Garfield Ridge Campsite and in a cold New England rain pushed on toward Ethan Pond, a campsite that included a six-man shelter and several tent platforms. Though none of us wanted to acknowledge concern over finding shelter space for the night—to have done so would have smacked of the competitiveness we had shunned in greater society—the rain inspired a quickening of our pace, and each of us discreetly counted heads and jockeyed for position over the last few miles to the pond lest we be left out in the rain.

By that stage of the trip, my rain fly, which had served as a groundsheet as often as a shelter, bore visible holes and admitted almost as much rain as it repelled. I didn't want to suffer a cold, clammy night beneath it.

When we arrived at Ethan Pond Campsite, we encountered six sullen faces peering out of the shelter into the rain. Dan managed to secure a space in the shelter after persuading a reluctant weekender to shift his body, along with his staggering assemblage of gear, over a few inches. If the shelter had been full of thru-hikers, I have no doubt they would have accommodated me too, but weekenders were notoriously protective of their personal space, and there clearly was no room for me.

I walked out to the tent platform, a ten-by-ten-foot elevated square of rain-soaked wooden slats, and began erecting my pitiful shelter. The task proved counterproductive in the rain, so I decided to wait and see if the rain would quit and walked back to dump my pack under the shelter's eaves. A while later, feeling crowded, I left the shelter and returned to the tent platform, somewhat reconciled to the notion that it would be my home for the night. Nearby, I noticed a large olive-drab tent mounted on another platform.

Just outside the tent, I met its occupant, a friendly, long-legged woman with brown hair topped by a blue wool watch cap. I eyed her ample shelter, and without presuming to ask if there was room inside for an extra boarder, I began complaining about my leaky digs for the night. Sensing my misery, she asked me to join her for a cup of hot tea inside the tent.

A large gas stove had heated the tent to a comfortable seventy degrees, and a steaming kettle sat on the burner. From it she poured two cups of herbal tea, and, as we sipped our drinks, we talked about her frequent trips to the White Mountains and about my experiences along the trail. She was a bright, cheerful woman whose knowledge of the wilderness amazed me. At dusk I rose to leave, but she seemed to sense my reluctance and asked if I'd like to stay the night in her tent. Without hesitating, I accepted her offer.

After we had finished our dinners, we sat close to a candle, and she showed me clippings from many of the edible plants that grew in the area: wood sorrel, a tart, tri-leaved plant that resembles clover and provides vitamin C; reindeer moss, a fungus of light green skeletal tines that boasts a musky mushroom flavor; and Labrador tea leaves, taken from a low-growing evergreen heath, which she steeped in boiling water and served to me with honey.

As we sat close over the candle, I wanted to move closer, to smell her hair, to kiss her. I wanted to hold her, not necessarily make love to her, but just hold her. For all of its gifts, the trail deprived us of that one thing—touch—which I believe we all craved. As we prepared to climb into our bags, I gently touched her back, and she drew away from me. I apologized and backed away, explaining how lonely for affection I had grown over the past few months and how much I enjoyed her company.

Moments later, with the candle out, I heard her slip from her clothes and enter her bag. I, too, lay naked in mine. Then I felt her hand reach for mine, and for an hour we lay silent, just stroking one another's hands. I reached over and kissed her, and she took me in her arms, kissing me back. Soon, we had rearranged our bags, laying one on the tent floor and covering ourselves with the other. We kissed and embraced through the night, sleeping and awakening in each other's arms, never making love but succumbing to blissful, innocent intimacy.

Near dawn she suggested that we walk outside to experience the cold rain against our skin, then return to the warmth of our sleeping bags. We did, and we ran naked and barefoot through the rain along the trail. Back in the tent, we climbed under our sleeping bags, still warm from when we had left them, and fell asleep. Soon, in spite of my desire to prolong the night forever, it was morning.

Over breakfast, she asked me if I would like some company for the morning hike. Yes, I told her, and in a dramatic overture that might have been lifted from a grade-B romance movie, I suggested that she accompany me to Katahdin. She hugged me, laughing at the suggestion. Once I realized how ridiculous it must have sounded, I laughed, too. I realized I was falling in love; *all* relationships, it seems, develop rapidly in the rarefied environment of the trail.

Together, we left Ethan Pond and descended into Crawford Notch. As we began the long, three-mile ascent to the Presidential Range, the sun emerged and the temperature rose. Midway up the climb, she stopped me and asked if I would be offended if she hiked topless, explaining that she didn't want to sweat in her last clean T-shirt. I hiked shirtless, so it seemed natural for her to do the same.

Besides, how could I pass up a chance to view her beautiful body in the daylight? She pulled her shirt off and slipped back into her pack, and we continued up the trail.

From time to time, as we ascended, I glanced back at her and admired her perfect, full breasts moving sensuously with her stride. I was struck by how her natural beauty complemented that of the wilderness.

As we neared the ridge, I spotted one of my fellow hikers, a quiet, contemplative Connecticut native whose face displayed little emotion, that is, until the day he caught a glimpse of a beautiful, topless woman bounding up the trail. The hiker, who sat on a rock munching trail mix, looked up, spotted me, nodded a silent hello, and returned his glance to the bag of trail mix on his lap. When his glance rose again, my hiking partner had come into view, and his eyes beamed like duel harvest moons. As we passed, the hiker, always a man of few words, was stunned totally speechless.

My friend left me at the Mizpah Hut, six miles short of Lakes of the Clouds Hut, our destination for the day. For the rest of the trip, I replayed our night together often in my mind as I walked alone through the woods, and I savor the memory even now. As it was, it was a perfect union of two free-spirited souls—a man and a woman—both searching for some meaning in the eastern wilderness and finding unexpected intimacy. If it had lasted longer, it might have lost some of its intensity. If it had not lasted as long, I would have regretted every second that was lost.

When I think of her, I think of a line from Whitman's "I Sing the Body Electric":

I have perceived that to be with those I like is enough,
To stop in company with the rest at evening is enough,
To be surrounded by beautiful, curious, breathing, laughing flesh is enough. . . .

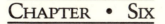

CHAPTER · SIX

Bad Company

We had our first encounter with lowlifes last night at Roan Highlands Shelter. A couple of gun-toting hoodlums in leather jackets and a drunken woman had hiked the half-mile from the road, and they commandeered the shelter for their private party. Only the Phillips brothers were bold enough to demand space inside. The rest of us were content to sleep in our tents.

A couple of weeks ago we heard a hiker tell a story about being abducted at a road crossing by some locals in a pickup truck. Apparently, they demanded that he help them rob other people or that he would himself become their victim. He was able to escape when the truck stopped at a backwoods road junction, as a car just happened to pass. He leaped from the truck, grabbed his pack, and ran into the woods. They searched for him for a few minutes, and he escaped unharmed. We've also heard stories from other hikers about moonshiners at backwoods road crossings who offer to sell them hooch. Seems that such encounters take place where roads intrude into the wilderness. Not much good results when their world and ours collide. Even in the face of such risk, I feel much safer out here on the trail than I would in any major city.
—May 26, 1979, Roan Highlands Shelter, Tennessee

It was a Sunday evening in the early spring 1987, and I shared Addis Gap Shelter in Georgia with a married couple, Kit and Candy, and their pit bull, A.T.

As we arrived at camp, the sun dipped behind the ridge. We quickly unrolled our bags and dressed in our camp clothes, ready to settle in for the night and enjoy the tranquil setting that had once been the site of the Addis family homestead. A grove of Carolina silver-bell trees sprinkled the ground with delicate white blossoms shaken free by the breeze. The slanting rays of the sun traced long shadows across the clearing, and a small brook sluiced away from the shelter down a hillside. Amid all the beauty, however, there was one unsettling feature: a gravel forest service road that wound up the mountain came within a few hundred feet of the shelter.

Most hikers have learned to apply the following postulate to their wilderness wanderings: the quality of people increases in proportion to the distance from the nearest road and the difficulty of the terrain. In other words, the bad guys don't have the gumption or stamina to hump heavy packs into the heart of the backcountry.

Service roads linked the backcountry with the outer world and invited intrusion, and occasionally they attracted an often belligerent corps of locals who drove their fat-tired 4X4s up into the mountains to fire their guns, drink beer, and sometimes harass foot travelers. Often such backwoods crossings were choked with discarded trash, littered with spent shotgun shells and empty whiskey and beer bottles, and gutted by all-terrain vehicles. We needed only to view the scattered refuse to know that our nemeses had been there, and we could only hope that our arrival would not coincide with theirs. I can't speak for other hikers, but I know that I always tensed when I approached such crossings, realizing that if I did emerge from the woods and face trouble, there wasn't much I could do to defend myself.

In all my days in the woods, I met only one hiker who had stowed a weapon in his pack. The rest of us felt that to walk armed would violate the true spirit of the trail. It also would have violated the law against carrying concealed weapons in national parks and forests. Besides, in view of our preoccupation with cutting weight, it would have been unconscionable to supplant one pound of food with one pound of steel.

During our night at Addis Gap, the road brought unwelcome visitors. As the three of us sparked our stoves and set about cooking our dinners, we heard a vehicle approach.

"That had better be a government truck," Kit said.

I hoped so, too, but realized that it probably wasn't. It was Sunday, late in the day. By that time most government employees were off the clock. Then we heard a volley of gunfire echo through the woods, which resolved any doubt.

A brown pickup truck soon rounded a bend and came into view. From the distance of several hundred yards, I noticed that the cab carried four people. As the vehicle drew nearer, I saw that it contained two men and two women. The truck continued until it reached the end of the road, thirty yards behind the shelter. Now out of our sight, the driver killed the engine. We heard the doors swing open.

"Oh, shit," I said under my breath. "We've got company."

I heard the two women giggling like adolescents. One of the men cursed them, telling them to shut up.

The four then stepped around to the front of the shelter. The two women—plump and in their midthirties, dressed in double-knit shorts and halter tops—stayed in the background giggling, while the men took seats at the picnic table perched in front of the shelter. I expected the protective pit bull to charge over my shoulder and confront the men, but I peered behind me—amazed—to find her snoozing peacefully at the back of the shelter.

The two men held beers in their hands and reeked of alcohol. The tall, gaunt man with dark eyes, a black beard, and stringy shoulder-length hair, glared into the shelter for a time before he spoke.

"You know these shelters are for everyone," he said, sternly. Then he smiled at his friend, a portly man with red hair and bloodshot eyes. The man smiled back. "They're not just for you backpackers."

We told him we knew that.

"Most hikers think they own these places," he continued. "But it ain't that way."

"Y'all want something to drink?" asked the friend, still wearing a queer smile. "We got some liquor and some beer. Done smoked up the pot, though."

There was a fresh ripple of giggling from the women.

"No, that's okay, but thanks," I answered.

"Naw, y'all gonna drink a beer," commanded the dark-haired man.

His friend returned to the truck. I suspected he might return with the beer *and* a weapon. While he was gone, his dark friend glared into the shelter at us without talking. I'm sure our apprehension was palpable. The redheaded man soon returned, proffering two beers.

As the women continued to giggle, the dark man snapped to his friend, "Hell, we ought to take them two out and shoot them!"

The redheaded man laughed, and I tried to muster a smile but couldn't. I knew that it was unlikely that the man would make good on his threat, but there was always a chance. These mountains were thoroughly isolated from the law.

The men stayed for nearly an hour, without talking much, but just glaring into the shelter. The pit bull continued to sleep. As night fell, they discussed staying at the shelter but finally decided to move on, saying they might be back later with some friends.

Relieved, we watched the truck wind away down the road and disappear around the bend.

"Think they were trying to scare us?" I asked.

"Well, they succeeded," Kit answered.

We discussed whether to move on up the trail or stay in the shelter and risk facing the men and a group of their hiker-hating allies later in the night.

Then we heard the truck stop and the doors open. Two shots rang through the trees, rousing the pit bull, who sat bolt upright growling.

There was no need for further discussion. Quickly, we were all on our feet, frantically stowing our gear. Within ten minutes we were racing north on the trail through the darkness. We spent a restless night on a mountain shoulder half a mile beyond the shelter, and I awoke several times through the night to hear the pit bull, tensed and alert, growling at shadows in the woods. From where we lay I spotted a string of lights marking faraway backwoods houses extending down through the valley, and in my sleepy daze I imagined a pack of militant rednecks stalking us through the woods with flashlights.

A few hundred miles farther north, I had confronted another weapon-toting yokel, not on the trail but in Erwin, a small trail town in northern Tennessee. Because of intolerance for hikers among some of the town's residents, in the late 1970s Erwin ranked as one of the trail's least hospitable stopovers. Erwin's most enduring legacy, it seems, involves the lynching of an elephant some years ago. As the story goes, during a circus in a nearby town, an elephant squashed a young spectator, and after a brief trial the town hired a crane operator in Erwin, who summarily executed the hapless creature by hanging.

Over the last decade the town has made great strides to clean up its reputation, and the Nolichucky Retreat Campground and Expeditions, a rafting outfitter located on the banks of the Nolichucky River. The town now offers hikers comfortable and friendly accommodations, but in 1979, in some ways Erwin seemed almost as inhospitable to hikers as it had been to clumsy pachyderms.

After we arrived in town, we found our way to the YMCA, a dingy edifice, and we welcomed the chance to take a hot shower and sleep under a roof, such as it was.

The shelters we had passed on our approach to town had posted warnings to hikers advising them not to interact with locals and not to divulge their travel plans. The signs made it clear that there had been trouble with some of the people from the area.

Though the town offered us little in the way of amenities, it was the first "wet" town we had passed through in many days, and after dropping our packs at the Y, Dan and I walked to one of the town's few taverns, several streets away. The tavern was nothing more than a long, dimly lit room with a chipped linoleum floor, a row of rickety stools, and a large cooler filled with iced quarts of Iron City Beer. Seventy-five cents bought a quart of beer and a styrofoam cup.

As soon as we crossed the threshold, I realized that we had made a mistake. Fifteen bleary-eyed patrons swung their faces toward the door, and as they did, conversation ceased. Most of the men wore work shirts and billed caps advertising chewing tobacco, fishing gear, or four-wheel-drive trucks. Some of the men had wads of tobacco bulging in their cheeks and sluiced the juice right onto the floor.

Clad in our hiking clothes and boots and with our long hair and beards—both emblems of the counterculture in 1979—we made ready targets. The men recognized us immediately as hikers or, worse, as hippie hikers who had chucked the work ethic to wander through the woods. Their values and ours, at least as they perceived them, were at odds, and I confess that I was guilty of making snap judgments about the men and their attitudes toward us myself. It turned out that my snap judgments weren't too far off.

Dan and I sidled up to the bar, ordered the house specialty, and soon sat in front of two frothy styrofoam cups.

"Hey, what the hell you fellows doin' walking when you can drive!" said one of the men. Laughter. "Wall, look at 'em boots! 'Em's some fancy boots!" More laughter. "You all walk in 'em cute little shorts?" Again, more laughter. I noticed that Dan's beer had vanished in one quaff, and he fixed me with a look that said, "Let's get the hell out of here. Now."

I took a long pull at my beer, hoping that the onslaught would end and that the men would focus their attention on something else. They didn't. The man on my left, who tottered unsteadily on his perch, turned a red, haggard face toward me and started raving about something. I'm sure he had a definite message in mind, but under the influence of a few dozen beers, all that came out was a string of garbled syllables. From the few words I could understand, I learned that the man was angry with a fellow named Rufus or Verl or some such, who had taken liberties with his daughter.

About that time, he rested his elbow on my shoulder and reached his free hand into his work pants and pulled out a small silver handgun.

I had had a terrifying experience in college when at a barn dance a drunken lunatic who had infiltrated the college crowd pulled a western-style revolver, poked it into my chest, pushed me back, and leveled the gun at my heart before someone wrestled the weapon from his hand. The experience left me with a dread of handguns.

Now, in this dingy Tennessee tavern as the sodden man waved the loaded gun in my face, I felt a twinge of panic. I looked at Dan, and for the first time since I'd known him, I saw he was frightened.

The man continued to bellow about this Rufus and how he was going to "kill that son of a bitch," when the man seated on his left intervened.

"Jack, you can't kill Rufus," he said. "He hanged hisself in prison last week!"

With his primary target gone, I imagined that the man might turn his sights on me. At that, Dan rose, sensibly figuring that this was an appropriate time to leave.

Just then our savior—a disabled young man with a vacant smile, a bum leg, and an atrophied right arm—entered the bar. He was, in the lexicon of this rural hamlet, the reigning village idiot, and the tavern denizens aimed their abuse at him. They jeered him and mocked him, but his smile indicated that he enjoyed the attention, derisive though it was.

The man's presence seemed to boost Jack's mood, and he called the crippled man over to the bar. As the young man approached, Jack pulled the clip from his gun and withdrew a single 22-caliber round. He then told the man that he had a game he could play, and he demonstrated how to pound the butt-end of the cartridge against the sharp metal edge of the bar with the slug pointed at his head. He handed the bullet to the man and backed away. As he did, Dan and I made our way toward the door.

My last memory of the tavern was of the pathetic man, the silly grin still playing across his face, pounding the bullet against the edge of the bar while the men stood clear of danger, laughing and waiting for the round to discharge.

Within a week, on May 26 at the Roan Highlands Shelter in Low Gap four miles north of the summit of Roan Mountain, we had another bizarre encounter. Six of us—the Phillips brothers; Mark, an eighteen-year-old thru-hiker from Maryland; Jeff, a Kansas native; and Dan and I—arrived at the shelter as it began to drizzle. Inside were two rough-looking men clad in black leather jackets who had hiked in the half mile from the nearest road. With them was an attractive woman with long dark hair and brown eyes. She and the men swilled whiskey from a Jack Daniel's bottle that sat on the floor beside a healthy store of tin cans.

The men seemed irked at our arrival and they made it clear that they planned on making good use of the shelter that night and did not welcome our company. The woman, though drunk, seemed happy enough with her two companions, and she sat fondling one of the men.

Most of us decided to avoid a confrontation and set up our tents and rain flies outside the shelter. The Phillips brothers, nonetheless, determined to wedge their way into the shelter, and after a few minutes of tense negotiation, the men grudgingly yielded. To insure their privacy, the men hung two rain ponchos from the shelter eaves, one dividing the shelter in half, and the other closing off the front.

Through the evening, as we huddled around a smoky fire, the three continued to party. At one point we dived for cover when we heard one of the men shout at the woman to put down the gun. Having discovered that the men were armed, we spent a restless night inside our nylon tents. The next morning we were packed and on the trail before the hung-over revelers awoke, and as we walked, the Phillips brothers shared what they had overheard from beyond the nylon partition.

"One of the men had sex with the woman a couple of times, and then he called his friend over," he said. "He told the girl that he wanted her to have sex with his friend." The woman, who was all but comatose at that point, initially resisted but then willingly accommodated the man's request. The men apparently took turns with her through the night.

As we distanced ourselves from the shelter, we wrestled with our judgment, wondering if we should have intervened on the woman's behalf. After some discussion, we decided we had done the right thing. The woman seemed to be a willing participant, and if we had intervened, what would the outcome have been if we had confronted the two burly, armed men in defense of a woman whose honor seemed as dubious as theirs?

The gun-wielding southern rogues were intimidating, but even they did not rattle us nearly as much as the illusive nocturnal demon that sent us fleeing from the shore of Tiorati Lake forty miles outside of New York City.

It was July 30, and I was traveling with Paul. Dan had pushed a day ahead, and Nick lagged a few days behind. We had veered off the trail ten miles south of Bear Mountain Bridge, where the trail crosses the Hudson River, and at dusk we found ourselves following the paved roads through Tiorati Circle.

At that point, we had become thoroughly at ease in the wilderness, yet the prospect of mixing with the denizens of the nation's largest city, which lay a scant forty miles away, left us spooked.

Initially, Paul and I had decided to camp on Tiorati Circle, a paved loop a few yards off the trail that ran along the shores of Tiorati Lake resort. When we got there, we encountered riotous commotion that left us feeling like backcountry immigrants newly arrived in a society devoted to noise, hedonism, and excess. One camper, a plump man in his early thirties, sat in a lawn chair basking in the glow of a Coleman lantern beside a small card table cluttered with a three-foot water pipe for smoking pot, a quart bottle of whiskey, and a massive sound system that blared disco dance music. In the site beside his, a family outfitted with an equally outsized boom-box blasted their hard-rock strains into the night. Several young men in souped-up cars had converted the circle into a racetrack, and they sped around the oval squealing their tires, shouting to other drivers and blaring their own music through open windows.

At the outset of my hike, I would have welcomed the security of having other campers—even such boisterous ones—gathered around me, but the three months on the trail had changed my perspective. These disrespectful urban campers seemed to violate the peaceful sanctity of the wilderness while they violated my own peace of mind, and Paul and I wanted nothing to do with them.

Before making camp, we decided to push up the road to find a less frenetic setting, even though it was now dark. Within a half-mile, we passed a group camp area where a dozen inner-city children—most of them from Harlem—sat clustered around a campfire grilling hot dogs and hamburgers. The delicious aroma of cooking meat tempered our wariness, and we ambled over to the fire. Soon we sat swapping tales with the children while sharing their dinner. Just before we left, a raccoon strayed into the camp, and the children scattered, screaming, from the fire. One young boy shrieked, "Bear! It's a bear!" as he ran.

Paul and I couldn't help but laugh at the irony. These kids had grown up on some of the meanest streets in America where they had no doubt witnessed muggings, shootings, stabbings, and other violent crimes. Yet, to them the wilderness and its harmless creatures were unfamiliar and strange, evoking fear and panic. A dozen armed gang members could have wandered into camp and not raised an eyebrow, but a ten-pound raccoon sent the children fleeing for their lives.

Paul and I thanked the children and their counselors for the kindness and pushed on. Faced with the prospect of bumbling through the brush in the dark looking for a suitable place to sleep, we opted instead to take our chances amid the noise and confusion back at Tiorati Circle.

We rolled out our bags along the fringes of the lake and decided not to hang our food, convinced that the noise from our neighbors would at least protect us from scavenging animals.

Minutes after we had climbed into our bags, we heard the horrible call. It wouldn't have been more unsettling if it had risen from the throat of a Godzilla. Instead, it was the call of the dread *homo sapiens intoxicatus,* and it came from the campsite nearest ours.

"Ahhhhhhh!" it began. "Ahhhhhhhhhhh! Somebody stole my fuckin' radio!"

Seconds later, a dark form was crashing through the bushes, and soon a bearded man in a white T-shirt and ball cap tottered above us as we cowered in our sleeping bags.

"I'm gonna kill the son of a bitch who stole my radio!" he shouted in our direction. "Yoos guys seen my radio?"

No, we explained, we hadn't. But we'd be sure to keep an eye out for it.

After scanning our Spartan camp, he seemed convinced of our innocence and staggered on through the weeds toward the next site. "Ahhhhhhhhhhh! Somebody stole my fuckin' radio! I'm gonna kill the fucker who stole my radio . . ."

Serenaded by the squealing tires, blaring music, and the mournful call of the radio-less man, we eventually fell asleep. But the urban reign of terror wasn't over for us quite yet.

About 3:00 A.M., after even the most devoted partyers had drifted off, I heard it. I shook Paul in his bag.

"Listen," I said.

It was the sound of something large, plunging with its paws and splashing through the water of the lake. It was moving toward our camp.

"What is it?" Paul asked.

"God, I don't know," I continued, "but I think we ought to hang our food."

Still half asleep, we slipped from our bags, and I fumbled through my pack for the fifty feet of parachute cord I carried for hanging our food. As I did, I could hear the strange creature plunging through the water toward us. I found the rope and, as Paul fixed his flashlight beam on a branch above us, tied a rock to one end of the rope before hurling it toward the branch. It missed. As I felt along the ground for the rope, Paul swung his flashlight toward the advancing creature.

"I can't see anything, but it's still moving toward us," he said.

"Yeah, and we'd better get this food up before it gets here," I said.

Before I could take another shot at the branch, the creature had cleared the shoreline and began moving through the brush.

I'm not sure if it was my imagination, but I swear I could see the whites of Paul's eyes bulging, and before I could stop him, he tore off through the trees in the opposite direction. Not one to face peril alone, I followed on his heels, and together we charged willy-nilly through the woods, peering over our shoulders to glimpse the mystery predator. Although we couldn't see what or who pursued us, we could hear it rustling through the brush a constant fifteen yards behind us, matching us stride for stride.

At one point I grabbed Paul's arm, and we stopped to listen. As soon as we stopped, the creature stopped. After a few seconds, we spooked again and sped off howling through the trees. The creature again was on our heels, fifteen yards behind us. I spotted the light of the bathhouse and raced toward it, thinking that we'd finally get a good look at our pursuer.

When we arrived under the light, we peered behind us. Still nothing. Then I cast a glance down at my boot and started laughing.

"What's so funny?" Paul asked.

"We are," I answered. "Look at my boot."

Looking down, he saw the parachute cord tangled around my ankle and started laughing too. I had been dragging the parachute cord through the weeds, and we had been fleeing from the dread rock monster I had secured to the other end while I was trying to hang our food bags. We may have identified one of our assailants, but the other, the bizarre aquatic demon that had plunged through the water toward our camp, remains a mystery.

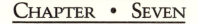
Wasted Along the Way

No matter how poorly prepared I feel for this trip, there is always someone less prepared, less well equipped, less conditioned. Some of the people out here are like harlequins in hiking boots. Some have never read a single word about this trail or hiked a single mile before setting out, and their misadventures tend to encourage me. Compared to some of them, I am a virtual expert on backwoods living. I've discovered, too, that there are a few hucksters out here, who seem to be preying on them.
—May 5, 1979, Fontana Dam, North Carolina

A white gauze bandage crusted with a yellow stain clung to Mark's forehead, a reminder of his rather inauspicious introduction to the Appalachian Trail. His eyes, glazed and distant, peered lifelessly from their sockets.

He curled in his cotton flannel sleeping bag in the recesses of the Springer Mountain Shelter, staring blankly out into the greening, rain-drenched forest while his partner, Don, a tiny man who stood five feet tall and weighed 105 pounds, set about building a fire. Don may have been small, but he was mightily armed. A massive hunting knife—a machete, really—hung from his belt and extended below his knee. In his right hand he held a full-sized axe, which he wielded fiercely against the unyielding trunk of a very large and healthy maple.

After assaulting the trunk for several minutes and with no results, he lowered the axe. Wheezing like an asthmatic, he scanned the woods for a more accommodating target, locating a smaller, though no less healthy, green maple. Straining to bend the small tree nearly double and struggling to secure the top to the ground with his foot, he grunted as he drove the axe into the midsection. The axe head rebounded like a Superball and struck Don square in the forehead, knocking him to his knees.

"Oh, shit," muttered Mark. "Now this."

The two of them were not having a good day. In fact, it had been a pretty miserable week. Only a few days earlier Don and he had had such high hopes for their journey on the Appalachian Trail. They had been planning for weeks, organizing their equipment, purchasing food, sharpening their axes and knives. But things hadn't worked out the way they had hoped, and their dreams, along with Mark's head—and now Don's—had been dashed.

Mark's head injury had occurred before they even reached the trail. After becoming entangled in his pack straps, Mark had stumbled off the bus that had carried them to Atlanta and had landed solidly on his forehead. The ambulance ride to the emergency room was an unexpected side trip, but Mark was relieved when the doctor glanced at the X-rays and reported that he had not fractured his skull. He had, however, suffered a wicked concussion, which had left him dazed and confused, and the medication they had given him to quiet his nerves had only compounded the problem. Against the doctor's orders, he had checked out of the hospital two days later. After purchasing two twelve-packs of Budweiser, Mark and Don had set out for Amicalola Falls.

The eight-and-a-half-mile hike up from the falls to the official start of the Appalachian Trail hadn't exactly met their expectations, either. Neither had trained for the hike, and the stiff uphill grade soon exhausted them. It also made them thirsty. They hadn't bothered to fill their canteens with water before leaving the park. Why bother? Each carried 144 ounces of beer, and as they struggled up the mountain, they left a trail of empty twelve-ounce aluminum cans behind them.

Near the halfway point, Mark began to suffer another spell. His vision blurred, and he spun and collapsed into a heap beside the trail. After Don assessed the situation, he became convinced that his partner was dehydrated and decided to go for water. Had they carried a map or guidebook, they would have realized that a perfectly good spring spouted water within a few hundred yards of their emergency bivouac, but the twelve cans of beer had already made their packs unmanageably heavy, and they had left the trail guide behind.

As his partner lapsed deeper into a daze, Don humped the four miles to the top of Springer Mountain, located the spring at the shelter, filled his canteen, then spun back down the mountain to his friend. By the time Don returned, Mark was sitting up, cradling his throbbing head. By now it was dark, and the two rolled out their sleeping bags—heavy cotton flannel models—in the brush and tried to ignore the rain that pummeled their faces and drenched their bags. It seems they had also neglected to bring a tent.

That was the end of day one.

The next morning, the two arose. Don arose, rather, while Mark, pale and wan, lay in his bag, his lifeless eyes cast toward the heavens. Don revived him with a tepid Budweiser, and after a breakfast of Fig Newtons, the two once again embarked for Springer more determined than ever.

Late that afternoon, long after they had exhausted their cache of beer, they arrived at the shelter, Mark tottering unsteadily and Don dragging his sodden sleeping bag behind him like a thick serpentine tail. While Mark lay in the shelter, his partner set out to build a fire to warm them and dry their wet clothes. Since no dead trees lay within two hundred yards of the shelter, in the interest of convenience, he opted to fell a few live ones, which was not proceeding well.

After Don thumped himself on the noggin with the butt end of his axe head, he soon staggered to his feet and turned his attention to yet another living maple, this one a mere sapling. On *this* diminutive twig his axe found purchase. Soon he had harvested a bundle of twigs and placed them in a tangled heap in the middle of the fire pit. But how to light them? Igniting green wood is tough enough; igniting *wet* green wood is nearly impossible. But the very enterprising Don doused the branches in a pint of white gas, struck a match, and at the cost of his eyebrows and forearm hair successfully kindled a fire that emitted a cloud of wet green smoke. Returning the axe to its sheath on his belt and swaggering like a gunfighter who had just dropped his arch nemesis, Don returned to the shelter.

Soon the dense smoke was billowing into the shelter, driving all of its occupants out into the rain, except Mark, who was too dazed to move. Squinting through tears, Don joined his partner at the back of the shelter where the two set about preparing dinner by peeling the plastic wrappers from a half-dozen SlimJims.

"What do you think?" Don asked, biting off a finger-length portion of his evening entree.

"About what?"

"About the trail."

"I dunno. What do *you* think?" asked Mark, still staring into the void.

"Do you think we can make it?"

"Where?" Mark asked, suddenly alert. "To Maine? Are you crazy! After all this!"

"No," Don answered. "Back down to Amicalola Falls."

"Well, if we rest up another day, I think I might be up to it."

And so, two days later, after the supply of SlimJims was spent and some of the color had returned to Mark's cheeks, the two again took up the blue blazes and retreated to Amicalola Falls, promising to return next year—better equipped, better prepared, better conditioned, in better health—to hike the entire Appalachian Trail.

Sadly, this tale of woe is true. I met Don and Mark on Springer Mountain while I was on the trail in 1987. They will forever epitomize the misadventures that often befall poorly prepared hikers who—eager but clueless—take up the trail.

As it turns out, the odds are against the hundreds of hikers who each summer leave Springer aspiring to reach Maine. During most summers, only about 20 percent will achieve their goal. Owing to a welter of possible complications, the others become wasted along the way, many before they even clear the seventy-eight miles to the North Carolina border. For one thing, there is injury. The Appalachian Trail is, in effect, a nearly continuous, five-month endurance event and, like any athletic pursuit, it poses limitless potential for injury. Rick, a hiker we had met in Georgia, who seemed to have the mental toughness and stamina to make it all the way, made it only as far as Virginia before he took a spill on a stretch of wet, rocky trail and opened a tendon-deep gash in his knee.

Victor wrenched a calf muscle in the Smokies and, after hobbling along and grimacing for a week, made the painful decision to depart the trail in Hot Springs, North Carolina.

There were less predictable obstacles, too, that led hikers to abandon their hopes. Byron, whom we had befriended in Tennessee, made it as far as New Jersey, we heard, before someone stole his pack while he was off in the brush relieving himself. Without a pack or the funds to buy a new one, Byron was forced to end his hike. One day in Shenandoah National Park in Virginia we discovered a note pinned to a wooden park service sign at a road crossing. The note, addressed to a hiker behind us whom we didn't know, read:

Dear ————,
Your father has died of a heart attack. Call your sister for details. Please return home immediately.

There were the psychological factors—boredom, loneliness—which also reduced our ranks. But more than anything else, it was poor planning and conditioning and

overloaded packs that led to failure. Springer Mountain
served as a magnet for legions of uninitiated hikers who
bumbled into the woods and who, often just as quickly,
bumbled back out. Incredibly, there were people who had
quit their jobs and drained their bank accounts to hike the
trail without ever having read about it or explored any of its
miles. They based their expectations on their own romantic
visions or secondhand information gleaned from friends
and acquaintances.

Though I never consciously derived pleasure from the
misfortunes of others, I confess that I did find solace in
their often ridiculous, sometimes humorous, misadventures. During my most difficult days, in fact, no matter how
unfit I felt for life on the trail, I found that reflecting on
some of the unforgivable gaffes of my colleagues could leave
me feeling like Kit Carson.

We met many of them face to face on the trail, and we
read the accounts of others in shelter registers. More often,
we learned about their desperate straits by the gear they had
left behind. All through Georgia, for instance, shelters were
cluttered with heaps of discarded items: axes, shovels, survival knives, shoes, boots, socks, shirts, pants, underwear,
bras, rain ponchos, canned goods, cook pots, gallon cans of
white gas, plant books, first-aid books, Bibles (full-sized
leather-bound editions), books of poetry, novels, bird books,
insect books, cookbooks.

Often the items were accompanied by notes that, with
some variation, expressed this sentiment:

> I am miserable. My pack is too heavy. My feet hurt. I've de-
> cided to cut weight by leaving behind this garden spade,
> cast-iron skillet, twelve-inch survival knife, and two-pound
> tin of Dinty Moore beef stew. I have not had the opportunity
> to use them but hope they'll be of service to someone. Head-
> ing north. Hoping things improve.

A hardliner would call such disposal of goods littering.
Most of the items became permanent fixtures in the shelters. After all, what reasonable hiker seeks to *increase* his
load once he's entered the woods? But then who condemned

the pioneers who lightened their loads by heaving their heirlooms and other expendable items overboard in hopes of successfully crossing the prairies?

We learned that there were other means of lightening one's load. One hiker Dan and I encountered less than one mile below Springer had kindled a trailside fire, which he stoked with heavy volumes on first aid, edible wild plants, birds, and bugs. We stood by watching him feed the flames. Like a backcountry merchant, he had set out his store of canned goods in orderly stacks, inviting passersby to take whatever they wanted. As if he hadn't suffered enough already under the weight of his pack, he tore the seat out of his trousers when he squatted to extract more extraneous items from his pack.

Then there were the two women I met as I neared the summit of Springer on a later trip. It was raining, and as I glanced ahead, I spotted the two of them shuffling along as if their legs were bound. In a sense they were. It seems that one of the women, a seamstress, had crafted "front" packs to supplement the storage capacity of their fully loaded backpacks. The packs, which fastened around the waist, had never been fieldtested, and after a few miles on the trail they had slipped down, settling around the women's upper thighs and reducing their strides to a series of baby steps.

But the women had other problems, too. Once in camp, I watched as each woman withdrew from her pack an entire spice rack, crafted from twelve-inch strips of Styrofoam and equipped with twelve or fifteen plastic bottles. Then came the stoves: propane torches and foot-tall iron tripods borrowed from a chemistry lab where one of the women worked. These were not modest propane burners, but heavy foot-long tanks with brass nozzles. The stoves were designed not to heat metal pots but to *melt* them. The cooking outfits also included a metal support for the torches, which directed the blue blade of flame through the ring of the beaker stand and onto the base of the cook pot. After twenty miles of abject misery, the women veered off the trail at the first crossroads, which led into Suches, Georgia.

Once in town, they dumped the "babies" and torches before buying more suitable gear and continuing on.

Then there were the two fellows from Atlanta who had set out under the mistaken assumption that once on the trail there was no means for egress or acquiring supplies. Their determination—and knees—gave out after twenty miles, and they too bailed out in Suches.

There was the sweet, naive woman from New York. Plump and in her early twenties, she had set out on the trail by her parents' choosing, not by her own. Her parents had hoped to help their daughter boost her self-confidence and drop a few pounds in the process, and they decided that a 2,100-mile hike along the Appalachian Trail might do the trick. So they bought her a pack, a pair of boots, and a bus ticket to Georgia.

Her first days on the trail were torturous, and it was remarkable that she made it as far as she did. Had it not been for Byron, who found her blubbering in the weeds on the trail in the Smokies, she might still be stranded there. Byron hefted her pack, along with his own, and led her, sobbing, to the next shelter. Once there, Byron assumed the role of big brother and urged her to bail out. She heeded his advice, sort of.

Over the next several weeks, she evolved from an Appalachian Trail hiker to an Appalachian Trail groupie. Frequently, we arrived in trail towns—through most of Georgia, North Carolina, Tennessee, and even into Virginia—only to find the woman waiting for us there. She had given up hiking, but not hitchhiking, and as we would pick up the trail out of town, she would hang her thumb for a lift into the next stop. Bryon repeatedly urged her to go home, fearing that some deranged motorist might take advantage of her, and he went so far as to buy her a bus ticket home, but she persisted. Eventually, she became the basis for a series of bets among hikers: would she or wouldn't she be waiting for us in the next town?

After Byron had purchased the bus ticket and extracted a promise from her that she would use it, he was so confident that he bet a group of us a milk shake each that when we arrived in Damascus, Virginia, she would be gone. When we entered town, we spotted her waving from a hotel and hoofed it directly to the local Dairy Queen to collect on our bet.

Where there are sheep, there are also wolves, and on the trail, where there are such poorly adapted hikers as the young woman from New York, there are hucksters out to take unfair advantage of them. The trail's reigning flimflam artist was a man known variously as Mack, Mountain Man Mack, and Ranger Mack. A portly, indigent man in his early twenties who hailed from some backwoods settlement, Mack had developed an ingenious scam.

Clad in a forest-service green uniform and wearing a pack, Mack would arrive on the trail in late April as the fresh corps of thru-hikers set out from Springer. He presented himself as an agent of the national forest service, and he carried a bogus badge and a small side arm. He explained that his mission was to serve as guide to hikers on the Appalachian Trail. Mack boasted that he had hiked the trail end to end, that he knew virtually every edible plant, and that he could steer a hiker safely through even the most formidable disasters. Having won the hikers' confidence, he would then amble along with them, gauging their gullibility as he inventoried their stores of cash and food.

To hikers ill-suited for the rigors of life on the trail and needing guidance, Mack was a godsend, or so he seemed. In exchange for a few dollars a day and a share of their food, he would shepherd them through the woods. Slowly. He stolidly refused to walk in the rain, and even on sunny days he seldom covered more than five or six miles.

Dan and I met Mack at Rocky Knob Shelter in Georgia the day after a tornado had ripped through the woods a few miles from our camp in Tesnatee Gap. Peering inside the shelter, we spotted Mack with four other hikers. Among them were the woman from New York and a bizarre, bearded man from Maine who seemed to be daft. Both posed perfect targets for Mack. They, along with the other two, had signed on with the shyster, who now sat fat and happy in the shelter eating their food. Why they never became suspicious of him or his alleged background I can't imagine. If he were an official of the forest service, why did he require food? If he refused to walk in the rain, how had he completed the trail? And if he had completed the trail and continued to spend his days hiking, why was he so fat?

We learned later that one morning near the edge of the Smokies, the hikers had awakened to find themselves alone in the shelter. Having bilked them out of money and food, Mack had vanished. It seems he had an aversion to the Smokies, and later in Hot Springs we would learn why.

A few days after we arrived in Hot Springs, Elmer, the owner of the Inn, explained that Mack, who lived off the kindness—or ignorance—of hapless hikers, was as much a part of spring in the southern Appalachians as the budding flowers. Years earlier he had been arrested for impersonating a government law enforcement official and for carrying a concealed weapon without a permit. Even now, Elmer explained, there was a warrant out for his arrest. It seems that while Mack felt comfortable working his scheme along the little-traveled trails of the national forests, he feared the trails of the national parks, which were populated with armed, *bona fide* rangers.

Elmer was right. Later, while on an early spring hike with a friend near Hot Springs in 1986, I arrived at Deer Park Mountain Shelter four miles south of town. We sat eating lunch when a shirtless hiker approached from the south, his gut flopping over the hip belt to his pack. He wore stereo headphones connected to a Walkman.

"Been damned hungry the past few days," he said, scratching his protruding belly after shedding his pack. "I hain't had a decent meal for the last four days, and I'm damned near starvin'." He flashed us a toothless grin as he eyed the bag of trail mix that lay on my lap. I offered him a handful, and when I did he snatched up the entire bag. Then his glance moved to the plastic bottle of whiskey beside me.

"That wouldn't be sippin' whiskey, would it?" he asked.

Though irked by his shameless mooching, I handed him the bottle. Then he spotted the tin of snuff in my shirt pocket. "And might I trouble you for a dip?" he continued. "Hain't had a dip for nigh on a week." Again, I obliged.

"God, I'm hungry," he continued.

"You know there's food in town," I suggested. "The Inn has some of the best meals on the whole trail."

"I hain't sure I can make it that far, I'm so darned weak, and my stomach's so empty it hurts," he continued, patting his healthy roll of flab. "And I hain't got no money. A couple guys robbed me back at the last shelter."

It had been years since I had last seen Mack, and though I didn't immediately recognize the face, his *modus operandi* was unmistakable. I decided to confront him.

"Your name wouldn't be Mack by any chance?" I asked.

An alarmed look spread over his face.

"Well, ah, some people call me that."

"Mountain Man Mack?"

"Well, yeah."

"Ranger Mack?"

"Uh-huh."

I started laughing. In seven years the trail hadn't changed one bit. The spring was just as beautiful—and Mack just as corrupt—as ever. The reason he was so reluctant to push on into Hot Springs, I surmised, was that he was known there by too many people, people who were wise to his game and might have turned him in to the authorities. He realized he would fare better, and eat better, if he stuck to the trail and plied hikers for food.

"Well, I think it's time to be moseying. Mack, I hope you get some grub," I said as I piled my gearack into my pack, stood, and climbed into the straps. My friend, who threw me a baffled glance, did the same. As we left the shelter, Mack tried one last ploy to separate me from my cash: "Hey, I'll sell you this Walkman for ten dollars." I ignored the offer and, still laughing, kept on walking. Over the few miles to our camp, I explained to my friend that he had met one of the trail's most notorious con men.

Initially, I viewed Mack—and others like him—as a

scourge of the trail, but in time I've come to regard him in a kinder light. In many ways he was the same as the mice, chipmunks, raccoons, skunks, feral dogs, and other opportunistic critters who lingered around the shelters and grew fat on our mistakes. But he was different from his four-legged counterparts in one regard: once I was on to his tricks, he seemed a lot less clever.

CHAPTER · EIGHT

Gear

> *I never imagined that existence could be so simple, so uncluttered, so Spartan, so free of baggage, so sublimely gratifying. I have reduced the weight of my pack to thirty-five pounds, and yet I can't think of a single thing I really need that I can't find either within myself or within my pack. The pack contains all essentials, as well as a few luxury items: a book, a Frisbee, a quarter-pint of whiskey, and a poem I photocopied at a library a few miles back. Today as I walked, I memorized the poem, "She Walks in Beauty" by Lord Byron, and tonight I will use the paper to kindle a fire and thereby reduce my weight by another ounce.*
> *—September 9, 1979, Poplar Ridge Lean-to, Maine*

I live with my wife and daughter in a century-old, two-story farmhouse in Tennessee. Our collective possessions occupy seven indoor rooms, a porch, and an outdoor shed. Together, they sprawl, they clutter, they choke. I open closets and confront boxes whose contents remain a complete mystery. I open drawers, searching for pencils or scissors, and sift through a chaos of knickknacks. In the work shed I forage for tools through a tangle of gadgets whose functions I have long ago forgotten.

Returning from the shed, I spot my former dwelling hanging on a nail in the enclosed porch. A green nylon frame backpack with a capacity of 2,500 square inches. It features one large main compartment, a front pouch, and four side pouches. The largest pouch—in the front—measures nine inches across, seven inches from top to bottom, and two inches deep. Below the pack bag is a vacant section of frame for my sleeping bag.

Eleven years ago, that pack was more than ample to contain the sum total of my worldly possessions—thirty-five to forty-five pounds worth. It included everything—absolutely everything—I really needed:

Two cotton T-shirts, two cotton bandanas, one pair of nylon running shorts, a pair of cotton army fatigue trousers, one wool shirt, a pair of wool gloves, a coated-nylon rain jacket, two pairs of wool socks, two pairs of thin liner socks, one pair of lug-soled boots for the trail and a pair of running shoes for camp, a stove and one-liter fuel bottle, a two-quart cook pot, a nylon foodbag, one plastic film canister filled with salt and another filled with pepper, a steel drinking cup, one metal spoon with bent handle, two one-liter plastic water bottles, a six-ounce plastic bottle for distilled spirits, one bottle of water-purification tablets, a toothbrush and small tube of toothpaste, a three-ounce bottle of biodegradable soap, a fifty-foot length of parachute cord for hanging food, a synthetic-fill sleeping bag rated to thirty-five degrees, a closed-cell foam sleeping mat, a first-aid kit, a trail guidebook, a paperback book, a spiral-bound notebook in which I recorded my journal, a billed cap, insect repellent, a Swiss Army knife, a butane lighter, and a partial roll of toilet paper.

How would I begin, I wonder, to prioritize what I own today and select thirty-five pounds from all this tonnage, thirty-five pounds that would answer my needs and leave me feeling as secure and well outfitted as I felt in 1979? I suspect I couldn't. Even if I were to fill my pack with the same items, I realize I could not resurrect the sense of self-sufficiency. Or the freedom that came from knowing that wherever I found myself at noonday or nightfall, my house and its goods rested beside me.

No. The years away from the trail have softened me, made me reliant on creature comforts. Certainly, I can and do release my hold on them when I return to the trail for a few days or even a week, but for five months? I would feel naked, vulnerable. I would, in spite of myself, imagine a host of dire what-if contingencies requiring the addition of first one item, then another and another, until my pack strained at its seams and refused to accommodate any more.

At one time my pack was an extension of myself. It accompanied me everywhere I went. When I carried it, it rode on my back as naturally as a flesh-and-bone appendage. And even after I took it off, my hands probed its pockets and hidden folds as precisely as I might have reached to scratch an unseen itch. I could locate any item, no matter how small or deeply buried, as quickly and surely as I might have raised a finger to touch my nose or flick an insect from my ear. I was like a snail or turtle whose den is a fixed companion along all the miles of its life.

Someone on the trail once shared with me a simple principle for reducing my pack to the bare essentials. "If you don't use an item at least once a day," he said, "get rid of it."

It was sound advice. With the exception of the items in my first-aid kit, some of which, thankfully, I never used, I abided by that principle. In the interest of economy, like most hikers I devised methods for extending the utility of the items I did carry.

My sleeping bag, for instance, fulfilled its primary task of insulating my body from the elements. It served almost as efficiently as a refrigerator. A quart of ice cream nestled at the core of a sleeping bag in its stuff sack would survive summertime heat and provide a refreshing dessert hours and miles out of town. My closed-cell foam pad served equally well as a beer or soda cooler or as a comfortable sleeping mat. I could roll three chilled cans tightly in the eight-foot-long pad, stopper the ends with wool socks, and enjoy a cold beer with dinner six or eight hours later. And when laid against a tree trunk, the pad served as a chaise longue for afternoon naps.

The plumber's candles I carried were effective fire starters, and when set on an overturned drinking cup, they provided ample light for reading or writing after dark. The flexible round screen—made from heavy-gauge aluminum foil—that circled my stove and shielded it from the wind, doubled as a lantern reflector. If I folded it in half, bent it into an arc, and then placed it behind a candle, it would illuminate an entire shelter. The windscreen also served as a spout if laid amid the rocks in a slow-moving spring that trickled down a hillside.

The fifty feet of nylon parachute cord I carried served several functions. Evenings, I tied a stone to one end, hurled it over a sturdy branch, secured the end to our nylon food bags, and hoisted it out of reach of raccoons and bears. The line served equally well as a clothesline, and I found that if I doubled the cord and twisted it before securing it to two trees, I could hang my socks, bandana, shirt, and shorts by threading the fabric between the twisted filaments. Even the stiffest breeze could not pluck them free. And once, when my pack bag tore from one of its grommets, I used the cord to secure the bag to the frame.

The needle and packet of dental floss I carried in my first-aid kit provided sturdy, waxed-nylon thread for repairing packs, clothes, and boots. My metal drinking cup held my evening tea, but it also served as a bowl for my morning oatmeal and a scoop for drawing water from pools too shallow to accept a water bottle or cook pot. My Frisbee provided postdinner diversion and served as a fine plate.

Once filled, my two-and-a-half-gallon waterbag, a plastic pouch housed in a purple nylon sack and outfitted with a rubber nozzle, contained ample water for evening meals and drinks. Once emptied of water and inflated with air, it made a comfortable pillow.

My two one-liter water bottles doubled as rehydrating containers, and a handful of dried beans or lentils dropped into a bottle of water in the morning would be swollen and ready to cook by the time I arrived in camp in the afternoon.

The rain fly I carried provided emergency shelter and doubled as a groundsheet, protecting my sleeping bag from damp earth. The coated nylon anorak, a heavy jacket I carried, repelled rain, and in cool weather I layered it over my wool shirt to retain body heat.

The three-and-one-half-ounce tuna tins I carried as my primary source of protein served, when empty, to thwart the critters who attempted to pillage our food bags at night. I baked the empty tin in the fire to remove the odor and then poked a hole in the can's bottom with my knife. Then I tied a knot halfway down the line from my foodbag and threaded the cord through the hole before I hung the bag. The upside-down can, situated midway on the hanging line, presented an impasse for the craftiest of mice.

Even my wool gloves served a dual purpose. They warmed my hands on chill, wet days, and they acted as hot pads for plucking boiling pots from the coals. Hikers caught by cold temperatures without gloves, found that wool socks doubled as warm mittens.

If the contents of our packs couldn't answer our needs, we turned to the forest for aid. Our ingenuity, combined with the wilderness' raw resources, resolved most problems.

Stiff rhododendron leaves or short sticks split in half and cleaned of their center core provided spouts when inserted into slow-trickling springs. When downed deadwood was drenched by rains, we could always find dry kindling by shaking the trunks of standing dead trees. The trunks telegraphed and amplified the swaying motion to the tops of the trees, which whipped furiously and cracked, releasing a hail of dead branches. Because of their vertical orientation, those top branches escaped the brunt of drenching rains and dried quickly in the air circulating through the treetops.

When our cook pots became crusted with baked-on food, we used nature's scouring pad, a handful of sand and pebbles from a streambed. A cook pot laid in a stream and anchored with a stone on its lid would cool instant pudding, and forked sticks driven into the ground near the fire and spanned with a wooden crossbar would provide a perfect drying rack for wet socks and clothing. We used the same spits for dangling pots over the flames. Flat rocks served as cutting boards for chopping vegetables and as dining tables.

If we weren't turning to the wilderness for solutions, we turned to it for amusement. Through the five months I spent on the trail, I do not recall ever once being bored for want of something to occupy my time in camp. There was always something to do or see.

Just before we reached the Lake Country in Maine, for instance, I had my parents send me my telescoping fishing rod, and I spent evenings angling for supplemental protein and for fun. The rod provided dinner for a half-dozen hikers when we reached Antlers Camp, an abandoned fishing camp on the shores of a pristine backwoods lake fifty miles south of Mount Katahdin. Situated on a rocky peninsula, the camp contained a series of old log cabins, the main cabin featuring a wood-burning stove and an iron skillet; it was perfect for a fish-fry. After arriving in the early afternoon, I pulled on my wool shirt, grabbed my fishing rod, and followed the curve of the shoreline three-quarters of a mile from camp. Perched on a rock and surrounded by flaming sugar maples and golden birches, I reeled in a dozen lake trout. Two hours later, when I arrived back in camp, I discovered that Dan, Paul, and two other two hikers who shared our camp had spent the afternoon harvesting freshwater clams from the rocky shore.

That evening Dan played chef, frying our fillets and mussels in butter, and we took our evening meal on the shoreline in front of a fire. As we ate, we watched the red sash of sunset ripple on the wind-buffeted surface of the lake.

Then there was stargazing, a diversion I could never get enough of. There were always mysterious specks—satellites, probably—floating in the seas of the heavens, which invariably led to discussion regarding life on other planets or extraterrestrials. And meteors. We would lie on our backs in open fields under the canopy of a real-life planetarium and fix on the star-flecked heavens. Although we had witnessed dozens of meteor showers, we could never contain the *ooohs* and *ahhs* that escaped as the bright orbs arced across black skies spilling trails of golden glitter.

Bird watching became another favorite pastime. I once sat at the base of a hardwood tree in Maine watching a pileated woodpecker probe the bark for grubs directly above me while his manic excavation showered me with wood chips.

And night hikes. As fearful as I had been in my first days in Georgia of the dark woods and mysterious night sounds, I later found in the dark woods a sanctuary where I could sit alone and think in the company of the animals. I often strayed away from camp, following the beam of my flashlight until I found a comfortable roost on a rock or fallen log. Then I switched off the flashlight and instantly was enveloped in the womb of darkness. Without my sense of sight, my hearing and touch became heightened, and I could follow the progress of large and small creatures as they moved around and past me. Chipmunks, skunks, mice, and squirrels scurried, while deer cracked and thudded. As deer approached, I could hear the branches snap and feel the ground vibrating under the heavy impact of their hooves.

But the night woods weren't always serene. One night in Connecticut I left camp and found a seat in a grove of hemlock along the Housitanic River. It was perfectly still when a hoot owl perched in the tree behind me suddenly unleashed its eerie call. From a distance of twenty feet, it boomed as if through an amplified speaker. Spooked, I started and jumped to my feet. Equally startled, the owl took flight, and I heard its wing tips slap the hemlock branches as it retreated.

Streams were favorite spots for evening reveries. They titillated the ears and the eyes. If we listened, we could hear the lapping water trace the entire musical scale in a random melody of ethereal notes and chords, and if we probed the water with our flashlight beams, we could watch scads of bizarre performers—nymphs, water spiders, crayfish, minnows—as they ducked and darted, scampered and scuttled in and out of the spotlight.

There were times, too, when we used the streams as aquatic sports arenas. In mid-May, for instance, Dan and I camped near a stream in Devils Creek Watershed in Tennessee, where we staged the Devils Creek Regatta. We used our pocket knife to carve small boats from dead wood. Rocks wedged into the boats' undersides provided ballast, and we even went so far as to gouge holes for masts. We established a starting line at the head of a thirty-yard stretch of flat water; a chute where the water narrowed to a falls marked the finish line. For two hours, until darkness made it impossible to follow the course of the boats, we ran the river, and before it was over, each of us skippered a fleet of six or eight boats, some built for speed, some built for stability, and others built for the sheer beauty of their intricate hulls.

There were other games, too. In Maine, after we had resupplied in Caratunk, we left town and covered thirteen miles before deciding to hole up in an abandoned barn near a road crossing. After we sat idle for half an hour, Nick discovered a length of wire, which he soon wound into four rings. We drove sharpened stakes into the ground, twenty yards apart, and engaged in game after game of Appalachian Trail horseshoes.

My favorite pastime, though, was reading. Along the trail, I read a dozen books, mainly on nature or the environment. Among them were Thoreau's *Walden*, Annie Dillard's *Pilgrim at Tinker Creek*, Whitman's *Leaves of Grass*.

I had read Whitman and Thoreau in high school, but in the classroom of the Appalachian wilderness, their writing came to life. I could peer up from any page and find living examples of the words.

I recall reading a passage from *Walden* while I was camped in the Lake Country of Maine less than one hundred miles from Katahdin. We were literally following in Thoreau's footsteps, he having visited the area in 1846. Though we explored those mountains 133 years later, the words were written about me, about us, about our carefree existence, and about anyone who seeks communion with the wilderness:

Remember thy creator in the days of thy youth. Rise free from care before the dawn, and seek adventures. Let the noon find thee by other lakes, and the night overtake thee everywhere at home. There are no larger fields than these, no worthier games than here may be played. Grow wild according to thy nature, like these sedges and brakes. . . . Let the thunder rumble; what if it threaten ruin to farmers' crops! That is not its errand to thee. Take shelter under the cloud, while they flee to carts and sheds. Let not to get a living be thy trade, but thy sport. Enjoy the land, but own it not. Through want of enterprise and faith men are where they are, buying and selling, and spending their lives like serfs.

CHAPTER • NINE

Stopping Along the Way

Last night in Port Clinton, Pennsylvania, Dan and I learned once again that the magic of comradeship does not end at the trailhead but often extends into the small towns along the route. We spent the evening at the Port Clinton Hotel bar in the small blue-collar town with Chuck the snake handler, the boom-pa lady, and a handful of other colorful personalities, and we departed town this morning with a new page of names in our address books.

Those hikers who blast in and out of town, stopping only long enough to fill their stomachs and their foodbags, are missing a vital part of the trail experience. But even though I've been on the trail for months and have on many occasions been greeted with warmth and acceptance by total strangers, I still occasionally struggle with feelings of mistrust. I'm left wondering why someone would open himself to me when all he stands to gain in return is my own trust and acceptance. Such feelings, I suspect, result from lessons we're taught from the time we're very young. I wonder if they'll survive beyond completion of my hike.

—July 21, 1979, Allentown Hiking Club
Shelter, Pennsylvania

April 24 introduced me to new extremes of experience. The previous night we had weathered a fierce thunderstorm that left the woods strewn with splintered branches and uprooted trees. The following day wasn't much better. After leaving camp, we trudged through cold rain and ankle-deep muck, and over the long afternoon my thoughts turned again and again to the comforts of town.

By early evening, when we finally slipped down an embankment and landed on paved Georgia Highway 75, we faced a decision: we could continue up the trail through more muck and cold rain, or we could follow the road to more inviting surroundings. Though we had not planned a town stop for another few days, we consulted our maps, hung our thumbs, and set out for Helen, Georgia, a tourist resort of alpine chalets and quaint restaurants nine miles to the south.

After scoring a ride from a sympathetic local in a big car, Dan and I, along with four other sodden hikers, were soon ensconced in a cut-rate motel room—twenty-six dollars a night for the bunch of us—and drawing lots for the shower. En route to the motel, we had cajoled our driver into stopping at a local package store and a pizza joint before he deposited us at the motel office.

Six showers and an hour later, the room lay in shambles. Fetid shirts, shorts, boots, and socks lay in dank, aromatic piles in corners and on counter tops. Pack covers and rain parkas dripped from curtain rods. Pizza boxes and empty beer bottles cluttered bedside tables. In the bathroom, dirt-smudged towels steeped in standing water, and a dark water stain crept along the all-weather carpet from the bathroom into the bedroom. The soil we had rinsed from our bodies formed a miniature delta at the drain in the bathtub.

But none of us seemed to notice the clutter, or if we did we didn't much care. We were too busy indulging our wanton appetites. It wasn't until we switched on the television that it occurred to us that our few days on the trail had already wrought some changes.

We watched a special program about the life of American novelist Thomas Wolfe. The story of Wolfe, a true icon oclast, appealed to our own sense of freewheeling independence. Then a commercial came on the screen. It was an unremarkable advertisement—for corn chips or glass cleaner or hair spray—but it had an unusual effect. We laughed. We roared. We howled. We cried. Not so much at the product itself but at the realization that the world of fresh-smelling houses, clean-shaven faces, sporty sedans, dutiful housewives, and industrious husbands no longer connected with ours. The commercial clearly had been directed at someone else.

The next morning we made a quick stop at a local grocery store, hitchhiked back to the trailhead, and again picked up the white blazes. Even though we faced another day of rain and muck, those things seemed much less dismal. Our twelve hours in town had restored us, but the town stop had done more than that. It had provided evidence that by following the trail we had strayed into a strange new realm where the attractions of civilization, though still appealing, had assumed a new role, and I realized that with months remaining ahead of us, this shift in attitude was only the beginning.

Helen, Georgia, was our first town stop, and over the next several months we visited dozens of villages, cities, back-road hamlets, and crossroads. As it turned out, those outposts of civilization were in some ways as vital to the trail experience as the mountains themselves.

The towns allowed us to phone friends and relatives to catch up on important news from home. News from home that did not reach us via the phone lines usually awaited our arrival at the local post offices, where postal clerks processed and held scores of boxes—boxes of supplies, care packages, and letters—addressed to us in care of general delivery.

Towns afforded us breaks from the routine of big-mile days, and we celebrated the long, steep descents that led us into those settlements just as working men and women might have welcomed the five-o'clock whistle that marked the onset of a holiday.

Towns also exposed us to the distinctive people and cultures of the various regions of the eastern United States. Along the way, we encountered open, slow-talking Southerners; circumspect residents of the populous mid-Atlantic states; and wry, taciturn New Englanders. Each region and town provided its own brand of succor.

Most important, towns provided needed supplies. Without them we would have been forced either to carry five months' worth of food on our backs or to subsist on roots and berries. The first option, I suspect, would have left us crippled; the second might have left us dead, owing to our familiarity with only a few edible plants.

Food. Though we cursed it for all the weight a five- or seven-day supply added to the pack on the stiff ascents out of town, we also celebrated it when, during the first days along a new section, the foodbag promised both plenty and variety.

Then, toward the end of that same stretch, when our reserves ran low and we subsisted on the dregs of the food sack, we became obsessed by food, talked about it incessantly, craved it, longed for it. Mountains of ice cream, bags of cookies, slabs of red meat, bowls of crisp greens, and boxes of pastries, cakes, and pies—these were the stuff of hikers' dreams during the last few days and nights before a resupply stop.

Consider that most long-distance hikers eat and metabolize as many as six thousand calories a day. After the first couple of weeks on the trail, when exertion tends to suppress a hiker's appetite, most end-to-enders succumb to an incurable case of "hiker's disease," an affliction characterized by an appetite that simply cannot be satisfied.

I could not count the number of times I confronted stunned expressions on onlookers' faces as they observed my colleagues and me wandering along the aisles of a food market dazed and bewitched by the abundance while trying to decide what to consume first, second, third. . . . We were, in effect, prisoners of want suddenly freed in a climate-controlled environment of excess, and in weaker moments my companions and I were likely to consume half-gallons of ice cream, pound bags of cookies, and quarts of fruit juice before returning to the store for the second course.

Our binge eating wasn't limited to grocery stores. In Elk Park, North Carolina, for instance, three other hikers and I arrived at a restaurant soon after it opened on a Sunday afternoon, paid our three dollars each, and single-handedly consumed the entire contents of a salad bar before the owner politely but firmly invited us to move on.

In a northern Virginia town, I spent five hours at an all-you-can-eat restaurant with another hiker, downing dozens of plates of steamed shrimp. We finally left the establishment more to ease the finger cramps that resulted from peeling so much shellfish than because we had eaten our fill.

The challenge we faced as caloric consumers, as I liked to describe it, was to "toe the fine line between bliss and nausea." Regrettably, I crossed that line on occasion and suffered the consequences. On one such night in Gorham, New Hampshire, after first visiting the local McDonald's, I ate five heaping bowls of a vegetable stew we had prepared in the kitchen of the Congregational church where we were permitted to stay. When I had choked down the last spoonful, I staggered out onto the church lawn, unbuttoned my pants to relieve some of the pressure on my bloated abdomen, and lay in the grass, moaning like a pregnant mare in the throes of labor. As I did, I prayed for the nausea to pass and vowed never to eat that much again. I kept my resolution only until we arrived in the next town.

Once we had purchased our supplies at a market, it was customary for us to sit on the store's stoop, alternately loading supplies into our packs and wedging morsels into our mouths. The process of taking products from the shelves and preparing them for the backcountry became known as "throwing away Madison Avenue." Essentially, the process involved stripping off the boxes, wrappers, bags, and canisters, which catered more to the whims of marketing executives than to the needs of backcountry travelers. Once we had removed the items from their packages, we deposited them in plastic bags. The bags were durable as well as flexible, and they allowed us to take full advantage of every available square inch of pack space. Eliminating Madison Avenue also spared us several pounds of useless heft.

Though at times it seemed that we hikers took more than we gave in each of those towns, filling our stomachs and food bags before moving on, I like to think that an equitable exchange took place when hikers visited civilization. Because many of the trail towns lay far off the main roads, townsfolk often embraced us as ambassadors of good will and seemed never to tire of our tales of adventure from the surrounding woods.

Local merchants welcomed our business, and they stocked their shelves with dietary staples—macaroni-and-cheese, pasta noodles, rice, peanut butter, English muffins, lentils, summer sausage, instant oatmeal, sardines, granola bars, honey—that were perfectly suited to our transient needs. Innkeepers often allowed us to pile as many as ten hikers into a room designed to accommodate two, and they often adjusted their rates to ease the jolt to our meager budgets.

Most townsfolk were accustomed to having legions of straggly foot travelers loose in their streets, and they afforded us all the courtesy of temporary residents. We brought curious stares from tourists unfamiliar with the trail, and they often seemed puzzled and fascinated by our peculiar avocation. Their questions seldom varied: Where do you sleep? What do you do when it rains? What do you eat? Seen any snakes? Seen any bears? Don't your feet hurt? Where did you start? Where are you headin'? Why are you doing this? Our responses soon became as pat and predictable as the questions themselves, but I, for one, enjoyed sharing my experiences with anyone interested enough to listen.

Along our journey, we logged a series of fond memories of

our stopovers, some because of novelty, others because of kindness shown us. A few were because of the rich relationships we enjoyed with our hosts.

At Wesser, North Carolina, a settlement set on the banks of the Nantahala River 137 miles north of Springer, we sat for hours in the rustic health-food restaurant eating fresh-baked herb bread and peering through picture windows at kayakers navigating the rapids below. In Damascus, Virginia, known as the friendliest town on the trail, we lodged in a two-story hostel dubbed The Place, which was owned and operated by the Methodist church. We spent the evening swapping tales with our brothers and sisters on two wheels—transcontinental cyclists—who had embarked on the Centennial Route that passed through town and continued on to the West Coast.

In Charlottesville, Virginia, Dan and I crashed in a dilapidated fraternity house with walls and doors pocked with fist- and head-sized holes, and we spent the evening in a local pub listening to live country music.

In Duncannon, Pennsylvania, on the Susquehanna River, we shared the basement of the city firehouse with a foursome of teachers who worked with mentally disabled children.

Dan and I arrived in Port Clinton, Pennsylvania, on a Saturday afternoon and found our way to a covered pavilion that the city had designated as an overnight area for hikers. By dusk, after cranking a hand pump and washing the grit from my face, arms, and legs, I wandered through the streets of the working-class town. The place looked drab and depressed, and had it not been for the experiences that awaited me, I would have forever viewed Port Clinton as a decaying, lifeless burg on the verge of economic ruin.

On the way back to the pavilion, I strayed into the lounge at the Port Clinton Hotel and took a seat at the bar. Once inside, I suspected I had strayed into another establishment of the Erwin, Tennessee, ilk. The working-class locals perched on bar stools studied me closely, but none acknowledged me directly. I ordered a beer, which cost me twenty-five cents, and as I sipped it, I noticed that the bartender had deposited a handful of small plastic tokens in front of me. I finished the beer and ordered another, but when I tried to pay for it, the bartender motioned toward the tokens. "Son, the rest of your beers have already been paid for."

These stone-faced locals, it seems, were not as sour as they looked. Once I realized that I sat surrounded by bene-factors, I hefted my mug and toasted them. Whatever doubts I had had about the character of those folks vanished with my next draught, and in minutes I sat surrounded by local men and women, all hungry for news from the trail.

After a half-hour of chatter about the trail, a woman in her mid-thirties entered the room carrying a curious con-traption that resembled a pogo stick adorned with cymbals, bells, a tambourine, a snare drum, and a squeeze horn. She greeted me, walked over to the juke box, and dropped a nickel into the slot. Soon Bobby Vinton's voice crooned the "Beer Barrel Polka" through the speakers. She then began lurching around the dance floor, bouncing the contraption, which unleashed a cacophonous din of clangs and crashes in time with the music. After a brief demonstration, she handed the device to me.

"This is called a 'boom-pa,'" she said. "And it's custom-ary for the guest of honor to play it on the first song."

I was both honored and mortified. By now the bar had attracted a standing-room-only crowd, and all eyes were turned on me. Again, she selected the Bobby Vinton tune on the juke box, and I tentatively stepped to the center of the dance floor and, laughing, began pounding and clanging with as much enthusiasm as I could muster. The bar's pa-trons soon encircled me, raising their beer mugs and cheer-ing me on. When the tune ended, I returned to my seat to a round of applause. I had been duly initiated.

The boom-pa's clamorous din and the crowd noise had apparently carried several city blocks to the pavilion and reached Dan's ears. Drawn by his curiosity, he followed the sound to the bar, and when he passed through the door, I announced to my newfound friends that it would only be fitting to afford Dan the same honor they had extended to me. Soon the polka tune roared through the speakers, and I sat back and laughed as Dan plied the boom-pa and received the same frenzied response.

Normally cool and composed, Dan sat with his mouth agape for some minutes after his boom-pa debut, and I felt obliged to explain our good fortune. As I explained the bargain beers, at twenty-five cents a draught, and the juke box, where a quarter bought five plays, he, too, began to amass the small tokens. Before long, both of us were gloriously drunk, sitting at the bar and hobnobbing with the other patrons as intimately as if we had shared the same parentage. Among them was a toothless fellow named Chuck, a self-described snake charmer who claimed to keep rattlers in his car as insurance against thieves. Though Dan and I were accustomed to providing tales of wild adventure, we yielded to a more masterful storyteller and passed the evening hours listening to Chuck relate fascinating—though unlikely—Indian legends, mountain ghost tales, and sorcery yarns.

When Dan and I departed Port Clinton the next morning, the town appeared much more vibrant and alive than it had when we arrived.

Several weeks later, we again encountered good fortune near Unionville, New York, at the lakeside home of Gary, a new age minister, and his wife and two sons. Dan and I—along with Paul, who had since joined our group—had met Gary at a road crossing a week south of Unionville when he stopped to give us a lift to the local grocery store. Back at the trailhead, he gave us his phone number and invited us to call him when we reached Unionville.

A few days later, we phoned him from the trailhead, piled into the back of his car, and soon arrived at his house. That evening, after we had enjoyed a lavish gourmet feast on the lakeside deck, Gary, an accomplished musician, uncorked a bottle of wine, lighted a candelabra, and serenaded us with beautiful classical music on his baby grand piano. It was the first music we had heard for weeks, and Paul and Dan, both musicians themselves, sat rapt through Gary's performance.

The next day we accompanied Gary and his wife to a formal lawn party. The host and his family occupied a massive country estate with manicured grounds and a private tennis court. A live rock band performed in a covered gazebo. Most of the few dozen guests sported designer-label togs. Dressed in our cutoff fatigue pants, rag wool socks, and tattered shirts, we looked like a trio of vagabonds who had strayed away from the local mission, but we soon discovered that our shabby dress, and our status as Appalachian Trail thru-hikers, only enhanced our romantic mystique among the hippie-turned-yuppie partygoers.

Paul and I borrowed a couple of rackets and spent the afternoon on the tennis courts. Between sets we raided the twenty-foot banquet table heaped with enough food to pitch a famished hiker into delirium. There were steamed clams and crabs, roast beef, ham, deviled eggs, salads, fresh fruit, fresh-baked bread, and kegs of iced beer.

After a two-day stay with Gary, we returned to the trail. Over the next several weeks we frequently found packages filled with books, food, and tidings waiting for us at post offices, courtesy of our zany friend.

Farther north we splashed in a lake with children from Pawling, New York. While in Pawling, on a dare I had my ear pierced. In Hanover, New Hampshire, we dined on five-star dormitory fare in Thayer Hall at Dartmouth—one of the more expensive colleges in the United States—and stayed at a former fraternity house that then housed both men and women and where the term *coed* applied even to the showers and the bathrooms.

Our passage through New Hampshire's White Mountains—the most punishing section of the trail—was fortified in part by a visit by Paul's mother, who lived in nearby Peterboro. When our gang—Nick, Dan, Paul, and Victor, the friend who had left the trail in North Carolina—reached Franconia Notch in North Woodstock, New Hampshire, we thumbed the few miles to a park at Profile Lake and met Mrs. Dillon, a jovial woman in her mid-forties. She had arrived in a station wagon brimming with things that trail life had deprived us of: a guitar, cold beer, and food. As we shuttled the food from the car, Mrs. Dillon confessed that she had been cooking for the better part of a week, and it showed. There were pans of fried chicken, plates of deviled eggs, a half-dozen cakes, cookies, and salads: potato salad, tossed salad, macaroni salad, Jell-O salad, cole slaw, fruit salad.

Throughout the long, sun-drenched afternoon, we sidled up to the picnic table, ate our fill, and rolled into the grass, only to begin the cycle again an hour later. Despite our efforts to find the bottoms of all the bowls, plates, and pans, there seemed to be no end to the food, and when we said good-bye to Mrs. Dillon, we loaded all the surplus we could carry into our packs and happily strained up the trail as if we had shouldered a load of gold bricks.

In Rangeley, Maine, the town of dowdy, vacationing retirees, a snooty teller in a posh tourist's bank glanced at my shabby clothes, refused to cash a one-hundred-dollar postal money order, and told me that no one should visit Rangeley without sufficient cash. A few blocks up the street, the teller at an austere, prefab workingman's bank cashed my check without a blink and for a half-hour engaged me in conversation about the trail.

Monson, Maine, is the last outpost of civilization for one hundred miles for hikers headed north, and a church converted to a boarding house provides lodging for most hikers passing through town. For some days prior to reaching Monson, we had heard stories about curious goings on in the town, which is situated on the fringe of the northern wilderness. There were stories about a haggard alcoholic—a resident at the church—who was prone to pestering hikers and pleading with them for spare change to feed his habit.

Though many stories grow with each telling as they're passed from hiker to hiker, the word on Monson was, if anything, muted compared with what we discovered when we arrived there.

Once in town, Paul opted to spend the extra money and stay at Shaw's Boarding House, a quaint bed and breakfast run by Mr. and Mrs. Shaw, while Dan and I, both watching our budgets, chose to stay at the church.

When I arrived at the church, a square-jawed man in his

sixties sat on the stoop. He wore thick glasses, seemed alert and well mannered, and asked me about the trail. After he helped me find a bunk in the church loft, he ushered me through the converted church while I kept an eye open for the belligerent drunk I had heard so much about.

I didn't realize it at the time, but I had already met him. After about an hour, the man approached me and asked me for seventy-five cents. Still disinclined to believe this was the man who had inspired the rumors, I handed him a dollar. He took it and walked directly to the local package store, where he bought a pint of Old Duke wine. By 2:00 P.M., he had finished his first bottle. Through the afternoon he systematically begged enough change from other hikers to buy his second, third, and fourth rounds.

By early evening, his eyes were bleary and glazed, his speech was slurred, and he had become the gruff, abrasive character we had been warned about.

"Break my arm, son," he muttered to me, thrusting his stout forearm in my direction. "Ain't no man can break my arm."

I learned later that he was challenging me to arm-wrestle. When I declined, he moved along and challenged other hikers. Soon one of the other hikers called his bluff and squared off with him over the kitchen table. In spite of the muscular physique he had developed while working as a logger, the drunk offered little resistance, and the hiker slammed his arm to the table. Tears welled in the old man's eyes, and he stumbled back to his room to the companionship of the Old Duke.

He emerged some time later as Dan and I fixed dinner in the church kitchen. Though he was still drunk, his disposition had softened somewhat, and he sat muttering unintelligibly at the table. As we ate our dinner, he disappeared and returned a few minutes later with a stack of ancient black-and-white photos. "This is my mother," he mumbled, pointing to an attractive woman in turn-of-the-century dress. "This is me," he continued, indicating a much younger, smiling version of himself surrounded by classmates in a grade-school photograph. A later photo showed him—young and strong—in a military uniform, his shoulders straining the seams of his shirt and his stout neck encircled by a tie.

"Then I could break any man's arm," he said, tapping the picture. He curled his arm and pointed to his biceps.

As he continued through the photos, he began to cry. The cry became a moan, and soon he sat alone in a corner of the kitchen, weeping, his eyes closed.

As I sat watching him slump, blubbering, into unconsciousness, I wanted to cry with him. The schoolboy he had pointed out to me in the photo had, no doubt, viewed his future with as much hope and promise as his classmates had. Where had he gotten off track? What had destroyed him?

That evening I climbed the loft to my bed at 10:30 P.M. and slept soundly for several hours. Then I heard a sound I'll never forget. It started at 2:00 A.M. from below the rafters and jarred me awake. It was, simply, the most pitiful sound I've ever heard. It began with the sound of retching, as if the old man were coughing up his heart and lungs. For a half hour, he gagged and vomited, and when the wave of nausea had passed, the retching was replaced by moaning and wailing. Then more retching. And more moaning. So it went through the night.

By dawn, he apparently had purged his guts and his emotional reserves, and I found him sitting in the kitchen early the next morning, his eyes clear. He was alert, and the belligerence was gone; he was the same polite, quiet man I had met upon arriving the previous day. He was ready to start a new day, to meet new hikers, to ply them for more change, to follow the same worn path to the package store, to run through his dog-eared photographs, and, finally, to pass the night gagging on bile and despair.

Out of town and back on the trail, I found a cluster of young ferns, picked a few sprigs, and rolled them between my palms. I held them to my nose, breathed in the sweet musk, and rejoiced in knowing that one hundred miles lay between me and the next town. As I walked, for the first time in my life I wondered what it would be like to grow old.

CHAPTER TEN

Hot Springs Rhapsody

We're back on the trail again, after spending ten days in Hot Springs, North Carolina. I've never been one to abide traditional religious values or to put much stock in spiritual transformation or rebirth, but I know that my stay in Hot Springs showed me more, taught me more, and changed me more than any other experience of my life. During our stay, after working in the fields and talking with Randall and Elmer, I felt as though I had awakened from a long sleep and for the first time began to experience the reality of the world around me. I left town today, not only renewed physically but utterly transformed spiritually. After this, I wonder what other experiences await me farther north.

—May 19, 1979, Spring Mountain Shelter, Tennessee

"'Tis a gift to be simple, 'tis a gift to be free, 'tis a gift to end up where you ought to be," Randall sang, giving life to an old Shaker hymn as he scratched the bow across the strings of his fiddle. I joined in the chorus. Dan did, too. The words seemed to capture the essence of what we had experienced since arriving in Hot Springs, North Carolina, a few days earlier.

As I stood at the edge of a furrowed field bristling with newly planted sorghum shoots, I was surrounded by friends: Dan, Randall, the proprietor of the farm, and Elmer, Randall's business partner, who operated a restored Victorian hotel three miles down the serpentine two-lane in town. The hotel, dubbed the Inn, had become a new age mecca for hikers where dinner time brought lavish five-course vegetarian meals and conversation that invariably explored philosophy, religion, and politics. Both Randall and Elmer, as ordained ministers and children of the sixties, were well versed in all three topics. Elmer had studied at Duke University, Randall at Yale.

Above and around the expanse of cleared farmland, the densely forested peaks of the Pisgah National Forest probed a cloudless blue evening sky. Randall, a tall, thin man in his mid-forties with a bushy beard that reached to his chest and shoulder-length hair coiled into a bun at the top of his head, continued his serenade, which he explained was more for the benefit of his crops than for his human audience. Randall's grandpappy, who had lived and died a farmer in these mountains, had told his grandson that fiddling to a newly planted field would ensure a healthy crop.

"'Tis a gift to be simple . . ." Randall continued.

The lyrics of the hymn might have been written about Randall himself and his bohemian lifestyle, and they characterized the wonderful dichotomy he represented. On one hand, he was a man who had traveled the world and had been educated at one of the nation's most prestigious universities. On the other, he was a man born and bred in the nearby mountains who had returned from his travels with a yen to regain his roots, to embrace the solitude provided by a back-country farm, to "wind up where he ought to be." In spite of his theological education, or perhaps because of it, he believed in the magic of such simple mountain folkways as fiddling to a field of fledgling crops just as fervently as he believed in the inherent goodness of the earth. Standing there beneath the mountains and in the company of friends, I began to believe in it too. Dan and I had spent the preceding five days in Hot Springs, at the Inn and on the farm, and in that time I had discovered that this small North Carolina hamlet was more than just another resupply stop. It was Eden, a place where hikers could find nourishment, love, acceptance, awakening. For me it provided all those things and more.

Randall and Elmer were two spiritual teachers who had risen out of the ashes of the sixties, preserving all the finest precepts of that era—brotherhood, sharing, love, peace, respect for nature—and carrying the banner into a new age. Because of them, my stay in Hot Springs showed me more, taught me more, and changed me more than any other experience on the trail. When Dan and I resumed our hike after a ten-day rest, I left the town renewed physically and awakened spiritually.

We had arrived in Hot Springs on May 11, tired and haggard from our first three weeks on the trail. Though our blisters had healed, we had encountered the second, and in some ways more debilitating, stage of physical afflictions that plague long-distance hikers. Under the pounding of fifteen- to twenty-mile days, our joints—knees and ankles—constantly ached; we had covered the sixty-eight difficult miles of trail through the Smokies in only four days. Making matters worse, the cuff of my boot had irritated the Achilles tendon of my left leg, and as I hobbled along, each step brought searing pain. I had been forced to walk in my running shoes, which provided little support, and I had tethered my boots—along with their five-pound heft—to my pack.

Then there was the fatigue. Our systems seemed to be wearing down, and each day left us more tired than the previous day. In short, we were ready for a break. We had learned from a southbound hiker that Hot Springs was a five-star stop, and in spite of our fatigue and my pestering leg pain, we pushed the last twenty-three miles into town in one day.

Once out of the woods, we arrived at the hiker hostel operated by the Jesuits, dumped our packs, and continued into town.

The town of Hot Springs consists of a main street, an eighth-mile stretch of hardware shops, grocery stores, a laundromat, and a couple of cafes. Populated by farmers and mechanics in work clothes, it looks like any other small southern crossroads town. That is, until you spot the Inn.

As I neared the main intersection in town, I peered off to the right and through the trees spotted a magnificent two-story Victorian edifice painted white and appointed with a sharp-peaked roof, ornate columns, and a verandah that circled the entire second floor. The building—surrounded by gas stations, modest frame houses, and streets lined with rusting pickup trucks—would not have looked more out of place if it had been set on Fifth Avenue in New York City.

I stepped onto a covered porch, cluttered with bicycles and hanging plants, and opened the door into the kitchen. Inside, Elmer, clad in faded overalls and a flannel shirt and with a bushy salt-and-pepper beard, stood poised over an antique black cast-iron stove that spanned the wall opposite me. Randall stood by the sink, washing greens—onions, lettuce, and spinach—grown on his farm. Once in the room, I was enveloped in a cloud of savory aromas. Dill, curry, sage, and garlic wafted away from a quartet of pots simmering on the stove, mingling with the scent of bread baking in the oven. As I stood breathing the aroma, Elmer approached, gripped me in a hug, and welcomed me to the Inn. Here, I learned, everyone was greeted with a hug. Then Randall introduced himself, and he, too, welcomed me with a hug.

After the greeting, Elmer invited me to explore the Inn, while the two returned to the task of preparing dinner for the twenty-plus hikers and other guests who would soon arrive for dinner.

I set out from the kitchen and made my way across a wood-paneled hallway and into a sitting room. The room had lost none of the Victorian charm it must have possessed when, near the turn of the century, the Inn catered to the wealthy clientele who journeyed to Hot Springs to bask in the town's natural mineral baths just two blocks away. A woven rug covered the hardwood floor; a wood-burning stove probed into the center of the room; and horsehair couches and easy chairs nestled in corners next to antique tables and lamps. Original art work from the 1920s hung between and above bookshelves that lined the walls. Many of the volumes were old leather-bound classics, and there were dozens of more modern coffee-table books of photography and art. But most of the books were devoted to nature, religion, philosophy, travel, and adventure. As I scanned the shelves, the ethereal strains of one of Bach's Brandenburg Concertos filled the room, reminding me of how much I had missed music while on the trail.

As I continued to explore, I found my way to the main dining room, outfitted with a half-dozen antique wooden tables and chairs. Two of the Inn's bedrooms opened off the main floor; the rest were upstairs. Most featured an antique four-poster bed draped with a patchwork quilt and a door leading out onto the verandah. At every turn I encountered more books, and arrangements of fresh-cut spring flowers sat on tables in each room.

At the time, a room for the night cost eight dollars, and four dollars bought a four- or five-course vegetarian feast of gourmet soups, salads, breads, stews, and desserts—all made from scratch and served family-style. After our self-guided tour, Dan and I quickly retrieved our packs from the Jesuit hostel and took up lodging at the Inn.

Our first dinner there began, as all of them do, with a welcome from Elmer. After a brief prayer he invited guests to introduce themselves to the group, and each hiker shared a bit of personal history and a general reaction to life on the trail. Then the steaming platters of food arrived: spinach salad with vinaigrette dressing, black-bean soup, rice stew, whole-wheat bread, and fresh apple and berry pies, all hot from the oven. We washed it down with iced herbal tea.

After dinner Elmer hosted a wine-tasting party, which drew a crowd of the artists and artisans—photographers, painters, poets, woodworkers—who had begun to settle in Hot Springs, turning it into a sort of backwoods Renaissance community with the Inn as its cultural epicenter. While Elmer entertained the more highbrow guests, Randall, whose cultural tastes were a shade folksier, hosted a collection of twelve hikers who lingered in the kitchen. The artists sipped wine and listened to classical music, while the rest of us pursued more down-home forms of amusement, sipping Tennessee whiskey and clogging to strains of mountain music from Randall's fiddle and the guitars of two of his friends. Soon the cramped kitchen erupted into a regular hoedown, with hikers swinging arm in arm and stomping the floor with lug-soled boots.

Later that evening, when only Dan and I remained, Elmer suggested we take a drive; he wanted to show us something. We climbed into a rickety, decades-old Rambler and set off up the mountain. A few minutes later we stopped at a pull-off on the quiet, two-lane highway and got out. Below us spread a scene of such stark beauty that I'll never forget it.

Several hundred yards below, miles away from the nearest incandescent light bulb, lay Randall's farm, its rolling fields shining silver in the moonlight. Above it rose the dark silhouettes of the mountains. In the center of the plot of cleared fields, a rustic two-room cabin perched on a hillside above a mountain brook. Moonbeams sliced through the skeleton of a rickety barn that stood beside it.

"We try to keep this place secret," said Elmer. "But it's so special that we like to share it with some of the people who come through town who we think might appreciate it."

Randall went on to explain, in his thick Carolina drawl, that he had purchased the farm several years earlier, and since then it had become his haven, his retreat, a place where he could pursue a simple, honest life of self-sufficiency that would keep him grounded in the earth. The cabin had no electricity or running water, and he worked the farm without chemical pesticides or motorized tools, tilling the fields with a horse-drawn plow and spreading cow manure as organic fertilizer. Oil lamps provided evening light, and he warmed his dwelling and cooked over a wood-burning stove.

As we stood mesmerized by the scene, Elmer broke in. "We've really enjoyed the two of you, and we'd like for you to consider a proposition. If you need a few days' rest, we'd love to have you stay with us. You can help around the Inn or work on the farm for room and board, and you're welcome to stay as long as you like."

As far as I was concerned, there wasn't much deciding to

be done. I needed rest, and the Inn and farm promised to expose me to a new way of life, one that my city upbringing had deprived me of. I voted to stay. Dan thought for a few seconds, then assented.

"This trail is about experiences," he said. "And I think there's a lot we could learn from this place."

So we took up residence in Hot Springs, like dozens of other hikers before and since who have wandered into town for a one-day stopover and wound up staying for days, weeks, or even years, living and learning from those two remarkable teachers.

And we did learn. For the next ten days, we shuttled between the Inn and the farm, working the fields through the morning and afternoon hours and in the evenings serving meals at the Inn. Each day brought new discoveries, new insights. For me, most of them occurred at Randall's farm, where I spent my nights, while Dan stayed at the Inn.

On the farm mornings began at dawn with plates of hot beans and cornbread Randall had cooked on his stove. After breakfast Dan and I, armed with hoes, acted as organic weedkillers, severing the necks of weeds that encroached on the tender, new sorghum sprigs. One day as we hoed, Dan and I sang choruses of old Negro spirituals, the sun warming our shirtless backs. When the hoeing was done, we rode a horse-drawn cart, spreading manure along uncultivated fields that Randall would soon till behind Bill, his chestnut-brown workhorse.

Afternoons always ended with a hike up the mountainside to a spring-fed stream dammed into a series of cool, thigh-deep pools where, naked, we splashed the sweat and dirt from our bodies before walking to the Inn to serve the evening meal.

Mornings, I hovered close to Randall as he entered the barn and soothed his cow, Molly, now nine months with calf. On Mother's Day morning Randall summoned me to the barn, where Molly lay licking her limpid, gangly offspring, which Randall named Daisy. She had been born only minutes earlier, and for the next several days Molly's milk was rich yellow with colostrum, which tasted heavy and sweet.

Other days, I worked little, instead spending the day with a fishing pole, rock-hopping along the mountain brook spanned by the rickety swinging bridge that separated Randall's spread from the quarter-mile dirt road that led to the highway.

Evenings were always special times. After we had finished our chores at the Inn, Elmer, Dan, and I walked or drove the three miles from the Inn to the rutted, quarter-mile dirt road that led back to the swinging bridge and Randall's farm. On one beautiful spring night the four of us sat on the front porch of the cabin on a dilapidated car seat salvaged from an old Volkswagen. We filled metal cups with whiskey mixed with fresh mint leaves and cold spring water dipped from an old barrel that sat on the side of the porch. A rubber hose led from a spring high up the mountain down across a field and onto the porch, where it constantly infused the barrel with ice-cold water. The barrel, which was outfitted with a hinged door and a series of shelves, served as Randall's refrigerator. There he kept Molly's milk stored in a gallon glass jar.

That night at dusk, the sun burned like fire when it touched the ridge line, and it spread into a beautiful horizontal blaze of red, pink, and magenta. We had front-row seats for the pyrotechnics, and after the sunlight began to fade, Randall took up his fiddle and, like a new-aged pied piper, led us out to the edge of the plowed field where he began stretching out the old Shaker hymn to encourage his crops to grow. Even today, when I hear the hymn, I fondly recall my days in Hot Springs.

That night, after Elmer and Dan had returned to the Inn, Randall lit the stove to heat water for tea, and we sat down over the small kitchen table draped with an oilcloth. A single oil lamp illuminated the scarred, rough-hewn walls hung with mementos from Randall's life. There were Japanese watercolors from his travels to the East to study Eastern religion during his years at Yale. There were photographs of his two sons, Randall, Jr., and Laird. There were mobiles crafted from bird bones or chips of quartz. There were shelves lined with hundreds of the knickknacks Randall had collected since moving to the farm: colorful stones, deer antlers, snakeskins, and turtle shells. They were, like the dwelling itself, beautifully austere, things most people would have swept aside to make room for more elegant furnishings. But they were Randall's most prized possessions, and not one of them had cost him a cent.

We had grown very close over the previous few days, and I had begun to feel like a student in the presence of a wise teacher who instructed through precept and example without ever seeming to teach at all. Randall had a way of asking questions—thoughtful questions—that inspired introspection.

We had talked easily for a half-hour or so, sipping tea, when Randall staggered me with an ostensibly simple question that begged for a deeper response. "Will you share with me who you are?" I laughed, but I realized that it was a question I had been asking myself daily since I started the trail.

As I began to answer, I sensed that I was on the verge of a cathartic outpouring. For the next seven hours we talked, and it was the most honest, revealing, illuminating encounter I've ever had. I traced my history, not only exploring important events, but finding myself realizing for the first time the impact of those events, their meaning, how they had shaped me, led me in one direction or another, and how, ultimately, they had led me to the trail and here to Randall's farm.

As the night passed and Randall refilled our tea mugs, I shared things about myself that I had never broached before. I confessed. I voiced regrets. I expressed hopes. I talked about the kind of person I wanted to become: a person who loved and trusted more, a person who gave more, a person who fully appreciated life's simple blessings. As I spoke, I began to believe that such changes were possible.

I talked about the trail and how in three short weeks it had dazzled me and introduced me to a new world, one I had never imagined existed. A world full of goodness and beauty.

After I finished, I asked Randall the same question, and he shared his story with me. About the incompatible lifestyles that had divided him from his wife, she being drawn to the city, he to his primitive farm. About his sons, whom he loved desperately and saw too infrequently. He talked about his spiritual search that had led him to Yale and later to the Far East. About his entry into the ministry and the rejection that resulted when his new-aged Christianity clashed with the Fundamentalist values of his conservative neighbors. Finally he talked about his decision to drop out, to abandon the mechanized world and sow his hopes for a better life here on the farm.

Near dawn Randall rose from the table and put his arm around me, thanking me for the soul-deep dialogue we had shared. After bidding him goodnight and with an oil lamp in hand, I climbed the ladder to the open-air loft where I slept. Before settling to sleep, I extinguished the lamp and walked to the edge of the loft, which looked out over the silent fields and shadowed mountains. The evening chill felt clean and good against my face, and I watched the steam of my breath billow and fade. Beyond, I could see the dew twinkling in the moonlight, and I detected the faint smell of manure, the sweet bite of hay, the perfume of clover. The rich tang of wood smoke hung in the air, and I heard Molly and her new calf lowing softly in the barn. I heard the water lapping over the stones in the stream. Suddenly, the boundaries separating me from the tranquil night world disappeared. The mountains engulfed me, and I began to feel as if I had just been born into a world filled with peace.

I experienced such an intense swell of emotion that I could hardly contain it, and for the first time in my life I knew that God and all His goodness lurked in every rock, in every tree, in every blade of grass, and in me. I walked to the mattress, climbed under the quilt, and lay—awake—until dawn, fearful that if I slept, I would awaken to find the feelings gone.

But several days later, when Dan and I said good-bye to Elmer and Randall and departed Hot Springs on May 19, those feelings were still as surely connected to me as my pack and walking stick. From then on the trail seemed different—more inviting, more filled with wonder, more charged with excitement. And as we picked up the white blazes, heading north, I realized that what I had discovered in Hot Springs was just the beginning. Hundreds of miles lay ahead, miles full of promise.

CHAPTER ELEVEN

Critters

I'm learning that nature can be as harsh as it is beautiful. I watched tonight as Randall's cat crept up into the open loft of the cabin, crouched, and uncoiled, seizing a bat that had been fluttering around the rafters in the lantern light. The cat then walked past me down the ladder with the bat still wriggling in her jaws. The act was so quick, so efficient, and yet so horrifying to me, perhaps because I haven't watched many living things die. Afterward, it occurred to me that predators like the cat are playing out their roles in this theater without malice or spite or cruelty, which we humans tend to ascribe to them and their killing acts.
—*May 16, 1979, Randall's Farm,*
Hot Springs, North Carolina

In many ways, the Appalachian Trail was a thriving biology lab or, more precisely, a biology theater where myriad critters—many I had no idea existed—bustled, stirred, buzzed, tittered, slithered, and scrambled about, entertaining and educating us with their antics. Through them we received a firsthand survival lesson.

But the animals offered us more than that. Over time, they became our colleagues, appealing to our sense of sight or sound through all of our days and nights on the trail and reminding us always that man, the animal, is never alone, never wanting for companions. There was the screech of the pileated woodpecker winging unseen through densely foliated tree tops. Graceful hawks and buzzards spiraled effortlessly on thermals. Barred owls or wild turkeys glided agilely on four-foot wings through dense hardwood forests. Woodchucks, chipmunks, squirrels, rummaged through the underbrush for seeds or insect larva. Skunks sauntered slowly across the trail with their young in tow.

There was the collective drone of millions of insects—the rhythmic tweep of crickets, the rasp of cicadas, the oscillating buzz of bumblebees weaving through the underbrush. The flutelike trill of the brown thrush and the incessant banter of the whip-poor-will violated the sanctity of night; and we could hear the tapping and pawing of white-tailed deer as they foraged through open meadows after dark.

In our daily and nightly encounters with the animals, it became difficult not to view them as paradigms, as living symbols of simplicity, contentment, and clarity of purpose in the often charitable, sometimes hostile, world of the wilderness. For the animals, to live was enough. Whitman captured that sentiment so well in *Leaves of Grass:*

> I think I could turn and live with animals,
>   they are so placid and self-contained,
> I stand and look at them long and long.
> They do not sweat and whine about their condition,
> They do not lie awake in the dark and weep for their sins,
> They do not make me sick discussing their duty to God,
> Not one is dissatisfied, not one is demented with the
>   mania of owning things,
> Not one kneels to another, nor to his kind that lived
>   thousands of years ago,
> Not one is respectable or unhappy over the whole earth.

I saw my first black bear in the Smokies as I hiked alone from Ice Water Springs to Cosby Knob in the northern section of the national park. He was a great three-year-old male, and he sat in the middle of the trail with his feet splayed outward, back erect like a Buddha in brown fur. Placid and self-contained, he seemed to embody the spirit of Whitman's tribute.

When I first spotted him, I wanted to shout, to share my excitement with my companions behind me on the trail, but I realized that to do so would have sent the animal fleeing through the trees. Instead, I stood trembling, like an adolescent who has just discovered sex, studying the bear as he swept the branches of a small bush into his gaping mouth.

The bear wasn't beautiful, and he wasn't majestic. In fact, he was somewhat waggish, with his abundant fat and baggy skin draped around him like an outsized black overcoat and with a vacant, blissful expression spread across his face. But he was also astonishing, astonishing because he was there at all: a massive wild beast pursuing his simple livelihood not forty yards in front of me.

After two minutes I ventured closer and snapped his photograph. Because I was positioned downwind, his powerful sense of smell—many times more acute than my own—didn't register my scent, and he was left to evaluate me through his rather feeble eyesight. After scrutinizing me for several seconds, he showed no alarm and remained where he sat until he had eaten his fill and decided to move on. I followed his clamorous passage down the mountain by tracing the heavy thud of his footfalls and the rustle of snapping branches.

When he was gone, I felt blessed to have been permitted such an intimate glimpse of one of North America's largest creatures, and I realized that our encounter was vastly more honest, more revealing, than ever might have occurred in a zoo. He and I had met on equal terms. No fences separated us; no manmade walls sealed him in or kept him out. He was free to roam as he pleased, freer in many ways than I, who adhered to established trails while he, guided by whim or instinct, created his own.

Taken alone, the encounter with the bear was enough to thrill me for weeks, but it was only one of three major wildlife sightings I had logged over the previous few days.

Two days earlier I had stood within ten yards of a six-point buck. I had left my backpack on the ridge at Spencer Field, at five thousand feet, and had wandered down a sunlit trail to fill my water bottle at a spring. As the chilly water tumbled over my hands, I heard a twig snap and looked up to see him peering at me.

My heart pounded as I watched him, certain that at any moment he would spook and vanish through the trees. But he never did. After several minutes, he strayed away at an easy pace, rooting for acorns as he went.

Then there were the wild boars. As I ascended from Spence Field toward the summit of Thunderhead late in the afternoon, I peered ahead to see an ample brown rump disappear into the brush. An eighth of a mile farther up the trail, I glanced thirty yards below me and saw an entire herd of twelve to fourteen wild boars—from three hundred-pound sows to cat-sized piglets—scampering through a thicket. I later learned that the boars were descendants of the Russian wild boars introduced to the area in 1910 by a lodge keeper who had imported them to serve as game for his clientele. The boars proved an elusive quarry, and the hunting lodge soon closed its doors, but the animals went on to thrive in the park.

Later that evening when I reached Derrick Knob Shelter, six miles north, I met a ranger on horseback. Slung over his shoulder was a shotgun mounted with a spotlight. He was boar hunting, part of a park-wide effort to eradicate the animals, which already had destroyed acres of foliage by rooting for acorns with their tusks. Above three thousand feet, the ranger would drag his kill off the trail and leave it as food for the carrion eaters.

Through the spring and summer, the ruffed grouse also became an important woodland symbol and a perfect emblem of the passing of the seasons. The game birds were always willing to share the secrets of their life cycle and their tactics of self-preservation with any passerby willing to look and listen.

I heard the birds long before I first glimpsed them. On our second night on the trail, for instance, I heard an eerie drumming sound that resembled the noise of a basketball being dribbled with increasing tempo on a carpeted floor. I heard that sound again and again over the next few days, yet neither Dan nor I had the slightest notion of what it was. We learned later that the dribbling sound arose from a male ruffed grouse beating the air with its wings to attract a mate.

Several days later as I ambled along a tranquil stretch of trail lost in thought, a sudden explosion of thundering wings jarred me to attention. Out of the corner of my eye, I spotted two birds the size of large game hens beating their wings and flying erratically through the trees. Their black, brown, and tan feathers provided perfect camouflage, and when they lit in trees several hundred feet away, they virtually disappeared into the background colors of the wilderness.

As the weeks passed, I found myself repeatedly startled by the grouse. Even though I encountered them every few days, I never learned to anticipate their frenetic, graceless retreat. Yet with each encounter I learned more about them. I soon learned, for instance, that when spooked, the male fled to a faraway tree, while the hen stayed near the nest. Though separated by some distance, the two birds maintained a constant communication of staccato squawks, perhaps a verbal assessment of their two-legged intruder. I also found that if I ignored their decoy and instead located the now-abandoned nest, I could glimpse tiny, perfectly camouflaged chicks darting for cover in the underbrush.

One day as I walked along the trail through the Blue Ridge of Virginia, I encountered a nest and, as usual, the male grouse scattered while the female clung to the ground. When she noticed that I had spied the nest, she employed her first diversionary tactic, which no doubt was intended to decoy predators. She hopped onto the trail in front of me, staggering drunkenly and feigning a broken wing. When she looked back and realized that I had called her bluff, she shifted to her second tactic, one that I still regard as the most perfect act of selfless devotion I've ever seen. Now twenty feet ahead on the trail, she turned to face me and billowed out her feathers until she had doubled in size. Squawking maniacally, she charged.

I held my position as the protective mother approached, but when she began nipping at my legs with her beak and thrashing me with her wings, I suddenly found myself fleeing down the trail—more amazed than afraid—with the enraged hen in hot pursuit.

As the spring yielded to summer, the chicks continued to grow with each sighting. By summer's end the chaos of dozens of thrashing wings greeted me whenever I encountered a nest, with father, mother, and offspring together taking wing in retreat.

Other birds had adapted more graciously to our presence and approached rather than withdrew from us. While I hiked through the Green Mountains of Vermont, for instance, one day I stopped in a spruce grove to have a snack. Pulling a granola bar from my pack, I sat on a rock, but no sooner had I peeled off the wrapper than a gray Canada jay landed squarely on my shoulder. At first I suspected that I had been visited by a winged demon, but soon the jay roosted on my finger and nibbled from my hand.

Through the north woods, the plump, round-headed birds, also known as scavenger jays or camp jays, became invited dinner guests and even entertainers. On the last night of our hike, in the twin shelters at Katahdin Stream Campground, one hiker in our group plugged both of his nostrils with bread, lay on his back, and soon catered a buffet for two jays. While the birds roosted on his chin and picked the bread from his nose, the rest of us howled, more shocked by the behavior of our own species than by that of the animals.

The jays were perhaps the most loveable among the camp raiders that abounded on the trail. The others engaged us in a never-ending battle of wits, but while we often disdained their efforts to pillage our supplies, we also marveled at their pluck and adaptability. They had learned to regard humans as hosts, not intruders.

Mice. When Dante described the inferno, rife with fire and darkness, he omitted one detail: mice. Millions of them, with rasping teeth and clattering claws.

I had my first encounter with mice on my third night on the trail. I had slept beside my foodbag in the shelter, certain that no creature would venture close to a sleeping human. I awoke to find a quarter-sized hole leading through the green nylon and into each of the half-dozen plastic bags inside. As it turned out, the stealthy mice had sampled from the bags, mingling their tiny brown droppings with the contents of each. The next night, I hung my foodbag from a nail driven into a shelter eave, thinking I had surely outsmarted them. I awoke the next morning to discover new ports of entry and freshly laid turds.

Determined to observe the rapscallions at work, the next night I lay in my bag, gripping my flashlight. As soon as I blew out the candle, the frantic chorus of scraping and gnawing began. The more brazen shelter denizens crisscrossed the shelter eaves, and when I clicked on my flashlight, their tiny eyes glowed red in the beam. Finally, one reached the nail that supported my foodbag and scampered down the line. Now in the spotlight, he gnawed insouciantly at the nylon until I drove him away with a well aimed stone.

I was baffled and prepared to offer nightly sacrifices—small heaps of food—in hopes that the mice would leave the larger portion alone. The next day a more experienced hiker taught me how to pierce a tuna can in the center, invert it, and suspend it midway along the line to discourage even the most enterprising rodents.

The barrier prevented them from reaching my food, but I soon discovered that the mice did more than assail foodbags. Once they realized our edible supplies were beyond their reach, they turned their sights on our wool socks and shirts and even raided our rolls of toilet tissue. The shredded tissue and frayed wool provided soft, warm batting for their dens, and close inspection between the shelter logs almost always revealed cushy nests heaped in colored wool and white tissue.

We soon learned to leave the pockets of our packs un-
zipped, to allow the critters free access. Otherwise, their
teeth would have made quick work of the pack cloth if a
pocket contained so much as a crumb of bread or a single
rolled-oat flake. I awoke one morning in a shelter to find a
trio of rigid mouse tails projecting from flaps and pocket
openings, and when I picked up my pack no fewer than a
dozen mice leaped for safety. Thankfully, because I had left
the pockets open, they had left my pack intact, though lib-
erally sprinkled with feces.

Though personal assaults were rare, they were not un-
heard of. The night we slept at Sassafrass Gap Shelter, seven
miles north of Wesser, North Carolina, one of the other
shelter occupants woke us all with a shout in the wee hours
of the morning. A mouse had blazed a path across his forehead, stopped near his nose, and emptied its tiny bladder
into his eye. And it wasn't unusual for an errant mouse to
take a wrong turn and wind up inside a bag occupied by a
slumbering hiker, an accident that usually resulted in a
chorus of squeaks and shrieks as man and beast scrambled
to escape their odd bedfellow.

While most of us faced the mouse menace with resignation and even good-natured fascination, others devised grim
methods for reprisal. One hiker, for instance, carried a supply of traps that he rigged each night before he turned in.
Within minutes of lights out, we would hear the clatter of
spring-loaded jaws; the hiker then slipped from his bag,
tossed the casualties out into the brush, and started the process over again.

Everyone soon began to consider his pesticidal mission
an exercise in futility. The mice were so populous that
while a few strayed into the traps, dozens of others pillaged
the shelter with impunity. Before abandoning his calling altogether, however, the hiker resorted to more drastic measures. He rigged a tiny hangman's noose and suspended a
dead mouse from the rafters in a Virginia shelter, a warning
to others that they might suffer the same fate. His mouse
lynching, like his efforts with the traps, backfired, and he
soon found himself besieged not only by mice but also by

fellow hikers who considered his tactics cruel and inhumane.

In the war against the mice, it seems the best we could hope for was a truce: if we stashed our socks and shirts and hung our foodbags properly, the mice contented themselves with the scraps spilled from our dinner pots.

Some shelters harbored larger, more daunting scavengers. Ice Water Springs Shelter in the Smokies, for instance, served as home to a resident skunk. While I slept in the shelter on the bottom tier of wire-mesh bunks two feet above the ground, I awoke at 3:00 A.M. to see the skunk's tail passing inches from my nose as he scoured the floor for food.

One evening in the Shenandoah National Park, Dan and I camped in an open field, and shortly after dark we heard a frantic rustling at the base of the tree that bore our foodbags. We soon trained our flashlights on an enterprising raccoon who spent the better part of the night devising tactics to reach our food, which dangled from a stout bough fifteen feet above the ground. First, the animal tried to untie the knot that secured the cord to the tree trunk. When that failed, he scampered up the tree and worked at the line where it draped over the branch. Finally, he suspended himself from the limb, grabbed at the line, and set the bags swinging back and forth. Though the animal never reached the foodbags, I had to resist a temptation to reward him for his perseverance and cunning.

Raccoons weren't the only animals that employed ingenious techniques. In the Smokies, a park ranger related a story about a notorious camp raider known as the Suicide Bear. The bear was known for hoisting himself into trees and, like a portly trapeze artist, flinging himself in the direction of the dangling foodbags. More often than not, the ranger explained, the bear would crash to the ground empty-handed. Undaunted, he would scale the tree and leap again and again until finally, bruised and battered, he limped off into the woods.

Occasionally his plan worked. He would leap, snatch the food bag in his paws, cling to it until the line snapped, and then scamper off into the brush with his pilfered dinner. According to the ranger, the bear's fur was a mass of scabs and bald patches, but he also sported an ample layer of fat, proof that his leaps into the void were sometimes productive.

Vermont was porcupine country, and the scavengers' teethmarks scarred everything that bore a trace of salt from hikers' sweat. The sharp edges of shelter planking, forest service signs, and even outhouse seats had been gnawed smooth. Pack straps, boots, and walking sticks posed equally tempting morsels, and we hung them along with our foodbags. Though I never saw a porcupine, the gnarled wood and piles of stones—antiporcupine artillery—left in shelters attested to bitter night battles between hikers and the bristling marauders.

The animals' behavior patterns weren't always as endearing as those of the grouse or as comical as those of the camp raiders, particularly when they embraced the harsh and sometimes gruesome world of predators and prey.

Near the streambed of Sages Ravine in Connecticut, for instance, I watched, horrified, as yellow jackets descended on a butterfly in such numbers that they completely obscured the body, covered the wings, and swarmed over the ground in a wriggling mass two feet in diameter. Initially, the butterfly struggled, but within seconds the battle was over. As the predators continued to work, the dead insect's wings waved pathetically as the wasps' mandibles gnawed through the tissue that attached the wings to the body. Perhaps the butterfly had strayed too close to the nest, or maybe the yellow jackets had sought him as food to be chewed to pulp and fed to their larva.

In Virginia I watched a giant cicada killer, a two-inch-long wasp with a bulbous, gold-spotted abdomen, swoop onto a cicada that clung to a tree trunk. The wasp arched its abdomen and drove in its stinger. When the cicada had stopped twitching, the insect dropped with its prey to the ground. It then lumbered into the air, still clutching its victim and flying like an overloaded transport plane to its den where, I learned, it would lay its eggs on the body of the paralyzed host. When the eggs hatched, the larva would enter the body of the cicada and eat the insect alive from the inside.

During my stay at Randall's farm in Hot Springs, North Carolina, I witnessed another staggering display of predatory skill. Nights at the cabin, I slept in an open-air loft with no walls separating me from the night air. One evening, as I poked my head through the trap door leading to the loft, I spotted a bat swooping through the open space under the eaves. An oil lamp dangled from my hand, and from its position below the trap door, it infused the loft with a faint, eerie glow.

As I watched the bat zig and zag along the rafters of the open room, Randall's tailless cat, Ichtar, slipped up the ladder, brushed past my chest, and crept onto the floor beside my head. Her body remained still while her head swiveled, tracking the bat's erratic course.

Though I had no idea what was about to happen, I was transfixed by the scene: a domesticated cat, but a predator, crouching, silhouetted against the dark walls of the loft, while the bat, seemingly drawn to the new life presence in the room, swooped closer with each pass. Finally, the bat flew within striking distance, and Ichtar's body uncoiled with such force and quickness that I missed the motion completely.

Still perched on the ladder, I lifted the lamp onto the loft floor and saw that the cat held the wriggling bat in her jaws. She moved back down the ladder, brushing past my chest, as serenely and purposefully as when she had arrived, while I, with racing heart and trembling hands, felt unnerved, as if I had just witnessed a murder.

Miles farther south, in Georgia, I had experienced a similar pang of disgust and frustration after I witnessed a suicide. Four of us sat by a fire and noticed a pale green luna moth—as large as a small bird—swooping close to the flames. Having watched countless insects scorch them-

selves in our candle flames, we knew what was likely to
follow. While we had had little concern for the self-destruc-
tive bent of smaller, less spectacular insects, the imminent
self-immolation of the luna provoked a response in all of us.
We rose, flailing our arms attempting to block the insect's
path back to the fire. But our protective efforts posed little
deterrent for the moth, and it easily maneuvered past us.

Inexorably programmed on its suicidal mission, the insect sputtered through the flames and careened to the
ground on the far side of the fire. Mortally wounded, it lay
on its back, wriggling its seared legs and fluttering its
singed wings until it had righted itself. No longer able to fly,
it limped along the ground, scaled one of the rocks ringing
the fire, and heaved itself into the pyre. There, without apparent fear or despair, it vanished in a brilliant flash of green
flame.

CHAPTER • TWELVE

Where I Live

I believe I have finally found my niche, and it's here in the woods. I thrive here. I relax here. I feel so right here. And I've begun to realize that I have become a resident of the wilderness: I no longer leave society to visit the woods. Rather, I leave the woods to visit society. When I'm in town, I feel uprooted and often suffer pangs of separation. When I'm in town, I constantly wonder what natural displays I'm missing, and it's also sometimes difficult to sleep because the air seems stale and all the familiar night sounds are muted by walls and windows.
—August 17, 1979, Little Rock Pond Lean-to, Vermont

None of us who ventured out on the Appalachian Trail for weeks at a time could resist being transformed by the experience.

Some of the changes were obvious. "There's something different about thru-hikers," Richard Bramley, the owner of a package store on the trail in Cornwall Bridge, Connecticut, once told me. Bramley, who offers free drinks to thru-hikers, has spent hours on his front porch listening to the stories of end-to-enders. "Once you've spent over two or three weeks on the trail, you're into a different head. You've begun to change. You've left the rest of the world behind, and it shows." People like Bramley who frequently encounter thru-hikers claim there is an unmistakable aura about them, a lean, hard look and a beatific demeanor.

Our clothes were perpetually soiled and often tattered, and the backs of our T-shirts bore permanent gray streaks where the aluminum crossbars of our packs had oxidized. Our boots were scuffed and scarred by rocks and roots, and our hair and beards grew unencumbered. By the time I reached Maine, for instance, I could no longer negotiate a comb through the tangle that billowed from my face.

Our leg muscles became sharply defined, and whatever fat we had carried along the early miles through the South soon disappeared. We covered miles—whether climbing or descending—at the same brisk, three-mile-per-hour pace. On long ascents we frequently blazed by weekend hikers who swore and grunted their way to the top. Our packs truly looked like mobile homes, with socks, bandanas, and surplus shorts and T-shirts tethered to the outside to dry in the sun.

Other changes were more subtle. After weeks on the trail, primitive instincts began to awaken. Away from the bombardment of loud music and the din of rush-hour traffic, our hearing became sensitized to the gentle cues of the wilderness. Never silent, the woods were constantly astir with the titter of birds, the rustle of wind through the leaves, the scurry of chipmunks scattering through the underbrush, the drone of buzzing insects, the rumble of distant thunder clouds, the crackling of approaching footsteps.

We developed a knack for predicting changes in the weather. By reading shifting winds, cloud formations, subtle changes in pressure, or the smell of dampness in the air, we could often forecast impending storms hours before they struck.

At the same time, the sounds, smells, and sensations of civilization became foreign and at times even threatening to us. The clamor of trucks and cars streaking along highways contrasted so starkly to the sounds of the woods, for instance, that I became edgy whenever the trail crossed a main road.

Other sounds pitched me into panic. I recall the night we

camped beside Pierce Pond in the wilderness of central Maine, miles from the nearest road. I had finished my dinner and had climbed out onto a large rock that jutted into the water, and as I lay on my back, gazing contentedly at the night sky, I dozed into a tranquil sleep only to be jarred awake as a fighter jet from Pease Air Force Base a few hundred miles away roared across the lake at treetop level, shooting flames from its afterburners. The incident left me shaken and disoriented, unable to sleep.

Other, less invasive, aspects of civilization disturbed us too. The stench of car exhaust burned our nostrils as we descended into towns from the fresh, clean air of the mountains, and the odors of perfume, deodorant, and soap on the well scrubbed people we encountered in towns almost sickened us at times. In one instance I was positioned in a line of a dozen tourists in a grocery check-out aisle in Rangeley, Maine, when the collective assault of a dozen bottled fragrances left me wondering if I could clear the register and exit with my supplies before I gagged. I suspect that my own rank aroma left my fellow shoppers wondering the same thing.

We could smell the acrid odor of tobacco smoke ahead of us on the trail from as far as a quarter-mile away. We also began to notice that day hikers carried on their clothes the distinct odor of their houses and the foods they had cooked for dinner. Often, as they passed me on the trail, I instinctively raised my nose to the air, reading their scents on the wind.

There were other changes, too. Over my five months on the trail, the very rhythm of my life settled down. I had no deadlines, no commitments, no job awaiting my return, no schedule to keep beyond reaching Maine before my cash reserves ran dry. I ate when I was hungry, slept when I was tired, hiked alone when I felt crowded or with friends when I felt lonely. I rose at dawn and covered my daily mileage with ample time to tarry at mountaintop vistas or soak my feet in streams and still make camp with enough daylight to roll out my bag, boil my noodles, write in my journal, and brew my evening cup of tea before sunset. My wrist watch became just another trinket to weigh me down and clutter my life, and I sent it home. Today, if I could revive any element of the trail experience, it would be that wonderful feeling of escape from mechanized timekeeping and the sense that the daylight hours provided more than ample time for fulfilling my obligations.

But the most notable change in me was the evolution from visitor to resident of the wilderness. It was such a gradual change that I can't say exactly when or where it happened, and I tried to explain it to Victor, the Massachusetts hiker who had departed the trail in North Carolina and joined us for weekends as we passed through New England. On an afternoon hike through the Green Mountains of Vermont he asked me what it was like to spend so many days away from civilization. As we walked through a fir grove, across exposed rock outcroppings, up boulder-strewn climbs, and finally to camp beside a tumbling brook, I explained that I felt as if I were ushering him through my home the way someone might walk a visitor through his house, pointing to the kitchen where he ate his meals, to the den where he sat with his evening tea, to the bedroom where he slept.

I explained to him that my layovers in town had become progressively shorter, and that I quickly became "homesick" for the woods. I told him that for every minute I dallied in town I realized that I chanced missing the natural wonders occurring in the mountains: hawks circling on thermals, bears lumbering away in retreat, scavenger Canada jays eating from my hand, deer pawing through camp at dusk, stellar sunsets rippling the horizon in waves of purple, red, and blue, and golden meteors blazing across black night skies that always left me with goose bumps no matter how many times I had seen them.

I explained to him that many of the trappings of my life in the city—electric can openers, microwave ovens, television sets, blow driers, daily hot showers—seemed excessive, wasteful. I explained that I had lost my lust for material things and could not think of anything I really wanted that wasn't already in my pack.

If the wilderness was my home, then many of the trail's 230 shelters served as my domiciles, linking passage through fourteen states and the 160 days of my trek. I could never resist the thrill of counting down the day's last mile, of feeling my pace quicken in anticipation, and finally glancing ahead and spotting the blue-blazed side trail or the shelter roof through the trees and knowing that the day's labor was complete, that it was time to rest.

The shelters were Spartan, fifteen-by-ten-foot open-faced lean-tos with sloping roofs and fieldstone walls or walls hewn from native timbers. Some of the shelters were spectacular relics of the 1930's, of the trail's earliest days and of the craftsmanship of the Civilian Conservation Corps. Some, like the squat Cable Gap Shelter seven miles south of the entrance to the Great Smoky Mountains National Park, were constructed of stout, two-foot-broad logs. A few of the shelters boasted four, not three, walls and included doorways, lofts, and shuttered windows. The Roan High Knob Shelter on the shoulder of Roan Mountain and the Blood Mountain Shelter, thirty miles north of Springer, were two such places.

Many shelters perched on the ridge line and afforded spectacular views of the surrounding mountains. Vandeventer Shelter, for instance, rests on a rocky ridge some one thousand feet above Watauga Dam, thirty-three miles south of the Virginia border. During our night on the ridge, we watched as the daylight waned and tiny lights shimmered like earth-bound stars, each marking a house or a barn or a church. The next morning we awoke to find the lake and her civilization gone. Instead we saw a stratus of dense silver clouds probed by the round green nobs of surrounding mountains.

Other shelters—Ice Water Springs, Russell Field, Spence Field, Derrick Knob, all in the Smokies—were crafted of fieldstone and equipped with indoor hearths and fireplaces.

Some, particularly those through the Lake Country of central Maine, nestled alongside pristine ponds whose tree-lined shores were scattered with rocks and driftwood bleached white in the sun. There the wild, maniacal laughter of loons echoed across the still water after dark.

Though simple, those accommodations afforded us more pleasure than a welter of more extravagant, more civilized, offerings ever could. A roof to keep off the rain. Three walls to block the wind. A timber platform on which to sleep or sit and watch the gradual arrival of nightfall. A sixteen-penny nail driven into the shelter eaves, a place to hang damp shorts, a waterbag, or a parcel of food. A spiral-bound register filled with pages and pages of hikers' tales, experiences, reflections, insights. A nearby spring spouting delicious fifty-degree water. A stout tree to cradle one's back.

Once at the shelter, I would slip from my sweat-soaked clothes and wander to the spring to fill my waterbag and splash the day's grime from my skin. Then I would pull on a pair of dry socks, a clean cotton T-shirt and wool shirt, a pair of long trousers, and a pair of ragged sneakers that seemed to weigh nothing at all after a day in hiking boots. If it was early in the evening, I might have four or five hours of daylight to do exactly as I pleased: to write, to read, to feed the fire, to talk with friends, to explore the environs of my temporary home. Or to do nothing at all and feel that the time was just as well spent.

CHAPTER THIRTEEN

Special Attractions

*Talk of mysteries! Think of our life in
nature—daily to be shown matter, to come in contact with
it—rocks, trees, wind on our cheeks! the solid earth!*
—Henry David Thoreau, The Maine Woods

Before assaulting Springer Mountain, I
had heard or read accounts of the trail's "special attractions," those sections that possessed the grandest vistas,
posed the most grueling ascents or descents, harbored the
largest and most varied populations of wildlife, boasted the
most exhilarating traverses, or offered other qualities that
made them especially memorable to hikers.

For the northbounder, the trail seems to arrange those
sections in perfect sequence. As hikers move north and develop physical and mental stamina, they encounter progressively more demanding terrain and more challenging
experiences.

It begins with Springer Mountain, an unremarkable peak,
really, at just over three thousand feet and shrouded in hardwood trees. For thru-hikers the mountain ranks as a major
milestone, marking either the outset or completion of their
months-long trek.

Some 165 miles farther north, hikers enter the Great Smoky Mountains National Park, which teems with wildlife—bears, boars, skunks, deer. As the most frequently visited national park in the country, it teems with human life, too. Through the park we ascended through rhododendron groves, along cascading brooks tangled in dense, rich underbrush, and across bald-topped mountains, and we scaled the tallest peak on the entire trail, Clingmans Dome, at 6,643 feet.

The 106 miles through Virginia's Shenandoah National Park led us through open meadows and over rocky promontories. In other places through Virginia we traced the trail past centuries-old carriage ruts past abandoned homesteads and settlements whose flower gardens still blossom and whose cherry and apple trees still yield fruit.

Much farther north, six and one-half miles beyond the Maine–New Hampshire border, the Mahoosuc Notch offers a mile-long scramble under, around, and between bus-sized boulders. The Notch is regarded as the trail's toughest mile, but for me it ranked as a gray, lichen-covered amusement park where we followed a series of white arrows that marked the *only* route through the jumble of granite blocks. The tight passages through the rocks frequently required us to shed our packs, tie them with parachute cord, and trail them behind us as we wedged through the cracks and fissures. Midway through the notch, we stopped to rest and dipped our drinking cups into a spring that courses under the rocks. As I withdrew my cup, the sides immediately fogged with condensation, even though the air temperature hovered in the fifties, and when I touched the cup to my mouth, the water was so frigid that it stung my lips.

Those were all special places, yet the trail offered three sections that, for me, represented emotional or aesthetic highlights of my trek: the White Mountains of New Hampshire, with their barren, windswept ridges that reach above timberline with the stark grandeur of the Swiss Alps; the Kennebec River, in southwestern Maine, an optional ford across 150 feet of roiling, waist-deep terror; and Mount Katahdin, the lone granite sentry that rises out of the Lake

Country of central Maine and which I regard as the trail's most perfect mountain.

The White Mountains

We have been blessed with beautiful weather for our passage along the Franconia and Presidential ridges where the trail reaches above tree line. Having heard descriptions of the rawer aspects of the weather in these mountains—and of the deaths that have resulted—we're both relieved and grateful. Crossing the Whites in fog, sleet, summer snows, dangerous winds, or any combination of those things would have made for tough going, but the worst part would have been exploring these mountains without being able to see them. We had heard that the terrain is challenging here, and I suppose that it has been, but I've been too absorbed in the grandeur and beauty that greets us at every turn even to notice.
—August 30, 1979, Lakes of the Clouds Hut,
White Mountains, New Hampshire

On April 12, 1934, the weather station on the barren summit of Mount Washington clocked winds in excess of 230 miles per hour, the stiffest winds ever recorded on the earth's surface. To put that figure into perspective, hurricane-force winds begin at seventy-five miles per hour. As the story goes, after the incredulous meteorologist confirmed the reading, the gauge broke, and winds continued to gain in intensity.

The winds and harsh winter weather have sculpted the ancient granite of the Whites into vast bowls, cirques, and windswept ridges stripped bare of all plant life but scrub vegetation, alpine flowers, and tundra grass. Along the Franconia Ridge and through the Presidential Range, the trail lopes above timberline and often stays there for miles, crossing the summits of Mount Lincoln (5,089 feet), Mount Lafayette (5,249), Mount Jackson (4,052 feet), Mount Pierce (4,310), Mount Eisenhower (4,761), Mount Franklin (5,004), Mount Washington (6,288), and Mount Madison (5,363).

For most of us who had passed the previous 1,700 miles cloaked in hardwood forests and shrouded in lush vegetation, our first forays above timberline seemed accompanied by magic. For every wonderful vista we had enjoyed through the twelve states leading from Georgia to Vermont, we had scrambled over hundreds of less spectacular peaks that, day after day, offered no vistas, no break from the often monotonous routine of ascents and descents. The Whites were different, in fact, majestic, a term I would be reluctant to apply to any of the other ranges we passed through en route. They were majestic because their stately summits towered as many as three thousand feet above tree line and provided unbroken, panoramic vistas in every direction.

The terrain above timberline boasts exaggerated proportions, where mountains swell like barren, well-muscled biceps; where clouds don't float, but shoot across the sky like ice splinters; and where the wind assaults you in sudden gusts that tug at your watch cap, billow your parka and pants, and leave you tottering and lurching for balance. Above timberline, the absence of trees scrambles your sense of distance and size. Open vistas make a dozen miles appear like a few hundred yards until you spot another hiker, a tiny black form advancing along a gargantuan crest, and your perspective returns and you begin to feel as small as the distant hiker appears.

Above timberline, the trails themselves meld into the Hobbitlike landscape. You can glimpse ahead a mile, five miles, ten miles, and follow the serpentine cut of the trail as it meanders across ridges, slumps into saddles, skirts around peaks, disappears, then emerges again as it strays back into your line of sight. The trails snake to the horizon, becoming ever more faint, narrowing with the distance, and you walk them with your eyes before you and you explore them with your feet. Ahead, you can see where you will stand in one hour, two hours, a day.

At the same time, the scale turns the landscape into a living relief map, and hiking becomes a lesson in living geography. You begin to understand how one peak links to the next, how streams follow the folds in the ridges and converge into rivers.

Our days along the Franconia Ridge and through the Presidential Range to the summit of Mount Washington were marked by blue skies and moderate temperatures. We visited several of the eight high-elevation huts operated by the Appalachian Mountain Club (AMC), which provide lodging and gourmet meals for short-term hikers who may spend several days to a week in the Whites, but none of us had the cash to pay the twenty dollars per night. Often we arrived at the huts just after breakfast and gobbled up left-over whole-wheat pancakes and muffins at five cents apiece.

On August 30 we reached Lakes of the Clouds Hut, a rustic T-shaped lodge sided with weathered cedar shakes. This, the largest of the AMC's eight huts, accommodates as many as ninety guests. Though we couldn't afford to pay for dinner and a bunk, the hut crew members allowed us to sleep on table tops in the dining room for two dollars. The next morning, the sun glinted through the windows, and we knew we were in for a beautiful summit day. Along the 1.4 miles to the top, we battled forty-mile-per-hour winds, which formed horizontal spikes of rime ice on the windward sides of trail signs and rocks, but the day remained clear. As we soon discovered, not everyone who explored the mountain had been so fortunate.

The same features that render the alpine ridges of the Whites majestic also make them deadly. Days earlier, as we neared the top of the three-thousand-foot ascent leading from Franconia Notch to the ridge, we confronted the first of several yellow warning signs posted at timberline. They read: "Attention: Try this trail only if you are in top physical condition, well clothed, and carrying extra clothing and food. Many have died above timberline from exposure. Turn back at the first sign of bad weather." The conditions are particularly harsh on Mount Washington. Later I would learn that the average June temperature on the mountain is forty-five degrees; in July it's forty-nine; and in August, forty-seven. The mountain routinely receives snowfall all months of the year.

The message did not strike home until we approached the summit of Mount Washington and encountered a series of weathered, wooden crosses wedged into the rocks. The crosses, we learned, marked the spots where hikers had died of exposure. One of the crosses, less than a quarter-mile from the summit house, served as a stark memorial to two hikers who had perished in a blizzard on July 18, 1958.

In the summit house a list hangs from one wall with the names of the mountain's victims. Since 1849 more than one hundred people have died of exposure on Mount Washington, nearly a quarter of them during the summer. Often their bodies were recovered only a few hundred yards from shelter. The scenario is often the same: fog materializes from nowhere or a sudden snowy whiteout descends, and visibility vanishes in minutes. Hikers clad in shorts and T-shirts, who might have been basking in warm sunlight only minutes earlier, suddenly find themselves drenched, shrouded in fog or snow, and buffeted by fifty- or sixty-mile-per-hour winds—the perfect recipe for hypothermia. The limited visibility leads to disorientation; the indistinct trails—snaking across boulder fields—disappear; and hikers stumble in circles. Soon their body temperatures plunge below critical levels, their mental faculties dim, and they lie down in the snow and yield to death.

Where there is death, there are tales of ghosts, and the Whites are no exception. Since 1979 I've returned to the Whites three times, and while on a magazine assignment there in 1987, I had what remains my only paranormal experience. I was working on a story about the high-elevation huts of the area and was on the trail with Charlie, a college-aged hut keeper who had spent the preceding summer working in Lakes of the Clouds hut. For the better part of a week, Charlie and I traced the Appalachian Trail through the region, stopping each evening at a different hut.

One evening we arrived at Mizpah Spring Hut, six miles south of Mount Washington, just before dusk. After the evening meal as darkness descended, Charlie and I sat with the few dozen guests in the hut reading and talking in the golden glow of propane lamps. At 8:30 P.M., the hut keepers extinguished the lamps, and we navigated our way to our bunk rooms with flashlights. Though ours was ample to sleep a dozen hikers, Charlie and I were the room's only occupants.

Soon after we climbed into our bunks, the mountain sounds became amplified in the darkness. As the wind surged against the sides of the hut, every sash whined and every rafter creaked and moaned. At the same time, I heard the distinct sound of someone—or some thing—pacing across the floor above us. I didn't know it at the time, but the storeroom was directly above us. With its steeply pitched roof and large stores of flour sacks and other dry goods, it was unlikely that anyone could have navigated across the floor, much less stood upright while doing so.

The footsteps continued. A rhythmic, light step moving from one edge of the ceiling to the other, turning and pacing back. I asked Charlie, who had spent several summers working in the Whites, if he had any notion of what it was.

"Mice?" he ventured, as perplexed as I.

"Uh-uh," I said. "If that's mice, they're damned big mice, and they're wearing shoes."

"What else could it be?" he asked after pausing to listen for a few seconds.

We drifted off to sleep to the sound of the incessant pacing.

At about 3:00 A.M., I had a dream. I call it a dream because I don't know what other term I could apply to it, but it was different from most dreams in that I experienced it in the semiconscious stage between sleep and wakefulness. It was too vivid to have been a dream.

It was night, and I was alone in an old abandoned house ascending a long stairway. At the top I arrived at a door that was ajar, and I pushed it open. Inside, the windowless room was dusky, not completely dark. There was no furniture on the scarred wooden floor, and on the right I spotted a brick fireplace smudged with soot. A rusted flour tin rested on the hearth, and as I spied it, it began to move, scraping in slow circles as if moved by an invisible hand.

As it moved, something across the room caught my attention. I peered to the left, across the floor toward an alcove at the far end of the room, and there I saw a shaft of gray light, like a translucent form, stretching from floor to ceiling. As I watched, it glided back and forth, tracing the width of the alcove. Though it had no shape—no discernible form, no features—I felt a strong presence in the room. Somehow, I knew—I just knew—it was a woman, a young woman. A tingle surged up my spine, and I felt my hair stand on end as if I had just passed into a strong electrical current.

That's when I awoke and called to my friend, who slumbered in the bunk across the room.

"Hey, Charlie, I just saw a ghost!"

"Huh? You saw what?"

"I'm telling you, man, I just saw the ghost of a woman!"

"Are you sure it was a woman?"

"Absolutely!"

"Wow," Charlie said. "Listen, in the morning tell the hut crew about this."

"Why?" I asked.

"I'd rather not say, but just do it."

The next morning, I recounted my experience to Mark, a hut keeper at Mizpah in his early twenties. After I had finished, he calmly explained that over the summer dozens of other hikers had reported the same experience: first the footsteps, then the ghost. "Her name is Betsy," he said.

Betsy, he explained, was a young hiker who had drowned in a rain-swollen stream several summers earlier. The hut keepers had found her body near the hut. Because they were unable to transport the corpse down the mountain in the dark, they wrapped her in a sheet and placed it in the hut basement overnight.

"A short time later," Mark said, "people began to complain about the ghost."

The Kennebec River

Paul, Dan, and I forded the Kennebec River today, and I have never experienced a more sustained or intense rush in my life. When I reached the northern side, I lay in the grass quaking for the better part of a half-hour, feeling exhausted and exhilarated at the same time. The exhaustion soon passed, but the sense of accomplishment has remained with me through the day and I suspect I'll carry it with me for months to come.

We had timed our crossing badly, as the dam upstream had already released its load, and when we reached the bank, the rapids churned and roiled. As we prepared to plunge in, my resolve began to waver, particularly when I watched some of the other hikers in our group climb into a ferryman's boat for a risk-free ride to the other side. As I watched the boat leave the shore, I realized that I was committed, and the reality of what I was about to do scared me shitless.

I'd been contemplating this day for hundreds of miles, wondering if I'd have the guts to follow through. The crossing was as difficult—more difficult, in fact—than I had imagined, but in a similar way, my strength and concentration exceeded my expectations, too.

—September 16, 1979, abandoned barn near Moxie Pond, Maine

The Kennebec River, which sluices south through the center of Maine toward the Atlantic Coast, cost me more adrenalin, and, once I had crossed it, left me with a greater sense of accomplishment than any other stretch along the trail. Since then, it has served as the yardstick by which I measure the extremes of fear and exhilaration.

After feasting on an all-you-can-eat pancake breakfast at the Carrying Place, a backwoods pancake house, we eased north to the banks of the Kennebec at 8:00 A.M. on September 16.

The Kennebec represented an important emotional passage for me, and it allowed me to measure the courage I had

gained over my months on the trail. Back in Georgia, I had
been frightened by chipmunks rattling the underbrush. At
that time, the notion of fording the Kennebec seemed
foolhardy and dangerous, and I probably would have walked
an additional 2,100 miles just to avoid it. But by the time I
reached Maine, my self-confidence had soared, and the Kennebec loomed more as a challenge than as an invitation for
disaster. I realized, too, that facing the Kennebec would put
my triumph over fear into a tangible perspective.

Positioned below a dam that releases thousands of tons of
water each morning, the river crossing is known for its unpredictable conditions. At times it is nothing more than a
shallow ford that laps at the shins. At other times it rages,
exposing hikers to a belt-deep channel of torrid rapids.

When we reached the river, we realized that our timing
was unfortunate. The dam had released its load, and the
150-foot-wide column of water was alive with riffles and
eddies.

Paul, Dan, and I eyed the surface and located a ragged line
of riffles breaking on the surface, which marked the shallowest crossing. The shallowest stretch, we realized, also
marked the fastest water. We clustered on the bank in the
weeds for fifteen minutes or more reviewing our strategy
and donned our fording gear. Because the riverbed was
strewn with rocks and boulders, we decided to leave our
boots on. To attempt the ford in bare feet would leave our
flesh tattered by the jagged rocks. There was another consideration, too. The current was so swift that without the
added support provided by the boots, if a foot had wedged
between submerged boulders, ankle or shin bones would
have snapped like green twigs, leaving us crippled *and* submerged.

There also was the question of traction. Along the trail
we had all careened into the weeds when our Vibram soles
had glanced off damp rocks, and we knew that wet Vibram
on wet, silt-covered stones would have provided us no purchase at all, never mind the tug of the current. So we opted
to pull on a pair of rag wool socks over our boots. The wool,

similar to the felt worn by fishermen on the soles of their waders, would provide at least some grab.

Next, each of us foraged through the brush for an additional walking stick to supplement the one we already carried. The notion was to form a tripod, with the anchored foot as one base, and the stick in either hand as the second and third. That way there would always be three points in contact with the bottom, and if we happened to totter, we would have a chance to arrest our fall using one or both sticks.

Then each of us unhooked his pack waistbelt. Over the years, the Kennebec has felled more than a few hikers. Those who were fortunate surrendered their packs to the current and reached shore drenched and shaken, but alive.

If our waistbelts had remained secured and we had taken a spill, the outcome would most certainly have been grim. The combined effect of the current, the unwieldy burden of a loaded pack, and the panic of being awash in a raging river would have left little hope of escape. With the belt unfixed, we stood a much better chance of jettisoning our packs if we submerged.

I chose not to dwell on those possibilities. In fact, I tried very hard not to think at all. If I had, I certainly would have pursued the sensible, risk-free means of crossing the river available to us at the time: as the three of us stood on the brink, a local boatman loaded several of our colleagues into his dinghy. For a few dollars, he would carry them safely across. Since 1985 when a woman drowned while fording the Kennebec, the Appalachian Trail Conference has admonished hikers to ferry across rather than ford, and the organization, in concert with the Maine Appalachian Trail Club, now subsidizes a ferry service through the summer months.

"Woooow, shit, Brill," shouted Dillon. "Do we really want to do this?"

"Just think about how great it will feel to get to the other side," I answered, as much to bolster my own failing confidence as to convince Paul of my commitment.

"Who's going first?" Paul asked. But even as we stood quaking on the shoreline, his question had already been answered.

Dan was twenty yards away from the bank and sinking up to his pack straps in rapids. As we watched, I noticed that for the first time since I had known him his motion had lost its grace. I could see that he was straining against the current, fighting it with everything he had. On his upstream side, the water curled like a hydraulic battering ram where it struck his body.

As Dan reached the halfway point, Paul stepped into the water, and I watched the water lap farther and farther up his thighs and finally reach near his waist. Then I knew that my moment of reckoning had come.

Paul and Dan were both endowed with long legs, while I am of a rather squat construction. My legs are strong, but they are also short. While the water reached just below Dan's and Paul's waists, it would reach to the middle of my own when I stepped into the deepest point.

As soon as I stepped in, I confronted an added hazard, one I hadn't anticipated. As I glanced at the rocks on the bottom through the rushing water, they seemed to waver, and within a few feet I began to suffer the effects of vertigo.

Within a few feet, I realized, too, that I had vastly underestimated the force of the current. It felt as if the combined force of all those millions of tons of water was piyoned against my thighs, threatening to pull me down, pull me under.

I soon lost perception of time and space. Was I moving? The distant shore didn't look any closer, but the water had gotten progressively deeper. Yes, I must be moving, yet progress was so slow, measured in inches. Lift the upstream—the left-hand—walking stick. Force it into the current. Plant it. Lift the left foot. Keep the thigh and knee stiff against the current. Advance it several inches. Ease the muscles enough to allow the boot sole to bounce along the bottom until it wedged against a rock. Plant it. Lift the right stick. Plant. Lift the right leg. Plant.

Soon a remarkable thing happened, something that I have

experienced neither before nor since: I became so thoroughly focused on my task that motion seemed to cease, and I became lost in such complete concentration that the surrounding woods disappeared and the roar of the rapids faded. There were only the water, the rocks, the current, and I, fighting against all of them. There was the feeling that if one muscle twitched, if the wind buffeted one strand of my hair, I would lose it. And there was the feeling, too, that there would be a release in surrendering, in letting go the fight and yielding to the current.

As I reached the halfway point, I heard voices and whistling coming from the northern bank, and I glanced up. Paul and Dan stood on the bank waving frantically toward my right—downstream. It seems that I focused too intently on the riverbed and had strayed upstream into deeper water. Now I faced the added burden of adjusting my course while continuing the ford.

Above the thunder of the water, I could hear my heart pounding in my ears. At the same time, I could feel surge after surge of adrenaline sparking my muscles.

Finally, the water began to inch down my stomach, then down my waist, my thighs, my knees. And I was safely across.

As I collapsed on the bank, the three of us recounted each step of the crossing like comrades who had survived the same battle. In many ways it was a battle—a battle against current, rocks, vertigo, and fear. I had just experienced a rush so intense, so sustained, that for a few minutes afterward my muscles refused to respond at all; they only twitched.

As I lay on the bank, I began to understand the addictive power of risk. I could fathom why skydivers, high-elevation mountaineers, race-car drivers—people whose relative risk was much greater than what I had faced—willingly laid their lives on the line. Yes, the experience had been frightening. But somehow the mental clarity I had experienced during the crossing overrode the fear, and a sense of peace and security settled over me when I finally reached the northern bank of the Kennebec.

Katahdin

Climbing Katahdin didn't produce the emotional catharsis I had expected it would. Instead, the climb was like the last frantic dash to touch home plate. With each step, my anticipation of triumph grew, but when I finally reached the summit, I felt a surge of sadness at realizing what I was about to leave behind. All of it: the rain, the cold, the mornings and evenings, the ascents and descents, the peaks, the friends, the seasons, the plants and animals, and the intimacy I've come to know with this world. I thought, too, about those things that I had already left behind. The continuum of my life has been broken. There are the events that occurred before the trail; then there is the trail. Those events seem thoroughly disjointed, as if from different lifetimes. The me of five months ago is a stranger. I am changed—forever.
—September 27, 1979, Mount Katahdin, Maine

I caught my first full broadside glimpse of Katahdin from the shore of Rainbow Lake Pond, twenty-seven miles and two days south of the trail's northern terminus. The sun shimmered off the fall foliage, and I could see where the ruff of red sugar maples and yellow birches yielded to scree and rock at the timberline. Katahdin was, and is, the most beautiful mountain I've ever seen, so perfect in shape and so solitary amid the sweep of flatlands.

As I viewed the mountain, I wanted to stop, to settle in and spend days or even weeks thinking about what those final few days meant. At the same time, there was an irresistible urge to confront the mountain, to trace its boulder-strewn shoulders, to reach its rounded, mile-high crown and complete the final leg of my journey. Katahdin had been the image in my sights for five months, especially in the early days when the peak seemed so distant and remote that we had little hope of reaching it, but when I actually beheld the mountain, I knew I would finish and realized that my days on the trail were coming to an end.

On September 26 we reached the twin shelters at Katahdin Stream Campground. By that point our ranks had swelled to nearly fifteen. Over the previous weeks we had left entries in trail registers urging our fellow thru-hikers to adjust their mileage so that we could make our summit bid *en masse*. Among those who joined our foursome were the Phillips brothers from Florida, Kansas native Jeff Hammons, newlyweds Phil and Cindy (who had honeymooned on the trail), Knoxville native Gary Owens, Jim Shaffrick from Connecticut, and Victor Hoyt, the Massachusetts hiker who had departed the trail in North Carolina.

We awoke on the morning of September 27 to clear blue skies. As we departed the shelters, the temperature hovered just above freezing.

The ascent to the summit of Katahdin is one of the stiffest along the entire trail: four thousand feet in just over five miles. In places the ascent requires hand-over-hand scrambling along boulder-strewn pitches, and in other places iron bars protrude from the rock and provide the only secure hand-holds.

But I think I speak for most northbounders when I say that the difficulty of the ascent is negated by the sheer excitement of reaching the end of the trail. But there were other factors as well that eased the strain of the ascent. For one thing, we were all in top physical form, having logged 2,100 miles of stiff ascents over the previous months. For another, before reaching the base of Katahdin, we had ambled through the rolling Lake Country without facing a major ascent for more than seventy miles, and our disdain for constant ascending and descending had passed. Our loads were much lighter than what we had become accustomed to, and we had supplanted our expedition packs with day packs since we would be following the same route to the summit and back down to Katahdin Stream Campground. Then there was the beauty of a perfect fall day. At every turn, autumn colors blazed, and as we emerged above timberline at three thousand feet, every foot of elevation gained brought new vistas of the surrounding sphagnum bogs and shimmering lakes that captured parcels of the azure sky on their surfaces.

Despite the beautiful surroundings, I soon found myself so thoroughly absorbed in a tangle of conflicting emotions that I felt as though I were climbing alone when in fact I was surrounded by companions. To reach the summit, I realized, would mean that I had achieved the goal, but then it occurred to me that I had already achieved other, more important, goals over all the miles that had led me there. Katahdin was a formality, a definitive end point.

Once we reached the rock cairn that marked the top, Dan and I embraced. We surveyed the vast flat Lake Country that sprawled for miles away from the mountain's base, and we studied the blue pockets of water fringed by acres of red and gold. Then we sat peering silently toward the south, back across five months and 2,100 miles to Springer Mountain. There were so many things to say, yet none of them could be articulated.

If the white blazes had led farther north, I'm certain that all of us would have followed them. But they didn't. We had reached the end of the trail. It was time to leave the wilderness and return home.

CHAPTER FOURTEEN

Coming Home

We've reached the end of the trail, and we're heading back home to people and things that once were so familiar. Yet I'm a bit apprehensive about how I'll respond to them and how they will respond to me. Will this experience make sense to anyone? Will things at home seem changed? Will I readjust? Will I remember all that I've seen, felt, learned, and shared over the past five months? Will I, in time, lose my intimacy with nature and begin to feel like a stranger when I visit the wilderness?

Tonight there are fourteen of us gathered in adjoining hotel rooms in Millinocket celebrating the completion of our trek. Tomorrow, I say good-bye to friends whom I've come to know and love so well. Then I will pile into a car for the trip home. The adventure continues. . .

—September 27, 1979, hotel room, Millinocket, Maine

Mount Katahdin represented the only peak along the Appalachian Trail that proved more difficult to descend than ascend, yet that difficulty had nothing to do with terrain. For me, the 2,100 miles from Springer Mountain north had represented an unbroken continuum, a journey along a ridgeline corridor that was neatly contained between woodland walls and the southern and northern endposts. As long as I remained within those boundaries, my foremost designation was that of Appalachian Trail hiker, and my primary goal remained to reach the trail's northern terminus.

Once I had reached Baxter Peak, I realized that my next footfall would stray outside those boundaries and would lead inexorably away from the trail and away from the white blazes that for 150 days had provided all the direction I needed. The next step would lead away from a world of simple routine, away from a world governed by weather and shifting winds where sun and seasons were the only time-keepers and where the measure of a day was in miles passed and insight gained. For the first time in more than five months, my path into the future was unclear.

As I reached the base of Katahdin, I confronted a tangle of conflicting emotions. I was proud of what I had accomplished, but I wondered what place my trail experiences would occupy in my life in the years that followed. I wondered if the lessons I had learned would be of use to me back home, and I wondered what I would do if I discovered that my new values clashed with those of civilized society. Would I have the courage to set off in my own direction? It would take me years to find the answers to those questions.

As daunting as the transition had been back in April when as a neophyte woodsman I had struggled for security in a foreign environment, I suspected the transition back would be more difficult still. And more abrupt.

Twenty-four hours after reaching the summit of Katahdin, I had said a painful good-bye to my trail friends, and was sitting in the passenger seat of a car cruising south along Interstate 95. As the car accelerated, I gripped the dashboard with white knuckles. Was it necessary to travel so fast, I asked the driver, a friend of Dan's who had agreed to shuttle us from Maine back home to Washington, D.C. He laughed and pointed to the speedometer. We were moving at fifty-eight miles per hour, yet compared to the three-mile-an-hour pace I had maintained along the trail, it seemed as though we had broken the sound barrier.

Once we were out of Maine and away from the mountains

and the accommodating residents of the trail towns, the people we encountered during our rest stops seemed to regard Dan and me, with our long beards and shabby clothes, as drifters or vagrants. Shopkeepers were abrupt, sometimes even rude. Diners at nearby tables glanced in our direction and muttered among themselves. As I confronted more and more suspicious faces, the pride that had evolved over the previous months began to ebb, replaced by self-consciousness and a feeling of being out of place. These people were clean and well dressed. I was filthy. After several consecutive showers, I began to notice my pack and clothes reeked of sweat and campfire smoke. While these people abided by rules of etiquette, I attacked my food like a famished savage. As we exited a fast-food restaurant in Pennsylvania, I recall joking to Dan, "Well, Toto, I don't think we're in Kansas anymore." It occurred to me then that if, after leaving the trail, I had strayed into a fairytale world peopled by dwarfs and witches, it wouldn't have seemed more skewed than this vision of mainstream America.

After a week back in Washington, the transition continued as I trimmed my beard, shed my trail clothes, and slipped into a navy-blue suit to be best man in a friend's wedding. Because I was penniless, the week after that I sought work through a temporary employment service. On my first assignment I spent four interminable days working as a file clerk and general lackey at a small corporate office. When a middle-aged woman chided me for misfiling a document, I wanted to explain to her that after five months in the wilderness, the disposition of a file didn't seem all that vital to me, but I didn't. Instead, I resigned myself to the fact that to the woman, my trail experiences were somewhat trivial while my ability to alphabetize files was of paramount importance.

Two weeks after that I returned home to Cincinnati and moved in with my parents. Though they had been supportive of my trail quest, they soon began to query me about my plans for the future. As it turned out, they weren't asking me anything that I hadn't been asking myself.

What followed was a slow, sometimes painful process of

reentry, marked by incidents that, taken together, made me wonder if my trek had been a tangential journey into the darkness rather than a pilgrimage toward self-discovery.

In October I attended a party with some friends. By then I had upgraded my wardrobe, and although, in the sartorial sense, I fitted in with the rest of the partygoers, my attitudes and theirs seemed at odds.

"What have you been up to?" asked a friend whom I had not seen for several years.

"Well, I've spent the past five months in the woods, hiking the Appalachian Trail," I said, somewhat tentatively.

"Oh, is that right?" he responded. "My wife and I spent ten days in Europe this past summer."

He detailed his trip, then described his job as a sales representative for a large corporation. He told me how well he was doing and asked if I had noticed his new car parked out in front. I hadn't. He insisted on leading me outside to show it to me.

Afterward, he returned to the party while I settled into a rocking chair on the front porch. It was a cool October night, and I found relief in the breeze rustling the fallen leaves, the crisp smell of fall, and the stars—the same stars that had adorned night skies while I passed through fourteen states. But beyond the glow of city lights, they seemed to have lost much of their luster, and I found myself wondering if my trail buddies had encountered the same difficulties. I wanted desperately to be with them. I knew Dan had abandoned his corporate career and had returned to Hot Springs. There, at the Inn, in the shadow of the mountains and surrounded by men and women who shared his trail values, he became an apprentice to a harpsichord builder. I regretted not having followed him there.

A couple of weeks later I shaved my beard and, clad in dress clothes, set out to find a job. A career counselor who helped me prepare a resume advised me not to include any mention of the Appalachian Trail among my accomplishments. He even suggested that I try to cover the gap it had created in my employment history.

"No one will see much value in your hiking experiences," he said. "They will only see that you were unemployed for those months."

I bristled at his suggestion that I should hide my adventure between lines on a resume or, worse, twist it into a nonevent, something that I should deny ever happened.

Despite his advice, I *did* include the trail on my resume, and it has appeared on every resume I've drafted since. I eventually landed a job in a backpacking shop, and though the position didn't pay much, it kept me in touch with people who, like me, lived for weekend forays into the woods.

During my tenure at the backpacking shop, in my years as a writer, and in all the relationships and roles that have occupied my life since 1979, I have drawn on my experiences from the trail. Though it took awhile to realize it, the trail had shaped me, had given me a philosophy and had toughened me in some ways, softened me in others, and taught me lessons I will never forget: lessons on survival, kindness, strength, friendship, courage, perseverance, and the ways of nature. Those lessons have affected everything I've done since.

From weeks of living out of a thirty-five-pound pack, I learned to find contentment in simple things and to rely on myself and my resources to surmount obstacles. From long days spent tromping through rain and cold, I learned that whenever I felt beaten, spent, exhausted, and ready to quit, there was always something left and that if I delved deep enough, I could always find the strength to keep moving forward. From watching the seasons yield one to the next, daylight surrender to night, and darkness give way to morning, I discovered that in the midst of chaos order and purpose are present for us. From the unqualified kindness shared among travelers in the back country, I learned that for all the cruelty loose in the world, people care deeply for their fellow creatures. And I learned that whenever I lose sight of those lessons, I can regain them by returning to the trail.

In the spring of 1987 I left my job as an editor with a large southeastern publishing company—a job that never really felt right for me—to pursue a full-time career as a free-lance writer. The transition was not as graceful as I had hoped, and I passed months of despondency when the assignments I sought didn't come. I decided to quit, but before I did, I loaded my pack and set out for Springer Mountain. The trail had answered my needs once before, and I had faith that it would do so again. Over the following weeks I mingled with the new class of thru-hikers and formed new, lasting friendships as I ambled along flower-speckled trails and savored the verdant arrival of spring. I also discovered that, though the circumstances of my life had changed, the trail had remained the same—just as charged with life and hope as I remembered it. A month after I began and 335 miles farther north, I was healed and returned to my chosen occupation more determined than ever. In time, I succeeded.

Since 1937 more than two thousand seekers have coursed along the trail's miles, each pursuing a personal mission, each in search of something enduring and real. Among those hikers I came to know, there was Elizabeth, who took up the trail seeking relief from the grief of losing her husband. There was Nick, who forged a new direction for his life after retirement. As for Paul, Dan, and the rest of us, fresh from college, we set out to learn the lessons of the wilderness before we learned the lessons of the professional world, and somewhere along the way, we all found what we were looking for. The answers may not have been exactly what we sought, but I believe they were precisely what we needed.

I suspect that the trail will continue to work its magic on the hundreds of future end-to-enders who in years hence will arrive at Springer, sign the log book, and point their boots and hopes north. I suspect, too, that years and years from now, after we have followed our new technologies and grand urban schemes into a new century, the trail will remain a sure route into our past, a route along which technology will always surrender to strength and spirit and the laws of nature.

Over the past eleven years, my memories of the months on the trail have survived as a time of sublime happiness, a time when I felt my neurons being switched on for the very first time. The mention of the trail still evokes images of lush, green mountains; of great gray clouds of mist wafting through virgin stands of hemlock and oak; of bald-topped mountains with views that roll out across miles and miles of blue-hazed hills; of hawks swirling above sun-drenched granite ledges; of springs that run so cold they made my teeth ache.

My other memories also grow more vivid and precious with time. No matter how many times I have hefted my backpack, picked up the white blazes, and trod my favorite sections of trail, the excitement—the sense of discovery—has never failed me. I doubt that any other event of my life will choke me with as much emotion, fill me with as much pride, or define more clearly who I am than my summer on the Appalachian Trail.

Appendix

For information about the Appalachian Trail

If you would like to learn more about the Appalachian Trail, write the Appalachian Trail Conference, Post Office Box 807, Harpers Ferry, West Virginia 25425-0807: or call (304) 535-6331.

Suggested Reading for Hikers

Appalachian Odyssey, Steve Sherman and Julia Older. South Greene Press.

Appalachian Trail Hiker, Ed Garvey. Appalachian Outfitters.

The Complete Walker, Colin Fletcher. Alfred A. Knopf, Inc.

Leaves of Grass, Walt Whitman. Modern Library.

The Man Who Walked through Time, Colin Fletcher. Random House.

The Monkey Wrench Gang, Edward Abbey. Avon Books.

The Nick Adams Stories, Ernest Hemingway. Charles Scribner's Sons.

On the Road, Jack Kerouac. Penguin Publishing.

Pilgrim at Tinkers Creek, Annie Dillard. Harper and Row Publishers.

Sand Country Almanac, Aldo Leopold. Ballantine Books.

The Snow Leopard, Peter Matthiessen. Penguin Publishing.

Walden, Henry David Thoreau. Doubleday & Company, Inc.

Walk across America, Peter Jenkins. Fawcett Juniper.

Walk West, Peter and Barbara Jenkins. William Morrow and Company.

Walking with Spring, Earl Shaffer. Appalachian Trail Conference.

A Woman's Journey on the Appalachian Trail, Cindy Ross. The Globe Pequot Press.

Zen and the Art of Motorcycle Maintenance, Robert M. Pirsig. Bantam Books.

American Prisons

A History of Good Intentions

BLAKE McKELVEY

Patterson Smith

Montclair, N.J.

Copyright © 1977 by
Patterson Smith Publishing Corporation
Montclair, New Jersey 07042

Library of Congress Cataloging in Publication Data

McKelvey, Blake, 1903–
   American prisons: A History of Good Intentions.

   Includes bibliographies.
   Includes index.
   1. Prisons—United States—History. I. Title.
HV9466.M29   365′.973   75–14556
ISBN 0-87585-704-3, cloth   ISBN 0-87585-804-X, paper

To the memory of
F. Lovell Bixby
and
Arthur Meier Schlesinger

CONTENTS

FOREWORD

American Prisons: A History of Good Intentions is an outgrowth of a work I published in 1936. The present volume enlarges on the earlier work (entitled *American Prisons: A Study in American Social History Prior to 1915*) by extending its period to the present day and by augmenting the account of the pre-1915 period with significant findings which have emerged in the last forty years.

Most of the grim walls of the century-old prisons that darkened the streets of several eastern cities when I first wrote are still standing. They were designed to be indestructible, and only the penitentiary at Charlestown in Massachusetts has been completely demolished. Fortunately all of the others of that early period — at Auburn, Richmond, Trenton, Baltimore, Columbus and Cherry Hill — have surrendered their major penal functions in whole or in part to other institutions. But if these drab symbols of punishment have given way to more modern prisons, recently renamed correctional institutions, the massive structures of masonry and steel that have arisen in practically every state perpetuate an unrelenting demand for retribution. Fires, riots, and renovations have caused the transformation of old and new interiors, into greatly improved housing facilities, but most of the thousands of inmates released annually, after varied sentences seem prone to return for repeated terms. The recidivism ratios provide a disillusioning judgment on the American penitentiary system."

Yet to the historian there is majesty as well as tragedy clustering around some of these old structures. The majesty is a product, not of their massive buildings and mounting statistics, but of the

ix

persisting efforts of many of their managers to achieve the goals proclaimed by the advocates and founders of penitentiaries two centuries ago. Successive generations of practical administrators and dedicated reformers have devised new procedures and treatment programs, generally with the best of intentions. Unfortunately their recurrent failures either to coordinate their efforts or to communicate with the prisoners have had many tragic results. Not only did the inmates sometimes suffer unexpected and perverse effects from meliorative programs, but their keepers were often brutalized in the process.

The goal of an ordered society has nevertheless persisted, and with it the challenge to develop a disciplinary system that will contain and to a degree harmonize man's vital energies. In America the penitentiary has played an historic role in this endeavor — historic in the sense that it has kept pace with the nation's successive eras of growth and maturation. Thus in the Colonial and early formative years of the young republic the colonists from England and the Continent brought not only disciplinary traditions but also pietistic and rationalistic concepts, which produced formalized penal as well as other governmental institutions that won recognition as models abroad. As the nation expanded, developing new and more populous states and a new industrial and dynamic society, new and larger prisons were required and new industrial and reformatory disciplines developed. And when in the early decades of the present century that era of expansion gave way to one of cultural growth and integration, stressing technological and scientific developments, the penal systems of the states and thereafter of the federal government as well took a turn in the same direction.

As we trace these developments in specific detail in the text we will see how the larger society continually imposed its interests and its points of view on the penal systems of the day. Thus a century and a half ago, when the states of the young republic discovered that their first congregate prisons, designed to dispense with earlier corporal and capital punishments, had in fact become dens of iniquity and violence, they replaced them with substantial penitentiaries equipped to house convicts in separate cells and endeavored to prepare them for a return to the community by labor in strict silence or in complete solitude in their cells. And when these regimens failed to produce the expected penitence, a more educationally motivated society produced reformers who devised indeterminate sentences to induce especially the youthful first offenders to cooperate in reformatory programs designed to speed their release under newly provided parole supervision.

Of course these well-intended projects were not developed in a vacuum, but in a turbulent society whose newly organized labor unions and struggling manufacturers resented the competition of cheap prison-made goods. As hostile labor laws progressively shut down successive systems of prison industries, creating vast pools of idleness, the prospects of reformatory penology faded amidst mounting disorder. Classical concepts of criminality as a willful infraction of the moral and civil order gave way to psychological and sociological explanations of delinquency and crime. At this point the emerging social sciences devised classification procedures to separate the defectives and the vicious malcontents from the tractable convicts. With new hope, prison administrators developed treatment programs to rehabilitate the inmates of their newly renamed correctional institutions. But again a dramatic change in the larger society brought a sudden rise in the number of blacks committed to prison, and the racial strife that resulted presented new challenges not only to the security forces but to the entire correctional system. The rights of prisoners became a crucial issue which revived the age-old debate concerning the nature of justice.

Thus American prisons, whether called penitentiaries, reformatories, or correctional institutions, have been part and parcel of the history of America. Yet they have never been totally or even far removed from similar disciplinary institutions in Europe. As the demographic and cultural migrations of Colonial days continued and increased mightily in the nineteenth century, so the trans-Atlantic flow of penal ideas continued, although in this field a more even balance of exchange developed. That balance continued into the technological and scientific era, as we shall see in the later chapters below.

Both the Americans and the Europeans developed distinctly different sets of institutions for juveniles and adults. Their provisions for the detention of suspects and of minor offenders also diverged, and so did their treatment of released convicts. The full history of juvenile institutions, of jails and houses of correction, of probation and parole and halfway houses, as well as the still unsettled questions concerning the nature of crime, are beyond the scope of this volume. Each merits a separate book and many have already been written. But all of these developments have had their influence on the main course of America's penal history, and we have noted their contributions as the occasion warranted.

Of course the divergencies in theory and practice between European and American developments, despite the constant interchange, are related to contrasting aspects of their societies. The diffusion of authority among many states; the heterogeniety of population, reemphasized recently by racial friction; and the greater emphasis on free enterprise and free will have all played a part in forming the American penal-correctional tradition and in distinguishing it from its counterparts abroad. Scholars on both sides of the Atlantic have long been aware of these differences, and social scientists among them have been eager to exchange ideas and to share insights in their search for a more effective correctional program. Perhaps an historical review of the development of America's correctional system, placing it in its changing national environment, rather than in a narrowly ideological or institutional setting, will contribute a degree of realism to our understanding.

In this work I have retained much of the detailed treatment of prison developments prior to 1915 from my earlier study of American prisons. For most of the states that account supplied the only historical review of the establishment and development of their prisons. In a day when prisons are standing before the court of public opinion as never before, it seems desirable that their record be reviewed in full.

My treatment of the developments of the last half century has not been so detailed. The increased number of state and national surveys and investigations and the lively journalistic commentary, both reportorial and critical, throughout this period have enabled me to recapture its history in broader outline. The developments here were still primarily in state institutions, but interstate and national trends were also establishing themselves. State boundaries and bureaucracies no longer exercised final control; transstate inmate attitudes as well as professional and labor movements played major roles and required careful analysis. Responsibility for action—for failures and accomplishments alike—had been widely shared. When a reassessment of the American correctional system is undertaken, its objectives as well as its shortcomings must be viewed in the full range of their development.

ACKNOWLEDGMENTS

I should like to express my indebtedness to the numerous persons who supplied generous help in earlier years and more recently in the preparation of this work. These include Dr. Sheldon Gleuck, Dr. A. Warren Stearns, former Commissioner of Corrections of Massachusetts, Dean George W. Kirchwey of the Russell Sage Foundation, Austin H. MacCormick, who after long years of experience in many responsible posts as administrator, consultant, and special investigator, serves today as executive director of the Osborne Association, and James V. Bennett, former head for many years of the Federal Bureau of Prisons.

I am indebted to the editors of the *Journal of Criminal Law and Criminology,* the *Journal of Negro History,* the *Pacific Historical Review,* and *Social Forces* for permission to use materials in the present work which first appeared in their respective publications.

The staffs of various libraries and historical agencies were most cooperative during the course of my research. I am especially indebted to the Massachusetts State Library (where I found a remarkably complete collection of official reports gathered during the previous century and a half from every state in the Union, and from which I was able to conduct my research on a first-hand perusal of all annual and special documents on prisons), the Widener Library, the Harvard Law Library, the New York Public Library, the various collections that formed the Russell Sage Foundation library, the Library of Congress, the Rochester Public Library, and the Rush Rhees Library of the University of Rochester.

I appreciate the kindness of Mrs. Elizabeth Croft for the opportunity to consult the special collection of books and sources assembled by the Rochester–Monroe County Criminal Justice Pilot City Program, and similarly to Mrs. Patricia Kingston for an opportunity to use materials from a special collection on penology she gathered at the Rochester Center for Governmental Research. I am especially grateful to Mrs. Croft, to Dr. Carlisle Dixon of the Pilot City Staff, and also to Mrs. Kingston and to Greg Thomas, formerly a special investigator for the McKay Commission and now a Senior Administrative Analyst, as is Mrs. Kingston, on LEAA projects with the Rochester Police Department.

Other Rochesterians who have served in key positions relative to this study and who have given generous assistance are Mrs. Dorothy Wadsworth, a member of the McKay Commission which investigated the Attica uprising, and Judge Harry Goldman, Presiding Justice of the Appellate Division, Fourth Department of the New York Supreme Court, and chairman of the Official Panel named to monitor and assure the prisoners' constitutional rights during the month following the takeover; each has read an early draft of my last chapter and given helpful suggestions for its improvement. I am grateful to Mrs. Virginia Mackey, of the Judicial Process Commission of Rochester for information concerning its activities in coordinating the programs of several regional groups concerned with the welfare of adult as well as juvenile offenders. Congressman Frank J. Horton, a member of the Committee on Government Operations with a special interest in reforms in the criminal justice system, has been most helpful in procuring federal documents and data of value to my researches.

Several administrators and research directors have responded generously to inquiries by letter and telephone. I recall with pleasure an interview with Dr. Howard B. Gill many years ago at the Norfolk Prison Colony, and I have again benefited from his responses to inquiries by letter and telephone. Professor Peter P. Lejins, Director of the Institute of Criminal Justice and Criminology at the University of Maryland, has been similarly helpful in response to questions at an interview and by telephone. E. Preston Sharp, Executive Director of the American Correctional Association, Daniel L. Skoler, Director of the American Bar Association Commission on Correction, and his assistants, Arnold J. Hopkins and Melvin T. Axilbund, have all been helpful. I am grateful also to Professor Albert Morris, research consultant of the Massachusetts Correctional Association, and to Hubert M. Clements, Deputy Director of the South Carolina Department of Correction, for materials supplied in response to inquiries concerning their research programs.

Several individuals have rendered special assistance. Professor Norman Johnston, author of a recent book on prison architecture, has answered technical questions on its historical developments. I am indebted to Robert E. Rodli, president of the John R. Wald Co. of Huntingdon, Pennsylvania, for an opportunity to examine several comparative reports compiled by that company on correctional industry and its production throughout the country during the last three decades. I am also grateful to Miss Armine Dikijian, librarian at the National Council on Crime and Delinquency, Hackensack, New Jersey, for her generous help, both with books sought and information offered, and to my brother-in-law Edward J. Holley, formerly an officer for several years at the Colorado State Prison at Canon City, for frequent letters and discussions on prison practices and traditions.

I am especially indebted to Thomas Kelly of Patterson Smith for the care he has given to the editing of this volume and to the staff at Patterson Smith for the help in assembling the illustrations.

I benefited enormously from frequent discussions with the late Dr. F. Lovell Bixby. As a psychologist who assumed administrative responsibilities, Dr. Bixby had participated in many of the key developments of the last half century, and the opportunity to review some of that rich experience and to prod his memory for insights on the many crucial questions with which he had dealt, has added much to the substance of my account and has greatly enlivened my all too somber researches.

Each of these and other friends has contributed much of value to this study, but of course the defects that remain are solely of my own making.

—Blake McKelvey

Rochester, New York

1.

THE ORIGINS OF PRISONS:
TO 1835

The penitentiary was one of the byproducts of the intellectual and humanitarian movements of the eighteenth century that contributed so generously to the founding of the American nation. The philosophical concepts of natural and equal rights as advanced by Montesquieu, Voltaire, Rousseau and their rationalistic followers were applied to the crime problem by the brilliant young Italian, Cesare Beccaria. But his famous essay *On Crimes and Punishments,* first published in his native Milan in 1764 and soon available in two English and several other translations, was, as he put it, an effort to compile and comment on the theories and practices slowly developed during preceding decades in creative centers in Western Europe. Intellectual stirrings dating back two centuries or more had joined with Protestant and Catholic moralities in challenging the vindictive attitude towards crime. William Penn had embodied an advanced expression of the new movement in his plans for the settlement of Pennsylvania in the 1680s, and although that aspect of his "noble experiment" had passed with him, the houses of correction in England and Holland that inspired Penn persisted and supplied centers for the development of new concepts and methods of handling criminals. When John Howard made his epochal tours of jails and workhouses in England and on the Continent in the mid 1770s, he recorded the achievements as well as the horrors of many lands in *The State of Prisons,* a seminal work that effectively launched the new era in penology.[1]

Intellectual and Institutional Antecedents

Beccaria and Howard provide significant starting points, but some scholars and contemporary activists sought earlier antecedents. Thus Thorsten Sellin, in his study of *Pioneering in Penology,* focused on the development of the House of Correction at Amsterdam in the late sixteenth century. He attributed its accomplishments to that city's rapid growth and its leadership in classical learning, which brought Plato's advocacy of imprisonment as a correctional device to the attention of Dutch scholars and prompted the Amsterdam city council in 1589 to establish a house of correction as propounded almost twenty centuries before in *The Laws.* On the other hand Max Grunhut, in his more widely ranging study of *Penal Reform,* traces the movement to the establishment in 1552 of the first house of correction in an old royal palace called Brideswell in London. Developed as workhouses for the confinement and correction of dissolute vagrants dislodged from their ancestral lands by the enclosure movement, bridewells, as they came to be popularly known, soon found a place in other British cities. In Grunhut's opinion they probably inspired the establishment of the Amsterdam House of Correction, which opened in 1595 and became the model for similar institutions in other European cities.[2]

Whatever their origin, all of the early houses of correction and workhouses were designed for the confinement of vagrants and other minor offenders whose crimes did not seem to justify capital or severe corporal punishments. As the joint influences of the enlightenment of the Renaissance and the humanitarianism of the Reformation took hold, an increasing number of more serious offenders appealed for and secured "benefit of clergy" status and were similarly confined until they could be transported under

---

[1] John Howard, *The State of the Prisons in England and Wales,* 4th ed. (1792; reprinted Montclair, N.J., 1973), and *An Account of the Principal Lazarettos in Europe,* 2d ed. (1791; reprinted Montclair, N.J., 1973). The first edition of *State of Prisons* was published in 1777; the second, revised, in 1780; the third, much revised and enlarged, in 1784. The first edition of *Lazarettos* was published in 1789.

[2] Thorsten Sellin, *Pioneering in Penology: The Amsterdam House of Correction in the Sixteenth and Seventeenth Centuries* (Philadelphia, 1944); Max Grunhut, *Penal Reform: A Comparative Study* (1948; reprinted Montclair, N.J., 1972), pp. 13–43.

terms of servitude to colonies abroad or housed in galley ships for work on public projects. Sometimes such convicts were held for brief periods in local jails ("gaols"), which likewise held pretrial suspects, debtors, and convicts awaiting corporal or capital punishments.

Apparently the first responsible leader to prescribe imprisonment as a corrective treatment for major offenders was the Quaker proprietor, William Penn. His "Great Law" for the government of the newly founded Province of Pennsylvania provided in 1682 for the confinement of both major and minor offenders in houses of correction where they would be required to perform useful work in compensation for, and in proportion to, their crimes. An amendment made murder a capital offense, the only one thus designated until 1700 when treason was added. Pennsylvania continued to rely largely on fines and imprisonment until 1718 when, following the death of William Penn, the assembly accepted a reimposition of the English criminal code, which increased the number of capital offenses to twelve and authorized whipping and other punishments common in the colonies as well as in Britain.[3]

Historians have not determined either the exact origins or the full influence of William Penn's experiment. It is uncertain whether his Quaker friends or a visit to Amsterdam had made him aware of the house of correction. An early Pennsylvania account presuming such a contact is disputed by Grunhut, who sees Penn's British antecedents and Quaker doctrines as the more significant influence.[4] In any event, several of the older colonies had already moved to establish both jails and houses of correction on the English model. In Massachusetts, for example, Boston opened its first jail in 1635 and its first house of correction three decades later. David Rothman attributes the early establishment of workhouses and houses of correction to the efforts of growing towns to check vagrancy and enforce their settlement laws. These institutions provided for the

[3] Harry E. Barnes and Negley K. Teeters, *New Horizons in Criminology*, 1st ed. (New York, 1943), pp. 463–465; Lawrence H. Gipson, "Criminal Codes of Pennsylvania," *Journal of Criminal Law and Criminology* 6 (1915): 323–344. Professor Barnes in an earlier study of the penal history of New Jersey describes a liberal penal code in that colony drafted by its Quakers a few years before that of Pennsylvania.

[4] Grunhut, *Penal Reform*, p. 44. Grunhut cites but does not agree on this point with George W. Smith, *A Defense of the System of Solitary Confinement of Prisoners Adopted by the State of Pennsylvania* (Philadelphia, 1833).

misdemeanants in congregate rooms within the local jail or closely adjoining it.[5] Little is known of the actual practice in Pennsylvania under its liberal code, but the construction of a new brick gaol and house of correction on High Street in 1721 provided facilities for the more stringent regimen of that later period.

No evidence has come to light of any knowledge in Europe of the Pennsylvania experiment. Beccaria relied almost exclusively on deductive reasoning in the formulation of his arguments against capital punishment and other forms of torture. He cited the rationalistic principles of Montesquieu rather than the practical experience of William Penn as the basis for his conclusions, but all three were part of the enlightenment that presaged the dawn of a new approach to crime. "The purpose of punishment," Beccaria declared, "is not to torment a sensible being, nor to undo a crime already committed. . . . The end of punishment, therefore, is no other than to prevent the criminal from doing further injury to society and to prevent others from committing the like offense." He further reasoned that while punishments must be severe enough to achieve these ends they must not be so severe as to brutalize the public. "There ought to be a fixed proportion between crimes and punishments," he maintained, and capital punishment should be reserved for the removal of men whose continued existence threatened the state. He did not regard imprisonment as a major form of punishment, however, and discussed it only as a method of detention prior to trial and sentencing. Occasional expressions of a preference for sentences to "slavery at hard labor" as more effective deterrents than capital punishment suggest, however, that Beccaria may have envisioned a form of imprisonment but neglected to specify its character. The decision to rebuild the original House of Correction in Ghent as a *Maison de Force* designed for the confinement of major offenders in individual cells represented a

---

[5] Edwin Powers, *Crime and Punishment in Early Massachusetts, 1620–1692* (Boston, 1966), pp. 214–223; Carl Bridenbaugh, *Cities in the Wilderness: The First Century of Urban Life in America, 1625–1742* (New York, 1938), pp. 72–75, 224–226, 384–386; Negley K. Teeters, *The Cradle of the Penitentiary: The Walnut Street Jail at Philadelphia, 1773–1835* (Philadelphia, 1955), pp. 5–11; David J. Rothman, *The Discovery of the Asylum: Social Order and Disorder in the New Republic* (Boston, 1971), pp. 25–29.

dramatic new step in the development of prisons.[6]

England, as Sidney and Beatrice Webb have shown, had an older tradition of imprisonment for minor offenses than Continental countries that followed the Roman civil law, but the gaols and bridewells, which numbered over two hundred by the 1770s, had lost their distinctiveness and become wretched jails. John Howard, appointed Sheriff of Bedfordshire in 1773, was shocked at the conditions he found in the county jail. When the reforms he suggested were resisted by the justices of the peace, he visited neighboring jails in a vain search for precedents. His journeys brought him into contact with other reformers, however, and won him a hearing before the House of Commons which he turned to good account. Encouraged, Howard pressed his prison inspections into Scotland and Ireland and crossed the Channel in 1775 for an examination of the jails and houses of correction of Europe. He was the first, as Grunhut has observed, to apply the empirical method of research to the field of social reform.[7]

Howard's Continental tours during the next two years focused attention on prison developments there that provided a pattern for penal programs in both England and America. The most significant was the House of Correction established by Pope Clement XI at Rome in 1704, but even more influential in several respects was the *Maison de Force* under construction at Ghent at the time of his visit in 1775. The Hospice of St. Michael in Rome was designed to care for two types of juvenile delinquents, incorrigible boys submitted to its supervision for discipline, and youthful offenders committed by the courts for a stint of hard labor and penance. The wing erected for the youthful offenders had small rooms or cells for the separate confinement of each boy, though most were permitted out for work in silence during the day. The reconstructed house of correction at Ghent likewise provided small, separate cells, arranged in pentagon clusters, around a control center. It was a new architectural model which could be adopted for the imprisonment of adults. Howard

---

[6] Cesare Beccaria, *An Essay on Crimes and Punishment,* with a commentary attributed to Voltaire, 3d ed. (London, 1770); James Heath, *Eighteenth Century Penal Theory* (New York, 1963); Marcello Maestro, *Cesare Beccaria and the Origins of Penal Reform* (Philadelphia, 1973).

[7] Sidney and Beatrice Webb, *English Prisons under Local Government* (London, 1922), pp. 3–40; Grunhut, *Penal Reform,* pp. 31–40.

discovered other interesting provisions for the housing and care of inmates in a few jails in Switzerland and Germany and in a new house of correction being erected at Milan.[8]

The meticulous detail with which Howard described each of the wretched jails he visited in England, as well as the foreign models, provided a sharp contrast that challenged Parliament to action. With his publication of *State of Prisons,* such able men as Popham, Blackstone, Bentham, and Romilly, all acquainted as well with the ideas of Beccaria and Montesquieu, rallied to Howard's support. Together they mounted a campaign for the reform of the criminal law and for a decision to replace the transportation system, which the revolt of the American colonies was just then interrupting, with national penitentiaries. Debate over the choice of a site for the first penitentiary delayed action, and the opening of new opportunities for the transportation of certain convicts to Australia again postponed for several decades the development of a penitentiary system in England. The model provisions laid down for penitentiaries in the law of 1779 were extended to local jails and houses of correction by a series of laws which culminated in the first general prison act of 1791. Although no central authority was yet available to see that these provisions were applied, several counties did proceed to build new institutions on the patterns approved by Howard and his followers. The most influential of the new structures was the model prison at Norfolk erected in 1784 and managed by Sir Thomas Bevoor.[9]

A Fresh Start in America

Philadelphia, the most important city of the New World, was the proper stage for statesmen eager to build a new penal system. Inspiration enough could have been derived from the programs of William Penn, but the city was the focal point for liberal European influences; Benjamin Rush, William Bradford, Caleb Lownes, and others interested in penal problems were in close touch with foreign leaders in this field, and, like Thomas Jefferson in his *Declaration,*

[8]Howard, *State of Prisons.* For an account of Howard's travels in Italy see pp. 106–123. A plate of the Rome House of Correction is at p. 114. The *Maison de Force* at Ghent is discussed on pp. 145–148, with a plate at p. 145. See also Grunhut, *Penal Reform,* pp. 17–22.

[9]Grunhut, *Penal Reform,* pp. 23–47; D. L. Howard, *John Howard: Prison Reformer* (London, 1958).

they were not concerned for originality. While William Bradford, an able jurist, drafted the code that was to inaugurate a new era in criminal jurisprudence, a group of Quakers and friends associated themselves in 1787 as the Philadelphia Society for Alleviating the Miseries of Public Prisons.[10] An earlier group, the Philadelphia Society for Assisting Distressed Prisoners had organized in 1776 to dispense food and clothing to prison inmates but succumbed when British forces entered the city in September 1777. The new society was the first in the modern world to assume the responsibility of planning a satisfactory penal system.

> When we consider [said the preamble of the Society's constitution] that the obligations of benevolence, which are founded on the precepts and example of the author of Christianity, are not cancelled by the follies or crimes of our fellow creatures, . . . it becomes us to extend our compassion to that part of mankind, who are the subjects of these miseries. By the aids of humanity, their undue and illegal sufferings may be prevented, . . . and such degrees and modes of punishment may be discovered and suggested, as may, instead of continuing habits of vice, become the means of restoring our fellow creatures to virtue and happiness.[11]

The immediate occasion for the formation of the new society was a popular reaction to the revised penal code of 1786, which substituted sentences of punishment at hard labor for capital punishment in all but two major crimes. That law, which followed Beccaria in theory and reflected the reform spirit of the newly organized state legislature, prompted the local sheriffs to send gangs of convicts out to work on the public roads and in the city streets. Secured by chains to each other or attached to heavy cannon balls and wearing pantaloons of bright colors to display their identity, the convicts provided a spectacle disturbing to many sober citizens. Opposed as most Quakers were to capital and other corporal punishments, the leaders of the new Society pressed a new resolution

---

[10] The organization was also known as the Philadelphia Society for the Alleviation of the Miseries of Public Prisons, *Pennsylvania Journal of Prison Discipline and Philanthropy* 1 (Philadelphia, 1845).

[11] Roberts Vaux, *Notices of the Original, and Successive Efforts, to Improve the Discipline of the Prison at Philadelphia* (Philadelphia, 1826), pp. 10–11: Orlando F. Lewis, *The Development of American Prisons and Prison Customs, 1776–1845: With Special Reference to Early Institutions in the State of New York* (1922; reprinted Montclair, N.J., 1967), pp. 13–24.

on the legislature. "Solitary confinement to hard labor and a total abstinence from spirituous liquors will prove the means of reforming these unhappy creatures," they argued. To achieve this end they persuaded the legislature to designate the Walnut Street Jail in Philadelphia as a temporary state prison to house convicts from throughout the state until other provisions could be made.[12]

The Walnut Street Jail, aptly described by Negley K. Teeters as "the cradle of the penitentiary," required additional facilities to meet its new responsibilities. Robert Smith, the city's leading architect, had designed it to serve the joint functions of a jail and house of correction. Built in the mid seventies of stone, it had an imposing two-story facade on Walnut Street and two wings extending back into a yard surrounded by a stone wall. Large rooms in the wings accommodated the misdemeanants and debtors on one side and the more serious offenders awaiting trial or sentence on the other. The workhouse at the rear end of the jail yard was converted into dormitory rooms for debtors and other misdemeanants, thus freeing their former accommodations for use by the newly sentenced convicts. A cellblock with sixteen inside cells constructed on the two upper floors of a new three-story building provided separate confinement for those sentenced to solitary imprisonment. Caleb Lownes, an iron merchant and leading member of the Society, had joined Dr. Benjamin Rush in urging provision of a cellblock patterned on Howard's proposals as applied in the county jail recently built at Norfolk in England. Lownes accepted the post of inspector and soon became the active manager of the work program in new sheds erected in the jail yard.[13]

Under the able direction of Caleb Lownes, the Walnut Street Jail prospered and attracted wide attention. He introduced a variety of handicrafts—"shoe-making, weaving, and tailoring; clipping logwood, grinding plaster of Paris, beating hemp, sawing and polishing marble . . . picking oakum" and the like, as he reported to the Society. His *Account of the Alteration and Present State of the Penal Laws of Pennsylvania*, written in collaboration with William Bradford and published in 1792, cited Beccaria, Montesquieu, and Howard and stimulated legislators in other states to reform their criminal codes. News of the success of the penitentiary house, where

12 Teeters, *Cradle*, pp. 29–32.
13 Teeters, *Cradle*, pp. 17–19.

convicts were confined in separate cells at night and released to work in the courtyard or shops during the day, attracted a stream of visitors. Members of the Philadelphia Society and delegations from other states and abroad were eager to study its program. The attention helped to maintain a state of excitement, and the friendly interviews by dedicated Quakers with the few inmates sentenced to solitary confinement helped to maintain inmate morale. Unfortunately, a flood of commitments soon overcrowded the cellhouse and other accommodations and so disrupted the work program that Caleb Lownes resigned in disgust in 1801.[14]

Prominent among the visitors to the Walnut Street Jail was Thomas Eddy, a New Yorker who became a key figure in the early development of American prisons. Prompted by outbreaks of disorder in the New York City jail, Eddy persuaded General Philip Schuyler to join him in 1796 in a visit to Philadelphia to inspect its jail. Back in New York they drafted and secured adoption of a bill substituting imprisonment for most corporal and capital punishments and authorizing the creation of a penitentiary for the confinement of criminals. Eddy became the commissioner in charge of its construction and erected Newgate in Greenwich Village, overlooking the Hudson River. He followed the plan of the Walnut Street Jail and gave chief emphasis, as in that structure, to the congregate rooms and workshops, cutting the number of solitary confinement cells to fourteen. Eddy, who was soon quoting Beccaria and Howard in his reports as chief inspector and agent, achieved a creditable discipline and work record in his first years. By 1802, however, a bloody riot and a mass-escape attempt that was frustrated only with military aid, Eddy became convinced, as he wrote to a friend in London, that the design of Newgate was a mistake that only an entirely new building could rectify. It should, he declared, be solely equipped after Howard's plan with single cells for the separate confinement of all inmates at night and with shops for their labor in strict silence on weekdays.[15]

[14] Caleb Lownes, *An Account of the Alteration and Present State of the Penal Laws of Pennsylvania* (Boston, 1799); Teeters, *Cradle*, pp. 39–104.

[15] Samuel L. Knapp, *The Life of Thomas Eddy* (New York, 1834), pp. 56–77; Thomas Eddy, *An Account of the State Prison or Penitentiary House in the City of New-York* (New York, 1801); W. David Lewis, *From Newgate to Dannemora: The Rise of the Penitentiary in New York, 1796–1848* (Ithaca, N.Y., 1965), pp. 29–34.

While Eddy was busily engaged in launching Newgate, delegations from other states, after visiting the Walnut Street Jail, planned prisons in Massachusetts, Maryland, and elsewhere. Eddy endeavored to persuade the Massachusetts officials who stopped off in New York to adopt a single-cell system—he even submitted a draft for such a design—but the Bay State authorities followed the Walnut Street model and built the first portion of the new prison at Charlestown on the congregate pattern. Similarly, in 1798, the first buildings of the prison at Trenton followed that model, as did the prison at Baltimore five years later. Connecticut continued to rely on an old copper mine as a makeshift prison. But in Virginia, Jefferson took the lead in establishing a prison at Richmond, designed in collaboration with Benjamin Latrobe, a French architect who had visited Ghent and made a sketch of its pentagonal cellblocks. Elsewhere the county jails, supplemented in a few places by houses of correction, sufficed to hold convicts until corporal or capital punishments could be administered, though humanitarians in Ohio, Pennsylvania, and Massachusetts were starting a movement to limit hangings to murder and one or two other crimes. As in Colonial days, and in accordance with the practice abroad, local sheriffs staged their occasional hangings in the public square where the spectacle sometimes attracted large crowds. Floggings, brandings and other mutilations, and the pillory persisted as punishments for lesser offenses, but a preference for jail sentences was spreading.[16]

Thomas Eddy, often called the John Howard of America, visited or corresponded with the managers of most of the country's prisons and was keenly aware of their problems. As in the case of Caleb Lownes in Philadelphia, Eddy saw the mounting wave of convictions overcrowd the limited facilities of Newgate; two years after the retirement of Lownes, Eddy too was ready to give up the management of Newgate but not to abandon the cause of prison reform. Instead, he launched a campaign for a second state prison, and when legislators from Auburn secured its designation as the site, he redoubled his efforts to persuade the authorities to construct it on the cellular plan, citing Howard and Bentham in support of

[16]O. F. Lewis, *Development*, pp. 53–70; Raymond T. Bye, *Capital Punishment in the United States* (Philadelphia, 1919); Herbert Falk, *Corporal Punishment: A Social Interpretation of Its Theory and Practice in the Schools of the United States* (New York, 1941).

separate night cells. Unfortunately the long-projected British penitentiary had not been built, and while Bentham's panopticon plan was attracting some attention in Pennsylvania, the contractors in New York, charged with the construction of Auburn in 1817, were content to follow the congregate models of Walnut Street and Newgate. Yet Eddy had planted the seed and within a few years his policies began to take hold.[17]

The Development of Rival Prison Systems

Whatever the intentions of the first generation, the years following the War of 1812 found the American states struggling with totally unsatisfactory prisons. Fortunately the increasing stability of the states enabled several of them to tackle their problems with new vigor, and four fairly distinct penal systems shortly emerged. The persistent faith of leaders of the Philadelphia Society in isolation as a prison discipline finally crystallized into the solitary system of Cherry Hill penitentiary. But before that model was securely established, the inspectors and administrators at Auburn achieved a practical compromise between separate confinement and congregate labor embodied in an architectural design supported by a disciplinary regimen that, with the aid of an aggressive society of reformers, won the country to its silent system. While these developments were in process, determined philanthropists in New York and Boston established separate houses of refuge to take children out of the jails and prisons. Other leaders in several major cities resurrected and reestablished houses of correction for misdemeanants to save them from the contamination of the crowded jails. The creation of these four institutional patterns provided models for the next half century of prison development.

Although Pennsylvania and especially Philadelphia still held a measure of primacy, the incessant growth of New York city and state forced its leaders to press ahead with the search for an adequate prison system. The establishment of the Auburn state prison, designed to relieve congestion at Newgate, was the first step, but its first buildings equipped with sixty-one single cells and twenty-eight congregate rooms, though more commodious than Newgate, soon proved inadequate. Eddy was still advocating the adoption of a separate-cell plan, and although most of his political friends at

[17] Knapp, *Thomas Eddy*, pp. 276–277, 285–286; W. D. Lewis, *Newgate*, pp. 34–46.

Albany were in disfavor, Eddy rallied support by taking the lead in forming the Society for the Prevention of Pauperism in New York, which among other causes helped to promote the single-cell system. A rapid increase in commitments forced action at Auburn, where mounting disorder in the congregate rooms favored a shift to separate cells, as Eddy had advocated. In recognition of this situation the legislature, in April 1819, authorized the inspectors "to alter or change the plan, originally adopted, so far as to render the same more suitable for confining each prisoner in a separate cell."[18]

In compliance with this directive William Brittin, the first agent (or warden), undertook the construction of a second or north wing equipping it with single cells. Neither the small block of solitary cells at Walnut Street jail nor those of Newgate, its counterpart, supplied an acceptable model. The cost of providing an outside window in each of the several hundred cells would have been prohibitive as well as a foolhardy safety factor. Brittin may have studied the plan of the Ghent House of Correction of 1773, as reproduced in Howard's *State of Prisons,* for on paper this appears to show a block of inside cells built back-to-back in one spoke of its octagonal structure. In fact, as Norman Johnston explains, they were interior cells opening into arcades on each level, but the concept of several tiers of cells opening onto galleries or catwalks could have been borrowed from the 1704 plan for the prison of St. Michael in Rome, also reproduced by Howard, although its cells were outside cells. If Brittin consulted these precedents he displayed ingenuity in combining their concepts into a double bank of back-to-back cells, each 7 by 3.5 by 7 feet in size, and opening onto narrow wooden catwalks, with the entire five-story cage encompassed by outer walls some six feet distant on all sides from the inside prison grill.[19]

As has frequently occurred in prison history, an outbreak of disorder changed the course of Auburn's development. When a fire kindled by some inmates gutted the new wing before it was

---

[18] W. D. Lewis, *Newgate,* pp. 56–60; Society for the Prevention of Pauperism, *Report on the Penitentiary System in the United States* (New York, 1822); Gershom Powers, *A Brief Account of the Construction, Management, & Discipline . . . of the New-York State Prison at Auburn* (Auburn, 1826), p. 30.

[19] G. Powers, *Auburn,* pp. 30–31; W. D. Lewis, *Newgate,* pp. 67–68; O. F. Lewis, *Development,* pp. 77–90; Norman Johnston to author, 29 May 1974; Howard, *State of Prisons,* pp. 114, 145.

completed, Brittin made several modifications in the design. The original cells, separated by brick walls one foot thick, had had floors and ceilings of wood which had enabled the fire to spread upward to the roof. To increase security he arched each cell with brick and topped the block with a cement ceiling twenty inches thick to prevent any access of fire or convicts to the roof. He at first lined each cell with wood and installed heavy wooden doors, but these features were soon altered, whether because of the excessive gloom or the excessive cost was not stated. Brittin's sudden death in 1821 brought the appointment of Gershom Powers as architect, and Powers, who completed the first block of 165 cells and a second of 120 similar cells, abandoned the wooden lining and substituted iron grates for the solid doors on the last of these cells. The increased security and economy provided by these small interior cells gave this cellblock pattern a double advantage and attracted immediate attention from penal authorities in other states.[20]

Frequent outbreaks of disorder in old Newgate and at Auburn during its construction prompted the legislature to create a commission to consider and propose proper action. The commission promptly despatched representatives to Philadelphia to study its famous jail. Although their reaction was favorable, subsequent reports told of serious outbreaks among the overcrowded inmates in the Walnut Street Jail, which its managers attributed to their inability to maintain the solitary confinement then in favor at Philadelphia. As a result of the commission's report, the New York Legislature, in April 1821, directed the officers at Auburn to divide its inmates into three classes. The act directed that the most hardened criminals be held in solitary confinement in separate cells. It stipulated that the less hardened criminals were to be confined in solitude until they gave evidence of repentance, when, though still kept in separate cells at night, they would be permitted to work at certain tasks in the daytime. A third group composed of "the least guilty" should be confined in separate cells at night but worked in prison shops in silence in the daytime.[21]

The plan reflected some of the reasoning of those who thought prisoners could be induced through penitence to reform their ways,

[20] G. Powers, *Auburn*, pp.31–34.
[21] New York Assembly, *Journal* (1820–1821), pp. 903–910; O. F. Lewis, *Development*, pp. 84–86.

but it also displayed a new determination to use imprisonment as punishment in a very real sense. Thomas Eddy had urged the adoption of individual cells and the use of solitary confinement for a brief period at the start of sentences for serious crimes as a form of penance, yet he opposed the plan advanced by many in Pennsylvania for long sentences to solitary confinement. But the demand for more severe treatment was mounting, and since the Pennsylvanians were already constructing a penitentiary at Pittsburgh to be equipped with separate cells for the solitary confinement of all inmates, that regimen was applied to eighty hardened criminals at Auburn in December 1821. The policy soon produced disastrous results, with several attempted suicides and mental breakdowns occurring among the men confined in idleness in the narrow cells. The increasing number of deaths among these convicts gradually became known and prompted a visit by the governor, who was so shocked by the conditions he found that he granted pardons in 1823 to most of those held for a year in solitude. The experiment with solitary confinement at Auburn had to be abandoned.[22]

Fortunately the men in control at Auburn—Gershom Powers, the agent, Elam Lynds, the warden, following the death of Brittin in 1821, and John Cray, the deputy keeper—had developed an alternate regimen for the remainder of the inmates that promised a measure of success. John Cray, a former army officer of the Canadian forces who had defected and settled in Auburn, devised a strict discipline which included such regulations as downcast eyes, lockstep marching, no talking or other communication between prisoners, and constant activity under close supervision of the guards when out of the cells. This strict discipline, coupled with a closely supervised work program in congregate shops, kept the convicts occupied throughout the day and, in addition to contributing to the maintenance of the prison, gave it an orderly atmosphere that attracted the praise of many visitors from other states. Confident of success, the New York authorities applied the separate-cell and silent system to the entire population at Auburn and, in 1825, launched the construction of a second state prison at Ossining-on-the-Hudson, where Elam Lynds led a crew of 100 carefully selected convicts in the building of Sing Sing.[23]

[22] W. D. Lewis, *Newgate*, pp. 64–70; Knapp, *Thomas Eddy*, 202–203, 244, 285–300.
[23] W. D. Lewis, *Newgate*, pp. 75–86; O. F. Lewis, *Development*, pp. 86–93.

Some inmates resisted the restraints of the silent discipline, but Warden Lynds was quick to demand their compliance. Legislators shocked at the disorders at Newgate had in 1819 authorized the re-introduction of flogging there and at Auburn, and Lynds made frequent use of the lash in the maintenance of order. So brutal were some of his punishments that Captain Cray resigned, and protests mounted among the citizens of Auburn disturbed by the reports of some of the floggings. When the harsh discipline at Auburn began to arouse criticism abroad, Thomas Eddy, while deploring the excessive use of the lash, wrote in defense of the Lynds regime, which he described in 1825 as the best of any prison in America. Local criticism had prompted Lynds' transfer from Auburn to Ossining, where, however, his strict discipline acquired an even wider exposure.[24]

A more effective defender and champion of the Auburn system appeared that year in Louis Dwight, founder and organizer of the Boston Prison Discipline Society. Born of devout New England parents and inculcated with stern Puritan morals, Dwight was diverted from the ministry when an accident in a chemical class injured his lungs. He found his calling a few years later when, on a horseback journey for the American Bible Society, he visited a number of jails and became shocked and indignant over the miseries of their inmates. Shortly after organizing the Boston Prison Discipline Society to correct these evils, he paid a visit to Auburn and became an enthusiastic advocate of its system.[25]

The failures of the earlier generation had left a fallow field for Dwight's cultivation, and the elaboration of the silent system at Auburn provided a program suitable to his tastes. The salvation of the convict, as conceived by Dwight and the Baptist and the Congregational ministers who rallied to his Society, was not the penitence of solitary souls but the redemption of unfortunate sinners, to be achieved with the aid of revivals and Sabbath schools and through the development of industrious habits under strict discipline in congregate shops. Unfortunately Dwight's strong

[24] W. D. Lewis, *Newgate*, pp. 45–47, 60–62, 85–90; Knapp, *Thomas Eddy*, pp. 298–321; Kai T. Erikson, *Wayward Puritans: A Study in the Sociology of Deviance* (New York, 1966), pp. 199–205. Erikson sees Lynds and his regimen as a direct product of Puritan ideology.

[25] O. F. Lewis, *Development*, 130–138, 290.

belief in the righteous nature of his cause made it difficult for him to tolerate disparate programs, and it was not long before he was engaging in an acrimonious controversy with the Philadelphians that seriously marred his reputation. Nevertheless, the Bostonian's influence spread rapidly, making him the first national figure in American prison reform.

Several of the American states had attained stability and were enjoying a measure of prosperity when Dwight took up his labors. As yet, however, only Auburn provided separate cells sufficient in number to accommodate its inmates and permit the silent system of prison discipline. Moses Pilsbury maintained a semblance of discipline under difficulties at Concord in New Hampshire. A few prisons in New York and New England had some minor provisions for the religious care of inmates. Baltimore had a fairly satisfactory arrangement for the segregation of the women with a matron in charge, and New York City was undertaking to establish a special institution for the care of juvenile offenders; these, however, were lonely forerunners of the elementary principle of classification. Dissatisfaction was rife, and forces were active that would enable Dwight to carry his program rapidly forward.

His first achievement was the establishment of a model prison at Wethersfield, Connecticut. Dwight's indictment of the vicious conditions in the old copper mine that had been used as a makeshift prison since before the Revolution had easily aroused the staunch puritanism of this commonwealth. The governor and the legislature undertook to replace the old Newgate horror by erecting a new prison on the Auburn pattern, and the first cellhouse, rapidly completed at Wethersfield, accommodated 135 prisoners in separate night cells, each 7 by 3½ and 7 feet high. Thereafter, as Dwight toured the states, interceding before the legislatures in behalf of their convicts, it was the Wethersfield structure built at a total cost of only $30,000, rather than the already politically corrupted Auburn, that served as his model. Connecticut had the good judgment to call the able warden Moses Pilsbury from New Hampshire to manage its prison; and for twenty years this self-made administrator, and his son Amos who succeeded him, maintained the best penal institution in the country. With the example of a practical achievement at hand, Dwight was able to persuade Massachusetts to erect a cellblock at Charlestown, and a half dozen other states—New Hampshire, Ver-

contact with each prisoner, would advance the reformatory objective.[29]

The debate reflected not only disagreement concerning the true purpose of the penitentiary but also uncertainty or ignorance of its design. Haviland's plan was patterned somewhat, whether consciously or not, on the Suffolk House of Correction designed by William Blackborn, a follower of Howard in England. Viewed from above, the seven cellblocks, branching out from a central rotunda, appeared like the spokes of a hugh stone wheel. Flanking the corridors that extended through each block were thirty or more large solitary cells, 8 by 15 and 12 feet high in the center of their vaulted roofs; each was adjoined by an exercise yard, likewise securely walled to prevent any communication between the convicts. The network of massive stone walls practically filled the twelve-acre plot of Cherry Hill, which was surrounded by an imposing outer wall with castle-like turrets at the four corners and an administration building in front that further accentuated the medieval design.[30]

The first reports of both inspectors and visitors to Cherry Hill were generally favorable, almost ecstatic. The apparent ease with which the simple disciplinary regulations produced subservience if not penitence among the inmates aroused the envy of some distraught officers from other prisons. Its reputation among convicts was less favorable and an inmate of the Walnut Street jail who feared a transfer urged his mother to do her best to secure a pardon for him and save him from transfer to "Bush Hill Penitentiary," as it was known to insiders. This reputation was not considered a disadvantage by the officials, and if it had not been for the $750,000 construction cost—a sum that staggered responsible state authorities in the 1830s—Louis Dwight would have encountered a more effective opposition. As it was, New Jersey built a cellblock on this pattern at Trenton in 1833, equipped with 192 outside cells, each 7 by 12 and 12 feet high, but neglected to provide individual exer-

[29]Edward Livingston, *Letter from Edward Livingston, Esq. to Roberts Vaux* (Philadelphia, 1828); Roberts Vaux, *Letter on the Penitentiary System of Pennsylvania, Addressed to William Roscoe* (Philadelphia, 1827), and *Reply to Two Letters of William Roscoe of Liverpool on the Penitentiary System of Pennsylvania* (Philadelphia, 1827).

[30]Teeters and Shearer, *Cherry Hill*, pp. 54–75; Norman Johnston, *The Human Cage: A Brief History of Prison Architecture* (New York, 1973), pp. 22–30; O. F. Lewis, *Development*, pp. 123–126.

cise yards. Maryland constructed small outside cells in a new building at the Baltimore prison but used them only for nighttime confinement and eagerly introduced congregate shops. Meanwhile, the decision at Harrisburg in favor of solitary confinement with labor called for the reconstruction of Pennsylvania's Western Penitentiary in 1829 equipping it with 170 large outside cells, which made it the third prison to adopt a genuine solitary system.[31]

Louis Dwight and his Prison Discipline Society continued to dominate the American prison scene. Bibles, Sabbath schools, and the preached gospel were prominent features of their reform program. The Boston Society in 1825 sent Jared Curtis and Gerrish Barrett as missionaries to the various prisons, maintaining them in successive institutions until the states were persuaded to provide for resident or part-time chaplains. The Society's agents joyfully reported revivals from time to time, and Sabbath schools became customary features in several prisons that welcomed the aid of visiting clergymen. The Society distributed thousands of Bibles and tracts, which later formed the nucleus of prison libraries, and secured the cooperation of some chaplains in encouraging inmates to commit passages of scripture to memory.[32] This program was perhaps more aptly fitted to prepare a responsive prisoner for a satisfactory adjustment to society after his discharge than the twentieth-century man might suspect. One chaplain, the Reverend Jared Curtis, was in fact so interested in the character of the inmates that he made the first known statistical study of a group of convicts. According to his report as chaplain at the Massachusetts State Penitentiary in 1832 he had interviewed 256 prisoners and tabulated their answers to a dozen questions. The answers pointed up a need for the careful training of youthful delinquents.[33]

No reformer could have selected a more fortunate plank than Dwight's program for the encouragement of prison industry. A half century had not diminished the American distaste for taxes, and

[31] Teeters and Shearer, *Cherry Hill*, pp. 73–86; O. F. Lewis, *Development*, pp. 120–129; Rothman, *Discovery*, pp. 85–86.

[32] Prison Discipline Society, Boston, *Third Report* (1828; reprinted in *Reports of the Prison Discipline Society of Boston, 1826–1854*, Montclair, N.J., 1972, hereinafter cited as P.D.S., *Reports*), pp. 60–63; *Fourth Report* (1828), p. 25. Rev. Barrett reported that one convict memorized 42 books of the Bible in 18 weeks.

[33] O. F. Lewis, *Development*, pp. 162–163.

the increasing burden of supporting idle convicts had become a major cause for popular dissatisfaction with the first prisons. The thriving handicraft labor of the early days of Walnut Street and Newgate prisons had soon been snuffed out by overcrowding and the resulting disciplinary breakdown; nevertheless, the prison at Auburn had scarcely been started when an enterprising citizen applied for a contract to operate a factory within the walls—a circumstance which played an important part in determining the nature of the compromise that gave rise to the silent system. The factory system itself was just then gaining a place in industry, and the merchant-capitalists who ventured into large-scale production in those early days turned eagerly to the permanent supply of cheap labor available in prison. By 1825 Auburn prison was a smooth-running industrial plant, and it was not long before this prison and those at Wethersfield, Charlestown, and Baltimore were realizing small surpluses over and above their expenses—an irrefutable economic argument in support of the silent system. Mechanics' associations raised protests in New York State, and a convention of ninety-nine of their delegates gathered at Utica in 1834, and in Albany in 1841, to fight the system. A legislative committee investigated the grievances and pressed the adoption of a regulatory measure in 1835. No changes occurred, however, as the authorities rejoiced over their successful reduction of the tax burden. Indeed, whatever their profits, the contractors considerably assisted the states in developing a stable penal system in America.

In addition to the rival penitentiary systems, the early reformers developed two correctional institutions which served to reduce the baneful influence of the common jail. Local groups took the lead in establishing juvenile reform schools and houses of correction to remove children and misdemeanants from the jails. These institutions were early attempts at penal specialization, and although the basis of classification was simple, the philosophy behind the reform was revolutionary in significance. Here was recognized for the first time in America the existence of crimes for which society rather than the individual was responsible. And the corollary easily followed that society had an obligation to train the neglected child and to rehabilitate the unfortunate vagrant or drunkard for a more wholesome life.

Religious or charitable bodies in a few European cities had developed reform schools for juvenile delinquents in earlier days, notably the Hospice of St. Michael in Rome, opened in 1703, but it remained for a group of humanitarians in New York City in 1824 to establish what became the first public institution of this character. The Reverend John Stanford, who had occasionally conducted a Sabbath school for children in Newgate prison and in the city jail since the early 1800s, had protested their confinement there, but it was not until the winter of 1816, when the number of poor waifs increased, creating disorder in the city streets, that a group of public-spirited gentlemen headed by Thomas Eddy, John Griscom, and Stanford met to form the Society for the Prevention of Pauperism.

The first task was to make a careful study of the problem. Griscom, a Quaker schoolmaster, assumed the direction of an investigation and after a preliminary report left to visit educational and correctional institutions in Europe. In London he visited a newly opened reform school for juveniles maintained by the London Philanthropic Society; he developed friendly contacts with Elizabeth Fry, William Roscoe, William Allen, and other British reformers before proceeding to the Continent. Back in New York he shared his new experiences and enthusiasms with the members of the Society. Charles Haines, who had continued Griscom's researches, had meanwhile informed the Society that there were 8,000 children of school age in New York City with no formal education and that many had served varied sentences in the city jail or penitentiary.[34]

The Society attracted several new members, among them Mayor Cadwallader Colden and a young lawyer named James W. Gerard, who became chairman of a committee on juvenile delinquency. The reports of Gerard's committee and those of a committee headed by Colden and later by Haines on the state of prisons attracted wide civic attention. When the Society assembled in 1823 to consider these reports, it hastily transformed itself into the Society for the Reformation of Juvenile Delinquents, whose purpose was to rally community support for the establishment of a House of Refuge for vagrant and depraved young

[34] Robert S. Pickett, *House of Refuge: Origins of Juvenile Reform in New York State, 1815–1857* (Syracuse, N.Y., 1969), pp. 26–38; John Griscom, *A Year in Europe*, 2 vols. (New York, 1823); Knapp, *Thomas Eddy*, pp. 276–277.

people.[35] The members present that evening contributed $900 to the cause; within a few months they had increased the sum to $17,000 and secured a site on the Old Post Road where abandoned barracks were remodeled and equipped with rows of inside rooms on each of the two upper floors. Stephen Allen, formerly an orphaned sailor boy and now mayor of New York and a new member of the Society, assured it some city support and helped Colden, now a state senator, secure a promise of $2,000 annually from the legislature for maintenance. Two years later the state assumed full responsibility.[36]

The links between the movements for reform schools and for penitentiaries were numerous. Not only were men such as Thomas Eddy, Cadwallader Colden, and Stephen Allen active in both fields, but Louis Dwight took an immediate interest in the promotion of reform schools and endeavored to persuade each institution to adopt at least a modified form of the Auburn separate-cell system. When Joseph Curtis, the first superintendent of the House of Refuge in New York, abandoned the silent system in an effort to develop a dynamic family relationship among his boys he was forced to resort to a frequent use of the lash to restore order. Louis Dwight not only criticized the lax discipline maintained by Curtis but deplored his poor work record and endeavored to commit the new houses of refuge opening at Boston and Philadelphia to the Auburn system. Both did construct or remodel buildings to provide separate cells or small rooms, and both developed active work programs, as did the New York House of Refuge under Nathaniel C. Hart, its second superintendent in 1826.[37]

But the reform school, even in America, was not exclusively of penal origin. John Griscom, Nathaniel C. Hart, and the Reverend E. M. P. Wells, in charge at Boston, were not only professional

[35] Pickett, *House of Refuge*, pp. 39–49; Joseph M. Hawes, *Children in Urban Society: Juvenile Delinquency in Nineteenth-Century America* (New York, 1971), pp. 27–51.

[36] O. F. Lewis, *Development*, pp. 294–299; Pickett, *House of Refuge*, pp. 50–66; Rothman, *Discovery*, pp. 57–78. Rothman relates the development of new penal institutions to the wider "discovery of the asylum." This he describes as a societal shift from local community and family care to a reliance on institutional treatment under state direction. He also sees it as a shift from a religious to a civic function. I regard the latter shift as the more soundly based.

[37] O. F. Lewis, *Development*, pp. 300–322; Pickett, *House of Refuge*, pp. 86–90; Rothman, *Discovery*, pp. 208, 214–216, 225–227.

educators but alert students of European educational reforms. The discipline which these men evolved contrasted sharply with prevailing penal customs. In New York the children were graded according to their conduct, and Wells in Boston added a marking system to encourage the children to strive for advancement to a higher grade. School studies for four hours a day alternated with industrial work in programs designed to keep body and mind busy. Merit badges and other rewards helped to eliminate corporal punishments. Unfortunately these inspired beginnings were discarded after a few years, thus failing to supply a model for prison reform.[38]

The local house of correction, the fourth distinct penal institution to be developed during the era, had long roots in the past. But most of the earlier attempts to maintain such institutions had failed after brief periods, and, although the use of the term "jail and house of correction" had kept the principle alive, no genuine house of correction existed in America at the opening of the century. New York City was gathering hordes of petty offenders into its jails, together with the hardened criminals awaiting trial, when in 1803 Mayor Edward Livingston proposed the construction of a city workhouse for the proper segregation of offenders. Several years passed before the city opened a bridewell, or workhouse, at Bellevue near the city hall. Its large congregate rooms, which soon became overcrowded, proved an abomination and prompted the city, at the behest of the Boston Prison Discipline Society, to seek a more suitable and adequate site. A workhouse on Blackwell's Island provided shelter for some debtors after 1826, and three years later the city purchased this 100-acre island in the East River and commenced the construction there of a city penitentiary or house of correction. Dwight's influence was strong enough to secure the adoption of individual cells, 250 of which were constructed in each of two wings. Auburn likewise supplied the model for its discipline and work program in the early years.[39]

Other cities faced similar problems as their jails and bridewells became seriously overcrowded. When Philadelphia opened a new jail on Arch Street in 1816, its security provisions proved so faulty

[38] Pickett, *House of Refuge*, pp. 67–85, 90–102; Hawes, *Children*, pp. 51–60.
[39] O. F. Lewis, *Development*, pp. 273–275, 287–288.

that the authorities restricted its use to debtors, witnesses, and petty offenders, but the congregate rooms defeated all efforts at correctional discipline. To assure a more adequate replacement for the old Walnut Street Jail, Philadelphia erected a new county prison at Moyamensing in the early 1830s, equipping it with 300 outside cells of large size for the solitary confinement of all sentenced to less than one year as well as of those held for trial and sentencing. The short terms hampered the development of a work program in the cells and forced an early abandonment of that effort. That failure also inhibited experiments with a correctional program.[40]

It remained for Boston to develop a model institution for misdemeanants. In 1822 Josiah Quincy as judge of Essex County recommended the establishment of a house of correction for the reform of petty offenders. Becoming mayor of Boston the next year, he designated one wing of the local jail for this purpose and introduced handicraft industries for its inmates. Increased commitments soon overcrowded these facilities, and the Prison Discipline Society described the Leverett Street Jail as "a scandal that cried to heaven." In 1831 the city council appropriated $20,000 to provide for the reconstruction of one of the buildings in an institutional cluster in South Boston as a house of correction. Supplied with a cellblock on the Auburn pattern and equipped with congregate workrooms, it soon became Louis Dwight's favorite model for city and county penitentiaries.[41]

The State of Prisons in 1835

After a number of bad starts the American states had finally enjoyed a decade of active prison development. Most of the states had revised their criminal codes, substituting imprisonment for the traditional corporal punishments. Groups of public-spirited citizens had banded together into societies that endeavored to secure satisfactory penal institutions. A score of prisons and a half dozen special institutions had appeared, and the time was ripe for the appraisement of these developments. Unhappily, local rivalries had grown to such a point that in the absence of standard measures of achievement the authorities were stooping to fruitless squabbles.

Fortunately by this time the theories of Beccaria had gained an ear

[40] Ibid., pp. 286–287.
[41] Ibid., pp. 281–283.

at European courts. Comprehensive plans were being made for European prisons, and responsible commissions were sent to study in the democratic laboratory across the sea. France sent Gustave Auguste de Beaumont and Alexis de Tocqueville in 1831; five years later Frederic Auguste Demetz and two companions came to check the earlier report. England sent William Crawford in 1832; and Dr. Nicholas Heinrich Julius came in behalf of Prussia two years later. Other official and unofficial visitors arrived, and, after making more or less careful investigations, returned with lengthy reports, most of them loud in their praise of the seemingly idyllic Pennsylvania system just then appearing for the first time in its pure form at Cherry Hill. This unanimity of judgment was partially responsible for turning England in 1835, Belgium in 1838, Sweden in 1840, and Norway and Holland in 1851 toward at least a partial adoption of the separate or solitary system for their new penitentiaries.[42]

But this very unanimity of judgment, running so directly counter to the general trend in America, deprived the European critics of the full measure of influence their surveys might have been expected to bear on American developments. Louis Dwight, whose reports circulated throughout the nation, was antagonized by the preference for Cherry Hill. However, Francis Lieber, a liberal German refugee serving on the faculty of the University of South Carolina, partially frustrated Dwight's conspiracy to silence the critics when he translated the report of Beaumont and Tocqueville for a Philadelphia publisher. The sober judgment of these brilliant Frenchmen informed Americans that their prisons had certain advantages over those of Europe: the American institutions checked the mutual corruption of the prisoners; they encouraged habits of obedience and industry; and they provided an opportunity for the reformation of the criminal. These critics considered the rival prisons in America as variants of the same system—confinement in solitude—some using walls, others depending on rigorous discipline; they concluded that "the Philadelphia system produces a deeper effect on the soul of the convict . . . while Auburn . . . is more conformable to the habits of men in society."[43] The pious Bostonians

[42] Grunhut, *Penal Reform*, pp. 40, 46–49, 52–53.

[43] Gustave de Beaumont and Alexis de Tocqueville, *On the Penitentiary System in the United States and Its Application in France*, translated, with an introduction, notes, and additions, by Francis Lieber (1833; reprinted Montclair, N.J., 1976), p. 59.

found little consolation in this contrast.

There were, of course, conditioning circumstances that helped to determine foreign opinion. Sing Sing, the most frequently visited institution of the Auburn class, was under the shadow of the harshest disciplinarian of its history, Warden Lynds. Moreover both Auburn and Sing Sing with their combined equipment of 1,770 cells seemed greatly overexpanded in contrast with Cherry Hill and the standards of the day. Wethersfield was a happier example of the Auburn system, and William Crawford, the English commissioner who in 1833 visited all but two of the prisons of America, generously recognized its merits but warned his countrymen against being "too sanguine as to its results," which he attributed largely to the genius of the two Pilsburys who had managed it from the start. The best he could say for the others was to commend their good intentions.[44]

But the Europeans were concerned with more serious matters than the dispute between the two rival penal systems. They lauded the states for their success in abolishing corporal punishments and limiting capital offenses[45] as well as for their general provision of institutions for the attempted correction of malefactors. They were, on the other hand, nearly unanimous in condemning the neglect of local jails, whose counterparts in England in particular were already receiving careful attention from reformers.[46] Crawford had some pertinent remarks to make concerning wholesale pardoning, but it must be noted that the flagrancy of the practice at the time—one-fourth of those discharged in New York were pardoned—actually represented a fair improvement over the enormity of the abuse as it had existed a short decade earlier when in many prisons half of the inmates were discharged through pardons. The sum of the foreign comments was that America had undertaken a large task with energy and had set a fine example to Europe, but that the time had not yet arrived for the states to rest content with their accomplishments.

[44] William Crawford, *Report on the Penitentiaries of the United States* (1835; reprinted Montclair, N.J., 1969), pp. 22, 32.

[45] Ibid. Crawford, abstracting nineteen state codes, finds only one capital offense in Pennsylvania, Ohio, and Tennessee; two in New Hampshire and Kentucky; three in New York, New Jersey, Maine, and Indiana; four in Illinois and Missouri; five in Vermont; six in Massachusetts and Connecticut; and seven or eight in five other states.

[46] Ibid. "There is far more injury resulting from confinement in the county gaols of any one of the States than benefit arising from its penitentiary." p. 23n; Playfair, *Punitive Obsession*, pp. 71–77.

*   *   *

Indeed many of the states were entitled to a little boasting over their penal developments during one short decade. Louis Dwight could now list ten prisons operating on the Auburn plan.[47] Each of these was adequately equipped with individual night cells, usually 7 by 3½ and 7 feet high. Two additional prisons already under construction would soon add one thousand to the existing total of over thirty-three hundred individual night cells.[48] Practically all these prisons were operating industrial departments, mostly under the direction of contractors or lessees, and several of them were regularly defraying their expenses. Fairly satisfactory women's quarters were being maintained at Auburn, Baltimore, Washington, and Wethersfield; and these four, plus Charlestown and Sing Sing, employed chaplains and conducted Sunday classes for the instruction of their illiterates. The rules of silence, downcast eyes, and the like were rigidly enforced in most of these prisons, but half of the states had abolished the use of the lash for prison discipline, and Richmond was at this early date experimenting with a system of honor badges and other rewards as incentives to good behavior. Unfortunately, the large numbers confined at Auburn and Sing Sing seemed to have made it necessary for the officers there to use brutal physical punishments, the iniquitous "cat" among them, in their efforts to maintain silence. As yet only Auburn, Baltimore, and Frankfort, Kentucky, had provided dining-room accommodations to ease the monotony of cell life. Such was the Auburn system at the end of the first decade of Dwight's ministry.[49]

The solitary system had been successfully instituted at Cherry Hill, Pittsburgh, and Trenton, but only the Pennsylvania penitentiaries were supplying sufficient handicraft industries to employ all their inmates. Each of the cells of these prisons was provided with a

[47] Auburn had 770 inside cells; Sing Sing, 1,000; Wethersfield, 232; Charlestown, 304; Windsor, 136; Concord, 120; and Washington, D.C., 214—all on the Auburn cell-block pattern; but Baltimore with 320 small outside cells, Richmond with 168, and Frankfort with 100 were following the Auburn system in all other respects.

[48] The first 200 cells at Columbus, Ohio, each 7 by 3½ by 7 ft., were opened in 1834, and the remainder of the 700-cell structure was already in process of construction; at the same time the 200-cell prison at Nashville, Tennessee, was well under way, following closely the Wethersfield model.

[49] P.D.S., *Reports 1–10* (1826–1835).

primitive sort of privy and a faucet that delivered a limited quantity of water every day—unique features in prison architecture for several decades. Chaplains made periodic rounds, encouraging each prisoner to read his Bible and to cleanse his soul through prayerful repentance, and the officers found themselves only rarely confronted with disciplinary problems. After a careful study of the records, Professor Teeters has concluded that Louis Dwight failed to substantiate his indictment of these prisons as insanity breeders, and indeed his attack seemed to have enhanced their deterrent value.[50] At all events, Pennsylvania was generally credited with two of the best prisons in the world in 1835. Yet an investigation only the year before of a scandal at Cherry Hill had disclosed a shocking amount of communication among the inmates and of fraternization between some prisoners and staff members. Evidence of the application of cruel punishments to suppress these disorders was also uncovered. Apparently even the best of prisons was far from perfect, but only the chairman of the investigating committee would admit it, while the rest took comfort in the knowledge that more damaging charges had frequently been substantiated against many of the Auburn-type prisons.[51]

Five other states had prisons that were anything but a boon to their self-esteem. Maine and Rhode Island were experimenting with their own adaptation of the solitary system. But the seventy-six underground pits at Thomaston, each 9½ by 4½ and 9¾ feet deep, were insufficient for the solitary confinement of Maine's ninety-one convicts in 1832, and fortunate it was, for the wretched fellows would have frozen to death without the warmth of a companion or two during the long winter months. Meanwhile the tiny inside cells that were being constructed in one wing of the Providence jail, with the object of housing the state's convicts in complete solitude, certainly belied the fair name of that city. Indiana and Illinois were still maintaining wretched structures after the style of the worst makeshift jails, and Georgia was vacillating between the trials of operating its equally unsatisfactory prison and the alternative of turning the prisoners over to the counties. The remaining states and the territories left the administration of justice entirely in the hands

[50] Teeters and Shearer, *Cherry Hill*, pp. 209–212.
[51] Ibid., pp. 95–107; Rothman, *Discovery*, pp. 101–108.

of local authorities—an arrangement which was proving, especially in the South, most unsatisfactory.[52]

The jails of the entire country were little better than those of the South. The criticisms of the Europeans prompted Dwight to seek for a model jail, but his search was without success until in 1836 Hartford erected one on the approved Auburn pattern. Philadelphia at the same time started the construction of its new city jail with large outside cells,[53] but these disparate patterns failed to arouse the rivalry among local authorities that was providing so much incentive to state prison officials. Instead, the wretched congregate jails remained to deteriorate with age and to contribute more to the making of criminals than toward their correction. Meanwhile the plan to create houses of correction, where misdemeanants could be confined and employed free from contact with the more serious detention cases, made little headway. Only Boston had succeeded in establishing a worthy institution of this type. New York's major contribution to jail reform resulted in 1831 from its abolition of imprisonment for debt, a measure adopted in Kentucky a decade earlier. Other states continued to crowd their jails with impecunious debtors. A move initiated in New York in 1830 to require sheriffs to perform hangings within the jail yards limited the size of the crowds that viewed these spectacles but added a new strain to the discipline of the many jails that acquired this function.[54]

Likewise, the movement for juvenile houses of reform had come to a stand with the creation of the institutions in New York, Philadelphia, and Boston. It was just at this time that several interesting developments in the treatment of juveniles were going forward in Europe, but another decade was to pass before these examples were to stir Americans to new efforts. Indeed, the New

---

[52] Crawford, *Report.* "In the Slave States, particularly, the county gaols are truly deplorable. It is the practice to commit a slave to the common gaol whenever it suits the convenience of the owner. . . . From the number and various descriptions of the prisoners, and the extremely limited space allowed them, these places of confinement exhibit scenes of great wretchedness and oppression." pp. 23–24n.

[53] Ibid., p. 17; American Prison Association, *Proceedings* (1928), pp. 217–219. No contemporary evidence has been found to support this print and description of the Burlington County jail and workhouse, allegedly built in 1808 on the plan later followed by John Haviland at Cherry Hill.

[54] Hugo A. Bedau, ed., *The Death Penalty in America*, 2d ed. (Chicago, 1968), pp. 9,

World, with its many opportunities for the young people who in Europe comprised the major portion of the delinquent classes, did not face very critical problems in this field until the development of industries and urban communities transformed the social landscape.

Thus the newly independent states were tackling their criminal problems with the energy of a young people, unhampered by rigid traditions. Old theories and methods of punishment had been swept aside. The penitentiary and its associated institutions were as legitimate offsprings of the age as the young democracies themselves. These developments were alike manifestations of the current belief in the free will of the rational man, they shared the same optimism for the future of the race, and they were animated by similar romantic ideals. Europe justly paid honor to the Americans for having established the first genuine penal system in the modern world—an achievement which was in large part due to the zeal of Louis Dwight and to his practical skill in fusing righteous impulses, a program of industry, and a rigid discipline into a cheap but secure structural pattern.[55]

BIBLIOGRAPHIC NOTE

Cesare Beccaria, *An Essay on Crimes and Punishment,* with a commentary attributed to Voltaire, may be consulted in the original or in numerous editions of several translations; John Howard, *The State of the Prisons in England and Wales,* 4th ed. (1792; reprinted Montclair, N.J., 1973) and *An Account of the Principal Lazarettos in Europe,* 2d ed. (1791; reprinted Montclair, N.J., 1973) are comprehensive firsthand surveys of European prisons. Jeremy Bentham, *An Introduction to the Principles of the Alteration and Present State of Penal Laws of Pennsylvania* (Boston, 1799). John Griscom, *A Year in Europe,* 2 vols. (New York, 1823). Gershom Powers, *A Brief Account of the Construction, Management, & Discipline . . . of the New-York State Prison at Auburn* (Auburn, 1826). Valuable reports of the prison officers are printed in the early legislative documents of most of these states, but full detail on all the prisons is available in *Reports of the Prison*

[55] Rothman, *Discovery,* pp. 294–295. Looking back 140 years later on these and related institutional developments in the Jacksonian period, Rothman was less certain of the achievements of these institutional founders. He suggests that "by incarcerating the deviant and dependent, and defending the step with hyperbolic rhetoric, they [the founders] discouraged—really eliminated—the search for other solutions." Rothman does not, however, question their good intentions.

Discipline Society of Boston, 1826–1854 (1855; reprinted Montclair, N.J., 1972), an invaluable source.

The best descriptive studies by foreign visitors are Gustave de Beaumont and Alexis de Tocqueville, *On the Penitentiary System in the United States and Its Application in France,* translated, with an introduction, notes, and additions by Francis Lieber (1833; reprinted Montclair, N.J., 1976); and William Crawford, *Report on the Penitentiaries of the United States* (1835; reprinted Montclair, N.J., 1969). The views of a dozen other visitors are canvassed in *Report of a Minority of the Special Committee of the Boston Prison Discipline Society* (Boston, 1846), and in P.D.S., *Eighteenth Report* (1843), pp. 40–103.

Harry Elmer Barnes, *The Evolution of Penology in Pennsylvania: A Study in American Social History* (1927; reprinted Montclair, N.J., 1969), is a scholarly treatment of the history of this important state and includes many rare documents. Orlando F. Lewis, *The Development of American Prisons and Prison Customs, 1776–1845: With Special Reference to Early Institutions in the State of New York* (1922; reprinted Montclair, N.J., 1967) is an exhaustive treatment of the institutional side of the developments down to 1845.

Other volumes of special value are: Harry Barnard, ed., *Reformatory Education* (Hartford, 1857); Harry Elmer Barnes and Negley K. Teeters, *New Horizons in Criminology,* an excellent text, of which the 1st ed. (New York, 1943) provides the student with the fullest treatment of the history of the subject; Hugo A. Bedau, ed., *The Death Penalty in America* 2d ed. (Chicago, 1968); Carl Bridenbaugh, *Cities in the Wilderness: The First Century of Urban Life in America, 1625–1742* (New York, 1938); Raymond T. Bye, *Capital Punishment in the United States* (Philadelphia, 1919); Alice M. Earle, *Curious Punishments of Bygone Days* (1896; reprinted Montclair, N.J., 1969); Thomas Eddy, *An Account of the State Prison or Penitentiary House in the City of New-York* (New York, 1801); Kai T. Erikson, *Wayward Puritans: A Study in the Sociology of Deviance* (New York, 1957); Herbert A. Falk, *Corporal Punishment: A Social Interpretation of Its Theory and Practice in the Schools of the United States* (New York, 1941); Katherine Fry and Rachel E. Cresswell, *Memoir of the Life of Elizabeth Fry: With Extracts from Her Journal and Letters,* 2d ed. (1848; reprinted Montclair, N.J., 1974); Lawrence H. Gipson, "Crime and Punishment in Provincial Pennsylvania," *Pennsylvania History* 2 (January 1935); Francis C. Gray, *Prison Discipline in America* (1847; reprinted Montclair, N.J., 1973); Max Grunhut, *Penal Reform: A Comparative Study* (1948; reprinted Montclair, N.J., 1972), a comprehensive work; Joseph M. Hawes, *Children in Urban Society: Juvenile Delinquency in Nineteenth-Century America* (New York, 1971); James Heath, *Eighteenth Century Penal Theory* (New York, 1963); F.

W. Hoffer, D. M. Mann, and F. N. House, *The Jails of Virginia: A Study of the Local Penal System* (New York, 1933); Marcus W. Jernegan, *Laboring and Dependent Classes in Colonial America, 1607–1783* (Chicago, 1931); D. L. Howard, *The English Prisons: Their Past and Their Future* (London, 1960); Norman Johnston, *The Human Cage: A Brief History of Prison Architecture* (New York, 1973); Cyrus K. Karraker, *The Seventeenth-Century Sheriff: A Comparative Study of the Sheriff in England and the Chesapeake Colonies, 1607–1689* (Chapel Hill, 1930); Samuel L. Knapp, *The Life of Thomas Eddy* (New York, 1834); W. David Lewis, *From Newgate to Dannemora: The Rise of the Penitentiary in New York, 1796–1848* (Ithaca, N.Y., 1965); Marcello Maestro, *Cesare Beccaria and the Origins of Penal Reform* (Philadelphia, 1973); William G. Nagel, *The New Red Barn: A Critical Look at the Modern American Prison* (New York, 1973); Bradford K. Peirce, *A Half Century with Juvenile Delinquents: The New York House of Refuge and Its Times* (1869; reprinted Montclair, N.J., 1969); Robert S. Pickett, *House of Refuge: Origins of Juvenile Reform in New York State, 1815–1857* (Syracuse, N.Y., 1969); Giles Playfair, *The Punitive Obsession: An Unvarnished History of the English Prison System* (London, 1971); Edwin Powers, *Crime and Punishment in Early Massachusetts, 1620–1692* (Boston, 1966); David J. Rothman, *The Discovery of the Asylum: Social Order and Disorder in the New Republic* (Boston, 1971); Thorsten Sellin, *Pioneering in Penology: The Amsterdam House of Correction in the Sixteenth and Seventeenth Centuries* (Philadelphia, 1944); also three excellent articles by Sellin in the *Journal of Criminal Law and Criminology:* "Filippo Franci: A Precursor of Modern Penology," 17 (1927): 104–112; "Dom Jean Mabillon: A Prison Reformer of the Seventeenth Century," 17 (1927): 581–602; "The House of Correction for Boys in the Hospice of Saint Michael in Rome," 20 (1930): 533–553; A. E. Smith, "The Transportation of Convicts to the American Colonies in the Seventeenth Century," *American Historical Review* 39 (1934): 232–250; Negley K. Teeters, *The Cradle of the Penitentiary: The Walnut Street Jail at Philadelphia, 1773–1835* (Philadelphia, 1955); Negley K. Teeters and John D. Shearer, *The Prison at Philadelphia, Cherry Hill: The Separate System of Penal Discipline, 1829–1913* (New York, 1957); U. S. Bureau of Prisons, *Handbook of Correctional Institution Design and Construction* (Washington, D.C., 1949); Sidney and Beatrice Webb, *English Prisons under Local Government* (London, 1922).

2.

FRESH THEORIES AND
FAILURES: 1835–1860

America had succeeded in establishing a penal system by 1835 but could boast of no great mitigation of crime. In the seventy years that had passed since Beccaria first formulated the rationalistic theories of punishment the New World had become the major arena for penitentiary developments. That original inspiration had, however, given place to religious and romantic sentiments before stable prisons had been secured. In the practical struggles of the succeeding years the zeal of the leaders had been absorbed in large part by the material and technical problems of establishing institutions. More than a score of prisons already stood as tangible accomplishments, but society's interest in the convict had simmered down to the bloodless passion for his salvation that still animated a few reformers.

Fortunately in the late 1830s the Western world was enlivened by a fresh current of humanitarianism. The interests of the common man were creating a host of generous reform movements that found expression in temperance campaigns, peace congresses, crusades against both wage and chattel slavery, and demands for education and equal opportunity for all men and women. In the midst of this ferment a more rounded program for the reformation of criminals was conceived. Like most of the idealistic programs of the day, the reformation of convicts was to enjoy a preliminary hearing, but its formal trial was deferred for several decades. Nevertheless, this era did witness the theoretical formulation of most of the principles that were to guide prison developments during the rest of the century.

The international exchange of inspiration and ideas played a large part in the new trends, but these revealed at the same time strong American contributions. Although the dominance of Louis Dwight continued in all practical matters, he had identified himself so closely with the propagation of the Auburn system that he began to appear as an obstacle to progress. The leaders who best represented the inspiration of the new generation were the erudite Francis Lieber, the engergetic Dorothea Lynde Dix, and the compassionate Samuel Gridley Howe. Theirs was, however, primarily a contribution of generous theories and programs, and even the auspicious outset of the New York Prison Association in 1844 failed to accomplish any considerable amelioration of the convicts. These intellectual stirrings awaited the development of a situation that would call their programs into being, and that occasion was not to arrive until after the close of the Civil War.

New Currents of Thought

American reformers have not always been as erudite as they were resourceful, and they have seldom buttressed their programs with the available European citations, but the leaders of this period, Lieber, Dix, and Howe, were frankly proud of the international horizons of their humanitarianism. On the other hand, it had not been homage for the young republic but determined agitation at home that had prompted Europe to send commissions to study prisons in America. The chief portion of the European agitation and of the programs advocated there differed little in spirit and character from those of the Pennsylvanians or of Louis Dwight and his school. A charitable concern for the oppressed and a religious interest in their salvation through penitence, prayer, and Sabbath instruction animated both movements.

There was, however, a new inspiration in England that envisaged a more agressive attack on the problem, one that was closely allied with the newer trends in education and social ethics. Scholars have traced back as far as William Paley's lectures in the late eighteenth century on moral and political philosophy to find the origin of the theory that a labor rather than a time sentence is the correct way of stimulating criminals to reform.[1] Archbishop Richard Whately reasserted the idea a half century later in his oft-quoted letter to Lord Grey, and direct lines can be traced from here through the ticket-of-leave to parole, the indeterminate sentence, and the whole reformatory system.

Two able administrators, acting independently and probably without knowledge of the earlier theorists, put these principles into practice with creditable results. First, Colonel Manuel Montesinos, who took charge of the old Spanish prison at Valencia in 1835, initiated a reformatory discipline coupled with a policy of releasing the men as soon as he became convinced of their reform. Unfortunately, after a few years of remarkable success, political interference took away his power to grant releases, and Montesinos resigned. A more influential experiment was that of Captain Alexander Maconochie at Norfolk Island, Australia. On accepting his appointment as commander of the penal colony, one of the last outposts of the English transportation system, Maconochie declared that a labor sentence was the only enlightened basis for the correction of offenders, and that it must be combined with a system that provides first "specific punishment for the past" and, in a second stage, "specific training for the future."[2] Although denied the authority to put the theory of labor sentences fully into operation, Maconochie's administration, by "providing a field for the cultivation of active social virtues" and thus "preparing for society in society," transformed some fruitful ideas into practical penological experience.[3]

England in the thirties, as in Howard's day, had been saved from commitment to a rigid penal system by the economy of transportation. The national penitentiaries finally erected in England on the

[1] Thorsten Sellin, "Paley on the Time Sentence," *Journal of Criminal Law and Criminology* 22 (1931): 264–266. Dr. Sellin quotes from William Paley's *Principles of Moral and Political Philosophy:* "I would measure the confinement not by the duration of time, but by quantity of work, in order both to excite industry and to render it more voluntary." It is interesting to note that several editions of Paley were printed in America before 1830. See also Max Grunhut, *Penal Reform: A Comparative Study* (1948; reprinted Montclair, N.J., 1972), pp. 85–88.

[2] Mary Carpenter, *Our Convicts,* 2 vols. (1864; reprinted Montclair, N.J., 1969), p. 96. Miss Carpenter is quoting from Alexander Maconochie, *Australiana: Thoughts on Convict Management* (Hobart Town, 1839).

[3] Alexander Maconochie, *Norfolk Island* (London, 1847); Grunhut, *Penal Reform,* pp. 78–80.

solitary pattern (Millbank in part but especially Pentonville) had become probationary prisons where convicts were confined for a year or two in solitude before transportation. But this simple method of distinguishing the punishment and correctional stages broke down when the indignant opposition of the colonies put an end to the transportation system, forcing England to solve its penal problems at home.[4] Maconochie received a hearty welcome when he returned to England in 1845, and his advocacy of progressive-grade treatment was endorsed by a large group of reformers, among them Frederick and Matthew Davenport Hill and Mary Carpenter. These leaders had gained faith in more aggressive reformatory methods from their experiences with juvenile offenders. The end of transportation brought them the opportunity to lead England, and especially Ireland, toward the development of a system of graded prisons, and their program was most successfully embodied a decade later in Sir Walter Crofton's famous Irish system. The new program called for four distinct stages of treatment—punishment in solitude for two years, followed by congregate labor under a marking system that regulated privileges and determined the date of discharge, then by an intermediate stage during which inmates were permitted to work on outside jobs, and finally conditional release under a ticket-of-leave. Unfortunately for England this promising experiment was emasculated after a few years by political interference, but not until after it had fructified developments in America.[5]

Several aspects of an educational penology were already developing in the New World. The Sabbath schools advocated by Louis Dwight had in many cases undertaken to educate the illiterates, and more elaborate programs of instruction were already in operation in the reform schools. Richmond penitentiary had experimented for a time with a grading system; Charlestown and a few other prisons were occasionally celebrating a holiday with entertainments. Scattered contractors were giving the convicts small bonuses for good work. Indeed, an increasing emphasis was being placed all down the line on positive aids to reform.

The most forward-looking programs of the era came from the theoretical reformers. Edward Livingston, dean of the group, had

[4] Giles Playfair, *The Punitive Obsession: An Unvarnished History of the English Prison System* (London, 1971), pp. 30–42, 59–64.

[5] Grunhut, *Penal Reform*, pp. 83–90.

outlined, in his model criminal code for Louisiana, a diversified system including reform schools for juveniles, houses of correction for minor offenders, and two grades of prisons. The proposed penitentiary system, which incidentally antedated the experiments of both Montesinos and Maconochie, envisaged a prison for punishment and labor in solitude, from which a convict by accumulating certificates of good conduct would earn his promotion to better quarters where he would enjoy the privilege of association in classes and at congregate labor. Although rejected by Louisiana, the code gained a deserved repute in the Northeast and in Europe.[6]

Livingston had likewise advanced, at least tentatively, another theory which, if seriously considered, might have significantly altered the course of American prison development. This theory followed as a corollary of the then popular "science" of phrenology and maintained that certain criminals could be detected by an examination of the lobes of their skulls. George Combe, an English visitor in the late thirties, was more actively committed to the theory, and if his lectures had stimulated scientific research rather than righteous indignation, he might have antedated the Italian Lombroso as the founder of modern criminology. Charles Caldwell of Kentucky, an early convert to phrenology, advocated its use in classifying criminals into correctional and custodial groups. But the scientific method, even in the natural fields, was gaining hesitant recognition only in a few universities, and the democratic belief in the equality of men together with the religious faith in salvation for all, was sufficient to reject the suggestion that most criminals were suffering from deformities and therefore were not responsible for their acts. Punishment, as a result, would have been inappropriate and futile, but not rehabilitation, apparently, for some phrenologists optimistically held out the possibility that educational and other correctional aids might stimulate the stunted brain to wholesome development.[7]

---

[6] Edward Livingston, *The Complete Works of Edward Livingston on Criminal Jurisprudence: Consisting of Systems of Penal Law for the State of Louisiana and for the United States of America,* 2 vols. (1873; reprinted Montclair, N.J., 1968).

[7] Charles Caldwell, *New Views of Penitentiary Discipline and Moral Education and Reform* (Philadelphia, 1829); Robert S. Pickett, *House of Refuge: Origins of Juvenile Reform in New York State, 1815–1857* (Syracuse, N.Y., 1969), pp. 107–108; Arthur E. Fink, *Causes of Crime: Biological Theories in the United States, 1800–1915* (Philadelphia, 1938), pp. 4–14.

* * *

The most dramatic attempt to apply these new theories occurred, strangely enough, in America's toughest prison, Sing Sing. An increasing number of female commitments in the early 1830s had overcrowded the limited facilities available to them at Auburn and prompted the state to build a separate cellblock for women in a partially isolated corner of the Sing Sing yard. The first matron who took charge with a staff of two female assistants in 1837 proved incapable of maintaining order, and her successor, aided by the harsh disciplinary support of Elam Lynds, back in charge of Sing Sing in 1843, proved no more successful. When reports of some excessive punishments inflicted by Warden Lynds reached John W. Edmonds, chairman of the board of control, the warden's resignation was requested as well as that of the matron. To replace the matron, Edmonds named Mrs. Eliza Farnham, a staunch admirer of Elizabeth Fry, the English penal reformer, and an accomplished school mistress who had also acquired an interest in phrenology. An independent spirit, Mrs. Farnham boldly dispensed with rules of silence and organized her charges into classes and choirs and congenial work teams in an endeavor to promote their rehabilitation. Unfortunately, by adding some phrenological and fictional volumes to the library, technically under the charge of the Reverend John Luckey, she aroused the hostility of the chaplain whose opposition, coupled with a change in politics, produced another reorganization that forced the resignation of Mrs. Farnham and reinstated a modified version of the Auburn discipline in the women's prison.[8]

Similar stirrings in Boston, had prompted a minority faction within its Prison Discipline Society to attempt to secure a hearing for foreign critics of the Auburn system. Samuel Gridley Howe and Horace Mann, the minority leaders, protested Dwight's policy of suppressing any mention of the several European studies that had praised the Pennsylvania prisons at the expense of the Auburn

---

[8] W. David Lewis, *From Newgate to Dannemora: The Rise of the Penitentiary in New York, 1796–1848* (Ithaca, N.Y., 1965), pp. 230–252. Marmaduke B. Sampson, *Rationale of Crime, and Its Appropriate Treatment: Being a Treatise on Jurisprudence Considered in Relation to Cerebral Organization . . . with Notes and Illustrations by Eliza W. Farnham* (1846; reprinted Montclair, N.J., 1973); Fink, *Causes of Crime,* p. 15.

system. When their protest was voted down by a committee whose report was widely publicized by Dwight, Mann wrote to Maconochie in England to secure his endorsement, and the minority published and distributed its own report. But Dwight's entrenched position enabled him to retain control over the Boston Society until his death in 1854.[9]

The revolt against the sterile argument over the respective merits of the separate (Pennsylvania) and silent (Auburn) systems produced a more immediate response in New York. A major result was the formation in 1844 of the New York Prison Association, but that accomplishment had other antecedents as well. Indeed a reaction against the severity of the Auburn discipline had commenced at an early date in that penitentiary itself when Elam Lynds was first pushed out as warden in 1824. He had moved on to establish his harsh discipline in Sing Sing but returned to reestablish it at Auburn in 1838. Lynds had been succeeded at Sing Sing by Robert Wiltse whose discipline if somewhat less brutal was equally vigorous and made Sing Sing in the opinion of some visitors into a virtual slave camp. A reaction to these harsh regimes occured in 1840 and brought the appointment of Henry Polhemus as warden at Auburn and of David Seymour at Sing Sing. Both were industrialists and endeavored to maintain productive industries but with less reliance on the lash. Seymour in particular ventured to trust some convicts for work in unguarded groups on the farm and developed educational and religious activities on Sundays that relaxed some old restraints. His chief aid in these endeavors was the Reverend John Luckey who as chaplain had won the confidence of many prisoners. Unfortunately their liberal regime encouraged some prisoners to press for more privileges and the resulting disorders shocked John W. Edmonds a newly appointed inspector late in 1843. As a former legislator he had voted to sustain the Auburn system, and he expected to find the discipline of strict silence in force. An appointee himself of the newly victorious Democrats, he

---

[9]*Report of a Minority of the Special Committee of the Boston Prison Discipline Society* (Boston, 1846). The minority consisted of Samuel Gridley Howe, Horace Mann and Charles Sumner. The work was also published the same year by Howe as *An Essay on Separate and Congregate Systems of Prison Discipline: Being a Report Made to the Boston Prison Discipline Society*. American Social Science Association, *Proceedings* (1874), pp. 12–16.

could not resist their pressure for reorganization and replaced Seymour with Lynds early in 1844.[10]

Warden Lynds promptly reestablished the regimen of silence with the aid of a renewed use of the lash. His regulations not only curtailed the activities of many inmates, but those of the chaplain as well, and Luckey was ready not only to reveal some of the details to Inspector Edmonds on his next visit, but also to fan his indignation at the excessive brutalities encountered. Surprised at the complexity of the responsibilities he had assumed as Chairman of the Board of Inspectors, Edmonds decided to secure wider counsel and issued a call for a convention in New York of citizens interested in planning a concerted program of penal reform. A variety of humanitarians and intellectuals responded, including Professor Johann L. Tellkampf, a visiting lecturer at Columbia College, and Isaac T. Hopper, a Hicksite Quaker who had been making regular visits to jails in the city and its environs for over a decade. A resolution calling for the organization of the New York Prison Association received hearty approval.[11]

Professor Tellkampf helped to lift the meeting above the old debate between solitary and silent regimes. He struck the keynote for many of those present when he declared that reformation, "the avowed object of penitentiaries," could not be realized by a complacent reliance on either silence or separation.[12] He proceeded to outline the system he and Dr. Julius had proposed to the king of Prussia the year before—a house of detention with strictly separate cells, a lunatic asylum for insane criminals, and three grades of penitentiaries through which the convict would advance from complete separation, after the Cherry Hill pattern, to strict silence but congregate labor on the plan of Auburn, and, finally, into a responsible association with a select group of reformed convicts where he would serve the remainder of his term under liberal regulations. With such a comprehensive formulation of many of the best theories of the day teasing the imaginations of the reformers at

[10] W. D. Lewis, *Newgate*, pp. 207–215; John Luckey, *Life in Sing Sing State Prison* (New York, 1860), pp. 25–30.

[11] New York Prison Association, *Report* (1844), pp. 11–20; ibid., (1849); W. D. Lewis, *Newgate*, pp. 220–223.

[12] N.Y.P.A., *Report* (1844), p. 45.

the convention it is no wonder that William H. Channing, the impulsive young Unitarian minister who became the first secretary of the Association, could assert with conviction that "the passion of overcoming evil with good is becoming everywhere superior to the vindictive spirit." Channing voiced the opinion of the convention when he concluded that "the community is itself, by its neglect and bad usages, in part responsible for the sins of its children; and owes the criminal, therefore, aid to reform."[13]

The Association was soon called upon by scattered reformers to father divers theories and programs. Letters arrived from various sources urging the society to endorse the reformatory sentence—the first expressions of this doctrine that have been found in American literature. Samuel Gridley Howe, recently returned to Boston after an extended study of European educational, penal, and asylum institutions, expressed the new theory most precisely.

> The doctrine of retributive justice is rapidly passing away, and with it will pass away, I hope, every kind of punishment that has not the reformation of the criminal in view. One of the first effects of this will be, I am sure, the decrease in the length of sentence and the adoption of some means by which the duration and severity of imprisonment may in all cases be modified by the conduct and character of the prisoners. What we want now—what no system that I know of offers— is the means of training the prisoner's moral sentiments and his power of self government by actual exercise. I believe that there are many who might be so trained as to be left upon their parole during the last period of their imprisonment.[14]

While this fresh whiff of Froebelian doctrine was not strong enough immediately to redirect penal trends in America, a group of Quakers, joining the Association, pledged it to some practical efforts in behalf of discharged prisoners. Friend Isaac Hopper was appointed special agent to help the prisoners find jobs and homes at the time of their release, and for many years this faithful Quaker continued to serve in that capacity, breaking the way for parole agents in the years to come.

The new society certainly did not suffer from a lack of ideas, but it

[13] Ibid., p. 31.
[14] Ibid., (1846), pp. 21–22; ibid., (1847), pp. 90–92, 128–130. These last citations refer to letters from Rev. Samuel J. May and Mrs. Eliza W. Farnham, matron of Sing Sing, each advancing views similar to those of Howe.

was handicapped by an overabundance of visionaries. A charter was secured from the legislature in 1846, granting authority to investigate the prisons of the state, but Judge Edmonds was not reappointed at the end of his term as inspector, and the new authorities refused to cooperate. John D. Russ, succeeding Channing as corresponding secretary, occasionally noted European developments,[15] yet his reports contributed very little to practical prison developments. The fact was that the Association found itself out of harmony with penal trends in America when the dominant Auburn system was still young and self-righteous. Losing its hold on the charitable resources of the community, the Association had to curtail its activities, and only the energies of Isaac Hopper kept it alive during the following decade as a local aid society. Thus, although the Philadelphia Society had meanwhile abandoned its traditional seclusion and was issuing and distributing public reports, Louis Dwight was able to continue his former domination of penological practice in America.

Institutional Expansion

The failure of the theoretical inspiration to take hold did not check the rapid development of prisons throughout the land. New prisons erected in the South and the West copied the Auburn pattern, or its Baltimore compromise of small outside cells, largely because of the relative economy of construction and the promise of profits from congregate labor. Several able wardens introduced disciplinary reforms, but usually as a result of practical problems of control, and the limited attention given to religious and educational matters was but an outgrowth of Dwight's program. The development of prosperous prison industries was the most earnest concern of the wardens, and indeed the rivalry between the officers of different prisons over their financial records gradually pushed aside the argument between the two systems, leaving it to the historians to settle if they could. Nevertheless, this era did witness the further development of several of the best ideas of the former generation, notably the construction of additional houses of correction and reform schools and the segregation of the women. In short the states were able at least to maintain former standards in spite of the

---

[15] Ibid., (1851), p. 312. Russ notes briefly Maconochie's proposal that labor sentences be substituted for time sentences.

tremendous growth in the area and population of their settlements.

In a very significant way the incessant growth of population and the rapid expansion westward were vital aids to prison reform. Together they necessitated the construction of new prisons, thus providing the reformers with opportunities for the application of their theories. But at this time the more advanced theorists did not have a program that was easily adaptable to frontier conditions, and in New York, where a growing penal population certainly afforded a splendid opportunity for an experiment with the system of progressive penal stages, politics was in the saddle. The program of Louis Dwight, with its relatively economical prison structures and its promise of prosperous industries, continued to dominate the officers charged with the responsibility of housing criminals. It was, nevertheless, a real undertaking for a frontier community to attempt to meet even this standard, and the erection of a dozen prisons was a creditable accomplishment.

The development of a penal system in the South and the Old Northwest was no simple task. In the late thirties these regions were still a part of the frontier in many senses of that illuminating term, and two additional decades were required before even the most advanced of these states was able to develop relatively stable prisons. The liberal criminal codes adopted at the start were quickly modified as the legislatures displayed a reckless willingness to add old-time punishments to a cumulative list of offenses.[16] The rapidly growing populations soon created serious housing problems in the new prisons, and several of the states were never able to provide the institutional equipment necessary to carry out the fine phrases of their laws. These frontier communities were preoccupied with the major problems of new settlements, and the authorities all too frequently shifted the burden of maintaining prisons to the first person who offered to assume it.

Frankfort, the oldest prison in the West, had struggled along for nearly three decades, neglected by the politicians, when in 1825 an energetic merchant, Joel Scott, offered to pay the state $1,000 a year for the labor of the convicts for five years. The authorities gladly shifted the whole burden to his care and in so doing originated the lease system that was to play an important part in the development

---

[16] F. S. Philbrick, ed., "The Laws of Indiana Territory, 1801–1809," *Illinois State Historical Library Collections* (c1930), 21: 35–50.

of American penology. Joel Scott's chief concern was to establish prosperous industries, but he was a canny man and realized that discipline and security were first essentials. Studying the reports of Louis Dwight, this first of lessees started the construction, with the aid of public funds, of 250 cells on the Baltimore pattern and paid more than nominal respect to the Auburn discipline. Kentucky gladly extended his lease, and, when he retired in 1832, gave it to T. S. Theobold on similar terms. In the midst of construction activities that provided a cellhouse, a dining room, a chapel, and several factories, Scott and Theobold carried on a profitable enterprise, creating an attractive pattern for many of the new prisons of the West and South.[17]

Ohio and Tennessee, already challenging the western political leadership of Kentucky, each built new prisons on eastern patterns during the early thirties. These institutions at Columbus and Nashville provided adequate accommodations for their growing populations until the mid fifties, and eager contractors vied for the opportunity to employ the inmates at prosperous industries that largely defrayed the prison expenses. The officers in both cases applied the Auburn discipline. After surviving a frightening epidemic of cholera, which took a toll of 115 inmates plus two physicians, one fourth the total population in 1849, the prison in Columbus developed rapidly and came to rival Charlestown for the blue ribbon among the larger institutions of this type during the fifties.[18]

Indiana and Illinois shifted along with jail-like structures at Jeffersonville and Alton until the late thirties when both states commissioned their contractors to build new cellblocks on the Auburn pattern. Wardens held a nominal authority for a time, but the contractors would brook no interference and secured the full rights of lessees at both prisons by 1850. Yet their building programs proved to be entirely inadequate. The 180 cells available at Jeffersonville in 1855 were crowded with 280 convicts, and the 160 cells completed a few years later failed to satisfy the needs of the expanded

[17] O. F. Lewis, *The Development of American Prisons and Prison Customs, 1776-1845* (1922; reprinted Montclair, N.J., 1967) pp. 253–259.

[18] Clara B. Hicks, "The History of Penal Institutions in Ohio to 1850," *Ohio Archeological and Historical Quarterly* 33 (Columbus, 1924): 377, 390–412. Prison Discipline Society, Boston, *Twenty-fifth Report* (1850; reprinted Montclair, N.J., 1972), pp. 38–43; O. F. Lewis, *Development*, pp. 267–268.

population. The first 88 cells at Alton in 1845 were already insufficient, and a decade later 300 prisoners were crowding 188 small cells. Not until both states undertook the construction of new prisons in the late fifties was there a reasonable hope that the wretched conditions would be corrected; unfortunately the outbreak of the Civil War defeated this expectation.[19]

The convicts of Missouri were crowded into a still more unsatisfactory prison. Early state laws had directed that criminals should be punished with solitary confinement at hard labor, and when the prison was first opened at Jefferson City in 1836, 40 outside cells seemed a reasonable equipment for 46 convicts. But the number of prisoners increased rapidly, and 40 additional cells failed to satisfy the needs. In 1847 the governor answered a petition for better accommodations with the argument that two and three prisoners had long occupied each cell with little difficulty. Another decade passed before the state resumed control of its prison, which had been surrendered to a lessee in 1842, and started the construction of a cellblock on the Auburn pattern with 236 small brick cells. But this program was likewise delayed by the war, and Missouri was never able to boast of possessing a satisfactory prison system.[20]

Meanwhile the Gulf states were cautiously experimenting with penitentiaries. The Carolinas still relied on the counties to administer justice, chiefly through corporal and capital punishments, but the law codes of the younger states of the Lower South frequently substituted terms of imprisonment for the older penalties. The regulation of the slaves who comprised the major portion of the population was usually handled in an extralegal fashion, but these growing states found it necessary to build small prisons in order to house the limited number of free-Negro and white convicts.

Administrative incompetence marred the good beginnings at the southern prisons. Georgia had established a prison in 1817 on the old congregate pattern, but Dwight's far-reaching agitation had helped to expose its evils, and in the late thirties the authorities erected a new building with 150 cells on the Baltimore pattern.

[19]Indiana State Prison, *Reports* (1849; 1856); Illinois State Prison Inspectors, *Reports* (1845; 1859; 1860).

[20]Missouri *Governor's Messages* (1837), p. 18; (1839), p. 14; (1848), pp. 24–25; (1859), pp. 25–28.

Although it was poorly located from the point of view of industrial activity, successive governors, complaining against large annual expenditures, forestalled improvements, and the structure remained in a neglected state until burned by the northern army during the war. Louisiana opened its new prison at Baton Rouge in 1835 and embarked upon a carefully planned industrial program. A cotton mill and a shoe factory were introduced not only to manufacture essential articles for slave wear but to train machine operatives and to fight the high prices of northern capitalists. The 100-cell prison was constructed on the Wethersfield model, and during the first years under a board of three directors the institution prospered. When its rapidly growing population increased expenses, the authorities leased the prison to an enterprising company. An addition of cells increased the number to 240, but the population grew more rapidly, and the outbreak of the war found the prison seriously overcrowded. Alabama turned its prison erected at Wetumpka in 1841 over to a lessee from the start; fortunately the 208 cells on the Baltimore pattern remained adequate for all demands.[21]

Mississippi and Texas satisfactorily met the moderate demands of their early years, while Florida did nothing, and Arkansas delayed until the end of the period to start its prison. The 148 cells erected at the "Walls" near the Mississippi state capital in the early forties proved adequate for all needs throughout this period, and a model cotton mill supplied labor for the well-disciplined prisoners and largely paid maintenance costs. When Texas prepared to erect a prison, one of its commissioners visited the Walls of Mississippi, as prisons in the South were generally designated, and returned with such a favorable report that the Lone Star State adopted this interpretation of the Auburn system. The 225 cells erected at Huntsville remained adequate until the eve of the war. The 85 similar cells erected at the Walls of Arkansas in 1858 were scarcely completed before the war brought an unexpected function to this as well as to most of the other prisons of the South—that of housing deserters and prisoners of war.[22]

It was little wonder that the South and the West did not follow

---

[21] O. F. Lewis, *Development,* pp. 265–266; Louisiana Penitentiary, *Reports* (1839; 1859); Inspectors of the Alabama Penitentiary, *Report* (1850–1851).

[22] Mississippi Penitentiary, *Report* (1858); Texas, *Governor's Message* (1853); N.S.P.A., *Report* (1868), p. 65.

Livingston's elaborate program or that of the theorists of the New York Prison Association. The settlers here were still engaged in the elemental struggle over land, slaves, and export prices, and the rapidly increasing population inundated all state institutions except in those parts of the South where the counties continued indifferently to manage these functions. With enterprising merchants eager to lease the cheap and sure labor supply in order to man a blacksmith shop, a cooperage, or a cotton mill it is surprising that so many of the states adopted the warden system before the end of the period. Most of these states were planning expansion along Auburn lines when the Civil War intervened, postponing construction in the Northwest and turning the convicts of the South back into the hands of irresponsible lessees.

The Auburn system was making a successful advance into a northern fringe of new states at the same time that it was establishing its sway throughout most of the older communities of the East. The advance into Michigan, Wisconsin, and Iowa carried with it a rich institutional heritage. Accordingly when Michigan territory established its prison at Jackson in 1839, Wethersfield served as the model, and a fair-sized cellhouse was erected. An agent was placed in control, empowered to install new cells as they were required, and when the 164 cells ready in 1850 were filled, others were added. Wisconsin, feeling unequal to the task of building a permanent prison at the start, erected a log structure at Waupun in 1851. But, unlike most of the makeshift prisons, Waupun was equipped with individual cells, each provided with an iron-grated door that was to be used in the stone prison when completed, and before the end of the decade the convicts had the latter well under way. Iowa apparently did not take such pains with its prison at Fort Madison after the first small cellhouse was completed on the Wethersfield model, for a new warden in 1857 reported the necessity of cleaning out the prison yard used by his predecessor to house a herd of cows. Nevertheless, these states had prisons with a sufficient number of cells and were ready to take an active part in the reform movement of the next decade.[23]

A renewed drive for the abolition of capital punishment won suf-

[23] Michigan State Prison, *Report* (1862), pp. 36–40; P.D.S., *Twenty-seventh Report* (1852), pp. 101–102; Iowa, *Governor's Message* (1860), pp. 19–21.

ficient success in several northern states to require the provision of additional cells in their prisons. Michigan was the first, while still a territory in 1846, to abolish the death penalty for all offenses except treason. Rhode Island and Wisconsin abolished it completely in the fifties and most other northern states reduced the number of capital offenses as antigallows societies spread westward from Pennsylvania and New England. But this campaign, like other reforms of the day, lost its momentum as the antislavery crisis mounted.[24]

As a final triumph for Dwight's campaign in New England, Maine and Rhode Island were persuaded to adopt the Auburn system. The authorities at Thomaston had repeatedly condemned their underground prison before the legislature was persuaded in 1836 to order the construction of a new cellblock on the Wethersfield pattern; delayed by hard times, the 108 cells of the new prison were not ready for occupation until the late forties. Rhode Island gave up its pretense of maintaining the solitary system when it introduced a congregate shop in order to mitigate the evil effects of confinement in small dark cells without labor. Dr. Francis Wayland, a former member of Dwight's Society and soon to be chosen president of Brown University, became chairman of the board of directors at the prison in 1851 and the following year commenced the construction of a new wing with 88 cells on the Auburn pattern. The Providence prison soon became a creditable institution. Meanwhile Dwight himself had been named as one of two commissioners empowered to plan the enlargement of Charlestown prison, and when the 150 new cells were opened in 1852, this old bastille had an equipment of 454 cells besides an old dormitory section that was soon to be refitted on the Auburn pattern.[25]

The Auburn system made some further advances in the Middle Atlantic States but generally along moderate lines. When, after the departure of Mrs. Farnham, the new matron at the women's prison at Sing Sing endeavored to reestablish the silent system she found that compromises had to be made in maintaining order among the inmates of its 98 outside cells and in the workshops and schoolrooms where some communication was essential. The wardens of all the major prisons, pressing their contractors for more profitable

---

[24] Hugo A. Bedau, ed., *The Death Penalty in America*, 2d ed. (Chicago, 1968), pp. 9–12.

[25] O. F. Lewis, *Development*, pp. 147–163.

returns, had to relax their regulations against communication within the shops. A mounting protest by newly organized labor unions, and by some struggling industrialists as well, against the unfair competition of prison labor brought the enactment of anti-contract and other laws in New York and elsewhere and complicated the operation of prison industries. It was in the search for non-competitive industries that the proposal was made· that a prison should be established in an undeveloped iron field in Clinton County, New York. The opening of the Clinton prison, named Dannemora after an iron center in Sweden, was widely hailed in 1845 as a real achievement. The operation, however, necessitated a modification of the regimen of silence, and although the location made such compromises less dangerous, the experiment failed to prove economically rewarding. While New York's third state prison gradually lost its distinctive character in the fifties, neighboring New Jersey, faced with a mounting population in its prison at Trenton, added a new cellblock on the Auburn pattern.[26]

Pennsylvania alone remained committed to the solitary system, but after 1842 it defined its plan as a separate rather then a solitary system. The Philadelphia Society annually appointed seven committees of lay visitors, one for each cellblock, and one or more members of each committee made an average of two visits a week to the inmates. This active and friendly communication, supplemented by the stream of dignitaries and other sightseers who numbered several thousand annually, effectively dispelled the monotony and solitude that most critics complained of. Yet even Cherry Hill could not escape some of the disciplinary problems common to all prisons, and when a diet of bread and water failed to produce obedience the officials chained men in ankle irons, inflicted the shower bath, or placed them in a dark cell, but the use of the lash was strictly forbidden. And throughout the fifty-three years when Richard Vaux, son of founder Roberts Vaux, was the principal inspector, secretary and president of the board, the penitentiary maintained the high standards of its separate regimen and did not find it necessary to confine two men to a cell until the late 1860s.[27]

---

[26] W. D. Lewis, *Newgate*, pp. 193, 250, 260–263; Harry Elmer Barnes, *A History of the Penal, Reformatory and Correctional Institutions of the State of New Jersey: Analytical and Documentary* (Trenton, 1918), pp. 514–529.

[27] Negley K. Teeters and John D. Shearer, *The Prison at Philadelphia, Cherry Hill* (New York, 1957), pp. 161–172, 195–200, 212–215.

*　　　　　*　　　　　*

By far the most important penal problems still centered in the local jails. Unfortunately the efforts of Louis Dwight, Dorothea Dix, and the many other reformers scarcely affected the character of these institutions. Petty politicians were still in control, reaping fat profits from the corrupt fee system. Food, heat, and clothing were frequently deficient. The bucket system, feeding in cells, poor ventilation, and an overabundance of bugs and mice all contributed to the wretched squalor of these institutions. The indiscriminate association of all classes in the corridors in complete idleness every day was, however, the crowning damnation of most jails.[28] The only feasible attack on this evil appeared to be the old one of removing special classes into separate institutions. The two most promising reforms of this sort were the campaign of Miss Dix for the removal of insane persons from jails and prisons and the widespread attack on imprisonment for debt. Miss Dix had commenced her investigation into the conditions of insane inmates in jails in Massachusetts in 1841. After a triumph there, she had extended her investigations into neighboring states, traveling over 30,000 miles between 1843 and 1847, inspecting 18 state prisons, 300 jails and 500 almshouses and other institutions. She played a major role in the establishment of five new hospitals for the insane and the expansion of several older asylums, and instigated improvements in other institutions.[29] No single individual played such a role in the struggle for the abolition of imprisonment for debt, but a resurgent labor movement and many civic leaders in scattered cities during the depression of the late 1830s pressed the campaign to a partial or full success in Michigan, Alabama, New Hampshire, and Tennessee, and in practically all states by 1857. Unfortunately, the relief provided by the removal of these groups from the local jails was more than offset in most towns and cities by the rapid growth of their populations and the increased police problems they faced.[30]

The petty offender was proving to be a decided nuisance in

[28] Dorothea Lynde Dix, *Remarks on Prisons and Prison Discipline in the United States*, 2d ed. (1845; reprinted Montclair, N.J., 1967), pp. 94–102. Miss Dix found only six jails worthy of honorable mention in 1845; three on the solitary pattern in Dauphin, Chester, and Philadelphia counties in Pennsylvania, and three on the Auburn pattern at Hartford, New Haven, and Boston.

[29] Helen E. Marshall, *Dorothea Dix: Forgotten Samaritan* (Chapel Hill, 1937), pp. 84–122.

[30] Charles Warren, *A History of the American Bar* (Boston, 1911), p. 467.

growing cities, especially during the winter months when he frankly sought refuge in the crowded jails. Albany determined in 1843 to correct this evil by building a local penitentiary for the confinement at hard labor of short-term drunkards and vagrants. The legislature hastened to grant the necessary authority, and Amos Pilsbury was called from Wethersfield to take charge. The achievements of this institution, notably its success in defraying expenses from the labor of the inmates, provided an attractive model for other cities. The New York Prison Association endorsed the program, and Rochester, Syracuse, and Buffalo in New York, as well as Cincinnati and Detroit, established such institutions during the next few years. Eleven counties in Massachusetts had meanwhile followed Boston's earlier example, but only two of these houses of correction were entirely separate from the county jails. Several other scattered cities built new workhouses, most of which did little more than provide labor for the inmates.

All these institutions except the Moyamensing workhouse in Philadelphia had adopted the Auburn-type cellblock, but no pretense was made of enforcing the silent system, and the absence of hardened criminals relieved them of the customary atmosphere of armed fortresses. Sabbath schools, libraries, and industry were standing these institutions off in sharp contrast with the great majority of the jails of the country, and a liberal discipline was differentiating them from the state prisons. Massachusetts, Michigan, and New York adopted the policy of sending most of their female convicts to these prisons, thus greatly relieving their state institutions. In 1856 New York passed a law permitting the commitment of young first offenders guilty of major crimes to the local penitentiaries and by this measure instituted a significant classification. But these institutions were only beginning to reveal their possibilities, though Zebulon Brockway, who had developed a successful work schedule and a rousing Sabbath-school program in the Rochester penitentiary only to become disillusioned over the recidivism of many of those discharged, was already studying the works of Maconochie and Crofton and speculating on the possibility of a reformatory sentence.[31]

*   *   *

[31] Zebulon R. Brockway, *Fifty Years of Prison Service: An Autobiography* (1912; reprinted Montclair, N.J., 1969), pp. 63–65.

An equally creditable advance was being made in the field of juvenile institutions. The three reform schools established in the 1820s had continued to develop in spite of the general diversion of interest to the state prisons. Now in the late forties an increasing recognition of public responsibility for the welfare of children brought a new impetus to the movement. State schools were established in Massachusetts and New York, but it was in the growing cities that this responsibility was most keenly felt, and Baltimore, Cincinnati, Pittsburgh, Providence, and Rochester were among the score of cities that established reform schools before the Civil War.[32]

The authorities had recognized from the first the desirability of distinguishing these schools from the general penal system, and the breach was widened during this era. In spite of an excessive amount of disciplinary repression in many places the silent system was never attempted, and supervised games became a regular feature in several schools. The obligation of the school to provide general elementary instruction was conceded if not always fulfilled, but the boast that the active trade departments provided a valuable industrial training was seldom justified; a school ship launched by Massachusetts in 1859 probably came nearer than any other reform school to achieving this latter objective. The children were usually committed to the care of the school authorities during their minority, but the managers were generally empowered to indenture them to tradesmen or householders as soon as their reform was evident; this arrangement, together with the experiments with internal classification, progressive grading, and honor systems, supplied precedents for similar innovations in adult prisons a few decades later, but the direct line of succession was to be very indistinct. Meanwhile Horace Mann, Calvin E. Stowe, and other American educators who explored the European field returned with glowing accounts of the cottage system of the Rauhe Haus in Germany and Mettray in France, and that pattern was adopted at Lancaster, Massachusetts, in 1855 and at Lancaster, Ohio, in 1857. But again the gap between the

---

[32] Robert S. Pickett, *House of Refuge: Origins of Juvenile Reform in New York State, 1815–1857* (Syracuse, N.Y., 1969), pp. 100–102, 180–182; Joseph M. Hawes, *Children in Urban Society: Juvenile Delinquency in Nineteenth-Century America* (New York, 1971), pp. 80–86; Blake McKelvey, "A History of Penal and Correctional Institutions in the Rochester Area," *Rochester History* 34 (1972): 6–9.

trends of the reform school and the penitentiary system restrained the latter from profiting by this innovation until in the next century the application of the cottage system to women's reformatories broke down the bars of the Auburn cellblock tradition.

Penology in Practice during the Fifties

The new currents of idealism that had enlivened penological theorists in the early forties failed to exert any considerable influence on prison practice. In Europe, where most of the countries were attempting to establish a penitentiary system somewhat after the Cherry Hill model, one or two significant experimenters were applying the new principles, most notably Sir Walter Crofton in Ireland; but Americans were at the time almost totally unaware of these developments. The American penitentiary had been projected and organized around the principle that each individual prisoner should be entirely cut off from his fellows. This simple negative program had early been modified in numerous respects, chiefly through the development of religious and industrial activities; now a moderate relaxation of the rigid disciplinary regulations and the introduction of new methods of control contributed to the same end. Nevertheless, the American prison system of the late 1850s was still very much as Louis Dwight had shaped it.

The dominant reform influences and reformatory agencies were, characteristically, religious. The campaign to supply Bibles, to provide chaplains, and to organize Sabbath schools had been largely successful. The growing power in the community at large of such denominations as the Methodists and the Baptists, with their emphasis on evangelism, was reflected in prison by an increasing number of revivals among the inmates; and, true to their higher responsibilities, many of the chaplains were more concerned over the soul of one condemned man than over the preparation of his fellows to return to society. No other incident sheds so much light on the reforms of this period as the heroic curtain call of Louis Dwight's career. Rising from his death bed in 1854, this forthright servant of God, long a leader in the morning prayer services in Old South Chapel, drove to the Boston Lunatic Asylum to deliver a comforting sermon to the inmates on "The Temptation of Christ."[33]

---

[33] P.D.S., *Twenty-ninth Report* (1854), pp. 27–28.

The general American temper of the day placed great reliance on religion, and it was not entirely as a figure of speech that wardens sometimes addressed their reports to "Our Father" as well as to the "Gentlemen of the Legislature."[34]

This widespread recognition of the function of religion in penology helps to account for the fact that Enoch Wines and Theodore Dwight, in their epoch-making investigation in the year following the Civil War, found that all the wardens agreed that a major object of imprisonment was the reformation of convicts. This was not lip service, for, in the tradition they had inherited from Louis Dwight, God was the great reformer of sinful men. The two investigators, reviving the long-dormant ideals of the New York society, were the heralds of a new era. While they praised the achievements of the past, noting especially the progress in Boston, Philadelphia, Detroit, and Albany, they nevertheless concluded "there is not a state prison in America, in which the reformation of the convict is the supreme object of the *discipline.*"[35]

A more absorbing concern of the wardens was to make the prisons pay their expenses. Louis Dwight had made prison industry one of his foster children. After the termination of his reports in 1854, the occasional interstate communications were little more than acrimonious arguments over the financial merits of the various prisons. Only the directors of Cherry Hill maintained a philosophical indifference toward large unearned expenditures, and the explanation of this exception may be found in the unique custom of charging the board of each prisoner to the county in which he was convicted.

Only such administrators as succeeded in making their institutions largely self-sufficient gained the opportunity to consider the other functions of imprisonment. In the incessant political turmoil none but financially successful wardens could live through a change in parties. It was not a chance circumstance that, with the sole exception of Cherry Hill, all the prisons gaining honorable mention from Wines and Dwight at the end of the period had outstanding

[34] Connecticut State Prison, *Report* (1870).

[35] Enoch Cobb Wines and Theodore Dwight, *Report on the Prisons and Reformatories of the United States and Canada* (1867; reprinted Montclair, N.J., 1976), pp. 287–288 (author's italics).

economic records. The Pilsburys, Haynes, Cordier, Rice, and Brockway, the ablest wardens of the day, had all won distinction in this respect before they did any experimenting in the reformation of their charges.

In the hard world of the prisoner this was not an indictment, and, when contrasted with the wretched idleness in local jails, it appears in its proper light as a genuine achievement. The abler wardens managed their prison industries with the aid of the institution's credit, but contractors dominated the scene in all but three or four of the prisons, frequently returning to the states more than enough to cover prison expenses, as was the case in 1852 when nine prisons reported a combined surplus of over $23,000.[36] The use of convict labor to help construct prisons, capitol buildings, and other public works was fairly general throughout the country but most frequent in the younger states of the West. The diversified methods of exploiting prison labor at the time enabled the authorities to avoid effective opposition, but the struggle to maintain prosperous industries frequently caused the authorities to lose sight of the interests of the prisoners; Wines and Dwight were disappointed to find that "one string is harped upon, ad nauseam—money, money, money."[37]

One of the inevitable results of this preoccupation with profits was a relaxation of the original methods of discipline. The construction program had provided a fairly adequate cell capacity so that most of the convicts, at least those of the Northeast, were supplied with individual cells throughout the era—a condition that was never to be realized on such a wide scale after the Civil War. Meanwhile the additional features of the silent system were receiving a more diversifed application, and the intrusion of educational and other activities was breaking down the rigid character of the old Auburn pattern.

Silence at all times, lockstep marching, downcast eyes except when addressed by an officer, no gazing at visitors, no clothing or other articles except as supplied by the prison, striped uniforms— these were the traditional features of the Auburn system, but

[36] P.D.S., *Twenty-seventh Report* (1852), p. 103. Wethersfield had annually reported small profits from 1833.

[37] Wines and Dwight, *Prisons*, pp. 265–268, 289.

Connecticut and New Hampshire were the only states to enforce all of them rigidly. The prison in Maine and that at Clinton, New York, went so far as to permit talking at labor "when necessary" and, together with Vermont, discarded the lockstep. Several of the wardens favored a radical modification of the whole system, and already complete "freedom of the yard" had been granted on national holidays in Massachusetts, Michigan, and Missouri. In most prisons discipline had become customarily lax on these special days; talking in the dining halls and the uproarious powwows in the cells at Sing Sing gained the authority of ancient custom. There was just a suggestion here of what the American prison system might have become, might yet become, if the prisoners were idle at all times. Wines and Dwight concluded as to the actual force of the silent system: "Communication, then, we must believe, takes place among convicts continually and in most prisons to a very great extent."[38]

The growing faith in public education and the popularity of circulating libraries had their influence on prisons. School classes had been a feature of juvenile institutions from their beginning; the Boston house of correction started classes in 1841, but the New York law of 1847 providing two instructors for each state prison was the first effective application of this policy to the major prisons. However, these teachers simply passed from cell to cell as occasional chaplains had done before, instructing in the three R's, and the periods between their visits were so long that the value of their services was questionable. By 1865 instructors in New York and Pennsylvania, as well as chaplains in Connecticut and New Hampshire, made their rounds in this fashion; only Ohio maintained regular classes conducted by the chaplain three evenings a week. Education in the other prisons rested with the Sabbath schools.

The provision for prison libraries was the next step in many prisons. Early chaplains had occasionally loaned books to trusted prisoners as a supplement to Bible reading. Probably the first prison library supplying more than Bibles and religious tracts was that established at Sing Sing in 1840 by Warden Seymour and Governor Seward. New Jersey and other states made similar provisions, but in 1847 New York was the first to start the custom of making annual

[38] Ibid., p. 177.

appropriations. When Wines and Dwight made their survey, they found libraries of a sort in all state prisons. Unfortunately, pious religious books, discarded by thrifty parsons, stuffed the shelves; their service was little more than that of providing an escape to readers bored with the drab realities of their prison home. Neither the libraries nor the elementary instruction can be credited with solving the indignant question of one convict: "Better thoughts! Where shall I get them?"[39]

The disciplinary problem was naturally more complicated in the prisons where the silent system held sway. The punishment records revealed that Maine, with its liberal policy toward talking, had the smallest percentage. A closer study showed that in the average prison the majority of punishments were for offenses against the rule of silence, and that short-term men and new arrivals received the largest share of these. The means of punishment were quite varied; the severe methods of earlier days had, however, been considerably modified. At least six prisons still permitted the lash and occasionally the "cat," but the trend was in the direction of leniency. New York had made the questionable reform of substituting the "crucifix," "bucking," and the "shower bath" for the unpopular lash. All the states permitted the dark cell with a bread-and-water diet, and this was the only punishment aside from the withdrawal of good time permitted in New England and Ohio.[40]

There were several developments during this period that represented positive achievements. Thus the introduction of the practice of commuting sentences for good behavior was a considerable advance over corporal punishment as a means of maintaining discipline. The provision of paltry sums for the aid of discharged criminals and the appointment of agents to assist these outcasts to make a new start in life were enlightened additions to the penal system. At the same time the success of the agitation of Dorothea Dix for public hospitals for the insane made it possible to relieve the jails and prisons of many of these unfortunates.

The principle of commutation was not original with this era. New York had had a good-time law as early as 1817, though it had

[39] Ibid., p. 221.
[40] James B. Finley, *Memorials of Prison Life* (Cincinnati, 1850); W. D. Lewis, *Newgate*, pp. 227, 251–253, 273–275.

not been applied. The early reformers had not distinguished clearly between commutation, the labor sentence, and the ticket-of-leave procedures that were being proposed in England during the period, all of which modifications of the simple time sentence had indeed been foreshadowed by Pennsylvania's action in 1790 in giving judges the power to release men they had sentenced in case they found them to be reformed before their terms were completed. But the distinguishing feature of commutation was the bid it made for obedience to prison rules, and Tennessee, beginning in 1833, was the first state to apply such good-time reductions of sentences over a period of years. The procedure did not gain wide popularity until, in 1856, Cyrus Mendenhall secured such a law in Ohio. Eight northeastern states followed within a decade, as the authorities quickly saw the disciplinary value of the scheme of granting the prisoners a few days' reduction of sentence for each month of good conduct. The reformatory value of these laws depended very largely on the character of the officers, but, at least during the first years of their application, commutation laws seemed to stimulate many convicts to try to become good citizens as well as good prisoners.[41]

Meanwhile the humanitarian temper of the age was directing attention to the problems of discharged prisoners. Quakers in and out of Philadelphia had early given aid and comfort to prisoners on their release from jail, but the New York Association was the first to organize the work under the kindly services of Isaac Hopper. Charles and John Murray Spear organized the Prisoners' Friend Association in Boston in 1845, and for several years, rallying friends to their assistance through the pages of their journal, *Prisoners' Friend,* these compassionate brothers aided the men discharged from the prisons of Massachusetts. The Philadelphia Society followed these leads in 1853 when it appointed William J. Mullen agent to care for the discharged and eventually secured government funds for his support.[42] Charitable citizens of Maryland, New Jersey, and Rhode Island likewise organized societies for this particular purpose. Massachusetts stepped forward into the next era when in 1845 the philanthropic John Augustus was appointed state agent and given government support in the care of the discharged. Another decided step in advance was taken in the same year by the New York

---

[41] W. D. Lewis, *Newgate,* pp. 280–281.
[42] *Philanthropist* (March extra, 1856).

Association when its women's branch founded the Isaac T. Hopper Home for discharged women prisoners, thus following the example of Elizabeth Fry in England. Amos Pilsbury, whose views on prison affairs carried weight, declared that this type of public charity had larger reformatory value than any amount of education within the prison.

Another forward-looking movement, the campaign of Dorothea Dix to persuade the states to undertake the cure of the insane, was beginning to exert an important influence on prison developments. As a result of the campaign the states, by the end of this period, had built asylums to a capacity that practically equaled that of the state prisons, and many serious cases were thus eliminated from the jails and prisons.[43] A few states provided that insane prisoners might be transferred to the asylums, but New York, troubled with the largest number of these cases, determined to erect a special asylum for insane criminals inside an extension of the walls at Auburn prison, and the new institution was opened in 1859.[44] Ohio and Illinois took steps in this direction a few years later, but unfortunately the buildings they erected followed the solitary-cell pattern rather than that of the asylum-ward already developed at Auburn and the better asylums. Another half century was to pass before more enlightened views concerning insanity were to make a contribution to penology.

Hardly anything had as yet been attempted in the most vital phase of prison reform—the organization of agencies for controlling policy. Except in Pennsylvania, politics was everywhere actively in charge. The selection of prison inspectors by the state Supreme Court had secured a stable, if conservative, administration in the Keystone State. Massachusetts, Vermont, and Maine claimed that their prisons were free from politics, but this was due either to the continued dominance of one party or to the economic efficiency of a given warden. No state had as yet vested control over its entire prison system in any central body as England and France had done. The Massachusetts Board of State Charities, organized in 1863, was only a timid step in this direction, while the New York Board of Prison Inspectors had long been a most disappointing experiment in

[43]P.D.S., *Twenty-seventh Report* (1852), pp. 103, 137. Dwight reports the population of seventeen prisons as 4,515, and that of twenty-four asylums as 4,943.
[44]W. D. Lewis, *Newgate*, pp. 281–283; Teeters and Shearer, *Cherry Hill*, p. 192; N.Y.P.A., *Report* (1868), pp. 154–164.

centralized management. Most of the prisons were controlled by an authority carefully suspended in good American style between a board of inspectors and a warden, each appointed separately and for varied short terms by the governor, legislature, or the two acting together. Massachusetts paid her warden $2,500, while all the others scaled from $2,000 down to $700.[45] Naturally these several features had discouraged able and honest men from seeking such insecure positions.

In the complex hierarchy of prison authorities there was yet another and most disturbing element—the governor's power to pardon. While it may have corrected many evils in the dispensation of justice, the frequent use of the pardoning power in an attempt to relieve overcrowded and unhealthy jails and prisons had undermined the discipline of many institutions.[46] The prisoners could see no certain standards of conduct where luck, religious "mush," or outside "pull" seemed to determine one's fate, and it appeared that the more desperate criminals got most of the "breaks." Discipline was difficult and reformation almost an impossibility where one out of six prisoners received a pardon. The wardens were all opposed to the practice, yet, when Wisconsin moved to require the recommendation of the warden, few of these practical officers considered the advantage worth the risk of the charge of favoritism. But at least the authorities were alive to the serious nature of the problem, which made them receptive to the parole system when it was brought forward in the next era.

Thus, before the outbreak of the Civil War, the American states had equipped themselves with an extended and somewhat diversified system of prisons. Except in Pennsylvania, the Auburn separate-cell pattern was predominant and, although modified in minor details, retained its strongly religious ideology and its active industrial program intact. However, its Baltimore architectural compromise had been copied extensively in the South and West, and the leasing arrangement of Kentucky was substituted in several of these outlying states for the more general contract system. Only in the Northeast were the prisons sufficiently equipped to provide most prisoners with separate cells, and only in a few of the larger states were facilities for the separate confinement of women and children

[45] Wines and Dwight, *Prisons*, pp. 77–82, 119.
[46] Ibid., p. 302.

available. But even the states of the West and the South, where these standards were seldom realized in practice, had laws and projected programs of construction that endorsed these precepts. It is true that the young states of the Far West and the wide-open territories shared few of these traditions, but on that rough-and-ready frontier practically the only criminals of consequence were the fast-shooting highwaymen and the half-breed cattle thieves whose careers frequently ended with their capture. "Strong jails" occasionally served there, as throughout the South, and still to a deplorable extent in the Northeast, housing an indiscriminate assortment of cases; only a score of local institutions in the more populous centers of the Northeast were struggling to correct some of the evils of this weakest link in the American penal system.

Yet despite the institutional and physical accomplishments of the American penal system, the frequent outbreaks of violence that marred the record of every prison and the reconvictions many of their dischargees experienced posed sharp challenges to their good intentions. Fortunately some forward-looking principles had found expression during the forties, and, although it was not suspected by the penal authorities even of the late fifties, the time was near at hand when these theories were to play a part in an extensive reorientation of the entire penal system.

BIBLIOGRAPHIC NOTE

Edward Livingston, *The Complete Works of Edward Livingston on Criminal Jurisprudence: Consisting of Systems of Penal Law for the State of Louisiana and for the United States of America*, 2 vols. (1873; reprinted Montclair, N.J., 1968); Alexander Maconochie, *Norfolk Island* (London, 1847); Mary Carpenter, *Our Convicts*, 2 vols. (1864; reprinted Montclair, N.J., 1969); William Paley, *Principles of Moral and Political Philosophy* (New York, 1860); and especially the early *Reports* of the New York Prison Association (1844–), are of primary importance for a study of the new theoretical trends. More of the annual reports of the prisons are preserved for this period, and they are supplemented by the *Reports of the Prison Discipline Society of Boston, 1826–1854* (1855; reprinted Montclair, N.J., 1972); Dorothea Lynde Dix, *Remarks on Prisons and Prison Discipline in the United States*, 2d ed. (1845, reprinted Montclair, N.J., 1967); George Combe, *Lectures on Phrenology* (New York, 1839), and his *Notes on the*

United States of North America (Philadelphia, 1841); and Enoch C. Wines and Theodore Dwight, *Report on the Prisons and Reformatories of the United States and Canada* (1867; reprinted Montclair, N.J., 1976).

In addition to a number of the volumes mentioned in the Bibliographic Note to Chapter 1, the following are of value to an understanding of the period: Harry Elmer Barnes, *A History of the Penal, Reformatory and Correctional Institutions of the State of New Jersey: Analytical and Documentary* (Trenton, 1918); Zebulon R. Brockway, *Fifty Years of Prison Service: An Autobiography* (1912; reprinted Montclair, N.J., 1969); Charles Caldwell, *New Views of Penitentiary Discipline and Moral Education and Reform* (Philadelphia, 1829); Rosamond and Florence Davenport-Hill, *A Memoir of Matthew Davenport Hill: With Selections from His Correspondence* (London, 1878); Arthur E. Fink, *Causes of Crime: Biological Theories in the United States, 1800–1915* (Philadelphia, 1938); James B. Finley, *Memorials of Prison Life* (Cincinnati, 1850); Clara B. Hicks, "The History of Penal Institutions in Ohio to 1850," *Ohio Archeological and Historical Quarterly* 33 (1924); John Luckey, *Life in Sing Sing State Prison* (New York, 1860); Helen E. Marshall, *Dorothea Dix: Forgotten Samaritan* (Chapel Hill, 1937); Marmaduke B. Sampson, *Rationale of Crime: And Its Appropriate Treatment; Being a Treatise on Criminal Jurisprudence Considered in Relation to Cerebral Organization . . . with Notes and Illustrations by Eliza W. Farnham* (1846; reprinted Montclair, N.J., 1973); Charles Warren, *A History of the American Bar* (Boston, 1911).

3.

THE DEVELOPMENT OF A
REFORM MOVEMENT
IN THE 1860s

The Civil War, ringing in a new era in many phases of social history, helped to coordinate in time and character the scattered strands of normal penological development. The compelling urgency of growing populations, the inspiration of native and foreign achievements, the zeal of new agencies for social control, and popular confidence in high ideals were opportunely brought together at the close of the war in time to assist a band of energetic reformers in an effective movement for prison reform. The first stage saw the best theories of the 1840s incorporated along with some new ideals into ambitious programs, and if the leaders were somewhat too optimistic, they nevertheless charted most of the developments of the next half century.

The war helped to bring the movement to a head in the late 1860s by checking a premature attempt at collaboration among prison officers. When Louis Dwight and his Boston Society ceased their labors in 1854, a real opportunity for new leadership had appeared. The New York Prison Association was handicapped at the time by poverty, and the mace passed to the hand of Frederick A. Packard of Philadelphia, editor of the quarterly *Journal of Prison Discipline*. Packard, however, was so firmly committed to the Pennsylvania system that, while greatly assisting the movement for reform schools,[1] he was unable to give hearty approval to the new ideas that his European correspondents called to his attention. His *Journal,* although widely circulated, could not buck the Auburn tradition in America.

Whether stimulated by these journals or propelled solely by a personal desire for guidance in building his new state prison, Edward M. McGaw, commissioner of Wisconsin prisons, corresponded with several wardens and reformers suggesting a conference in Philadelphia. When the convention of Friends of Penal Reform gathered in September 1859, eight states and three prison societies were represented. Gideon Haynes and five other wardens were among the thirty-two delegates. Most of the time was spent debating the relative merits of the Pennsylvania and Auburn systems, and, although the delegates lacked enthusiasm, they organized the American Association for the Improvement of Prison Discipline and called a second convention to meet in New York the following year.[2]

Several of the outstanding men in the field were present at the second gathering. Judge John W. Edmonds, John H. Griscom, and Francis Lieber from New York, together with William Parker Foulke and Frederick Packard from Philadelphia, were all old in the service; Zebulon Brockway, down for the occasion from his county penitentiary in Rochester, was just making his reputation as a thrifty warden. Again the old debate raged between the rival systems, and a long philosophical discourse by the aged patron of the past, William Parker Foulke, failed to stir the creative genius of the young Brockway.[3] There is no evidence that the third convention under the presidency of Dr. Griscom ever convened as scheduled in Baltimore in 1861. Meanwhile Packard's quarterly, with its resources diverted by the war, was taken over by the Philadelphia Society, and, as an annual journal, became the official report of that organization. All articles now had to be approved by a vote of the Society, and Philadelphia was saved the embarrassment of nurturing a move-

[1] *Journal of Prison Discipline and Philanthropy* 13 (April 1858): 104; ibid., 14 (April 1859): 92.

[2] Ibid., 14 (July 1859): 184–187; ibid., 15 (January 1860): 137–140. The prisons of Indiana, Maryland, Massachusetts, Michigan, New Jersey, New York, Pennsylvania, and Wisconsin and the societies of Baltimore, New York, and Philadelphia were represented at this conference.

[3] Ibid., 16 (January 1861): 34–36. At this meeting the organization was renamed the American Association for the Improvement of Penal and Reformatory Institutions.

ment that might outgrow the faith of the fathers.

The war helped in another way to unify and to time the movement. Whether the army had absorbed the potential criminals, afforded a refuge for fugitives, or supplied a convenient commutation of sentence, the result was the same—a decided reduction of male commitments in all the states of the North. In the summer of 1865 Wines and Dwight found most of the prisons equipped with reasonably adequate housing accommodations and fairly prosperous industries. The sudden increase in commitments following the close of the war crowded the prisons, placed penal problems on the front page in both popular and legislative journals, and presented all the prison administrators of the country with a common housing problem.

The Emergence of New Leadership

The war had failed to absorb all the energy of the Northerners, and in New York, in particular, philanthropists as well as capitalists and laborers had their minds on other matters. After several lean years, during which the New York Association had been almost forgotten by the rapidly changing city, new friends began to rally to its cause. Judge John David Wolfe joined and became president in 1861. Although at first inclined to wait until the war had been won before pressing his cause, within a year the new president was pounding at the doors of the legislature, hat in hand. The real leadership, however, was to come from E. C. Wines, the new corresponding secretary appointed in 1862.

Dr. Enoch Cobb Wines was ripe with experience when the Civil War snuffed out the City University of St. Louis, of which he had just been chosen first president. After leaving his father's New England farm and graduating from Middlebury College, Wines had instructed in boys' schools, on a naval training ship, and, after several years of ministry in a Congregational church in Vermont and later in a Presbyterian parish on Long Island, had become a lecturer at Washington College, Pennsylvania. For a short time in the 1830s he had edited the *Monthly Advocate of Education*, urging the need for state normal schools and free public education. Added to all these rich experiences was the strength which comes to a man who, in the memory of his son, "never had a religious doubt." When he was called to the New York Prison Association as its new secretary in 1862, Wines responded in the spirit of a laborer assigned to a new vineyard, and he soon proved himself to be worthy of his hire.

Most of his fellow workers had had long experience in the work. Francis Lieber and Judge Edmonds were still active members. Dr. John H. Griscom, son of the noted founder of the first house of refuge, was carrying on in his father's spirit, while Abraham Beal was faithfully bearing the mantle of Isaac Hopper. Theodore W. Dwight, scion of the noted Dwights of Yale and soon to become first head of the Columbia Law School, joined the group shortly after the arrival of Wines. But these kindly spirited citizens and their growing Association needed the zeal and organizing ability of Dr. Wines to translate their high ideals into action.

Like his predecessor in Boston, Wines was essentially a pulpit reformer and for eighteen years used his post to proclaim many and varied ideals, all looking toward the reformation of criminals. Again and again he called for more earnest support, declaring, "Our work is mainly a work of humanity and benevolence. . . . It is a philanthropy akin to that divine benevolence that calls backsliders to repent."[4] Animated by a persistent zeal himself, Wines instilled a new enthusiasm into the New York Association and won for it the leadership it had failed to gain in earlier days.

But zeal and organizing ability never of themselves create great movements, and energetic leaders are fortunate when they find scattered forces in the field, ready for guidance toward coordinated expression. Wines found an abundance of such forces active in the early sixties, and rejoiced with Theodore Dwight over the many signs of growth noted on their tour. Wardens such as Cordier in Wisconsin, Rice in Maine, Hubbell in Sing Sing, as well as Haynes and Brockway were struggling to solve their growing problems; if there was to be any genuine reformation of criminals, it would be their job, and each was busy with his experiments.

Dr. Wines was not content to wait and see if criminals could be reformed: he was determined to move mountains to achieve it. Dissatisfied with the faltering efforts of New York State prisons, he persuaded the leaders of his association to authorize a nationwide investigation of penal methods in search of the most promising

[4] New York Prison Association, *Report* (1863), p. 51.

techniques for the reformation of convicts. Securing the eager collaboration of Theodore Dwight and a letter of introduction and endorsement from Governor Fenton, he set forth on a protracted tour of the state prisons from Thomaston, Maine, to Waupun, Wisconsin, to Jefferson City, Missouri, to Baltimore, and visited the fifteen penitentiaries, sixteen reform schools, and many of the numerous jails and houses of correction scattered throughout the intervening northern states. They also made a brief jaunt into neighboring Canada, visiting the prison at Kingston and a few local jails.

In order to keep their assignment within reasonable limits Wines and Dwight collected documents as they progressed for more careful study after their return and compiled seventy bound volumes of such documents from the states visited and others beyond their travels. They prepared a probing questionnaire of 26 pages, which they mailed to prison authorities throughout the country, and secured returns from 45 such correspondents. Finally from field notes and documents they produced a 570-page *Report on the Prisons and Reformatories of the United States and Canada,* which was to have an impact on penal developments in America and Europe second only to John Howard's *State of Prisons.*[5]

The report brought several unsuspected developments to light and promoted a healthy rivalry between the states. The touring inspectors were welcomed as visiting dignitaries and made several warm friendships with wardens and chaplains of kindred spirit. The interest they displayed in the evening schools conducted by the chaplains of the Ohio and Indiana state prisons pointed up opportunities for instruction that the more traditional Sabbath schools could not realize. They welcomed a proposal by Warden Cordier of Wisconsin that prisoners should be rewarded by a share in the proceeds of their labor and praised his recognition of them as men and his grant of the privilege to write and receive letters and to have a visitor once a month. Wines and Dwight awarded accolades to other wardens for similarly unusual innovations, but they did not find a single prison that merited recognition as a reformatory. Instead they repeatedly held up the principles and practices of the Irish system of Sir Walter Crofton as the most worthy model. The

---

[5] Enoch Cobb Wines and Theodore Dwight, *Report on the Prisons and Reformatories of the United States and Canada* (1867; reprinted Montclair, N.J., 1976).

nearest approach they found to this idea was in two or three reform schools and in Brockway's Detroit House of Correction.[6]

Wines and Dwight were generally disappointed in the prisons they visited, but they enthusiastically commended Gideon Haynes for the progress made at Charlestown. To start with, they liked the design of the cellblock with its tall windows that admitted more light than the small windows of the Auburn model. Haynes, moreover, was making important modifications in that discipline. He had, they reported, abolished the dehumanizing striped uniforms and the lockstep marching with downcast eyes. His efficient industrial program, although in the hands of contractors, was supplying healthy activity to the prisoners. A liberal interpretation of the rules of silence, a careful application of the commutation system, and the practice of granting occasional holidays in the yard to those in good standing had eliminated the necessity for the use of the lash and greatly reduced the problem of discipline. In 1867 Haynes added a good library, an active Sabbath-school program, and a third educational feature in the form of lectures once or twice a month. When in the following year the legislature appropriated $1,000 for these purposes, he purchased schoolbooks and conducted classes for illiterates two evenings a week. There was ample justification for ranking Charlestown as the model state prison in the land in the late sixties.[7]

The best expression of the point of view of wardens awake to their opportunities came from Zebulon Brockway, and Wines and Dwight proclaimed his institution in Detroit the model house of correction. Few men are able to project their future careers so concisely as did Brockway in 1865, revealing as well a clear understanding of the factors that were to bring success.

> I feel [Brockway wrote to Wines] that there are very gross defects in the prison system of the land, and that, as a whole, it does not accomplish its design; and that the time has come for reconstruction. There are doubtless in operation in the prisons of this country, religious and moral agencies, physical and hygienic regulations, and a system of employment for prisoners which if combined in the management of one institution, would produce a model prison indeed. To find them, combine them, and apply them, is, in my mind, the great desidera-

---

[6] Ibid., pp. 145–153, 162–165, 281–286.
[7] Ibid., pp. 154–156, 162–164.

tum. . . . In my own quiet corner here, I am at work at this and trust that by next year the practical operation of our system of labor and partial gradation of prisoners will add at least a mite to the progress of prison reform. . . . This is an age of demonstration, and the practicality of the improvement proposed must be demonstrated at every step to secure its adoption.[8]

Thus the movement enlisted sturdy officers for its field activities. All the congresses, investigations, and reports, all the "I was in prison and ye came unto me" sermons, were significant only in so far as they helped awaken and enrich the experimenting imagination of the wardens and secured for them a free hand, a stable tenure, and public support. But this was service enough for any reformer, since without it enduring progress was impossible. Already Franklin B. Sanborn and Samuel Gridley Howe in Massachusetts, Richard Vaux in Pennsylvania, Dr. Francis Wayland, the elder, in Rhode Island, and less prominent men in other states were busy at the task.

The tour of Wines and Dwight in the summer of 1865 and the organization that winter of the American Association for Promoting the Social Sciences[9] officially launched the movement. By 1868 Wines was able to report that "more has been published in the quarterly, monthly, weekly and daily journals of the country within the last two years than during the ten years preceding."[10] To this literature should be added the comprehensive report of Wines and Dwight, the publications, now fat volumes, of the New York and Pennsylvania prison societies, of the Massachusetts Board of State Charities, and of several special investigating commissions in New Jersey, Pennsylvania, and other states. A growing appreciation of the public's responsibility for its criminals was an encouraging feature of this literature, and the need to place control in capable and nonpartisan hands was clearly expressed.

Organization for Control

The decentralized American democracy was being knit together in post–Civil War days as problems of control received attention in

[8] Ibid., pp. 343–344.
[9] N.Y.P.A., *Report* (1866), p. 35. This organization was later renamed the American Social Science Association.
[10] N.Y.P.A., *Report* (1868), p. 63.

industry and politics, and the fields of charity and correction profited from this trend. A growing concern over poverty, insanity, and crime and a popular reaction to cruelty, debauchery, and corruption acted in varying proportions in different states to prompt the creation of central authorities for inspection and control. Politics, a desire for economy, and the hangover of local traditions frequently retarded developments, but the commanding necessities of housing and other problems pushed reforms ahead in those states where the march of affairs was gaining momentum. Massachusetts, New York, Pennsylvania, Ohio, and Illinois each organized its board of charities before 1879. Rhode Island, Michigan, Wisconsin, and North Carolina quickly followed their example. These boards were to have a quite varied influence on prisons, but the trend toward central control had nevertheless set in.

Civic pride, social righteousness, and public charity have always been considered strong points of the Bay State, but the creation of the Board of State Charities was frankly conceived as a move toward economy. An earlier board of commissioners of charities created in 1856 with restricted authority over almshouses had proved inadequate, and the new board with seven members was organized in 1863 and empowered to investigate all public charitable and correctional institutions in the state and "to recommend such changes and additional provision as they may deem necessary for their economical and efficient administration." Franklin Benjamin Sanborn, neighbor and disciple of Emerson, was chosen secretary, and the venerable Samuel Gridley Howe was shortly made chairman. In the midst of many other responsibilities Sanborn found time to canvass the world's literature for ideas on correction and brought together in a special report on prisons in 1865 the first complete surveys in America of the English ticket-of-leave and the Irish-Crofton systems.[11] Howe and Sanborn quickly made their board the model governmental agency of the decade.

New York had long been struggling with the problem of prison control, but both the board of inspectors and the New York Prison Association had failed to perform this function. The three inspectors, one elected each year, had large powers of control, but in practice each assumed full authority over one of the three prisons

[11] Massachusetts Board of State Charities, *Special Report on Prisons and Prison Discipline* (Boston, 1865).

and proceeded to give his henchmen their share of the jobs, the orders for supplies, and the contracts for labor and construction. In 1859 Governor Morgan had recommended that complete authority be given to one inspector who should be appointed for a long term by the governor. When the legislature failed to act, Morgan undertook to demonstrate the value of the procedure by appointing Amos Pilsbury as his special investigator in 1862; but the regular inspectors blocked the work of even this seasoned veteran, claiming that they, rather than the governor, were responsible for this function. Central responsibility was impossible in such an arrangement.

It was largely due to this impasse that Enoch Wines and Judge Wolfe found the legislature responsive in 1863 to their appeals for funds to aid their inspection of prisons.[12] Good fortune had placed a friend on the board of inspectors and Hubbell as warden of Sing Sing, thus opening prison doors to frequent inspection. When these friends were removed within a year or two, Wines became convinced that progress was impossible while politics was in the saddle. At his suggestion the Association began to prepare for New York's periodic constitutional convention, the reformer's heyday, just around the corner. It named a committee to draft an amendment providing centralized control over the prisons, and Wines and Dwight made their famous tour in order to collect facts and experiences for its use.

This committee, comprised of Dwight, Lieber, Griscom, Gould, and Wines, was supported by Judge William F. Allen and Mayor John T. Hoffman, soon to become governor. They drafted an able amendment, designed to eliminate politics from prison control. A prison commission of five members, one to be appointed every two years for a ten-year term, was to have full charge of all state prisons, to appoint and remove the chief officers, to make regulations and grant orders and contracts. The constitutional convention appointed its own prison committee, and, following Governor Morgan's proposal, a majority of this group recommended a single, all-powerful, prison superintendent; but vigorous lobbying on the part of Wines persuaded the convention to substitute the Association's amendment for that of the committee. With victory so near, it was a

---

[12] N.Y.P.A., *Report* (1870), pp. 157–164. Wines raised $12,770 in 1863, $5,000 each from the city and from the state; the average expenditures of the Association during its first seventeen years had been $2,350.

considerable disappointment when the entire constitution was rejected at the polls in 1869. Nevertheless, a high standard had been raised and an ideal program had received favor and endorsement by a responsible authority; the New York reformers were still optimistic of final success.[13]

Ohio, like New York, was experiencing tremendous development. Her state prison at Columbus, with its 1,050 cells, had the questionable distinction of ranking with Sing Sing as the largest in the land. Already it was becoming crowded. Several attempts to perfect its management culminated in the law of 1867, which applied the New York idea to the board of directors, providing six-year appointments for its three members, one every two years. This body acquired the power to select the major officers, to create the rules, and to let the contracts. Meanwhile the seventy-seven counties with their dilapidated jails urgently needed central supervision, and, following the lead of Massachusetts, Ohio created a state board of charities in 1867. Its five nonsalaried members, appointed for three-year terms, enjoyed powers of inspection and recommendation for all penal and charitable institutions in the state. As no funds were supplied to employ a secretary, the prison lent the services of its chaplain, Albert G. Byers. For several years thereafter this Methodist minister and onetime army chaplain secured free passes on the numerous railroads and traveled his extended circuit throughout the state, visiting jails and almshouses, insane institutions and reform schools, and occasionally returning to his home base at Columbus. In company with the president of his board, Byers visited major institutions in New York, Pennsylvania, and Massachusetts, and worked out a well-considered program for the expansion of the state penal system; their most noteworthy success was in the counties where they stimulated the erection of new structures on a model borrowed in part from Boston.

The favorable reputation of central boards of supervision was spreading, and in 1869 three more states created such boards. In Pennsylvania the Philadelphia Society called attention to the valuable work of the Massachusetts Board, and the legislature finally moved to create a similar one. Unfortunately its influence was dissipated by responsibility for the inspection of all eleemosynary

[13] The New York Board of Charities, created in 1867, does not come into this discussion because it had nothing to do with either jails or prisons.

institutions, and with few powers it could do little more than undertake the education of county and state officers. In Illinois, where the number of state charitable institutions had increased from three to eight during the decade, emphasizing the need for central management, the state created a board of public charities in 1869 with authority to inspect all public institutions except the state prison. Frederick Howard Wines, son of the New York reformer, became secretary for the board, and in succeeding years the county jails and especially the several correctional institutions of Chicago profited greatly from his persistent prodding. In Rhode Island a legislative committee, appointed to consider the state's need for an insane asylum, proposed in 1868 that such an institution be built together with a state house of correction on a state farm and further recommended that a single board be created to supervise them. These proposals met the approval of the legislature, which created a board of charities and correction and gave it not only supervisory authority but full power to establish a new state farm and to manage it thereafter. Thus was created the first board of control in America; its scope was gradually extended as additional institutions were erected on the 400-acre farm, and a decade later, when a new prison was built at the farm, that institution as well was brought under its control.

Other states were shortly to follow these leads, and in the meantime public-spirited citizens were organizing prison societies. Maryland, New Hampshire, and far-western California witnessed the formation of societies on the New York pattern, and at least one, that presided over by G. S. Griffith in Baltimore, was destined to exert considerable influence over local penal developments. Agitation for reform in New Jersey and Indiana found vent in special investigating commissions, but their comprehensive reports suffered from the lack of the follow-up work of the boards of charities in other states. Much more remained to be done in 1870 than was realized at the time, but progress in the direction of central inspection and control had at least been encouraging.

Origin of the Reformatory Program

One of the first results of reorganization was the emergence of a class of men who quickly came to regard themselves as professional penologists. The members of the several boards of supervision, and especially the secretaries, usually saw longer service than the earlier managers had enjoyed, and several of them became active leaders of the reform movement. Enoch Wines and his son Frederick, as well as Richard Vaux, Albert Byers, and G. S. Griffith made their reputations in this work; Franklin Sanborn, the two Francis Waylands, Samuel G. Howe, and Theodore Dwight served the cause faithfully in spite of their larger interests in other fields. Brockway, Cordier, Rice, Haynes, Felton, Vail, and the Pilsburys among the wardens enjoyed longer tenures and advancement from one position to another, partly as a result of the influence of the new controls. These were some of the men that gave the movement form and personality, making its history much more than a statistical abstract.

Among the men who were presuming to show the American public how to reform its criminals, very few considered it necessary to make a protracted study of the problem. They had the feeling that their natural equipment of Christianity and common sense required only the baptism of experience to secure them good standing in the calling. They quoted the Bible to prove the reformability of criminals, but their faith more frequently came out of a warm experience; Brockway was one of many who gained strength at the altar.[14] This element was so prominent in the early days that its importance can scarcely be overestimated; its practical disappearance in the course of the next fifty years was to be a significant factor in the story.

Many of the leaders were already so old in prison service that the new organizations at first brought simply a greater zeal and force to ideas inherited from a century of reformers. Wines and Dwight in their report had applauded several new developments, but most of their attention was directed toward the stimulation of the old programs for education, religion, industrial activity, and human kindness.

Efforts to improve the educational facilities opened weekday classes in Wisconsin, Ohio, and New Hampshire prisons and in the Detroit house of correction. Following the example of Haynes in Massachusetts, these and other state prisons provided occasional

[14]Zebulon R. Brockway, *Fifty Years of Prison Service: An Autobiography* (1912; reprinted Montclair, N.J., 1969), pp. 63–65. Brockway tells about his conversion in Rochester, the "city of revivals," in the late fifties.

lectures on advanced subjects. Connecticut, as well as New York and Pennsylvania, now had instructors going from cell to cell each evening, while many others continued to conduct Sunday-school classes. Prayer meetings, first introduced in 1862, numbered five within a half dozen years. A general improvement of the libraries brought the total number of books in all the prisons up to 15,000 by 1868.

A similar agitation for improved living conditions was showing results. The several boards and societies, especially those of New York, Massachusetts, and Ohio, published elaborate plans for model prisons and jails, and these not only influenced the builders of new prisons or cellhouses but also encouraged the remodeling of old structures. The full-length windows introduced at Charlestown replaced the dingy windows of the old Sing Sing pattern, and most of the prisons installed gas lights. The drive for larger cells and for more adequate ventilation was already active before the New York Prison Association published Dr. Griscom's essay on prison hygiene,[15] but Griscom's argument for a ventilating system that would supply four cubic feet of fresh air per minute to each prisoner appeared to enlist the authority of science behind the reform. Although no prison realized the recommended ideal, the larger cells of the Joliet pattern became the order of the day.[16]

Wines and Dwight hailed with enthusiasm the good-time laws and other innovations discovered on their tour. Commutation of sentences for good behavior quickly spread into twenty-three states by 1869, when only Indiana among northern states had failed to adopt such a law. The New York Association won its first national victory when President Johnson signed a federal commutation act it had sponsored. Meanwhile agitation for the better care of women in prison was prompting the appointment of matrons in an increasing number of prisons. Massachusetts and Michigan removed their women entirely from the state prisons and confined them in local houses of correction. New York continued to maintain its women's prison at Sing Sing as the only separate prison for women in the country; but Wisconsin and Illinois provided women's buildings

[15] John H. Griscom, *Prison Hygiene* (Albany, 1868).

[16] N.Y.P.A., *Report* (1867), pp. 44–65. Incidentally, the cells of Joliet were 7 by 7 feet and contained 196 cubic feet in contrast with the 169 cubic feet in Sing Sing cells, and the 315 cubic feet in the new cells being erected at Elmira.

and yards within the walls of their state prisons, although the latter never used the structure for this purpose. Massachusetts and Indiana were already considering radically new innovations.

This was an era of remarkable prosperity for prison industries. Machines with steam power were replacing the old handicrafts and became for a few years the basis for a healthy prison atmosphere. Many wardens developed a zest for the reformation of their prisoners when successful industries brought freedom from concern over tenure. Growing populations at first favored the industries by supplying more laborers and reducing overhead costs, but the prisons soon became congested, thus seriously handicapping efficient production. At the same time protests were arising again from the struggling labor organizations, and both the professional reformers and their sympathizers began to criticize the profiteering contractors.[17] Meanwhile the problems of overcrowded cells and congested factories joined to supply the urge that prompted several states to build new institutions, thus providing the reformers with a fighting chance to win the adoption of some of their best ideals during the succeeding decade.

In other words, there was a native substance to the reform movement, a program and a technique that was growing up within the four gray walls of American prisons. But this was only part of the story. While most of the new leaders were men of affairs, depending on their common sense and the heritage of tradition, a few of them, notably Wines and Sanborn, sought far and wide for new methods and theories. The movement was in this way considerably enriched and stimulated by foreign influences.

The expanding horizon of Dr. Wines was characteristic of the movement. His first reports reveal a close study of the earlier reports of his Association and the Boston Society and disclose a knowledge of the writings of the European critics of the 1830s. By 1864 Wines was corresponding with the venerable Frenchmen, Lucas, Tocqueville, and Beaumont, and with the English inspector of prisons,

---

[17] E. T. Hiller, "Labor Unionism and Convict Labor," *Journal of Criminal Law and Criminology* 5 (1915): 851–879.

[18] Walter L. Clay, *The Prison Chaplain: A Memoir of the Rev. John Clay, With Selections from His Reports and Correspondence and a Sketch of Prison Discipline in England* (1861; reprinted Montclair, N.J., 1969).

Colonel Jebb. The following year he prepared a paper on the "Progress of Prison Reform in England," using the excellent memoir of John Clay as a prime source.[18] Wines did not begin to correspond with the Hill brothers, Sir William Crofton, or Mary Carpenter, until after his extended tour of American prisons, and his first reaction to their ideas was colored by the prejudices of his first English correspondent, Colonel Jebb. Beginning in 1866, however, the reports of the New York Society were full of Crofton's system. Gaylord Hubbell, former warden of Sing Sing, while on a trip to Europe in that year made a special visit to the Irish prisons, and his account beggared the most enthusiastic reports of its European friends. During the next decade all the descriptions and criticisms of American prisons by Wines and his Society were strongly under the influence of the Irish ideal.[19]

This was not the first knowledge of the Irish system to reach America. As early as 1856 the *Journal of Prison Discipline*, still a liberal quarterly as edited by Frederick A. Packard, had a note on the ticket-of-leave idea; two years later it presented a fair discussion of the Irish system. The merits of the new methods were recognized, but even the liberal Pennsylvanians could see no possibility of improving their system, and nothing more was heard of Ireland.[20] The real apostle of the Irish system was the young Emersonian, Franklin B. Sanborn. As secretary of the Massachusetts Board of State Charities he learned of Crofton's work sometime during 1864 or 1865, thus antedating Wines by a few months. But the matter of priority of discovery was not so important; it was in the zeal of his apostleship that Sanborn excelled. His impatience for a demonstration of the ideal in Massachusetts produced no little hard feeling in Charlestown, proud of having the best prison in the land.

The Maconochie-Hill-Crofton group had more influence on the

[19]The influence on Americans of English writings during this era must not be overlooked. Preeminent among these were the works of Mary Carpenter, notably *Our Convicts* (1864; reprinted Montclair, N.J., 1969) and *Reformatory Prison Discipline: As Developed by the Rt. Hon. Sir Walter Crofton in the Irish Convict Prisons* (1872; reprinted Montclair, N.J., 1967); Walter L. Clay's memoir of his father *The Prison Chaplain*, cited above; Frederic Hill, *Crime: Its Amount, Causes, and Remedies* (London, 1853); and Matthew Davenport Hill, *Suggestions for the Repression of Crime* (1857; reprinted Montclair, N.J., 1975).

[20]*Journal of Prison Discipline and Philanthropy* 11 (January 1856): 53; ibid., 13 (January 1858): 16–25. From Volume 1 through Volume 11 (1845–1856) this journal was called *Pennsylvania Journal of Prison Discipline and Philanthropy*.

development of penology in the New World than in the Old. While the forms of this system were adopted in several places in Europe, they were shortly discarded or corrupted. America, on the other hand, never exactly copied the Irish system, but its methods and theory of punishment came at just the right time to enrich and inspire a strong native movement. The Americans were the aggressors; their movement appropriated these foreign theories and made them the basis of its new gospel. The grading of criminals according to the degree of reformation; the use of a mark system as a check on this process and as a restraint against disorders; the recognition of religion, education, and congregate labor as reformatory agents; and finally the release on ticket-of-leave as soon as reformed—no single one of these measures was wholly new to America. Crofton's significant service was to combine them into a unified experiment on adult prisoners.[21] His achievement fired the imaginations of American reformers and provided a new pattern free from the old rivalry between the Auburn and Pennsylvania systems. The new pattern was fortunately in harmony with American trends and helped to knit them together into an elaborate reformatory program.

The humanitarian idealism of the forties came to dominate the movement, supplying it with a charitable attitude toward the criminal. The frequent use by Wines of the term "backsliders" rather than "sinners" when referring to convicts was indicative of the changed attitude that regarded prisoners as potential citizens deserving to be educated for the society into which they were to be released as soon as their satisfactory readjustment was assured. This last conception, although arising as a common-sense interpretation of the function of imprisonment, made a clean break from the traditional ideal of justice, which sought to make the punishment fit the crime. The elaborate legal and judicial technique that had grown up in the administration of the older ideal stubbornly resisted the advance of the newer conception; yet several practical modifications of the older procedure helped prepare the way for the adoption of the reformatory sentence in the next era.

[21] Walter Crofton, *A Few Remarks on the Convict Question* (Dublin, 1857); Max Grunhut, *Penal Reform: A Comparative Study* (1848; reprinted Montclair, N.J., 1972), pp. 83–88.

The free use of the pardoning power, long a vicious feature of state government, was steadily undermining the tradition that courts should mete out carefully measured sentences for specific crimes. Reformers, seeking to modify the effects of the system on prison discipline, proposed that at least politics might be eliminated by the creation of pardon boards, but many feared that such a recognition of the power would encourage jail-deliveries. Massachusetts re-enacted in 1867 an old common-law provision for conditional pardon, and this attempt to curb one of the dangers of too frequent pardons provided an instructive precedent for the parole laws of the next generation.

The increasing concern for discharged prisoners was likewise important in this connection. In 1866 Massachusetts provided a special agent to visit the boys and girls released on permits from its juvenile institutions. Regular police officers had previously performed this function in Ireland and a few other places, but Gardiner Tufts, the new agent, was the first special parole officer, and in 1869, when he was further directed to inspect the cases of children before trial, he acquired probationary functions as well. The humanitarian labors of John Augustus, dating back to 1841, when he had first "bailed out" the Boston jail, had antedated the probationary functions of Gardiner Tufts, but when Augustus was made state agent to aid the discharged, his energies had been diverted. Thus the recognition of the state's responsibility to supervise the readjustment of released offenders first developed under Gardiner Tufts in connection with the evolution of juvenile treatment in the late 1860s; it was not to be many decades before all criminals would gain the status of state wards.[22]

This new attitude received its first application to cases of drunkenness, vagrancy, and prostitution. It was becoming clear that the states, in branding liquor and certain practices as social evils, forfeited the right to hold the victims entirely responsible. Again a Massachusetts law of 1866 led the way by authorizing magistrates to release persons committed to houses of correction for vagrancy as soon as such an individual "had reformed and is willing and desirous to return to an orderly course of life."[23] In 1869 Rhode

[22] Warren F. Spalding, "Colonel Gardiner Tufts," *Proceedings* (N.P.A., 1891), pp. 263–266.

[23] Massachusetts Board of State Charities, *Report* (1870), p. 13. The earlier law of 1860 had suggested this provision, but its vague instructions had not been applied.

Island established its state house of correction and conferred the power to release reformed inmates on the board of state charities and correction.[24]

Meanwhile, working with a similar class of prisoners in Detroit, Brockway complained of the futility of short sentences. Two years of agitation finally secured the adoption in 1869 of his famous "three year law" giving him the power to detain Detroit women sent up for sex offenses until they were reformed—not exceeding three years. Brockway had urged in behalf of the law:

> Experience has demonstrated that to sentence such persons (prostitutes, vagrants, confirmed pilferers, and those whose persons and appetites are beyond their control), to imprisonment for definite periods of time frequently subverts the purpose in view. . . . To commit these persons to the House of Correction until they are reformed will be a strong inducement for them to enter immediately upon the work of self-improvement.[25]

These developments, as well as the commutation laws, were all pointing in the direction of reformatory sentences. They were deviations from the simple method by which a blindfolded goddess was supposed to measure out punishment in proportion to the gravity of the offense. They had come about as practical adjustments to actual problems, but they were disjointed practices, foreign to the system of which they purported to be a part. It remained for the leaders of the reform movement, inspired by liberal theories, to coordinate them into a new reformatory system.

Possibly some of these beginnings had been stimulated by foreign theories. Sanborn had advocated the Irish system a year before the Massachusetts vagrancy law was adopted. But it was a far jump from the one system to the other; the Irish program dealt only with long-term prisoners, and after 1864 it had lost its indeterminate-sentence clause and was stressing the reformatory discipline of its intermediate prison; Massachusetts, on the other hand, was facing a totally different problem with a very special class of prisoners. In Detroit

---

[24] Rhode Island Board of State Charities and Correction, *Report* (1870), p. 24. The board asserted that "The object of the sentence to the Workhouse is not punishment but reformation. . . . The persons committed are the wards of the State and the sole object of their commitment should be reformation. It is not expected that those committed will remain for the whole term of their sentence, and in practice this is rarely the fact."

[25] Detroit House of Correction, *Report* (1868), pp. 11–12.

Brockway cited English precedents in recommending his house of shelter in 1868 but did not refer to the Irish developments in connection with his three-year law.[26] These vagrancy laws meanwhile had a long ancestry, and plenty of precedents could be found in English and colonial law for the principles here adopted. The significant point was that these ideas were now applied to offenders against newly enacted laws by officers who were soon to be in a position to extend the application of these principles to a broader class of criminals.

The far-reaching significance of these practical developments did not appear, however, until foreign theories helped to enliven American thinking. This was notably true in the case of Enoch Wines and Franklin Sanborn. The latter had not been advocating tickets-of-leave very long before he discovered the little-used conditional-pardon law and hailed it as a possible means to his end. In 1867 he secured an amendment of the law, giving the warden the responsibility to recommend candidates for such pardon and the duty to order the arrest of any released man who failed to conform to the conditions imposed. Gideon Haynes, fearful of showing favoritism, hesitated to assume the responsibility, and the governor's council proved unable to resist demands for full pardon, so that it was several years before a workable parole system was developed. But the reform was gaining support elsewhere, and in 1869 Enoch Wines rejoiced to note that recommendations had been introduced in the Michigan, New York, and Ohio legislatures favoring the indeterminate sentence. His report quoted with pleasure from the official message of the kindly governor of Ohio, Rutherford B. Hayes:

> It may seem to be in advance of the present day, but it is, as we believe, but anticipating an event not far distant, to suggest that sentences for crime, instead of being for a definite period, especially in cases of repeated convictions, will, under proper restrictions, be made

[26] Among the Brockway papers deposited in the Russell Sage Foundation Library in New York was a copy of Joseph Adshead's *Prisons and Prisoners* (London, 1845) with occasional marginal notes by Brockway; these notes were possibly made at the time of his first reading of the work, evidently in 1860. While Adshead urged the adoption of grades, tickets-of-leave, rewards for good discipline, and industrial training, Brockway's notes are all related to the attack on solitary confinement as a sufficient aid to redemption. Of course this would not prevent the natural infiltration of the other and more constructive ideas.

to depend on the reformation and established good character of the convict.[27]

Antecedents of the Reformatory

A movement begins to reveal real strength when costly institutions are erected and dedicated to its ends. The excellent discipline of Haynes at Charlestown and Hubbell at Sing Sing passed away with these wardens, but the building of Elmira Reformatory was a lasting achievement. The American reformatory institution was a mutation resulting from the junction of developments in two distinct classes of prisons. A growing demand that the states undertake the reformation of misdemeanants encouraged the creation of institutions on the pattern of the better local houses of correction. In some instances the agitation resulted in distinct institutions of this character; more frequently it combined with a growing campaign to remove the youthful offenders from the state prisons, thus producing the typical adult reformatory. The enthusiasm for the indeterminate sentence and the other correctional devices predisposed the leaders to favor the development of special institutions where these methods could be applied under the most favorable conditions. Finally it was the insistent demand for more adequate prison accommodations that provided the opportunity for the creation of a radically new type of institution.

The remarkable developments at the Detroit house of correction made significant contributions to the development of adult reformatories. This institution had resulted from agitation begun by prominent citizens in 1856 against the abuses and expenses of the local jail. Brockway's reputation as the head of the self-supporting Monroe County (New York) penitentiary had spread, and he was called to Detroit in 1861 as the first superintendent to organize the new enterprise. The first concern was the industrial program, and for this Brockway was well fitted; but the young superintendent had recently gained a strong religious conception of the higher nature of his calling. With the cooperation of sympathetic friends in the city, he promised jobs to all who maintained good disciplinary records and in 1865 granted wages for over-stint production. Brockway organized a Sunday school for the men and helped the matron establish an evening school for the women; in 1866 he called a

[27] N.Y.P.A., *Report* (1869), p. 162.

chaplain to his assistance and provided morning chapel services in both departments. Most significant of all, he developed an experimental grading system in the women's branch in 1865, the first application of the theory to adults in America.[28]

But all these efforts were greatly handicapped by the short terms of confinement, and accordingly Brockway began the campaign for longer sentences which resulted in the three-year law of 1869. A house of shelter, opened adjacent to the prison in this year, provided a home where discharged women could labor until they found respectable positions. This he soon converted into a secondary prison to which the better behaved women could be removed and detained under a more liberal and homelike discipline until the expiration of their sentences. It became in a sense the first women's reformatory in America. With the able assistance of Miss Emma Hall, the head of the house of refuge, and of Professor H. S. Tarbell, superintendent of the union schools of Detroit, Brockway, by providing lectures of lyceum character and experimenting with reading assignments, made his educational department more than a dull reading-and-writing school. When his proposed comprehensive indeterminate-sentence law was defeated in 1871, Brockway resigned, but the institution was so well established that, in spite of the abandonment of the house of shelter, it continued for many decades as one of the outstanding penal institutions in the country.

These houses of correction were essentially city rather than county institutions. Even in Massachusetts only the two or three counties containing large cities developed institutions worthy of the name, notably the Boston house of correction on Deer Island. They were largely concerned with drunkenness, vagrancy, and prostitution—offenses against local order and decency, social evils for which society considered itself in part responsible. Just as in the case of public education, so now in jail reform the cities were the first to assume responsibility; nevertheless, Francis Wayland agitated for a state house of correction in Rhode Island, and a few other states considered such proposals. Massachusetts was the first to establish a state workhouse when it appropriated the almshouse at Bridgewater for this purpose in 1866. Other New England states followed this lead, partly because most of the laws there gave more attention to this kind of offender, and partly because states were small enough to

[28] Brockway, *Fifty Years*, pp. 58–125.

permit the gathering of short-term prisoners to one site without bankrupting the state with transportation charges. The proposals brought forward in other states did not get very far at this time.[29]

The other root idea of the reformatory had gained recognition in America as early as 1822 when the Society for the Prevention of Pauperism had proposed that criminal youths should be taken out of the penitentiaries. The reform schools that resulted were primarily for misdemeanants although the judges had usually been given discretionary authority to commit very young criminals there as well. Several states had made sixteen the minimum age at which a person could be convicted of crime, but the first legislative recognition of a class of young male criminals occurred in 1856 when New York directed that all under twenty-one years who were convicted of the first offense should be sent to the local penitentiary where such existed. By 1872 there were three hundred young men segregated in this way. When the Detroit house of correction was being erected, Michigan adopted a law committing all its male first offenders under twenty-one to this institution; however, a judge of the state Supreme Court declared the law unconstitutional, and Brockway's experiments with this class were delayed until 1877.

The Empire State with its teeming criminal classes was the cradle for the adult reformatory. In 1863, anticipating the end of the war and a flooding of the prisons, A. B. Tappen, one of the state inspectors, proposed the building of a new institution. After collaborating with the leaders of the Prison Association he suggested that it be called a state penitentiary and be used as an intermediate link between the county penitentiaries and the state prisons, and further that it might house the younger and less vicious criminals without elaborate walls or bars in a location where convenient industries would supply a valuable training. The Association endorsed the proposal suggesting the addition of a grading system and rewards. The reformers gradually elaborated their ideal until in 1868 they saw it as an opportunity to introduce the Irish system and to create a truly model institution.

Forced to action by the expanding prison populations, the legislature created a commission to select a site and recommend plans for a reformatory. Theodore Dwight and Gaylord Hubbell

[29]Wines and Dwight, *Prisons*, pp. 337–338; Brockway, *Fifty Years*, pp. 86–135.

were both named to the commission, thus assuring the influence of the Association. A 250-acre farm outside of Elmira was chosen for the site, and a most progressive program was outlined in the report of the commissioners to the legislature in 1869:

> It is apparent that the law under which we act [said the Commissioners] does not contemplate simply another State Prison. In referring to a reformatory we assume that the design of the Legislature was that there should be a selection from the mass of convicted criminals, of such persons as are most likely to yield to reformatory influences. . . . We recommend that no person be sentenced to the proposed reformatory whose age is less than sixteen or more than thirty years, or who shall be known to have been previously convicted of any felonious offense. . . . He [the inmate] will learn that a record will be kept from day to day of his conduct, and that it will be made to tell in his favor. . . . Privileges will be conceded to him. . . . A portion of his earnings may be set aside for his use on the expiration of his sentence. . . . It has been a favorite theory . . . of Mr. Recorder [Matthew Davenport] Hill of England that criminals should be sentenced not for a definite term of years, as at present, but until they are reformed, which may, of course, turn out to be for life. While we do not propose to recommend this rule in full, yet we think that it has much to commend it in principle and that it may safely be tried in a modified form.[30]

The commissioners further recommended that a special agent be appointed to supervise the young men after their release until their final discharge. One of the most valuable proposals was that the institution be placed under the control of a nonpartisan commission to be organized along the line of the Association's proposed prison commission. Thus all the best ideas of the day were woven into the plans for Elmira reformatory. Unfortunately financial difficulties in the state delayed construction, and the institution was not opened until 1877.

Nevertheless, the prison-reform movement appeared at full flood in 1870. The gradually accumulating heritage of a half century of builders and reformers had been enlivened by a new spirit since the war. A rapid increase in the number of convicts had forced prison problems before the public eye. New and impartial agencies of inspection had brought a clearer understanding to the problem.

[30] Commissioners of New York State Reformatory, *Report* (1870), pp. 2–3.

Foreign experiments had been hailed as showing the way for a more satisfactory solution of the difficult task of reforming criminals. Scattered achievements in a few state prisons and in several progressive city institutions were adding to the enthusiasm of optimistic idealists. One very considerable undertaking had already been endorsed by New York State, and great things were expected from the new reformatory being erected at Elmira. Great things were hoped for all along the line, and all that these forces seemed to lack was a central coordinating agency to direct their proper fulfilment. Enoch Wines was already planning a vast gathering at Cincinnati which should formally inaugurate the new era. Nobody suspected the disillusionment just around the corner.

[For Bibliographic Note see end of Chapter 4.]

4.

COURSE OF THE
MOVEMENT:
1870–1880

The imagination of Enoch Wines had been stirred by the widespread clamor for reform. Inspiring theories quickened his spirit. He would not have been true to himself had he been content, after his tour of 1865, to settle down quietly in Bible House, New York. His thoughts soared above annual reports into a glamorous dream of a world organization in which conscientious leaders of all nations would join to plan an ideal prison system. And indeed the records reveal how he carried his American and European friends off their feet with him and how, in the space of a few years, they convened several congresses and sent resounding calls for prison reform around the world. But these men overestimated the power of the idea. The organizations they established were poorly designed to force their theories upon governments, and the first suggestion of their futility practically disbanded them. The death of the bolder leaders left to the generation that followed little but a heritage of idealistic programs set forth in a voluminous literature. Nevertheless, a few younger men had gathered inspiration from the heights and were patiently building for the future.

Organization of the Movement

Wines determined that the first step toward an international gathering of prison reformers was the organization of an American association sufficiently representative to call such a convention.[1] In response to an inquiry sent out in 1868, forty replies from various states favored the gathering of a national congress. The New York and Philadelphia societies hesitated to assume responsibility, but Wines and a few friends took the initiative and sent invitations to all parts of the country for a congress on prison reform to meet in Cincinnati in 1870.[2] Governor Rutherford B. Hayes welcomed the 130-odd delegates who gathered from twenty-four states, Canada, and South America. Wardens, chaplains, judges, governors, and humanitarians—they made a distinguished assembly; and the conspicuous absence of the eastern Pennsylvanians freed the convention from the usual acrimonious debate over the rivalries of the fathers. Indeed, the delegates concerned themselves largely with the future, and after eagerly discussing many papers and addresses they unanimously adopted a declaration of principles so forward-looking that for several decades their successors were able neither to better it in theory nor to exhaust its possibilities in practice.

There were some very remarkable papers among the forty presented to the congress. Several had been written by English and French reformers, but the majority were by budding American penologists. The Irish system was ably described by its foremost developer, Sir Walter Crofton, as well as by its enthusiastic American admirers, Sanborn and Hubbell; Matthew Davenport Hill sent a fine paper on the indeterminate sentence, elucidating its theoretical aspects. Such age-old problems as executive pardon, jail systems, aftercare of juveniles and adults, and prison hygiene

[1] National Congress on Penitentiary and Reformatory Discipline at Cincinnati, *Transactions* (New York, 1870), pp. 253, 267–275. The earlier international congresses on prison reform—the first at Frankfort-on-Main in 1846, the second at Brussels in 1847, and the third and last again at Frankfort in 1857—undoubtedly influenced the thought of Enoch Wines. Other unofficial gatherings had discussed international standards for statistics of crime and charity at Brussels in 1853, Paris in 1855, Vienna in 1857, and London in 1860. The United States was represented only at the first Frankfort congress, where Louis Dwight, its sole delegate, won few if any converts.

[2] "Minutes of the Acting Committee of the Philadelphia Society," manuscript (Philadelphia Society Library, 1867–1873), pp. 125–128, 146–151. These records show the cool reception Wines received from this old society at the same time that his own associates in New York were hesitating to act. Nevertheless, such diverse leaders as Daniel C. Gilman, F. B. Sanborn, Theodore Dwight and Amos Pilsbury endorsed the call for the convention.

received considerable attention. Dr. Wines, true to his major purpose for convening the congress, read a paper advocating an international gathering.

The most able address of them all, however, was Brockway's "Ideal for a True Prison System for a State." Here the best thinking of the New York group and of the foreign experimenters was gathered into one system along with the practical experience of a skilled administrator. Brockway proposed that a nonpolitical commission, such as that recommended in New York, be created and given full power to build and control juvenile reform schools, district reformatories or houses of correction, reception prisons for male adults in which each convict would be examined and the incorrigibles retained for life while the others would be transferred to industrial or intermediate reformatories, and lastly reformatories for women. He recommended that discipline be regulated by grades and marks and that these be administered in connection with indeterminate sentences so as to release each prisoner as soon as he was reformed. Brockway's paper, with its inspiring ideals full of revolutionary significance, soon became the center of a stormy discussion; in the end the declaration of principles approved most of his recommendations.[3]

The convention was in the hands of reformers who had arrived with prepared speeches while the traditions had no spokesmen. Overwhelmed with inspired addresses, with prayer and song and much exhortation, even the hardheaded wardens were carried up for a mountaintop experience.[4] In their enthusiasm for the ideal they rose above the monotony of four gray walls, men in stripes shuffling

[3]Cincinnati Congress, *Transactions* (1870), p. 54. Brockway recommended that "all persons in a state, who are convicted of crimes before a competent court, shall be deemed wards of the state, and shall be committed to the custody of the board of guardians until, in their judgment, they may be returned to society with ordinary safety and in accord with their own highest welfare."

[4]National Prison Association, *Proceedings* (1887), pp. 311–312. Brockway at this time looks back over the seventeen years intervening and recalls that at Cincinnati in 1870 he had had an experience similar to that of the disciples on the Mount of Transfiguration. He had felt himself strengthened by "a mysterious, almighty, Spiritual force. . . I was going to have a grand success . . . but it did not work. . . . I found that there was a commonplace work of education to do with these persons whom I hoped to inspire. . . .That did not suffice. The industrial training of prisoners was taken up, and that is drudgery. Getting down to drudgery, and even lower than that. . . ." Thus he warns the younger men that hard work must follow inspiration.

in lockstep, sullen faces staring through the bars, coarse mush and coffee made of bread crusts, armed sentries stalking the walls. They forgot it all and voted for their remarkable declaration of principles: Society is responsible for the reformation of criminals; education, religion, and industrial training are valuable aids in this undertaking; discipline should build rather than destroy the self-respect of each prisoner; his cooperation can best be secured with an indeterminate sentence under which his discharge is regulated by a merit system; the responsibility of the state extends into the field of preventive institutions and to the aid and supervision of prisoners after discharge; a central state control should be established so as to secure a stable, nonpolitical administration, trained officers, and reliable statistics.

Wines was in fine feather when the leaders of the convention and prominent men throughout the nation signed up as charter members of the National Prison Association. Congress was persuaded to adopt a resolution inviting the nations of the world to send delegates to an international congress on prison reform to meet in London in 1872, and an appropriation of $5,000 was made to provide for a commissioner to carry forward the American part of the program. Wines resigned his New York post in order to accept the secretaryship of the new Association and the appointment as United States commissioner tendered him by President Grant. In his new capacity Wines made a special visit to many of the European capitals and national penitentiaries in 1871, and it was largely as a result of his campaign that twenty-two nations sent official representatives and a total of four hundred delegates gathered from all parts of the world to London in July of 1872.

The Americans took a prominent part in the sessions. Representatives from nineteen states joined Wines, and when the voluntary visitors were added the delegation totaled seventy. Several European countries and Japan as well were stimulated to new efforts in behalf of their convicts. But the Americans who contributed so much to the congress were able to take back from the meetings little more than the satisfaction to be derived from the delegates' halfhearted endorsement of their Irish gospel. The numerous reports made to the legislatures, including that of Wines to Congress, might have produced larger results had it not been for the changing economic and political scene of the mid seventies. Nevertheless, the London congress had all the appearances of a glorious success when the National Prison Association gathered in its second convention six months later.[5]

Horatio Seymour, governor of New York, presided over representatives of twenty-one states gathered at Baltimore. As corresponding secretary Wines had invited Mary Carpenter and Sir Walter Crofton, the British experts on juvenile and reformatory techniques, to submit papers which he read to the assembled delegates. He had invited each state to prepare a report on its penal developments and to designate a representative to present it. Twenty-five states and the territory of Utah complied, and the reading of their reports added to the interest and substance of the four-day congress. The congress made no attempt to draft a new set of principles, for the declarations at Cincinnati and London were quite satisfactory to the leaders. Moreover, with the largest delegation hailing this time from Pennsylvania, some dissension had developed on certain principles, and neither faction wished to risk a challenge to its faith.[6]

Brockway, absent because of sickness, sent a report for the committee on prison discipline urging the indeterminate sentence with conditional release under police supervision, but this time, in the discussion that followed, the weight of opinion was on the side of older traditions.[7] Richard Vaux, chairman of the directors of Cherry Hill, and delegates from Ohio, Missouri, and New Jersey assailed the proposals with vigor. Dr. Wines as secretary reported the proceedings, but most of his friends of Cincinnati and London were absent, and he found himself and his program somewhat pushed aside by the new men representing the changing authorities in the states. Yet the Baltimore meetings brought the varied reformers,

[5] The International Congress was held in London, July 3–13, 1872, and was called the International Congress on the Prevention and Repression of Crime, Including Penal and Reformatory Treatment. For reports of the congress see Edwin Pears, ed., *Prisons and Reformatories at Home and Abroad: Being the Transactions of the International Penitentiary Congress* (London 1872) and Enoch Cobb Wines, *Report of the International Penitentiary Congress of London* (Washington, 1873) [to which is added] E. C. Wines, ed., *Transactions of the National Prison Reform Congress: Held at Baltimore, Maryland, January 21–24, 1873, Being the Second Annual Meeting of the National Prison Association of the United States* (Baltimore, 1873).

[6] For the reports of the twenty-five states and the territory of Utah see E. C. Wines, ed., *Transactions* (Baltimore, 1873), pp. 375–460.

[7] Wines, ed., *Transactions*, pp. 331–336.

practical administrators, and responsible political leaders from many states onto the same platform and despite divergent views prompted an agreement to meet a year later in St. Louis.

The St. Louis congress represented a bold effort by Wines and his followers to press their reforms on a hostile frontier. Invited by Governor Woodson's spokesman at Baltimore to come to Missouri and see a modernized lease system in operation, the National Prison Association accepted and held its third reform congress in St. Louis in May 1874. In the absence of Governor Seymour, Richard Vaux was elected president and presided over a succession of lively meetings in which papers by American and foreign reformers were delivered and debated. So animated was the discussion, with twenty-three varied prison officials rising to express their views on the question of prison discipline on the first day, that the congress was not able to hear all the papers submitted and accepted thirteen for publication in its official transactions.[8]

The published *Transactions* provided perhaps the most significant contribution of the St. Louis congress. Indeed the volume recalls the monumental *Report* of Wines and Dwight published seven years before. Instead of devoting two sessions as at Baltimore to state reports, Wines prepared a lengthy summary for publication describing the prisons of thirty-seven states and two territories, quoting in each case from official reports or the governor's message, and in many instances adding his commendation or criticism as the subject seemed to warrant. He followed this review of the state prisons with a similar account of the houses of correction in eleven states and the reform schools in these and ten additional states and the District of Columbia. The pious flavor of the comments and strictures of Dr. Wines must have grated on the sensibilities of some officials, but the candor with which he wrote and the assurance with which he accepted and praised reports by local chaplains, telling for example of the prayer meetings held daily in Connecticut prisons or reporting that every inmate of Oregon State Prison had read his Bible from cover to cover at least once during the year, serves to document a reform era now a full century past. That Wines was in

[8]National Prison Association, Enoch C. Wines, ed., *Transactions of the Third [1874] National Prison Reform Congress: Being the Third Annual Report of the National Prison Association of the United States* (New York, 1874), pp. 157–272. The congress was held in St. Louis, May 13–16, 1874.

step with his age is demonstrated by a report from the chaplain of the state prison in Wisconsin who told of a prison church organized in 1867 which had admitted 183 convicts into full membership and was happy to report that only one of the 101 discharged had backslid and been sentenced to another prison.[9]

But if the zeal Wines displayed for certain religious practices appears dated, his respect for objective data was equally strong and resulted in the preparation of a succession of invaluable tables. Of each of the forty-four state prisons we learn not only the number and size of their cells, the number and nativity of their inhabitants, the character and value of their products, and the nature of their educational and religious practices, but also the type and frequency of disciplinary punishments. In comments following the tables Wines does not hesitate to record his criticism of the six states that entrusted their convicts to leasees, of the seven that had a mixed lease and contract system, and of the several states that gave the contractors almost a free hand in the labor of their inmates. But he does note that ten of the eleven states that reported earnings in excess of expenditures had prisons that merited commendation in other respects as well.[10] Similar tables on the houses of correction and reform schools show the institutional and reformatory advances already achieved in the urbanized states of the North and East.[11]

The Fourth National Prison Congress met in New York City in June 1876. With Governor Seymour again in the chair and Dr. Wines securely in charge, it devoted its major attention to plans for the International Congress to be held at Stockholm in 1878. Several sessions and over half of the pages in its published *Transactions* were devoted to reports of prison conditions and developments in foreign lands. These reports, supplying details on most of the countries of Europe and on Brazil in South America, displayed the broad extent of the movement Dr. Wines had launched. But the papers that elicited the greatest interest, as displayed by the number of delegates who rose to add to the discussion, were several dealing with American problems. Enoch Wines and his son Frederick and

[9] Ibid., pp. 273–466; see especially pp. 285, 352, 372.
[10] Ibid., pp. 375–389.
[11] Ibid., pp. 415–418, 454–463.

Franklin Sanborn each contributed one or more papers, as did two chaplains and the secretaries of three local prison reform societies, while several wardens spoke up in the discussion periods that followed. They were especially interested in the papers on prison discipline, reformatory techniques in juvenile institutions, and programs of industrial training. Aid to the discharged and the care of women in prison were likewise discussed. But in the excitement over the forthcoming international gathering at Stockholm plans for a fifth meeting of the National Prison Congress were forgotten.[12]

Legislative Achievements

After all, the real goal of the reformers was not the national organization, with its mutual edification, but the reformation of prisoners. The program envisaged the enactment of new and more liberal methods of punishment, the erection of prisons suitable for the new objects of confinement, and the practical development of a reformatory discipline under stable administrations. The central association, with all its high-flown speechmaking, was much less important in the struggle of the various states toward these ends than the plodding local bodies.

Unfortunately the state boards of charities, although they increased in number during the seventies, failed to fulfil the expectations of their founders, at least in respect to state penal institutions. Michigan, Wisconsin, and Connecticut were the first to create such boards during this era, and, like most of their predecessors, their major concern was the inspection of county institutions. Kansas, on the other hand, created a board of trustees of state charitable institutions, but this board of control had no authority over the prison. This shift toward control was characteristic of the period, although it was not carried into effect in many states for some time.[13]

Franklin Sanborn had early recognized the need for real control

[12]National Prison Association, Enoch C. Wines, ed., *Transactions of the Fourth* [1876] *National Prison Reform Congress: Being the Fourth Annual Report of the National Prison Association of the United States* (New York, 1877). See also Peter P. Lejins, "Penal Reform and the American Correctional Association," *Proceedings* (A.C.A., 1957), pp. 8–22. I am indebted to Dean Lejins for the discovery of the published *Transactions* of the Fourth National Prison Congress.

[13]Anderson W. Clark, *State Control and Supervision of Charities* (Lincoln, Neb., 1905).

over all the prisons of Massachusetts, and his first report had recommended the creation of a responsible prison commission. Various conditions, especially the plight of the female prisoners, forced the general court to act, and a prison commission was created in 1871. Its original powers were, however, limited to local correctional institutions and responsibility for the care of the women, and not until the reorganization of 1879 was its authority extended to include the prison. Massachusetts thus achieved a centralized system of management for its prisons that was rivaled only by that of its tiny neighbor, Rhode Island, when the erection of a new prison on the state farm in 1879 brought all charitable and correctional institutions under the responsible control of the state board.[14]

Meanwhile reformers in New York did not accept as final the defeat of 1869 when the entire constitution had been rejected. Governor Hoffman as well as Enoch Wines proposed that the prison amendment be submitted separately for a popular vote. While the legislature procrastinated, the county penitentiaries, under stable administrations and largely free from politics, continued to defray their expenses in sharp contrast to the growing deficits of the three state prisons, mounting as they did from $366,000 in 1867 to $588,000 in 1874. Accordingly, when the amendment was finally submitted and approved, the model commission of five, aiming primarily at nonpolitical statesmanship, was discarded in favor of the more efficient single superintendent. Other factors, such as the scandals centering around the old Canal Commission, had made the public suspicious of such independent bodies. The withdrawal of Wines from the New York Association and the death of other prominent leaders weakened the influence of the disinterested reformers and permitted the politicians to centralize the system without freeing it from party control. Louis D. Pilsbury, son of the "Nestor," was to make a creditable financial record as the first superintendent, but that was about the extent of his control over state prisons, and he had no jurisdiction over the many and important local institutions.

Meanwhile the trend toward centralization was scarcely evident in

[14] Massachusetts Board of State Charities, *Reports* (1866, 1870, 1875, 1879); Massachusetts Prison Commissioners, *Report* (1879).

the remaining states. The Ohio board of charities, failing to secure financial support, discontinued its activities during several critical years, and, when it was revived by Governor Hayes in 1876 and a salary of $1,200 provided for its hardworking secretary, the board had to remain content with its former powers of inspection. The North Carolina board likewise failed to gain financial support and remained dormant for many years; no other state in the South made even a beginning in this direction for another decade. New Jersey and Indiana were equally inattentive to their needs for central control, while Illinois failed to bring its state prisons within the scope of the board of charities, and its citizens remained ignorant of many evils in these supposedly model institutions. Only California, by a reorganization in 1880 in which it adopted verbatim the New York Association's model for a nonpolitical commission, acquired a system of control that ranked it with the more efficient states of the Northeast.[15]

Nevertheless, the waning of the national movement and the failure of many states to achieve central control over their prisons did not entirely check the advance of the new ideology. Both the belief that criminals would become better prisoners with the assurance of friendly assistance after their discharge, and the theory that they should be discharged as soon as they were reformed, gained increasing favor, and the country was prepared for an endorsement of these programs in later decades.

The discharged prisoners received increasing attention from both state officers and charitable societies during the seventies. While several prisons slightly enlarged the meager sums designed to provide an outfit and a ticket home for each of its discharged, Pennsylvania in 1870 supplied funds to employ an agent at each penitentiary to supervise this system, thus matching the earlier appointment of a state agent by Massachusetts. In New York, when an 1877 amendment prohibited the use of public funds in support of incorporated organizations, the state assumed full responsibility for the extensive work of John Russ, the New York Association's agent for the discharged, and Superintendent Pilsbury named him state agent. The prison societies in these states did not discontinue their

[15] Clark, *State Control*, pp. 25–29.

aid to the discharged, and at least one new society, that organized by the younger Francis Wayland in Connecticut, undertook the job in a new field.

Meanwhile the theory and significance of the indeterminate sentence was being noised about. New York had tentatively adopted the principle for its new institution under construction at Elmira; Brockway, rejoicing over the passage of his three-year law at Detroit, made a gallant fight for a comprehensive indeterminate-sentence law in Michigan, and although defeated in 1871 was able to enlist many supporters who later carried the measure through in a compromised form. Proposals for comprehensive reforms in Connecticut, Illinois, Ohio, and Wisconsin incorporated the indeterminate sentence as a main feature, but none of these programs was adopted at the time. Many responsible authorities held back until the new theories should have an opportunity to demonstrate their merits in actual practice, and for this service everyone looked hopefully to Brockway as he took charge at Elmira in 1876.[16]

Institutional Expansion

The major concern of the era was the housing problem. At no other time during the second half of the century did the prisons suffer so persistently from serious overcrowding as during the ten years following 1868. A few of the states, notably New Jersey, Indiana, Illinois, and Missouri, never succeeded in freeing their prisons from the evil of two or more men to a cell, but most of the other northern states approximated the standard of a cell for each man except during this decade. Furthermore, overcrowding was more of a problem for management at this time than in the early years of the next century, for the silent system still had a strong hold on prison traditions during the seventies. The attempt to correct overcrowding gave the reformers an opportunity, and where they were strongly organized they were able to secure new institutions after their own mind. Everywhere expansion occurred, and by the close of the decade most of the states of the Northeast were equipped with prison structures that were to serve them for the rest of the century with only occasional additions.

The slow progress of construction at Elmira, delaying the

---

[16] Wisconsin State Prison Commissioner, *Reports* (1866), pp. 2–21; (1868), pp. 6–7.

opening of the reformatory until 1876, deprived the reformers of a model which might have tipped the balance in favor of their programs in Ohio, Illinois, New Jersey, and California, each engaged in the expansion of its regular prisons. A more favorable result rewarded the reformers in Michigan, Indiana, and Massachusetts. Brockway's long agitation in Michigan, supported by Governor John Bagley, prevented the enlargement of Jackson prison and secured instead the creation of the Ionia house of correction and reformatory to relieve congestion at Jackson. When the first cellblock was opened in 1877, the three hundred cells, each 8 by 5 by 7 feet high, soon duplicated in a second cellblock, provided a creditable equipment. But a shift in politics left the legislative and administrative organization of the institution in inexperienced hands, and neither indeterminate sentences nor grades and marks were provided for. Ionia soon became in practice a prison for young men where an active industrial program was the only reformatory device.[17]

Meanwhile, as prison populations increased beyond capacity, the problem of segregating the women from the men became more difficult. Numerous scandals roused popular indignation in several states, adding incentive to the move for complete separation. Thus Indiana's success in building the first entirely separate institution for women was the fortuitous result of a series of scandals, rather than the work of reformers. Yet it takes leaders to direct public indignation, and the annual meeting of Friends in 1866 started the public protest. Two of their number were chosen to investigate, and the report of Charles and Rhoda Coffin was instrumental in rousing Governor Conrad Baker and the legislature to action. A long postponed plan for a girls' reform school reinforced the movement, and in 1869 a reformatory for women and girls was created. Sarah Smith, a prominent Friend, placed in charge when the new institution was opened in Indianapolis four years later, introduced a kindly, maternal discipline. But there was no board of charity or other instrument in the state to bring in new ideas, and the continuing interest of a committee of Friends succeeded only in

[17] New York Prison Association, *Report* (1869), p. 106; Ohio Board of Charities, *Report* (1868) 11: 515, 647; Illinois State Penitentiary, *Report* (1868), pp. 67–69; Zebulon R. Brockway, *Fifty Years of Prison Service: An Autobiography* (1912; reprinted Montclair, N.J., 1969), pp. 71–75.

100 American Prisons: A History of Good Intentions

preserving the human touch. For many years the major concern of the officers was to prevent the older women from corrupting the younger girls.

The fortunes of women convicts in other states varied considerably. While Connecticut and Missouri were erecting new cellhouses with separate yards for the women, Illinois was crowding them into the fourth story of the warden's house and using the admirable women's building for the overflowing male population. Except for New York and Massachusetts, the other states continued their earlier arrangements, usually with a matron in charge of the dormitory or small cellhouse located within the state prison. Michigan's provision in 1872 for the removal of all women to the Detroit house of correction lost the character of a satisfactory solution when Brockway and Miss Emma Hall retired from control there, and the adjacent house of shelter was soon abandoned. Except for the Cincinnati women's jail and the provision for misdemeanant women in Detroit, Indiana, New York, and Massachusetts, no attempt was made at this time to remove the women from local jails.[18]

Overcrowding was one of the factors that forced the removal of the women from Sing Sing. The one hundred outside cells in a separate building on the hill above the main prison had been overcrowded almost from the start, and the law of 1856 permitting the courts to sentence women felons to the county penitentiaries had failed to solve the problem. In 1872, when Mrs. Van Courtland assumed the duties of volunteer agent for the women's branch of the New York Association, she found 133 hopeless women crowded in the Sing Sing prison while many of the same class were as securely confined in several county penitentiaries without suffering the stigma of a Sing Sing record. On the basis of these facts she renewed the agitation for a women's reformatory, but the state was too busy building Elmira and enlarging Auburn and Clinton to consider another institution at the time. The superintendent compromised by removing all the women from the infamous association with Sing Sing to Kings County penitentiary. Two more decades were to pass before New York provided for the care of some of its women felons in special reformatories.[19]

[18] Lucien V. Rule, *The City of Dead Souls* (Louisville, 1920), pp. 94–111.
[19] Helen W. Rogers, "Digest of Laws Establishing Reformatories for Women in the United States," *Journal of Criminal Law and Criminology* 8 (1917): 518–553.

The development of an enlightened program for the care of women prisoners in Massachusetts was closely bound up with the careers of two Christian women. Hannah B. Chickering, as a young woman, had felt a strong urge to use her talents in public service but did not find the channel until a visit to Quaker friends in Philadelphia opened her eyes to the many needs of women in prison. Back home in Dedham, Miss Chickering established a library in the local jail and in 1874 opened an asylum for discharged females. Her efforts to extend the services of this institution to women from all parts of the state attracted the cooperation of F. B. Sanborn, the secretary of charities, and of Mrs. Ellen C. Johnson whose interest in the hardships of homeless and vagrant women had been aroused by her contact with them during war work. Together these reformers stirred up a statewide agitation for a women's prison. The general court chose to sidestep this demand by creating a prison commission, another of Sanborn's proposals, with power to transfer the women to a suitable house of correction. Sanborn selected Greenfield jail in 1871 for the use of the women of the western part of the state and named Miss Chickering one of three women advisers in cases of transfer; but the local jail authorities refused to cooperate, and the makeshift failed. Continued growth of state and local prison populations forced a return to the earlier proposal, and a women's prison was provided for in 1874 and opened three years later at Sherborn. Its three hundred outside rooms and two fifty-bed dormitories were soon crowded with major and minor offenders from all parts of the state; fortunately a new law soon permitted the transfer of certain cases to the jails, thus relieving congestion. But it was not until 1884 when Mrs. Johnson finally assumed control that a stable discipline based on a graded system was developed, making Sherborn the model institution for women in America.[20]

The main construction activities of the seventies were directed toward the enlargement of the older prisons. The state authorities were still striving to provide a cell for each prisoner, and while this standard was fully maintained only in New England, the majority of

[20] Massachusetts Board of State Charities, *Report* (1870), pp. 101–105; Massachusetts Commissioners of Prisons, *Report* (1880), pp. 29–34; Rogers, "Digest of Laws"; Eugenia C. Lekkerkerker, *Reformatories for Women in the United States* (Groningen, 1931), pp. 90–96.

the northern states were fairly adequately equipped by the end of the decade. The construction of additional institutions on the Elmira pattern was put off until the next era.

Charlestown, model prison of the sixties, suffered from serious overcrowding during most of the following decade. The institution was cramped by its narrow confines, and, as the land values were high, the general court decided to sell the old site and build a new and larger prison at Concord with the proceeds. The arguments of the reformers for two small prisons with limits of 450 convicts each, in order to facilitate the segregation of the young, the accidentals, and the drunkards from the vicious and the repeaters, were defeated by the prospect of securing one large and economical prison at little or no cost. Meanwhile the removal of the women from the jails to Sherborn opened the way for a compromise; all men with sentences of three years or less were committed to the local institutions, and the plans for Concord were reduced from 1,000 to 750 cells. The prison commission, hoping that this law was but the first step in the transformation of all local prisons into state district institutions, proposed that the Fitchburg house of correction be altered for use as a young men's reformatory. But the value of the Charlestown site suddenly declined, and the state, faced with the necessity of paying hard cash for Concord, refused to consider additional outlays for prison reform. Massachusetts had sufficient cells by the end of the decade, but the rearrangement of the penal system that converted Concord into a young men's reformatory was not achieved until the next era.

Each of the other New England states made a fairly satisfactory solution of its population problem. Rising land values in Providence induced Rhode Island to sell the city jail and build its new prison at the state farm; the desire for a better industrial location prompted New Hampshire to erect a new 248-cell prison at Concord; and Vermont provided equivalent accommodations by completing its partially constructed prison at Windsor. Connecticut and Maine were content to enlarge their older prisons to satisfy the needs of slowly growing populations. Rhode Island and Vermont each built state workhouses to correct unsatisfactory jail conditions, following the earlier lead of Massachusetts. Vermont, inspired by the Elmira pattern, renamed its workhouse a state house of correction and admitted the less vicious young felons at the discretion of the directors and judges, thus preparing the way for the development of a real reformatory when circumstances became favorable.

Four additional states in the North made advances toward the solution of serious housing problems. New York opened Elmira and expanded Auburn and Clinton, and only the isolation of the latter in the Adirondacks prevented the full utilization of its facilities to relieve Sing Sing, where the flood of commitments continued to crowd two men into many of its tiny cells. In a similar manner Michigan, adequately equipped after the completion of Ionia, tolerated a faulty distribution of state and local offenders. Ohio provided a sufficient number of cells at Columbus by the close of the decade, but this achievement equipped the state with the largest prison in the world, and the state board of charities found little cause for elation over this unwieldy institution. Meanwhile a reorganization of the board of the Western Penitentiary in Pennsylvania placed Edward Wright in the warden's office, where he shortly secured permission to build a shop to house congregate labor and a new cell building on the Auburn pattern, thus satisfying the population demands by a break from the state's traditional pattern. At the same time Allegheny County built a new workhouse and brought Cordier from Wisconsin to organize its industry and discipline, with the result that it soon became a model local prison, the rival of Detroit, and shamed the reformers of Philadelphia into establishing a new house of correction for the eastern city.[21]

Serious overcrowding in the prisons of Indiana, Illinois, and New Jersey continued in spite of repeated indictments by progressive investigators. Missouri likewise belonged to this group but as its most renegade member. Possibly these states would have done better had they provided permanent boards responsible for the supervision of prisons, but scandals and corruption absorbed the attention of their politicians. The Quaker agitators in Indiana were fortunate to get a women's prison. Illinois, after long delay, was forced by the danger of insurrection at the overcrowded 1,024-cell Joliet prison to start a new institution at Chester, but her politicians failed to heed the suggestion that it be made a reformatory. Chicago built a new

[21] Harry Elmer Barnes, *The Evolution of Penology in Pennsylvania: A Study in American Social History* (1927; reprinted Montclair, N.J., 1969), pp. 206–209, 306–310.

house of correction and imported the able Charles E. Felton from the Buffalo penitentiary to take charge, but the cells were so tiny and convicts were so continuously crowded—two, even three, to a cell—that the institution deserved rather the title of house of corruption.[22]

Of all the northern states, Missouri maintained the most diabolical prison conditions. The intense feelings and hostile factions inherited from the Civil War still dominated state politics. As power shifted from radical to liberal Republican and then to the Democrats the major concern in regard to the prison was that it should be as small a financial burden as possible. And yet, when the state was head over heels in debt, it did enlarge its old prison and erect a women's building outside the walls. The Democrats regained political control in 1873 and turned to the lease system that was rapidly becoming popular in the South. After two years of bad management the bankrupt lessee surrendered the disorganized institution to the state authorities, but renewed efforts to organize discipline and industry were handicapped by a steadily increasing population, which by 1878 numbered 1,333 men in 460 cells and rooms, besides 164 women in the separate 146-cell building.

Wisconsin, Minnesota, Iowa, Kansas, and West Virginia were still in many respects on the frontier of the advance of northern penological institutions; nevertheless, they were able during the decade to equip themselves with fairly adequate prisons. The Wisconsin authorities failed to carry through a comprehensive reorganization of their penal system along lines similar to those advocated by Sanborn in Massachusetts, and yet the end of the decade found the prison at Waupun only slightly overcrowded. Minnesota had no difficulty in expanding the recently established prison at Stillwater to meet the slow growth of its criminal population. Iowa, boom state of the era, started a second prison before the first was completed, only to face the difficulty of supporting two inadequately staffed and partially occupied institutions. Kansas stuck doggedly to what many had considered an overambitious program and was able to report in 1880 the completion of the entire prison structure. With 688 up-to-date cells patterned after those of Joliet it was, without a rival, the best prison west of the Mississippi. Nevertheless, so serious were the social

[22] Max Stern, "The Chicago House of Correction" (Master's thesis, University of Chicago, 1932).

problems of this frontier state that the convicts had constantly overcrowded the available cells as they were completed and now exceeded the capacity by at least one hundred—a condition which was to be aggravated as the next era advanced.

The leaders of West Virginia faced north from the first. When in 1866 the legislature appropriated $50,000 for a state prison, the pattern of the new cellhouse at Pittsburgh was adopted, and the state energetically pressed the construction of its prison at Moundsville. By 1880 it had finished the wall, one of the cellblocks, and a small women's building, as well as a dining hall and several shops. The 223 cells here provided were sufficient at the time for the needs of the state and represented the only genuine Auburn prison south of the Mason and Dixon line. In the interests of economy the southern lease system was frequently proposed but it was always defeated, and this state became in respect to penology a true daughter of the North.

Thus the northern states in the decade of the seventies opened eleven new state prisons or reformatories, at least four of which were dedicated to a special class of criminals. When taken in connection with the considerable additions to older prisons and with the new houses of correction, this era of construction might well be regarded as successful in spite of the disappearance of the organized movement—successful, that is, in supplying fair accommodations in most of the states and in clearing the ground for other reforms in succeeding years.[23]

When in 1873 Mary Carpenter visited prisons in the United States, she quickly discovered the weakest part of the American system:

> The existing jails are insufficient both in size and number, and the overcrowding of the prisoners necessarily causes great demoralization among them. . . . The female prisoners are not properly separated from the males, nor are they under proper supervision. . . . I saw in the cells two or three prisoners together, without anything to prevent them spending the whole day in idleness and injurious conversation.[24]

[23] Frederick H. Wines, "Twenty Years' Growth of the American Prison System," *Proceedings* (N.P.A., 1890), pp. 79–104, is a concise review of some of the developments recorded here. My record is based on what I have gleaned from the original state prison reports as published in the respective state documents.

[24] N.Y.P.A., *Report* (1872), p. 119.

The few jails that she visited suffered by contrast with institutions of the same grade in England, for it was in this very important class of prisons that the mother country was making the greatest improvements. While there was some resentment among American reformers who would have liked to have Miss Carpenter visit Detroit and a few other prisons they proudly named, they were nonetheless aware of the truth of her indictment, and many of them were earnestly facing the problem.

The attack on the jail evil came from two directions. The first problem was to find competent leadership. County government was generally lax unless the community had become so populous that vital interests made for strong party factions. In such cases the critical nature of the jail problem played into the hands of the reformers, and some excellent houses of correction were the result. The other attack was through the state authority over all local political divisions. But local self-government was a strong tradition, and even the best of the boards of charities and prison commissions found it difficult to get any real power over local jails. Nevertheless, great improvements in inspection and standardization were made in Massachusetts, Michigan, Ohio, Wisconsin, Illinois, and to a degree in Pennsylvania and New York. But excellent comprehensive proposals brought forward in New York, Massachusetts, and Wisconsin were not seriously considered.[25]

The best of the local reforms were not very impressive. In spite of a law against sending children to jail, the Massachusetts commission found ninety-seven so confined in 1869, and only with the most persistent agitation was it able to reduce the number to twenty-five three years later. The New York Association found in 1878 that but five out of sixty jails had carried out the mandatory regulations for the segregation of women, children, and witnesses; a strenuous campaign the following year brought only ten more jails into line. When such was the performance in the most advanced state, the Americans had little response to make to their candid English visitor. The Michigan penal commission might well have spoken for the whole country when it reported that "the jails . . . have

[25] Illinois Board of State Commissioners of Public Charities, *First Biennial Report* (1870), pp. 1–7. This board like seven in other states established in the late sixties, had the power to inspect local jails and other institutions except the state prison in this and several other cases. See also Clark, *State Control*, pp. 25–29.

escaped reform and are in Michigan today as wretched as they have
been in England or America at any time in their existence."[26]

Improvement of Discipline

When all the legislatures have had their say, when their laws have
been interpreted and their appropriations have been spent, the final
problem still remains. The impact of these measures on the internal
life of the prison is the alpha and omega of penology, and it is with
this that the prisoner is chiefly concerned. If the old "cons" had not
heard of it through speeches and sermons, it is certain that many of
them, whose terms spanned the era, would scarcely have known of
the worldwide reform movement. Many of them must have told their
younger buddies of the good old days. Yet the story was not one-
sided, and on the whole the prisoners got the better "break" at the
end of the period.

The general standards of prison schools gradually rose during the
era. Unfortunately several of the more promising experiments were
either discontinued or considerably modified. Thus the excellent
school system which Brockway had developed at Detroit deteriorated
sadly after he and Miss Hall departed. In a similar fashion the
lecture system of Haynes at Charlestown was modified by his
successor, sacrificing much of its educational value. A lesson had
nevertheless been learned by the administrators concerning the
disciplinary value of school classes. Accordingly when the depression hit prison industry in Massachusetts and many of the
contractors laid off their men, Warden Chamberlain relieved the
strain of idleness by expanding the evening schools into day schools;
but a revival of trade two years later converted even the regular
schoolrooms into factories. Meanwhile the occasional evening
schools of 1865 had spread until all the state prisons in New
England and those in Michigan, Illinois, and Iowa, as well as New
York and Pennsylvania, provided such opportunities to learn to
read and write. New York appeared the model of generosity,
spending $7,500 a year on teachers, chaplains, and books, but when
this was divided among the teeming populations of New York
prisons and administered cell to cell, as was the normal practice, it
did not transform much gray matter.

The prison library was another department potentially of large

[26] Michigan Penal Commission, *Report* (1876), p. 9.

value to the convict. Wines and Dwight had found libraries in all the state prisons of the North, but the books had been contributed by charitable persons, and were for the most part antiquated religious treatises, of little interest or value. Some of the states were already assuming responsibility for supplying small annual sums to replenish the libraries. This custom spread, but there was little care to apportion these funds, ranging between $25 and $200 so as to secure desirable books and magazines. In 1877 the New York Association compiled a catalogue of one thousand suggested titles covering a wide variety of interests, listed so as to guide chaplains seeking to provide a library of fifty to one thousand books. This might have had a large influence had it come when the reform movement was in full flood, but no record has been found of any prison that used it. Many of the prisons did work out reasonably efficient distributing systems, enabling the convicts to make use of the books available, but no adequate accounts were kept of the expenditures, and, with petty graft on the one hand and thrift drives on the other, even the meager funds provided did not always reach the library shelves. The chaplains, who generally had supervision of the prison library as well as the educational program, were the pioneer representatives of the correctional staff that would later appear in many prisons. Among the chaplains of this period were Hickox in Michigan, Mitchell in Kansas, and Carleton in Massachusetts as well as Luckey in Sing Sing.[27]

The county jails supplied plenty of education, but it was as "seminaries of vice and crime." Outside of Massachusetts almost no organized instruction was provided; the commissioners of that state worked diligently and succeeded in establishing a library in every jail and in developing good schoolroom instruction in Lowell, Lawrence, and South Boston houses of correction. Sabbath schools and libraries existed in scattered jails elsewhere, but the former were usually dependent on the whims of local parsons. The work of Linda Gilbert in establishing libraries in the large jails of such cities as Chicago, New York, St. Louis, and Buffalo during these years was of great service to the thousands of prisoners who flocked through those portals. Nevertheless, in the great majority of the jails, if the idle unfortunates wished to occupy their minds they had to depend

---

[27]Daniel C. Gilman, *The Charities and Reformatories of Connecticut* (Middletown, Conn., 1870); N.Y.P.A., *Report* (1868), pp. 396–401.

on books or papers supplied by their friends, and this was a privilege not always granted.[28]

The rudiments of education were about all that any prison supplied. Their contribution was more in relieving the monotony of prison life than in fitting men for society. Possibly the better prisons through these agencies were helping to Americanize an increasing number of aliens, but the schools and libraries were in favor with the wardens largely because of their disciplinary value. They supplied a basis for a system of rewards, while in another important respect they aided in the relaxation of the silent regulations, so difficult a problem for untrained officers. Prison education for its own sake was not yet the reformatory panacea that it was to become a decade or so later.

The one reform which all the wardens praised during these years was the commutation system. This was one of the few practices that spread not only throughout all the northern states but into the Far West and South as well. Many of the laws were carefully administered and possessed a disciplinary value that they were to lose in time. However, only Michigan and Vermont tried to carry out the full intent of their laws, going so far as to add wage payments to the good-time earnings.[29]

There were many other scattered changes in prison discipline, although they fail to reveal any general trends. On the one hand, Michigan removed John Morris, whose strict discipline in attempting to stamp out the use of tobacco had made Jackson prison notorious, and inaugurated an era of liberal discipline under Warden Humphrey and Chaplain Hickox; in the same year Indiana replaced Warden Shuler, who had eliminated the "cat" from Jeffersonville, and gave control to A. G. Howard, a strict disciplinarian who used the lash freely. In general, the punishments applied were much the same as in earlier years, for, while several of the states had regulations against the "cat" or the "shower bath," Sanborn

[28]Linda Gilbert, *Sketch of the Life and Work of Linda Gilbert: With Statistical Reports* (New York, 1877).

[29]N.Y.P.A., *Reports* (1867), pp. 25–27; (1868), pp. 154–164; Negley K. Teeters and John D. Shearer, *The Prison at Philadelphia, Cherry Hill* (New York, 1957), p. 192. Pennsylvania in 1869 became the eighteenth state to adopt good-time or commutation laws.

was of the opinion that these regulations were not strictly followed.[30]

The most important disciplinary trend, the gradual relaxing of the silent system, was not so much the work of reformers as the inevitable result of overcrowding. Silence was possible as long as each man could be locked in a separate cell and carefully supervised at labor; but with two in many cells or with scores sleeping in corridors or in the chapel, silence was no longer pretended. The system remained in its worst possible form—a law not generally obeyed but which could be enforced at the whim of an officer. In this form it became a major cause for the prison atmosphere of repression. The frank abandonment of these regulations in the higher grades at Detroit and Elmira was to be a significant contribution to reformatory discipline in later years.

Prison industry was a major concern of administrators and reformers alike. From the first penitentiary days, when fierce debates raged over the merits of labor in solitude versus labor in association, there had always been conflicting theories. Industry gained its place in prison discipline because where it was omitted revolts, mutual corruption, and waves of insanity always appeared. A few hard-headed reform wardens, as Amos Pilsbury and Zebulon Brockway, grasped the equally significant fact that the only sure basis for a permanent administration was relative economic self-sufficiency. The Wines school, on the other hand, took the theoretical stand that, as the purpose of prisons was the reformation of criminals, the first concern should not be the economic one.

A sharp argument had occurred during the first day at Cincinnati between Enoch Wines and Amos Pilsbury over this difference of opinion. It was never settled. Wines failed to persuade a single state government to support a prison administration that sought only the reformation of its inmates; even Elmira did not slight the economic factor during the first years. On the other hand, the prosperity of prison labor came to smash in 1873, and during the following years in the North only rare administrations were able to insure their tenure by paying all the prison expenses. The dispute was in reality

---

[30] George H. Hickox, "The History of Michigan State Prison," *Biennial Report* (Michigan State Prison, 1898), pp. 40–42; Indiana State Prison South, *Annual Report* (1868–1869).

only a tactical one and it was soon overshadowed by the agitation against contract labor.

The right of way of the contractor had long been a characteristic of the prison world, and so it remained for many years, in spite of the reformers. The New York Association started a campaign to stop this exploitation of penal servitude, and, in the hard times following the panic, their arguments were reinforced by the petitions of the competitors of prison contractors, both employers and workers. One result was a series of state investigations of the prison-labor problem in the late seventies. Several of these shed considerable light on the subject, but while they condemned the contract system, they hesitated to recommend its abolition until some other system had been partially introduced.[31] As any other system seemed to demand large state appropriations to start with, no one of the responsible boards was very definite in its recommendations. A few suggestions, such as that aiming to prevent concentration in one industry by limiting the percentage to be employed in each trade, were happy inspirations to quiet the protests of the competitors; on the whole no permanent contribution to the solution of this problem was made during the decade. The only law of any consequence was that in New York centralizing control in the hands of the state superintendent and directing him to diversify production. The war against contractors was a total failure. Even Wisconsin abandoned the state account system and called in contractors to manage her industries. Nevertheless, the very zeal with which the undaunted contractors pushed their cheap goods onto the public market helped to call down on their heads the storm of laws that dominated the next period.[32]

In spite of a partial realization of its objectives, the organized movement gradually disintegrated. The constantly changing personnel was an influential factor in this decline. Prison officers had never enjoyed secure tenure, and although in the period following the Civil War a few able wardens had served year after year, most of

[31] U.S. Commissioner of Labor, *Second Annual Report, 1886: Convict Labor* (Washington, D.C., 1887), pp. 307–368. Carroll D. Wright, the author of the report, reviews the many state investigations, notably those in New York in 1841, 1867 (Wines), 1871 (Wines); 1879 (L. D. Pilsbury); Ohio in 1877; Pennsylvania in 1877; Massachusetts in 1878 and 1880; New Jersey in 1879; and Connecticut in 1880.

[32] Henry C. Mohler, "Convict Labor Policies," *J.C.L.C.* 15 (1925): 530–597.

them were turned out by political shifts in the mid seventies. The death of several of the unofficial reformers crippled the movement even more seriously. Thus the passing of Francis Lieber, Abraham Beal, and Judges Edmonds and Wolfe was a serious blow to the New York Association. Wines, Sanborn, and Byers unfortunately withdrew from their key positions at a critical time in the mid seventies. The removal of Gideon Haynes from Charlestown after he had sold his soul for five thousand greenbacks, the removal of Shuler and Sullivan in Indiana, the transfer of Cordier from Wisconsin to Pennsylvania, and the resignation of Brockway from Detroit—all seriously checked important developments. The death of Amos Pilsbury carried away an important link between the theoretical reformers and the hardfisted wardens. Only Brockway remained, and his job, as he accepted his new post at Elmira, was to build for the future.[33]

The views of many of the new officers were aptly expressed by the new Ohio board of directors in their 1873 report:

> The management of penitentiaries has, until lately, attracted very little attention, except so far as pecuniary results were concerned. Some excitement was created a few years since in regard to crime generally and the reformation of criminals, and several conventions have been held at which a number of subjects were discussed. We are not aware that our officers have derived any practical benefit from these conventions. The excitement and the discussions have passed away leaving a very slight impression in the world.[34]

But the Ohio directors were badly misinformed. Dr. Wines was already a world figure, and the movement he had organized in America was stimulating important developments in Europe, South America, and Japan. As president of the International Prison Association he was busy arranging for its second congress, to convene at Stockholm in 1878, and, in last-moment preparation, he called the Prison Reform Congress at Newport in the early part of that year. However, Wines admitted his American defeat by failing to invite all prison men to this gathering; only his select friends had an opportunity to vote on resolutions of still a broader nature than those of 1870. The gathering had little significance and its

[33] Brockway, *Fifty Years,* pp. 68–150, 154–174.
[34] Ohio State Penitentiary, *Report* (1873), pp. 31–32.

resolutions are interesting only because, even at this date, they idealized the Crofton system, long since abandoned in Ireland.

In his presidential address at Stockholm, Dr. Wines reviewed the progress of prison reform. In almost every nation the newer principles had had some effect, but the veteran reformer was a bit overpleased with these achievements. A large share of credit was due to the state of external and internal peace which the European countries were at last enjoying. Yet, as penal systems were developed, the movement, coming at an opportune time, exerted its influence. However, in place of the practical experimenters taking charge of American prisons, a legalistic profession was gaining control of the prisons on the continent, and had Wines lived long enough he would have seen the Europeans become skeptical of the optimistic claims of the American reformatories. Already he noted the passing of Matthew Davenport Hill, Mary Carpenter, and other outstanding members of the group that had organized the world-wide reform movement. Enoch Wines was almost the last of the unshaken idealists; fortunately he remained long enough to finish *The State of Prisons* and leave it as a monument to the era that had ended.[35]

An era had ended indeed—that is, provided the history of institutions ever lends itself to procrustean terminology. Perhaps it would be better to say that a generation had passed. What a generation it had been! All but Sanborn and Brockway had been men of advanced years, and yet such had been their idealistic enthusiasm that they had defied the old Hebrew prophecy. Marvelous were the visions they had seen: contrite convicts working earnestly for merits with which to gain their freedom; conscientious officers serving their states as long as they could create a new spirit in their prisoners; Christian friends administering public aid to released prisoners and helping them toward useful citizenship; and great national and international conventions pointing the true road to life. Their compassionate idealism had carried them not only far ahead of contemporary attitudes toward the criminal but somewhat out of the realm of practical penology; nevertheless, they succeeded in implanting their major principle—that the criminal was an

[35] Enoch Cobb Wines, *The State of Prisons and of Child-Saving Institutions in the Civilized World* (1880; reprinted Montclair, N.J., 1968).

erring brother deserving of society's special care until he should be refitted for a normal life in its midst—in the newly established Elmira reformatory, "free college" for the criminal youth of New York State.

The rise of Enoch Wines and his movement had been attended by many fortuitous circumstances. Not only did this generation profit from the experiences of a century of reformers, but the older rivalries and traditions were waning as the new leaders came upon the stage, leaving them free to make fresh combinations of old principles. The opportune discovery of the Irish model supplied an ideal pattern at the same time that the newly created organizations for inspection provided agencies for the advancement of reform programs. The industrial boom of the late sixties gave many of the wardens the opportunity to enjoy the zest that comes from running a thriving concern, thus raising them above the drab worries of repressive discipline and supplying them with the two essentials for success: optimism and long tenure. By the same token the prisons were advanced in the public esteem, and an eager rivalry in the construction of adequate plants took place. The erection of new prisons was largely a response to the pressure of population growth, but here again circumstances played into the hands of the reformers, who in several cases succeeded in shaping the building programs.

By the late seventies, however, fortune was turning against the reformers. Political upheavals were playing havoc with their friends; economic reversals were blighting their optimism; legislative defeats were compromising their programs; and finally death was claiming its own. The generation passed, but it left a clearly formulated program, a few promising experiments, a rich literature, and a quickened public responsibility for the reformation of criminals.

BIBLIOGRAPHIC NOTE

The sources are enriched, beginning with this period, by the regular reports of the newly created state boards of charities and corrections, notably those of Massachusetts, Ohio, and Michigan, in these years. The official reports of all the northeastern state prisons are also available, and those of the Detroit house of correction are important. The New York Prison Association, *Reports*, especially after 1862, the *Journal of Prison Discipline and Philanthropy* (Philadelphia, 1845–); the National Congress on Penitentiary and Reformatory Discipline [Cincinnati], *Transactions* (1870); the National Prison Association, *Proceedings* (1873; 1874; 1876); and the International Penitentiary Congress, *Transactions* (London, 1872; Stockholm, 1878) are all of primary importance. *John Augustus, First Probation Officer* (1852; reprinted Montclair, N.J., 1972) is Augustus' own account of his early work in probation. Linda Gilbert, *Sketch of the Life and Work of Linda Gilbert: With Statistical Reports* (New York, 1877); Gideon Haynes, *Pictures from Prison Life: An Historical Sketch of the Massachusetts State Prison* (Boston, 1869) give two contemporary accounts of workers in jails. Enoch Cobb Wines, *The State of Prisons and of Child-Saving Institutions in the Civilized World* (1880; reprinted Montclair, N.J., 1968) is a comprehensive source for nineteenth-century correctional fact and theory. Charles Richmond Henderson, ed., *Correction and Prevention*, vol. 1, *Prison Reform* (1910; reprinted Montclair, N.J., 1976), contains biographical sketches of the leaders, and a survey of the reforms, of this period.

Cited earlier, but of value for this period, are the works of Harry Elmer Barnes, Zebulon Brockway, Mary Carpenter, Enoch C. Wines and Theodore Dwight, and Max Grunhut. Other works of special interest are Benedict S. Alper and Jerry F. Boren, *Crime, International Agenda: Concern and Action in the Prevention of Crime and Treatment of Offenders, 1846–1972* (Lexington, Mass., 1972) is a comprehensive overview of worldwide penal congresses; J. Estlin Carpenter, *The Life and Work of Mary Carpenter*, 2d ed. (1881; reprinted Montclair, N.J., 1974); Mary Carpenter, *Reformatory Prison Discipline: As Developed by the Rt. Hon. Sir Walter Crofton in the Irish Convict Prisons* (1872; reprinted Montclair, N.J., 1967); Anderson W. Clark, *State Control and Supervision of Charities* (Lincoln, Neb., 1905); Walter T. Clay, *The Prison Chaplain: A Memoir of the Rev. John Clay, With Selections from His Reports and Correspondence and a a Sketch of Prison Discipline in England* (1861; reprinted Montclair, N.J., 1969); Sarah E. Dexter, *Recollections of Hannah Chickering* (Cambridge, Mass., 1881); Daniel C. Gilman, *The Charities and Reformatories of Connecticut* (Middletown, Conn., 1870); John H. Griscom, *Prison Hygiene* (Albany, 1868); Frederic Hill, *Crime: Its Amount, Causes, and Remedies* (London, 1853); Matthew Davenport Hill, *Suggestions for the Repression of Crime* (1857; reprinted Montclair, N.J., 1975); Eugenia C. Lekkerkerker, *Reformatories for Women in the United States* (Groningen, 1931); Sir Evelyn Ruggles-Brise, *Prison Reform at Home and Abroad* (London, 1924); Lucien V. Rule, *The City of Dead Souls* (Louisville, 1920).

5.

CONVICT LABOR AND PEDAGOGICAL PENOLOGY: TO 1900

American prison developments became increasingly complex in the northern states as the nineteenth century entered its last quarter. The heritage of a century of reformers and a half century of builders had supplied a considerable equipment of customs and cells. Recent building programs had measurably allayed the demands of expanding populations, and in several instances reformers had successfully directed construction toward the creation of promising institutions. These new reformatories together with a number of forward-looking organizations found themselves in the eighties in the midst of a complex play of forces, dominated by the struggle of organized labor and "free" industry for legislative protection from prison competition. State after state adopted anticontract laws that exerted a far-reaching influence on prison developments.

The survivors of the older generation found the younger men eager to join in reviving the National Prison Association in order to discuss their mutual problem, the anticontract threat. Zebulon Brockway had by this time sufficiently elaborated his reformatory discipline at Elmira to provide a model for new institutions, and the revival of the reform movement was greatly aided by this practical demonstration of its ideology. The annual congresses, resumed in 1883, became increasingly popular and supplied a convenient agency for the education of the officers and inspectors regularly brought into power by political changes within the states. Thus pedagogical penology, elaborated in the reformatories, became the standard for all prisons by the end of the century, and many of them were to meet the emergency resulting from labor laws by a partial application of the new technique.

The Domination of the Labor Problem

The Industrial Revolution was already at full tilt in America. Two of its phases in particular exerted a large influence on prison developments: the substitution of machine industry for handicraft production, and the organization of the labor forces. Both developments had been in process for some time, and already the former had transformed prison industry and given it into the hands of contractors. Many of the prisons had become prosperous factories and remained such, at least for the contractors, except when the depressions of the mid seventies and the mid eighties destroyed their markets. Many of the reformers, who, a few years before, had bitterly attacked the subversive influences of the contractors, now elaborately defended the system. The public, for its part, hesitated to trust the transient politicians in charge of the prisons with the management of large industries.

The question might have been tabled in this fashion had it not been for the constant growth of organized labor during a period of sharp political rivalry. It was one thing for the National Labor Party to insert an anticontract clause in its platform, and for the Knights of Labor as well as the Federation of Organized Trades and Labor Unions to follow this lead; but it was quite another thing when the district assemblies of the Knights and the state federations took up the agitation. State politicians had their ears to the ground in the early eighties, and they revealed some ability at *Realpolitik* if not in penological statecraft.

The industrialization of America was taking place chiefly in that belt of nine states reaching from Massachusetts to Illinois. Led off by New York in 1864, all but two of these had state federations of labor by 1889, and Pennsylvania and Ohio, the two exceptions, were centers of the growing Knights of Labor with its energetic local and district assemblies. All except Indiana had, before 1887, appointed special commissions for the investigation of prison labor, and as for the Hoosier State, it remained, until the nineties, not only the most backward in prison reform but the least advanced industrially of the group. But the old subterfuge—commissions for investigation—did not suffice. The parties in power in Illinois and New Jersey hearkened to this demand of the labor forces, as did the Democrats, when in the early eighties, with the aid of many labor votes salvaged from the Greenback-Labor party, they turned out the Republicans in Massachusetts, Pennsylvania, New York, and Ohio. The same party, capturing the White House, was able by 1887 to pass a law forbidding the contracting of any federal criminals.[1] This legislative onslaught was shaking the foundations of the prison system of Louis Dwight. In desperation the wardens and responsible reformers turned to the national association and also convened congresses where they could share their concerns and debate possible solutions. There was little hope of returning to the happy circumstances of the early seventies when eleven states had annually defrayed the expenses of their prisons from the returns on the labor of the inmates. Dr. Wines had deplored the emphasis placed on such production, but now all agreed that the prisons could not be administered properly without labor to fill the long hours of the convict's day.[2]

In the midst of this hubbub Zebulon Brockway proposed a piece-price scheme to the National Association in 1883, proclaiming it as the long-sought-for solution. Indeed from the point of view of the warden it had great advantages. It proposed to eliminate the disturbing influence of the contractor within prison walls by giving the officers full control over discipline of the convicts and management of the industries. On the other hand, it proposed that the warden contract with outside companies to supply machinery and thus free himself from the necessity of waiting on state appropriations. The scheme would make possible as large a diversification of industry as the warden saw fit or his managing ability allowed; further than this, it avoided the ill repute of the contract system and insured a rich market.

The new proposal received a varied reception. Many of the leaders hailed from states where the current of opinion disregarded labor protests, and they were naturally little inclined to encourage even a

[1] U.S. Commissioner of Labor, *Second Annual Report, 1886: Convict Labor* (Washington, D.C., 1887), p. 368. For the laws of all the states on convict labor quoted in full see Part II, pp. 507–604.

[2] National Prison Association, *Transactions* (1874), pp. 379–381.

modification of the existing system; thus Professor Francis Wayland from Connecticut and various leaders from Michigan were constant critics of the proposed plan. Michael Cassidy joined in this attack but from entirely opposite premises; his Philadelphia prison was still operating on the old solitary system, supplying handicraft labor, and unaffected either by the necessity for self-support, the machine age, or the labor unions. On the other hand, leaders from Ohio, New Jersey, and Illinois were immediately attracted by Brockway's scheme, and politicians were plentiful who, after satisfying labor with laws against contractors, agreed to save the public taxes by permitting the prisons to earn a part of their expenses at piece-price agreements. In fact, of the states that abolished contracts, all but Pennsylvania very quickly reorganized their prison industries on this new plan.

The prisons weathered the severest phase of the storm of labor agitation before the end of the eighties. The growing disharmony within labor ranks, the return of the Republicans to power, and the public awareness of the magnitude of the costs of idle prisons brought a lull in anticontract agitation. At the same time the weight of the reports of numerous special investigations and of the several state labor commissioners and finally, in 1886, of the United States labor commissioner, was all on the side of cautious, moderate regulation rather than complete abolition of contracts. Most of these minimized the importance of prison labor as a competitor of the free workers. Carroll D. Wright, the United States commissioner, made a special study of the quantity and value of products displaced and concluded that $28,754,000, the total product of 45,300 convicts in 1885, was a very small figure when compared with $5,369,579,000 produced by 2,732,600 free laborers five years before.[3] This rapidly became a major argument and was not seriously challenged until the end of the century.

But the labor forces were not the only interests that had to be pacified. It has been seriously questioned whether the agitation from the beginning was not simply a cleverly devised campaign on the part of the industrial competitors of the contractors to destroy the latter's advantages.[4] At all events the labor attack had no sooner been checked than the manufacturers rallied to the cause and formed their

[3] U.S. Comm. Labor, *Convict Labor,* P. 295, and tables on pp. 192–199.

[4] Philip Klein, *Prison Methods in New York State: A Contribution to the Study of the Theory and Practice of Correctional Institutions* (New York, 1920), p. 296.

national anti-convict-contract association. Presidents of wagon factories, shoe, furniture, and stove companies, chiefly from Wisconsin, Michigan, Iowa, and Missouri—all at the time lacking anticontract laws—gathered in Chicago in 1886 to hold their convention. Here they frankly unveiled their interest in eliminating the unfair competition of their rivals and voted to send their president, Colonel W. T. Lewis, on a lecture tour to urge their cause.

Several schemes were proposed in these years that were designed chiefly to curb prison competition. One that made considerable headway was the requirement that all products be stamped "prison made." Another proposal, revealing a curious assortment of motives, suggested that prisoners should be employed exclusively at labor with hand tools and manpower machinery. Carroll D. Wright was especially active in agitating this solution which he considered to be the secret of the success of the Cherry Hill penitentiary. At his prompting, Massachusetts adopted a modified form of the plan by forbidding the purchase of new machinery after 1887, and this remained a thorn in the side of her prison administrators for many years. New York in 1888, prohibiting all manufacture by motive power, succeeded in disjointing her entire prison system until a new law righted it. Heedless of this lesson, Pennsylvania politicians sold their state's penological birthright for labor votes in 1897 by adopting an extreme form of this scheme. This reactionary policy, combining the desire to retard prison production and the more general wish to check the speed of mechanization in America, revived the old notion that the prisoner might thus learn a useful trade.

Another proposal designed to limit the competitive range of prison industries urged the prohibition of interstate traffic in such goods. The O'Neill Bill aiming at this end was introduced and almost carried through Congress in 1888. The wardens who gathered that year at the annual congress in Boston were greatly disturbed over the prospect and passed a resolution recommending a special convention of prison officers and state legislators to determine a just solution of the difficult problem. That resolution was soon forgotten, however, as the decline of the labor influence in the late eighties and the disappearance of the anticontract association sufficed to stave off immediate legislation.

*   *   *

While the fury of the storm of labor legislation relented somewhat in most of the states toward the close of the decade, in New York it continued unabated. Situated at the center of much of labor's political agitation, New York experienced from the first the full gamut of forces playing around the problem. It devised the legislation that formed the basis for much of the discussion and practice of its neighbors in succeeding years.

The acute nature of the problem in the Empire State was due in part to its industrial environment. But the remarkable efficiency of prison industries after the creation of the all-powerful superintendent in 1877 aggravated the situation. Lewis Pilsbury's success in cutting prison costs to one-fifth of their earlier average entailed the development of extensive industries, and many competitors began to protest.[5] Governor Alonzo B. Cornell expressed this growing hostility in 1880, and in the following year the legislature sent a committee to investigate industrial conditions at Sing Sing. The report favored the contract system, but the legislature hesitated to meddle with the ticklish problem and referred it to the people. Amid a confusion of issues the contract system was condemned by a small majority. Again the Republican legislature refused to act, but that astute politician, David B. Hill, attacked the problem during his governorship with energy, insisting that the popular will be respected and that "unnecessary interference with outside industrial interests" be eliminated.[6] The amendment prohibited new contracts but failed to provide an alternative system. Fortunately for the prisons, as well as for the state treasury, most of the contracts extended ahead several years, but gradually, as they expired, the situation became critical. Finally the legislature created the Prison Labor Reform Commission to plan a new system and authorized, in the meantime, temporary piece-price agreements. These measures came none too soon, for unemployment at Auburn was desperate, and Brockway at Elmira was almost at his wit's end. The commission made a careful study and concluded in 1887 that the piece-price system was highly admirable, but, as popular opposition must be met, a special effort to diversify the industry would be

[5] Ibid., pp. 336–368; New York Superintendent of Prisons, *Report* (1879). The cost was reduced from $317,000 in 1876 to $67,800 in 1878.
[6] New York, *Governor's Messages*, ed. C. Z. Lincoln, vol. 8 (Albany, 1909), pp. 12, 165.

necessary, and arrangements should be made for sale to public and charitable institutions. This last suggestion, an early expression of the idea that later developed into the public-use system, appeared at the time as an effort to dodge the issue. Disregarding this moderate advice, the legislature adopted the Yates Law prohibiting contracts of any kind and abolishing all manufacture that used motive power. Only production by hand labor was allowed, and then only for the use of state institutions. Immediately surpluses became enormous deficits, and the superintendent protested against this destruction, not only of the industries but of the whole prison discipline. Only in Elmira was the industrial stoppage made an occasion for constructive measures.

The state finally realized that the problem could not be left in the hands of greedy interests. Professor Charles A. Collin of Cornell, formerly associated with Brockway at Elmira, drafted the bill which Senator Jacob S. Fassett of Elmira introduced in 1889, the high-water mark of prison-labor legislation of the century. The new law sanctioned both the piece-price and state-account systems, but provided that no industry should employ more than five percent of the number working at that occupation in the state; a few industries were further restricted to one hundred laborers and required to produce for state use only. Of larger significance, the law definitely abandoned the idea that industry should be organized primarily for self-support and accepted the reformatory motive. The convicts were to be divided into three classes: those with good prospects of reformation were to be instructed in trade schools and employed at these trades with no idea of profit to the state; the repeaters who were at least good prisoners and possibly reformable were to be assigned to industries at which they could earn a living after discharge and their keep in the meantime; the desperate criminals who were to be rewarded with all the drudgery and menial labor rather than the choice jobs which their long terms and professional standing had formerly assured them. In addition, a wage not to exceed one-tenth of the earnings was to be paid to meritorious prisoners.

Unfortunately the state and its officers were poorly prepared to administer so good a law. Neither the abilities of the officers nor the structural equipment of the prisons permitted the genuine classification called for. Meanwhile many industries lobbied for the same protection granted to the shoe and stove hollowware trades where only one hundred prisoners could be employed. Impatient with the persistence of the problem, and possibly stimulated by the rigors of the depression of 1893, the constitutional convention of 1894 advanced an amendment which was shortly adopted fixing 1897 for the end of all forms of contract labor. A prison commission was created to organize a new system on the state-use principle, already partially applied, and its jurisdiction was extended over the county penitentiaries which had so long escaped state interference. A law of 1896 carried out these constitutional provisions and required the several state departments to purchase from the prisons as long as their needs could adequately be supplied.

New York thus finally evolved a system with great possibilities. It excluded the prisons from the haggling of the market place but opened a rich, if unexplored, field for their enterprise. Yet it was no foolproof scheme and in succeeding years, while the state prisons were able to carry on, for the time at least, fairly satisfactory industrial programs, the county penitentiaries, with their former industrial efficiency blasted, and with no law giving them a preemption on any market, fell back into the class of mammoth city jails, condemning their inmates to noxious idleness. When the New York Prison Association made a comprehensive survey in 1900, it found a discouraging industrial lassitude, incompatible with any purpose of reformation, permeating the entire prison system of the state; and only the adult reformatory was avoiding its vicious results by other devices.

New York's pioneer legislation had been observed with interest by her neighbors, but only Massachusetts was ready to follow the new lead. The developments in the Bay State were less complex in their political aspects but hardly less so as far as the prisons were concerned. After repeated reverses the anticontract forces finally secured a law in 1887 creating a superintendent of prisons to administer the industries at state account. Yet, by failing to provide the necessary credit and by prohibiting the acquisition of new machinery, the law prevented efficient reorganization and at the same time, by banning contractors, wiped out the overtime payments which had been such an important incentive to efficient labor in the old days. Several of these mistakes were corrected in the following year as a new law permitted each prison to make piece-price agreements, but this in turn undermined the authority of the superintendent and made central management difficult. Unemployment was gradually eliminated, but repeated recommendations for a wage system to revive the interest of the convicts in their labor roused no response.

After several more or less unsatisfactory years with this system the general court was again persuaded to follow the example of New York. It abolished all contracts in 1897 and gave the necessary power to organize a state-use system to the superintendent. He soon developed an efficient administration and while Massachusetts never adopted an elaborate system of labor classification, her prison equipment was such that she achieved its object more nearly than did New York. The three-year minimum for state prison commitments generally excluded all but the hardened convicts from Charlestown; the likely candidates for reformation were sent to Concord, and, when the existing piece-price agreements expired, they were given trade instruction; the county houses of correction took care of the remainder and provided fair labor conditions. At the close of the century the authorities were looking ahead to large developments of outdoor labor, and while Pettigrove's proposal that prison labor be used to build a canal across Cape Cod was not followed, the companion proposal that a state camp for inebriates be opened on a large tract of waste land was carried into effect in 1902.

When in 1883 the Democrats captured the Republican stronghold in Pennsylvania, they hastened to reward their labor allies with an anticontract law. In this state, where the district assemblies of the Knights were so strong, no politician could propose to dodge the law by piece-price agreements, but, as the Eastern penitentiary had long depended on handicraft industry at state account and as the Western prison had long-term contracts, the effect was not immediately disastrous. A complex system of wage payments was instituted to make the best of the existing industry, and the Democrats, again in power in 1891, demonstrated their liberalism by enacting an eight-hour limit for the convict laborer. Two parties could play this game, and in 1897 some Republicans paid for their mess of pottage by pushing through the devastating Muehlbronner Act abolishing the use of power machinery in the manufacture of goods produced elsewhere in the state and seriously limiting the number of men employed at any one industry in each prison. This crippled the industry in the Eastern as well as in the Western penitentiary and only the reformatory, already turning to trade schools and farming, escaped serious injury. The act made a farce of prison labor in Pennsylvania for the next thirty years and did more than any other factor to degrade the two great penitentiaries of the Keystone State from the first rank of American prisons.

The other states did not find it necessary to follow these leaders until the beginning of the next century. New Jersey, Ohio, and Illinois had all abolished contracts in the early eighties, but the administrative authorities had almost immediately turned to the piece-price compromise and were able to continue their fairly prosperous industries. In Illinois it was not until the radical Democrat, John P. Altgeld, became governor that conscientious effort was made to put into effect the intent of the amendment of 1886. He directed the introduction of industries to be operated on state account, and soon over half of the prisoners were laboring at these. Nevertheless, his Republican successor reversed the policy, charged the enormous outlays for machinery to Democratic graft, and returned to piece-price agreements. Gradually the labor forces regained their influence, both here and in Ohio, and with the aid of outside merchants they were able, in the early years of the next century, to exclude prison products from the open market. Indiana, partly because of the inefficiency of her prison industries, escaped the labor attack of the eighties. Accordingly in 1888, when for the first time her prisons reported self-support, it was an occasion for public congratulation, and it was not until the last year of the century that a law was finally passed calling for the gradual abolition of contracts.

That Michigan, rapidly becoming industrialized, escaped the fury of labor legislation was partially a result of the fact that her major prisons were already operating largely on public account. The Detroit house of correction continued to pay its full expenses under Superintendent Nicholson, but, as in the days of Brockway, it operated all its industries without any outside interference. Meanwhile Jackson prison was extending its mining activities into additional state-owned coal lands and experimenting with hog-raising and trucking on its sixty-five acre lot. When in the nineties an attack was again made on the contractors, Warden Otis Fuller was able to report to the National Prison Congress that he had successfully defended the industries of Ionia against the assault of outside companies, making no mention of labor unions.

The anticontract agitation did not affect the labor of prisoners in all parts of the country, although it had some surprising reverberations. In the South efforts to restrict and even to abolish the lease system and to substitute farming and road labor were coincident with but entirely independent of the northern agitation; yet there were serious labor troubles in Kentucky and especially in Tennessee over prison labor, and, in the latter, violent outbreaks persuaded the state to terminate its coal lease in the early nineties. Meanwhile in the West the anticontract law of the federal government, prohibiting such employment for federal convicts, practically eliminated industry from the territorial prisons. When new states were formed here, this provision was usually imbedded in their constitutions, and indeed hardly a prison in the Rocky Mountain area provided any productive labor for its inmates, aside from a little stone-quarrying, until the development of the honor road camps in the present century.

Labor problems, however, were rife in three western prisons. The lease of Nebraska's prison in 1877 was bitterly assailed until replaced by contracts in the nineties. Oregon, on the other hand, abandoned state-account industries and in 1895 leased its penitentiary. California's earlier action prohibiting new contracts after 1882 was more to be expected in view of its active labor forces, and it affords a clear example of the speed with which an organized force can get results in a young state. This wide-spreading activity of the anticontract agitation suggested the expanding horizon of the northeastern prison system, but it was not until the next century that the development became significant.

A few protests occurred in such border states as West Virginia, Missouri, and Kansas, but on the whole their prisons attracted praise rather than censure as they developed profitable industries. In fact practically everybody in Missouri and Kansas rejoiced when their respective prisons began in the early eighties to operate nearby coal mines, thus gradually becoming sources of profit to their states. Protests that arose were brushed aside by the authorities. Similarly in West Virginia the governor pointed out that if labor should insist that the profitable contracts at the prison be abandoned, the alternative would be either work on the public highways or some lease system as in the South.

Meanwhile Minnesota was doing some constructive experimenting of its own. When its law of 1889 made one-half of the prisoners available to contractors an agreement was made with the recently organized Minnesota Thresher Company to produce its binder twine. It was a new thing for a state prison to get in on the ground floor of an expanding industry with a great market in the community. Whatever labor problems might have developed were forestalled as the state took over this industry in the early nineties and established the model state-account system of the nation. Producing and selling cheap in an almost unlimited market to the benefit of the chief portion of its electorate, and at the same time paying its prison expenses, Minnesota had an unassailable system.

The nonindustrial states of the North largely escaped this problem. Wisconsin gave it no attention until the depression of 1893 caused the contractor to lay off most of his laborers and roused the authorities to the danger of dependence on such a system. An investigation was made and a change to the New York system proposed, but returning prosperity solved the problem, and it was not until 1907 that a new system was adopted, patterned after Minnesota.[7] In Iowa, except for the successful action of button companies to secure protection from prison competition, little attempt was made to regulate the use of prison labor. Aside from Massachusetts none of the New England prisons experienced any hardships due to anticontract agitation. Maine, however, seriously hampered her prison industry, carried on for many years at state account, by limiting the number to be employed at any one trade to 20 percent of the convicts. The sole industry, a wagon factory, was seriously handicapped until the warden hit upon the trick of dividing the industry into several trades; but the prison never regained its old prosperity for, symbolical of most prisons, it was putting its money on the horse in a railroad era.

The controlling factors in the convict labor problem of the nineties were thus local rather than national in character. Only in

[7] E. Stagg Whitin, "Prison Industries in the State of Wisconsin," in "Good Roads and Convict Labor," *Proceedings of the Academy of Political Science* 4 (1914): 309–332.

such states as New York, Pennsylvania, and Massachusetts were the
interests sufficiently organized to secure their full desires, and it was
fortunate that these states were able to bear the burdens of
nonproductive prisons. The neat penological rationalization of the
legislation in these states attracted both the interests and the
reformers throughout the country, and gradually the old American
tradition of prisons supported by the labor of their inmates gave
place to a new standard of convicts working to learn trades but
avoiding the public markets. If its negative aspects were most
prominent, both in the causes and in the results, the new industrial
program nevertheless contributed much to the spread of the
reformatory function of labor.

Organized labor, strong throughout the North in the mid
eighties, lost much of its political influence after the decline of the
Knights. Whatever its defects for the economic struggle, this
national body exerted through its state and district assemblies a
powerful influence on state politicians. It not only claimed to fight
the whole cause of labor but was quick in this instance to defend the
welfare of a small portion of its members. When the strength of the
Knights declined, the American Federation of Labor eagerly took
over this plank of its predecessor's program, but the cautious
political activity of its subsidiary state federations prevented them
from attaining the influence of their predecessors over prison
developments. Nevertheless, the continued growth of the power of
the national A. F. of L. and its unswerving adherence to the attack on
penal servitude, did much to prepare public opinion and especially
the politicians for the new function of prison industry.

The Republicans as well as the Democrats began to see the light
toward the end of the century. Carroll D. Wright, as commissioner
of labor under Cleveland in 1886, had defended the contractor, but
by 1896 he had become aware of the existence of unfair competition.
The final crystallization of the new attitude appeared in the
recommendations of the United States Industrial Commission of
1900, created by a Republican House. Its report strongly endorsed
New York's recently elaborated state-use system; in fact, twelve out
of thirteen resolutions urged the superiority of this system over all
others. A considerable array of statistics revealed greater profits from
the contracts, but the commission took higher ground, asserting:
"The most desirable system for employing convicts is one which
provides primarily for the punishment and reformation of the

prisoners and the least competition with free labor, and, secondarily, for the revenue of the State."[8] Both of these reports justified rather than complained of the decline in the earning capacities of the prisons, and they rejoiced in the comparative expansion of the public-account industry; in the later of these investigations even the piece-price system was frowned upon.

The new theories did not always have clear sailing. The national reports showed an irresponsibility for state budgets that stood in sharp contrast with several state investigations. An Illinois commission, originally favorable to the New York plan, was frightened from it by a discovery of the failure of even the well organized administrative agencies of that state to secure employment for more than one-third of the state prisoners and for but few of those in the counties; it was especially cautioned by the discouraging financial results. Nevertheless, the day of self-supporting prisons was passing, and the states were at the same time becoming accustomed to larger budgets. The recommendations of the Industrial Commission were to be widely quoted in succeeding years.

The one resolution of this commission that proposed definite action by Congress revived the old agitation for the restraint of interstate traffic in prison-made goods. The old O'Neill Bill had been repeatedly agitated, but it had always been tabled. Several of the states had undertaken to secure the same end by laws regulating the importation of prison products from other states, requiring branding or an importer's license, or some such restraint.[9] Congress itself forbade the importation of such goods from foreign countries. But the state laws were being attacked in the courts, and already the more extreme New York and Ohio laws had been set aside.[10] The problem had a clear affinity with the regulation of the interstate

[8] U.S. Industrial Commission, *Report . . . on Prison Labor* (Washington, D.C., 1900), Part III, p. 11ff. See also U.S. Comm. Labor, *Convict Labor*, Bulletin no. 5 (Washington, 1896), p. 446ff.: "The total income in forty-one states in 1885 has been $24,271,078 and this fell to such an extent that they reported only $19,042,472 in 1895, while at the same time the number of convicts increased from 41,877 to 54,244 between these dates. The problem of comparison is complicated because the sum is the value of the goods, not of the work."

[9] U.S. Indust. Comm., *Prison Labor*, pp. 141–166, for a complete summary of convict labor laws. New York and Ohio were the first in 1894, but Kentucky, Indiana, and Wisconsin followed in rapid succession, and Colorado shortly adopted a moderate law.

[10] Ohio law set aside in *Arnold* v. *Yanders* (1897), 47 *N.E. Reports*, p. 50; and New York law in *People* v. *Hawkins* (1898), 51 *N.E. Reports*, p. 257.

liquor traffic, and the Industrial Commission favored a Wilson Act
for prison labor instead of the complete federal prohibition of such
commerce proposed by the O'Neill Bill. Three decades were to pass
before Congress passed the Hawes-Cooper Bill, which was in effect a
response to this earlier recommendation.

The prison-labor problem had arrived at the zenith of its
influence by the close of the century. While the aggressive activity of
organized labor had turned to the economic field, politicians eager
to attract votes still campaigned, and competing industrial interests
were gaining a hearing. Only a few of the states had carried their
legislation far enough to gain political stability, but already their
measures were the center of agitation in many of the other states.
Even the federal government had mounted the band wagon and was
considering taking the driver's seat with a questionable federal
police power.

The larger significance of the problem was just beginning to
appear. Most of the states, escaping the rigors of the agitation, had
been able by one means or another to provide employment for the
large majority of their convicts, and, in spite of brief crises, the old
system had been able to hold its own in their prisons. In
Pennsylvania, New York, and to a lesser degree in Massachusetts, a
new situation had developed; the major reliance of the disciplinarians could no longer be a good day's hard labor. This was fortunate
for the reformatories, in that they were encouraged to develop to the
full their trade schools, their military organizations, and all the
other features of their discipline which, in an earlier era, might have
been abandoned as the need for economy urged self-support. The
regular prisons in these states were in a quandary. The labor system
in Pennsylvania had become a farce; in New York the lax
administration supplied scarcely one-third of the convicts with
work; in Massachusetts the prisoners were idling about antiquated
machinery, and no officer pretended to maintain the old silent
system. Should the prisons adopt the reformatory methods and strive
to provide a constructive social program; should they study to
provide conditions that would keep the convicts fairly contented and
orderly; could they maintain obedience in the face of idleness by a
return to brutal punishments—these were some of the questions that
labor legislation was forcing on the attention of the authorities in
1900. These questions were destined to become more insistent as

organized labor grew in strength and saw more clearly its place in a competitive capitalistic society that faced frequent periods of contraction.

The Early Development of Adult Reformatories

Fortunately the young men's reformatory, child of the imagination and the housing problem of the seventies, was already making a creditable development when the labor problem became the dominant consideration in prison affairs. Brockway had successfully established a reformatory discipline at Elmira before the anticontract laws effectively attacked prison industry, and he was able to take advantage of the new emergency to transform Elmira into an industrial training school, free from the responsibility of self-support. The anticontract movement joined with the population problem in strengthening the campaign for reformatories in other states, and additional institutions were established, several of them on the now well integrated pattern of the industrial reformatory at Elmira.

Louis Dwight and Enoch Wines had dominated their eras by organizing the propaganda for reform; Zebulon Brockway won his laurels by service in the ranks. Amos Pilsbury and Gideon Haynes before him, and at least a half dozen wardens in his day and later, fully equaled Brockway in administrative ability, and a few officers have revealed similar capacities for experimentation, but no other man had so successfully united all these qualities with a long life of practical service. Although not as widely famed as the elder Wines, Brockway during at least twenty of his fifty years of service was the most significant laborer in the prison field.

After his conversion in the late fifties Brockway retained a strong religious faith. He wanted religion to help him reform convicts, and if not always as serviceable in this respect as he desired, it did strengthen Brockway's zest for his job and provided him with an armor of righteousness that made him, in his later years, impervious to the darts of wise, as well as foolish, critics. His dominant personality and strong conviction earned for him by the close of his career the reputation of a tyrant, but by that time the venerable superintendent was able to bear the distinction with dignity, along with many another graduate of the school of hard knocks. Quite different features were prominent during the long years of his labors.

Eagerness to confer with other reformers and to give their ideas a trial, readiness to enlist and work with men of various specialties and to adapt their programs to his needs, brilliant ingenuity in devising solutions for critical situations, practical ability in handling men and in winning their loyalty, scrupulous honesty in the administration of public funds—such were the qualities that persuaded the New York reformers to trust their new reformatory to his care. Brockway was no Captain Ahab stubbornly chasing an elusive ideal through a half century; rather he was a determined commander ever scanning the horizon for the blowing of a new idea that might help to put character into the young men in his charge.[11]

When he assumed his new duties at Elmira in 1876, Brockway prepared the bill which became the controlling act of the institution. Indeterminate sentences were provided for all commitments, and the board of managers was empowered to release the inmates on parole as soon as a grading system or some similar device indicated their reformation. The sole amendment added by the legislature provided that no one should be detained longer than the maximum sentence provided in the criminal code for his crime, thus fortunately safeguarding against the danger that a few excessive terms served by unruly or feebleminded prisoners might rouse the public to abolish the experiment before it should have a fair trial. The age limits for commitments were fixed at sixteen and thirty, and only men convicted of their first felony were to be received.

The major task remained—that of developing a system of grades and marks that would maintain discipline, encourage reformation, and determine the date of its accomplishment. This latter was the crucial point and neither Maconochie nor Crofton was an adequate guide; Brockway had to devise his own program. Accordingly, as soon as the buildings were sufficiently completed to provide separate quarters, the rapidly increasing population was divided into three grades. The first was the honor grade to which a man had to earn his way by securing a specified number of marks in the second, or reception, grade. These marks were to be earned by satisfactory performance in school and shop and by good conduct; a perfect record during six months would accumulate sufficient marks for

[11] Zebulon R. Brockway, *Fifty Years of Prison Service: An Autobiography* (1912; reprinted Montclair, N.J., 1969). Brockway began as a guard at Wethersfield in 1848 under Amos Pilsbury.

promotion, and a similar performance in the first grade made the young man eligible for parole at the end of his first year. Very few proved able to demonstrate such an immediate reformation, and any serious misconduct or aggravated loss of marks demoted the inmate to a lower grade from which he had to earn his promotion if he desired parole. Brockway hoped to retreat behind his marking system and to substitute for the customary hostility between prisoners and officers the atmosphere of a school in which the instructor encourages the pupils to grapple with their records. In addition to developing self-control by marking the performance of the daily activities, Brockway sought to cultivate the inmate's self-respect by grading the privileges and accommodations so as to make the man in the first grade proud of his standing.

The reformatory was happily situated in a college neighborhood, and in developing his educational department Brockway soon disclosed a penchant for working with specialists. In 1878 he placed several able first graders in charge of elementary classes that met six evenings a week. He engaged Dr. D. R. Ford of the Elmira Women's College to conduct courses in physical geography and natural science for the more advanced young men. The next year he gave Dr. Ford charge of the entire department and employed six public school teachers and three attorneys as instructors for the elementary classes. He expanded the advanced section to include classes in "geometry, bookkeeping, human physiology and sanitary science." When D. P. Mayhew arrived from Michigan State Normal School to assume the duties of moral director he organized a third educational division offering classes in Biblical teachings, ethics, and psychology. The instructors awarded marks for successful work in their classes, but no artificial relation existed between the three grades and the three educational divisions; the stimulus to advance to the higher divisions came from the popularity of their courses. This incentive was especially strong in the early eighties when Charles A. Collin took charge of the ethics and economic courses and Professor J. R. Monks lectured on history and literature. Possibly stimulated by the fame of the Chautauqua summer schools, Brockway and his educational coworkers organized a summer session in 1882 with such gratifying results that it was made a regular feature.[12]

[12] New York State Reformatory, Elmira, *Report* (1880), p. 27.

But it was becoming evident that all the young men did not benefit equally from these classes, and in the summer of 1883 Brockway brought Professor N. A. Wells from Syracuse University to conduct a class in industrial arts for the dullards. Fifty backward students were selected for the experiment, and ten capable inmates were appointed as monitors to aid Wells supervise a course in terra-cotta modeling. The results were so encouraging that the thirteen-week course was repeated during the following summer on an enlarged scale, including classes in plumbing, tailoring, telegraphy, and printing. Another year saw the experiment grow into a year-round department, one of the pioneer trade schools of the country, and in 1886 a special building was provided for this activity. The purchase of a printing press in 1883 for the more economical publication of institutional reports quickly attracted some of the ablest inmates to this trade, and a plan was hit upon of printing a weekly leaflet to digest the news of the daily papers that were excluded from the reformatory. Thus the *Summary,* the first and for several decades the best of a long line of prison papers, grew out of a desire to train selected inmates in a useful trade and at the same time to keep the others informed of developments outside the prison.

Brockway's ready experimentation with new ideas was further illustrated in 1886 when he encouraged Dr. Hamilton D. Wey, a visiting physician, to organize a special class of twelve low-grade, intractable convicts for intensive physical training along the lines of the recently imported Swedish technique. The training included carefully planned and measured diets, steam or hot-water baths with rubbing and kneading of muscles by an expert trainer, and extended drills in calisthenics. A special early-morning school period rounded out the program and supplied a gauge for judging results. When the treatment was discontinued after several months owing to the loss of the trainer, both Dr. Wey and Brockway were gratified to find that ten of the twelve patients were ready to take an active part in the normal institutional life.

Amid such experiments it was no wonder that both inmates and officers thrived. Brockway had early dispensed with the services of a regular chaplain and was entertaining a succession of prominent and able speakers. These visitors, numbering thirty-six in 1885, were a fruitful source of stimulation to the officers as well as to the prisoners, but, what was more important for American penology, they carried away with them a most favorable impression of the new reformatory. Champions were sorely needed, for many critics were protesting against the newfangled methods of pampering criminals. Brockway, on one occasion, responded that he was trying to give his boys "something to pull at," something hard to do that would call into use their best faculties.[13] Charles Dudley Warner, a frequent visitor, proclaimed Brockway's work to be a remarkable demonstration of the educational theories of Froebel. In 1885 he declared that

> the rose-water method, the rewards and punishment method, the sanitary method, are alike and all united inadequate to touch the great criminal mass. . . . I firmly believe there is a way. . . . That way, is education. . . . And by education I do not mean the teaching of knowledge, the imparting of information, learning from books or any other source. I mean . . . a training and bringing out of all the powers and faculties that go to make up a man, sound in mind, in morals, in body.[14]
>
> It is the fundamental thing in Froebel's system of education [Warner added more than a decade later] that the only way to awaken powers is by creating activity . . . that makes something, that does something. . . . The whole Elmira system is based on that ability to form and change habits.[15]

Thus Brockway and his coworkers developed the educational provisions of Elmira far beyond those of any other prison. The reformatory was well established before the tornado of labor laws hit the state upsetting the industrial systems so laboriously developed in other prisons. A quite unexpected result of these laws was the new prominence forced upon the educational activities at Elmira. Compelled to shift from one to another of five different industrial systems during the first twelve years, only the most versatile of administrators could have maintained a distinct institutional character; Brockway, by emphasizing the educational features, succeeded in establishing a coordinated industrial reformatory.

The industrial program had been a major feature of the reformatory from the beginning. Brockway, with a reputation for making his institutions pay their way, had organized the first

---

[13] N.P.A., *Proceedings* (1887), pp. 281–282.

[14] N.P.A., *Proceedings* (1885), pp. 232–233.

[15] N.P.A., *Proceedings*, (1898), pp. 261–263.

industries with borrowed money, operating them himself, as was his custom. But the legislature refused to back this system with the necessary credit and in 1881 directed the managers to make suitable contracts. Regulations were adopted limiting the hours of labor to eight on each weekday and providing for an over-task bonus in cash and marks for the grading system. Brockway, however, soon became dissatisfied with the contractors and, as the agitation against that system was coming to a head in the legislature, proposed the piece-price system as a means for eliminating their interference and satisfying the amendment of 1884. Support for this scheme grew and it was partially introduced in 1887, only to be terminated by the Yates Law in the following year. Responsible men recognized that this last measure offered no real solution, but, while Charles A. Collin was drafting the excellent Fassett Law, Brockway was busy working out his own solution. Fourteen hours after the sudden cessation of all industries in 1888 he had a military-training department in operation, and within a month all the inmates were organized into companies and were drilling several hours each day. Meanwhile the trade school activity was shifted from its two evening sessions to fill the six mornings of the week; the literary school was convened every evening except Sunday; and the physical education department, formerly handling only a few abnormals, was expanded so as to provide calisthenic exercises to the entire population. A touch of drama was added to this remarkable transformation when the fife and drum corps was enlarged into a brass band. Because of the emergency, these pioneer developments of the penal curriculum were safeguarded from attack, and when the Fassett Law freed Elmira from the necessity of self-support the few productive industries permitted to the institution were readily coordinated with the trade-school department. The erection of a gymnasium in 1890 established the physical culture and military departments as year-round features and gave them, together with the evening school, a coordinate place with the trades department in the now completely evolved reformatory technique.

Unfortunately Brockway's remarkable success in these adminis-trative details was prompting judges in all parts of the state to inundate Elmira with new commitments. Additions to the original 504 cells were made in 1886 and again in 1892, raising the total to 1,296 cells but without adequately accommodating the growing population. Overcrowding continued to harass the institution until a branch reformatory was built in the next century, and this situation, more than any other factor, served to plague and darken the latter days of the great superintendent.

It was difficult to check Elmira's hardy development, and new innovations were made in its technique during the nineties. A succession of able inmate editors of the *Summary* made some pioneer efforts at penological research. One of them in 1893 made the first scientific study of prison diets, and his report, with its consideration of the calories and grams of the various types of nourishment and its comparison of the rations at Elmira with those of the American and German armies, contrasts sharply with the usual pound-and-quart analysis, chiefly concerned with economy. But the most important disciplinary development of the decade was the introduction in 1896, following Concord's example, of organized sport. Games had been organized spontaneously in a few prisons at earlier dates when the prisoners had been given the freedom of the yard on special occasions, but no prison, not even the Massachusetts reformatory, developed this feature to the point that Brockway now carried it in his endeavor to foster self-control and team spirit at Elmira. This feature was to prove one of the most popular of the reformatory's contributions to prison discipline in the next century, although only a few institutions were able to derive other than entertainment value from it.   .

The industrial reformatory at Elmira was now successfully established, attracting sometimes the praise and sometimes the ridicule of prison administrators, aspiring politicians, newspaper alarmists, and foreign critics, who may or may not have walked in the shade of its late-Victorian turrets. Its well coordinated discipline, centering around the grading and marking system, was animated by an honest application of the indeterminate sentence. With an industrial activity subordinated to trade and academic schools, and a military organization and calisthenic exercises supplemented by intensive physical culture for the defectives, keeping the men fully employed; with the weekly *Summary* for the world's news, an extensive library, and the frequent Sunday lectures by prominent visitors, all prodding the flagging intellect; and above all with the stimulation and kindly encouragement of Professors Monks, Ford, Collin, and Wells, of Dr. Wey, and, last but not least, of Zebulon

Brockway—Elmira, "College on the Hill," was surely supplying its inmates with something more to pull on than their own bootstraps when they wished to lift themselves out of the gutter. A large percentage of success was reasonably to be expected as long as society afforded the released men ample opportunities for constructive citizenship.

There was in the atmosphere of Elmira something vital, and yet so intangible as to escape many a scribe and copyist. It may have been the power of faith or the force of inspiration which came to Brockway because he believed in the reformatory value of his methods. Whatever it was, he passed it on to his coworkers and to the men under his care. It created the "will to pull," which was the one element that no reformatory discipline could dispense with and which would become a lost art as more sophisticated penologists emphasized clinical classification and prognostications for reform. It was one of those realities which later generations discredit because they cannot reproduce them. It made all the difference in the world between the reformatories, such as Elmira at its high tide in the early nineties, and their disillusioned remnants which paraded the youth of a new era down the ruts of tradition. While vital statistics frequently achieve little better than a consummate jest, considerable credence is due the investigation in 1888 which reported 78.5 percent of the 1,125 men already paroled to be reformed and laboring as good citizens for the support of themselves and their families.[16] The more favorable economic opportunities in the years before 1893 further increased the percentage of success.

By the nineties Elmira had become the model for other reformatories, demanding imitation rather than originality; but the institutions already established did not quickly conform to its pattern. Thus the Ionia house of correction or Michigan reformatory, especially during the long years of Otis Fuller's administration, made no attempt to introduce what Fuller regarded as Brockway's reformatory frills. Elementary instruction was provided and the

---

[16] N.Y. State Reformatory, Elmira, *Report* (1888), p. 26. Modern skeptics should not overlook the fact that the probation system had not yet come in to exclude from the reformatories the most likely candidates for reformation. See also Anthony M. Platt, *The Child Savers: The Invention of Delinquency* (Chicago, 1969), pp. 64–74, for a somewhat different version of the development of the reformatory in America.

lockstep was abandoned, but the traditional rules of silence were retained and the institution in both theory and practice placed its major reliance on good hard labor as the best method of reformation. Meanwhile at Sherborn, in spite of the determination of Mrs. Ellen C. Johnson, superintendent for many years after 1884, the presence of both major and minor offenders made the application of a system of grades and marks difficult. The poorly coordinated provisions for the release on permit, indenture, and parole of the various types of cases further complicated the situation, while the failure to develop industrial activities limited the educational possibilities of the institution. The one real accomplishment was the development of a farm with its opportunities for both exhausting labor and varied occupations, including the privilege of caring for pets and flowers. The planting of a mulberry grove, although it failed to provide the intended silk industry, supplied an attractive setting for Sunday afternoon lectures; and many visitors were to become entranced by the quaint scene as they spoke or sang to rows of primly dressed women seated in the shade. The undesirable overcrowding of the first years resulted in measures shunting more and more cases into local institutions, and Sherborn's population dwindled far below its accommodations, making the general court reluctant to answer appeals for appropriations for new developments. Nevertheless, in an unobtrusive way Massachusetts continued to give a large portion of its female prisoners a friendly care that greatly excelled the treatment of women in all other states until New York took a fresh lead at the end of the century.

The Bay Commonwealth was in these years developing a much more successful institution in its young men's reformatory. A decline in the commercial value of the site of old Charlestown prison scheduled for replacement in the early eighties, prompted the state to designate the prison under construction at Concord as a reformatory. When organized in 1884 it placed no age limits on commitments and many major and certain minor offenders were admitted. The Elmira pattern was already gaining repute, and a new law of 1886 provided for indeterminate sentences with two-year maximums for misdemeanants, five-year maximums for major offenders, and a grading system to determine the date of parole. But Concord was prevented, by the mixed character of its population, from adhering strictly to the Elmira pattern, and the ingenuity of its officers made it in some respects an additional experiment station.

The reformatory was fortunate in securing as its first superintendent Colonel Gardiner Tufts,[17] and equally fortunate in his young assistant, Joseph Scott. Both were educators with a strong religious bent, and they secured the faithful cooperation of Chaplain William J. Batt in making this force a major feature of the discipline. The grading system and many of the educational features of Elmira were introduced, and *Our Paper* followed the *Summary*, although it gave greater space to original compositions by the inmates. Industrial and manual training departments and physical exercises were introduced after their value had been demonstrated in New York, but this was also after the slightly tardy labor laws of Massachusetts had made it necessary to find a substitute for productive industries. Concord authorities were the first to develop a program of organized sports but its open-air gymnasium, unlike Elmira with its better equipment, could not be used throughout the year. The most original achievement at Concord was the organization of several societies or clubs to one of which all convicts who had advanced to the first grade were eligible for election. Little restraint was placed on the activities of these organizations at their weekly meetings, and in many cases the club members and the institution reaped many of the advantages to be derived from the self-government schemes that were to arouse so much controversy two decades later.[18]

When Colonel Tufts died in 1891 his able assistant, Joseph F. Scott, succeeded to control and continued the reformatory policies of the institution with even greater success. After the example of Mrs. Johnson at Sherborn, farming activities were extended, and a 200-acre tract was put under the plow. Among other improvements an up-to-date hospital was erected in 1900. The establishment of a state farm for misdemeanants relieved the reformatory of many commitments for drunkenness, but hundreds of these charges continued to crowd the cells at Concord, and their two-year-maximum sentences

[17] N.P.A., *Proceedings* (1891), Appendix I.

[18] Massachusetts Prison Commission, *Concord Report* (1887), pp. 19–28, 61–72. The societies included a Reformatory Prayer Meeting with 30 members, a Y.M.C.A. with 187 members, a Catholic Debating Society with 225, a Saturday Scientific and Literary Club with 75, a Baseball and Literary Society with 45, and a Chatauqua Club with 15 members. The Saturday-afternoon games included baseball, football, wrestling, and leaping; neighboring towns frequently sent teams to play against the reformatory on special days.

occasioned the rapid turnover that released 2,465 between 1885 and 1889 in contrast with the 2,674 parolees from the larger Elmira during its first thirteen years. Although the fullest realization of the reformatory influences was thus prevented, Concord had become a most creditable addition to the institutional equipment of Massachusetts by the end of the century.

The further extension of the reformatory pattern was in large part the work of the National Prison Association. Its sessions provided a parade ground for the various disciplines, and Elmira invariably carried off the blue ribbon. Even the strong self-righteousness of the eastern Pennsylvanians could not resist this influence, and the proposed middle penitentiary of that state, patterned after Cherry Hill in 1878, was transformed, while still on paper, into a young men's reformatory. Huntingdon was built during the eighties on the Elmira model, adding the farming activities of Sherborn and Concord as a major feature, and when Major R. W. McClaughry, warden at Joliet but formerly a professor of Latin, was called to take charge, an efficient reformatory discipline was organized. A half dozen additional states took steps toward the establishment of young men's reformatories before the end of the century, and, although their programs were in many cases delayed, the Elmira model had gained full recognition as the correct penitentiary pattern. Thus in place of the generous dreams and ambitious resolutions of the earlier generation, a practical interest in Brockway's achievements had become the chief growing point of penology.

The Revival of the National Movement

The success of Elmira and the rising clamor of the labor forces, occurring simultaneously in the early eighties, were large factors in the revival of the National Prison Association. The passing of the earlier generation had not put an end to the general agitation for prison reform, for the National Conference of Charities had voted in 1879 to enlarge its scope so as to include problems of correction; but the secretaries of state boards of charities and other interested reformers who had gathered to these conferences failed to enlist the collaboration of prison officers, and their sessions had little practical effect. It was at Brockway's suggestion that W. M. F. Round, secretary of the New York Prison Association, and Franklin Sanborn, president of the American Social Science Association, joined in calling the preliminary gathering at Saratoga Springs in 1883 of those interested in reviving the National Association. In spite of the imminent danger of anticontract legislation, prompting the wardens to gather together to work out a solution for threatening unemployment, it proved to be a difficult task to weld the various elements together into a united association. The wardens, usually hardheaded Civil War veterans with some political connections, were not eager "to sit at the feet of the Gamaliels who were running the machine." But the reformers were not the kind of men to take back seats, and Sanborn, Brinkerhoff, the younger Wines, Round, Byers, and Francis Wayland quickly monopolized the platform. Brockway was an old comrade, but most of the other wardens did not feel at home in this company, and the first regular congress in 1884 had scarcely closed before a group of prison officers gathered separately at Chicago. William Round, secretary of the revived Association, hurried to Chicago and was greatly relieved when he learned that they were not bolting from the reform movement.

Possibly the factor that did more than anything else to hold the Association together was the personality of its president, Rutherford B. Hayes. His record of faithful cooperation in the earlier period, combined with the prestige of being a former president of the United States, prompted his annual reelection until his death in 1892. But, while the Association might have held together, it would have accomplished little had not a number of able wardens been so situated that they enjoyed unusually long terms of service. Such officers as Brockway at Elmira, Joseph Nicholson who had succeeded him at Detroit, Charles E. Felton at the Chicago house of correction, Ellen Johnson and Gardiner Tufts at the two reformatories of Massachusetts, and Michael Cassidy and Edward Wright at the two Pennsylvania penitentiaries, were in charge of institutions never subjected to politics. At least one warden, McClaughry, enjoyed a long career in several institutions because of his distinguished work. A. A. Brush, whose eleven years at Sing Sing created a record for that political football not broken until the arrival of Lewis E. Lawes, and of H. F. Hatch and E. C. Coffin at Jackson and Columbus helped to provide the successive congresses with an atmosphere of realism that kept their speculations within the bounds of practical affairs. A few outstanding chaplains, notably George Hickox at Jackson, John Milligan at Pittsburgh, and William Batt at Concord, served to keep the religious tradition alive although it no longer stood forth as the dominant inspiration. The annual deliberations of these men as they traveled from city to city helped to coordinate prison developments throughout an expanding section of the country and supplied instruction for the new officers—wardens for a year or two—thus preventing the anarchy of politics from swamping the few achievements already made in the field of penology.

Preoccupation with practical affairs was an outstanding feature of most of the earlier congresses. The term "reform" gained a genuine disrepute as the crusading zeal of the leaders of the seventies was disclaimed, at least among a group of self-styled practical wardens led by Michael Cassidy of Cherry Hill. Although the sessions usually opened with a large popular assembly on Saturday evening at which visiting and local dignitaries lectured on the public's responsibility for the criminal, and although a symphony of sermons filled the next day as chaplains and local pastors celebrated prison reform throughout the convention city, the real work of the congress did not begin until Monday brought the wardens out in full force, airing the soiled garments of the prison system. Strange alignments developed during the debates over various issues. Brockway defended the "rod" against Cassidy, Brush, and others who maintained that a solitary cell with bread and water was the best way of taming the intractable. When Judge Wayland urged that the moral welfare of prisoners should be safeguarded to the extent of denying the use of tobacco, Warden Brush was quick to retort that he was not striving to make angels out of his charges. When Brockway urged that prisons be limited to six hundred inmates as against Brush's contention that they should be prepared to house one thousand, the delegates supported Brockway, but the states, here as in so many cases, continued to build as economy and population dictated, exceeding even Brush's standard in a dozen institutions by 1900.

The Association undertook to stimulate federal action in the collection of penal statistics and in behalf of federal prisoners. Frederick Wines, as criminal statistician for the census bureau, complained of irregular prison records. Every warden appreciated the difficulties in the way of statistical comparisons, and Joseph Nicholson introduced a resolution in 1890 calling upon the federal government to establish a bureau to gather annual statistics—a practice already operative in several European countries but not to be adopted in America for several decades. Meanwhile the makeshift arrangement of boarding federal prisoners in the various state and local prisons without supervision or adequate records was still more reprehensible. General Roeliff Brinkerhoff's agitation on this point, beginning in 1885, continued for a decade before a faltering start was made toward the development of a federal penal system. His election as president of the National Prison Association in 1893 following the death of President Hayes prolonged the noncontroversial leadership of Ohio for another five years and enabled Brinkerhoff to maintain pressure for federal action.

Lively discussions occurred at the congresses on most aspects of the penal problem. The care of the discharged, the influence of education, and of course the power of religion were considered in an attempt to evaluate their aid to reformation. Occasional reports were made on the nature of developments in Europe, praising the centralization achieved there or attempting to account for the remarkable decline of crime in England.[19] But the two subjects which received most attention were the convict-labor problem and the challenge of reformatory technique. Only death could silence such critics of Elmira as Michael Cassidy, but, as the number of reformatories and the experiments with release on parole increased, objections to the new procedure were pushed aside, and discussion centered on the respective merits and defects of the various adaptations of the technique.

The wardens, never quite content with their place in the Association, organized a subsidiary body in 1886 to take charge of the sessions at which their special problems were considered. Joseph Nicholson of Detroit was chosen president and McClaughry of

---

[19] N.P.A., *Proceedings* (1891), pp. 80–106, 237–249. Warden Cassidy, after a visit to England, attributed this enviable record to the migration of discharged convicts to America. Captain Massie of Canada credited the achievement to the large amount of Christian work among the poor and middle classes. C. E. Coffin gathered statistics to show that the reduction in commitments was largely due to a substitution of fines for prison sentences.

Joliet, secretary. The latter was charged by his fellows to find a scheme for identifying prisoners in order to settle the old argument as to the number of allegedly reformed men released from one institution only to be gathered into another.

McClaughry received his commission at an opportune time. Alphonse Bertillon had recently elaborated a scheme for the identification of recidivists, or "back-sliders" as F. H. Wines translated the term, based on the theory that while the bone structure of the body does not change after reaching maturity, individual variations are so elaborate that a series of minute measurements provides an infallible identification. The city of Paris had adopted the scheme in 1883 in order to aid in classifying its unwieldy file of criminal photographs, and four other French cities were introducing the system when McClaughry ordered instruments from Bertillon. The demonstration of the novel scheme before the Association at its Toronto session in 1887 attracted keen interest. Skepticism was allayed but feelings were aroused, and A. A. Brush, the hardfisted warden of Sing Sing, joined with the sentimentalists who considered the convict's past his own affair. Nevertheless, the Bertillon system gained wide approval, and in the course of two years a central bureau was set up at Joliet under the direction of the wardens' association with fourteen prisons pledged to cooperate. Unfortunately only a few states provided funds to purchase instruments, and no assistance was given to the central bureau, thus forcing its abandonment. The scheme was saved from complete discard when in 1896 New York established a bureau of identification at Sing Sing, staffed to supply service to any prison officer in the country, and the association of chiefs of police opened a similar clearinghouse at Chicago. By the end of the century seventeen states and Canada were cooperating more or less efficiently through these two agencies, and the wardens' association was content to see its self-appointed task in more capable hands.

Meanwhile the chaplains had likewise formed a subsidiary organization in order to maintain their position in the movement. George Hickox of Jackson was chosen president, and the association undertook to secure general observance of the third Sabbath in October as Prison Sunday, a special occasion for chaplains and Christian wardens to invade the public pulpits and for ministers far and wide to try their hands at prison reform. But while this campaign was winning much success, the chaplains were under fire within the profession, where the old faith in the conversion of convicts was rapidly waning. Brockway dispensed with the services of a chaplain and even moderate-tempered Hastings H. Hart of Minnesota urged that "no convict ought to be allowed to feel for a minute that he can make a gain of godliness."[20] Some chaplains felt constrained to justify their calling before the congresses by lengthy perorations on "The Ideal Chaplain," but many were content to perform their kindly functions in an unobstrusive fashion among the friendless men behind the bars.

A fundamental transformation occurred in the national movement during the early nineties. New vistas were appearing, and the redirection of attention became especially evident at the St. Paul congress in 1894 where a host of professors and doctors almost pushed the practical wardens off the platform. Professor Charles R. Henderson of the new University of Chicago presented his first paper, debating the existence of a criminal type and introducing his audience to the contemporary European speculations on that subject.[21] Professor Charlton T. Lewis of New York analyzed the theoretical and practical implications of the indeterminate sentence, while Charles A. Collin, now a professor of law at Cornell, described the recent achievements of Elmira. Eugene Smith presented a paper on criminal law reform, and Charles H. Reeve again attacked the problem of a national standard for criminal statistics. The reports of Dr. J. B. Ransom, physician at Clinton, and Dr. M. V. Ball of Cherry Hill on the results of experiments in the care of tubercular prisoners revealed that the most recent scientific discoveries concerning that troublesome malady were being used.

A changing social landscape was favorable to the leadership of the professors. The development of departments of sociology in the colleges brought into action a new group of specialists, among whom Henderson of Chicago was the most active. The flood of laws regulating convict labor took the problem of determining the proper

---

[20]Hastings H. Hart, *The Reformation of Criminals* (Oberlin, Ohio, 1890), p. 23.

[21]Only Dr. Hamilton D. Wey of Elmira had made a previous reference to the theories of Lombroso before a national congress. Arthur E. Fink, *Causes of Crime: Biological Theories in the United States, 1800-1915* (Philadelphia, 1938), pp. 179-184; Platt, *Child Savers*, pp. 18-28.

industrial policy for prisons out of the hands of the wardens and made occasion for comprehensive studies of the situation by such national authorities as Carroll D. Wright. A growing attention to the care of the discharged rendered especially timely the information Barrows gathered in 1895 from Europe. The appointment of Samuel J. Barrows as the United States commissioner on the International Prison Commission in 1895 marked a revival of federal interest, dormant since the days of Enoch Wines, and paved the way for the visit of the international association to America fourteen years later. All these activities were a bit beyond the range of busy wardens.

Of course the Association could not survive without the wardens, and to assure their participation at the top level it determined at Austin in 1897 to rotate the presidency and other leading offices among the practical administrators in the field. Zebulon Brockway was the first to win election as president and served at the Indianapolis congress in 1898. McClaughry succeeded to that post the next year and presided both at New Orleans and at Hartford. Warden Edward S. Wright of the Western Pennsylvania Penitentiary followed at Cleveland in 1900, and so the succession continued drawing leaders from varied regions and types of institutions as the years progressed.

Meanwhile the accumulating mass of statistics was adding fuel to many old controversies. The mounting criminal ratios called forth hoarse cries against "collegiate and hotel prisons."[22] The dispute over the percentages of the reformed and the broader rivalry between institutions which attempted to make much of education and those which still clung to the cleansing influence of hard labor gained in feeling as labor laws threatened the latter. The debate over indeterminate-sentence and parole laws took on a new aspect as statistics convinced the reformers that they had either to secure mandatory laws or to awaken the proper officials to a fuller appreciation of those already on the statute books. In justifying their programs to the general public the leaders continued to rely upon appeals to humanitarian sentiments and to the state's interest in deflecting as many individuals as possible from criminal activities— justifications which were possibly as reasonable as could be made in a society which had not undertaken the responsibility of securing to

[22] *The Forum* (October 1891); Howard Association of London, *The Collegiate and Hotel Prisons of America* (London, 1891).

every citizen the opportunity to realize the fullest development of his capacities.

The Association was becoming conscious of a larger audience. The lecturers were preparing their addresses for the judges, legislators, and editors of popular journals—authorities who wielded the real power in prison affairs. The warden's annual seminar was developing into a migrating chautauqua and responded to more than one appeal to come over into Macedonia. Such were the Association's visits to Denver and Austin, but the new spirit was most dramatically expressed when an extra session was convened in New Orleans in response to an earnest call from Michael Heymann for aid in his fight for reform in Louisiana.[23] These wide-ranging travels extended the influence of the northern movement into the relatively foreign Southland and the virgin West. In the process, new and promising methods of farm and road labor were uncovered and introduced into the North. At the turn of the century the isolation of the major sections of the country was only in part broken down, and the South continued to maintain a characteristic system of its own. The Association did not gain a truly national character until the first decade of the new century when it helped to round out the growth of the pedagogical penology it had nurtured so long.

BIBLIOGRAPHIC NOTE

The revived National Prison Association, *Proceedings* (1884–) are of primary importance, as are the New York State Reformatory, Elmira, *Reports* (1876–) and the official reports of the other early reformatories. Connecticut, *Contract Convict Labor Commission* (1880), a report of the special commission, provides a convenient summary of the reports of similar commissions in other states. U.S. Commissioner of Labor, *Second Annual Report, 1886: Convict Labor* (Washington, D.C., 1887); ibid., *Annual Report, 1905: Convict Labor* (Washington, D.C., 1906); ibid., *Convict Labor*, Bulletin no. 5 (Washington, D.C., 1896); U.S. Industrial Commission, *Report . . . on Prison Labor* (Washington, D.C., 1900); Massachusetts Superintendent of Prisons, *Report on the Various Methods of Employing Prisoners* (1898); Carroll D. Wright, *Hand Labor in Prisons*

[23] N.P.A., *Proceedings of the Adjourned Meeting at New Orleans* (1899), pp. 357–366.

(Boston, 1887). National Anti-Convict-Contract Association, *Proceedings of the National Convention* (Chicago, 1886).

Cited earlier, but of value for this period, are the works of Zebulon Brockway and Arthur E. Fink. Frederick C. Allen, *Hand Book of New York State Reformatory* (Elmira, 1927) and Alexander Winter, *The New York State Reformatory in Elmira* (1891; reprinted Montclair, N.J., 1976) shed light on this subject. Hastings H. Hart, *Reformation of Criminals* (Oberlin, Ohio, 1890) presents an excellent summary of prison reform. E. R. Beckner, *A History of Labor Legislation in Illinois* (Chicago, 1929); Mollie R. Carroll, *Labor and Politics* (Boston, 1923); T. V. Powderley, *Thirty Years of Labor* (Columbus, 1890); and E. T. Hiller, "Labor Unionism and Convict Labor," *Journal of Criminal Law and Criminology* 5 (1915): 851–879, all supply important materials on this crucial problem. Philip Klein, *Prison Methods in New York State: A Contribution to the Study of the Theory and Practice of Correctional Institutions* (New York, 1920) and Anthony M. Platt, *The Child Savers: The Invention of Delinquency* (Chicago, 1969) present two pictures of the development of the reformatory in America.

6.

REFORM IN THE
NORTHEASTERN STATES:
TO 1900

Although the revival and increasing strength of the national movement were important aspects of prison history, it was up to the states to determine the success or failure of the reform programs. The outstanding problem facing prison officials in the last decades of the century was the labor dilemma; but the two controlling factors of the previous era, population growth and the struggle to develop nonpartisan agencies for central control, continued to influence developments. Meanwhile the remarkable growth of the country with its improved living conditions was raising the standard of decency considered proper for prisons. Propelled by these forces, many northern states made reasonable progress toward introducing reformatory technique into the strongholds of the earlier penology of Louis Dwight, yet the total effect on the mass of the prisoners remained obscure.

The Struggle for Centralization

The efforts of the states to develop more satisfactory administrative agencies in the correctional field persisted in the directions suggested during the seventies. Experience continued to demonstrate the folly of trusting prisons to the control of transient politicians. An attempt to secure candid reports led to an extension of the spheres of the existing nonpolitical boards of charities and to the creation of such boards in additional states. A move to give genuine powers of control to these boards or to other central agencies made considerable headway in at least a half dozen northern states.

Massachusetts and New York had played the pioneer roles in this field during the seventies and now continued to reveal abilities for leadership. As before, it was the former that made the greater progress toward stable centralization. Although its prison commission, organized in 1879, was second only to the Rhode Island board of charities in the extent of its control, the Bay Commonwealth found, with changing conditions, that many of its features were unsatisfactory and that other functions had to be added. Thus, when the state provided for indeterminate sentences to Concord reformatory it gave the prison commissioners the responsibility of determining when to grant a release permit in each case. The habitual-criminal act of the following year conferred on them the discretion of releasing men sentenced under its provisions after they had served at least five out of their twenty-five years; again in 1895 the general parole and indeterminate-sentence act unwisely placed this same function on their overburdened shoulders. It was no wonder that the proposal was frequently made that these volunteer servants be made full-time, salaried officers.

The struggle for central control was unexpectedly aided when labor laws upset the prison industrial system. A superintendent of prison industries was provided in 1887, following the New York precedent, to organize state-account trades in all the penal institutions in the state. The decision in the following year to permit piece-price contracts lopped off the major functions of the new officer, but a decade later a new act abolished all forms of contract labor and reestablished his responsibility for the organization—this time—of state-use industries. The appointment of the able secretary of the prison commission, Frederick G. Pettigrove, as superintendent in 1898 brought harmony between the two authorities, but it was not until 1901 that a new reorganization combined these authorities into one commission with full authority to appoint and remove officers of state institutions, to order transfers or new construction in both state and local institutions, and to manage industries. With Pettigrove as chairman and each of the members receiving a full-time salary, this board became the most efficient correctional authority in the country.

The throttling hold of politics was much tighter in New York, yet rivalry between the parties in the end carried centralization to a point not far behind that of Massachuetts. The successive superintendents of the state prison industry made notable financial records, but political considerations limited most terms to five years. The New York Prison Association, experiencing a revival of activity in the nineties similar to that of Enoch Wines' day, continued its services as semiofficial inspector of the prisons of the state until 1896. A political upheaval in the previous year and the resulting investigation of prison management had disclosed considerable corruption.[1] The legislature, finally persuaded by this scandal to adopt the old proposal of Enoch Wines, created a prison commission composed of eight nonsalaried members and gave it authority to inspect all state and local prisons, to recommend desirable change and to enforce its policies in local institutions by court orders. Unfortunately the superintendent of industries was left independent of this body which in practice did not prove to be as effective as the Massachusetts commission in controlling either the state or local institutions.

The drive toward central control was making greater progress in the states of the Upper Mississippi Valley. The simpler problems of young states enabled them to gather all their charitable and correctional institutions under one authority. With the example of the Kansas board of charitable institutions in mind, the authorities of Wisconsin in 1880 abolished all its separate boards of directors and created one board of supervision, going beyond Kansas by including the prison under the board's control. The older board of charities continued to make annual inspections until 1891 when friction between the two authorities prompted the state to merge them into one board of control with full powers over state institutions and duties of inspection in the case of county jails. Wisconsin thus completed an organization that should have secured

---

[1] Subcommittee on Investigation of State Prisons, *Report* (New York Assembly, Doc. 76, 1895), pp. 1–27. The Democratic boss of the city of Auburn had supplied the prison with meat during the terms of the last two wardens at excessive prices, and the evidence indicated that he had secured the appointment for one of these men.

her leadership in penal developments.

But other factors intervened, and Minnesota stepped forward as the real leader in this section. The state was fully equipped with institutions by 1883 when it first considered the necessity for centralization, and the problem did not appear to call for more than a board of charities. Fortunately the board secured the services of the young Rev. Hastings Hornell Hart, and his persistent labors not only laid the basis for a distinguished public career but directed the development of correctional and charitable institutions along sound and progressive lines. The reorganization of these activities under a board of control in 1901 merely institutionalized an influence that had long been dominant. Iowa, after considering the rival procedures of its neighbors for at least a decade, chose the more authoritative instrument of government when it created a board of control in 1896; but here, as in other western states that established similar authorities after the turn of the century, the organizational advantage did not offset Minnesota's gain from Hart's leadership.

Of the remaining states of the North not previously equipped with some such form of central supervision, only Indiana took effective action in that direction. The old boards of charities continued to make annual inspections and to offer helpful suggestions on all correctional matters in Connecticut, Pennsylvania, Michigan, and Ohio. In Maryland and the northern New England states the governors undertook to perform this function. But in New Jersey, Illinois, and Kansas existing state boards had no responsibility for the state prisons, and, except for emergency investigations, the public was dependent on the reports and the policies of the political authorities. Missouri alone took no steps toward freeing its correctional activities from political dominance. Indiana was roused to action only by a scandal in its southern prison under Warden Howard in the late eighties; nevertheless, its board of charities, created in 1889 under the leadership of Timothy Nicholson, assumed an aggressive policy and supplied enlightened leadership in correctional affairs for several decades.

These boards provided a permanent body of recruits for the national movement. Even in states where they were not effectively in control, they helped to propagate the theories and programs discussed at the congresses. Several of the state boards staged annual conferences gathering the officials of state and local charitable and correctional institutions together for mutual discussion of their problems in the light of the more advanced theories of the day. Michigan, which staged the first conference in 1881, profited greatly from these educational gatherings, and the convening of annual conferences quickly spread into several neighboring North Central states. Their boards, relatively free from partisan control, struggled to remove the blight of politics from prison administration, and while their success in this direction was very limited they deserve much credit for the improvements made in the prison system.

Reforms Approved by the Legislatures

The last quarter of the nineteenth century witnessed a steady drift of opinion toward the conclusion that "a prison without reformatory influence is but a nursery of crime."[2] Much that was said on this subject in innumerable reports was little better than official cant, but the advantages offered by the new methods and the disruptive effects of the labor laws were compelling many officers to take the new theories seriously. When critics complained that it was distorted philanthropy if not sheer injustice to "take money from honest labor to make dishonest idlers comfortable, teach them trades, furnish them books, papers, and teachers," Charles H. Reeve responded that it was not philanthropy but sound public policy to redeem rather than to damn offenders.[3] While many of the theoretical reformers attempted to clothe their proposals in the terms of practical policies, some of the wardens did not hesitate to speak out boldly for the claims of sentiment and Christian brotherhood, thus dodging the demand that these public welfare measures be sacrificed to the dominant philosophy of individualism. The reform doctrine was aptly phrased in 1890 by the new board of charities of hitherto backward Indiana when it declared: "It is the criminal and not the crime that justice must consider. . . . Not what the man has done, but what he will do, should determine the length of his imprisonment."

The indeterminate sentence had long since become a familiar principle, and its successful application at Elmira had dispelled many doubts as to its practicability, but it was a political upheaval

---

[2] Indiana Prison North, *Report* (1886), p. 15.
[3] Charles H. Reeve, *The Prison Question* (Chicago, 1890), p. 148.

in Ohio that first brought the principle into the realm of major prisons. When the Democrats captured the state in 1883, they not only redeemed their pledge to the labor forces by abolishing prison contracts but undertook in one fell swoop to apply the whole reformatory technique to the penitentiary. They created a new board of directors and appointed new and inexperienced officers to introduce a grading and marking system and administer paroles at the prison. The board of charities was overwhelmed by this sudden adoption of its principles, and its fears that the reform program would be discredited seemed to be well grounded as the $50,000 annual income of the prison was turned into a deficit of $150,000. Fortunately the Republicans, who recaptured control at the next election, were persuaded by General Brinkerhoff to improve rather than to abolish the new system. They placed a fresh set of officials in control and negotiated new piece-price contracts, but limited their amendments of the parole law to its obvious defects. Under the new law only those serving sentences for their first felony, in case it was not first-degree murder, were eligible for parole after the minimum sentence for the crime had been completed; questions of guilt and arguments by attorneys were barred from consideration by the board of directors charged with issuing paroles; and the applicant was required to have reached the top grade in the prison and to show the promise of a job awaiting his discharge. Many were surprised at the approval which greeted these measures. Criticism was more freely showered upon a companion law that provided life sentences for habitual criminals and those sentenced for their third felony; popular sentiment supported the courts in their failure, except in rare cases, to prosecute such offenders, even after the introduction of the Bertillon system at the penitentiary made identification possible.

But Ohio's effort to apply reformatory discipline in the old state prison, overcrowded with 1,600 felons, was encountering difficulties. The officers and guards were poorly selected for the task of applying the marking system, and attainment of the first grade was not always made a prerequisite for parole. The requirement that a job be available was working to the advantage of a favored few with influential friends on the outside. At the same time the irregular application of the habitual-criminal act was creating an atmosphere of resentment inimical to the reformatory aspirations of the prison. These handicaps were accentuated by the repeated changes in management at Columbus, resulting in turn from the continued seesawing of politics in Ohio.

The admitted limitations to Ohio's success did not restrain other states from following her lead. The distinction between indeterminate-sentence laws and parole laws was not yet clearly appreciated, and their constitutionality was still in doubt. The two sentiments— to "sock" the repeater and to succor the first offender—were inconveniently confused, and when, as in Ohio, they were drafted into law at the same time and the enforcement of both attempted in one prison, the diffuculties were indeed multiplied. Few wardens suspected the obstacles that would have to be overcome before they could report that the Elmira technique was functioning smoothly in their old prisons. Not only the traditional-minded judges and lawyers but a large section of the public and most of the criminals were still blind to the justice of the new correctional philosophy that concerned itself with the criminal rather than with the crime. European visitors were amazed at the hardihood with which the Americans ventured to experiment in spite of these unsettled issues.

The first batch of laws applying the principle of the reformatory sentence to the mass of criminals came to grief in one way or another. The attorney general of New Jersey advised against the use of the state's 1889 parole law on the grounds that the legislature could not tamper with the authority of the courts to fix sentences. Michigan's indeterminate-sentence law of the same year was held invalid by the court as an infringement of the governor's power to pardon. Optional indeterminate-sentence laws in New York and Wisconsin were but seldom applied, as the judges hesitated to surrender to the prison officers the power of determining the length of sentences which they themselves had so long been accustomed to mete out with judicial poise. Legislative affirmation in Kansas and Vermont of the governor's power to grant conditional pardons had some effect on the pardoning procedure of the latter state where the small population made possible such direct executive supervision.

Meanwhile Massachusetts, already busy with plans for the reformatory treatment of its less vicious men and women, took up the attack on the repeaters. It adopted a habitual-criminal act in 1887 which prescribed twenty-five-year sentences for men convicted of a third felony but permitted parole after five years provided their reformation was evident to the commission. The ancestry of such laws goes back at least to Edward Livingston; Virginia, Louisiana, and New York had adopted such laws before the Civil War, although only that of Louisiana had been given effect. Europe's more extensive use of the principle was now attracting the attention of American travelers. Encouraged by the promise of accurate identifications through the use of the Bertillon technique, Wisconsin and California quickly adopted the measure. But events soon demonstrated the unwillingness of attorneys and judges to apply these laws. Massachusetts, by far the most conscientious in its enforcement, had convicted only twenty-five under this law by 1895, the majority of them as a result of a special drive against criminals in 1894.

In spite of these early discouragements the advocates of the reformatory sentence returned to the attack with renewed determination in the mid nineties. A succession of court decisions upheld several of the older laws and removed barriers to new ones. Under the inspiration of Hastings H. Hart, Governor William R. Merriam and Warden Henry Wolfer successfully applied the reformatory technique at the Stillwater prison in Minnesota in 1892, granting conditional pardons, with restraint, to the worthy men in the top grade. A parole law passed by the legislature in the following year was so efficiently administered that it attracted the interested attention of the delegates at the St. Paul congress of the National Prison Association in 1894.

Massachusetts and Illinois made additional improvements in the application of these principles to the mass of their criminals in the mid nineties. A law of the former state in 1894, authorizing the commissioners to parole any reformed first offender after two-thirds of his fixed sentence had expired, was followed the next year by a mandatory indeterminate-sentence law requiring the courts to give maximum and minimum sentences to all except the habitual criminals already provided for. A survey in 1896 discovered that the average leeway between the maximum and the minimum sentences was three years and six months, thus revealing that many judges were ready to give the principle a fair trial. Governor John P. Altgeld secured the adoption of a parole law in Illinois and directed the introduction of a grading system at Joliet. A conservative parole policy saved the reform from discredit and Warden McClaughry, rich with reformatory experience, persuaded the returning Republicans to extend the principle. An indeterminate-sentence law was passed in 1897, patterned after that of Massachusetts but taking a step forward by creating a special board of pardons to administer paroles.

Encouraged by these examples several additional states endorsed the reformatory sentence in the late nineties. Backward Indiana awoke with a start in 1897, led by its new board, and adopted sweeping reforms. Among other reforms, it made provision for the parole of first offenders in each of the men's prisons, and two years later extended this to the women's prison as well. Even before Indiana took these rapid strides forward to the front rank of penal reformers her northern neighbor had discovered that she could quietly dodge her court decision by extending to the prison officers the power to release the reformed men on licenses to be at large. While this was by no means satisfactory, it sufficed until replaced by a comprehensive parole law in 1903. Connecticut, another leader of the earlier days, failed to respond to the petitions of its prison association until 1897, and the parole law adopted at that time was poorly drafted and seldom applied. Vermont went further, adopting both indeterminate-sentence and parole laws in 1898 and applying them to all at the state prison and at the house of correction. Although the state court shortly declared the parole law unconstitutional, the governor stepped forward and granted conditional pardons to all deserving them under the unchallenged indeterminate sentences.

The influence of this profuse legislative activity was not as far-reaching as might have been expected. Aside from those fortunate enough to be committed to one of the better reformatories, the great majority of prisoners gained little of value from the laws. The courts neglected to give the indeterminate sentences in New York and Wisconsin; the boards rarely used their parole authority in New Jersey, Michigan, and Connecticut; none of the new principles applied to any of the convicts of Pennsylvania outside of Huntingdon reformatory. Finally in Massachusetts, where the reformers had achieved their most complete successes, new legislation in 1898 directed that release be granted automatically at the expiration of the minimum term if the prisoner's record showed no black marks, thus changing the admirable law of 1895 from a reformatory to a disciplinary measure. It was no wonder that the courts steadily increased their minimum sentences, greatly reducing the margin that was to serve as an incentive to reform. In a similar fashion the courts of Illinois fixed the maximum and minimum sentences so close together that a new law was necessary in 1899 taking this power completely out of their hands. Ohio, Indiana, and Minnesota were developing stable parole policies, but at least in the first two of these the great majority of the prisoners were not kept awake nights by prospects of parole, for the additional requirement that applicants for release show the promise of a job was not easily met.

If the entire penal system had not been revolutionized, it was not due to the inactivity of the legislatures. The reformatory sentence had at least won its way into the statutory law. Twenty-five states had some form of a parole law in operation in 1898, and these scattered all the way from Massachusetts and Vermont in the Northeast to California in the West and Alabama in the South. If the administration was almost everywhere unsatisfactory, a few enlightened experiments were being made, and the courts and the public as well as the prisons were having an opportunity to adjust to the new theory.

Massachusetts, prize laboratory of nineteenth-century reformers, was pioneering in still another direction, making discoveries that were destined not only to contribute much to the technique of reformatory penology but also to revolutionize the entire prison problem. The custom of releasing individuals on probation, when circumstances suggested that they might be saved from a life of crime without a term in prison, had a wide, extralegal practice throughout the world, especially in juvenile and minor cases. It was in Boston as previously noted, that John Augustus had extensively applied this practice in the 1840s. Gardiner Tufts had expanded the program in the 1860s, to be followed by Rufus W. Cook in the early seventies.[4] The legislature in 1878 authorized the mayor of Boston to appoint an officer to probate both juveniles and adults; two years later it extended this authority to all other mayors in the state.

[4] John Augustus, *A Report of the Labors of John Augustus in Aid of the Unfortunate* (1852; reprinted Montclair, N.J., 1972, as *John Augustus: First Probation Officer)*; Warren F. Spalding, "Colonel Gardiner Tufts," *Proceedings* (N.P.A., 1891), pp. 263–266.

Boston, at least, gave it a fair trial when it placed its former chief of police, Edward H. Savage, in charge. In the course of fourteen months Captain Savage provided bonds for 536 persons, only 43 of whom failed their trust and had to be committed to prison. As experience brought confidence in this treatment, its application was expanded. In 1890 the cases totaled 2,050 in greater Boston and 196 in the rest of the state. Already 1,000 of these cases involved persons over twenty-five years of age.[5]

England in her Probation and First Offenders Act of 1887 began to explore the possibilities of this treatment; Australia, New Zealand, and finally in 1891 France, adopted somewhat the same program. Massachusetts, however, maintained its leadership by developing a well-organized administration for the new treatment. A few months before the French legislation went into effect the Bay State reorganized its system, taking the function from the local executives and making it mandatory for county courts to appoint probation officers. It directed these agents to investigate not only the juvenile cases but all those involving drunkenness as well. Some agents found themselves nearly swamped in this inexhaustible social problem but were able to demonstrate so many advantages of outside treatment that the state extended the system to major offenders and directed the superior courts to provide themselves with probation officers. In 1890 the prison commission, securing the power of central supervision over this activity, assembled the scattered officers into the first annual conference and worked out schemes for co-operation in locating straying probationers. The superiority of this method of supervising outside treatment to the plan of requiring the men to report by letter recommended itself to parole administrators and prepared the way for the appointment of parole officers in several states in the next century.

Reformers in other states were watching the Massachusetts experiment. As early as 1880 R. L. Dugdale had recommended that New York adopt the scheme, but no action was taken until 1893 when the legislature affirmed the common-law power of the judges to suspend sentences. An increasing use of this power developed in an informal fashion in cooperation with the charity organizations of

---

[5] Edward H. Savage, *Police Records and Recollections: Or, Boston by Daylight and Gaslight for Two Hundred and Forty Years* (1873; reprinted Montclair, N.J., 1971), p. xiii.

several large cities, and by 1898 agents of the Philadelphia and Baltimore prison societies, an officer of the Chicago Woman's Club, and volunteers in each county under the direction of the board of charities in Minnesota, were all functioning as active if unofficial probation officers. This new feature of the correctional system was destined for extensive use in later years.

New Reformatories and Special Institutions

Some of the states were endorsing the reformatory theories by more substantial action. The unceasing growth of the criminal class, outstripping population growth in many states, was forcing the construction of new prisons, and the remarkable success of Elmira and the example of Sherborn, Concord, and Huntingdon encouraged imitation. Already in the nineties it was no longer a matter of experimenting with new devices, for Elmira was the unchallenged model. The establishment and satisfactory organization of a half dozen such institutions were the largest practical achievements of the states in penal reform during this decade. But the peculiar problems presented by certain classes of misdemeanants likewise demanded attention, and several states provided special institutions to house them, partly but not entirely on the reformatory model. Meanwhile the wider application of the elaborate reformatory technique was having the unexpected result of emphasizing the inability of demented and insane criminals to adjust themselves to the normal institutional activity, and several states undertook to establish special institutions for their proper care, thus advancing a step further the classification of institutions that had originally helped to differentiate the reformatory from the penitentiary.

The reformatories established during the seventies and eighties continued their development in the nineties. Elmira, Ionia, Sherborn and Concord had already attained a fairly stable character, and their problems were now essentially those of continued administration, although Elmira was faced with the additional problem of accommodating a steadily growing population. Pennsylvania, on the other hand, was busily engaged in organizing its recently opened reformatory at Huntingdon, a task beset by difficulties since the adoption of the indeterminate sentence had aroused opposition in the eastern part of the state. Fortunately

McClaughry remained in charge long enough to commit the institution thoroughly to the reformatory doctrine, and T. B. Patton, a former inspector, beginning a long term of service in 1891, continued his predecessor's program, minus his inspiration. Restricted by the drastic labor laws of Pennsylvania, the idyllic prison on the banks of the blue Juniata turned to farming and nonproductive trade schools and became the penal showplace of the Quaker State in the industrial era.

Minnesota was one of those states where prisons and almost everything else were built ahead of traffic. The aspiring community at St. Cloud was determined that it should have a state institution, but all it could secure was the promise of the second prison when one should be built. With the small population exhausting neither the accommodations nor the possibilities at Stillwater prison this was a chimerical prospect even in a boom state. The reformers saw an opportunity to enlist the local interest in their programs and in 1887 persuaded the legislature, with the help of an appeal to state pride to vote $100,000 to erect a reformatory at St. Cloud. Albert Garvin, trained under McClaughry at Joliet, opened the institution with its 128 up-to-date cells in 1890. The 139 young men who first moved in had already received indeterminate sentences; and they were soon organized into grades under a system of marks based on educational, labor, and disciplinary activities. Within a short period Garvin added other features of the Elmira system, such as a military organization in 1892, a course of lectures in ethics two years later, and a trade-school department built around institutional activities. The reformatory acquired a 446-acre farm that became an important adjunct. The one great drawback to the development of this institution was the reluctance with which the people of the state turned to crime.

Few indeed were the states that faced this handicap! Overcrowding had long been most serious in Illinois. When McClaughry returned from Huntingdon in 1891, full of enthusiasm for reformatories, he found Governor Joseph W. Fifer and others eager to join the movement. Together they persuaded the state to convert Pontiac "boys' prison," as the court had termed it, into a young men's reformatory. The transition was started under the direction of General F. B. Sheets, but when Governor John P. Altgeld came to power he persuaded McClaughry to take charge. Again the veteran

warden introduced the reformatory system with all its trappings—
literary and trade schools, military organization, inmate newspaper,
band, farm, and, of course, grades and marks with which to
determine the date of release. The speedy construction of the first
large cellblock to accommodate five hundred was beggared by the
rapid growth of the population; even the five hundred additional
cells completed by 1897 were inadequate for the 1,200 youths
confined there at the end of that year. Pontiac reformatory was
unique in that it was forced to receive boys as young as ten years of
age. While these boys were always in the minority, the problem of
keeping them separate from the young men was a serious handicap
to the development of the proper treatment for each class, and the
difficulty was not solved until the next century. Nevertheless,
Pontiac was securely established—the only major institution in the
Great Valley to be fully geared to reformatory penology during this
era.

Ohio had every reason to be among the first states to build a
reformatory. Second only to New York in seriously considering the
proposal back in the sixties, its able board of charities and successive
wardens and directors had persistently emphasized this measure as
the proper solution for congestion at the overgrown penitentiary in
Columbus. The legislature did provide in 1884 for a commission to
plan and locate a young men's reformatory at Mansfield, but in the
close contest for political supremacy neither party dared add to the
tax burden by appropriating for the construction of a "dude
factory." Finally in 1896, when the 1,600 antiquated cells at
Columbus were crowded with 2,100 men, Ohio opened temporary
buildings at Mansfield, and transferred some two hundred young
men there. The permanent buildings were not sufficiently completed
to permit a thorough organization of the institution on a reformatory basis until J. A. Leonard took charge in 1901.

The establishment of a young men's reformatory did not receive
responsible consideration in Indiana until the newly triumphant
Republicans decided to give the penal system a thorough overhaul-
ing in 1897. The two prisons were seriously overcrowded, but
economy ruled that the aged prison at Jeffersonville should be
transformed into a reformatory; transfers were made, and soon its
536 wretched cells were crowded with over nine hundred men under
thirty years of age; the building program to provide proper housing

did not make progress until the next century. Fortunately the appointment of a prominent politician as superintendent was balanced by the selection of Albert Garvin of Minnesota as deputy, and, spurred by the expiration of old industrial contracts and restrictions against new ones, he rapidly introduced genuine reformatory measures.

Several additional reformatories were provided for in the last years of the century although their satisfactory organization was delayed a few years. Kansas had taken the first step in 1885, accepting the donation of a 640-acre farm near Hutchinson for the site of its reformatory; but the opening of profitable mines at the state prison had discouraged a division of the labor supply, and it was not until the prison became excessively overcrowded in 1895 that thirty young men were transferred to Hutchinson to start the development of the reformatory. Neither here nor at Green Bay reformatory, established by Wisconsin in 1897, was a reformatory discipline developed until the opening years of the next century. While these states were using their young men to build reformatories, New Jersey turned the job over to contractors in 1895, yet the urgent need for relief at Trenton prison did not prevent delays, and Rahway reformatory was not opened until 1901. Meanwhile the reputation of Elmira was spreading into the South and West. Kentucky, Texas, and California each made legislative gestures in the reformatory direction, but obstacles intervened, and Buena Vista reformatory in Colorado, opened in temporary buildings in 1892, was the only genuine adult reformatory established outside the northeastern states in the nineteenth century.

All these reformatories received major offenders and some of them, following Ionia and Concord, opened their doors to special classes of misdemeanants as well. In the meantime additional cities were developing houses of correction to relieve their overcrowded jails, and most of these institutions were able to supply their short-term inmates with some form of occupation. Three New England states went further and established state workhouses that provided many genuinely reformatory features to these classes. New York established some excellent institutions for women misdemeanants that pioneered in new fields of correctional activity, but their full significance was not realized until major offenders were admitted at the turn of the century. The same state provided some special institutions for another class of criminals—the insane—a development which represented a significant modification of the trend to make all prisons into reformatories of the same type. Other states, following this lead, helped to prepare the way for the emphasis on classification that was to become the dominant characteristic of penology in the early twentieth century.

Massachusetts, Vermont, and Rhode Island had each created its house of correction during the seventies, but little use was made of them until this period. The Bay State first took its workhouse seriously in the late eighties when it was casting about for a solution of the problem presented by the increasing number of drunkards before the courts. A law of 1889 renamed the workhouse at Bridgewater the state farm and directed that a hospital for inebriates be erected there. Delays ensued, and the hospital was not opened until 1894 and not provided with a special indeterminate-sentence law until 1898 when the elaboration of a special treatment was making headway. Vermont's efforts to develop correctional activities at its house of correction were repeatedly obstructed by the many tramps that crowded the institution in the winter months, but the use of this labor to erect a new cellhouse in 1895 and the visit of the officers in that year to Elmira provided new inspiration. Military drill, calisthenics, educational features, and a liberal discipline were introduced, and the institution was opened to young felons with indeterminate sentences at the discretion of the courts, thus giving it a more genuine reformatory character.

The most significant development in connection with the minor offenders of New York State was made in behalf of a small number of its females. Reformatory penology had almost overlooked the women during the last decades of the nineteenth century, possibly because their number in most states seemed too insignificant to demand special care and they fitted readily into the household economy of both jails and prisons. This was, however, not the case in New York, and the agitation of Mrs. Josephine Shaw Lowell in 1881 prodded the state to establish the Hudson house of refuge for women convicted of certain misdemeanors, chiefly those involving sex morality. Hudson, opened in 1887, and a similar institution at Albion in the western part of the state, opened in 1893, served chiefly wayward women. New York finally established a reformatory for young women at Bedford Hills in 1900. Under the management of Dr. Katherine B. Davis it adopted the Elmira discipline. The inmates here were the first women to receive the complete reformatory treatment—indeterminate sentences, grades and marks, literary and trade instruction, and wholesome farm labor—and the provision of separate cottages for the accommodation of those of the top grade added a significant feature to the environment of adult reformatories. Although antedated by the institutions at Detroit, Indianapolis, and Sherborn, if they are to be regarded as women's reformatories, the New York Reformatory at Bedford Hills absorbed the adults from Hudson, which became a girls' reform school in 1904. Bedford Hills, which accepted women of all ages committed on indeterminate sentences for major offenses, rapidly emerged as the pioneer in reformatory discipline. It not only heralded a new day for female prisoners but led the next generation in its attempts to improve on the Elmira technique.[6]

The recognition of a public responsibility for the care of the defective and the insane was one of the humanitarian achievements of the mid nineteenth century, but it was several decades before many states came to recognize a special responsibility for those both afflicted with insanity and convicted of crime. New York, driven to action by her expanding prison populations in the late fifties, had erected an asylum for insane convicts in a walled addition to Auburn prison. This institution, equipped with the latest methods for ward treatment, had been placed under the independent control of an able physician in 1876, but it was soon overcrowded, and in 1892 under the guidance of William P. Letchworth a new penal insane asylum with adequate provision for security was built at Matteawan. Matteawan, in turn, became so popular with wardens desiring to rid themselves of unbalanced inmates and with judges wishing to avoid passing sentence on demented prisoners at the bar that the state was persuaded to erect a second institution at Dannemora in order to provide adequate and separate accommodation for these two distinct groups. When the latter institution was opened in 1899 to receive

---

[6] Eugenia C. Lekkerkerker, *Reformatories for Women in the United States* (Groningen, 1931), pp. 101–106; Estelle B. Freedman, "Their Sisters' Keepers: An Historical Perspective on Female Correctional Institutions in the United States, 1870–1900," *Feminist Studies* 2 (1974): 82–86.

transfers from the prisons, New York was able to achieve an advanced standard of classification in penal treatment.

Only a few states followed this lead at the time. Frederick Wines persuaded Illinois that the twenty-four solitary-punishment cells at Joliet were unsatisfactory accommodations for the insane, but the 150-man hospital started in the early eighties near the prison at Chester was not ready for occupation by the criminal insane until the mid nineties. Michigan provided a similar though less satisfactory institution near the Ionia house of correction in 1885. Massachusetts gave up its practice of transferring insane prisoners to the regular asylums in 1895 when it converted the asylum on the state farm at Bridgewater into an institution for the criminal insane; by the end of the century over three hundred were securely housed there. Ohio, Indiana, Iowa and Kansas equipped makeshift wards at their prisons for the insane, but only the separate ward Connecticut provided at Wethersfield supplied the medical attendance necessary to free these departments from the prison atmosphere. In spite of provisions for transfer to the asylums, most of the insane prisoners of the remaining states continued to blunder through the prison routine, to the injury of themselves and the disruption of institutional discipline.

Several factors were involved in the campaign for special asylums for insane criminals. As prison discipline became more complex with the introduction of grades and marks, the demented found themselves less able to make adjustments. On the other hand, desperate criminals were frequently attempting the ruse of insanity in order to take advantage of the laws providing for transfer to the insecure asylums from which they might effect their escape. Hardfisted wardens, naturally reluctant to see their prisoners put something over, frequently attempted by means of the strap or other device to discourage such stratagems. Meanwhile serious overcrowding at both the prisons and the asylums was the most influential factor in forcing the construction of the new institutions. But there was, in addition, a very significant theoretical aspect to the problem. The debate as to how far insanity exonerated a criminal had long been of interest to the medical and legal professions, yet the public did not begin to show concern until new theories were imported from Europe suggesting the inherent insanity of a large portion of the criminals. Richard Dugdale's study of the Jukes in the seventies stood practically alone in America as a consideration of criminal heredity, without, however, establishing any clear conclusions along this line. The dominant belief that all men were reformable presented a stubborn opposition to the Lombrosian theories and admitted only the moderate concession that the violent insane should be given special attention.

The close of the century found reformatory penology triumphant. Not only had its chief tenets been accepted by the responsible leaders of the many official and semiofficial bodies concerned with prisons but they had been widely recognized in the statute law of the North. If this had not yet greatly transformed the outlook of the common run of prisoners, substantial gains had been made in the struggle to bring correctional treatment closer to the lives of the convicts. Ten or more special institutions had been erected in the last quarter of the century and dedicated to the methods and purposes of the pedagogical penology worked out by Brockway at Elmira. This system had been actively applied for at least a decade in several places, and the faith of its advocates was still strong—so strong, indeed, that its introduction elsewhere was being rapidly advanced.

But the first stage of the application of reformatory penology was drawing to a close. Zebulon Brockway, the one vital genius of this development, retired from his post in the closing year of the century. Elmira, product of his labors, had grown unwieldy owing to forced expansion to more than twice its intended size and was now inadequate for its charges, so rapid had been their increase. Brockway's technique, ingeniously elaborated and integrated according to the best knowledge of the day, was helping to regenerate prison discipline, but at the same time it was failing to transform the lives of all the young men under its charge. Critics, some sentimental and some statistical but all incapable of understanding his problems, gathered to heckle the old man, now gray with fifty years of service. Strangely enough, he was accused of cruelty; the founder of the reformatory was paddling young misfits who could not or, as he thought, would not profit from the more subtle persuasion of the best grading system in the country. A thorough investigation more than vindicated Brockway, but he had become tired of breasting the criminal problems of an ungrateful world and was glad to hand his job over to younger men. The several universities that were assuming the responsibility of recognizing exceptional merit in the community missed an opportunity to prove themselves superior to the common understanding, for no honorary degrees were conferred on the creator of pedagogical penology. Nevertheless, Brockway stands without rival as the greatest warden America has produced.

The first stage of reformatory penology was closing in other respects as well. Younger wardens were taking charge in several of the institutions, and their jobs as well as their abilities were largely administrative in character. At the same time social statesmen with a scientific turn of mind were displacing the experimenting wardens as the spearhead of reform. Suggestions of a special treatment for inebriates, for women, and for the insane and new methods of outside supervision were opening larger horizons for reformatory activity. The extension of the movement into the outlying sections of the country and the application of the new discipline in the old penitentiaries were drawing men outside the reformatory field into action. While the task of pressing these varied activities to their logical fruition was to be left to the next generation, considerable effort was already being devoted to the rejuvenation of state prisons.

[For Bibliographic Note see end of Chapter 7.]

7.

THE STATE OF PRISONS
IN THE NINETIES

American prisons have developed through a succession of fairly clearly defined eras, much like a great unfolding pageant, and the central theme has been the evolution of penological realism. Each era has had its special set of actors, its peculiar stage properties, and its dominating problems, but in an important sense the underlying plot can be detected only by observing closely the relation of these factors to the changing background. Stocks, whipping posts, and grim gallows cluttered the background during the eighteenth-century prologue; the scenes of the first act, running through several decades of the early nineteenth century, were staged in front of the massive walls of rival prisons; now in the second act the walls have been pushed aside, and we watch the officers and reformers debating before the open face of towering cellblocks in which the figures of convicts can be seen crouching silently behind the bars; in the next era the convicts will file out onto the front stage and take a major part in the drama; finally, in an epilogue an individual convict will remain standing in center stage while keepers, teachers, doctors, psychologists, divines, and judges will make up a speechless background. Neither the sentimental persecution stories of tortured convicts nor the record of boodling activities by officers and contractors but rather the persistent quest by society for penological realism has been the central drama of the penitentiary.

All the earnest argumentation and recital of experience, the dickering for office and its spoils, the agitation against the competition of convict labor, the diversified lawmaking and formulation of discipline—all the complicated activities which occupied center stage in the last quarter of the nineteenth century took place in the imminent presence of great tiers of overcrowded cells. So tumultuous was the babble of the actors in the foreground that the setting was too frequently obscured. The curious citizen could have examined the extended tables of standard symbols that were annually presented to the legislatures, reporting the numbers of convicts and cells, the receipts from the labor contracts, the pennies in the daily budgets, and the pounds of food distributed; he might have taken account of the wild stories that constantly leaked out *sub rosa* from the wretches behind the bars; but it was to be many years before anybody in America became much interested in reporting the nature of the convicts. The second phase of penological realism was coming to a close in the nineties, but still the curious citizen, as well as the prison authorities, believed loyally, if vaguely, in the equality of men and was confident that most criminals, if given a fair chance, would reform; therefore he inspected the prisons.

The numerous books and pamphlets written by convicts during this era lacked the candor of several of the better ones of the next century. They were chiefly concerned over the injustice of their trials or with the coarseness, corruption, and brutality of their keepers, but by this very preoccupation they reveal much concerning the atmosphere of the great walled cages called penitentiaries. The reforms and improvements that occupied such a large place in official reports were seldom noted by convict annalists. Instead a long procession of wretched beings shuffled past in close step, a large portion of them still in stripes, all of them dreary with long days of sullen waiting, too frequently in stupid idleness. In place of the paternal indulgence so loudly condemned by the public press, these accounts revealed a reign of fear and deceit—soft-footed guards sneaking along the cell range to catch men talking through the pipes and to hurl them into the dungeon for a day or two; treacherous "stools" or trusties goading the new arrivals and carrying tales to the deputies; overtaxed doctors gruffly dosing the daily sick list, fakers and diseased alike, or giving the dread hospital assignment from which few were reputed to return alive; the ever present "shyster" ready to fleece the guileless with hopes of pardon or parole; above all, fear of the "cracked ward" to which so many unlucky comrades had graduated after a siege in the dungeon with straight jacket or repeated cuffings. In place of the achievements in reformation these stories were loaded with incidents of "bootleg" activities involving opium, liquor, and tobacco; here were also morbid accounts of the "kid business," implicating both officers and prisoners, and occasional birth notices in the many prisons where the female convicts were inadequately segregated.[1]

More or less aware of the vicious evils which these accounts displayed, the reformers could discover no simple method of routing them. They continued, however, to beat around the bush in the best fashion of the day. They strove to eliminate political influences and to secure impartial supervision in order to assure the public that the prisoners were enjoying the primary decencies for which it was paying. They democratically undertook to apply the reformatory disciplinary measures to all convicts. In a few places they even made enlightened attempts to deal with specific problem groups, thus foreshadowing some of the major concerns of the next century.

Politics in Prison Management

It was one thing to create impartial boards of nonsalaried inspectors and quite another thing to keep politics out of prison. Not only did the one or two well-paying jobs attract spoilsmen, but the large and expanding institutions had many lucrative contracts to distribute, and patronage was apparently indispensable to party solidarity. The continued dominance of one party, as in Minnesota

---

[1] Alexander Berkman, *Prison Memoirs of an Anarchist* (New York, 1912), especially pp. 240–262, 304–307. Berkman, aided by other convicts, gathered evidence to present to the board of charities at Riverside penitentiary in the nineties but was prevented from doing so when his plan was reported by a "stool" and he was placed in the dungeon. His evidence included *(a)* dope, dice, cards, cigarettes, and knives—proving smuggling; *(b)* prison-made beer—proving theft of potatoes and yeast supposedly used for the prisoners' food; *(c)* names and numbers of men engaged in the "kid business"; (d) graft, specific instances of which included the disappearance over a term of ten years of all the fees collected from visitors for the library fund; *(e)* favoritism, "stool" and trusty espionage—all contrary to law; *(f)* "basket," dungeon, cuffing, chaining up by the wrists, punishment of the insane. Whether this indictment of Warden E. S. Wright, generally considered a reformer, and the Riverside penitentiary, frequently listed among the best in the country, was accurate or not, it was probably not a very extreme picture of the seamy side of prisons in general.

and northern New England, and the presence of successful wardens there and in a few other prisons, especially those with excellent financial records, safeguarded their institutions from the disturbing effects of political upheavals. Pennsylvania, however, was the only state with a well-established tradition of prisons free from politics, but Massachusetts and Connecticut succeeded in organizing their prison management on this principle by the end of the era. Elsewhere the state prisons suffered considerably from the rack of politics.

After the retirement of her great reform warden under a cloud of scandal in the seventies, Charlestown prison saw a succession of five wardens come and go as their political support dictated. Warden E. J. Russell complained in 1890 against the chicanery of the investigations which were regularly made the excuse for political dismissals and which at the same time undermined even the best efforts at discipline. The Massachusetts prison commission, long a critic of the situation, finally, in 1891 gained the authority to appoint the wardens, and retained Benjamin F. Bridges, the last of the political appointees, thus at least nominally making Charlestown free of politics—as the two reformatories had been from the start.

Strictly speaking, the Connecticut state prison had never been a political plum. From Moses Pilsbury down, its wardens had been able officers, many of them called from other states. Changes had, nevertheless, frequently occurred when political supremacy passed from one party to the other. Thus the Democrats in 1893 conducted an investigation and removed S. E. Chamberlain, formerly at Charlestown, appointing in his stead J. L. Woodbridge of the Rhode Island state farm; the recovery of the Republicans a few years later prompted a new investigation with the inevitable discovery of graft. Although the warden this time was cleared of responsibility his discipline had been undermined, and he soon resigned. Fortunately the state in 1899 called Albert Garvin, one of the ablest wardens of the day, from Indiana and Wethersfield was soon enjoying a stable administration and renewed fame.

Politicians elsewhere were not so circumspect, nor were they so easily eliminated. It was an era of sharp political rivalry, and from New York west to the Rockies only Missouri experienced the unbroken sway of one party throughout the period, although

Illinois, Iowa, Minnesota, and Wisconsin approached that record. Even the creation of central authorities in New York State merely concentrated control over patronage. Individual wardens, such as A. A. Brush at Sing Sing and Isaiah Fuller at Dannemora, retained office under successive superintendents as a result of their efficient administrations, but they had become, in fact, little more than disciplinarians. The managing authority changed practically every five years in response to political shifts, and with it went the important contracts and other advantages of control.

In Ohio, scarred battleground of politics, the penitentiary suffered probably more than any other institution from repeated pillaging. The loud rejoicing on the part of the reformers over the law of 1874, with its provision for a board of five directors, one to be chosen every year, was hardly justified by results. The Democrats who won control in 1884 passed the same law a second time with slight changes, thus creating the occasion to appoint an entirely new board. This procedure was repeated four times within the next twelve years, and the only warden able to win even a second appointment when his own party returned to power was E. C. Coffin.

No other state quite equaled Ohio's record, although several were not far behind. Indiana's boards of directors served only two-year terms, but the fact that they appointed the wardens for four years added something to the stability of their administrations. The state board of charities secured the passage of a bill in 1895 for the removal of public institutions from politics, yet at the last moment the prisons were excluded from its jurisdiction. The five-year terms of wardens in New Jersey and Maryland were considerable assets to their prisons, and John H. Patterson and John F. Weyler could each boast ten years of unusually successful administration when the Republicans captured both states in 1896. Although Weyler retained his post for fifteen more years to gain international fame for his industrial achievements at Baltimore prison, the politicians of New Jersey decided that they could easily afford to lose a good warden, and the interests of party were satisfied. Similarly, although Republican control in Michigan and Kansas was shaken only for short periods in the mid eighties and again in the mid nineties, each of their prisons suffered a double change of wardens on these occasions, and the resulting instability was a major factor in depriving these states of the leadership in penal development which their institutional equipment might have earned for them.

The states where party rivalry was not so close enjoyed an initial advantage over their neighbors but made varied use of it. Minnesota alone maintained a stable and progressive administration, importing two of McClaughry's ablest officers, Albert Garvin and Henry Wolfer, to manage her prison and reformatory, and it was no coincidence that Stillwater was the best state prison in the country throughout the era. On the other hand, the prison at Jefferson City carried off the honors at the bottom of the list in spite of Missouri's lack of political upheavals. In Illinois McClaughry served the state well, making Joliet for a time a model prison in spite of serious overcrowding; but opportunity called the Major and his best officers elsewhere, and when the Democrat, John P. Altgeld, carried the state, he found and removed from control a lesser grade of Republican politicians. Altgeld proceeded to demonstrate that his motives for reform were not entirely Jacksonian by calling McClaughry back to serve as superintendent of the new reformatory at Pontiac. When the party of the full dinner pail recaptured the state, the prisons were taken over as part of the reward; fortunately McClaughry was persuaded to take charge again at Joliet.

Real stability depended upon nonpartisan control. Thus while Iowa and West Virginia enjoyed considerable political stability, the administrations of their prisons changed as rapidly as that of any Methodist church. The successive wardens at Moundsville remained at the beck and call of their party, but Iowa took steps to correct a similar situation by creating its board of control in 1898. Wisconsin had led off in this direction in 1891, although the Democrats, who created the first board, secured most of the advantages for their supporters, and the Republicans, returning to power, appointed an entirely new board in 1895 and secured a new distribution of benefits. Nevertheless, these boards, slowly gaining prestige, freed themselves from political entanglements, and in the next century several of them provided able leadership in public welfare developments, particularly in the midwestern states.

Civil service reformers were making another attack on the spoils system, and their measures were already affecting the prisons of the more progressive states. New York and Massachusetts each had laws dating from the eighties which covered the minor prison officers.

The Wisconsin board of control adopted merit tests for many of its employees, and after 1897 the authorities of the Indiana reformatory required its guards to pass certain tests of fitness. Yet these laws did little more, in practical operation, than to guarantee the tenure of office of aged Civil War veterans long after their efficiency as guards had become doubtful. Some of the unsettling effects of politics were inherent in the type of democracy then current in America. The principle that any man who helped build the political strength of a party was able to fill, and had a right to demand, any administrative post he chose, largely controlled the selection of wardens, and as long as this principle was maintained elaborate reformatory programs were doomed.

Prison Standards of Living

Americans in these years were making considerable improvement over the makeshift living arrangements of their frontier days. They were building more modern homes in which plumbing fixtures and other conveniences were receiving attention. But this was the work of an individualistic economy, and it was some time before the new standards began to influence the discussions of prison housing conditions. Nevertheless, the growing size of the institutions forced attention to sewage disposal, sanitary bathing, ventilation, and standardized diets. As mounting populations compelled new construction, better provision was made for these accessory features of the housing problem.

The building programs of the seventies had considerably relieved the desperate crowding in most of the prisons, but the rapid growth of the population in the tier of states reaching from Massachusetts to Kansas kept this problem in the foreground. Only a few states were able to provide separate cells for every prisoner throughout this era, and for long periods several states continued to crowd two into a cell, thus becoming inured to the evils of the practice and preparing the way for a break from the Auburn traditions in other respects as well.

The New England states were the most assiduous adherents to the old standards. In its struggle to provide for a growing convict population, Massachusetts not only built new institutions at Sherborn, Concord, and Bridgewater, but remodeled Charlestown prison and raised their total cell capacity to over 2,300 by 1896. Serious consideration of plans for another prison was delayed only as the

Spanish-American War checked commitments for a year or two. The prisons of Maine, New Hampshire, and Vermont adequately met the demands of these languishing communities, but Rhode Island had to erect barracks in 1893 to house the overflow from its 126-cell prison at the state farm. Connecticut disregarded the advice of Charles Dudley Warner, chairman of its special investigating committee in 1885, and erected a new cellhouse at Wethersfield instead of a totally new prison; however, even an additional expansion in 1898 brought the total up to only 550 cells, which fortunately proved adequate for the time. The close of the century thus found all the states of New England living up to the old standards of Louis Dwight.

Wisconsin and especially Minnesota had a surplus of cells, and the critics failed to explain why the model 573 cells at Stillwater could not attract sufficient lodgers from the less considerate states. Maryland, Michigan, and Iowa were the only other states outside of New England able to approach this standard. When the old Baltimore prison became crowded in the mid nineties, John Weyler was already building a model addition, and the completion of the new building with its 820 steel cells, each 9 by 5½ and 8 feet high and equipped with a basin, toilet, ventilating shaft, and sliding door, enabled the state in 1899 to boast of one of the best prisons in the world. In Michigan, when Ionia failed to relieve congestion at Jackson in the eighties, the temporary expedient of stringing a row of cots in the corridor was first applied in order to avoid confining two in a cell; but continued growth in population persuaded the authorities to erect a branch prison at Marquette, thus increasing the state's cell capacity to 1,774 by 1896. The cell capacity at Waupun, now increased to 500, adequately met the needs of Wisconsin until the end of the period when the newly erected reformatory supplied necessary relief. Iowa, during the eighties, completed Anamosa prison, which together with the older prison at Fort Madison, supplied sufficient cells until the prisoners approached the thousand mark in the late nineties.

New York could have approximated the old standard if its convicts had been satisfactorily distributed between its three major prisons and its reformatory, for each had by the end of the period over 1,000 cells, and the total was near 5,000. Unfortunately Sing Sing's location near New York made it the destination of a disproportionate number of commitments, and large transfers from there and from Elmira failed to relieve their congestion. Agitation commenced at the turn of the century for a new prison to replace Sing Sing and a new reformatory to relieve Elmira. In sharp contrast Ohio was unable to decide on a site for even a second prison, and continued to add new buildings at Columbus until the cells totaled 1,800, greatly exceeding any other prison in the world. Many of these cells were too cold in winter, and others were too hot in summer, but the authorities did not begin to transfer batches of the younger men to the unfinished reformatory at Mansfield until the main population had exceeded the two thousand mark in 1896, and the continued development of Mansfield did not relieve congestion at Columbus.

Pennsylvania built more extensively than any other state during this era but failed to keep pace with its needs. The 732 "solitary" cells at Cherry Hill were forced to house an average of 1,100 prisoners during these years, thus finally defeating the old tradition, although Warden Cassidy and Inspector Richard Vaux stubbornly refused to recognize the fact. The expansion of Pittsburgh compelled the abandonment of its old penitentiary and the construction of a new one at Riverside during the eighties, and its 1,160 modern cells, each 8 by 5 and 8 feet high, were soon filled to capacity. The abandonment of the plan for a new prison in the center of the state and the construction in its stead of the Huntingdon reformatory, although providing an additional 500 cells, delayed for several decades the relief of the Eastern Penitentiary. But, if two convicts were to be housed in a cell, certainly they could live more comfortably under such an arrangement at Cherry Hill than anywhere else in the country.

Several other states made attempts to provide the accommodations required by their laws but were defeated by the steady growth of their populations. New Jersey frequently enlarged the prison at Trenton, yet the population persistently registered 200 ahead of capacity. West Virginia made good progress with the construction of Moundsville during the eighties, but when the original plan for 404 cells was completed in 1894, the population already stood at 500 and continued to grow unchecked. Indiana built 760 Joliet-sized cells at its Michigan City prison and 200 fine new ones at Jeffersonville; again the prisoners multiplied more rapidly, and the warden determined to admit the inevitable and announced that the new cells were double ones.

But Illinois was more responsible than any other state for

shattering the Auburn tradition. The imposing structure at Joliet, together with the growing reputation of its able warden, made it a model for many western prisons; however, since its 1,024 cells, each 7 by 4 and 7 feet high, were continually crowded with around 1,500 prisoners, many of them eagerly admitted as lodgers from the federal government and western territories, the example was not in the Auburn tradition. When in 1884 Illinois completed the first 400 cells in its southern prison at Chester, the authorities announced the capacity to be 800, and the population exceeded even this limit before the close of the century. The construction of 1,000 cells at the young men's reformatory at Pontiac in the nineties failed to relieve the situation, and in 1898 the prison commissioners finally expressed strong condemnation of its evils.

> When one thinks of two men spending never less than fourteen hours each day during six days of the week and on the seventh day nearly twenty-one hours in a space so reduced, and with a slop bucket in the cell for their use . . . he is compelled to ask what excuse the great State of Illinois can offer for compelling men . . . [to] eat, rest and sleep in quarters so repellent, so utterly unfit for the purpose that their very existence is a disgrace to the State that permits it.[2]

Kansas, likewise, whether prompted by the Illinois example or the zest for profits, crowded lodgers from outside the state into its already overcrowded 688-cell prison at Lansing and failed to relieve the situation by the tardy construction of 200 cells at Hutchinson in the nineties. But Missouri was the state that maintained the most wretched prison in the country, rivaled only at times by Virginia, Kentucky, and California. The prison at Jefferson City, already crowding 1,200 convicts into 500 old cells in 1880, permitted the population to reach 2,300 before adding 236 small "congregate rooms" in 1898. It had become, as one governor described it, "the largest school of crime" in America.

Thus the last quarter of the century witnessed the constant expansion of prison accommodations. The adult reformatory had become a major factor in the situation, and eleven institutions of this type, more or less fully constructed, were housing around 6,000 inmates by 1900. By the same date a dozen prisons in the northern states were confining in excess of 1,000 prisoners each, two of them

[2] Illinois State Penitentiary, Joliet, *Report* (1898), p. 14.

over 2,000, and the old ideal of the 500-cell prison was forgotten. Not only had the solitary system of Pennsylvania finally passed out of existence in practice, but several midwestern states were regularly confining two men in a cell with complete equanimity, thus heralding the end of the Auburn tradition as well.

A new responsibility assigned to many state prisons in these years was the task of executing the death sentences. This function, traditionally performed by the county sheriffs, was increasingly transferred to prison wardens in the northern states, especially after New York first substituted an electric chair for the age-old gallows in 1888. Sing Sing and all other prisons thus designated had also to provide accommodations for men awaiting execution, and the "death row" or "death house" added a gruesome feature to the prison environment. In several states, where the legislatures gave local juries discretionary authority to grant life sentences in place of the death penalty, the prisons received an additional influx of longterm inmates.[3]

An interest in the equipment of prisons was taking the place of concern over the number of cells. Thirty or so years after the "floating palaces" of America's western waters began to advertise wash basins in their staterooms, prison officers started an agitation for such conveniences for their grimy lodgers. Very little, however, was accomplished in this direction until after the growing popular interest in sanitation had produced laws requiring minimum health standards in the tenements of the larger cities. Meanwhile industry was equipping itself to meet the new demands, and the J. L. Mott Iron Works issued a catalogue in 1881 announcing a simple and efficient plumbing device ready for installation in prison cells. The new prison cell was gradually transformed into an efficient cubicle during this era as iron and steel became the materials of construction, but prisons are substantial structures, and once built even industrial revolutions do not readily alter them. Thousands of prisoners continued to drowse away the hours in musty old brick or stone cells heavy with layer on layer of whitewash.

Bathing requirements had long been among the most unpopular features of prison discipline. It was with a touch of irony that one of the most severe of prison punishments was nicknamed the "shower bath." Tub bathing was almost as fearful and certainly much more

[3] Hugo A. Bedau, ed., *The Death Penalty in America*, 2d ed. (Chicago, 1968), pp. 17–19, 28–29.

vile than the punishment. Joliet's announcement in 1884 that sixty wooden tubs had been installed in a new bathroom gave it the right to boast the best equipment for bathing convicts in the country. The fourteen hundred men could now each have a tub to himself once a week, a great luxury when compared with the prisoners forced to jump into a large tank with a hundred of their fellows once or twice a month. Other prisons followed Joliet's example, until in 1892 Clinton prison set a new standard by introducing the first equipment for shower bathing. The physician reported that the men now enjoyed bathing, and other prisons became interested; when Baltimore opened its model cellhouse in 1899, it was the sixth prison to provide showers. Several prisons had meanwhile accomplished the more difficult job introducing running water into each cell. The Riverside penitentiary, built by Pennsylvania in the eighties, was the first Auburn structure to provide this convenience, and most new construction followed its example. There was one very considerable problem that had to be solved before any of these sanitary devices were possible, and that was the provision of an adequate water supply. The ideal site of the early days had been a high spot near a town with possibly a stream flowing by a corner of the plot. But the rapid expansion of most institutions had soon outgrown the services of the first wells, which in many cases were abandoned only after their waters had been contaminated owing to the imperfect disposal of the prison sewage. The struggle to solve this problem demanded repeated attention from many prisons.

The night bucket maintained its disagreeable place in most of the cells. Efforts to correct some of its evils led to the substitution of enameled iron for wooden buckets, as the former could be more easily and thoroughly cleansed. Illinois was the first to provide bucket chambers, and these enclosures in the cells at Chester were connected by air ducts to the ventilators in the roof. Maryland's new cellhouse in 1899 was the first Auburn prison to introduce toilets with running water into each cell. Although most of these devices were adopted by later builders, only the most costly reconstruction could instal them in the old structures. When J. B. Ransom made a study of prison conditions responsible for the spread of tuberculosis, a visit to seventy-seven prisons in the early 1900s revealed that the great majority were still using the old bucket system.

Similarly, in the closely related problem of ventilation, most of the prisons continued to rely on the old "law of the diffusion of gases." Charlestown prison converted every pair of its small cells into one, thus securing for each cell a door and a window as well as greater air space. Open grated doors of steel gradually displaced the heavy iron or wooden ones of the past, and new prisons built cells on larger patterns than the first Auburn standard, although this fact encouraged the doubling up that more than offset the advantage in increased air space. Some wardens installed fans to drive the foul air that gathered at the top of the cellhouse out through ventilators in the roof. Most new prisons provided air ducts leading from each cell to the fans and ventilators, but the convicts were quickly arrayed against this system, preferring foul air to the armies of crawlers that constantly campaigned through these highways. Many a warden installed and gave generous praise to a new ventilating system, but his successor a year or two later usually discovered the fan to be out of commission and the pipes stuffed shut by the convicts. Ventilation was proving to be about as difficult a problem in prison as in the large-city tenements of the day.

The coal stoves and kerosene lamps in the corridors aggravated the problem by polluting the atmosphere without fulfilling their own functions. The wide introduction of steam and hot-air systems during the eighties and nineties was a considerable improvement. When electric lighting gained a commercial basis, Elmira was quick to instal an expensive equipment of incandescent bulbs, thus becoming in 1892 the first adequately lighted prison. Nevertheless, for many years even such a well-equipped prison as Riverside continued to depend on candles.

In most of these matters the prisons were slowly improving their living conditions, but in the dining arrangements there was a decided regression. Enoch Wines had found dining rooms in almost all state prisons in his day, but several factors had contrived to close most of them. Population growth rendered the old rooms inadequate at the same time that it demanded their space for new cells or shops. The occasional prison outbreaks usually occurred when the men were all gathered together in these halls, thus prejudicing wardens against them. Even the economy of the dining room failed to prevent prisons from returning to cell feeding. When the directors of Joliet made an investigation in 1900, they found scarcely a dozen major prisons equipped with dining halls, and most of these served the evening meal in the cells. This additional use of the cells gave increased significance to the problems of overcrowding and sanitation.

Meanwhile the standard of prison diets was slowly rising. Scurvy and other forms of undernourishment were practically eliminated, and yet the science of dietetics received almost no attention from prison authorities. Diets were frequently compared, but the outstanding conclusion was that a reasonable budget was ten cents for each man each day. Mush, milk, bread, potatoes, vegetables, pork, beef, apples, beans, and coffee, made chiefly of bread crusts, were the staple foods. There was constant complaint against the condition of the bread and particularly of the meat. Prisoners were usually drafted as chefs, and their concoctions did not always display skill. These facts, combined with the absence of fruits, sugars, and fats, made the meals anything but pleasant or wholesome. Possibly however, the convicts missed their liquor and, in the many prisons where it was prohibited, their tobacco, more than they suffered from the meals.

A western convict recorded an instructive sample of prison humor, which now began to find its way into these bastilles as the silent system was relaxed. According to the story, a young farmhand on his arrival at prison received his equipment and was heading for his cell when an old "con" asked if he had not been cheated of his sheets; the youth took the hint and went to the officer with his complaint; the tale further has it that he got sheets. If the story may be relied upon, these were about the only sheets ever distributed in prison during the era. Towels and soap were not so rare, but they were expected to last. Few prisons followed Elmira's policy of supplying a comb, toothbrush, and fresh mattress to each new arrival.[4]

The newspapers and politicians who cried out against luxurious penal hotels were sadly misinformed. The prisons were tardily following the general rise in the standards of sanitation, but only in the new buildings were real improvements achieved. The critics would have had a genuine issue had they condemned the single

[4] Julius B. Ransom, *Tuberculosis in Penal Institutions* (Washington, D.C., 1904), p. 14. "The straw ticks or mattresses of many institutions are seldom disinfected, are not protected by sheets or pillow covers. The bedding . . . is left in the cell to be occupied by another. . . ." (This report was prepared for the Seventh International Prison Congress, 1905, and published separately in 1904 as House of Rep. Doc. 142, 58th Cong., 3d sess.)

standard of security, which was the major cause of the enormous expenditures, or had they stressed the state of idleness resulting from the labor laws. It was this latter factor rather than the number of the cells or their alleged sumptuousness that dominated the life of the prisoner in this era.

Schemes for Discipline and Reformation

Overcrowded prisons threatened with the cessation of their industrial activities presented their officers with a problem that the Auburn tradition could not solve, and they were thus prompted to turn to the Elmira technique for assistance. The older educational and religious activities were not overlooked, but the newer features received greater emphasis. The extension of the parole system to the state prisons joined with the disciplinary problem to encourage the introduction of grades and marks but without supplanting the older devices for maintaining order. A new atmosphere took the place of the traditional restraint in many prisons, yet only one or two wardens succeeded in developing the spirit as well as the technique of Elmira at their institutions.

Most of the prisons maintained some sort of an evening school during the winter months, but none of them attained the standards achieved at Charlestown in the days of Warden Haynes. Warden Hatch developed a comprehensive program at Jackson in the eighties which, however, was discontinued by his successor. Jackson and a half dozen other prisons provided school buildings and laid in a stock of children's textbooks, which frequently proved serviceable to new wardens wishing to inaugurate their administrations with a generous flourish. The slowly accumulating stocks of the libraries, aided in an increasing number of prisons by modest annual grants, provided greater comfort to a few lonely intellectuals, and Joliet was able to boast at the turn of the century that its library of 16,271 volumes was the largest prison library in the world, but no librarian or chaplain was prompted to congratulate his prison on the nature of these collections.

Book learning was not after all the chief need of the convict, and a few officers found occasion to note that Victor Hugo's dictum "that he who opens a school closes a prison" was not verified by American experience. But there was in these years an increasing appreciation of the broader aspects of education, and wardens began to refer to their industrial establishments as trade schools. The fact that Lynn,

Massachusetts, gained local notoriety as the home of discharged prisoners because of the number of its craftsmen who learned their trade in prison shoeshops helped to substantiate the claim in one instance, but prison industries had rarely been selected with this object in view. Indeed, further to obstruct this possibility, many of the laws regulating prison labor undertook to ban those industries in which a convict might find employment in his state after discharge. Industries were not all excluded, however, for the prison officers succeeded in circumventing the regulations in most cases, and the increasing number of reformatories usually developed some trade school departments. Many prisons acquired printing presses, as at Elmira, providing valuable trades to a few selected inmates and prompting the publication of prison journals in four prisons and four reformatories during the early nineties.

Sunday continued to serve as a day of rest in prison. The libraries afforded about the only relief from the boredom of the long hours spent in the cells from Sunday noon to Monday morning. The Sunday morning service was a fairly regular feature, and many of the prisoners were at least grateful for its diversion. A few of the chaplains attempted to make the day more congenial for a portion of their flock by organizing special societies which were in some cases permitted to meet in the afternoon hours. Such were the Christian Endeavor groups at the prisons in Wisconsin and Indiana, the Chautauqua circles in four or five prisons, and the Mutual Aid League at Jackson. In most of the institutions, however, even the favored trusties could not be permitted out of their cells on Sunday afternoon, for this was the one time when the guards received a respite from their long hours of thankless vigil.

New tones enlivened many of the chapel services during this era as friends supplied additional instruments to support the traditional prison choir and organ. Several prisons developed orchestras, and these, together with the bands of the reformatories, added a feature that was to become more prominent in the next century. Chapel services were generally under the direction of full-time, Protestant chaplains, but Catholic priests were permitted to minister to inmates of their faith; by the end of the period some of the states with increasing Catholic populations were officially naming Catholics as assistant chaplains.

In the late nineties Mrs. Maud Ballington Booth strode into the midst of this prosaic clericalism waving the banner of evangelism.

Mrs. Booth came to America under the auspices of the Salvation Army and gained her first interest in convicts during visits to the Army's prison-gate missions. After her break with the Army in 1896, she formed the Volunteers of America with a subsidiary branch, the Volunteer Prison League. Her labors began in Sing Sing and spread rapidly to many of the major prisons. Stirring emotional appeals were the foundation of her strength, but Mrs. Booth followed her first success in each prison by gathering her converts into permanent League units. Each member pledged to pray and read his Bible daily, to use clean language, form cheerful habits, and obey the prison rules; for this he was given a badge, and the League's paper, the *Volunteer Gazette,* was sent to him weekly. Mrs. Booth undertook to answer all letters the prisoners wrote to her, and established Hope Halls in New York, Chicago, and San Francisco to which the members were invited to come for aid after their discharge. The League units in nine of the largest prisons numbered a total of 2,679 Volunteers by the end of the century.

But the abler prison officers were pinning their reformatory hopes on disciplinary rather than on emotional methods. The progressive grading system became the favorite nostrum of the day. When Warden E. S. Wright moved his prisoners into the new penitentiary at Riverside in the eighties, he reorganized an earlier grade system after that of Elmira. The warden at Columbus introduced a similar system when the adoption of parole and labor laws provided an incentive. Old Charlestown prison instituted a grading system when the reformatory at Concord was opened, and Warden Hatch brought Jackson in line too. But, except at Elmira and Concord, these first experiments were not coupled with an indeterminate-sentence system, and, deprived of the vital function of determining the date of discharge, they were soon abandoned or permitted to degenerate into meaningless routine. The revival of the agitation for parole systems in the nineties was accompanied with a more effective development of the grading system, first at Stillwater in 1891 and then in quick succession at Charlestown, Jackson, Joliet, Columbus, Jefferson-ville, and Wethersfield. Several other prisons also introduced grades as did all the new reformatories but without the elaborate agitation that accompanied the programs in the above institutions.

Faced with this widespread stampede to their ideas, veteran

reformers began to rub their eyes and soon discovered that their prize reformatory device was degenerating into a shield for lax discipline. The Indiana state prison was the first to make open recognition of this fact by providing that all new arrivals should enter the top grade and only lose the privileges it accorded them when they were detected in some offense. By the late nineties the reports of most prisons showed fully nine-tenths of their inmates as members of the top grade, enjoying the full privilege of talking, playing games, reading newspapers, and engaging in whatever additional activities the warden had seen fit to develop. Brockway, whose reports showed that the majority of his boys still had much to do before they could be considered reformed and accorded full privileges, had become a cruel disciplinarian in the eyes of many of his associates and finally retired in disgust. Only Stillwater prison under Henry Wolfer and Wethersfield under Albert Garvin were able to maintain grading systems on the genuine reformatory basis that encouraged the men through self-control to earn privileges of freedom and responsibility. Elsewhere, except in the reformatories, the grading system not only lost its capacity for stimulating individual development but failed to afford the parole authorities any real assistance in selecting men for conditional release. Nevertheless, it performed one real service—that of civilizing prison customs by restricting the use of striped suits, head-shaving, lockstep marching, and similar practices to the punishment grades in most prisons.

Wethersfield, long the most stubborn stronghold of the principles of Louis Dwight and the discipline of Amos Pilsbury, led the revolt in the mid nineties by devoting one hour each day to calisthenic exercise and granting the members of the top grade the privilege of organizing literary societies and enjoying free association one hour each fortnight. At about the same time Michigan permitted conversation at mealtimes in its prisons and gave the inmates in the top grade a daily recess in the yard, while Indiana permitted conversation in the cellhouses for two hours each evening. The public did not always approve of these concessions, and residents of New Hampshire decided at the polls that the old rules requiring downcast eyes and silence should not be abandoned. Nevertheless, Warden Hunter was applauded when he announced at one of the Iowa quarterly conferences of superintendents in 1899 that his experience in granting freedom of the yard on public holidays encouraged him to follow the example of Joliet, Columbus, Jackson, and Wethersfield and grant the privilege once a week. But the extensive development of organized sports on these occasions did not take place except in a few reformatories until well into the next century.

The abandonment of the old rules of silence greatly simplified the job of discipline in one respect but opened the way for favoritism and intrigue and encouraged the development of espionage. The barriers which the Auburn system had erected against mutual corruption were let down, and few of the prisoners or the officers made a constructive use of their greater freedom of intercourse. Many wardens declared that if given enough rope most criminals would hang themselves, and some wardens then proceeded to let the rope slip through their fingers.

The legislators frequently tried their hands at prison discipline, filling the statute books with laws abolishing all sorts of punishments, but the legal rights of prisoners had long served as the stock joke among cynical convicts. A few years after New York abolished corporal punishment in prison an investigation at Clinton revealed the frequent use of paddling, tying up by the wrists so that the toes barely touched the floor, confinement in dark cells, and the like. Warden Howard was dismissed in Indiana when evidence leaked out proving that he had made frequent and sometimes cruel use of the "cat" although it had been abolished six years earlier. When Ohio prohibited the lash and the "shower bath," the authorities invented the "humming bird," a device for administering electric shocks which was even more feared than the former tortures. In the opinion of most wardens, the determination of the proper punishments was not the function of a legislative majority. Prison officials often attributed the outbreak of riots or fires to the announcement of the abolition of certain punishments or the relaxation of disciplinary measures. Certainly the number of knifings and bloody encounters between inmates increased when they secured the freedom of the yard, and some wardens hastened to withdraw the privilege.[5]

[5] Charles L. Clark and Earle E. Eubank, *Lockstep and Corridor: Thirty-five Years of Prison Life* (Cincinnati, 1927), pp. 50–55. Clark reports that the riot of 1896 at Jackson prison, which followed a relaxation of discipline in Michigan prisons, prompted the warden to return to rigid controls. See also *Chicago Tribune*, 1 January 1893, for an account of a conservative reaction in the Indiana State Prison.

Public opinion, sometimes acting through the legislature, had its influence, but so did the particular conditions of each prison. When the industrial activity was sluggish and there was no great demand for the labor of each convict, the bread and water, or "Pennsylvania diet," sometimes combined with confinement to a dark cell, was the mainstay for serious cases; or an intractable convict might be handcuffed to the door of his cell and forced to stand through the day looking at a gray wall while his fellows idled in the shop. On the other hand, the model prison in Baltimore, with more use for its labor, retained the "cat" until 1905 when the physician discovered that the blood of one victim remaining on the cords of the lash infected succeeding victims with syphilis. Meanwhile greed for profits in Kansas invented another deviltry designed to bring the prisoner to terms quickly. The culprit's hands and feet were bound and drawn together behind his back, and he was then deposited, face down, on a stone floor with his feet held above him by a wooden "crib," and here he remained until he fainted or made a convincing cry for mercy.

In the midst of viciousness, brutality, repression, and varied outcroppings of insanity it would have been surprising if personalities and techniques had not frequently become mixed up in tragic episodes. Rare investigations and more frequent reports by former convicts told appalling tales of prisoners who were relentlessly driven down the entire gauntlet of punishments until with broken health they landed in the "cracked ward," possibly with, and possibly without, shattered intellects. Penology still had a considerable distance to go before it could boast that it encouraged as well as permitted every inmate and every officer to develop only the better faculties of his manhood.

These were the extraordinary punishments that seemed indispensable to many of the men in charge of prisons, no matter what grading system they might maintain. Nevertheless, in spite of the fundamental flaws that these exceptions revealed, the rigid regulations of the past were giving place to the technique of the reformatory, and, although the spirit and the motivation that animated Elmira in its best days were sadly lacking, new privileges and customs had transformed the activities of many prisons and had made them much more tolerable places in which to live.

*   *   *

The Care Given Special Groups

With the major forms of pedagogical penology more or less clearly worked out and widely endorsed, prison officials devoted greater attention to the peculiar problems of special groups within their care. The movement had enlisted the support of diverse elements of the population, and several of its new programs grew out of the special interests of some of these allied groups. Prison physicians took the initiative in projecting new treatments for the tubercular as well as for the insane. Local philanthropic societies helped to provide more generous aid to the discharged. The federal government was at last aroused to undertake the care of some of its own prisoners. Only the city and county authorities, except in rare instances, continued to shirk their responsibilities.

The prisons were profiting along with the country at large from the gains made for the science of medicine in these years. Resident doctors had for some time been on the staffs of the larger and more progressive institutions, but the visiting physician was still the mainstay elsewhere. The periodic examination of the sick list remained hopelessly inadequate in most prisons and disheartened many an unfortunate criminal with a genuine ailment. The influence of most visiting doctors on the development of higher standards of sanitation and dietetics was not as great as it might have been, nor did they take an independent stand and assert any responsibility for safeguarding the health of prisoners receiving corporal punishment. Their most significant service was performed in connection with the campaign for the proper care of special groups, such as the tubercular and the insane; in time some were to assume large responsibilities in the study of the individual criminal.

Several prison physicians were fully abreast of the medical profession in its attack on tuberculosis. When the doctor in attendance at Wethersfield prison reported in 1881 that only one prisoner had died during the preceding year from pulmonary consumption and congratulated himself that only a few of these cases had developed, "due to the grace of God," he was, for his day, no old fogy. Gradually, as discoveries occurred in Europe and America concerning the nature of this malady, a new interest in its treatment developed among prison physicians. In 1888, shortly after the first tuberculosis congress gathered in Paris, McClaughry's physician at Joliet segregated thirty-odd consumptives of that prison into an idle shop where they worked at light tasks during the day and where they slept in an airy dormitory at night. But it was Dr. J. B. Ransom, physician at Clinton prison, who made the first permanent contribution to the treatment of tuberculosis in prison. Possibly stimulated by Dr. Trudeau's success at Saranac Lake, Dr. Ransom conducted experiments with the care of selected cases in dormitories near the prison and demonstrated that the high altitude and pure air of this choice site in the Adirondacks were admirably fitted for the treatment of tubercular prisoners. The superintendent soon began to transfer convicts suffering from this malady to Clinton, and ordered special fresh-air wards constructed for their accommodation. Since a study of the reports of a dozen major prisons revealed that about 45 percent of the deaths in prison were attributable to this disease, the successful development of a program at Clinton in the early nineties provided a pattern for other prisons, but the general provision of real hospital wards and of open-air wards on the roof did not come until the next century.

The spread of the parole laws attracted public interest to the problems of the discharged prisoners. The strongest prison-aid societies of the earlier period, notably those in New York, Philadelphia, Maryland, and Connecticut, continued to perform their valuable services. About the only truly active organizations to join this group were the society and home of Agnes d'Arcambal in Detroit and the Massachusetts Prison Association, both started in the late eighties. Additional homes were founded in Chicago and Providence, and societies existed in several other states, but none of these attracted wide support. The state agents in New York and Pennsylvania continued to function, and most of the reformatories appointed special officers to perform the similar service of finding jobs and homes; the reformatory agents frequently tried, in addition, to maintain a friendly contact with their boys. Practically all the states supplied their released prisoners with a few dollars, a ticket home, and a suit of clothes. While these added up to considerable sums in the eyes of the taxpayers, they were as necessary a part of justice as the meager meals fed to the prisoners; unfortunately this last "handout" aroused about as little gratitude from the friendless derelicts as had the daily meals; the self-conscious former convict always tried to scrap the suit as soon as possible.

A few new friends rallied to the cause of the "down-and-outer" during this period. The Salvation Army's prison-gate movement started in the mid nineties, and the Volunteers of America and the Central Howard Association commenced activities not long afterward, although these bodies did not become fully effective until the next period. Indeed, little real work had yet been done in any of the states or by any agency toward helping the criminal at the most critical point in his entire career—a failure which contrasted sharply with the record of England and parts of the Continent.[6]

If the Americans were falling down at the close of their penal treatment, they were making diabolical blunders at its beginning. European critics who found American democracy most rotten at the bottom certainly could not have been gainsaid by an indignant local patriot who knew anything about his county jail. The hundreds of thousands of offenders who paid forced visits to these institutions, year after year, almost without exception returned the worse for their experience. Here one could find the inmates inadequately separated by sex, age, criminal experience, and state of health; here the inmates continually idled about the enclosures with almost no disciplinary restrictions except occasionally those of the insidious "kangaroo courts" under which guise the oldtimers preyed upon the new arrivals until all illusions about public justice were shattered.

The reformers of the day did not leave it to visiting Europeans or to the students of a later generation to condemn this situation. A half dozen of them surveyed the problem on successive years before the national gatherings, exposing the evils with caustic remarks; nevertheless, their major interests were in other matters. No sheriff's association appeared to rank with that of the wardens, chaplains, and physicians; in fact, practically none of this class of officers appeared at the congresses. Their tenure was too short and insecure to permit many of them to develop professional interests, since the sheriff's job remained one of the most lucrative spoils of local party victory. The fee system still reigned supreme, permitting a thrifty man to extract a large profit between the sum paid by the county for the support of each "head" and the pittance paid out for food; well-

---

[6]Hastings H. Hart, "Prisoners' Aid Societies," *Proceedings* (National Prison Association, 1889), pp. 270–288. Hart lists and describes nineteen of these societies.

to-do inmates added to these profits by renting the more comfortable cells and buying their own food and clothing. Boarders were naturally in demand, and, as profits were large enough to permit their division into several shares, it was not unknown for constables to "run men in for revenue only." The wheels of justice appeared always to be clogged.

Efforts to correct these evils were not lacking. Possibly Massachusetts made the most effective reforms by centralizing its jail system under the prison commission and by authorizing that body to determine institutional standards, thus creating an authority to remove undesirable officers, to transfer from one jail to another, and even to close an unsatisfactory institution. Meanwhile the Minnesota board of charities planned a model jail and directed the erection of forty of these institutions, and the Ohio board almost equaled that achievement. A few new houses of correction were erected, notably that in Milwaukee, but none of these did much more than provide an opportunity for labor and possibly a smattering of schooling— none came up to the Detroit house of the old days. Moreover, New York's labor laws, by destroying the fine industry and discipline of its county penitentiaries, condemned their thousands of inmates to desultory idleness, offsetting any gains the generation may have made in the field elsewhere. Wherever a good system did develop, the jail was almost immediately crowded beyond capacity by neighboring cities or counties eager to house their criminals as safely as possible—a procedure which the fortunate sheriff was usually glad to encourage. These evils were everywhere obvious, and inspections repeatedly brought them to the attention of the legislatures, usually holding up England and Scotland as the shining examples of how the job should be handled.[7] But it was not until the next century that Hastings H. Hart and Joseph Fishman were to force this problem before the public with a fanatical persistence that produced some results.

[7] Wisconsin Board of Charities, *Report* (1890), pp. 10–11. "We have found a very large part of the jails of the state at one time or another in a deplorable condition, filthy, swarming with vermin, without bathing facilities, with foul bedding, and with disgusting and disease breeding privies right in the jail. . . .We have found women and men given the liberty of the same corridor, and we have frequently found boys in unrestricted intercourse with hardened criminals. Even in those jails built for classification we have frequently found all the inner doors thrown open and indiscriminate association of all prisoners allowed."

The difficulties presented by the task of moving the decentralized local authorities to effective reform were not as surprising as those encountered by the reformers in their attempt to persuade the federal government to assume its obvious responsibilities. General R. B. Brinkerhoff's attempt to get a report of the number of federal prisoners was blocked for a time, but finally an appeal to President Cleveland produced results, and information was supplied showing a total of 1,027 federal prisoners lodged in state prisons and about 10,000 in county jails in 1885. A steady increase in the number of these prisoners, reaching 2,516 and about 15,000 respectively by 1895, underlined the demand for a penal program. Congressman Samuel J. Barrows, assisted by Brinkerhoff, secured the adoption in 1891 of a law directing the purchase of three sites for federal prisons. But no funds were supplied, and nothing was done until Congress in 1894 provided for the temporary conversion of the military prison at Fort Leavenworth into a civil prison and directed that a new prison be erected near that site. Cleveland placed Warden J. W. French, formerly at Michigan City prison, in charge at the fort, and 500 federal prisoners were shortly gathered there. When McKinley and the Republicans took over the government, they cast about and selected the best Republican warden in the country—the veteran of Joliet. Under Major McClaughry's able direction a model penitentiary on the Joliet pattern was slowly erected at Leavenworth, but the second institution, planned for the site selected at Atlanta was delayed until the next era.[8]

As the nineteenth century was drawing to a close, the movement for prison reform was girding itself for a more effective realization of its principles and programs. The northern states had finally recognized the reformation of criminals to be a part of their responsibility for maintaining public safety. They had enacted laws, built institutions and developed customs directed toward the desired end. The old compulsion for self-support had been widely relaxed as a result of the labor laws, and a more liberal discipline was being applied in an attempt to handle the problem of increasing idleness. Everywhere the continued growth of the country had forced and made possible the erection of new institutions, usually on a grander scale. Better living conditions and an abandonment of old traditions

[8]Roeliff Brinkerhoff, *Recollections of a Lifetime* (Cincinnati, 1900), pp. 262–263.

were, it is true, more in evidence than a genuine application of the pedagogical penology of the reformatory, but the wide introduction of the forms of Brockway's technique at least indicated the aspirations of the younger generation that was taking over the task of prison management for the next era.

Professional penologists were coming to the fore, and they were challenging the authority of politicians in prison control. But if the political placemen who still manned the majority of the prisons were pathetically incapable of appreciating the high aspirations and positive features of the reformatory discipline, the august members of the well-schooled bar showed little better understanding of the significance of the indeterminate-sentence laws they were applying. Most attorneys and judges continued to play the part of old Shylock, demanding the exact pound of flesh that the old contract-theory of society considered the prisoner to have forfeited when he committed his crime. The law schools, with their newly perfected case method of instruction, were failing to consider the most important factor in the criminal case—the criminal—and their emphasis was according-ly on the standardization rather than on the individualization of criminal law. Penal reformers were not to make much headway against this rival educational trend until the development of a science of criminology in the next century enabled a few of its experts to invade the schools.

Thus stupidity and the lack of imagination were not only the chief sources of cruelty in prison, as Oscar Wilde had discovered, but major obstacles to a full realization of the positive values of reformatory penology. Yet these obstacles did not appear insur-mountable to the new generation coming forward at the turn of the century. Zealous advocates, such as Samuel J. Barrows and Hastings H. Hart, and thorough analysts, such as Charles R. Henderson, were assuming leadership. The application of pedagogical penology and the extension of its influence into the West were to be the dominant features of their program for at least the first decade of the new century.

BIBLIOGRAPHIC NOTE

The official reports of the institutions, of the state boards of charities and correction or the state boards of control, of the prison commissions, and, where these are not adequate, the messages of the governors, supply the main source of information on this period. The National Prison Association, *Proceedings,* and the New York Prison Association, *Reports,* are of exceptional value during these years. Frederick H. Wines, *Crime, Pauperism, and Benevolence in the United States at the Eleventh Census, 1890,* 2 vols. (Washington, D.C., 1895-1896), provides statistical analyses of correctional trends.

In addition to the works of Harry Elmer Barnes on Pennsylvania and New Jersey and Philip Klein on New York, cited earlier, Frank W. Blackmar, "Penology in Kansas," *Kansas University Quarterly* 1 (1893): 155–177; J. E. Briggs, *Social Legislation in Iowa* (Iowa City, 1914); Harry H. Jackson, *The Michigan State Prison* (Jackson, 1928); and Frederick G. Pettigrove, *An Account of the Prisons of Massachusetts* (Boston, 1904), supply historical treatments of developments in individual states. Other volumes of special interest are: John P. Altgeld, *Our Penal Machinery and Its Victims* (Chicago, 1894); Samuel J. Barrows, *The Criminal Insane in the United States and in Foreign Countries* (Washington, D.C., 1898), and, among others, his *Prison Systems of the United States* (Washington, D.C., 1900); Alexander Berkman, *Memoirs of an Anarchist* (New York, 1912); Maud B. Booth, *After Prison, What?* (New York, 1903); Roeliff B. Brinkerhoff, *Recollections of a Lifetime* (Cincinnati, 1900); Charles L. Clark and Earle E. Eubank, *Lockstep and Corridor: Thirty-five Years of Prison Life* (Cincinnati, 1927); Henry M. Hurd *et al, The Institutional Care of the Insane,* 4 vols. (Baltimore, 1916-1917); F. R. Johnson, *Probation for Juveniles and Adults* (New York, 1928); Joseph N. Larned, *The Life and Work of William Pryor Letchworth* (1912; reprinted Montclair, N.J., 1974); Eugenia C. Lekkerkerker, *Reformatories for Women in the United States* (Groningen, 1931); A. R. Macdonald, *Prison Secrets: Things Seen, Suffered, Recorded During Seven Years in Ludlow Street Jail* (New York, 1893); D. J. Morgan, *Historical Lights and Shadows of the Ohio Penitentiary* (Columbus, 1893); Julius B. Ransom, *Tuberculosis in Penal Institutions* (Washington, D.C., 1904); Charles E. Reeve, *The Prison Question* (Chicago, 1890); Lucien V. Rule, *The City of Dead Souls* (Louisville, Ky., 1920); Salvation Army, *Broken Souls* (New York, 1929); Edward H. Savage, *Police Records and Recollections: Or, Boston by Daylight and Gaslight for Two Hundred and Forty Years* (1873; reprinted Montclair, N.J., 1971); William R. Stewart, ed., *The Philanthropic Work of Josephine Shaw Lowell* (1911; reprinted Montclair, N.J., 1974).

ILLUSTRATIONS

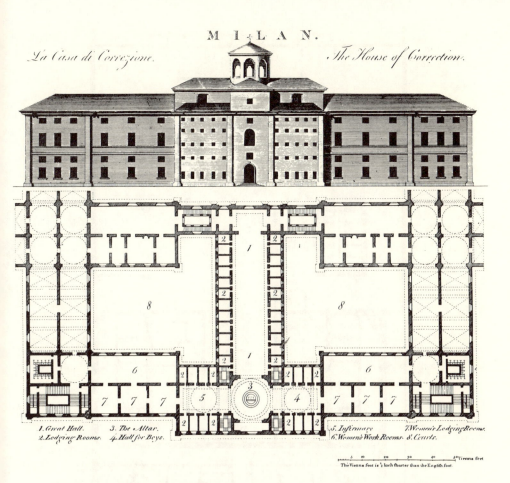

MILAN.

La Casa di Correzione.

The House of Correction.

1. Great Hall.
2. Lodging Rooms.
3. The Altar.
4. Hall for Boys.
5. Infirmary
6. Women's Work Rooms.
7. Women's Lodging Rooms.
8. Courts.

The Vienna foot is ⅓ inch shorter than the English foot.

1. House of Correction, Milan, about 1760. Described by the influential English reformer John Howard as "noble and spacious," it was one of several European institutions that supplied models for early American penitentiary design.

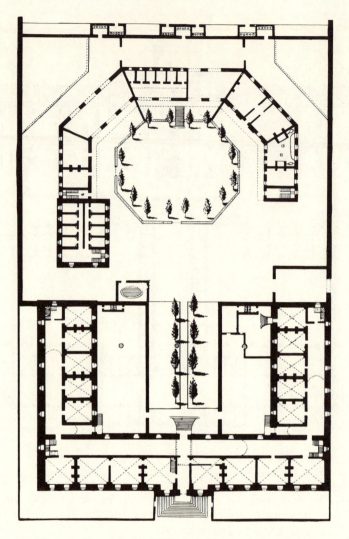

*2. Walnut Street Jail, Philadelphia, as it appeared to-
ward the end of the eighteenth century. Known as the
Cradle of the Penitentiary, it provided both individual
and congregate cells and workhouses, mixing elements
of the two rival prison systems which were to emerge.*

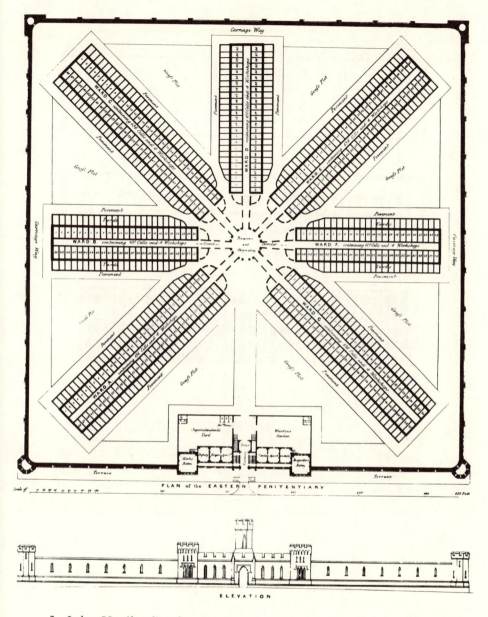

3. John Haviland's plan for Eastern State Penitentiary at Cherry Hill, Pennsylvania, erected 1823. In this archetype of the Pennsylvania system, the moderately large individual cells, each with its adjoining exercise yard, provided total isolation throughout the prisoner's term to encourage "penitence."

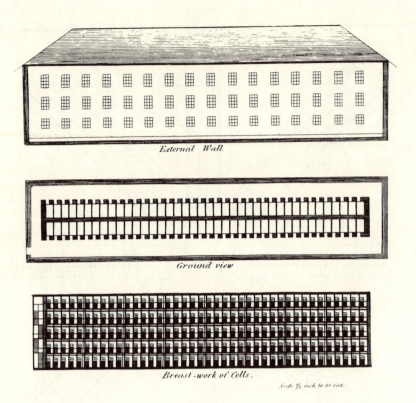

External Wall

Ground view

Breast-work of Cells.

Scale ½ inch to 10 feet.

4. Cellblock at Auburn, New York, about 1820. Under the Auburn system, the rival to the Pennsylvania system, the prisoners worked together by day in congregate workshops and were confined at night in the small cells shown above. Note that the cells do not adjoin the external walls but are separated from them by walkways—an innovation at the time.

5. *Dining hall at Sing Sing Prison, 1878. Striped uniforms and lockstep marching were key features of the Auburn system, which sought to induce obedience through rigid discipline and the rule of silence. When these severities were relaxed in the 1880s, many wardens abandoned the large dining rooms as too conducive to mass disturbances and resorted to small messhalls or feeding in the cells.*

6. *The iron gag was a punishment to which disobedient prisoners at Eastern State Penitentiary were subjected (one fatally) in the 1830s. It was an example of the sanctioning of cruel and illegal punishment which has often occurred even in institutions with a general history of humane government.*

7. *Receipt of pardoned prisoner, Mount Pleasant Prison (Sing Sing), 1833. Illiterate like most convicts of his day, this man signed with an "X" for the receipt of expenses for returning home. The pardoning power was much abused in the early nineteenth century.*

8. *Thomas Eddy (1758–1827). Eddy advocated the use of imprisonment in place of corporal punishment and championed reform schools for youths. A Quaker businessman (like many reformers of his time), he was often referred to as the John Howard of America.*

9. *Amos Pilsbury (1805–1873). Warden Pilsbury's prison at Wethersfield, Connecticut, was noted for its strict (although humane) discipline and productive labor. He and his father Moses are often considered the first professional prison warders in America.*

10. Shoemaking at Eastern Penitentiary, about 1880. When this prison became crowded, the rule requiring complete separation was relaxed and prisoners were permitted to work together at certain handicrafts.

11. Charlestown (Massachusetts) Prison, about 1890. As the inmate population grew, the prison was remodeled and expanded. Tall windows were introduced (on the wing at the right) to admit more light into the traditional Auburn-type cellblock.

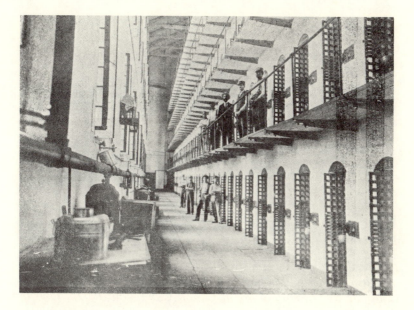

12. *Cellblock, Ohio Penitentiary, about 1890. The added light did not carry far into the interior cells of this typical Auburn cellblock with its highly stacked tiers and closely slatted doors.*

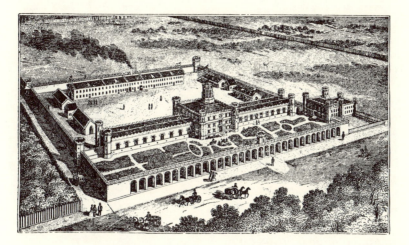

13. *The Wisconsin State Prison at Waupun, built in the late 1850s, was one of many American prisons to follow the successful Wethersfield version of the Auburn plan. Here the cellblocks are within the castellated wings in the foreground and the shops in the buildings at the rear of the prison yard.*

14. *Persistent population growth has been a burden to prison administrators across the nation since the Civil War. This view of the Colorado State Penitentiary at Canon City (about 1900) shows the prison yard cramped by the erection of new cellblocks and workshops.*

15. *Enoch Cobb Wines (1806–1879), after brief careers as educator and theologian, found his true calling in penology. As an author and the chief organizer of national and international prison associations in the 1870s, he wielded great influence in America and abroad. His son Frederick Howard Wines followed in his footsteps.*

16. *Zebulon Brockway (1827–1920) was a leading proponent of the indeterminate sentence, then hailed as a great advance but now under attack as arbitrary and capricious. Brockway founded the Elmira Reformatory (1876), which soon became a model for the rest of the world.*

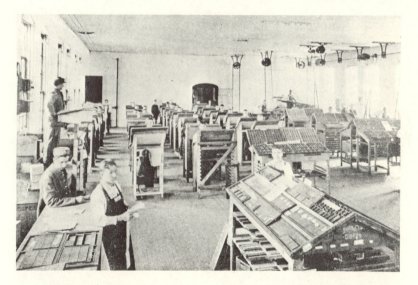

17. *Printing and bookbinding shop at Elmira Reformatory, about 1900. Printing, a common trade in American prisons, was only one of about twenty skills taught in Elmira's trade school program, which, together with military drill, was a major feature of Brockway's reformatory system.*

18. *As growing pressure from organized labor forced the curtailment of prison industry, some warders turned to elementary education programs to fill idle hours. The top drawing, by an inmate, shows teachers standing before their students at the Ohio Penitentiary (Columbus) as guards watch from chairs on high. Pictured in the inset is the penitentiary's "Superintendent of Schools." The bottom drawing shows the prison library about 1895, when it boasted five thousand volumes.*

19. *After the Civil War most convicts in southern states were sentenced to county road camps where they labored in chain gangs under armed guards. Often they were locked at night in movable cages, shown here in a North Carolina camp (about 1920). In the lower picture the tarpaulin has been dropped to protect against the weather.*

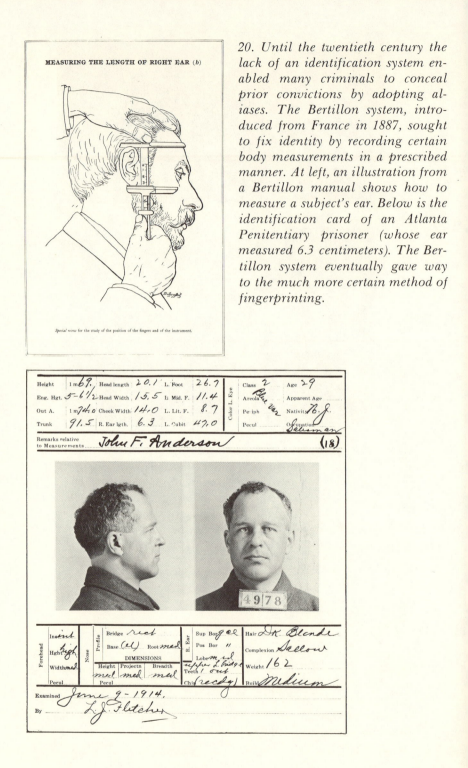

20. Until the twentieth century the lack of an identification system enabled many criminals to conceal prior convictions by adopting aliases. The Bertillon system, introduced from France in 1887, sought to fix identity by recording certain body measurements in a prescribed manner. At left, an illustration from a Bertillon manual shows how to measure a subject's ear. Below is the identification card of an Atlanta Penitentiary prisoner (whose ear measured 6.3 centimeters). The Bertillon system eventually gave way to the much more certain method of fingerprinting.

MEASURING THE LENGTH OF RIGHT EAR (b)

Special view for the study of the position of the fingers and of the instrument.

21. *In its search for new architectural patterns, Illinois in the 1920s chose the "Panopticon" ("inspection house") model devised by the English philosopher Jeremy Bentham in 1791. This prison at Stateville employed four giant circular prison houses in which all cells could be supervised from a central guard tower. Experience proved the Panopticon plan to be of limited practicality, however, and the warden caused the fifth unit to be built on the Auburn plan.*

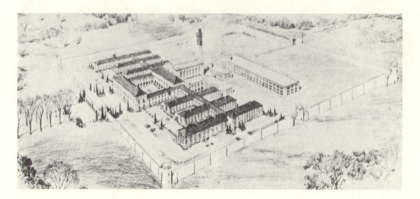

22. *Adapting a European model, the American architect Alfred Hopkins popularized the "telephone pole" design, shown here in the Federal Penitentiary at Lewisburg, Pennsylvania (1932). The arrangement of cellblocks and workshops at right angles to a central corridor provided both flexibility in layout and coordination of elements for supervision and control.*

23. *In this new federal minimum-security prison at Butner, North Carolina, adult males are confined in "cottages," an architectural arrangement first employed in juvenile reform schools and women's reformatories.*

24. *The "classification" of prisoners according to their characteristics has been a feature of modern penology. It has led not only to the construction of entire prisons for special kinds of offenders but also to plans such as this at San Luis Obispo, California (1974), wherein each cellblock has its own exercise yard.*

25. *F. Lovell Bixby (1901–1975). An able administrator first in the New Jersey and then in the federal prison systems, Dr. Bixby was also a proponent of new methods in correctional treatment, many of his own devising. He was responsible for the introduction of an important rehabilitative technique known as "guided group interaction," in which a small group of offenders meets repeatedly to discuss their problems in an unstructured manner under the guidance of a group psychologist.*

26. *One hundred years after its founding in 1870, several former presidents of the American Correctional Association pose beneath a plaque commemorating its first congress in Cincinnati. From left to right, Richard A. McGee, Professor Walter Reckless, Myrl Alexander, Austin H. MacCormick, Sanford Bates, Edward R. Cass, James V. Bennett.*

27. *In New York's Attica Prison yard, Correctional Services Commissioner Russell Oswald (lower left) negotiates with a committee of inmates. The Attica uprising of 1971 brought into dramatic public focus the racial and prisoner's rights issues lately troubling American prisons.*

SOURCES OF ILLUSTRATIONS

1. John Howard, *The State of the Prisons in England and Wales,* 4th ed. (1792; reprinted Montclair, N.J., 1973).

2. Negley K. Teeters, *The Cradle of the Penitentiary: The Walnut Street Jail at Philadelphia, 1773–1835* (Philadelphia, 1955).

3. William Crawford, *Report on the Penitentiaries of the United States* (1835; reprinted Montclair, N.J., 1969).

4. Gershom Powers, *Report of Gershom Powers, Agent and Keeper of the State Prison at Auburn, Made to the Legislature, January 7, 1828* (Albany, 1828).

5. *Frank Leslie's Illustrated Newspaper,* February 23, 1878.

6. [Thomas B. McElwee], *A Concise History of the Eastern Penitentiary of Pennsylvania* (Philadelphia, 1835).

7. Collection of Patterson Smith.

8. Samuel L. Knapp, *The Life of Thomas Eddy* (New York, 1834).

9. Zebulon R. Brockway, *Fifty Years of Prison Service: An Autobiography* (1912; reprinted Montclair, N.J., 1969).

10. Amos H. Mylin, comp., *State Prisons, Hospitals, Soldiers' Homes and Orphan Schools Controlled by the Commonwealth of Pennsylvania,* vol. 1 (Harrisburg, 1897).

11. Massachusetts Commissioners of Prisons, *Special Report . . . upon a New State Prison Combining the Congregate and Separate Systems of Imprisonment, March, 1894* (Boston, 1894).

12. E. G. Coffin, *Souvenir of the Ohio Penitentiary* (Columbus, 1899).

13. Wisconsin State Board of Control of Reformatory, Charitable and Penal Institutions, *Second Biennial Report for the Two Fiscal Years Ending September 30, 1894.* (Madison, 1894).

14. Colorado State Board of Charities and Correction, *Ninth Biennial Report . . . for the Period Ending November 30, 1908* (Denver, 1909).

15. Charles Richmond Henderson, ed., *Prison Reform* (New York, 1910).

16. Zebulon R. Brockway, *Fifty Years of Prison Service: An Autobiography* (1912; reprinted Montclair, N.J., 1969).

17. Fred C. Allen, comp., *Handbook of the New York State Reformatory at Elmira* (Elmira, 1906).

18. E. G. Coffin, *Souvenir of the Ohio Penitentiary* (Columbus, 1899).

19. Jesse F. Steiner and Roy M. Brown, *The North Carolina Chain Gang: A Study of County Convict Road Work* (1927; reprinted Montclair, N.J., 1969).

20. Alphonse Bertillon, *Signaletic Instructions: Including the Theory and Practice of Anthropometrical Identification* (Chicago, 1890). Identification card, collection of Patterson Smith.

21. U.S. Bureau of Prisons, *Handbook of Correctional Institution Design and Construction* (Washington, D.C., 1949).

22. U.S. Bureau of Prisons, *Handbook of Correctional Institution Design and Construction* (Washington, D.C., 1949).

23. U.S. Bureau of Prisons.

24. California Department of Corrections.

25. Blake McKelvey.

26. Austin H. MacCormick.

27. Wide World.

8.

SOUTHERN PENAL DEVELOPMENTS: 1865–1900

The southern states from a penological point of view scarcely as yet belonged to the Union. Their halting developments looking toward a penitentiary system had been cut short by the Civil War, and the turmoil of reconstruction created social and economic problems and standards of cruelty that continued for several decades to vilify the penal practices of the South.[1] While the northern prisoner may have grown pale and anemic gazing through the bars in the gloom of towering cellblocks, his southern brother dragged his chains through long years of hard labor, driven by brutal physical torture, oftentimes to his grave. A half century was not sufficient to efface this institutional estrangement.

Practically all the forces and conditions controlling northern developments were absent in the South. Men and women, preoccupied with the task of rebuilding their homes and communities, did not organize to carry on the patient humanitarian labors that blossomed so fruitfully in prison societies and boards of charities in the North. The incessant lash of increasing convict populations that drove the northern states to build new and better institutions was certainly not lacking here, but the South had no Auburn tradition of

[1] The most detailed account of Southern prisons in the early 1870s, covering all except Arkansas and Louisiana, appears in E. C. Wines, "Annual Report of the Secretary," *Transactions* (National Prison Association, 1874), pp. 273–400.

one man to a cell to compel sober consideration of new plans at each overflowing; the authorities simply lengthened the chains binding man to man, and the railroads and other companies that leased such labor gladly pushed their construction camps farther into the mountains, the swamps, or the mining regions. No strong unionism raised its voice to order the convicts out of the construction field, and in the few cases where violent struggles did occur, as in the Tennessee coal fields, the stable political situation of the South forestalled effective legislation.

Indeed the penal developments south of the Potomac were dominated by rather special problems. Evidence that reconstruction helped to aggravate race conflicts was graphically presented by the rapid increase in the number of Negroes in the criminal population. In the Deep South they soon exceeded 90 percent of the total, making the traditions and methods of the old slave system seem more logical patterns for southern penology than the costly methods of the North. The prostrate South had to rebuild its railroads as well as its prisons, both considerably demolished by northern troops, and the tax-laden citizens were only too eager to hear of large profits coming to the state from convicts busy constructing the highways of commerce and the foundations of industry. When most citizens believed that the end justified the means, it was not surprising either that poor Negroes, facing long sentences for unlucky escapades, should make desperate breaks for freedom or that their guards should adopt brutal measures to curb them. Thus race hatred, slave-driving traditions, desires for economy, public ignorance of the facts, and desperation among the convicts—all combined during the first trying years of reconstruction to saddle a damnable lease system on the southern states.

Rare criers in the wilderness protested; and, although their idealism failed to turn the tide, the lease system gradually receded of its own accord. Several of the forces, such as the railroad boom, spent themselves, and, when the agrarians captured political control in the nineties, a more wholesome plantation life became a major feature of a still distinctively southern penal system. But while these latter developments were taking place in the Lower South, the border states had detached themselves and were adapting many northern methods to their peculiar needs, thus further demonstrating the sectional character of southern penal developments. The contrasts between the two southern sections and the northern states in penological developments became apparent when the National Prison Association visited Nashville in 1889 and Austin in 1897, attracting a large outpouring of southern participants to its sessions and exposing their conflicting views to open debate.

Dark Days in the Black Belt

The defeat and surrender of its armies opened an era of partial chaos in the governmental functions of the South. Several of the prisons, such as they were, had been dismantled by northern troops, and something had to be done to provide for the punishment of the increasing number of vagrant and sometimes desperate freedmen. Something had to be done quickly, whether the government was temporarily in the hands of a faction of southern patriots, southern unionists, or northern army officers. Accordingly an adaptation of the old lease system of Joel Scott of Kentucky and his imitators appeared in several places, and with the exception of Alabama and Texas all the Gulf states quickly turned unreservedly to this system. When the Democrats regained control during the seventies, their determination to cut the tax burden prompted them to exchange the first leases for others more favorable to the state treasuries. The exploitation of convict labor thus became an established tradition, with the lease system as its first standard pattern.

Georgia's penal developments were typical of the section. When in 1868 General T. H. Ruger took over the state government, he found a hundred convicts on his hands and, with the old prison in ruins, promptly leased them to an enterprising railroad builder. The first carpetbag governor, Rufus Bullock, was easily persuaded to continue the policy to the benefit of the railroads of his associate, H. I. Kimball. When Bullock lost control in 1870, a Democratic investigation revealed, among other shocking facts, that only 380 of the 496 convicts could be located. Nevertheless, as the major concern was economy, the legislature hastened to endorse the system and agreed to lease 500 convicts to seven different contractors. By 1876, when its prisoners numbered 1,110, Georgia had developed a leasing program under which it distributed its convicts among three companies on twenty-five-year contracts. Each company agreed to pay the state $25,000 a year for the labor. Governor J. M. Smith congratulated the state in 1877 upon its happy solution of a perplexing problem.[2]

Penal developments in Mississippi followed practically the same course. The military government leased the convicts in 1867 for three years, and the carpetbaggers extended the term. A partial reorganization of the government in 1872 brought to power some critics of the lessee who was receiving $20,000 a year from the state, and they made an attempt to restore the old penitentiary system with a superintendent in charge. But the superintendent, noting that the dilapidated state of the prison, with its locks and machinery demolished by the troops, could be corrected only at great expense, determined to keep only the young, the infirm, and the sick at the "Walls" and leased the able-bodied to a railroad on terms favorable to the state. When the Democrats gained full control in 1876, a proposal for a new penitentiary was quickly voted down, and the entire population was leased to the Hamilton and Hebron Company on what appeared to be favorable terms; the company, however, soon discovered that it could sublease the convicts at even higher rates, and no check was maintained over the cruel fate of the penal slaves.

In a similar fashion Louisiana, with the prison at Baton Rouge sufficiently dismantled to discourage its repair, created a board of control to supervise the leasing of the convicts. It negotiated a twenty-year contract providing for increased returns to the state and requiring the lessee to enforce any regulations which the board should adopt for the discipline of the prisoners. But this slight improvement over the other leases proved of little value, for the board found that it could neither enforce its regulations nor collect the annual payments. A Prison Reform Association, organized at New Orleans in 1886, failed to oust the lease system; it did, however, secure more lucrative payments to the state and the appointment of a state board to supervise conditions in the chain-gang lease camps.[3]

Arkansas and Tennessee likewise turned their prisons over to lessees at the close of the war. Their first contracts required that the

---

[2] Edward Grubb, *Methods of Penal Administration in the United States* (London, 1904), pp. 38–39; Wines, "Annual Report, 1874," pp. 288–291.

[3] Mark T. Carleton, *Politics and Punishment: The History of the Louisiana State Penal System* (Baton Rouge, 1971), pp. 20–87.

convicts be employed within the walls, as in most border states, but circumstances soon prompted them to permit the development of work camps at the discretion of the lessees. Arkansas paid a small fee for the support of each prisoner in the late sixties and permitted the lessee to incur a huge state debt for the construction of additional cells which he then proceeded to fill with federal convicts to his own profit. A political overturn finally compelled the lessee to pay an annual rental of $25,000 to the state but permitted him to employ the inmates as he chose.[4]

Tennessee, finding its old 356-cell prison at Nashville over-crowded in the early seventies, leased the excess in batches to various companies. Reports of numerous escapes and numerous deaths among the men sent to the lessee camps prompted a revision in 1884 granting the Tennessee Coal and Iron Railroad an exclusive lease to the entire convict population for a payment of $100,000 a year. The company soon had the majority of the convicts housed at three mining camps and boasted that the deaths in 1886 and 1887 had been cut to "only 93 out of an average of 1,350" prisoners. When a reform faction protested, the company negotiated a new contract in 1891 agreeing to pay $250,000 annually and to build new and more sanitary stockades to house the men at its mining camps. With the onset of the depression, when the company cut the work day and pay of its free miners, while maintaining full production at its prison camps, a mob of free miners set fire to one of the convict stockades, loaded the prisoners into boxcars, and dispatched them to the Nashville prison. To maintain its lease the company undertook to rebuild the state penitentiary, equipping it by 1898 with 800 modern cells, each 6 by 8 by 8 in size, on the improved Auburn pattern. It provided workshops for the labor of some 400 men at various trades but employed another 200 in work gangs on the prison farm and some 600 at its reconstructed Brushy Mountain mining camp. In describing this system to the National Prison Association gathered at Austin, Texas, in 1897, T. J. Hill, the company's superintendent in charge, detailed the benefits not only in profits to the state and to industry, because of the increased supply of fuel, but also in industrial training to the convicts. The great majority of the convicts, he reported, were unskilled Negroes who thus learned a trade and work habits that assured them jobs in the mines on their

[4]H. C. Gill, "State Prisons of the United States," *Proceedings of the National Conference of Charities and Corrections* (1883), p. 264.

discharge. Curiously enough the managers of the Austin Congress scheduled Hill's address for the end of the last session and followed his rosy report not with the usual discussion but with hasty resolutions of thanks to the local committees and officials before singing the doxology in adjournment.[5]

But Florida took the prize for corruption and cruelty in penal affairs during this period. The federal government had loaned the arsenal at Chattahoochee for a state prison, and during the eight years of reconstruction the boodlers in charge housed an average of eighty-two convicts there at a total cost of $234,473. When the federal troops were withdrawn, the Democrats quickly cut expenses by leasing the prisoners to a construction company for the nominal sum of $100 a year. Succeeding years saw a shift of leases almost every year as the state sought to improve its bargain, thus shuttling the convicts about in a haphazard fashion, with never any permanent quarters. The prisoners were held together only by a barbarous discipline enforced at the point of the gun, and the system was aptly described as "the American Siberia."[6]

Neither Alabama nor Texas had suffered so cruelly from war or reconstruction, and their earlier traditions resisted the new trends for a time. The first reconstruction government in Alabama had leased the prison at Wetumpka for six years, but when the state recovered the institution in 1872, it placed a warden in full control. The buildings were unfortunately in a wretched state of repair, and as the legislature provided only a small appropriation for maintenance, the warden found it desirable to hire out the able-bodied in order to meet expenses. The legislature agreed to sanction the policy but required the warden to station an officer at each camp to supervise discipline. A little experience revealed that the lessees were shirking all responsibility for guarding the convicts and safeguarding their health. As the number of escapes and the ratio of deaths mounted, Alabama followed its neighbors in placing full responsibility upon the lessees. A striking hint as to the origin of the technique of the lease system appeared in 1880 when the warden advertised three

[5] Tennessee Penitentiary, *Report of the Superintendent* (1888), pp. 9–15; Tennessee Board of Prison Commissioners, *Report* (1897-1898); T. J. Hill, "Experience in Mining Coal with Convicts," *Proceedings* (N.P.A., 1897), pp. 388–405.

[6] Gill, "State Prisons," p. 264; J. C. Powell, *The American Siberia: Or, Fourteen Years' Experience in a Southern Convict Camp* (1891; reprinted Montclair, N.J., 1970).

grades of prisoners for contract, asking $5.00 per month for the "full-hands," $2.50 for "medium-hands," and nothing but their keep for "dead-hands," thus borrowing some well-known terms from slave traditions. A move toward the abandonment of this system during the eighties was blocked by financial considerations, which prompted a shift in lessees to the Tennessee Coal and Iron Railroad, which agreed to construct a model camp at its Pratt mines. Dr. R. M. Cunningham, the physician in charge at the "Walls" and later at the mines, delivered a vigorous defense of the lease system before the Nashville Congress in 1889. He endeavored to explain the high death rate as a result of the feeble health of many of the black convicts on their arrival, but he concluded by admitting that the lease system was not the most ideal.[7]

Texas with its great area and rapidly growing population found the 225 cells at the Huntsville prison hopelessly inadequate during the first years after the war. The first expedient of employing the overflow on state railroads was terminated when the state sold the railroads to private interests and leased the entire prison. The first lessee soon defaulted. A new lessee was found who built a second prison with 400 cells at Rusk and equipped it with a foundry to develop the product of nearby mines. This structure was finished when the lease expired in 1880, and 50 additional cells became available at Huntsville, but the total of 675 cells could not accommodate the 2,000 convicts who were, at the time, scattered over a wide area, laboring at railroad and bridge construction, iron-blasting, and plantation-farming. The state superintendent accordingly felt compelled to contract out the majority of his charges but succeeded in maintaining efficient inspection and regulation, thus eliminating many of the worst evils of the lease system.

Warden Whatley frankly admitted, however, that he could not maintain discipline either at Huntsville or in the more crowded work camps without a frequent use of "the strap." He believed, as had his predecessor Major Goree, that a prompt application of corporal punishment had a greater disciplinary effect than confinement in dark cells or other protracted punishments. He was glad to report at the Austin meeting that a good-time law was proving helpful, and that he was planning an early trip north to see the

[7] R. M. Cunningham, "The Convict System of Alabama in Its Relation to Health and Disease," *Proceedings* (N.P.A., 1889), pp. 108–141.

model prisons there. Major Goree added that the system's success in meeting its annual expenses over a period of years had been supported by a policy of paying small sums to the convicts for overtime work as in a few northern prisons.[8]

Penal Systems in the Border States

Institutional developments in America have had their sectional variations but never any sharp boundary lines. The sectional variations are particularly noticeable in penal history, possibly because prisons have been more closely tied to state political affairs than have been the educational and charitable institutions. Thus there was a belt of states stretching from Virginia and the Carolinas to Missouri that scarcely fell in with the general penological trends of either the North or the Deep South. In the Carolinas, where, before the war, the administration of justice had been entirely in the hands of the counties, the state authorities now built penitentiaries. Events soon converted these prisons into little more than penal hospitals. The Carolinas, like Tennessee, soon leased the able-bodied convicts to outside contractors. Virginia, Kentucky and Missouri, on the other hand, developed prisons to house most of their convicts, but they were slow to respond to the penal reform movement. West Virginia alone, and only for a time, turned its back on the southern influences and attempted to maintain a penitentiary.

The reconstruction government in North Carolina decided in 1868 to build a penitentiary on the Auburn pattern. After a scandal occasioned by the disappearance of the first commissioners with $100,000 paid them for eight thousand acres of worthless pine barrens,[9] a second commission chose a 22-acre site near Raleigh and hired an architect from Ohio to build a prison on the model of the new construction at Pittsburgh. When the Democrats captured the state and appointed still a third commission, it expanded the plan to provide a total of 1,000 cells and supplied temporary wooden huts to house the prisoners while construction proceeded slowly. But as the number of convicts increased more rapidly than funds were provided

[8] L. A. Whatley, "Corporal Punishment in Texas," *Proceedings* (N.P.A., 1897), pp. 59–61; Thomas J. Goree, "Corporal Punishment," ibid., pp. 64–67; "Some Features of Prison Control in the South," ibid., pp. 131–137.

[9] North Carolina Commission of Inquiry, *Report* (N.C. Sen. docs., 1868-1869), pp. 1–9.

for construction, the authorities turned to the lease system and placed 500 men on contracts to various railroads in 1877. The construction of the first 500-cell block and encompassing wall was completed by 1882, but the failure of an experiment with a shoe factory left many inmates at the prison idle and prompted its officials to treat it as a reception center and hospital for the sick and other weaklings rejected by the lessees. In 1883 the warden reported that returns from the lessees, who held 800 able-bodied convicts in labor camps on six railroad systems, were sufficient to pay the full expenses of the penitentiary. Although his records revealed that 100 had escaped during the year, in spite of the efforts of the officers, who had shot eleven others fleeing from the chain gangs, he was able to congratulate the state on its $678 surplus.

South Carolina made an equally poor start in the development of its penitentiary. It erected a stone prison on an eleven-acre plot on the outskirts of Columbia in the late sixties. The first building with 200 cells soon proved inadequate and the state authorized additional construction increasing the total to 625 cells during the eighties, but the number of convicts grew even more rapidly. To relieve congestion the prison leased a farm and developed a camp to house its workers, but a drive for economy prompted Governor Wade Hampton to negotiate a lease placing 200 able-bodied convicts in chain-gang camps on a railroad construction project. When Captain J. G. Guignard, a director of the penitentiary, accepted an invitation to attend the National Prison Association Congress at Nashville, he "came to learn, not to instruct." He was impressed by the industrial school for juvenile delinquents he saw at Nashville and concluded that South Carolina might profit from the removal of many youths from its penitentiary. He was happy to report that the state had abandoned the old lease system a year or two before and had assumed the task of feeding, clothing, and guarding its convicts whether in the penitentiary or in the labor camps along the Columbia canal on which they were laboring in scattered chain gangs. Although the casualties and the escapes were high, the penitentiary was successfully defraying its expenses.[10]

In similar fashion the prisons of Virginia and Kentucky, though fairly in line with northern penal standards before the war, became

[10] J. G. Guignard, "Prison Work in South Carolina," *Proceedings* (N.P.A., 1889), pp. 245–247.

desperately overcrowded after that conflict and soon adopted some southern traditions to fit their needs. The prison in Richmond, with 168 outside cells in a semi-circular block designed, as previously noted, by Benjamin Latrobe, had been perhaps the best in the South before the war, and though partly demolished was quickly reconstructed in the late sixties. Again the increasing number of inmates overtaxed the facilities, and the state sent many in chain gangs to help with the reconstruction of the railroads. When the state turned the railroads over to private companies, it leased gangs of convicts to their supervision. Criticism of this system prompted the warden to negotiate with a shoe company, for the construction of a contract factory at the prison. The profits realized from this operation in the late seventies encouraged the warden to keep many able-bodied men at the prison, crowding two into each cell and housing others in large dormitories. The lease system continued, offsetting to a degree the mounting congestion, which was not remedied until the completion of a new cellblock in 1905 and the construction of a new stockade at the prison farm relieved the pressure.[11]

The Kentucky prison at Frankfort, birthplace of the lease system, had remained in the hands of private operators until a decade following the war. An increasing population compelled the lessee, who confined his operations within the prison, to undertake the construction of additional cells, again on the Baltimore plan. The new total of 700 cells failed, however, to accommodate all the convicts, who numbered 1,000 by the end of the decade, while the increase was clogging the narrow confines of the hemp factory. Disturbing rumors of cruelty roused Governor Luke P. Blackburn to cancel the lease and place a warden in full charge at Frankfort and to project a second institution on the Elmira pattern at Eddyville. But as the state was not prepared to operate prison industries, contracts were let for this purpose, one of them to a railroad company permitting the use of 250 men in its construction camps. The railroad soon acquired the other contracts and increased the numbers at its prison camps to 650 by 1885. But this action roused popular indignation, and, when free labor stormed one of the camps and released the convicts, the state was again prompted to assume control. It despatched some convicts to Eddyville to speed construc-

[11] Virginia Penitentiary, *Report* (1905), pp. 5–9.

tion of the new prison, but the old prison was still so seriously crowded that a disastrous uprising occurred among the idle convicts. The disillusioned state authorities again turned the prison over to a lessee in 1889. It was not until the completion of the second prison in the early nineties that Kentucky finally assumed full responsibility for the management of its prison system.

By 1880 all the former Confederate states and Kentucky as well had surrendered a major portion of their criminal populations into the hands of lessees. Alabama and Texas were attempting to supervise the lease camps, while Virginia, Kentucky, and the Carolinas were maintaining prisons for a portion of the prisoners; but in each of these states, and in Missouri as well, the dictates of economy had given rise to a wretched system of penal slavery that was little better than that of the Black Belt. Occasionally the voice of a reformer was heard above the sound of the moneychangers, but the taxpayers soon reasserted their interests. Although the most critical years of poverty in the South were over by 1878, the convicts continued to pay retribution, not only for their own sins, at a time when that old principle was losing force in the North, but also for the public crimes of Civil War and reconstruction. Many thousands of happy-go-lucky Negroes awoke from rosy dreams of freedom and forty acres and a mule to find themselves shackled to the task of rebuilding the wealth of the South in hopeless penal slavery.

Convict Life in the South

Sentimental proposals for the reformation of criminals found little support during the years when the New South was in process of formation. The struggle between the races and the factions was so fierce during the first years that cruel penal conditions could have aroused hardly any surprise. In the eighties George W. Cable urged that the just treatment of the convicts be recognized as a public responsibility, but, with the public schools and charities struggling to survive with inadequate support, the criminal could not escape the demand that he at least earn his keep. In place of the religious and educational ideals that were inspiring the development of the adult reformatories in the North, the old slave system was supplying traditions and customs to the penology of the South. Unfortunately the lease camps never saw the development of the paternalism that had been the saving grace of the old plantation system, and no private-property interest in the life of the laborer safeguarded the convict from injury. New laws that horrified idealists in the North gathered the most restless and independent from among the freedmen and gave them hopelessly long sentences. The discipline which had kept the relatively docile slaves in the fields before the war could have no effect now; the penal slaves had to be herded about their camps by armed guards and shackled in the "cribs" at night. The interests of the lessee in the largest possible return from the least outlay too frequently determined the policy of the state.

There were no standard living arrangements in the southern prison camps. Yet one strong factor, the demand for economy, brought them all practically to a common level—scarcely that of subsistence. None of the lease camps ever tried to introduce any of the Auburn traditions, and the penitentiaries that did have individual cells seldom attempted to apply rules of silence. Wooden huts of one story usually housed a hundred or more on crude bunks strung around the walls. The danger of escapes frequently compelled the authorities to shut these up tight at nightfall, and they soon became very foul. Water was usually scarce, and bathing almost impossible; other sanitary arrangements were invariably crude, and disease was rampant. Food was plentiful or scarce as the economy of the lessee determined. Heat was usually lacking although rickety stoves or open fires sometimes added much smoke and a little warmth during the cold nights of the winter months. The fear of escapes was the controlling factor in discipline. The lessees tried various devices for shackling the feet and sometimes in desperate cases attached heavy iron balls to the chains. Striped garments were everywhere in use, and the convicts had no such picayune tastes regarding their footwear as northern prisoners had; they were glad to get any at all. Tobacco chewing was everywhere in evidence, but smoking was prohibited because of the fire risk. Southern newspapers did not cry out, as in the North, against the hotel accommodations of their prisoners, but the criminals failed to migrate north.

Religious influences, though not absent, had little effect. It was difficult to secure white chaplains, and it was out of the question to hire Negroes. However, plenty of the latter turned up in the camps by legal proceedings, and these dusky but fluent souls usually practiced their calling without restraint on the one day of rest.

Sunday schools were popular among the prisoners, and occasionally outside workers added to the value of these feeble attempts at regeneration. When the religious forces did bestir themselves, they usually attacked such popular devices of the devil as card playing. Arkansas passed a law against that vice in 1890, but the warden reported that he found it impossible to stamp out the most popular Sabbath pastime.

Such were the living conditions of the great majority of the southern convicts in the first two decades following the war. Even when Alabama determined to make the lease system as respectable as possible, the model camps constructed at the mines did little more than improve the sanitary and eating arrangements. After fourteen years' experience in charge of convict camps in Florida, Captain J. C. Powell was inspired to compare that system with the horrors of Siberia. If his information was limited to the very worst system of the South, his account certainly depicted villainy that surpassed any responsible picture of the situation in Siberia. Warden Bankhead in Alabama was more to the point when he called on local analogies:

> I am prepared to demonstrate that our system is a better training school for criminals than any of the dens of iniquity that exist in our large cities. . . . The first lesson taught is that the state cares nothing for the criminal, nor his well being. . . . You may as well expect to instill decent habits into a hog as to reform a criminal whose habits and surroundings are as filthy as a pig's. To say there are any reformatory measures at our prison, or that any regard is had to similar subjects, is to state a falsehood.[12]

Death or escape were the only quick methods of relief available to the convicts. Before the lease system was well established, and where the convicts were let out to numerous lessees, escapes were very frequent. Both the concentration of the convicts into the hands of one lessee and the demand that the guards be held responsible for the escape of men under their supervision were measures taken to check the evil. Yet as late as 1882 a survey of the reports revealed that a total of 1,100 men had made successful breaks for freedom in the two previous years in southern states, in contrast with sixty-three escapes from among 18,300 northern convicts in one year. A similar study of

[12] Alabama Penitentiary, *Report of the Inspectors* (1882), p. 15.

convict mortality revealed that, while the average death rate of twenty-eight northern prisons was 14.9 per thousand, the average in the South was 41.3 per thousand.[13] The appalling conditions which these statistics reveal were partly the cause and partly the result of the brutal practices of the lease system.

Southern discipline was not complicated by elaborate schemes for reformation. Cable described it as "such as provides for efficiency in labor, and against insurrection and escape." No rules of silence gave occasion for petty punishments as in the North; in fact, there were no written rules of any sort in many cases where complete control was entrusted to the lessee. Punishments were usually administered with the lash or the strap, but ingenious guards sometimes devised special forms of torture, such as the notorious "watering" penalty in Florida, during which a convict would be stretched on his back and a stream of water poured into his mouth until he was nearly drowned.[14] Alabama and Texas were the only states to regulate punishments by law during the period; elsewhere the only check was the interest of the lessee in seeing that punishments did not impair his labor force.

The chief reliance for security was on the chains, the dogs, and the armed guards. In the early days guards did not always shoot at escaping prisoners. To stamp out such laxity some states levied fines on the lessee for every escape, and the guard's job was made to depend on his vigilance. Scores of fugitives were shot down every year in some of the states, and yet, with conditions as they were, desperate men were always ready on the slightest occasion to "hang it on a limb" in the hope of freedom.

Cruel as was the fate of the convicts, southern courts showed no sentimental hesitancy in meting out the full penalty of the law. There were no habitual-criminal laws here; none were needed. Massachusetts courts might consider a twenty-year sentence for a third felony too harsh to be applied, but of the 1,200 convicts in Georgia in 1880 only 150 had terms as short as three years, and over 500 had terms of ten years or more. Everywhere in the South sentences were unreasonably long, and the Negroes got more than

[13] George W. Cable, "The Convict Lease System," in *The Silent South* (1889; reprinted Montclair, N.J., 1969). This enlarged edition published for the first time eight heretofore uncollected essays by Cable on prison and asylum reform.

[14] Powell, *American Siberia*.

their just share. The social hatreds engendered by years of strife were still rampant, and it continued to appear a social good to take idlers off to construction camps long after the notorious vagrancy laws were forgotten. There was no check, as in the North, where cells rapidly became crowded and compelled the construction of costly bastilles if convictions were too frequent. There were, in fact, no saving circumstances to protect the unfortunate southern convict from hopeless oblivion until the first era of large-scale construction came to a close in the early nineties.

Even more than in the North the great majority of the prisoners remained under the control of the counties. These authorities had no more adequate housing than the states when the new constitutions abolished branding, whipping, and the stocks in favor of fines and imprisonment. While the states were experimenting with their leasing systems, the county sheriffs showed no lack of initiative in making use of their new labor forces.

The many responsibilities of southern counties provided them with ample use for cheap labor. The employment of convicts in cleaning the streets was introduced by many cities at the close of the war, but the construction and repair of rural wagon roads soon became the chief task for such labor. Counties in the North as well as in the South had experimented with road labor from early times; it did not become a regular activity, however, until reconstruction days in the South. Carroll D. Wright found county convicts laboring on the public roads in eight southern states in 1886. Even West Virginia, striving to develop a northern penitentiary system, permitted its counties to labor 25 percent of its total criminal population on the roads in that year.

There was seldom any clear distinction in southern law between state and county offenders. Judges usually had the discretion of committing their prisoners to the state prison or to the county chain gang, although North Carolina and a few other states limited the county sentences to ten years. The arrangement usually worked to the advantage of the counties, for in districts failing to make profitable use of this labor supply the judges handed the great majority over to the state; but when a sheriff was building roads or leasing the men to advantage, the courts kept the able-bodied at home and sent only the aged and infirm to the state prison. The state authorities, eager to meet the largest demands of their lessees, made frequent protests, but little was done until the states themselves began to take over the responsibility of road construction at a later date.

Such rivalry sometimes called forth damning indictments of the county systems. As county camps were less permanent or substantial than those of the state and as the authorities were, if possible, less responsible, the conditions were much more wretched. Many of the sheriffs, rather than superintend the labor themselves, leased their charges to private companies to work the roads, drain swamps, operate lumber camps, or perform other local functions for which free labor could not readily be secured. There was no adequate state regulation or inspection and seldom any responsible local supervision, and the scanty records at the court houses considered only the financial accounts, the convictions, escapes, deaths, and discharges. Again chains, dogs, and guns were the chief means of preserving public security, while the interests of the convicts were disregarded. The evils of this system joined with those of the state leases to supply arguments to the tardy agitators for reform in the late eighties.

New Influences in the Nineties

After two decades of reconstruction the South began to develop a new sense of proportion. The common man with the aid of his various Populist organizations was crowding the old gentry out of politics, and, as long as the Negro accepted the inferior status to which he had been reduced, the common man in politics was willing to consider his welfare, even the welfare of those convicted of crime. But the lease system was doomed by its decreasing usefulness to the state rather than by the growth of a strong humanitarianism, and it was not abandoned until profitable substitutes were perfected. First the women, the children, and the sick were moved into separate quarters; then experiments with plantations, industrial prisons, and road camps supplied promising patterns for a new southern penal system by the close of the century.

Humanitarian and economic interests joined to intercede in behalf of the women and the boys in the later eighties. The North had made the care of juvenile delinquents a charity distinct from the penal system before the war, and the segregation of the sexes had been accepted as a principle since the days of Louis Dwight, but the

South had largely escaped these problems until Negro women and boys began to appear in large numbers in the criminal lineup after the war. The slave traditions of the lease system recognized no distinctions until the practice of dividing the convicts into "full-hands," "half-hands," and "dead-hands" revealed the advantage of separate treatment for the women and the boys. Attention was at last given to the recommendations of the charitable-minded that special farms be provided by the state where these classes could earn their keep free from evil influences. Few lessees were willing to take such "dead-hands" and left them to clog the prisons. Texas, North Carolina, and Virginia, whose prisons were becoming centers of industrial activity, were the first to provide asylum farms, and Alabama soon followed their example. The interests of the Populists in the practical education of the "forgotten man" strengthened the movement, and by the close of the century only Tennessee and Louisiana had failed to provide for the removal of at least a portion of the women, the children, and the sick from the mass of the prisoners.

These experiments with small penal farms came at an opportune time for southern penology. The new political leaders were anything but partial to the large leasing companies whose political ties were usually attached to their predecessors. Sharp bargains pressed many of the lessees to the wall just as the railroad boom on which they had depended was drawing to a close. Long contracts and new opportunities in mines and swamps preserved the lessees of the southeastern states, although more abundant returns were gradually extracted from them and more careful regulations enforced, but elsewhere the lease system was gradually replaced.

The first extensive use of adult prisoners on large farms and plantations occurred in the southwestern states of this period. In Texas the criminal population was expanding rapidly beyond the capacity of the two state prisons and beyond the demands of the construction lessees, prompting the authorities in the mid eighties to experiment with sharecrop farming. By 1888 one-third of the 3,000 state prisoners were employed in this fashion on private farms, and the state was itself organizing the work on the newly purchased 2,700-acre Harlem farm. Texas continued to enlarge its penal plantations by a gradual acquisition of scattered farms, but Mississippi made a bold and complete shift to the new system. The people of the state, discouraged by failure of the authorities to collect profits from the lessee, adopted a constitutional provision ordering the termination of all leases by 1895. Accordingly the authorities, after experimenting for a few years with sharecrop farming, purchased the 15,000-acre Sunflower plantation and developed on it the model penal system of the South. Only Louisiana adopted this program wholeheartedly before the end of the decade, but most of the other southern states made farming an important accessory to their other penal activities, much as several northern states were to do a decade or so later. At the turn of the century the penal plantation appeared to be the ideal goal for southern penology.

A considerable number of northern traditions crossed the border and traveled down the Mississippi Valley in these last years of the century; unfortunately in penological matters they were chiefly the castoff techniques of a former era. Thus the contract-labor system, in the years of its expulsion from several northern prisons, received a ready welcome in the prisons of Kentucky and Tennessee and was given more intensive application in those of Virginia and Missouri. When Kentucky opened its branch prison at Eddyville in 1890, state officers took full charge at both prisons, terminating the long leasing tradition, but the original intention to make Eddyville a reformatory was forgotten, and contractors were brought in to make an active industrial program the main feature of both prisons. Similarly in Tennessee, labor and Populist agitation persuaded the legislature to abolish the old lease under which the Tennessee Iron and Coal Railroad had used convicts to break strikes in its mines; the state replaced its old prison with a new one on a large plantation near Nashville, and completed its equipment of 800 cells, each 8 by 6 and 8 feet high, in 1898; but the state also erected log dormitories on public coal lands at Brushy Mountain, and the major portion of the convict population continued to labor under the contractors who operated these mines for the state. The state profits from these activities were rivaled only in the other border states—Virginia, Maryland, Missouri, and Kansas.

The only genuine intrusion of current penological theory from the North occurred in New Orleans. A prominent resident of that city, Michael Heymann, had been thrown into close association with Frederick Howard Wines at the World's Fair in Chicago, and returned to New Orleans determined to organize a prison society to fight for the adoption of reformatory penology. Heymann's society succeeded in persuading the state constitutional convention, then in session, to incorporate progressive principles into its clauses providing for the abolition of the lease system, but even the assistance of a special visit from the National Prison Association failed to induce the legislature to follow up these northern leads. Lousiana rejected reformatory penology in favor of the new southern pattern evolved in Mississippi and purchased Angola, eight thousand acres of good land sixty miles north of Baton Rouge, to replace her abandoned lease.

But the increase of state control represented by these shifts to plantation and industrial prisons and by improved supervision of the lessees in the other states was counteracted in many localities by an increased use of the convicts on county roads. Farmers in politics were partial to this use of convict labor, and the uncertain distinction between county and state offenders permitted the courts, especially in Georgia, Alabama, and the Carolinas, to sentence an increasing proportion of the able-bodied to hard labor on the local roads. No supervision was provided, and the chain gangs on the roads, lodged in boxcar cages and surrounded by dogs and armed guards, became a notorious symbol of southern justice—a greedy heir to the technique of the lease system it helped to displace. The widely boasted reduction in the death rate of southern convicts did not take these county chain gangs into consideration, and indeed for a time their fate was entirely overlooked by the state authorities.

Thus by 1900 all the penal programs that were eventually to replace the lease system were in active operation in the South. The prospect, in spite of its darker aspects, was the most encouraging the section had envisaged during the previous century. But there was a total absence of men studying the problem in any thorough fashion, and there was almost as great a dearth of public-spirited citizens organized to safeguard the interests of prisoners. Public authorities never for a moment slaked their thirst for profits from convict labor, and the first three decades of the twentieth century were to witness public greed defeat the hopes of the late nineties. The penal systems, whether centering around plantations as in the southwestern part of the section, specializing in road labor as in the southeastern states, or developing contract industries as in the border states, remained strangely isolated from the vital influences active in northern penology.

BIBLIOGRAPHIC NOTE

The printed documents of the states contain but few reports by the lessees, and, except where wardens or superintendents were appointed, the student is forced to rely on the brief comments on penal affairs in the governor's messages. The development of state control or supervision in the eighties and nineties brought with it regular official reports, usually of a statistical nature. Special legislative committees or special messages from the governor, at times when one lease was being discarded or other revision made, supply fuller detail. This situation renders the occasional address on southern conditions before the National Prison Association of great value, and the address of George W. Cable, "The Convict Lease System," delivered before the National Conference of Charities in 1883 and reprinted in his *The Silent South* (1889; reprinted Montclair, N.J., 1969), is indispensable to the student. Frances A. Kellor, *Experimental Sociology, Descriptive and Analytical: Delinquents* (New York, 1901), for the same reasons, is of value for a study of conditions in the nineties.

Works of special interest are: Mark T. Carleton, *Politics and Punishment: The History of the Louisiana State Penal System* (Baton Rouge, 1971); Frank W. Hoffer, Delbert M. Mann, and Floyd N. House, *The Jails of Virginia: A Study of the Local Penal System* (New York, 1933); Collis Lovely, "The Abuses of Prison Labor," *Shoe Workers' Journal* 6 (July–October) 1905; Albert D. Oliphant, *The Evolution of the Penal System of South Carolina from 1866 to 1916* (Columbia, 1916); J. C. Powell, *The American Siberia: Or, Fourteen Years' Experience in a Southern Convict Camp* (1891; reprinted Montclair, N.J., 1970); William C. Sneed, *A Report on the History and Mode of Management of the Kentucky Penitentiary, From its Origin, in 1798, to March 1, 1860 (Frankfort, Ky., 1860); Jesse F. Steiner and Roy M. Brown, The North Carolina Chain Gang: A Study of County Road Work* (1937; reprinted Montclair, N.J., 1969); Elizabeth Wisner, *Public Welfare Administration in Louisiana* (Chicago, 1930).

9.

PENOLOGY IN THE
GREAT WEST:
TO 1900

The Great West was the third fairly distinct section of America during the last half of the nineteenth century. The normal advance of the frontier had come to a halt at the edge of the plains, and the building of states on the Pacific coast and in the vast mountain areas was in many respects a new phase of American development. The settlers brought a large heritage of eastern culture with them, but the barrier of plains and mountains severed many of the connecting links that might have kept them in touch with new developments in the East, and they quickly revealed an easy freedom from older traditions. This freedom was particularly evident in the case of penal institutions, for neither the traditions of Louis Dwight nor the programs of Enoch Wines influenced these territories and states during their formative years. Indeed, the frolicsome cowboys and carousing miners who enjoyed their practical jokes at the expense of zealous missionaries and energetic drummers would have doubled up in boisterous laughter if a kindly spirited easterner had appeared to urge the reformation of cattle thieves and highwaymen. The surprising fact was the speed with which these scattered settlers built their homes, schools, churches, and finally their prisons, universities, and asylums.

Thus the establishment of prisons in the Great West was a phase of the institutional conquest of the last frontier. A rough-and-ready, oftentimes desperate, struggle to curb lawlessness determined the character of the early instruments of justice. The federal government, holding the territories in tutelage, was quite innocent of penal experience, and many of the officers sent west to administer its functions were political adventurers, frequently described in the territories as "carpetbaggers." Prison techniques and patterns were imported, but unfortunately the channels of influence, whether by way of California or the Missouri Valley, were dominated by several of the worst prison structures in the country. Thus, as thick patches of population crept up the valleys, through the passes, and along the railroads during the last quarter of the century, their newly elected and inexperienced officials hastened to provide makeshift prisons, but except in a few instances it required a decade or two to bring their institutions into line with penal developments in the East.

A major handicap was the lack of ready opportunities for employment in the far western prisons. The scarcity of local industrial enterprise on this rapidly advancing frontier, and the adoption of federal anticontract laws in the 1880s combined to keep most of the prisoners in idleness, thus creating a situation that made the introduction of rules of silence impossible. Only in the few states which devised an adequate industrial program and where the creation of boards of charities provided leadership did a stable penal system emerge during this era.

Prison Developments in California

California, the outstanding state of the Far West, was beset by major criminal problems from the start. El Dorado of the world's adventurers, its population of 90,000 in 1850 grew tenfold by 1880, ranking it on a level with Minnesota, Kansas and a dozen older states, but the criminals increased at an even greater rate. The old Spanish jails had become inadequate during the first turbulent prospector days, and when the San Francisco Committee of Vigilance rallied the inhabitants to the support of law and order, the legislature voted to build a penitentiary. Following frontier traditions, it committed that task, together with the care of the convicts, into the hands of a lessee. The lessee selected a site near some clay pits on Point San Quentin and erected with convict labor two buildings, one equipped with forty-eight cells and the other providing rooms for the housing of groups of prisoners. In 1855, when over 300 men crowded these quarters, reports of numerous deaths and escapes and of the brutal discipline of the guards prompted the state to assume control. When the unexpected costs and a political shift turned the prison back to the lessee a year later, continued corruption forced the state to reassert its control finally in 1858; but California's penal problems were just beginning.[1]

Eastern traditions gained some recognition from the new authorities. The governor, lieutenant governor, and secretary of state constituted a board of directors, which appointed a warden and introduced contractors to run the industries. The Rev. James Woodworth, a recent migrant from New England, organized a prison association, corresponded with Enoch Wines in New York, and pressed the state to erect two additional cellhouses that increased the total to 444 by 1873 when the population at San Quentin had reached 915. To relieve congestion the prison authorities contracted with the Natoma Company to supply convicts for construction work on its dam and canal at Folsom in return for the erection there of a second prison on the Auburn pattern. Work progressed in the mid seventies, but the first cellblock was not ready to receive inmates until 1880, by which date over 1,300 convicts so crowded the San Quentin prison that it prompted an investigation that pronounced it among the worst "colleges of crime" in the land.[2]

A move for reform was developing, backed by forces similar to those in the East. A strong workingman's party, outgrowth of the battle for the exclusion of Chinese labor, launched a campaign against penal contracts and, in the close balance of forces between the major parties, prompted the adoption of a constitutional provision in 1880 prohibiting future contracts and excluding from the prisons all industries that competed with free labor in the state. The California Prison Association had secured the appointment of a "moral instructor" at San Quentin and the organization of a reading class for young boys confined there. Moreover, the report of Wines and Dwight had found its way into the hands of some delegates to the constitutional convention who pressed for the successful adoption there of the amendment New York had rejected providing

[1] Tirey L. Ford, *California State Prisons: Their History, Development and Management* (San Francisco, 1910), pp. 13–24.

[2] California Special Commission of Inquiry Into the General Administration of the State Prisons of California, *Report* (Sacramento, 1881)

for a long-term nonpolitical board of managers.[3]

But the politicians entrusted with the task of serving the cards could not resist the temptation to favor their own hands. The Republicans, who had been able to oust the Democrats because of the presence of the labor party, proceeded to man the entire prison system with their henchmen. The new board of managers sent one of their number to visit the better prisons of the East and proceeded to formulate an advanced program in several respects, but this show of forthrightness failed to appease the ousted Democrats. When the labor forces discovered that the contracts were quietly being continued, they joined with the Democrats to drive the Republicans from control. Two investigating commissions—one appointed by the Republican governor in an attempt to head off the opposition, and the other by the legislature when the Democrats regained control—made careful studies of the situation and roundly condemned the political affiliations of the board of managers. The governor's commission did not hesitate to brand the existing prisons as inadequate but offered no real solution. Yet the commission created by the legislature was bipartisan and, when its report recommended the removal of the board of managers, the legislature readily determined to name the commission members as the new board. It installed Democratic officers at San Quentin but left the Republicans in charge at Folsom. Thus by the mid eighties California had achieved a system of bipartisan control, and, since the managers were acquainted with the most advanced theories of the day, the prospect for enlightened developments was encouraging.[4]

The labor problems were the first to demand attention. In response to the constitutional ban against contracts, the board adopted Brockway's piece-price compromise, which functioned until the Federated Trades Council forced the complete abandonment of the system in 1889. A jute factory, started a decade earlier with state funds, provided an alternative and highly useful industrial activity. There were no local competitors to oppose this industry, and the increasing demand of the farmers for burlap sacking assured the prison officials of a prosperous market.

[3] Frank Roney, *Frank Roney, Irish Rebel and California Labor Leader: An Autobiography* (Berkeley, 1931), pp. 391–399; California, *Constitution of 1880*, Article 10.

[4] California State Board of Prison Directors, *Report* (1882), pp. 13–21; California State Penological Commission, *Report* (1885), pp. 1–60.

Meanwhile the convicts at Folsom labored under the old arrangement with the Natoma Company until its dam and canal were completed in 1892. The contract had pledged the company to supply the prison with power for its industrial establishments, but the isolated location of the prison combined with the labor laws to block the development of industries. Aside from those engaged in construction work and the few employed at stonecrushing, the majority of the men here were confined in idleness until the development of highway construction in the next era provided increased demand for crushed stone.[5]

California made considerable advance in line with eastern trends in management and industry, but here the development stopped. The bipartisan managers failed to show the expected zeal for the solution of other problems, yet it was not entirely their fault, since their frequent recommendations received scanty attention from the legislature. The fact was that no strong local interests concerned themselves with housing or other problems, as had been the case in respect to labor and management. After the demise of the California Prison Association in the eighties, there was no public-spirited organization to rally popular sentiments in behalf of the reformation of the criminals.

California's worst failure was in the matter of prison accommodations. With a generous allowance for doubling up, the authorities at San Quentin were able to report a capacity of 700, and 413 cells were provided at Folsom; but the total convict population hovered around 2,000 during the nineties, and appeals for new cells were disregarded. Statistics fail to tell the complete story, for California was gathering a much larger portion of its lesser offenders into these "colleges of crime" than was the custom in the East. An early attempt to provide for intramural classification failed as the suggestion that Folsom be converted into a reformatory was forgotten. No pretense was made of enforcing the restraints of the Auburn tradition, and no other system of correctional discipline was applied in its stead, with the result that these prisons, especially when employment was slack, became great seminars in vice and crime.

Fortunately the strength of the campaign for public education helped to bring tardy success to the agitation for a reform school.

[5] Calif. Bd. Pris. Drtrs., *Reports* (1890; 1894).

The boys' department at San Quentin, started in 1875 under the supervision of the chaplain, had been gradually disbanded as the officers became convinced of its futility. The legislature was finally persuaded in 1888 to provide for the construction of the Preston School of Industry for Boys at Ione, though it was 1894 before the first boys were moved there from the prison. But Preston and Whittier, a second reform school opened in 1891, were for juveniles, and when they became well established as progressive institutions in the next decade, the demand for a young men's reformatory was still unanswered.

The managers had evidently arrived at their final conclusions on penal problems at the time of their comprehensive investigation of their predecessors in the early eighties. About the only additional innovation they sponsored was the Bertillon system of identification, which was adopted in 1890 at the time of its high favor with eastern wardens. When the legislature in 1893 granted the managers limited powers of conditional discharge, these officials, having studied the problem when tickets-of-leave were still considered impracticable, declined to exercise their new powers. California, however, was facing some unique criminal problems; not only was its convict population disproportionately large, but its prisons were the first to be seriously troubled by the opium traffic. The last decades of the century saw this problem attain major importance at San Quentin, and M. G. Aguirre, the new warden in 1899, was to make a considerable reputation as a prison reformer as a result of his vigorous efforts to stamp out this vice.

Prisons in the Northwestern States

The half dozen more or less thriving settlements in the Northwest revealed the wide assortment of influences that stem on the frontier. The first three to attain statehood contrasted in almost every respect except in their failure to develop satisfactory prisons. Nebraska, the most accessible and most populous of the group, quickly forgot the idealism of its early days when a succession of droughts and pests brought defeat and disillusionment. The trail to Oregon witnessed a motley rush of home seekers to that distant settlement, providing the state with ninety thousand people by 1870, but in the confusion all distinctive penal traditions were lost by the way. Nevada in her boom days was prompted to undertake an ambitious penal program, but the quick disillusionment concerning the state's future relegated this program, together with many other rosy dreams, to the scrap heap. Colorado, Utah, and the Dakotas were more successful in developing stable penal institutions and in maintaining connections with eastern movements, although the size of the problem in Colorado made the struggle a most difficult one.

Nebraska in the early days had close ties with the Northeast, and the agitation of Enoch Wines readily attracted attention. The newly organized state inherited a penal stockade at Lincoln from the federal authorities of its territorial days but commenced the construction of a stone prison on the Auburn pattern at Lancaster, three miles from Lincoln, in 1867. Under the direction of a state board of public lands and buildings, Warden Campbell supervised the work of the convicts in the construction of the wall and a cellblock with 400 small cells. Campbell and his successor pressed the construction program and maintained a cell capacity equal to the population growth, but they failed to develop sufficient industries to employ all the men. The mounting cost of mainte- nance finally prompted the officials to lease the prison in 1877 to a company that agreed to provision and guard the inmates at forty cents a day and their labor. The lease was patterned after one negotiated in Kansas in this depression year. A warden retained nominal charge, but since he was forced to rely on the guards supplied by the lessee he had little real authority. When the first ten-year lease expired, the state issued a second to an individual who was shortly lodged behind the bars of his own prison under the management of his assignees. The death of a feebleminded inmate as a result of brutal punishment in 1892 brought criticism of the situation to a head. A legislative investigation revealed shocking conditions, including the total neglect of sanitation, the improper association of women and boys as well as the insane with the rest of the population, and the use of physical torture as a penalty for failure to complete the labor tasks.[6]

It was not so easy to correct as to condemn these evils. Two years passed before the state was able to buy out the rights of the lessee, and then the board of public lands was only prevented from

[6] Nebraska Joint Committee of Investigation of the State Prison, "Legislative Documents," (1893), pp. 6–9; National Prison Association, *Transactions* (1874), pp. 340–341.

contracting a new lease by the intervention of the governor through the courts. When the warden was finally secure in his control, he brought contractors in to operate the industries, and the authorities rejoiced that the prisoners were at last earning a part of their cost to the state, for the fees required of the state under the terms of the lease had added weight to the demands of the reformers. In the midst of the discussion of penal affairs in 1893 the legislature adopted a parole law, and the governor, upon whom the parole authority had been conferred, was able to work in cooperation with the warden after 1895 not only in selecting worthy parolees but in developing a better discipline within the prison. The governors, however, were busy men, and these first happy results did not continue for long. On the other hand, the wretched conditions in the old cellhouse remained until fire destroyed the entire structure in 1901, compelling the state to make a fresh start in penitentiary matters.[7]

Oregon had a longer but hardly more satisfactory experience with prisons. The territory had erected a log structure in the early fifties at Portland, but rumors of corruption soon involved the officers in charge, and the legislature leased the prison to a private company. Shortly after statehood was acquired, this system was discontinued, and the governor became ex officio warden. In 1866 the legislature transferred the penitentiary from Portland to Salem and despatched one of its members on an eastern tour to study prison and other institutional designs. On his return the state commenced the construction of a stone prison on the Auburn plan. The 88 cells, completed by 1873, proved reasonably adequate for the 95 inmates, and Warden Holsclaw was able by employing the men at brickmaking, shoemaking, and farming to defray part of the maintenance cost. With the aid of a chaplain he started an evening school, a circulating library, and developed a satisfactory discipline that attracted the notice in the mid eighties of H. H. Bancroft, the historian. Unfortunately the slowly mounting population, coupled with labor difficulties in the late eighties and the depression of the early nineties, prompted the governor in 1895 to turn the entire responsibility for the prison over to a lessee. Protests were numerous, but practically the only improvement made before the end of the century was the removal of the juveniles to a farm several

---

[7] Nebraska, *Governor's Message* (legislative doc., 1895) pp. 23–24; Samuel J. Barrows, *Prison Systems of the United States* (Washington, D.C., 1900), pp. 96–100.

miles distant from the prison and the gradual establishment there of a reform school.[8]

During its boom days Nevada made great plans for its state institutions. The log structure erected as a territorial prison fortunately burned to the ground shortly after statehood was acquired, and the warden employed the convicts at the construction of a stone prison with 43 cells, each 8 by 4½ and 8 feet high. But the state was thronging with desperadoes, and overcrowding forced the authorities in 1874 to plan the construction of an ambitious penitentiary on the Joliet pattern at Reno in the western part of the state. It soon became apparent that Nevada boosters had overshot their mark, for the population of the prison as well as that of the state declined rapidly. Construction at Reno was halted and so rapid was the decline of the population that the old prison at Carson City soon found its accommodations practically equal to the state's needs. But the spirit was taken out of the reform element. Unfortunately the relaxed pressure brought a lassitude that resulted in an abandonment of the formerly thriving shoe industry and a reliance on stone quarrying as the sole productive occupation. This activity, however, saved the day in a most unusual way; as the work progressed the laborers with pick and shovel uncovered some prehistoric tracks in the quarry. Reports of this discovery attracted thousands of visitors whose fees supported a library and a chaplain and whose presence dispelled the atmosphere of stagnation that had threatened to settle upon the institution. The warden, meanwhile, was elected by the legislature, and so important was this political plum that one man had to be removed from the post by force of arms, while another more influential politician held the titles of warden, governor, and warden successively. Nevada had not solved its penal problem, but depopulation had practically eliminated it.[9]

Several other settlements in the Northwest achieved more creditable penal developments. The hard times of the late seventies did not blight the development of Colorado, Utah, and the Dakotas, as had been the case in Nebraska, and fertile lands supplied a basis

---

[8]N.P.A., *Transactions* (1874), pp. 350–352; Hubert Howe Bancroft, *History of the Pacific States of North America*, vol. 25, *Oregon* (San Francisco, 1888), pp. 644–645; Prisoner no. 6435, pseud., *The Oregon Penitentiary* (Salem, 1917).

[9]Nevada State Prison, *Reports* (1873–1874; 1883–1884; 1893).

for permanent growth after the mining rush had spent its force. The channels of eastern influence were kept open, and before the end of the century these states were taking an active part in the National Prison Association congresses.

Colorado voted to erect a prison ten years before it attained statehood, and, although the federal authorities took charge of construction, the state thus inherited a prison equipped with 90 cells when it joined the Union in 1876. As the convicts already exceeded the capacity, the warden commenced the construction of new cell-houses on the Auburn pattern, increasing the equipment to 444 cells by the end of the century. He engaged a contractor to develop a shoe industry, adopted rules of silence, appointed a chaplain, and helped him organize a library and a school in an effort to match eastern penal standards. But the problems increased too rapidly for the authorities who suffered from the state's unstable political situation, which shifted the prison back and forth between partisan appointees and undermined its discipline. When organized labor persuaded the legislature in 1890 to copy New York's model anticontract law, it made no provision for the introduction of state-account industries. The prison authorities soon found that the small amount of quarrying possible on the twenty-five-acre prison lot at Canon City was entirely insufficient. Experiments with the labor of convicts in small gangs on the roads near the prison and on a state irrigation canal had to be abandoned when the public protested against the use of armed guards to check escapes. The continued growth of the population had persistently exceeded the cell capacity and reached 600 by the end of the period, thus considerably aggravating the problems of idleness and discipline.

Colorado took decisive action to correct these deficiencies in 1891 when it created a state board of charities with authority for corrections as well. The board was soon advocating several eastern reforms. It persuaded the legislature to adopt a parole law and to give it the authority to release prisoners on parole when they attained the proper grade in the state prison. The board promoted the development of an industrial school for delinquent boys previously established at Golden and made it one of the best institutions of its kind in the West. And although funds were not available for permanent construction, the board persuaded the state in 1889 to establish a reformatory for young men at Buena Vista in temporary buildings. When Colorado entertained the National Prison Association on its first visit to the Mountain States in 1895, its leaders were able to boast not only the first adult reformatory and the first board of charities, but also the only separate building for women, the only effective parole law, and the only genuine grading system west of the Mississippi River. The legislature was shortly to take a lead over most eastern states as well by adopting a mandatory indeterminate-sentence law applicable to all but a few exceptional offenses.[10]

During Utah's long apprenticeship the prison was one of many points of friction between Mormon and federal authorities. In the early days the thrifty Mormons had farmed out their occasional criminals to enterprising individuals. Several of the convicts were not members of the church, and, when the federal authorities took control over the settlement, the marshal demanded that all prisoners be turned over to his care. For a time the Mormons bitterly contested this claim of jurisdiction, but the erection by the federal authorities of a fine prison with 224 cells at Salt Lake City brought them to terms. When statehood was finally granted in 1896, Utah inherited this fully ample prison and made immediate efforts to develop a stable and progressive system. It placed a board of corrections in control with full powers of parole, and under its direction a grading system was developed on the Elmira pattern. The board provided a library and school and organized diversified industries to produce for state-use and to provide trade instruction. A happy find was the cotton-sock factory which developed into a profitable concern, since it enjoyed a large market with no competitor within the state to raise objections. These accomplishments, plus the establishment of a reform school at Ogden in 1896, helped to persuade many eastern critics that the Mormons had fully demonstrated their capacity for statehood.[11]

The Dakotas, enjoying a freer hand in the development of their territorial institutions, were ready for statehood when the Republican victory cleared the way to that goal in 1889. South Dakota's delegate, already in attendance at the prison congress, could boast of

[10] Colorado Board of Charities, *Reports* (1892–1894; 1894–1896); N.P.A., *Proceedings* (1895), pp. 14–23. Minnesota and one or two other states anticipated Colorado in a few of these reforms but not in all.

[11] Utah State Board of Charities, *Reports* (1896; 1897).

a complete array of state institutions in full operation, and the state hastened to create a board of charities and to endow it with powers of control. The 128 fair-sized cells at Sioux Falls were more than adequate for the small demands of this orderly community, and the prisoners found employment at a stone quarry and on the eighty-acre farm attached to the prison. A parole law was adopted in 1890 but repealed two years later, and the reformers could not secure its readoption or the introduction of grades at the prison until the early years of the next century. But the reform school at Plankinton was successfully maintained, and, when at the close of the era the population at the prison finally approached the capacity, plans were projected for expansion.[12]

North Dakota in like fashion enjoyed a slow but well-considered development. The 160-cell prison at Bismarck proved adequate throughout the period, and this circumstance may have helped to discourage the use of the parole law adopted in 1891. A harness factory, operated with the aid of a contractor, was closed by an anti-contract law in 1897, but labor on the new capitol building, on the 800-acre farm leased by the state, and at a state brickyard supplied employment during the summer months, and preparations were made for the introduction of a twine factory at state account, following Minnesota's successful experiment with that industry. No reform school was needed at this time, for the state lodged its occasional juvenile delinquents at Plankinton in South Dakota. Successive governors gave close attention to penal and charitable problems, enabling the state to handle these affairs quite successfully during its first decade of self-government without the aid of a board of charities.[13]

Makeshift Penology in the Territories

The remainder of the West retained its great open spaces throughout the century. The era of the frontier was officially closed by 1890, and the national Republicans hastily carved four additional states out of the northern territories to buttress their power in the nation's capital, but it was some time before respectable northeastern traditions were able to dominate the institutional life of these

[12] N.P.A., *Proceedings* (1889), p. 251; South Dakota Board of Charities, *Report* (1900–1902), pp. 70–76.
[13] North Dakota Penitentiary, *Report* (1896–1898).

sparsely settled communities. The example and patterns of Missouri, Kansas, and Nebraska on one side, and those of California and Texas in other directions, conflicted with those of Colorado and the Northeast, while local exigencies played the part of arbiter. Everywhere a makeshift penology held sway.

The federal government had the opportunity to supply leadership but was ill fitted for the task. The only federal measure that exerted a controlling influence was the anticontract law of 1887, secured by eastern labor in its own interests. This law, by restricting the employment of federal prisoners, checked the federal marshals in charge of most of the territorial prisons from developing industrial activities. Anticontract restrictions found their way into most of the constitutions hopefully put forward by the territories when seeking statehood, and few of the prisons in these later mountain settlements provided any regular employment until after the turn of the century. Over against the questionable value of this influence stood the federal government's liberal land donations, which considerably aided most of these states in erecting public institutions.

Washington and Montana experienced many trials with their convicts before they took their places on the omnibus bill of 1889. Washington Territory leased its prisoners in 1877 to a mill owner in Seatco, now called Bucoda, who made the best of their labor during the day and herded them through a trapdoor into a log pit to spend the nights in mutual corruption and suffocation. This structure was possibly the worst prison in America since the closing of Connecticut's old copper mine nearly a century before. The federal authorities built a prison on McNeil Island and offered to take the territorial convicts as lodgers, but the lessee was sufficiently influential to retain his profitable labor force until the territory erected a new prison at Walla Walla in 1886. The cellblock arrangement of the new prison represented the first triumph of northeastern traditions, but anticontract laws discouraged the development of industries, and the inexperienced officers were unable to apply any but the crudest of disciplinary regulations to their idle prisoners. The attainment of statehood brought little change aside from the customary expansion. Washington authorities built four additional small cellblocks at Walla Walla, increasing the total to 450 before the turn of the century, but an attempt to introduce the jute industry proved unsuccessful and idleness predominated. The state provided a reform school for youthful offenders at Chehalis in 1891 and a few years later created a board of control with authority to grant paroles and organize an industrial program at the prison, which promised better conditions for the future.[14]

Montana shifted along with a small prison erected by federal authorities at Deer Lodge in the southwestern part of the state and ready for occupancy in 1871. The federal marshal in charge was soon forced to crowd three men into each of the 28 cells. Although he doubled the number of cells, the crowded condition remained when the state inherited the prison in 1889. The new authorities quickly leased their unwanted responsibility, agreeing to pay forty cents a day for the keep of each prisoner. The constitution prohibited contract labor, making it illegal for the lessee to develop any industries, and the resulting idleness rendered it impossible to enforce the rules of silence in the overcrowded institution. Liberal land grants fortunately enabled the state to establish a reform school at Miles City in 1894 and to project plans for a new prison at Billings in the central part of the state. The lessee, however, was able to persuade the authorities to build the new prison at Deer Lodge instead, and the erection there of a modern cellblock with 288 steel cells at least provided some occupation for the convicts at the old prison. A board of charities, organized in 1899, found the prison still in the hands of the lessee, seriously overcrowded, and devoid of any regular system of labor or discipline; and thus it remained for another decade.[15]

Wyoming made even more diverse makeshifts before achieving a stable penal system. In the early seventies the federal authorities erected a wooden prison at Laramie, but excessively high charges roused criticism. The territorial legislature was advised of better terms at the Nebraska state prison, and the convicts were sent there. A still better bargain was soon made with Joliet, and during the mid eighties the large majority of Wyoming's criminals were delivered to this greatly overcrowded penitentiary in Illinois where

[14] George W. France, *Struggles for Life and Home in the North-west* (New York, 1890), pp. 223–426; Ezra Meeker, *Seventy Years of Progress in Washington* (Seattle, 1921), pp. 104–105, 309; Washington Board of Control, *Report* (1903–1904), pp. 44–50, 109–115.

[15] Montana, *Governor's Messages* (legislative docs.) (1891), pp. 5–7; (1893), pp. 12, 22; (1897), p. 32; (1901), pp. 15–16.

they earned their keep by hard labor. The sheriffs, meanwhile, were growing fat on the fees allowed for transporting these prisoners, and the territory finally determined to build its own prison at Rawlins. In 1890 Wyoming attained statehood and inherited the prison at Laramie and, like Montana, leased the entire institution to a private party, reserving only the right to appoint the warden. This compromise was of little advantage since it proved impossible to find an able man willing to stick to the job; indeed, for some time there was an average of more than one warden a year. Plans for the new prison had meanwhile progressed and by 1898 an Auburn structure with 234 cells was completed at Rawlins. A dispute with the lessee delayed occupation until, in 1901, the state reluctantly permitted the lessee to take charge at Rawlins for the balance of his contract. An adequate prison was about all that Wyoming could boast, but that was not so bad for the first decade of the least populated state of the Union.

The territory of Idaho was forced to content itself with the small federal prison. The legislature complained against the charge of seventy-five cents a day for each prisoner, and no wonder, since it required one-third of the taxes to support the convicts. As no alternative presented itself, idle convicts soon crowded the forty-two stone cells, and the construction of an equal number of steel cells in 1890 brought only temporary relief. When Idaho inherited the prison, it gave full control to the warden, but unfortunately ten men succeeded one another in this office in as many years, and discipline remained chaotic. A Chautauqua reading circle, organized in 1887, provided some diversion for favored prisoners, but the majority, except for a three-hour drill in the prison yard under armed guard, remained idle in their locked cells day and night. Affairs took a turn for the better in 1900 when a renewed threat of serious overcrowding prompted the legislature to appropriate funds for expansion. The warden employed some of the inmates in the construction of a new cellhouse and devised a grading system to promote discipline and facilitate the application of a newly adopted parole law.[16]

Three southwestern territories, New Mexico, Arizona, and Oklahoma, remained under federal authority throughout this period, but no effective steps were taken to build prisons. New Mexico contented herself for a time with the old Spanish jails, until

[16] Idaho Penitentiary, *Reports* (1900), pp. 4–14; (1903–1904), pp. 5–12.

in 1884 the legislature voted to erect both a capitol and prison, anticipating a statehood that did not materialize for nearly three decades. No pretense was made at the Santa Fe prison, or at the Yuma prison in Arizona, of providing a cell for each man; in fact all of the 40 cells at Yuma were built to hold four inmates, and six were sometimes crowded into them. No industries were introduced into either of these prisons, and the convicts whittled away their time making trinkets to sell to visitors. Arizona created a board of control in 1896, empowered to supervise the labor of convicts outside the walls, and a partial lease system resulted, helping to relieve the prison congestion but introducing methods that were already being discarded in most of the southeastern states. Religion was the only reformatory influence in either of these prisons, and there was not much of that. The wardenship was one of the few lucrative posts open to local politicians, and it was greatly sought after by men hoping to be in the lineup when statehood was attained. Apathy to wretched penal conditions characterized the territorial period.[17]

Oklahoma, on the other hand, shirked its penal responsibilities entirely. Its criminals, who multiplied even more rapidly than its citizen body, were packed off, young and old alike, to the penitentiary in Kansas, where they were jammed into overcrowded cells and left to learn the folly of their ways while digging coal in the mine pits. Oklahoma, scene of the last land rush, required another decade of growth before it was ready to assume the obligations of a settled community.[18]

Thus, in a limited sense, penological technique had moved west. A few of the states, notably Colorado, Utah, and the Dakotas, had fairly caught up with their older neighbors to the east in legal and institutional equipment. These four and one or two other states adopted the parole and indeterminate-sentence laws with which the eastern states had been experimenting for over a decade, but nowhere in the Great West were the principles fully understood or applied. Some of the new states created boards of charities, established juvenile institutions, and constructed new cellblocks on the Auburn pattern; unfortunately, in most cases their cell

[17] Arizona Territorial Prison, *Reports* (1885), pp. 135–142; (1893), pp. 226–229; (1899), pp. 447–456.

[18] Oklahoma, *Governor's Message* (legislative doc., 1899). Kansas charged twenty-five cents a day for each prisoner in 1891, raised it to thirty-five cents in 1898, and to forty cents a few years later.

accommodations were desperately overcrowded. But the general failure to provide any industrial activity or other form of employment was neutralizing the best efforts toward reform. Probably only Utah and the Dakotas had sufficiently considered this problem to achieve moderately satisfactory systems. The exploitation of penal labor, so prevalent in the Northeast and so unrestrained throughout the South, had been largely avoided in the Great West, except in California and Nebraska, but at a great price—the practical surrender of the objectives of the penitentiary as distinguished from the single purpose of secure confinement. Only a few of the institutions, notably those of the Dakotas and Utah, had succeeded in developing labor and disciplinary activities that justified a comparison with the newer reformatory penology of the Northeast; elsewhere the unrestrained intercourse of idle convicts was the dominant feature of the daily life in the majority of the prisons.

BIBLIOGRAPHIC NOTE

The messages of the territorial governors to their legislatures or to the Secretary of the Interior are practically the only firsthand sources available before the settlements became states; then regular prison reports are included in the state documents, while the governors' messages continue to be of value. The reports of the three special investigations in California in the early eighties, the regular reports of the board of managers in that state, and the reports of the boards of charities in Colorado, South Dakota, and Utah are of great value. George W. France, *Struggles for Life and Home in the North-west* (New York, 1890), and Frank Roney, *Frank Roney, Irish Rebel and California Labor Leader: An Autobiography* (Berkeley, 1931), shed light on the development in Washington and California. Prisoner no. 6435, pseud., *The Oregon Penitentiary* (Salem, 1917) and Tirey L. Ford, *California State Prisons: Their History, Development and Management* (San Francisco, 1910), are convenient historical surveys. Hubert Howe Bancroft's volumes on the several western states, compiled in the late eighties contain many useful details on their prisons; and Samuel J. Barrows, *Prison Systems of the United States* (Washington, D.C., 1900), describes most of these western prisons.

10.

THE HEYDAY OF REFORMATORY PENOLOGY: 1900–1915

The turn of the century witnessed the opening of the third phase of the evolution of pedagogical penology. For a decade or two America was to enjoy a moderate although uneven prosperity, and many formerly retarded states were able to establish more respectable penal systems. The national reform movement, strengthened by the fresh vigor of the younger men who were shouldering its responsibilities, undertook to till the whole of America, and Europe again became distinctly visible on the horizon. The controlling influences of earlier days, such as the problems of labor and population and the organization and talents of the leaders, unfolded in unexpected ways. In the course of the first decade or so the old Auburn system was totally discarded except for its hollow architectural shell; new methods of labor and discipline were developed, and the reformatory technique, as a result of its wider application, acquired a radically different character. Improved statistical methods provided a sounder basis for the appraisal of achievements and encouraged a skepticism that turned almost into cynicism among a younger generation advancing to control during the World War period. Meanwhile the contributions of related sciences to the study of the individual and of crime causation opened the way for the development of the modern analytical science of penology.

234

The Maturity of the Profession

The era of experimenting wardens had virtually passed with the old century, and the young men who pushed forward to fill vacancies, as well as the older men who advanced to better jobs, were primarily concerned with the more extensive application of a system already fully developed. They were forced to make numerous adaptations and in fact transformed the system more radically than had their predecessors, but this was the result of unfolding circumstances. The movement had acquired stability, integration of tradition, and organization; when radically new methods and theories appeared at the close of the era, they simply provided new viewpoints for the mature profession.

By 1900 the congresses had ceased to be roundtable discussions and had become lecture tours for the education of new recruits both in prison management and in control. There was a wealth of leaders and a striking accord among them. Frederick Howard Wines, Samuel J. Barrows, Hastings H. Hart, Charlton T. Lewis, Fredrick J. Pettigrove, and Amos Butler differed little from the leading wardens—Joseph Scott, Albert Garvin, Henry Wolfer, and the venerable Major McClaughry—in their interpretation of the programs and the objectives of the movement. Foreign papers full of commendation were received chiefly from German admirers. The number of the delegates rose above the five hundred mark; thirty-five states were represented at Albany in 1906, thirty-nine at Chicago the next year, and thirty-four at far-west Seattle two years later. As the Association thus traveled up and down and across the continent, it revised its name to the American Prison Association in 1908, and sheer size lent weight to its theories, while the wider experience served to enrich its program. The evils of the southern lease system were discovered to be quite distinct from the possibilities for healthy outside employment, and the new plantation system received hearty approval. Colorado's honor camps on the roads attracted loud praise and helped to prepare the way for a new kind of education for citizenship. A growing appreciation of European developments stimulated more careful attention to both the causes of crime and the fate of the discharged. Thus the movement opened channels for development in the future, although its major interests continued to center around the campaign for the adoption of reformatory penology.

*   *   *

The reviving interest in foreign developments raised the question as to the relative merits of foreign and American achievements. The delegates of the various nations, meeting every five years in the international prison congresses started by Enoch Wines, could report few penal developments worthy of comparison with the American reformatory, but, when their more satisfactory jails and their more generous assistance to the discharged were taken into account, and especially when their less disturbing criminal trends were considered, the comparison was not so favorable to the Americans. The discussion became acrimonious when the newer criminologists of Italy, France, and Germany entered the fray, prompted by their theories of criminal types and crime causation, to belittle the service of the reformatory and to attribute the American claims of success to the optimism of the frontier. Charles R. Henderson was loudly applauded at the American Prison Congress of 1908 when he outlined and then refuted the criticisms of the European scientists. It was clear to his hearers that these men, by their emphasis on the born criminal, were seeking to justify the passive technique of the prisons of their lands. Samuel J. Barrows, the other leading American student of European developments, was likewise unimpressed by the scientific contribution and remained content to detect notes of accord between the two continents. The full impact of these ideas was not felt in America for another decade.[1]

The Germans were the first to appreciate the merits of both contributions. It was proving difficult for some of the smaller states of the empire to build adequate prisons on the approved Pennsylvania model, and the authorities of several of the institutions were developing positive disciplinary devices to control the prisoners they were unable to keep in solitude. It was also in these years that the Borstal system was developing in England for the care of offenders under twenty-one years of age, applying devices suggestive of Elmira. As these various beginnings were discussed at the international congresses in 1895 and 1900, the Europeans began to awake to the significance of the American activities.[2] Dr. Wolfgang Mitter-

[1] National Prison Association, *Proceedings* (1908), pp. 135–149; Isabel C. Barrows, *The Sunny Life: The Biography of Samuel June Barrows* (Boston, 1913), pp. 206–208; Negley K. Teeters, *Deliberations of the International Penal and Penitentiary Congresses: Questions and Answers* (Philadelphia, 1949).

[2] For a list of American and international congresses see Appendix.

maier of Heidelberg was especially discerning. He saw that, while the German interest in penology grew out of general scientific progress and therefore was primarily concerned with the philosophy of punishment, the Americans had been attracted to the problem out of a spirit of "compassionateness," and their activity was directed by their "passion for education"; he explained further that it was easy for a young people to think of criminals as individuals rather than as a distinct class, that it was natural that they should turn prisons into "institutions" and treat criminals as "inmates." He thought that, as the scientific development of his own country continued and as the contributions of anthropology and psychiatry were fully appreciated, German authorities would not hesitate to give the principle of the indeterminate sentence and the methods of the reformatory a genuine application to at least a part of their prisoners.[3]

Some of the European states did adopt a few of the forms of reformatory penology. Indeterminate sentences of a sort, and particularly probation, found an increasing application. But the probation laws were usually suspended-sentence laws and, along with those providing indeterminate sentences, were chiefly designed to detect and penalize the recidivist. When the international gathering at Washington in 1910 voted approval of the indeterminate sentence, the resolution specifically applied only to the young and the moral degenerates. The Americans, glorying in the vindication of their principles, did not fully appreciate that their visitors had admitted the value of reformatory treatment only for the young and at the same time were indicating a desire to hold indefinitely those who were criminal by nature. The Europeans did not share the optimism of the founders of the American reformatory movement, but by this date there was not so much optimism left in America.[4]

The national congresses frequently took cognizance of the lessons to be learned abroad, such as jail reform, the care of the discharged, and the improvement of the statistical records, but the Association was not equipped to handle these problems, especially not the jail

---

[3] Sir Evelyn Ruggles-Brise, *Prison Reform at Home and Abroad: A Short History of the International Movement Since the London Congress, 1872* (London, 1924), pp. 91–133; New York Prison Association, *Report* (1894), pp. 190–198.

[4] Charles R. Henderson, *Modern Prison Systems* (Washington, D.C., 1903), pp. xxxiii–xxxvi.

situation. The congresses did, nevertheless, provide publicity and encouragement to a growing array of charitable societies interested in the discharged. The Central Howard Association, formed at Chicago in 1900, undertook to aid men in all states where there was no agency at work, and its activities soon came a close second to those of the New York association which was now spending around $11,000 each year in aid of the discharged. Citizens of Kansas organized a society in that same year which promptly despatched agents who organized affiliated societies in seven neighboring states. Mrs. Maud Ballington Booth continued to expand the work of her Volunteer Prisoners League units, and Commander Evangeline Booth, who had taken charge of the Salvation Army in the United States in 1904, organized Brighter Day Leagues in many prisons. One important aspect of this activity was the general disappearance of prisoners' "homes"; aid societies now generally gave assistance under the supervision of visitors, following the trend of general charity work.[5] Homeless convicts might find shelter in the increasing number of religious institutional dormitories, but these were not in any sense the criminal headquarters the old homes had frequently become. One survey listed thirty-nine aid societies active in 1911, yet they hardly scratched the surface of the problem, and their services did not begin to compare with the more efficient work in this field in several European countries.[6]

The upward trend of prison populations was again accelerated in these years by a renewed drive for the abolition of the death sentence. Ten additional states, lead by Kansas in 1907, abolished capital punishment within a decade for all but a few exceptional cases, and although most of them repealed these laws a few years later, as the violence of the prohibition years mounted, the pressure of new commitments was not relieved. Moreover, the execution of some 1,800 convicts between 1901 and 1917, as tabulated by the *Chicago Tribune*, added to the tensions in many prisons and increased the demand for institutional reforms.[7]

The problem of criminal records and penal statistics was a double

[5] N.P.A., *Proceedings* (1904), pp. 182–207; (1906), pp. 311–318.

[6] Salvation Army, *Broken Souls* (New York, 1929), pp. 13–19; American Prison Association, *Proceedings* (1912), pp. 244–254.

[7] Hugo A. Bedau, ed., *The Death Penalty in America*, 2d ed. (Chicago, 1968), pp. 10–14, 30–31, 35–38.

one, and no single authority seemed to have jurisdiction over either branch. The attempts of the National Association to secure a standard pattern for prison reports was of little avail, and the intermittent surveys of the United States census investigators failed to stick to a satisfactory standard, rendering a comparative use of their successive tables most difficult. The problem of criminal identification received more attention, but the Bertillon system was proving to be very cumbersome. A new impetus was given to this activity in 1901 when New York authorities imported the finger-print system from New Scotland Yard.[8] Mark Twain's *Pudd'nhead Wilson* had popularized the system, and many prisons and police departments quickly adopted it. Again the problem of securing a central bureau appeared, and in 1907 the federal government established a clearinghouse on a voluntary arrangement, accumulating 925,000 fingerprint records by 1925. It was not until this later period that America began to develop records and statistics comparable to the more efficient systems of Europe.

The reform movement continued to rest primarily on the state organizations for supervision and control. Considerable improvement in these organizations occurred throughout the country during this period, but Europeans still regarded administration as one of the weakest points of the American system, chiefly because of the irresponsibility of the counties. The federal government was at last assuming responsibility for the care of some of its convicts but had no adequate agency for the direction of its program and thus failed to supply leadership to the movement.

Most of the northern states had already developed some agency for the central supervision of their prisons. The state boards of charities remained the customary organization in this section, and in spite of limited powers several of them provided effective leadership, notably the relatively new board in Indiana. New Jersey still failed to create a satisfactory permanent organization, but a special commission on dependency and crime made a valuable study of the field in 1908.

[8] The Chinese had used fingerprints for centuries in connection with passports, and the English police department in India had adopted the system about 1860; Francis Galton proved it to be a reliable factor for identification in 1888; but E. R. Henry, who came from the police department in India to New Scotland Yard, was the first to solve the many difficulties of classification, perfecting his system in 1897. N.P.A., *Proceedings* (1900), p. 383; (1901), pp. 71–78; (1904), pp. 56–60; (1925), pp. 98–105.

The reorganized Massachusetts board of prison commissioners of 1901 was the most efficient and powerful board of control in the country. New York, on the other hand, profited as much from the revival of its prison association under the secretaryship of Samuel J. Barrows as from its imperfectly coordinated central prison authorities.[9]

The Middle West advanced but did not complete its swing toward state boards of control. The boards of Iowa and Minnesota, created at the turn of the century, assumed full responsibility, as had that of Wisconsin a decade earlier, while the board of charities in South Dakota continued to perform control functions. Nebraska and North Dakota created such authorities toward the end of the era. Illinois, Missouri, and Kansas failed to develop central control over their prisons; fortunately Charles A. Ellwood in Missouri and Frank W. Blackmar in Kansas provided valuable if unofficial leadership to their states. The liberal uprising that upset the old political machines in several of these states had a good effect on prison developments, notably in Iowa and Nebraska where there was much to be done, but Governor J. W. Folk and his successors in Missouri proved unable to carry out the Herculean reforms they recognized as necessary in Missouri. Kansas and Illinois inaugurated new central administrations during the second decade.[10]

Many of the southern states had established central state penal authorities in the nineties, but none of them was independent of political control. West Virginia created a board of control on the northern model in 1909, and Virginia and Tennessee created a board of charities and a board of trustees respectively. Together with the revived board of charities in North Carolina, these agencies provided inspection and some leadership, but the diversion of large numbers of the convicts from state to county authorities, where they were largely beyond the ken of inspectors, destroyed any gains the section might claim in the matter of administration reform.[11]

In the Great West, agencies for control established before or at the

---

[9] Henderson, *Prison Systems*, pp. 152–180; N.Y.P.A., *Report* (1916), pp. 200–202.

[10] Henderson, *Prison Systems*, pp. 155–161; Frank W. Blackmar, *Report on the Penitentiary to Governor George H. Hodges* (Topeka, 1914); Charles A. Ellwood, *A Bulletin on the Condition of the County Jails of Missouri* (Columbia, 1904).

[11] Frank Tannenbaum, "Southern Prisons," has been reprinted in Frank Tannenbaum, *Wall Shadows* (1922; Montclair, N.J., 1976), pp. 169–203; Edward Grubb, *Methods of Penal Administration in the United States* (London, 1904), 38–39.

turn of the century gained efficiency with age, especially in the Mountain States where the settlements were gradually acquiring stability. Washington made a thorough reorganization in 1901 when an efficient board of control was placed in charge of state institutions; Oregon followed this example a decade later. The model board of prison managers in California had long failed to supply leadership, but the formation of a conference of charities and correction in 1901 and the creation of a board of this type two years later brought fresh vigor to the cause of reform. When Oklahoma was admitted as a state, Kate Barnard became the first commissioner of charities and started a vigorous campaign for reorganization, and the state, awaking to its responsibilities, created a board of control to direct the construction of a state prison and an adult reformatory.[12]

Thus throughout the nation the penal systems were being institutionalized. The central authorities were by no means free from political influence, but in many states its disturbing power was removed a space or two from control over the major prison officials, and the application of civil service standards and tenure to the minor positions brought greater stability there as well. These changes favored the formal adoption of the program of the movement but militated against the development of new methods, and the inspiration necessary for the application of reformatory technique was not engendered by the process of standardization. The members of the profession were becoming practitioners, and any radically new theories or techniques evolved in the future would have to come from beyond their ranks.

The Triumph of Reformatory Technique

Almost all the indications were propitious for reformatory penology in 1900. The well-established profession was pledged to its tenets, and many of the liberal popular journals were lending their support. At least a dozen institutions had already been dedicated to its application, and while these grew in size and stability others were added and secured a fine start in the same undertaking. Not only were indeterminate-sentence and parole laws spreading throughout the North and West, but court decisions were dispelling all doubts as

[12] Henderson, *Prison Systems*, pp. 161, 169–175; California State Board of Charities and Corrections, *Report* (1906), pp. 33–35; "Cleaning Up the Kansas Penitentiary," *Charities and Commons* 21 (6 February 1909): 772–773.

to their constitutionality, and the laws were winning a larger application to criminals generally. Probation laws affecting adults were gaining approval in many states, riding on the crest of the wave of radical reform in the treatment of juveniles. About the only discouraging tendency of the era was the standardization and devitalization of these measures, particularly in the case of the administration of parole. But it was not until near the end of the era that new facilities for statistical analysis made possible a reevaluation of these devices and introduced a spirit of skepticism.

The adult reformatory was now a stable feature of institutional penology. The institutions at Concord, New Hampshire, Huntingdon, Pennsylvania, St. Cloud, Minnesota, and Pontiac, Illinois, were all fairly established on the Elmira pattern; each had its indeterminate-sentence law and parole officer, each its graded system with marks rewarding proficiency in academic and industrial schools as well as excellence in deportment. Such accessory features as military units, calisthenics, organized sports, institutional band and weekly paper, and special societies among the men of the top grade were fairly prevalent, and farming activities on a partial honor basis were becoming a standard feature. The institutions at Lansing, Kansas, Mansfield, Ohio, Green Bay, Wisconsin, and Buena Vista, Colorado, were rapidly developing along these same lines. Indiana was making extensive and fairly successful efforts to convert its old prison at Jeffersonville into a genuine reformatory, and the authorities at the Vermont house of correction were like-minded although seriously handicapped by an overabundance of short-term misdemeanants. Even the three earlier women's institutions were taking up some of these methods, and Ionia alone held unswervingly to its old program of reformation by hard labor, unhindered by "pedagogical fads." Only the women's reformatory at Bedford, New York, was making radical innovations in this program.[13]

Meanwhile several new institutions of this sort were being successfully established. New Jersey opened an imposing structure at Rahway in 1901, and able officers rapidly introduced all the best

---

[13] Henderson, *Prison Systems*, pp. 195–199; Ohio State Reformatory, *Report*, (1908); Kansas Reformatory, *Report* (1910); Wisconsin Board of Control, *Report* (1902), pp. 380–383; Colorado State Board of Control, *Report* (1902), pp. 34–35; Indiana Reformatory, *Report* (1916); Vermont House of Correction, *Report* (1907–1908).

features of the older reformatories, thus supplying the long-backward state with a first-rate institution. Persistent agitation in Iowa finally produced results in the middle of the decade when the agrarian politicians captured control and among other reforms transformed the prison at Anamosa into a reformatory. Washington, awakening to the larger responsibilities of statehood, provided for a reformatory at Monroe, and this admirable institution was in operation one year when the state hosted the National Association in 1909. Oklahoma started a reformatory at Granite in 1909 and Connecticut at Cheshire in 1913. A reformatory was opened in Worland, Wyoming in 1915 and at Lincoln, Nebraska in 1921. Cheshire, in particular, soon became an excellent institution. After long years of agitation Kentucky finally in 1913 provided for the conversion of its old Frankfort prison into a reformatory. Each of these several institutions was provided with an indeterminate-sentence law, and the officers undertook to introduce the standard reformatory technique; most of them were fairly established before the war terminated the reformatory era.[14]

Two specialized types of institutions experimented in new directions during the latter years of the period. Dr. Katherine B. Davis took charge of New York's reformatory for women at Bedford Hills in 1900 shortly after it was opened to major offenders and proceeded to make it the most active penal experiment station in America. She developed a cottage system to supplement the older buildings and provide a more homelike environment; she introduced a trade department to train the women for occupations open to them after discharge. She gave special attention to the treatment of sex offenders and in 1911 secured funds for a clinic to study the character and problems of individual inmates. Here was a new pattern for reformatories, soon to be followed by New York's other institution for women at Albion and by New Jersey's women's reformatory opened in 1913 at Clinton. Mrs. Jessie D. Hodder, assuming charge at Sherborn in 1911, likewise took advantage of

---

[14] Harry Elmer Barnes, *A History of Penal, Reformatory and Correctional Institutions of the State of New Jersey: Analytical and Documentary* (Trenton, 1918), pp. 610–618; Iowa Board of Control, *Report* (1909), pp. 13–14; Washington State Board of Control, *Report* (1916), pp. 270–285; Connecticut State Reformatory, *Report* (1912–1914); Kentucky Board of Prison Commissioners, *Report* (1913). See the governor's messages in the other states.

some of the experiments of Dr. Davis.[15]

The second group of specialized institutions represented a revitalization of the old houses of correction. Massachusetts continued its experiments with the care of drunkards on the state farm, and Boston enlarged its house of correction at Deer Island. New York City created a reformatory for misdemeanants in 1905, but failed to develop a constructive program until Lewis E. Lawes arrived a decade later and moved the institution out of the city to New Hampton Farms. Before this date several other large cities were undertaking to give their minor offenders a more enlightened treatment, somewhat after the character of the reformatory farm, and some of these applied indeterminate sentences. Several of the older city penitentiaries were extensively renovated—that of Buffalo was moved out onto a fine farm; but the new correctional farms at Kansas City, Cleveland, and Washington, D.C., became the model institutions of this type. Thus the reformatory theory at last broke the barriers that had kept the treatment of women and misdemeanants from its fructifying influences, and the next era was to see a greater extension of this activity.[16]

The reformatories in these days were frequently called upon to give an account of their achievements. Special investigations, sometimes prompted by reports of mismanagement, sometimes arising from complaints against country-club treatment for criminals, made old-style surveys of the character of the institutions as viewed by a committee of observers. But the Europeans were asking for statistical reports of the performance of the reformatories, and Joseph Scott, now at Elmira, made two such investigations of the post-institutional histories of one thousand discharged Elmira boys. Many faults would later be found in the methods of these investigations and of the others of a similar character, but the reformers were encouraged at the time by the conclusion that about

[15] Eugenia C. Lekkerkerker, *Reformatories for Women in the United States* (Groningen, 1931), pp. 96–106; Anthony M. Platt, *The Child Savers: The Invention of Delinquency* (Chicago, 1969), pp. 75–100. Platt credits the women with a much wider influence as they imposed their middle-class ideology on the juvenile and reformatory as well as on the women's institutions. He sees the introduction of the cottage system as a strategy to enhance their maternal control.

[16] Massachusetts Prison Commission, *Report* (1900), pp. 280–281; New York Prison Association, *Report* (1918), pp. 20–22; George M. Kober, comp., *Charitable and Reformatory Institutions in the District of Columbia: History and Development*, (Washington, D.C., 1927).

nine-tenths of the boys were reformed. Meanwhile, as the original burst of enthusiasm passed, many of the reformatories fell under the control of men less able than the founders, and most of the new officers failed to reveal the ingenuity in overcoming obstacles that had been the chief genius of their predecessors. There were, at the same time, increasing obstacles in the form of less tractable inmates, for the probation laws were beginning to free many of the others from confinement even in a reformatory. Later studies of the achievement of these institutions would reveal a much lower percentage of success than that claimed at this time.[17]

The main forms of reformatory penology continued to win their way into the state prisons. Massachusetts, Colorado, Indiana, and Illinois had already made their indeterminate-sentence laws mandatory for all but life sentences, although the judges, by allowing only narrow margins between their maximum and minimum commitments, were in large part defeating the laws. Of the other states only Minnesota gave its law any considerable application to convicts sent to the state prison. The reformers found the task of educating the judges to an appreciation of the full spirit of the laws to be very difficult. They secured better results from the legislatures as Wisconsin, Minnesota, Michigan, and Connecticut adopted new laws extending the application of this principle to most convicts. But none of the states succeeded in hurdling the obstacle of unsympathetic judges who clung to the opinion that they were the proper authorities to measure out punishment.[18]

The general failure to solve the problem of the supervision of parolees undoubtedly helped to cause as well as to justify judicial conservatism. Rarely did the methods of selecting men for parole from prison inspire confidence. The reformatories, with a more satisfactory technique of choosing parolees, still had generally but one parole officer to supervise their graduates scattered throughout the entire state. The arrangements for supervising parolees from state prisons were still less satisfactory. The parole authorities in Massachusetts cooperated with local probation officers to some extent; in Indiana the scheme of requiring the employer to send part

[17] N.P.A., *Proceedings* (1904), pp. 158–165; A.P.A., *Proceedings* (1910), p. 275.
[18] Wisconsin Board of Control, *Report* (1908), p. 19; N.P.A., *Proceedings* (1907), pp. 81–93.

of the earnings of his parolee to the prison officers for safekeeping until final discharge created a strong economic tie between the authorities and their charges; but Minnesota developed possibly the best supervision in connection with the local units of the state conference of charities. The authorities elsewhere relied largely on the monthly reports of the parolees sent in by mail, usually with the signature of a "best friend" attached.[19]

Notwithstanding the failure to secure its genuine application, the principle of the indeterminate sentence made its way into the statute law of all the other northern states by 1915. New Hampshire took it up in 1901 and applied paroles with care for some years; Maine and Rhode Island rounded out New England's endorsement toward the end of the period. The liberal movement in politics brought the remaining states of the Middle West into line; Iowa in 1907 and Nebraska, Kansas, and the Dakotas at the end of the decade each adopted first or new laws applying this principle. Congress in 1910 finally passed a parole law applicable to federal prisoners, thus taking its place among the last straggling northern authorities to pledge themselves to the reformatory sentence.[20]

The penological conquest of the Great West advanced apace during the first decade of the twentieth century. Colorado was the only state already equipped with a working parole system at the turn of the century, although several others had made a late beginning, but all the states here provided themselves with some sort of a parole system before 1915. Indeed, outside of California, the percentage of convicts reached by these laws compared well with that of the Northeast. Washington, Oregon, Wyoming, and Utah as well as Colorado made as extensive use of paroles during the latter years of the period as any state in the country.[21]

These theoretical aspects of northern penology did not have much influence on the practice or legislation of the South. Kentucky's reluctance to grant paroles under the old law of 1888 was not changed by the revised law of 1900, and only the reorganization of

---

[19] Mass. Pris. Comm., *Report* (1907), pp. ix–x; Minnesota State Prison, *Report* (1911–1912).

[20] A.P.A., *Proceedings* (1911), pp. 221–238; U.S. Bureau of the Census, *Prisoners and Juvenile Delinquents in the United States, 1910* (Washington, D.C., 1918), p. 45 and Table 28, p. 47, which shows the percentages committed under indeterminate sentences in each state.

[21] N.P.A., *Proceedings* (1905), p. 189; A.P.A., *Proceedings* (1910), p. 275.

Frankfort prison as a reformatory brought the principle into effect there. Virginia and West Virginia adopted parole laws, and the former put its law of 1904 to good use in relieving congestion at Richmond. Several of the states of the Lower South applied the principle to their juvenile offenders, but Louisiana, late in 1914, was the first among them to grant paroles to adults. Retributive justice still characterized the South and when the authorities in Georgia in 1907 reported that only 666 out of her 2,464 convicts had sentences of five years or less and 1,677 of them had terms of ten years or more, there was no popular protest.[22]

But even in the North and the West, where the reformatory sentence had become a standard feature of the penal law, the situation was anything but satisfactory. The 1910 census reported that about fifteen thousand indeterminate sentences had been granted in the year surveyed, or about 14 percent of the total number of felons sentenced—not a very large figure considering the prevalence of the laws. Indeed, the failure of the courts to apply the available laws was to some degree a result of the growing popular disfavor which the unsatisfactory methods of administration were earning for the reform. No effective attack was made on this problem until after the war.

Probation, an even more radical modification of the penal standards of justice, was nevertheless gaining popularity. The pioneer activities of Massachusetts in this field, extending over a half century, had attracted worldwide attention. A few other states had made cautious experiments with the system, and the popular campaign for a more enlightened treatment of juvenile delinquency helped to carry this reform ahead with surprising rapidity. At the same time the reform promised economy, and many states welcomed the relief it promised to overcrowded institutions. The public appeared more ready to grant a convict a second chance at the time of his trial than an early parole from prison; the press was generous with praise; and the federated women's clubs took an active interest in furthering the measure. As a result every northern state except New Hampshire adopted probation laws for both juveniles and

[22] A.P.A., *Proceedings* (1910), pp. 275–278; Mark T. Carleton, *Politics and Punishment: The History of the Louisiana State Penal System* (Baton Rouge, 1971), pp. 171–172.

adults by 1910, and almost every western state did likewise by 1915. A significant new development, the juvenile court, prompted increased reliance on probation for the treatment of delinquent children. The early efforts of John Augustus to probate the cases of youthful offenders in Massachusetts had removed many from the normal sentencing procedures, as noted earlier. Similar practices in a few other states had treated delinquent children informally before the first juvenile court was officially established in Chicago in 1899. Several large cities developed similar courts for the separate hearing of misdemeanant charges against juveniles in the early 1900s, and most of them engaged probation officers. The first such officers were generally supported, as in Chicago, by interested citizen groups. The states increasingly assumed that responsibility as the decade advanced, and several followed Illinois in establishing courts of domestic relations or family courts to substitute counselling for litigation in that broader field as well.[23]

Probation was one reform that did not suffer from the growing disillusionment that was beginning to hang like a shroud over the penal system. Its timely development made probation appear to be a substitute for imprisonment, which indeed it was. Another asset was the more generous provision for the supervision of probationers, made possible by the immediate economy secured through outside care. The fact that probation developed in connection with the courts rather than out of the penal system seemed to be a point in its favor, and at all events the judges were not lined up against the system by any threat to their prerogatives. But this circumstance of its development presented the states with a new problem of centralization, and again Massachusetts and New York led the attack as they attempted to coordinate and direct the activities of local court probation officers. A national probation association was organized in 1907, and the establishment of probation systems throughout the country—juvenile probation, but not adult, spread into the South— added a valuable branch to the penological profession.[24] At the same time the development contributed indirectly to the difficulties of prison and reformatory administrators. Not only were many of the

---

[23] Fred R. Johnson, *Probation for Juveniles and Adults: A Study of Principles and Methods* (New York, 1928), pp. 6–12; Wiley B. Sanders, ed., *Juvenile Offenders for a Thousand Years* (Chapel Hill, 1970), pp. 373–376, 416–429, 444–453.

[24] Mabel A. Elliott, *Conflicting Penal Theories in Statutory Criminal Law* (Chicago, 1931); Massachusetts State Board of Charities, *Report* (1908), pp. 149–151.

more likely candidates for reform kept from the institutions, but those committed no longer regarded the reformatory as the best "break" they might have received, and their disgruntled attitudes had to be overcome before the work of reformation could go forward as in the earlier days. The fact that so many could be successfully handled on the outside reenforced the argument that the apparent achievements of the reformatories were little better than the costly education of young men who were not really criminal. The answer that such men would quickly have become criminals if sent to the prisons did not save reformatory penology from the jolt which the success of the probation movement brought to its already unsettled equilibrium.[25]

Nevertheless, the ideology of the reformatory had finally gained an established place in American penology. The old theory, that a man could be made penitent by giving him a just measure of punishment to balance against the gain he had received from his crime or the injury society had suffered, had been radically qualified. Unfortunately neither the judges, the prison officers, nor the criminals had in many cases grasped the full meaning of the new principles, and the general public remained largely ignorant of the subtle revolution that had taken place in the theory of punishment. Under these circumstances the portentous reformatory experiment was not receiving a fair trial and suffered from the growing impatience of the public toward sentimentalists and their talk of reform. A shadow was cast over the reformatory technique so carefully elaborated during fifty years of patient experimentation, but it takes more than a vague feeling of disillusionment to scrap a well-established institutional equipment. The reformatory and its technique, handicapped by a loss of optimism, continued into the era of clinical penology as its most valuable heritage.

The Passing of the Auburn System

The half century that witnessed the growth of the reformatory saw also the gradual disintegration of the Auburn system. The principles and technique of the reformatories helped to reshape the older prison program, weakened because the population and labor problems had in the course of several decades destroyed the even

---

[25] A.P.A., *Proceedings* (1919), p. 186; (1924), pp. 238–245; Georgia State Board of Public Welfare, *Report* (1925–1926), pp. 47–48.

balance of that rigid system. By the opening of the twentieth century the authorities were everywhere turning from the old silent discipline, and many of them were attempting to introduce reformatory technique in its stead. Unfortunately the task of applying these devices in the major prisons was too much for untrained staffs; except in a few cases the final result was a lax discipline that tolerated almost everything but violence. In place of the elaborate technique of the reformatory, many officers fell back upon the fiction of a square deal as a means of controlling, if not of reforming, their prisoners. Amid the wide diversity of prisons and programs all that could safely be concluded was that the Auburn traditions had passed.

At the beginning of the century only the prisons of New York, Pennsylvania, and Massachusetts had as yet felt the full impact of the industrial upheaval. Other northern states had dodged the issue for the time, and the South was turning from its lease system in response to entirely different forces; the states and territories of the Great West had found anticontract laws a major impediment to the development of stable prisons, but the limited number of their convicts had enabled them to shift along. Legislation against the sale of the products of penal labor became more effective during this era, yet the delay had permitted the elaboration of several substitute labor systems. New York laws had outlined a model state-use system which the authorities had implemented in part; Minnesota and California had developed successful state-account industries; experiments with minimum-security farm and road camps were shortly to increase in number; finally, Maryland was rehabilitating the old contract system. The prisons were dominated by the struggles of their officers to develop one or another of these sytems, usually with indifferent success.

The attack on the sale of prison products was now receiving the hearty support of state and national labor commissioners. The United States Industrial Commission of 1900, accepting the views of the critics of prison contractors, even went so far as to frown at the piece-price system, still respectable in that day, and hailed the New York state-use system as the most satisfactory. The report of the United States Commissioner of Labor on prison industry in 1905 elaborately reenforced this stand. His careful statistical analysis disclosed the tendency of prison contractors to specialize in industries that were suffering a declining market. The situation was especially grievous for the manufacturers of brooms and brushes, stove hollowware, overalls and farm shirts, harnesses and wagons, cooperage, and certain grades of shoes. The investigators further discovered that prison products, manufactured at low labor cost, served to fix unreasonably low price levels in these industries.[26] The American Federation of Labor continued to pass resolutions, and special unions, notably the Boot and Shoe Workers' Union, made aggressive attacks against the large companies operating in the prisons of several states. They protested against the system that permitted the employment of 4,253 convicts in shoe factories in twelve prisons at an average labor cost of forty-eight cents a day, dumping twenty-five thousand low-priced shoes on the market every day; they protested against the depression of industrial standards and the exploitation of the convicts.[27]

The anticontract agitation finally began to have its way. Illinois, Indiana, and Iowa considerably limited the number that might be contracted and required industrial diversification. Ohio, Kansas, Michigan, and New Jersey in the North, as well as Oregon and Wyoming in the West, and Georgia and Texas in the South joined the leaders of the earlier period in abolishing all forms of contract labor. More than a dozen states passed laws of one kind and another to check the importation of prison-made goods from other states, but such laws had little effect until the Hawes-Cooper Bill came into effect two decades later. Only the smaller New England States, Alabama and Florida in the South, and the belt of states stretching from Maryland and Virginia to Missouri and Oklahoma stood by the old contract system with scarcely any restraint.[28]

Industrial readjustment was a distinct problem in each prison, but various trends were dominant in different sections. Production for state use was the most usual scheme adopted in the large industrial

[26] U.S. Commissioner of Labor, *Twentieth Annual Report, 1905: Convict Labor* (Washington, D.C., 1906).

[27] Collis Lovely, "The Abuses of Prison Labor," *Shoe Workers' Journal* 6 (July, August, September, October, 1905): 3–9, 5–14, 5–12, 5–11; E. T. Hiller, "Labor Unionism and Convict Labor," *Journal of Criminal Law and Criminology* 5 (1915): 851–879.

[28] Illinois State Board of Prison Industries, *Report* (1914), pp. 74–89; National Committee on Prison Labor, *Prison Labor in the Party Platforms of 1911–1912*, leaflet no. 17 (New York, 1913) reviews the platforms in some twenty states.

communities, following New York's lead. The state-account system was most popular in the Middle West and along the Pacific coast as the prison authorities attempted to duplicate the success in Minnesota and California in developing industries that were enjoying a growing local market. While several of these western prisons organized thriving state-account industries, most of those of the Northeast encountered difficulties in persuading the public authorities to purchase the products they were equipping themselves to produce. New laws were passed directing the state departments to order their supplies from the prison industries, but these laws were never adequate, and prison officers had to devise other activities unless they were willing to permit the labor supply to rot in the cells as Pennsylvania was doing. More and more this became the sorry state of affairs, but many efforts were made to avoid it.[29]

Prison farms offered the most convenient relief from the situation. The adult reformatories had for years been cultivating institutional farms, and certain western prisons had early developed such opportunities. The reclamation project started by Massachusetts on nine hundred acres at Rutland in 1900 proved the feasibility of employing certain classes of misdemeanants at such labor. City and county correctional farms were taking advantage of this form of employment, and the southern shift to plantations was dramatizing the opportunities of the system. Ohio purchased fifteen hundred acres in Madison County as a site for a new penitentiary, and, although considerations of economy defeated the plans for permanent buildings, the farm provided the base for a camp to which men were removed from the overcrowded prison and given healthy labor. In a similar way Illinois acquired a large farm as a site for a new prison in 1907, and, while the construction of Statesville was deferred, the farm provided a valuable branch for Joliet in the intervening years. Kansas and other western states put many of their convicts to work on the lands that had long been lying fallow about their prison walls, but it was Michigan that inaugurated the most extensive farming activities among northern prisons when in 1914 the 1,600-acre farm near Jackson prison was made the center of an

---

[29] William N. Gemmill, "Employment and Compensation of Prisoners," *J.C.L.C.* 6 (1915): 507–521.

active trucking and canning enterprise for the supply of state institutions.[30]

The Lower South had in the meantime turned almost completely to the plantation system, although Alabama, a rising industrial state, still kept the majority of her convicts working in the mines. Texas made the most extensive investment in farms and by 1917 had a total of seventy-eight thousand acres; Oklahoma provided large farms at both her prison and reformatory; but when Georgia turned finally from the lease system, although at first putting many on farms, she soon turned the great majority into still another form of outside labor—the road gang.[31]

The successful application of prison labor to road building was an achievement of the West. Warden Thomas J. Tynan of Canon City possibly deserves the credit for solving difficulties that had long obstructed this development. Colorado, as well as other states in the West and hundreds of counties in the South, had made earlier attempts to use the convicts on the roads, and the South was persisting in this activity, but the conditions had always been most unsatisfactory. Escapes were numerous, and cruel devices had been applied to check them. Living conditions were not only crude but unsanitary; only in the South did public indifference tolerate such a system. But the West was beginning to feel a greater demand for roads, and the increasing number of idle convicts prompted renewed efforts to solve the two problems together. Colorado was the first to work out a solution.[32]

The new system of road labor was in several important respects an outgrowth of reformatory penology. Colorado's early adoption of northeastern reforms had been frustrated by overcrowding and idleness, but, when Warden Cleghorn in 1906 determined to make

[30] Mass. Pris. Comm., *Report* (1905), pp. xvi–xvii; A.P.A., *Reports* (1913), p. 32; (1916), p. 13; Jesse O. Stutsman, *Curing the Criminal: A Treatise on the Philosophy and Practices of Modern Correctional Methods* (New York, 1926), pp. 107–109 where are listed farming developments and acres cultivated in American prisons.

[31] U.S. Bureau of Labor Statistics, *Convict Labor in 1923* (Washington, D.C., 1925), pp. 94–103.

[32] A.P.A., *Proceedings* (1910), pp. 12–19; Sydney Wilmot, "Use of Convict Labor for Highway Construction in the North," in "Good Roads and Convict Labor," *Proceedings of the Academy of Political Science* 4 (1914): 44–67.

another experiment with road labor, he was able to take advantage of the earlier measures. Twenty-five of the men of the top grade were selected on the basis of their approaching eligibility for parole, and with promises of parole within a few months these men were stationed at a road camp some miles from the prison with but one unarmed guard as manager over them. The experiment was successful, and additional camps were sent out the next year, aided by a new highway law passed by the legislature to provide funds for this activity. Twenty escapes in 1907 discouraged Cleghorn, but Thomas J. Tynan, who succeeded him as warden, injected new enthusiasm, and the honor camps rapidly became so popular that the counties ready to pay the small expenses assigned to them under the law were forced to compete for the privilege. The prisoners were equally eager to earn the special parole and monetary allowances accorded them under the 1907 law, and the state soon had an average of two hundred men employed in these honor camps the year around. The West had at last found a constructive labor policy. Arizona, New Mexico, Nevada, Wyoming, and Utah quickly developed convict road camps on this pattern, but Montana made a larger use of honor road camps than any other state after 1912. Most of these mountain and other far-western states developed similar honor camps on farms some distance from the main prisons.[33]

The good-roads movement was active throughout the nation in these first years of the automobile. Occasional counties in the Northeast employed their prisoners on the roads, and 1913 saw convicts in Illinois, Iowa, Wisconsin, North Dakota, and even New York laboring in this fashion. But it was in the South that convict road labor became most popular, threatening to displace all other penal systems. In the Carolinas the counties retained increasing numbers of the able-bodied convicts for their local chain gangs, while other states, notably Georgia, leased their prisoners to the counties for road construction. Louisiana was driven out of farming in the early part of the second decade by the ravages of the boll weevil and two disastrous floods, and the authorities leased the convicts for levee construction in order to earn funds to pay off the heavy losses in agricultural funds. The direction of these southern

[33] Colorado State Prison, *Report* (1908), p. 67; (1916), pp. 3–6; Joseph M. Sullivan, "'Notes' on 'Good Roads and Convict Labor,'" *J.C.L.C.* 5 (1915): 777–783: A.P.S., "Good Roads and Convict Labor," pp. 6–92.

trends was, indeed, back to the old lease system in so far as the treatment of the convicts was concerned, for the standards of the honor camps of the West were nowhere realized. The entire development was a fearsome demonstration of the fact that, however far the South may have traveled since the dark days of reconstruction, black convicts had no secure safeguards against exploitation. The good-roads movement offered a desirable outlet for penal labor only in those states where the social controls over the penal system were strong enough to make the road camp a minor feature of the reformatory program of the prison; such was the achievement for a time in most of the western states and in many of the instances where this employment was developed in the North.[34]

Meanwhile the old border states between the North and the South largely escaped these shifting experiments. Most of them stuck to the old contract system, to the great profit of their treasuries and the lucky contractors. Warden J. F. Weyler was even able to win a new respectability for the system by combining a discipline of rewards with small wages for active labor in the model surroundings of his new Baltimore prison, prompting many visitors to acclaim it the best reformatory prison in the country, but a more careful investigation in 1913 disclosed many disturbing defects. No fortuitous array of merits, however, could down the odious notoriety of the old contract system, not so long as a half dozen wretched examples of that system still flourished from Virginia west to Missouri. Aside from their profits and the confinement they provided for criminals, the only advantages these prisons could boast were those of hard labor over "sterile tasks" and "aimless idleness"—the characteristics of many of the reform prisons of the day, as leaders in these border states were wont to remark.[35]

Advantages of industry and economy were, nevertheless, real merits. The retrograding tendencies of the Pennsylvania prisons and

[34] Jesse F. Steiner and Roy M. Brown, *The North Carolina Chain Gang: A Study of County Road Work* (1937; reprinted Montclair, N.J., 1969); John Lewis Gillin, *Taming the Criminal: Adventures in Penology* (1931; reprinted Montclair, N.J., 1969); A.P.A., *Proceedings* (1919), pp. 172–176, 186–195; James E. Pennybacker *et al*, *Convict Labor for Road Work* (Washington, D.C., 1916).

[35] Maryland Penitentiary, *Report* (1905), p. 13; (1913); Julian Hawthorne, *The Subterranean Brotherhood* (New York, 1914), pp. 24–26, 150; A.P.A., *Proceedings* (1919), pp. 120–130; (1926), pp. 158–162.

the county penitentiaries in New York when their industrial systems broke down, and the new vitality which came to western prisons with the development of road and farm activities amply demonstrated this truth. Indeed, the industrial factor was the most determining influence in penology throughout the nation in these years. The rapid elimination of the contractors forced the officers to reorganize the industries and disciplines of their prisons, but they had to do this in the face of hostile economic interests and in the midst of party rivalries for patronage that had by no means been eliminated by the elaborate development of administrative bodies. Few wardens were able to measure up satisfactorily to these new responsibilities. The result was that, instead of carrying out the reformatory theories of pedagogical penology so widely endorsed by the laws, the prisons were driven before the wind to such an extremity that their officers adopted a live-and-let-live policy and strove to keep the convicts contented within the walls.

Prison discipline seemed to be within reach of its goal in 1900. Major prisons in all parts of the North were turning to the methods of the reformatory; even in the South and the West the omens were propitious. The system seemed on the verge of attaining the destiny so hopefully mapped out by the inspired leaders of 1870. In the course of the decade the prisons of the North, with few exceptions, did achieve most of the forms of that program, and those of the Great West came into their inheritance; even the South followed its rising star for a time. But the striking changes in the industrial and population problems upset the calculations, and numerous statistical surveys began to suggest to the leaders that their goal had eluded them. New disciplinary trends brought fresh enthusiasm, but the profession was not a little inclined to skepticism as it passed on to the next generation a penal system finally freed of all the old Auburn traditions except the architectural shell.

Grading and marking devices gained for a time almost universal acceptance in penitentiary discipline. A dozen prisons had already applied this reformatory device before the old century closed. Now most of the other prisons of the North, the federal penitentiaries, and several prisons in the West likewise introduced grades. But it had taxed the ingenuity of the best reformatory officers to administer the system where the sentences were of a uniform indeterminate character; prison wardens, often inexperienced and with uncertain tenure, naturally met many difficulties in applying grades to a population variously under indeterminate sentences, definite sentences with and without eligibility for parole, and life sentences. Again and again these grading systems had to be amended, suspended, or abolished; where they persisted, institutionalization sapped their vitality. As in Indiana, the great majority of prisoners were soon enjoying the privileges of the first grade.[36]

The greatest improvements of the period were made in the western prisons. Several of these carried out fine construction programs in the first decade—programs that were nominally, but only nominally, in line with the Auburn traditions. Prison buildings or no prison buildings, the real penological developments of this area waited upon the introduction of a labor system. When the road camp and the farm finally came into use toward the end of the decade, not only had the heyday of rigid reformatory discipline passed, but the outside labor favored a much freer technique than that of either Auburn or Elmira. These states turned rapidly to the newer recreational discipline that was so much more in keeping with their traditionally lax regulations. Their example provided an influential stimulant to the spread of the newer methods of discipline throughout the nation.

The South failed to realize in penology the full promise of its new beginnings in the nineties. Its penal history continued to be identified with the history of convict labor systems, and these took an unfortunate turn during the first decade. There were a few improvements in the border states—notably the new cellhouse erected at Richmond prison, the conversion of Frankfort prison into a reformatory, the great expansion of the farming activity in Texas, and the building of a prison and an adult reformatory in Oklahoma—but these were exceptions to the general trend. From the Carolinas south and west the convicts were largely put out in chain gangs on the roads. As these were usually under the inefficient control of the counties, most of the important gains of the nineties for central control were lost. The section was very much like the convict who was aptly described, when returning from a thorough

[36] Indiana State Prison, *Biennial Report* (1904); *Rules and Regulations for Governing and Disciplining the United States Penitentiary* (McNeil Island, Wash., 1911).

lashing, as full of correction up to the neck.[37]

If the penal authorities of the South were hard pressed for a justification of their system, many of those of the North were suffering from a strange illusion. The new officers who took charge of the New Hampshire prison in 1910 were not alone in their view that their predecessors had left "little in the way of improvements for us to do." Little to do—with the prisons jammed with criminals, most of them recidivists! Penal practitioners had traveled far from the spirit of the experimenting wardens of twenty years before. The widespread protests that were arising from the discharged prisoners did not endorse this opinion.[38]

The prisoners were, in fact, gaining a voice in their control. They wrote as never before, describing the corruption and the horrors that still remained, but especially the stupid "slouching about their sterile tasks" that had become the prime factor of the prison environment. The whole weight of a flood of prison memoirs beat against the disciplinary traditions of the previous century and helped to push them out of the prison system.[39] The silent opinion of the mass of the convicts was even more influential, forcing the authorities to admit practically all prisoners to the top grade and its privileges, inducing the parole boards to release men automatically at the end of their minimum sentences, and encouraging the officers to develop a more lenient discipline. But this mass opinion was not always silent, and for the first time in the age of penitentiaries a wave of prison riots broke the monotonous routine. More than ever before the wardens had to bid for the confidence and cooperation of their prisoners.[40] The experiments with self-government that were to gain so much notoriety at the end of the period were not the frivolous

[37] Virginia Penitentiary, *Report* (1905), pp. 5–9; Kentucky Prison Commission, *Report* (1913), pp. 15–20; Oklahoma State Prison, *Report* (1917), pp. 193–204; Prison Reform League, *Crime and Criminals* (Los Angeles, 1910), pp. 117–125.

[38] New Hampshire State Prison, *Biennial Report* (1910), p. 429.

[39] Russell C. Arnold, *The Kansas Inferno: A Study of the Criminal Problem, By a Life Prisoner, A Description of the Kansas Prison As It Is and As It Should Be* (Wichita, 1906); *Life in Sing Sing, By Number 1500* (Indianapolis, 1904); Joseph Kelley, *Thirteen Years in the Oregon Penitentiary* (Portland, 1908); Donald Lowrie, *My Life in Prison* (New York, 1912).

[40] Nevada State Prison, *Report* (1913–1914), pp. 5–8; Michigan Joint Prison Boards, *Proposed Legislation* (Lansing, 1913), pp. 16–22, presents a survey of recent riots and proposed remedies.

experiments in prison discipline they were sometimes considered to be, but the result of a union between idealistic officers and the upsurging desire of the mass of the criminals for more tolerable conditions. The prison populations had acquired a new character, whether as a result of changing social conditions outside or because of the disappearance of the Auburn restraints, and this new character played its part in the development of the modern prison customs under which almost everything but violence is tolerated.

Prison conditions were undergoing a slow improvement during this period. The federal government completed Leavenworth and Atlanta prisons and reopened a third at McNeil Island, housing 1,514, 1,184, and 239 in these institutions in 1915; Warden Henry Wolfer built the new model prison at Stillwater, the best penal structure in the country for many years; New York, Nebraska, and Oklahoma built new prisons, and Virginia and California constructed badly needed additions.[41] But cell construction occupied a minor place beside the efforts to make the old prisons more tenantable. New sanitary arrangements, dining halls, shower bathing, and outdoor exercise, as well as expanded library facilities, prison journals, and more liberal mailing privileges were the order of the day. The old lockstep, shaved head, and striped uniform practically disappeared for good. A more extensive provision for separate treatment of the insane and the tubercular was made in these years; even the South finally began to give attention to the problem of tuberculosis so rife among its Negro convicts. It was vain to claim any ideal solution of these problems, but virtually throughout the country the efforts of the past century to make the prisons comfortable—in a very narrow sense of the word, to be sure—went steadily forward. Only in the matter of the provision of individual cells was little done, and even here large plans were projected, only to be held up by the war and other changing forces.[42]

The county jails continued to maintain their deplorable features. Vigorous indictments of their conditions appeared from time to time, but little improvement resulted. Only those few northern states

[41] Minnesota State Prison, *Biennial Report* (1916); A.P.A., *Proceedings* (1925), pp. 179–196.

[42] J. J. Sanders, *Prison Reform* (Arizona, 1913), pp. 8–12; A.P.A., *Proceedings* (1912), pp. 85–92; Henry M. Hurd *et al, The Institutional Care of the Insane in the United States and Canada*, vol. 1 (Baltimore, 1916), pp. 348–351; Corinne Bacon, comp., *Prison Reform* (White Plains, N.Y., 1912), pp. 70–73.

where persistent inspection by state boards had kept the facts before the public presented fair conditions, and most of these states were crowding their jails with drunkards to the questionable advancement of the public morals. The jail thus continued to be the weakest link in the penal system, and the fee system its most insidious feature; European critics were convinced that the American criminal problem demonstrated what happens to a chain with a weak link. The only genuine improvement was in the case of those half dozen cities that created farm colonies for their misdemeanants. Hastings H. Hart among others saw clearly that a possible solution lay in the development of jail substitutes, such as these farms, or, in many cases, fines and probation. The "passing of the county jail" was, however, a very futuristic dream as yet.[43]

The remarkable transformation of prisons in the second decade was the natural conclusion of the forces that had long been playing on their development. Reformatory methods had broken down the old traditions, but the prisons were failing to give the new methods the sturdy application they required. Idleness and the liberties of the top grade gave the convicts greater opportunity to make their wishes felt in prison affairs. It became difficult to intimidate them as individuals, much more so in the mass; prisoners had to be cajoled into orderliness. Fortunately the men taking charge of the prisons had the wit to see that by taking the initiative in creating a positive recreational system they retained leadership over their men.

The new recreational activities had long roots in prison customs. Since the days of Gideon Haynes, fifty years before, holiday privileges had increasingly become a feature of prison life. The "freedom of the yard" thus occasionally granted was an indefinite term, and its application had varied greatly with the nature of the prison structure and the officers in charge. Occasional lectures, musicals, and theatricals had supplied entertainment in prisons, and the reformatories had developed such features to a considerable extent during the winter months as a substitute for their outdoor military drills and organized sports. The farm and road camps were

[43] N.P.A., *Proceedings* (1900), pp. 291–293; (1907), pp. 94–114; Calif. Bd. Char. and Corr., *Biennial Report* (1914-1916), pp. 50–55; Stuart A. Queen, *The Passing of the County Jail* (Menasha, Wis., 1920); Joseph F. Fishman, *Crucibles of Crime: The Shocking Story of the American Jail* (1923; reprinted Montclair, N.J., 1969).

nurturing a new type of associate life, particularly in the western prisons. All these departures from the strict rule of silence culminated during the early years of the second decade in a recreational movement that swept the last vestige of the old Auburn technique out of the prisons.

The final transformation was a sudden and rapid process. The occasional half holiday of the former era gradually became a regular Saturday or Sunday feature during the first decade in scattered prisons. Frequently the newly organized institutional bands, introduced into the prisons now that their value had been demonstrated in neighboring reformatories, provided a concert as the main feature of these half-holiday occasions. The abler wardens gave close attention to this development, but the prisoners, by their evident appreciation of the afternoon in the yard and by their spontaneous organization of games, helped to guide the final development. Beginning about 1910 regular organized sports became an accepted part of the prison curriculum in the Middle West, and by 1915 this feature had spread into practically all the prisons of the Northeast as well as those of the Great West.[44]

Prison athletics not only proclaimed the end of the Auburn system and the triumph of one feature of reformatory technique, but presaged a new era in prison discipline. Organized sport was in direct line with the attempt to make prison life more tolerable, and its welcome was doubly enthusiastic because the lax industrial activity was failing to occupy the full time and energy of the prisoners. The wardens, through cautious experiments with their first graders, had discovered their ability to control men in masses, and, as athletics opened a new horizon in correctional therapy, many officers felt inspired to attempt to "re-create the man in prison," a popular slogan at the congresses of the day.

But this hurried shift to entertainment activities marked the abandonment of many of the pedagogical principles and undertakings of the reformatory. Grandstands were erected, indicating that the recreational possibilities of athletics were to be sacrificed to the entertainment feature of league games; the wide introduction of the movie a few years later, and of the radio still later, further

---

[44] Kansas State Penitentiary, *Report* (1910), p. 14; Philip Klein, *Prison Methods in New York State: A Contribution to the Study of the Theory and Practice of Correctional Institutions* (New York, 1920), pp. 193–195.

emphasized the transition from the recreational program of the reformatory, with its educational motivation, to the amusement program of later prisons, seeking to keep their inmates contented.

Thomas Mott Osborne made a similar and much more startling application of a reform technique to prison discipline at old Auburn in 1913. A former mayor of that city with many public interests, Osborne had been moved the previous year by reading Donald Laurie's *My Life in Prison*, and he was ready to accept appointment by Governor Sulzer as chairman of a State Prison Reform Commission. But to inform himself as to the nature of the problems, he determined not simply to visit but to live for a week among the convicts in Auburn prison. Securing the consent of the warden and the state superintendent of prisons, he announced his plan to the assembled prisoners at a chapel meeting on September 28, 1913. His astonishing request that the men treat him as fellow inmate Tom Brown was greeted with incredulity but interest by the 1,400 prisoners and with ridicule and cynicism by most of public press.[45]

But it was the inside reaction and the experience he gained that chiefly interested Osborne. A few days in prison garb, walking from cell to mess hall to workshop, and performing the routine tasks and roles of an inmate, quickly won this warmly dynamic man the respect and confidence of many of his fellows. Among the host of suggestions he received was one of trusting the prisoners to assume a share of the discipline and management of life within the walls. His own earlier contact with the George Junior Republic, of which he had served as a director in the nineties, had prepared him to entertain such a proposal, which he had himself formulated in an address before the National Prison Association at its meeting in Albany in 1904. Now the suggestion that the prisoners be permitted to form a Good Conduct League, which would assume responsibility for supervising some inmate activities, seemed worth a try.

A few weeks after the dramatic conclusion of his stay in prison, Osborne was back with the consent of the warden and superintendent ready to assist in the organization that December of what became

[45] Thomas Mott Osborne, *Within Prison Walls: Being a Narrative of Personal Experience During a Week of Voluntary Confinement in the State Prison at Auburn, New York* (1914; reprinted Montclair, N.J., 1969); Thomas M. Osborne, *Society and Prisons: Some Suggestions for a New Penology* (1916; reprinted Montclair, N.J., 1975); Frank Tannenbaum, *Osborne of Sing Sing* (Chapel Hill, 1933).

the first Mutual Welfare League in any prison. The prisoners cast secret ballots in their workshops electing 49 delegates to a constitutional convention that met on December 28 and drafted the bylaws for their new organization, which in succeeding weeks and months assured responsibility for orderly marching, for programs in the chapel, and finally for activities in the prison yard.

The unexpected demonstration of a capacity for self-discipline and the transformation the League brought in the life of Auburn prison attracted wide interest. When difficulties at Sing Sing forced the warden there to resign, the governor and superindtendent offered the post to Osborne. Accepting the challenge, he proceeded to encourage the prisoners there to organize a Mutual Welfare League and gave it an increasing share of the responsibility for prison discipline and inmate activity. Soon a lively program of social and educational activities was developing. But under the intense glare of external publicity several disciplinary problems acquired a lurid character and because of a shift in state politics prompted an investigation of the Osborne administration.

George W. Kirchwey, dean of the Columbia Law School and a friend of Osborne, accepted an appointment as acting warden of Sing Sing during the investigation and saved the Mutual Welfare League from extinction. Osborne was eventually cleared of all charges, but the experience had been so trying that he shortly resigned and the future of his experiment with penal democracy remained in doubt. Its deviation from the pedagogical techniques of Brockway's reformatory penology was clear, yet it had a greater affinity with the spirit and purposes of that movement than with the newer techniques of the analytical students of criminology who were bidding for control. The fact was that prison discipline was again in flux, at the outbreak of the First World War, and the determination of new directions would await its conclusion.

Reformatory penology completed its cycle about 1910. For half a century it had run its course, an integral phase of American life. Developing within the old Auburn system, the reformatory technique had slowly displaced the older traditions so that by the end of the era only the architectural shell of Louis Dwight's system remained. Reformatory theory held society responsible for the regeneration of its criminals, and a large-souled optimism had enlivened and added power to its educational devices—both of which features the Europeans were quick to recognize as characteristically American. The old theory that years of imprisonment were to be meted out to fit the crime had been almost entirely erased from the statute books; in its place had been written the right of the convict to his freedom, within certain limitations, as soon as he could be reformed. The organization of the system had been so elaborately carried forward that scattered wardens were leaning back in their chairs and blandly reporting that all reforms had been adopted, but already several radically new considerations were appearing, indicating different trends for the future.

The creation and application of reformatory penology had been the work of three generations spanning the years from 1865 to 1910. A group of eclectic idealists of the late sixties had contributed the fundamental principles, but the actual formulation of the technique had been accomplished by the succeeding generation of experimenting wardens. The reformatory program had gained its opportunity when Louis Dwight's older system was thrown out of gear by critical population and labor problems. The development of new agencies for public supervision and control had supplied a more effective leadership for reform. But so great were the growing pains of the nation that pedagogical penology scarcely received a fair trial in any state. Now the third generation, after winning a formal triumph by pledging practically the whole nation to the program, was forced to hand on its responsibilities amid a growing feeling of disillusionment.

The almost nationwide acceptance of the reformatory program had been disastrous to its record. The majority of prison officers were miserably failing to apply Brockway's carefully balanced program; growing populations were taxing the already overexpanded institutions beyond their capacities; labor laws were restricting the opportunities for industrial activity; and improved statistics were revealing a startling number of repeaters whose prison and reformatory terms seemed only to have briefly interrupted their criminal careers. Reformatory penology had sought to individualize the criminal at least to the extent of fitting his term of imprisonment to his peculiar reformatory needs, but the effect of the general adoption of the technique had been quite the reverse. The striped figures of the earlier days had been called forth from the partial seclusion of separate cells only to be submerged in the stagnant pools of humanity that characterized the idle, overcrowded, and undisciplined prisons of the day. Osborne's bold attempt to give a measure of self-government to the mass of criminals had produced two startling demonstrations of uncertain significance. A new school of penologists, though pointing in another direction, would have to coordinate these divergent trends to achieve effective leadership after the war.

BIBLIOGRAPHIC NOTE

·The regular reports of the prison officers, the boards of charities, or boards of control are available for almost every state during this period. These are supplemented in some states by special investigations, such as Frank W. Blackmar, *Report on the Penitentiary to Governor George H. Hodges* (Topeka, 1914); Charles A. Ellwood, *A Bulletin on the Condition of the County Jails of Missouri* (Columbia, 1904); Maryland Penitentiary Commission, *Report* (1913); Pennsylvania Penal Commission, *Employment and Compensation of Prisoners in Pennsylvania* (Harrisburg, 1915); reports of the various investigating committees of the Texas legislature, 1910–25; the annual *Proceedings of the National Prison Association,* (from 1908–1954 *American Prison Association),* the successive issues of the *Journal of Criminal Law and Criminology* (1910–) and *Mental Hygiene* (1917–) show the trends in both theory and practice. The U.S. Bureau of the Census, *Prisoners and Juvenile Delinquents in the United States, 1910* (Washington, D.C., 1918) and U.S. Commissioner of Labor, *Twentieth Annual Report, 1905: Convict Labor* (Washington, D.C., 1906) provide valuable statistical surveys.

Among the many volumes dealing with some phase of the developments during this period may be mentioned: Russell C. Arnold, *The Kansas Inferno: A Study of the Criminal Problem, By a Life Prisoner, A Description of the Kansas Prison as It Is and as It Should Be* (Wichita, 1906); Corinne Bacon, comp., *Prison Reform* (White Plains, N.Y., 1912); Isabel C. Barrows, *The Sunny Life: The Biography of Samuel June Barrows* (Boston, 1913); Hugo A. Bedau, ed., *The Death Penalty in America,* 2d ed. (Chicago, 1968); Henry M. Boies, *The Science of Penology: The Defense of Society Against Crime* (New York, 1901); Mabel A. Elliott, *Conflicting Penal Theories in Statutory Criminal Law* (Chicago, 1931); Joseph F. Fishman, *Crucibles of Crime: The Shocking Story of the American Jail* (1923; reprinted Montclair, N.J., 1969); Benjamin O. Flower, *Progressive Men, Women, and Movements of the Past Twenty-Five Years* (Boston, 1914); John Lewis Gillin, *Taming the Criminal: Adventures in Penology* (1931; reprinted Montclair, N.J., 1969); Edward Grubb, *Methods of Penal Administration in the United States* (London, 1904); Hasting H. Hart, *Social Problems of Alabama*

(Montgomery, 1918); Julian Hawthorne, *The Subterranean Brotherhood* (New York, 1914); Charles R. Henderson, *Modern Prison Systems* (Washington, D.C., 1903); Charles R. Henderson, *Tendencies Towards Centralization in Foreign Countries* (Washington, D.C., 1903); Paul Herr, *Das moderne amerikanische Besserungssystem* (Berlin, 1907); Henry M. Hurd *et al, The Institutional Care of the Insane in the United States and Canada,* vol. 1 (Baltimore, 1916); Fred R. Johnson, *Probation for Juveniles and Adults: A Study of Principles and Methods* (New York, 1928); Joseph Kelley, *Thirteen Years in the Oregon Penitentiary* (Portland, 1908); George M. Kober, comp., *Charitable and Reformatory Institutions in the District of Columbia: History and Development* (Washington, D.C., 1927); Collis Lovely, "The Abuses of Prison Labor," *Shoe Workers' Journal* 6 (July–October) 1905; Donald Lowrie, *My Life in Prison* (New York, 1912); Thomas Mott Osborne, *Society and Prisons: Some Suggestions for a New Penology* (1916; reprinted Montclair, N.J., 1975); Thomas Mott Osborne, *Within Prison Walls: Being a Narrative of Personal Experience During a Week of Voluntary Confinement in the State Prison at Auburn, New York* (1914; reprinted Montclair, N.J., 1969); Prison Reform League, *Crime and Criminals* (Los Angeles, 1910); Stuart A. Queen, *The Passing of the County Jail* (Menasha, Wis., 1920); Richard F. Quinton, *The Modern Prison Curriculum* (London, 1912); Sir Evelyn Ruggles-Brise, *Prison Reform at Home and Abroad: A Short History of the International Movement Since the London Congress, 1872* (London, 1924); Salvation Army, *Broken Souls* (New York, 1929); J. J. Sanders, *Prison Reform* (Arizona, 1913); Wiley B. Sanders, ed., *Juvenile Offenders for a Thousand Years* (Chapel Hill, 1970); F. C. Sharp and M. C. Otto, "Study of the Popular Attitude Toward Retributive Punishment," *International Journal of Ethics* 20 (1910): 341–357: Jesse O. Stutsman, *Curing the Criminal: A Treatise on the Philosophy and Practices of Modern Correctional Methods* (New York, 1926); Frank Tannenbaum, *Osborne of Sing Sing* (Chapel Hill, 1933); Frank Tannenbaum, *Wall Shadows* (1922; reprinted Montclair, N.J., 1976); Negley K. Teeters, *Deliberations of the International Penal and Penitentiary Congresses: Questions and Answers* (Philadelphia, 1949); Ernest S. Whitin, *The Caged Man* (New York, 1913).

The several historical surveys of specific phases of the development by Harry Elmer Barnes, J. E. Briggs, Mark T. Carleton, Harry H. Jackson, Philip Klein, Eugenia C. Lekkerkerker, Anthony M. Platt, Jesse F. Steiner and Roy M. Brown, and Elizabeth Wisner have been noted in earlier chapters. Further bibliographic references may be found in the exhaustive and indispensible August F. Kuhlman, *A Guide to Material On Crime and Criminal Justice* (1929; reprinted Montclair, N.J., 1969).

11.

NEW PENOLOGICAL
UNCERTAINTIES:
1915–1930

A sense of uncertainty if not disillusionment gripped many penal officials in the late teens and twenties. The wide adoption of the tenets of reformatory penology had displaced the old Auburn silent system with varied pedagogical and recreational programs but with questionable results. Indeterminate sentences, probation, and parole had modified if not replaced the old concept of sentences measured to fit the crime. But the steadily mounting crime statistics and the increasing degree or at least awareness of recidivism dispelled much of the assurance that had long characterized the more idealistic reformers. Several responsible wardens and other professionals, frustrated by the disquieting evidence, were prompted to reexamine some of their basic theories and practices. Some urged a return to the sterner and simpler methods of the classical era of Beccaria, Howard, and Louis Dwight. Others gave a more attentive ear to the theories of the positivists, and although few in America were ready to accept Lombroso's original concept of the "born criminal," a new emphasis developed on the need to study and classify convicts not only as first offenders or repeaters, but as individuals with varied propensities and tendencies that might require specialized treatment. More accustomed to the discussion of practical programs and procedures, few wardens grasped the conceptual significance of the new trends as the "soft determinism" of the psychologists displaced the "hard determinism" of the biologists as well as the classicism of Beccaria and his followers. Yet despite a paucity of theory, the skepticism many expressed at Columbus, Ohio, in 1920, when reviewing the accomplishments of the Prison Association's first half century, strengthened their desire for the establishment of clinics and laboratories to achieve a fuller understanding of criminals and their problems.

New Vistas in Criminology

The American emphasis on the more practical services of penology had contrasted with the greater attention some Europeans had long given to the theories of crime causation. Many American penologists were convinced, as we have noted above, that the Lombrosian concept of natural or born criminals was a corollary of the more passive penal techniques of the Pennsylvania system most European countries had adopted. But the more activist approach of the Americans, which had enabled them to graft the indeterminate sentence and reformatory techniques onto the old classical penology, had also prompted them to distinguish between varied classes of criminals—misdemeanants, juveniles, women, first offenders, hardened criminals, and both demented and feebleminded convicts. To assist in identifying members of the last two categories, prison officials had called on the services of the newly emerging psychiatrists, and these and other professionals precipitated a renewed discussion of the causes of crime.

Successive European critics had considerably modified the original Lombrosian doctrine before the Americans gave it much attention. Enrico Ferri, a disciple of Spencer as well as of Lombroso, his Italian compatriot, had stressed sociological aspects of the personality of criminals.[1] Several French scholars had also emphasized the social factors in crime causation, and even Lombroso, in his later years, had recognized the existence of criminals by accident or passion. But the great Italian founder of the positivist school of criminology died in 1909 before the publication of Dr. Charles Goring's study of English convicts, which refuted the Lombrosian contention that confirmed criminals had characteristic and easily observable features. Goring's careful head and body measurements

[1] Enrico Ferri, *Criminal Sociology* (Boston, 1917).

of 3,000 second and third termers, when compared with similar measurements of 1,000 university students, failed to reveal any striking distinctions and finally disposed of the phrenological aspects of criminal anthropology. But his research also employed a new statistical approach to the study of criminals, which intensely interested several American scholars.[2]

Despite their sturdy faith in the equality of men, on which the reformatory doctrines were in part based, scattered Americans had explored divergent views of crime causation. Robert Dugdale's study of the Jukes in the 1870s had disclosed more evidence of hereditary criminality than Lombroso uncovered, while several prison physicians had written and published papers suggesting physiological and psychological causes of crime.[3] Pioneer sociologists, notably Professor Henderson, who served as president of the American Prison Association in 1902, stressed social causation. The organization of the American Institute of Criminal Law and Criminology in 1909 not only climaxed these early developments but also heralded the new era. It provided for the translation and publication of outstanding European treatises and launched the *Journal of the American Institute of Criminal Law and Criminology* to focus attention on the "new spirit of research and investigation."[4]

Dr. William Healy, in surveying these developments in 1915, declared that "it is quite fair to speak of most of the previous work

[2] Charles Goring, *The English Convict: A Statistical Study*, unabridged ed., together with *Schedule of Measurements and General Anthropological Data* (1913; reprinted Montclair, N.J., 1972). The *Schedule* contains the raw data on which the study was based. Charles A. Ellwood, "The Classification of Criminals," *Journal of Criminal Law and Criminology* 1 (1910): 536–548.

[3] Richard L. Dugdale, *The Jukes: A Study in Crime, Pauperism, Disease, and Heredity*, 5th ed. (New York, 1891); George F. Lydston, *Addresses and Essays* (Louisville, 1892), pp. 65–108.

[4] The Modern Criminal Science Series, under the editorship of Professor John H. Wigmore, translated and published the works of nine European criminologists: C. Bernaldo de Quiros, *Modern Theories of Criminality* (1911); Hans Gross, *Criminal Psychology* (1911; this and the subsequent five titles reprinted Montclair, N.J., 1968); Cesare Lombroso, *Crime, Its Causes and Remedies* (1911); Raymond Saleilles, *The Individualization of Punishment* (1911); Gabriel Tarde, *Penal Philosophy* (1912); Gustave Aschaffenburg, *Crime and Its Repression* (1913); Raffaele Garofalo, *Criminology* (1914); Willem A. Bonger, *Criminality and Economic Conditions* (1916); and Enrico Ferri, *Criminal Sociology* (1917). In 1931 the name of the journal was changed to *Journal of Criminal Law and Criminology*.

on this subject as theoretical." Yet some exceptions were in order, notably the work of his own Juvenile Psychopathic Institute in conjunction with the juvenile court in Chicago. Established in 1909, it had conducted varied research projects, including a study by Healy and Miss Edith Spaulding of 1,000 youthful repeaters, which tended to discredit the claims of hereditary criminality. Dr. Henry H. Goddard's pioneer efforts to test the intelligence of the boys at the Training School at Vineland, New Jersey, was another early example of empirical research. Patterned after the work of Dr. Alfred Binet in France, observed on a tour in 1908, Goddard's researches enabled him to classify the inmates at Vineland into various categories and prompted other scholars to launch forty similar studies, most of them in juvenile institutions, before 1914.[5]

While most of the early mental testers were finding evidence of idiocy and feeblemindedness among the inmates and concluded that significant causal relationships had thus been revealed, Dr. Healy who with Miss Grace Fernald conducted such a study at his Chicago institute reported that less than ten percent showed mental defects. Dr. Healy had designed the study to assist in developing a classification that would facilitate correctional programming. He was forced to conclude that the evidence was too complex for simple classification and that more careful study of individual delinquents was required before adequate provisions for treatment could be made.[6] Several other institutional clinics were joining in this effort. Dr. Katherine B. Davis secured a grant from the Rockefeller Foundation in 1912 for the continuation of her clinical studies of the problems of sex offenders in the Women's Reformatory at Bedford Hills, New York. In Massachusetts, Dr. Guy Fernald established a clinic at Concord, and Dr. A. Warren Stearns at Charlestown, while Dr. Victor V. Anderson developed the first clinical service for an adult criminal court at Boston. But the new era of clinical criminology was finally opened with the establishment of a clinic

[5] Edith R. Spaulding and William Healy, *Inheritance as a Factor in Criminality: A Study of 1000 Cases of Young Repeated Offenders* (Chicago, 1914); William Healy, *The Individual Delinquent: A Text-Book of Diagnosis and Prognosis for All Concerned in Understanding Offenders* (1915; reprinted Montclair, N.J., 1969), p. 15ff.; see Stanley P. Davies, *Social Control of the Mentally Deficient* (New York, 1930), pp. 51–57, for a discussion of Dr. Goddard's researches and conclusions.

[6] Healy, *Individual Delinquent*, pp. 15, 25, 31, 159–160.

headed by Dr. Bernard Glueck and supported by Rockefeller funds at Sing Sing in 1916.[7]

The early clinical findings, like the first mental tests, failed to develop a solid foundation for classification or theoretical analysis. Most of them had proceeded without any reliable knowledge of norms or control groups. That defect became abundantly evident when the outbreak of war in Europe prompted recruiting efforts that assembled an army of young men and spurred the officials to employ mental tests to assist in utilizing their talents. The results of the army tests in 1918 soon revealed the need for new standards of gradation and supplied a more reliable norm for further tests of both juvenile and adult delinquents. As a result the high ratio of 40 or 50 percent feebleminded, as reported by Goddard and some other early testers of delinquents, was scaled down to a median of 20 percent in a summary by Edwin H. Sutherland of 150 such studies made during the 1920s.[8]

Several factors contributed to the proliferation of clinics and special studies in the postwar years. A half dozen leading universities developed sociological and psychological courses dealing with crime and punishment, and at least three law schools introduced a discussion of clinical research into their criminal law courses. The organization of the National Committee for Mental Hygiene in 1909, and the formation of state committees in a score of states within its first decade, assured support for numerous studies and prompted the establishment in 1917 of the new journal, *Mental Hygiene*, to provide an outlet for their findings. Prodded by these committees, the newly appointed superintendent of prisons in Illinois created the post of state criminologist and called Dr. Herman Adler from Harvard to direct the study and classification of its convicts. Not to be outdone, the Boston Juvenile Court invited Dr. Healy of Chicago to assume charge of its research clinic. Massachusetts adopted a law in 1924 providing for the examination

---

[7]*Mental Hygiene* 1 (1917): 160–161; 3 (1919): 157–167; Edith R. Spaulding and William Healy, "Inheritance as a Factor in Criminality," *J.C.L.C.* 4 (1914): 837–858; "Report of the Department of Research in the Jeffersonville Reformatory," *J.C.L.C.* 5 (1915): 757–761.

[8]Winfred Overholser, "Clinical Study of Adult Offenders," *Social Work Year Book* 1 (1929): 87–89.

of all persons sentenced to local jails as well as to its prisons and reformatories, thus achieving the most complete coverage in America.[9]

But the most significant work in this field was that of Dr. Bernard Glueck at Sing Sing. Financed by the Rockefeller Foundation, this first clinic organized by the National Committee for Mental Hygiene undertook a comprehensive examination of all inmates received there during the reform administrations of Osborne and Kirchwey. Dr. Glueck, a psychiatrist who had stressed the necessity to explore the whole life history of an individual criminal before devising a therapeutic treatment, proceeded to undertake such a research program. He accepted the indeterminate sentence as a valuable feature but regarded it as applicable to only a limited portion of the prison population to be selected not by a grading system but by clinical examination. After several months of study, during which 608 new arrivals were carefully examined, 28 percent were found to have a mental age of twelve or less, 18.9 percent were found to be psychopathic, and 12 percent were diagnosed as suffering from a mental disease. He recommended that this 59 percent receive special care either at the Dannemora asylum for insane convicts or at a new institution to be built for defective and psychopathic inmates. Sing Sing, he proposed, should be converted into a classification and distribution prison, as Samuel J. Barrows had suggested several years before; but now with the aid of science an effective classification was, he believed, possible.[10]

While this pioneer classification clinic still lacked official status and responsibility, other efforts in this direction were gaining acceptance. Dr. Herman Adler had more real authority in Illinois, as Drs. Healy and Stearns did in Massachusetts, while similar testing was beginning in Michigan, Ohio, and Pennsylvania. As the twenties advanced, the national and state committees for mental hygiene pressed successfully for the appointment of psychiatric consultants in over a hundred courts and for the employment of full-

[9] Robert H. Gault, "On the Teaching of Criminology in Colleges and Universities," *J.C.L.C.* 9 (1918): 354–365; L. F. Barker, "The First Ten Years of the National Committee for Mental Hygiene," *Mental Hygiene* 2 (1918): 557–581.

[10] Bernard Glueck, "A Contribution to the Catamnestic Study of the Juvenile Offender," *J.C.L.C.* 3 (1912): 220–244; see also his articles in *Mental Hygiene*, 1 (1917): 171–195; 2 (1918): 85–151; 3 (1919); 177–218.

or part-time psychiatrists on the staffs of many prisons. An increasing number of major offenders were being examined, but except for the women in a few states and juveniles before the courts and in some institutions the treatment was not greatly altered.[11]

A partial explanation of the greater impact of the clinical examinations on the treatment of women and juveniles was the more careful attention given in their cases to social and environmental factors. Community studies, such as that of the Misses Breckinridge and Abbott at Chicago in 1912, had established a relationship between broken homes and juvenile crime. Frederick M. Thrasher's study of the propensity of city youths to run in neighborhood gangs helped to make their delinquency seem less willful. The researches of Dr. Davis into the sex life of inmates at the women's reformatory at Bedford related them to their social and economic environment and made proposals for special treatment more persuasive.[12]

A major impediment checking the application of the new theories was the prevailing legal system. Dr. Glueck's desire to substitute clinical evidence for the traditional grading system in determining the proper time for release under the indeterminate sentences found no support in law. Dean Roscoe Pound of Harvard clearly perceived the difficulty when he observed that, while the new scientific advance "calls for individualization, the traditional spirit of the law calls for generalized penalties." Moreover the political and ethical tenor of American traditions favored an insistence on the complete equality of men before the law. The American Bar Association was nevertheless ready on occasion to cooperate with the American Psychiatric Association and supported the National Committee for Mental Hygiene in its campaigns for the appointment of psychiatric consultants for the courts. And young Professor Sheldon Glueck of the Harvard Law School urged that the blindfold be removed from

[11] Guy E. Fernald, "The Psychopathic Laboratory in Criminology," *J.C.L.C.*, 9 (1918): 413–419; Winfred Overholser, "Psychiatry as an Aid to the Administration of Criminal Justice," *Annals* 145 (September 1929): 23–30.

[12] Sophonisba P. Breckinridge and Edith Abbott, *The Delinquent Child and the Home* (New York, 1912); Mable R. Fernald, Mary H.S. Hayes, and Almena Dawley, *A Study of Women Delinquents in New York State* (1920; reprinted Montclair, N.J., 1968); Frederic M. Thrasher, *The Gang: A Study of 1,313 Gangs in Chicago* (Chicago, 1927); Eugenia C. Lekkerkerker, *Reformatories for Women in the United States* (Groningen, 1931), pp. 111–130.

the eyes of justice before she be permitted to wreck vengence upon intractable wills.[13]

These questions raised again the old debate as to the proper treatment of criminals. As the traditional conception of crime as sin gave ground during the nineteenth century, some theorists drew an analogy between delinquency and disease. John H. Wigmore rejected such an analogy but asserted that "modern science, here as in medicine, recognizes that crime also (like disease) has natural causes . . . and that penal or remedial treatment cannot possibly be indiscriminate or machine-like, but must be adapted to the causes, and to the man as affected by those causes." Such views were not readily accepted by the public, however, which continued, as Wigmore put it, to see crime as caused by "the inscrutable moral free will of the human being." This doctrine and the demands for harsh punishment it fostered were vividly demonstrated in the public response to the sensational Loeb and Leopold trial. Yet even Wigmore could see the value of severe punishment in this case as a deterrent and justified it as an expression of the public's moral conscience. Numerous psychiatrists hastened to respond, some labeling such views archaic not only because punishment does not deter but because it also fails to produce a cure.[14] In reviewing the situation for the National Commission on Law Observance and Enforcement (Wickersham Commission) at the end of the period, Morris Ploscowe concluded that the "inherent complexity of the problem" of criminality was so great that more research was essential before causation could be determined and adequate treatment prescribed.[15]

Prison Administration in the Twenties

Of course the practical administrators of the `prisons and reformatories could not await the perfection of such a program.

[13] Bernard Glueck, "A Study of 608 Admissions to Sing Sing Prison," *Mental Hygiene* 2 (1918): 85–151; Roscoe Pound, *Criminal Justice in America* (New York, 1930), p. 197; S. Sheldon Glueck, *Mental Disorder and the Criminal Law* (Boston, 1925).

[14] John H. Wigmore, chairman, "General Introduction to the Modern Criminal Science Series," in Saleilles, *Individualization*, p. vi–ix. See also John H. Wigmore, "Relation between Criminal Law and Criminal Psychiatry," *J.C.L.C.* 16 (1925): 311; and his statement on "The Loeb-Leopold Case," in *J.C.L.C.* 15 (1924): 400–405.

[15] Morris Ploscowe, "Some Causative Factors in Criminality: A Critical Analysis of the Literature on the Causes of Crime," in U.S. National Commission on Law Observance and Enforcement (Wickersham Commission) *Report No. 13: On the Causes of Crime*, vol. I (1931; reprinted Montclair, N.J., 1968), pp. 136–142.

They had the responsibility for making immediate decisions concerning the care and treatment of a host of convicts. Generally the established practices appeared the easiest if not the best course, but several unsettling factors compelled the officials to entertain new proposals during the twenties. The war and its aftermath bringing new conceptions of crime, the resultant growth in the criminal population, and the mounting pressure against prison industries combined with several lesser influences to make the postwar period one of innovation and transition in penal developments. Advocates of reform, both humanitarian and scientific, received a hearing and won opportunities to demonstrate some of their schemes, but the increased independence and intransigence of the inmates rendered most of the experiments indecisive and at the same time heightened the pressure for reform.

The American Prison Association continued its traditional function of bringing the new political appointees into annual conclaves with the older wardens and other professionals. New ideas and programs received a hearing at these congresses, and although the association never assumed the championship of research, as the Institute of Criminal Law and Criminology did, or of reform as the National Committee for Mental Hygiene and the newly formed Osborne Society did in their fields, its successive presidents included some of the most distinquished men in the fields of administration, research, and reform, as the names of Frederick G. Pettigrove, George W. Wickersham, and Hastings Hart testify. Moreover, the list of its standing committees and affiliated societies, which exceeded a dozen in these years, afforded scope and support for all interested members.[16]

One topic discussed at practically every Congress from 1910 on was the movement for extramural road and farm camps. Colorado's success in developing honor camps on the roads in 1906 had prompted a dozen western states and several in the Northeast to organize similar camps within a decade. This activity prospered without the aid of a special committee because of the eager backing of the good-roads lobby and the constant pressure of overcrowding in many state prisons. In the South the ill repute of the old chain gangs turned state authorities to the development of penal

---

[16] John W. Wilson, "The American Correctional Association and Organizational Activities in Corrections," *Proceedings* (A.C.A., 1959), pp. 249–258.

plantations, as in Mississippi and Louisiana for example, and a dozen large prison systems in the North acquired farms to help relieve congestion within the walls and provide useful labor. A federal digest of convict labor laws in 1923 revealed that all the states permitted the employment of prisoners on institutional farms and on road work or other construction outside the walls.[17] Although the development of heavy road machines and of construction companies eager to take over the job reduced the demand for road camps in many states during the late twenties, the continued pressure of overcrowded prisons and the development of state authorities equipped with classification clinics eager to find minimum security places for low-risk convicts helped to keep the road camps in use.[18]

Somewhat related in theory to the honor camps, Thomas Mott Osborne's experiments with self-government in prisons were more dramatic but less permanent. The mutual welfare leagues he established in Auburn and Sing Sing persisted after his departure but in modified form and the efforts of scattered wardens to develop similar leagues in other penitentiaries generally stopped with the organization of inmate committees to supervise recreational and other special programs. But Osborne, as superintendent of the U. S. Naval Prison at Portsmouth during the war, not only developed a third successful inmate league there, but also inspired a number of able assistants, among them Austin H. MacCormick and William B. Cox, whose careers displayed and prolonged his influence. Further to promote his concern for the welfare of convicts, several friends of Osborne joined to found the National Society of Penal Information, which promptly named Osborne as chairman and undertook the investigation of prison conditions throughout the country. The publication in 1925 and 1926 of the first two *Handbooks* covering most state penal institutions for adults set a high standard of objective description and analysis.[19]

[17] American Prison Association, *Proceedings* (1916), pp. 410–418; (1917), pp. 104–109; U.S. Bureau of Labor Statistics, *Convict Labor in 1923* (Washington D.C., 1925), pp. 4–23, 167–265; Jesse O. Stutsman, *Curing the Criminal* (New York, 1926), pp. 108–109.

[18] Joseph M. Sullivan, " 'Notes' on 'Good Roads and Convict Labor,' " *J.C.L.C.* 5 (1915): 777–783; James E. Pennybacker *et al, Convict Labor for Road Work* (Washington, D.C., 1916).

[19] Thomas Mott Osborne, *Society and Prisons: Some Suggestions for a New Penology* (1916; reprinted Montclair, N.J., 1975); Frank Tannenbaum, *Osborne of Sing Sing* (Chapel Hill, 1933); A.P.A., *Proceedings* (1926), pp. 192–198, supplies a list of inmate leagues; National Society of Penal Information (1933 on, Osborne Association), *Handbook of American Prisons* (New York, 1925; 1926).

One of the Prison Association's most active committees, later organized as an independent affiliate, was the committee on jails, which Hastings Hart served for many years as chairman. Its repeated exposures of jail conditions were well documented. Only a few cities or urban counties, notably Washington in 1913, followed such former leaders as Milwaukee in establishing institutions for the care of misdemeanants separate from their jails for detention charges. Several of the earlier county houses of correction had forgotten their original inspiration, but a few such as Detroit were reviving it. Indiana, Illinois, and California followed an earlier Massachusetts lead in providing a state farm for misdemeanants. Many unfortunates, however, continued even in these states to reside in jail, and the great majority in other states suffered many of the evils so vividly described by Joseph Fishman in his sensational book, *Crucibles of Crime*, and by other inspectors and critics.[20]

There was considerable legislative approval in this period for the payment of small wages for convict labor. Prison contractors had early hit upon this device for stimulating penal workers to greater production, and it was the fear of losing such payments, small as they were, that prompted many convicts to oppose the introduction of state controlled industries. A combination of motives, including increased production, an additional disciplinary check, and the object of enabling convicts to aid their families encouraged the payment of small wages. Governor Alfred E. Smith among others urged this reform at the annual congresses and before the legislatures, several of which endorsed the principle. Few states, however, provided the funds needed to put the program into effect, but the returns on state production enabled some prisons to pay nominal wages, enough to maintain a disciplinary effect and to keep the program alive.[21]

The only reform that achieved full effectiveness was the shift from the cumbersome Bertillon system of identification to the newly perfected fingerprint system. Several states followed New York's lead

[20] Joseph F. Fishman, *Crucibles of Crime: The Shocking Story of the American Jail* (1923; reprinted Montclair, N.J., 1969); A.P.A., *Proceedings* (1923), pp. 282–303; George M. Kober, comp., *Charitable and Reformatory Institutions in the District of Columbia: History and Development* (Washington, D.C., 1927).

[21] William N. Gemmill, "Employment and Compensation of Prisoners," *J.C.L.C.* 6 (1915): 507–521.

in 1902 in establishing a central clearing house for such records, and Congress finally created a Federal Bureau of Identification to assemble and coordinate the records of all participating states.[22]

A widespread trend towards the centralization of control within the states greatly benefited administrative reform. An earlier effort to eliminate politics had resulted in the creation of the state boards of charities and corrections, but their powers of inspection and recommendation had often proved ineffective, and several states chiefly in the northcentral district moved to create boards of control. Most of these boards had authority over welfare as well as correctional institutions. Responsibility, however, was diffused, and to correct that situation Illinois in 1917 created a department of public welfare headed by a director who was politically responsible to the governor. The director, a member of the governor's cabinet, had authority over five superintendents of correctional or charitable institutions, parole, and welfare research. The efficiency achieved quickly attracted the attention of officials in Ohio and a half dozen other states. Both Massachusetts and New York, where the reformers had developed separate departments of correction under non-partisan control, now gave authority to individual commissioners responsible to the governor. This resumption of political leadership proved advantageous, except in Ohio where frequent political shifts created instability. To avoid this, New Jersey created a state board to appoint and supervise the single administrative head of its department of welfare.[23]

Centralization brought improved administration but generally left some gaps. In New Jersey the new commissioner failed to secure control over the state prison, since the "keeper" under the constitution received his appointment directly from the governor. Michigan and Pennsylvania, which transformed their boards into departments, also failed to give the new commissioner full control over the state prisons. By contrast, in Georgia and Mississippi, where the prison boards were elected by the voters, their jurisdiction was limited to the state prison system, as it was in Oklahoma and

[22] A.P.A., *Proceedings* (1925), pp. 98–102. The F.B.I. had a total of 925,000 fingerprints by 1925.

[23] Ibid., pp. 320–325; Sophonisba P. Breckinridge, *Public Welfare Administration in the United States: Select Documents*, 2d ed. (Chicago, 1927), pp. 557–560; Clair Wilcox, "State Organization for Penal Administration," *J.C.L.C.* 22 (1931): 51–60.

other southern states, where the wardens were appointed, by, and responsible to, the governor. Only Colorado required that candidates for board membership pass a civil service test. Only Massachusetts gave its commissioner full responsibility over the local jails, but that policy won sufficient praise to become a leading plank in the campaign for a federal prison system as the decade drew to a close.[24]

The move towards centralization focused increased attention on the administration of the parole system. A survey in 1915 of a dozen statistical reports revealed estimates of parole success ranging from 74 to 97 percent, but critics were quick to point out numerous flaws in these computations. The lack of a standard concept of parole violation was patent; more serious was the dearth of parole supervisors in many states, and the limited qualifications of most of those employed. It was quite appropriate therefore that the first effective project of the newly created department of public welfare in Illinois should be the establishment in 1919 of an elaborate system of parole supervision.[25] The reorganized authorities in New Jersey likewise accepted the task of establishing an effective parole system as a first responsibility. California under its indeterminate-sentence law of 1917 established a central system with full-time parole agents, and Minnesota, which had previously relied on volunteer agents, determined under its new board of control to employ parole officers. Massachusetts, on the other hand, permitted its pioneer parole system to deteriorate under a board that adopted the policy of granting paroles automatically upon the fulfillment of formal conditions. In a probing survey in Pennsylvania and elsewhere, Professor Clair Wilcox pointed up the need for more effective supervision by trained agents of limited numbers of parolees, and the Pennsylvania legislature in 1929 endorsed, though it did not adequately fund, such a program.[26]

[24] N.S.P.I., *Handbook* (1926; 1929); Breckinridge, *Public Welfare*, pp. 557–580; A.P.A., *Proceedings* (1925), pp. 322–325.

[25] Robert H. Gault, "The Parole System a Means of Protection, "*J.C.L.C.* 5 (1915): 799–806; Clair Wilcox, *The Parole of Adults from State Penal Institutions in Pennsylvania and in Other Commonwealths* (Philadelphia, 1927), pp. 194–220.

[26] A.P.A., *Proceedings* (1923), pp. 116–129; California State Board of Prison Directors, *Report* (1916–1918), p. 12; Minnesota State Board of Parole, *Report* (1924–1926); Wilcox, *Parole of Adults*, pp. 35–37, 139–141.

Several of the reorganized authorities were meanwhile considering another aspect of the problem—the selection of men for parole. It was at this point that the new school of criminologists began to score. Their psychiatric testing of individual convicts and their sociological compilation of case histories encouraged them to take a hand in selecting candidates for parole. The old prerequisites—that a man have the offer of a job, that his disciplinary record be clean, that his crime not have been too heinous or his earlier criminal record too bad, and that his former neighbors, the minister, and the judge should favor his parole—no longer seemed compelling. Under the newer theories of crime, moreover, these strictures had failed to produce the desired results. To be sure, no state had applied these older standards conscientiously for any great length of time, for the necessity to relieve overcrowding usually supplied the chief argument for an early grant of parole, while the desire to avoid the appearance of favoritism had prompted the parole officials to release most men automatically at the expiration of their minimum sentences. Widespread criticism of this practice now prompted the authorities to turn to the professionals for advice.[27]

Most states had adopted parole laws by the mid twenties and many had appointed one or more psychologists to the prison staff, but the task was overwhelming. A New York crime commission discovered that the state parole board established in 1926 was able to give each case only about five minutes and had no time to consider elaborate reports. The paroles granted from Elmira and Bedford reformatories were more carefully considered, as was true in other state reformatories. As a result of the Lewisohn commission report, New York strengthened and gave its parole board independent status. State parole boards in Massachusetts, Illinois, Kansas, and Connecticut provided for the preparation of psychological studies of each applicant, but even there the tendency, as Professor Wilcox discovered, was to grant the parole automatically at the expiration of the minimum sentence unless the scientists made a vigorous protest. Wisconsin sent case workers out to check the candidate's home environment, and Pennsylvania, in response to the Wilcox study, endeavored to improve its paroling procedures.[28]

[27] Wilcox, *Parole of Adults*, pp. 129–143; Edward Lindsey, "Historical Sketch of the Indeterminate Sentence and Parole System," *J.C.L.C.* 16 (1925): 8–69.

[28] Wilcox, *Parole of Adults*, pp. 151–165; New York State, *Report of the Special Commission on the Parole Problem* (New York, 1930), p. 12.

Confronted by this new responsibility, criminologists began to speculate on the possibility of devising predictability tests. Sam B. Warner, who made the first deliberate effort in 1923 when he studied the parole records of 600 men released from Concord Reformatory, half of them successes and half failures, failed to identify any significant criminal characteristics. Hastings Hart in a restudy of Warner's data reached a more optimistic conclusion. Ernest W. Burgess at Chicago checked the records of 3,000 Illinois parolees against a list of twenty-two selected factors and produced a schedule of prognostic scores that spurred students elsewhere to join the search for prediction techniques.[29]

Public confidence in the effectiveness of parole was considerably shaken in the late twenties by a number of studies of the ratio of success. Most of the disappointing results could be blamed, in the opinion of Professor Wilcox, on the lack or inadequacy of supervision, and a session on parole at the Association congress in 1920 produced a list of ten recommended standards to assist the states in correcting this situation. Hastings Hart was so confident of the ultimate success of parole that he actively promoted its extension to misdemeanants, citing promising moves in that direction in a dozen states.

The courts used the somewhat parallel provision for probation more freely in misdemeanant cases, and here the need for supervision was repeatedly emphasized. The National Probation Association, organized in 1907, took up the campaign for state supervision, and in 1924 reported the employment of 2,658 salaried probation officers in thirty states. But, with upwards of 200,000 probationers released each year, the degree of supervision left much to be desired. A study in 1923 of the results of probation in Massachusetts, where the provisions for supervision were most extensive, concluded that 83 percent had successfully completed their terms.[30] Several other early studies of the results of probation in New York, Illinois and elsewhere, reported ratios of success that hovered around 70 percent, which, though disappointing, was much better than the ratios of

[29] Sam B. Warner, "Factors Determining Parole from the Massachusetts Reformatory," *J.C.L.C.* 14 (1923): 172–207; Hornell Hart, "Predicting Parole Success," *J.C.L.C.* 14 (1923): 405–413; Ernest W. Burgess, "Factors Determining Success or Failure on Parole," in Andrew A. Bruce *et al, The Workings of the Indeterminate-Sentence Law and the Parole System in Illinois* (1928; reprinted Montclair, N.J., 1968), pp. 203–249.

[30] A.P.A., *Proceedings* (1921), pp. 8–10; (1924), pp. 238–245.

reformatory and parole success as revised downward by the Gluecks and others in the late twenties. The effect was to emphasize the need for a better classification of offenders before the courts and on reception by the penal authorities and for improved supervision on probation and parole.[31]

New Construction and Operation

The persistent problem confronting most states was the relief of overcrowded prisons. The slack building programs of the war years left prison officials unprepared to cope with the mounting populations of the twenties. Several states launched ambitious building programs, but the budgets these projects forecast, both for construction and upkeep, dismayed all but the most affluent legislatures. Fortunately the scientists were ready with an alternative. Their studies of individual convicts suggested the practicability of classifying inmates for confinement in maximum-, medium-, and minimum-security prisons with the assurance of economy and the probability of reduced recidivism. Experiments with road and farm camps fitted into this program and encouraged new innovations in prison architecture. Promising developments commenced in several states, but before their merits could be tested in the midst of growing inmate hostilities the onset of the great depression presented new and unexpected difficulties.

Faced with the reality of mounting prison populations, several states engaged in a contest, the folly of which later became apparent, to build the largest penitentiary. In 1914 Warden Edmund Allen of Illinois had protested that the proposed new outsize prison at Stateville, to replace the old one at Joliet, would be more costly and less efficient than a cluster of widely scattered medium-security cottage units. Before he had a chance to initiate that proposal a shift in politics cost him his job. His successor launched construction in 1917 of a mammoth penitentiary on a design that reflected Bentham's Panopticon. The design called for eight circular cellhouses clustering around a central dining hall. When a riot erupted shortly after the first three were completed in the early twenties, it

[31] New York State Probation Commission, *Probation in New York State: A Review of the Development and the Use of Probation from October 1, 1907 to September 30, 1921* (Albany, 1922); Charles L. Chute, "State Supervision of Probation," *J.C.L.C.* 8 (1918): 823–828; Wickersham Commission, *Report No. 9: Penal Institutions, Probation and Parole*, pp. 153–161.

was discovered that the supervision provided from a central guard post left much to be desired. A design change equipped a fourth circular house with dormitory units for low-risk inmates, while a new, maximum-security, inside cellblock, on the traditional rectangular design, brought the total capacity, two in a cell, up to 3,250 by the late twenties.[32]

California erected new cellblocks at its two old prisons, adding 500 at Folsom and 800 at San Quentin. The new cells were 10.5 by 4.5 by 7.5 feet in size and of modern construction with a toilet, lavatory, and double-deck bunks in each, thus increasing the capacity of these prisons to 1,700 and 3,500 respectively. Only insane inmates enjoyed the luxury of a single cell.[33] Michigan was content to crowd its mounting population of over 2,000 inmates into the less than 1,000 cells and rooms of old Jackson prison in the mid twenties, while construction of a new penitentiary to house 5,510 prisoners progressed within a 64-acre enclosure on the outskirts of the city. With the aid of prison labor, half the structure was ready for occupancy by the end of the decade when the convict population already exceeded 3,000.[34]

Ohio and Missouri met the convict-housing problem by overcrowding existing facilities. In 1925 Ohio had over 2,500 convicts jammed into 840 old cells and dormitories at Columbus. Its reformatory was crowding two men into each of its 900 cells while rushing construction of a new dormitory for farm workers outside the wall. The situation in Ohio worsened as the decade advanced, but it did not rival that in Missouri, which in 1925 confined over 2,800 convicts in the 970 cells of its old prison at Jefferson City. Its reformatory at Boonville was likewise overcrowded. So many parolees were being recommitted that the judges sent most new commitments to the penitentiary, which developed three camps on outlying farms as its population climbed to 4,000 during the decade.[35]

[32]Gladys A. Erickson, *Warden Ragen of Joliet* (New York, 1957), pp. 95–98; N.S.P.I., *Handbook* (1926), pp. 191–193; U.S. Bureau of Prisons, *Handbook of Correctional Institution Design and Construction* (Washington, D.C., 1949), pp. 69–70.

[33]California State Board of Prison Directors, *Reports* (1914; 1918; 1924); N.S.P.I., *Handbook* (1926), pp. 108–109, 120.

[34]N.S.P.I., *Handbook* (1926), pp. 286–288; (1933), pp. 439–442; U.S. Bur. Pris. *Handbook Design*, pp. 67–68.

[35]Ohio General Assembly. Joint Committee on Prisons and Reformatories, *The Penal Problem in Ohio* (Columbus, 1926); Missouri Department of Penal Institutions, *Report* (1929–1930), pp. 6–7, 151–152; N.S.P.I., *Handbook* (1926), pp. 324–326, 462–463; (1933), pp. 780–782, 808–810.

These five states had equipped themselves with one or more security prisons, one or more adult reformatories, and numerous farm camps. Each had also achieved a measure of administrative centralization and had undertaken studies of the inmate population. Illinois, as we have seen, had appointed a state criminologist. But none of the five had undertaken to redistribute its swollen population of inmates among a range of specialized institutions as several eastern states were endeavoring to do. Perhaps the explanation lay in part in the growing influence of the psychologists and sociologists who were engaging in penological research in the colleges and universities of the northeastern states and in part in the stable political traditions of the area.

New York, already equipped with a variety of institutions, made the first moves toward a classification program. The long agitation of reform groups, notably the New York Prison Association, and the criminological studies of Dr. Davis at Bedford and Dr. Glueck at Sing Sing had prepared the state for a forward step in this direction. The scattered prisons that already dotted the landscape of this most populous state and the old practice of transferring convicts from one prison to another facilitated the adoption of scientific principles of classification. With the opening at Comstock of Great Meadow prison without walls in 1911, and the conversion a decade later of the branch reformatory at Napanoch into an institution for defective delinquents, New York had acquired a diversified group of nine adult penal institutions. Zealous efforts on the part of backers of several of these institutions to secure desired improvements, however, delayed the conversion of Sing Sing into a central classification clinic. Instead, the state provided for the construction of two of four proposed new cellblocks there, started work on a new cellblock at Auburn, and launched reconstruction of an old block at Elmira to equip it with outside cells. The state built a wall around the yard at Wallkill to improve its security and constructed dining halls and remodeled other facilities in every institution. Mounting impatience for the creation of a central classification system prompted the appointment of Dr. Walter N. Thayer as commissioner of correction in 1930 and the creation of a temporary investigating commission under Sam A. Lewisohn to recommend forthright action.[36]

[36] New York Commission to Investigate Prison Administration and Construction, *Report* (1931); N.S.P.I., *Handbook* (1926), pp. 402–441; (1933), pp. 586–764.

While New York procrastinated on classification, Massachusetts supplied new initiative. The Bay State, with a long tradition of leadership in penal reform, rivalled New York in the early creation of specialized institutions. Under the able administration of Sanford Bates, appointed commissioner of corrections in 1919, the state remodeled the oldest cellblock at Charlestown, converting each pair of two small cells into one and reducing the population by transfering the younger men to Concord Reformatory and placing others in road camps. In addition to its farm camp for misdemeanants, the state opened an institution for defective delinquents at Bridgewater in 1922, a year after New York's pioneer action in this respect. State-appointed psychiatrists examined convicts on their arrival at each prison and reformatory and at the local houses of correction as well. Bates resigned in 1928 to become director of the newly created U. S. Bureau of Prisons, but before he left Massachusetts he launched preparations for the development of a new state prison at Norfolk and late in 1927 appointed Howard B. Gill as superintendent. Dr. Gill, formerly the purchasing agent for federal prisons, was acquainted with the plans for new institutions such as the Federal Reformatory for Women built that year at Alderson, West Virginia, and the new construction at Rockview in Pennsylvania. In planning his new medium-security prison he adapted the so-called cottage pattern of Alderson and incorporated some of the open-cell and glazed-tile construction of the second cellblock at Rockview, creating a uniquely new penal design. With a contingent of convicts transferred from Charlestown, he commenced construction of a wall and the first cottages in 1928. A program of psychiatric interviews and social case studies, commenced with the aid of the state psychiatrist, soon attracted a special grant from the Bureau of Social Hygiene and set the stage for the development of a classification clinic in the early thirties.[37]

Pennsylvania, after shifting along for half a century with two outmoded prisons, Cherry Hill and Riverside Western, made several promising new starts. An ambitious plan to gather the entire convict population into one gigantic penitentiary at Rockview near State College was checked in 1913, and, after considerable debate, only

[37] Massachusetts Commissioner of Corrections, *Reports* (1927), pp. 4–6; (1928), pp. 4–8; (1930), pp. 4–40; U.S. Bur. Pris., *Handbook Design*, pp. 99–103, 133; Sanford Bates, *Prisons and Beyond* (New York, 1936), pp. 1–15.

one maximum-security cellblock was built. The administration of its 500 cells was attached to the western penitentiary. The establishment of a department of welfare in 1921 brought the management of prison industry, education, and parole under its authority but failed to centralize the eastern and western branches of the penal system. The department did, however, extend its supervision in 1927 over the county jails and promoted the development of psychiatric examination in all state institutions. A rapidly growing convict population in the western districts prompted the construction at Rockview in 1927 of medium-security cellhouses with 512 outside rooms lined with colored glazed tile to enhance their cleanliness and avoid the customary prison palor. The combination of maximun-, medium-, and minimum-security accommodations at this farm colony encouraged the development there of a classification clinic that made good use of professional talent at the nearby State College.[38]

It was New Jersey, however, a state that had never before aspired to penological distinction, which assumed leadership in the first decade after the war. A shocking regime of brutality at the state prison in Trenton, exposed by the *New York Post* in a series of articles in 1916, prompted the appointment of an investigating committee. Headed by Dwight Morrow, ably supported by Professor George Kirchwey, it made a probing study and recommended basic reforms, including the establishment of a State Board of Control with authority over both the penal and the welfare agencies. That board named as its first commissioner Burdette G. Lewis who soon enlisted the assistance of Dr. Edward A. Doll as director of classification and parole in developing a classification procedure. With the aid of Calvin Derrick they devised a plan for a centralized parole bureau. The state board authorized the appointment of a psychiatrist, a psychologist, and an educational director at each institution and outlined the procedures they should follow in examining new commitments and preparing recommendations for classification. But the board recognized the authority of the local board of managers of each institution to fix the date and conditions

---

[38]Pennsylvania Secretary of Welfare, *Reports* (1928), pp. 79–92; (1930), pp. 4–5, 114–125; U.S. Bur. Pris., *Handbook Design*, pp. 35–36, 39, 96–97.

of parole. Commissioner Lewis had some difficulty in establishing a centralized authority, but the detailed directions prepared under his leadership helped to coordinate the classification efforts at the several institutions.

The appointment of Dr. William J. Ellis as commissioner after a political overturn in 1925 brought a new surge forward. Ellis had been the assistant and then the successor of Dr. Doll as director of classification and enlisted his assistance in formulating a policy of institutional differentiation to accommodate various classes of inmates. He speeded the construction of permanent buildings at Leesburg, the prison farm, in order to relieve the pressure of overcrowding at Trenton and to permit a test of minimum-security treatment. He pressed ahead with the building program at the women's reformatory at Clinton, and launched the more substantial development of a new reformatory for men at Annandale. He engaged a young professor of psychology, Dr. F. Lovell Bixby, to head the revitalized division of classification. Although the warden at the state prison at Trenton retained a measure of independence, Bixby, backed by Ellis, was able in the late twenties to develop a procedure for classification that standardized the testing of newly sentenced convicts throughout the state's increasingly diversified penal facilities.[39] Together they perfected a marking system designed to enlist the cooperation of convicts in speeding their own parole.

Several of the newly centralized authorities elsewhere likewise developed diversified penal institutions and endeavored to provide classification programs to service them. A comprehensive survey of the penal system of Texas in 1924, spurred by dismaying deficits in its farming operations, prompted the state to construct an industrial prison at Sugar Land and to erect new dormitories at its large Eastham farm, but a proposed plan to develop a central clearing-house to classify and distribute the convicts more effectively was forgotten. Alabama, stimulated by an investigation of its jails by

[39] New Jersey Prison Inquiry Commission, *Report* (1917), pp. 12–77; New Jersey State Prison *Report* (1920–1921), pp. 18–20, 74–102; National Society of Penal Information (1933 on, Osborne Association), *News Bulletin* 1 (August 1930): 5–8; James Leiby, *Charity and Correction in New Jersey: A History of State Welfare Institutions* (New Brunswick, 1967), pp. 251–259; F. Lovell Bixby, "Classification, Credit Marking and Parole: The New Jersey Plan," (Typescript, 1930, courtesy of the author.)

Hastings Hart during the war, erected a new prison at Kilby on the old Baltimore model, and, when the old coal company leases expired in 1928, acquired a third large penal farm and organized a number of road camps but made no effort to classify its prisoners scientifically. Virginia achieved a greater diversity of institutions, including a farm camp for defective delinquents, another for aged convicts, and still another for women. It remodeled its old penitentiary at Richmond and established several model road camps. In the process it discovered a need to classify its convicts and turned to New Jersey and New York for assistance. In Maryland, Harold E. Donnell, formerly an assistant of Osborne at Portsmouth, not only developed diversified housing units at a new state penal farm at Roxbury but also secured the aid of several scholars in a study of the social background and psychiatric character of new commitments in an effort to place them in appropriate units.[40]

Most of the other states fell into one or the other of two categories. Some, like Wisconsin and Minnesota, had achieved fairly adequate penal systems before the war and by increasing their road or farm camp facilities met the needs of stable or slowly rising convict populations without difficulty. Connecticut and other New England and several Western states belonged to this group. In contrast, another group of states, while escaping the acute problems confronted by Ohio and Missouri, faced their mounting convict populations with surprising equanimity. Indiana and Kansas developed farm colonies; West Virginia and North Carolina placed increasing numbers in road camps; Mississippi and Louisiana added new facilities on their penal plantations, while Florida and Oklahoma crowded new arrivals into existing cells or dormitories that were already overcrowded a few short years after their construction. Many of these states, by defraying most of the cost of their penal systems from inmate production on state farms or under varied leases and contracts, avoided serious challenges until the onset of the depression and the passage of the Hawes-Cooper Bill

[40] Texas Committee on Prisons, *Summary of Texas Prison Survey* (1924), pp. 8–47; Texas Joint Legislative Committee on Organization and Economy, *Report* 8 (1933): 22–27; Hastings H. Hart, *Social Problems of Alabama* (Montgomery, 1918), pp. 69–70; Virginia Penitentiary, *Report* (1932), pp. 939–947; *News Bulletin* 1 (October 1930): 7–11; 4 (August 1933): 6.

disrupted their systems and forced new decisions in the early thirties.[41]

The most promising new beginning of the late twenties was the organization of the United States Bureau of Prisons. An increasing number of federal offenses in the postwar years under the prohibition laws and the interstate social and economic regulations had crowded the three federal prisons and prompted the Hoover administration to shoulder its expanding responsibilities. It established and commenced the construction of a women's reformatory at Alderson and laid plans for a men's reformatory. To assure the proper management and development of these activities President Hoover invited Sanford Bates to come to Washington as superintendent of prisons. Shortly after his arrival Bates received a report from James V. Bennett of the Federal Bureau of Efficiency, who had been asked to study the needs of the federal prisons, recommending the creation of a bureau of prisons within the Department of Justice. The proposal, endorsed by Hoover as well as Bates, was soon adopted by Congress and the president and Attorney General William D. Mitchell appointed Bates as the first director of the new bureau. Bates secured the appointment of Bennett and Austin H. MacCormick of the National Society of Penal Information as his chief assistants and together they developed a program of classification, education, industrial production, and administration that would provide a model for penal developments during the thirties.[42]

One incentive for responsible federal action was the poor treatment many federal convicts were receiving in scattered county jails. Joseph Fishman, who had served for several years as a federal inspector of the jails where federal convicts were boarded and had published a scathing indictment of the conditions that prevailed in most of these local institutions, joined the staff of the National Society of Penal Information to press for local as well as national reform.[43] Long before the federal bureau began to take effective action a number of urban counties expanded and diversified the

[41] N.S.P.I., *Handbook* (1926; 1929).

[42] Bates, *Prisons and Beyond*, pp. 14–20; Federal Penal and Correctional Institutions, *Report* (1930).

[43] Fishman, *Crucibles*.

activities of their workhouses and houses of correction. A workhouse and reformatory at Washington, D.C. commenced construction of permanent buildings on a 1150-acre farm in 1923, and several county penitentiaries in New York and Pennsylvania expanded their facilities. But the most striking improvements were achieved in a half dozen states that followed the example of Massachusetts in developing state farms for misdemeanants and assumed the responsibility for the inspection and psychiatric services at their local jails.[44]

The federal prison system was likewise responding to the mounting demand for separate and adequate accommodations for women prisoners. In an effort to end the practice of boarding women convicts in any one of the five state prisons for women or nine women's reformatories, Congress in 1924 appropriated funds for the purchase of a 300-acre farm in Alderson, West Virginia for a women's reformatory. Constructed in 1927 on a cottage plan adapted from the New York State houses of refuge for women misdemeanants, it provided a new architectural model for five additional women's reformatories soon undertaken in other states, and for medium-security prisons for men as well.[45]

Changing Prison Atmosphere

The interest in psychological testing and classification was further accentuated by the changing atmosphere of most prisons. The tenets of the reformatory had widely displaced the old Auburn silent system with varied pedagogical and recreational programs but with uncertain results. Overcrowding had eradicated many of the advantages of the modernized facilities, and the relaxation of discipline had increased internal violence, especially between inmates, and had resulted on occasion in riotous outbreaks. Since increased freedom of movement and expression had released hostilities rather than producing cooperation, even hardheaded administrators began to look to the scientists to weed out the incorrigibles and perfect methods of treatment for their more hopeful charges. Unfortunately the widening effect of the anti-convict labor laws was reducing the revenue of many prisons and

[44] Kober, comp., *Charitable Institutions*, pp. 49–78; Louis N. Robinson, "The Relation of Jails to County and State," *J.C.L.C.* 20 (1929): 396–420.

[45] Lekkerkerker, *Reformatories*, pp. 117–119, 291–293.

discouraged state legislatures from backing new penological programs. Mounting crime ratios in the affluent postwar years compounded the difficulties in several states, and the onset of the depression, instead of relieving this situation, brought new fiscal problems. Fortunately the new display of federal responsibility offered some hope for the future.

Many of the striking changes that occurred in American prisons during the twenties were superficial in character but they had a profound cumulative effect. Striped uniforms and lockstep marching were the memories of an earlier decade, as was the compulsion to produce, but the drab, ill-fitting garments and the often aimless shuffling from one prison yard to another seemed an uncertain gain. Most of the formal educational programs, designed originally to assist illiterate convicts of immigrant origins to learn to read and speak English, no longer served a wide need, and a survey in 1920 revealed that even in the reformatories most of the academic and industrial instruction was administered by poorly trained instructors, few of whom had ever entered college.

For the mass of convicts the prospect was dull, but alert individuals could find reading matter in the prison libraries, and at Waupun in Wisconsin and a dozen other prisons they could enroll in university extension courses. In an increasing number of prisons capable inmates could participate in the compilation of an occasional or regular prison journal. All but two of the twelve reformatories visited in 1920 had inmate bands, and numerous prisons were similarly provided before the end of the decade. Even more popular was the practice of showing motion pictures once or twice a week, a feature reported by 85 of 109 prisons surveyed in the late twenties.[46]

Yet the freer movement and the doubling up in the cells brought hazards as well as advantages. As opportunities for violence and abnormal sex activities increased, the attempt to maintain order became more difficult, and while many vicious disciplinary practices

---

[46] Frank F. Nalder, *The American State Reformatory: With Special Reference to Its Educational Aspects* (Berkeley, 1920), pp. 320–422; Florence R. Curtis, *The Libraries of the American State and National Institutions for Defectives, Dependents, and Delinquents* (Minneapolis, 1918); Philip M. Hauser, "Motion Pictures in Penal and Correctional Institutions" (Master's thesis, University of Chicago, 1933.)

were now officially banned, the deprivation of privileges did not always suffice, and confinement to "the hole" and other outmoded practices continued in many prisons. The Prison Association devoted a session to a discussion of the treatment of venereal disease in women in reformatories at its Boston congress in 1923 and endeavored three years later at Pittsburgh to refute a popular cry against the pampering of criminals.[47]

The biggest change in the internal life of American prisons was the rapid decline in the number of inmates employed during the twenties. Between 1895 and 1923 anti-contract laws had effected a gradual drop in the percentage employed from 72 to 61. Now suddenly the employed dropped to 52 percent. The situation was more critical where the majority of those employed were engaged at makeshift maintenance jobs devised merely to occupy the inmate's time. As the campaign of organized labor and other groups to stop the exploitation of prison labor progressed, additional states abandoned the contract and piece-price systems and turned to public-account industries, as in Minnesota and California, or to the state-use system on the New York model. Organized labor and some management groups were also opposed to the lucrative public-account systems, but some prison officials were able to find industries with large local markets and little or no competition within the state. Only the state-use system had the full approval of organized labor and of many reform groups that sought to reduce the influence of contractors and independent industrial managers on prison administration. The percentage employed at state-use increased from 33 to 65 in this decade and a half, but much of this employment was nominal since the other state departments preferred to purchase their supplies on the open market. New York State, with the longest experience and a record of innovative enterprise, had only slightly over a fifth of its convicts employed as the decade drew to a close.[48]

Despite its stringent laws, labor in New York and in other states with similar laws felt threatened by the convict production of the

---

[47]A.P.A., *Proceedings* (1923), pp. 107–115; (1926), pp. 78–81.
[48]A.P.A., *Proceedings* (1919), pp. 120–126; (1926), pp. 153–157; U.S. Bureau Labor Statistics, *Convict Labor 1923*, pp. 94–104; "Prison Labor in the United States," in "Notes," *J.C.L.C.* 24 (1933): 615–618; New York Prison Association, *Report* (1931), pp. 97–101.

more permissive states. Efforts to check the transport of prison-made goods across state lines failed until the Hawes-Cooper Bill, adopted by Congress in 1929, extended such power to the states. Illinois and several northeastern states hastened to take advantage of the act. This safeguarding of industrial interests increased the number of convicts made idle in other states. Only in the South, where many prisoners worked on state-owned farms or at road and levee construction, were the great majority productively employed; elsewhere the prisons were forced to multiply the maintenance jobs to reduce the evils of complete idleness.[49]

Two aspects of the mounting convict population of the postwar years reflected the impact of that epochal conflict. The war had drastically reduced the influx of immigrants to America prompting heavy industries in Northern cities to turn to the South for replacements for the constant supply of unskilled labor they needed. A new migration of Negroes to the North brought a rapid increase in the number of blacks in the prison populations of such states as Illinois, Missouri, Ohio, Michigan and Pennsylvania. Their high rate of commitment was partly due, Professor Sellin discovered, to the discrimination practiced by social and legal agencies against the Negroes because of their poverty and color. Moreover the prejudice that contributed to their conviction followed them into the many prisons where they encountered hostilities from inmates and guards, which gave rise to a new form of friction.[50] The number of men imprisoned for murder was also increasing, and whether confined on "death row" or, where capital punishment had been abolished, quartered with the rest of the prison population, their presence added tension within the inmate society and between inmates and the guards. The fact that blacks accused of such crimes were more likely to be convicted than whites tended to increase their proportion and to compound the difficulties.[51]

The rapid introduction of organized sports into American prisons represented another effort to absorb the time of unemployed inmates

[49] U.S. Bur. Labor Stat., *Convict Labor 1923;* E. Stagg Whitin, "The Employment of Prisoners," *News Bulletin* 1 (August 1930): 3–6; U.S. Bureau of Foreign and Domestic Commerce, *Prison Industries* (Washington, D.C., 1929), pp. 34–40.

[50] Thorsten Sellin, "The Negro Criminal," *Annals* 140 (November 1928): 52–64; Louise V. Kennedy, *The Negro Peasant Turns City-Ward: Effects of Recent Migrations to Northern Centers* (New York, 1930), pp. 182–191.

[51] Harrington C. Brearley, *Homicide in the United States* (1932; reprinted Montclair, N.J., 1969), pp. 21–22, 27, 97–116.

in peaceful activities. Intramural baseball games and special games with visiting teams from neighboring institutions attracted participation and grandstand interest and in some cases developed an institutional spirit that served to check if not to eliminate outbreaks of violence. These activities proved most constructive in prisons where, as in Missouri, Warden Painter was able to entrust the conduct of recreational programs to an inmate council somewhat after the model of Osborne's welfare leagues.[52]

One decided benefit of administrative reorganization was a more responsible attention to sanitary and health matters. A survey in 1927 revealed that 97 physicians, of whom 57 were part time, had charge of the medical departments of all the prisons and reformatories in the country and that all but five made medical examinations of all new commitments. The survey found also that prison hospitals had only minimal facilities and that less than half supplied any dental treatment. The wide introduction of the Wassermann blood test for detection of syphilis constituted a positive advance during the twenties. Increased evidence of drug addiction in several prisons presented another concern to the medical authorities. Psychiatric and other researches conducted by staff and visiting professionals in a few of the women's reformatories and in several progressive prisons with rudimentary clinics helped to create a new attitude of concern for the individual prisoner.[53]

But few of these efforts won any mention, let alone commendation, in the increasing number of inmate accounts of prison conditions. Eugene V. Debs, the era's most celebrated prisoner, condemned the whole penal system as a prop for capitalism. Charles L. Clark, an habitual criminal looking back after thirty-five years in various prisons, blamed the inability of most prison officers to dispell the hostility of convicts for the failure of practically all

---

[52] Tannenbaum, *Osborne*, pp. 125–134; Austin H. MacCormick, *The Education of Adult Prisoners* (New York, 1931), pp. 292–310; Frank L. Rector, *Health and Medical Service in American Prisons and Reformatories* (New York, 1929), p. 223.

[53] Rector, *Health*, pp. 59–68, 102, 163–185; Edith R. Spaulding, "The Importance of Adopting the Wasserman Test for Syphilis as a Routine Measure in the Examination of the Inmates of Penal Institutions," *J.C.L.C.* 4 (1914): 712–715; Amos O. Squire, "Penal Institution Hospital Treatment of Venereal Diseases," *J.C.L.C.* 9 (1918): 253–259; Lawrence Kolb, "Drug Addiction in Its Relation to Crime," *Mental Hygiene* 9 (1925): 74–89.

reformatory programs.[54] Several inmate accounts supplied lurid details of prison conditions and reported sensational brutalities such as the electric shock "humming bird," which some officers resorted to when the lash and other corporal punishments were banned.[55] All reported the continued use of forbidden penalties in hidden torture chambers, but two inmate authors emphasized other matters. Robert Joyce Tasker writing from inside San Quentin, and Victor F. Nelson from Charlestown, agreed that neither the existing brutalities nor the persistence of torture properly characterised prisons, but the degrading "suppression," the deadening "habit," and the enervating "monotony" which combined to produce the prevailing prison stupor that vitiated all correctional efforts. Nelson included a candid discussion of the inmate's sex problems which led to the destruction of the social standards on which rehabilitation depended.[56]

Inmate accounts reflected the views of a literate minority, but numerous disturbances, incendiary fires, and riots expressed the mounting mass protest. Fires and work stoppages as a result of machine breakages had been endemic to the penal system even under the restraints of the Auburn ststem. Desperate breaks for freedom had been frequent especially in the South, and some had resulted in wider disturbances or riots. But the concerted riots that broke out in Joliet in 1918 and in a half dozen prisons during the next three years marked the reaction of men in crowded prisons to frustrations and brutalities suffered under the partly relaxed discipline of the reformatory era. A second series of concerted riots in 1929 spread from Leavenworth in Kansas to Canon City in Colorado, to Auburn and Dannemora in New York. These distrubances, and some of lesser magnitude in other prisons, protested the bad food, the overcrowding, the enforced idleness, the tolerance of violence alternating with seemingly arbitrary punishments, and the shifting policies of prison boards which by denying expected benefits or paroles often aroused vocal individuals. Even as wardens, such as

[54] Eugene V. Debs, *Walls and Bars* (1927: reprinted Montclair, N.J., 1973); Charles E. Chapin, *Charles Chapin's Story Written in Sing Sing Prison* (New York, 1920); Charles L. Clark and Earle E. Eubank, *Lockstep and Corridor: Thirty-five Years of Prison Life* (Cincinnati, 1927).

[55] Ernest Booth, *Stealing Through Life* (New York, 1929); Albert Wehde, *Since Leaving Home* (Chicago, 1923); Wickersham Commission, *Report No. 9*, pp. 31–36.

[56] Robert Joyce Tasker, *Grimhaven* (New York, 1928); Victor F. Nelson, *Prison Days and Nights* (Boston, 1933).

A.L. Bowen at Joliet, suppressed these outbreaks with force and the renewed use of many old restraints, they recognized that repression was not the answer and that more meaningful jobs, more constructive training, and a more scientific classification were needed to develop effective penal programs.[57]

BIBLIOGRAPHIC NOTE

The *Proceedings of the American Prison Association* provide continuing commentary and analysis of correctional developments as do many useful articles in the *Journal of Criminal Law and Criminology*. The reports of a number of special state and federal commissions are of excellent documentary value to the study of the criminal justice system in these years. Among these are Cleveland Foundation, *Criminal Justice in Cleveland,* Roscoe Pound and Felix Frankfurter, eds. (1922; this and the subsequent three titles reprinted Montclair, N.J., 1968); Illinois Association for Criminal Justice, *The Illinois Crime Survey,* John H. Wigmore, ed. (1929); Missouri Association for Criminal Justice, *The Missouri Crime Survey* (1926); and— of particular importance—U.S. National Commission on Law Observance and Enforcement (Wickersham Commission), *Reports,* 14 vols. (1931).

The nine titles in the Modern Criminal Science Series, translated and published under the editorship of Professor John H. Wigmore, are important for an understanding of the work of those European criminologists who influenced American penology. The works are: C. Bernaldo de Quiros, *Modern Theories of Criminality* (Boston, 1911); Hans Gross, *Criminal Psychology* (1911; this and the subsequent five titles reprinted Montclair, N.J., 1968); Cesare Lombroso, *Crime, Its Causes and Remedies* (1911); Raymond Saleilles, *The Individualization of Punishment* (1911); Gabriel Tarde, *Penal Philosophy* (1912); Gustave Aschaffenburg, *Crime and Its Repression* (1913); Raffaele Garofalo, *Criminology* (1914); Willem A. Bonger, *Criminality and Economic Conditions* (Boston, 1916); and Enrico Ferri, *Criminal Sociology* (Boston, 1917).

Two works which offer a philosophical treatment of punishment are Alfred C. Ewing, *The Morality of Punishment: With Some Suggestions for a General Theory of Ethics* (1929; reprinted Montclair, N.J., 1970) and Heinrich Oppenheimer, *The Rationale of Punishment* (1913; reprinted Montclair, N.J., 1975).

[57]*Social Work Year Book* 1 (1929): 319–320; A.L. Bowen, "The Joliet Prison and the Riots of June 5," *J.C.L.C.* 8 (1917): 576–585; Wickersham Commission, *Report No. 9,* pp. 34–36; *New York Tribune,* 18 February 1935.

Other works of value to a study of this period include: Sanford Bates, *Prisons and Beyond* (New York, 1936); Ernest Booth, *Stealing Through Life* (New York, 1929); Harrington C. Brearley, *Homicide in the United States* (1932; reprinted Montclair, N.J., 1969); Sophonisba P. Breckinridge, *Public Welfare Administration in the United States: Select Documents*, 2d ed. (Chicago, 1927); Sophonisba P. Breckinridge and Edith Abbott, *The Delinquent Child and the Home* (New York, 1912); Andrew A. Bruce *et al*, *The Workings of the Indeterminate-Sentence Law and the Parole System in Illinois* (1928; reprinted Montclair, N.J., 1968); Charles E. Chapin, *Charles Chapin's Story Written in Sing Sing Prison* (New York, 1920); Charles L. Clark and Earle E. Eubank, *Lockstep and Corridor: Thirty-five Years of Prison Life* (Cincinnati, 1927); Stanley P. Davies, *Social Control of the Mentally Deficient* (New York, 1930); Eugene V. Debs, *Walls and Bars* (1927; reprinted Montclair, N.J., 1973); Richard L. Dugdale, *The Jukes: A Study in Crime, Pauperism, Disease, and Heredity*, 5th ed. (New York, 1891); Gladys A. Erickson, *Warden Ragen of Joliet* (New York, 1957); Mabel R. Fernald, Mary H.S. Hayes, and Almena Dawley, *A Study of Women Delinquents in New York State* (1920; reprinted Montclair, N.J., 1928); Joseph F. Fishman, *Crucibles of Crime: The Shocking Story of the American Jail* (1923; reprinted Montclair, N.J., 1969); S. Sheldon Glueck, *Mental Disorder and the Criminal Law* (Boston, 1925); Charles Goring, *The English Convict: A Statistical Study*, unabridged ed., together with *Schedule of Measurements and General Anthropological Data* (1913; reprinted Montclair, N.J., 1972) William Healy, *The Individual Delinquent: A Text-Book of Diagnosis and Prognosis for All Concerned in Understanding Offenders* (1915; reprinted Montclair, N.J. 1969); George M. Kober, comp., *Charitable and Reformatory Institutions in the District of Columbia: History and Development* (Washington, D.C., 1927); James Leiby, *Charity and Correction in New Jersey: A History of State Welfare Institutions* (New Brunswick, 1967); Eugenia E. Lekkerkerker, *Reformatories for Women in the United States* (Groningen, 1931); George F. Lydston, *Addresses and Essays* (Louisville, 1892); Austin H. MacCormick, *The Education of Adult Prisoners* (New York, 1931); Frank F. Nalder, *The American State Reformatory: With Special Reference to Its Educational Aspects* (Berkeley, 1920); National Society of Penal Information (1933 on, Osborne Association), *Handbook of American Prisons* (New York, 1925; 1926); Victor F. Nelson, *Prison Days and Nights* (Boston, 1933); Thomas Mott Osborne, *Society and Prisons: Some Suggestionns for a New Penology* (1916; reprinted Montclair, N.J., 1975); Roscoe Pound, *Criminal Justice in America* (New York, 1930); Frank L. Rector, *Health and Medical Service in American Prisons and Reformatories* (New York, 1929); Jesse O. Stutsman, *Curing the Criminal* (New York, 1926); Frank Tannenbaum, *Osborne of Sing Sing* (Chapel Hill, 1933);

Robert Joyce Tasker, *Grimhaven* (New York, 1928); Frederic M. Thrasher, *The Gang: A Study of 1,313 Gangs in Chicago* (Chicago, 1927); U.S. Bureau of Labor Statistics, *Convict Labor in 1923* (Washington, D.C., 1925); U.S. Bureau of Prisons, *Handbook of Correctional Institution Design and Construction* (Washington, D.C., 1949); Albert Wehde, *Since Leaving Home* (Chicago, 1923); Clair Wilcox, *The Parole of Adults from State Penal Institutions in Pennsylvania and in Other Commonwealths* (Philadelphia, 1927).

12.

CLASSIFICATION AND REHABILITATION: 1930–1950

Despite the traditionally close alignment of prison management with politics, a number of scholarly studies had an impact on penal developments in the 1930s and 1940s comparable to that of the far-reaching New Deal. Successive studies by the Gluecks and others of the subsequent careers of reformatory graduates revealed a shocking amount of recidivism. And when Austin MacCormick, after several probing investigations of the nation's prisons and reformatories, reported that few if any had effective educational programs, the disillusionment increased.[1] The outbreak of a half dozen riots in 1929 and a disastrous fire a year later in the Ohio state prison at Columbus, which took 322 lives, added to the disillusionment. It was in fact shattering enough to prompt reformers and some practical wardens alike to reexamine their respective theories and practices and to seek new insights and procedures. Fortunately the psychiatric studies, the experiments with classification in New Jersey and with convict participation in New York, all supplied suggestive hints to a new group of federal prison administrators whose programs soon provided models for penological advances.

Again the papers and discussions at the annual meetings of the American Prison Association highlighted the trends. These sessions

[1] Sheldon and Eleanor T. Glueck, *Five Hundred Criminal Careers* (New York, 1930); Austin H. MacCormick, *The Education of Adult Prisoners* (New York, 1931).

rarely reflected disillusionment, and yet the Gluecks' recently published study was cited on four occasions by the speakers at the 1930 congress in Louisville. George W. Wickersham, a former president of the Association and chairman of the recently appointed National Commission on Law Observance and Enforcement, cited the pessimistic findings of Drs. Sheldon and Eleanor Glueck concerning the recidivism of 80 percent of 500 graduates of Concord Reformatory as a "striking demonstration of the need for a thorough review of the whole subject."[2] But Austin MacCormick hastened on the first morning of that congress, in a paper on "Education and the Library in the Prison," to reveal that his critical judgment on the performance of reformatory programs did not imply defeatism; instead it pointed up the necessity for a more positive and individualized approach. And as a follow up at the last session, young Dr. F. Lovell Bixby read a paper describing the development of classification in New Jersey from a passive plan to separate dissimilar inmates into a positive effort to promote individualized treatment.[3]

Federal Leadership

But the outstanding contribution of that congress was its demonstration of the capacity of the Federal Bureau of Prisons to render positive leadership. James V. Bennett, an assistant director, in a paper on "Prison Industries," outlined the problems confronting state as well as federal prisons. Both faced the impending restraints of the Hawes-Cooper Bill as well as the industrial retrenchment enforced by the depression. Bennett described the efforts the federal bureau was making to develop diversified industries to produce articles for use in other federal departments; he urged the states to establish similar state-use programs. Sanford Bates, as director of the federal bureau, reported on the success of the American delegates to the Tenth International Prison Congress at Prague in amending a resolution favoring solitary confinement to permit the flexibility required under a classification system that seeks to treat prisoners individually according to their needs. Bates in another paper described the efforts of the federal bureau to

[2] American Prison Association, *Proceedings* (1930), pp. 104, 108, 186, 313.
[3] Ibid., pp. 35–48, 391–397.

develop diversified institutions and programs to meet the needs of the expanding federal system.[4]

But of course the vigorous enunciation of positive programs did not assure their immediate adoption, much less their practical success. The issues debated at the 1930 congress continued to command attention at later congresses. And in 1933 when the Association met at Atlantic City and heard a number of papers describing the classification procedures and educational programs of that state's pioneering program, the haunting question again arose, "Have Our Prisons Failed?" Under the presidency of Dr. Walter N. Thayer, commissioner of the N. Y. Department of Correction, the Association heard a series of addresses by specialists in psychiatry, psychology, education and social work, as well as by law enforcement officials and penal administrators. The speakers included such men as Dr. Edgar A. Doll, Dr. William J. Ellis and Dr. Bixby all active in New Jersey, Dr. James L. McCartney, Dr. Howard B. Gill, Professor Edwin H. Sutherland and MacCormick among many others.[5] Sanford Bates, who attempted to answer the haunting question in the negative, recalled years later that when he delivered that address under the same title at a forum in Boston, a member of the audience had arisen in the question period to ask, "Have our prisons failed?" His reply as he recalled was, "No, but I have."[6]

Many prison administrators had no doubt reached the same conclusion on frustrating occasions, but in the early 1930s several hopeful new developments were appearing. And most of the advances were occurring in the federal system under the leadership of Sanford Bates. With the assistance of Dr. Hastings Hart, now with the Russell Sage Foundation, Bates had organized a training school for prison officers in 1929 in conjunction with the federal detention jail in New York.[7] While his chief assistants, MacCormick and Bennett, were busily engaged in upgrading the educational, disciplinary, and industrial programs at the three federal penitentiaries and the two reformatories in various stages of construction, Bates was formulating plans for expansion. New federal offenses

[4] Ibid., pp. 135–136, 308–320, 377–391.

[5] Ibid., (1933), pp. 160–179, 189–192, 221–225, 290–297, 305–312.

[6] Ibid., pp. 114–120; *American Journal of Correction* 19 (November-December 1957): 6.

[7] A.P.A., *Proceedings* (1930), pp. 170–174.

had boosted the inmate population from 7,170 in 1925 to 13,103 in 1930. To meet this challenge Director Bates established a number of penal camps at old World War I army posts where numerous bootleggers and moonshiners received an opportunity to perform useful services, and in the process demonstrated the viability of "open" or minimum-security institutions. Bates and his assistants also worked with Alfred Hopkins on plans for a new medium-security prison to be erected at Lewisburg, Pennsylvania.[8]

Alfred Hopkins, a New York architect who had prepared the plans for several county and state institutions in the postwar years, had made a study of penal designs abroad as well as in the states. His plans for Wallkill, which was reaching completion near Newburgh, New York, in 1930, supplied medium-security facilities for 500 inmates in outside rooms in four three-story blocks that avoided the traditional prison appearance. A prison without walls, it stirred new interest in penal design and helped to win Hopkins the contract to plan and build Lewisburg. Bates and the other American delegates to the Prague congress, who visited five modern prisons in Europe, were especially impressed with one in Brandenburg, Germany, which also had outside rooms or cells in small blocks, as at Wallkill, but grouped them to serve three classes of prisoners.[9] Hopkins, whose book on prison architecture appeared that year, was ready to incorporate that feature in his new plan together with still another European innovation, the "telephone pole" design first introduced in the Fresnes prison in France in 1898. The visit to Brandenburg, where he found a plan by Hopkins on exhibit, prepared Bates for a receptive consideration of his architect's innovative proposals for Lewisburg, which became the model for many new prisons.[10]

Lewisburg broke with earlier penitentiary design in more than one respect. The telephone-pole pattern featured a long connecting corridor, which extended from the administrative building past dining rooms, shops, and other essential facilities, and bisected the cellblocks or housing units. It provided for convenient and easily supervised interior circulation and facilitated the differentiation of

[8] Sanford Bates, *Prisons and Beyond* (New York, 1936), pp. 127–136.

[9] U.S. Bureau of Prisons, *Handbook of Correctional Institution Design and Construction* (Washington, D.C., 1949), pp. 93–94; A.P.A., *Proceedings* (1930), pp. 318–320.

[10] U.S. Bur. Pris., *Handbook Design*, pp. 70–78; Alfred Hopkins, *Prisons and Prison Buildings* (New York, 1930).

housing facilities and other services while maintaining centralized control and security. The Lewisburg plan called for three cellblocks on one side, two equipped with medium-security outside cells and one with maximum-security inside cells, and on the other side three dormitory blocks, one fitted with 140 honor rooms for inmates who earned special treatment. Built of brick and in the Italian Renaissance style, the new penitentiary not only contrasted sharply with old prison architecture, but also permitted the flexibility of administration desired by the advocates of classification.[11]

Bates and his assistants in formulating plans for the new federal bureau had committed themselves to an attempt to treat convicts as individuals. Several of MacCormick's educational and health programs had taken account of individual rather than mass needs, and to assure their full application at Chillicothe he had resigned as assistant director to become warden of that model new reformatory. But it was in 1934, when Bates appointed F. Lovell Bixby as assistant director, that the bureau embarked on a full program of classification. Dr. Bixby, in charge of the pioneer classification program in New Jersey after 1929, had perfected its examining procedures and prepared a series of reporting forms to standardize the scientific and environmental researches conducted on each new commitment. In addition to tabulating some of the personality traits, work skills, and educational needs of each inmate, Bixby had endeavored to determine the degree of their acceptance of penal discipline and had pragmatically proceeded to divide them into groups that respectively seemed to require minimum-, medium-, and maximum-security provisions. Having left the New Jersey department in 1933 to make a number of field studies for the Osborne Association, Bixby was eager on their conclusion to get back into active administration and welcomed an invitation from Bates to succeed MacCormick and develop a federal classification program.[12]

The comprehensive report of the Wickersham Commission had meanwhile appeared emphasizing among other matters the desira-

[11] U.S. Bur. Pris., *Handbook Design*, pp. 72–73.

[12] Bates, *Prisons and Beyond*, pp. 159–164; William J. Ellis, "Practical Results of the Classification Program," *Proceedings* (A.P.A., 1940), pp. 227–232; James Leiby, *Charity and Correction in New Jersey: A History of State Welfare Institutions* (New Brunswick, 1967), pp. 257–259.

bility of classifying inmates for treatment and differentiating institutions to meet inmate needs. It endorsed the action of the federal bureau in developing a penal farm for narcotics at Lexington, Kentucky, and a hospital for defective delinquents at Springfield, Missouri, and commended the establishment of a half dozen road and farm camps for the housing and employment of minimum-security inmates outside the walls. The mounting stream of federal commitments favored institutional diversification, but the vast distances that separated the federal institutions, requiring the assignment of guards and officers for several days in each transfer operation, encouraged the development of classification and treatment programs to handle a variety of inmates in each institution.[13]

Bixby accordingly developed classification committees in each prison. Composed of a psychiatrist, a psychologist, a social worker, and parole officers as well as the chaplain and industrial, educational, and disciplinary officers, they conducted separate examinations but conferred jointly on the assignment of each new commitment. As in New Jersey, the classification committee followed reports on each case, met for a reclassification at stated intervals depending on the sentence, and made recommendations for reassignment or for consideration by the parole board, which, however, had to make its determination of the date for each man's conditional release within the narrow limits set by the law. Only youthful offenders received indeterminate sentences under the federal Juvenile Delinquency Act of 1938.[14]

The upgrading of the parole service was a major aspect of the reform program both in New Jersey and in the federal service. Although the state board in New Jersey did not exercise full control, and, in fact, relied on the local boards to grant parole, and on the state prison to name its parole officers, the central board maintained more effective supervision over the rest of the system than had been attained in any other state. The federal parole system was more successfully centralized in 1930 under a paid board of parole, which

[13]U.S.National Commission on Law Observance and Enforcement (Wickersham Commission), *Report No. 9: Penal Institutions, Probation and Parole* (1931; reprinted Montclair, N.J., 1968), pp. 65–67.

[14]Osborne Association (formerly National Society of Penal Information) *News Bulletin* 7 (June 1936); James V. Bennett, *I Chose Prison* (New York, 1970), pp. 43–44.

increased the numbers of parolees from 2,644 that year to 7,964 in 1949. A probation act in 1930 launched this new federal service under the jurisdiction of the federal courts, which assured a regional coverage. It made the probation officers responsible for probationers from their courts and for the supervision of men paroled by the federal parole board to their care. Despite the wide diffusion of the locally appointed agents, the federal parole board served as a model for the states, six of which developed supervised parole systems by the close of 1937.[15]

Federal leadership was most effective in the field of prison industries. James V. Bennett, whose original investigation of federal prisons had proposed the establishment of the bureau with the object of promoting rehabilitation through work, had been given charge of this phase of the program. The impending application of the Hawes-Cooper Act had prompted Bennett and Bates to secure the enactment of a bill making it mandatory for federal departments to purchase their supplies from the prisons when and if they produced them. A major argument had been the need to keep the increasing number of federal convicts occupied in order to maintain discipline and promote rehabilitation. But Congressman Fiorello LaGuardia and others, who wished to save all jobs for free workers and to compel the government to repeal prohibition and other regulations responsible for the mounting convictions, blocked appropriations necessary to implement the prison industries. To circumvent this obstacle, Bennett, with the assistance of Eleanor Roosevelt, secured the president's backing in 1937 for a bill creating the Federal Prison Industries, Inc., a semi-independent corporation similar to the Reconstruction Finance Corporation, with power to introduce and operate prison industries on a nonprofit basis. Under its vigorous management a group of diversified industries was developed which not only met all production costs, including modest wages to the prisoners, but returned a profit of $567,698 in the second year.[16]

[15] Leiby, *Charity*, pp. 258–259; Bates, *Prisons and Beyond*, pp. 247–266; Winthrop D. Lane, "A New Day Opens for Parole," *Journal of Criminal Law and Criminology* 24 (1933): 101–104; Charles L. Chute, "The Progress of Probation and Social Treatment in the Courts," *J.C.L.C.* 24 (1933): 67–70; *News Bulletin* 9 (February 1938).

[16] Bennett, *I Chose Prison*, pp. 85–99; Bates, *Prisons and Beyond*, pp. 90–110; James V. Bennett, "Prison Industries," *Proceedings* (A.P.A., 1930), pp. 135–142.

The Response of the States

The federal example provided leadership to struggling wardens of state institutions. Few responded when Bennett warned in 1930 and again in 1934 of the possible effects of the Hawes-Cooper Act. Many expected the act to be set aside by the courts or to remain inoperative in most states. But the states, as we have seen, acted to restrict imports from out-of-state prisons, and the courts upheld the laws, driving contractors from most prisons and creating vast pools of idleness.[17] Even the adoption of a Prison Labor Code under the provisions of the National Recovery Administration, though signed by the proper officials in 21 states, failed to check the anti-importation laws. New York, one of the pioneers in resorting exclusively to production for state use, was encountering so much resistance from departmental purchasing agents that the great majority of its convicts remained idle. Nevertheless a dozen additional states turned completely to the state-use system and several others increased the number of prisoners assigned to farm and road camps.[18]

When the prison industries code lapsed, along with other N.R.A. codes following the Supreme Court decision abolishing that program, President Roosevelt issued an executive order establishing the Prison Industries Reorganization Administration. Supported by funds from the Emergency Relief Appropriations Act, its staff, headed by Louis N. Robinson, made surveys of the needs and potentialities of the prisons of 22 states and recommended construction or industrial projects to supply the desired employment. Unfortunately by the late thirties when these reports were ready the mood of the country had changed. Although E. R. Cass, general secretary of the Prison Association made an earnest effort to obtain federal grants-in-aid to the states for the development of prison industries, no such funds were forthcoming. Several states did organize industrial corporations comparable to that in the federal system, but idleness continued to blight most prisons until the

[17] Bennett, "Prisons Industries," pp. 135–142; James V. Bennett, "Prison Labor at the Crossroads," *Proceedings* (A.P.A., 1934), pp. 241–249.

[18] James V. Bennett, "Prison Labor Code," *News Bulletin* 4 (October 1933); U.S. Bureau of Labor Statistics, *Laws Relating to Prison Labor in the United States as of July 1, 1933* (Washington, D.C., 1933); A.P.A., *Proceedings* (1940), pp. 365–371.

outbreak of World War II created a new demand.[19]

Bennett, who succeeded Bates as director on his resignation in 1937, had supported Mrs. Roosevelt's efforts to promote the use of federal funds in maintaining educational programs in state prisons and reformatories. The Osborne Association, which was formed by merging the National Society of Penal Information and the Welfare League Association in 1932, was an active backer of these programs, and successfully urged the continuation of their support by the Works Progress Administration. A dozen states took advantage of these funds to establish industrial training programs to relieve the blight of idleness in penal institutions, and several improved their library services or acquired additional band instruments. Bennett did not need to resort to New Deal agencies to maintain federal services, but to make fuller use of the resources available he extended the official daylight time to permit prisoners to use the libraries and recreation rooms in the evening hours. Austin MacCormick, who had resigned his post as warden of Chillicothe in 1934 to accept an appointment under Mayor LaGuardia as Commissioner of Corrections in New York City, had renewed his ties with the Osborne Association and, with William B. Cox its director, pressed the efforts of its *News Bulletin* to promote educational and training programs in prisons throughout the country.[20]

Most of the states, hard hit by the depression, had difficulty in maintaining earlier penal standards. A few, however, seized the opportunity to secure Public Works Administration funds to aid in the construction of new buildings at an old prison as at Jefferson City, Missouri, or to speed the erection of a new prison as in Georgia. That state was at last able to abolish its vicious chain gang system and to gather all state and county convicts into its new prison on a 2000-acre farm at Reidsville. There a classification clinic selected some for assignment to minimum-security work camps scattered about the state, some who were defective or "deranged" for

[19] Frank T. Flynn, "Employment and Labor," in *Contemporary Correction,* ed. Paul W. Tappan (New York, 1951), pp. 242, 250–252; Howard B. Gill, "The Future of Prison Employment," *Proceedings* (A.P.A., 1935), pp. 179–185.

[20] Bennett, *I Chose Prison,* pp. 85–96; *News Bulletin* 6 (December 1935); 9 (April 1938): 3–6; 11 (February 1940); Osborne Association, *Handbook of American Prisons and Reformatories,* vol. 1 (New York, 1933), xxvi–xli.

transfer to the old prison at Milledgeville, but retained most of the security risks at the new prison.[21] North Carolina made eager use of P.W.A. funds to assist in building two systems of work camps, one for misdemeanants gathered from the former county chain gangs, and one for felons judged ready for assignment to road camps. With the completion in 1939 of brick cellhouses and dormitories to accommodate 85 units of 110 to 150 each in scattered but well built and secure camps, the state was able to remodel its central prison as a reception and classification center and prison hospital and won commendations from MacCormick for its accomplishments.[22]

The availability of federal funds provided the incentive in some states; the investigations of the Osborne Association stimulated action in others. In Michigan, for example, some critical comments by Cox and Bixby in 1934 prompted Governor Frank Murphy to launch an investigation which led to the appointment of a reform commission and warden in an effort to correct some of the mistakes at the mammoth new prison at Jackson. But before Warden Joel R. Moore, formerly the head of probation field services in the federal system, could complete his disciplinary changes, a new political shift brought his dismissal and the restoration of repressive measures.[23] Michigan, like Illinois, had embarked on the construction of a mammoth penitentiary before the development of classification theories and techniques made such institutions virtually obsolete. Although they provided some cellblocks with outside and some with inside cells and some with dormitories, their architects, who failed to sense the potentialities of the telephone-pole design for the development of diversified groups of convicts, had constructed almost indestructible molds for mass rather than individualized treatment. New York State had developed several diversified institutions, but its new maximum-security prison at Attica, which represented the last word in correctional repression, opened in 1931 with only limited provisions for diversification.[24]

New York City narrowly escaped the same mistake. The decision to build a new city penitentiary on Rikers Island to replace the

[21] *News Bulletin* 9 (April 1938); U.S. Prison Industries Reorganization Administration, *The Prison Labor Problem in Missouri: A Survey* (Washington, D.C., 1938).
[22] *News Bulletin* 9 (August 1938).
[23] A.P.A., *Proceedings* (1939), pp. 287–292; *News Bulletin* 11 (December 1940).
[24] Osborne Assoc., *Handbook 1933*, pp. 133–146, 439–457, 594–608; U.S. Bur. Pris., *Handbook Design*, pp. 62–70.

antiquated workhouse and penitentiary was made in 1931, and work had commenced prior to the appointment of MacCormick two years later. Designed on the traditional cellblock pattern, it was not prepared to handle different types of inmates, and the steady influx of short termers, 15,000 of whom arrived in 1936, discouraged efforts to treat them individually or in other than cellhouse groups. MacCormick, however, persuaded Richard A. McGee, the able vocational director at Lewisburg penitentiary, to take charge of the new penitentiary, and the skills he developed as an administrator won him an enviable reputation and brought a call in 1941 to move to Washington to assume direction of the state's correctional and welfare institutions.[25]

Several other metropolitan county penitentiaries occupied more adequate plants, some planned by Alfred Hopkins as in Weschester, New York, and Bucks County, Pennsylvania, but none managed to develop more than a rudimentary classification system. The rapid turnovers made distinctions other than of age, sex, and degree of sobriety hard to determine; most county superintendents were content when order was maintained and the housekeeping chores performed. Several additional states gave their prison boards authority to inspect jails, and great improvements occurred in the South when, as in North Carolina, several states took over the operation of county road camps and abolished the chain gangs that had blighted the lives of countless misdemeanants, most of them black, for decades. The organization of the National Jail Association as an affiliate of the American Prison Association in 1938 reflected the growing concern but produced few realistic gains. Hastings Hart continued his campaign for the eradication of the fee system, the substitution of fines or probation for most jail sentences and the confinement of convicted misdemeanants in institutions separate from those for detention cases awaiting trial. The states of California, Wisconsin, and Virginia established new farm camps for misdemeanants, following the earlier action in this field in Massachusetts and a few eastern states, but elsewhere the gains were minimal.[26]

Meanwhile in Texas the state prison board, alerted by a visit of the Prison Association to Houston in 1934, accepted the offer of the

---

[25] *News Bulletin* 8 (August 1937); A.P.A., *Proceedings* (1939).

[26] Robert J. Wright, "The Jail and Misdemeanant Institutions," in *Contemporary Correction,* pp. 311–322.

Bureau of Research and Social Science of the University of Texas to establish a classification clinic backed by the Laura Spellman Rockefeller Foundation. The clinic, opened at the penitentiary in Huntsville in 1935, classified all white inmates into six groups on the basis of age and the probability of rehabilitation. The state, which took over the clinic two years later, assigned these men to one of six specialized residential units on its penal plantation and distributed the Negroes and Mexicans among three other units. The women and some of the men with industrial skills were kept at the penitentiary, and plans were considered for the development of two more specialized units for feebleminded and homosexual inmates.[27]

No state, not even Texas or New York, rivaled California in the growth of its convict population. The legislature decided in 1935 to separate the tractable inmates from the hardened criminals and to remove them from San Quentin and Folsom to a new penal institution to be developed on a 2600-acre farm near Chino. The women's clubs of the state secured a provision for a separate prison for women at Tehachapi to be patterned after the model federal prison for women at Alderson, West Virginia. Dr. Norman Fenton and the Bureau of Juvenile Research took the lead in developing special camps for juveniles. Dr. Kenyon Scudder, named superintendent of the new prison under construction at Chino in 1940, transformed it from a maximum-security to a medium-security institution by recruiting a professional staff and developing a correctional program which involved the inmates and avoided the expense of building and guarding a wall.[28]

The Threat of Prisonization

The publication in 1940 of Donald Clemmer's *The Prison Community* focused attention on the inmates' rather than the officers' or reformers' versions of that community. A sociologist serving as a correctional officer in a medium-sized state prison at Menard, Illinois, he made a careful study of the character traits and group association of the inmates under his charge. He concluded that most of them, arriving from varied backgrounds, had a deep fear of the other inmates and a fear and suspicion of the guards,

[27] *News Bulletin* 9 (August 1938); A.P.A., *Proceedings* (1934).
[28] *News Bulletin* 10 (August 1939); Joseph W. Eaton, *Stone Walls Not a Prison Make: The Anatomy of Planned Administrative Change* (Springfield, Ill., 1962), pp. 44–70.

which soon aligned them into small protective groups and started a process he called *prisonization*, that made them progressively hostile to any correctional program. Other studies of the inmate community at about this time, one by Hans Riemer as a volunteer "inmate" for three months in the Kansas state prison in 1938, reached similar conclusions and raised critical and skeptical questions as to the effect and value of many reformatory schemes.[29]

This startling and disturbing view of the prison community started a series of probing researches by scholarly penologists.[30] At the same time it focused attention again on the need to select and segregate inmates amenable to rehabilitation before they became prisonized. Professor Edwin H. Sutherland had developed a theory of "differential association" in the third edition of his *Principles of Criminology*, published in 1939, to explain the process by which criminality was acquired. A few of his followers began to devise methods to check that process at least for convicts who had stumbled into crime accidentally or impulsively.

Other scholars were seeking positive programs to dispel the penal apathy and breach the hostility that inured convicts to correctional efforts. While psychiatrists were baffled by their inability to probe the distorted attitudes of more than a few individual convicts, some psychologists and sociologists were considering the possibility of developing programs in group therapy. Dr. William A. White had chaired a seminar on group psychotherapy in Philadelphia in 1932 at which Dr. J. L. Moreno had expounded his theories of psychotherapy and roll playing.[31] Among those present was the young Dr. Bixby who would have occasion to experiment with group programs at crucial points in succeeding years. Early in 1933, in fact, as a field investigator for the Osborne Association, he visited Elmira and was impressed by a "special training class" for intractable young men held in a separate cellblock and conducted under psychiatric supervision separate from the main body of inmates. After discussing the advantages of that procedure with Dr. Frank L. Christian, the superintendent, Bixby was eager to apply

[29] Donald Clemmer, *The Prison Community* (New York, 1958); *News Bulletin* 11 (October 1940).

[30] Fred E. Haynes, "The Sociological Study of the Prison Community," *J.C.L.C.* 39 (1948): 432–440.

[31] Jacob L. Moreno, *The First Book on Group Psychotherapy*, 3d ed. (n.p., 1957).

the separate-group approach to malcontents at the Rahway, New Jersey, reformatory. With the assistance of Dr. Benjamin Frank, the psychologist there, Bixby and Superintendent Mark Kimberling segregated a group of troublemakers in a separate cellblock and provided for their employment and recreation in an isolated part of the yard. The experiment unfortunately had to be abandoned because most of the boys involved felt it necessary to maintain their reputation as tough guys.[32]

But Bixby was not defeated and a few years later he tried again. As superintendent at Chillicothe in the early forties he gathered a group of 20 boys with serious pre-trial records and placed them in a separate building erected for the purpose and called Dormitory No. 7. With the assistance of an able psychiatrist and a psychologist supplied by the Public Health Service, and with the help of part-time teachers from the Chillicothe schools, Bixby gave these boys an intensive treatment before they had a chance to establish a reputation for hostility. His six-month program offered the boys successive stages of work assignments, vocational exploration, and group discussions that encouraged them to achieve progressive goals and fitted most of them in his opinion for release. When the federal parole board proved unwilling to grant such early releases, Bixby was ready to accept a six-month leave, proffered by Director Bennett, to help California launch its Adult Authority. A subsequent call from the army to serve as director of military prisons prolonged his leave and made Bixby at one point an interested observer of an experiment conducted by a young sociologist, Sergeant Lloyd McCorkle, in a rehabilitation center at Fort Knox where delinquent service men were motivated to rehabilitate themselves by group discussions. On retirement from military duty, Bixby sought an opportunity to promote such a treatment program in civilian prisons and soon found it in New Jersey, again under Sanford Bates.[33]

Classification had been first applied in a pragmatic fashion in New Jersey, as we have seen, and had won the collaboration of most of the local institutional boards despite the continued independence of the state prison. When Sanford Bates accepted appointment as commissioner of Institutions and Agencies in New Jersey in 1945 he

---

[32] Osborne Assoc., *Handbook 1933*, pp. 670, 678; Leiby, *Charity*, pp. 254–260.
[33] Interview with Dr. F. Lovell Bixby, September 1974.

persuaded Bixby to return to the state to direct its penal and parole divisions. He was able at last to bring the parole services at the state prison under central administration with that of other institutions. He launched and supervised the development of a diagnostic center at Menlo Park for the examination and classification of juvenile delinquents, sex offenders, and cases submitted by judges seeking advice. A pioneer in what would later be called "soft determinism" he was formulating basic procedures for the psychiatric treatment of convicts no longer considered to be equal in all respects. But Bixby's more significant accomplishment was the establishment of a residential treatment center for youths at Highfields, the former home of the Charles Lindberghs. To direct it he engaged Lloyd McCorkle, who had now secured his doctorate in sociology. Together they launched an epochal experiment based on a technique they called "guided group interaction" to distinguish it from psychiatric group therapy.[34]

Before Highfields actually opened its doors in 1950, other states had pressed forward in several aspects of classification. Dr. Walter Thayer, as commissioner in New York, had promoted the efforts of Dr. Bernard Glueck and his successors at Sing Sing to develop psychiatric guide lines to distinguish the varied classes of criminals. Some states followed that lead, but in the federal bureau Frank Loveland, who had succeeded Bixby in charge of classification, renamed that process case management and assigned each inmate a correctional team that included custodial, industrial, and professional personnel.[35]

The American Law Institute had meanwhile proposed a plan whereby youthful offenders, rather than being sentenced to penal institutions, would be sent to statewide authorities or clinics. California was the first to enact such a law in 1941, giving its Youth Correctional Authority the responsibility of studying offenders between the ages of 16 and 21 to determine the nature and place of their treatment and the time for their parole. New York, prodded by

---

[34] Leiby, *Charity*, pp. 291–292, 302–313; Lloyd W. McCorkle, Albert Elias and F. Lovell Bixby, *The Highfields Story: An Experimental Treatment Project for Youthful Offenders* (New York, 1958); H. Ashley Weeks, *Youthful Offenders at Highfields: An Evaluation of the Effects of the Short-Term Treatment of Delinquent Boys* (Ann Arbor, 1958).

[35] Bennett, *I Chose Prison*, pp. 200–204.

the report of the Lewisohn Commission, established a reception and classification center for youths 16 to 21 at Elmira in 1945. Located in a cellblock equipped with 352 outside cells, a separate recreation yard, and an auditorium, it held new arrivals for a period of seventy-five days during which a team of experts determined their special characteristics and needs prior to assigning them to Elmira, Wallkill, the vocational institution at Coxsachie, or one of the state prisons or mental hospitals. The center did not have authority as in California to determine the length of confinement, but it could select individuals for inclusion in a new industrial training program at Elmira, or those able to benefit from the Institute for Training and Rehabilitation opened at Wallkill in 1932. Both the Service Unit, as the institute at Wallkill was identified, and the diagnostic center at Elmira, had authority to transfer youths from one institution to another as their deportment dictated.[36]

The publication by the American Prison Association in 1947 of the *Handbook on Classification in Correctional Institutions* provided a convenient manual for alert prison officials. Prepared by its committee on classification, with a major contribution by Frank Loveland, it supplied guidance for classification programs in Michigan, Kentucky, and several other states. Minnesota and Texas followed California and created youth authorities, based in well-staffed classification centers, which were empowered to determine the length as well as the character of treatment. Only New York and California proceeded to develop central classification clinics for adult convicts, and their clinics at Sing Sing and San Quentin respectively were still in the experimental stage in the late forties.[37]

The reassurance some prison officials derived from the classification programs of the mid forties was due partly to improvements in prison industry. Classification enabled wardens to select the better prospects for industrial assignments and fortunately this possibility developed in several states just as the outbreak of the Second World War created a new demand for production in many fields. And as the

[36] Tappan, ed., *Contemporary Correction*, pp. 124–155; Glenn M. Kendall, "The New York State Reception Center," *Federal Probation* 12 (September 1948): 42–47.

[37] A.P.A. Committee on Classification and Case Work, *Handbook on Classification in Correctional Institutions* (New York, 1947); Frank Loveland, "Classification in the Prison System," in *Contemporary Correction*, pp. 91–123.

war brought a relaxation of restraints against prison industries, it also aroused a latent spirit of patriotism among the inmates, many of whom tackled their jobs with vigor, hoping perhaps, to shorten their terms and to secure an opportunity to enlist.

Before the outbreak of the war the Federal Prison Industries had developed 21 industrial plants in various branches of the system and the 3,421 men they employed produced products which grossed $5,500,000 when marketed to the other federal departments. These shops soon became "small war plants," as Bennett described them, and not only doubled in number but quadrupled their output by the close of 1942. The bureau increased the modest daily wages, added overtime pay, and enabled some skilled inmates to earn as much as $75 a month.[38] Few states enjoyed such opportunities, but a presidential executive order issued in July 1942 eliminated legal obstacles to prison industries and enabled many prisons to negotiate war contracts and to dispell idleness for many inmates during the next two years. Federal aid for industrial training programs also materialized, and the excitement over the war's progress not only diverted attention from old grievances but also stirred a desire among prison officials, as revealed at the 1943 and 1944 congresses, to plan for postwar improvements. Unfortunately the sudden cancellation of war contracts in 1944 halted many prison industries and accentuated the disciplinary problem at the same time.[39]

The Professionals and the Career Men

The canceling of the war contracts lowered the curtain on what Dr. Gill, formerly in charge of the industrial division of the federal bureau, called the industrial prison. No longer would the state or federal prisons focus their efforts on the maintenance of productive industries and no longer could state officials rely on the returns of prison labor to maintain or render large support to their penal institutions. A few southern states with fertile plantations, and a few northern states with lucrative industries, such as a binding-twine factory in Minnesota which was free of competition within the state, were the exceptions that proved the rule. Even there, the prison

[38] Bennett, *I Chose Prison*, pp. 89–91.
[39] A.P.A., *Proceedings* (1942; 1943; 1944); Frank T. Flynn, "Employment and Labor," in *Contemporary Correction*, pp. 238–252.

officials had to pay modest wages to insure production, and elsewhere they had to develop activity programs to take the place of the vanishing industrial assignments.[40]

Most of the leaders of the Prison Association were focusing on the positive rather than the negative aspects of this change. The increased time available for educational and recreational programs, for classification interviews, and group counseling promised greater flexibility and improved results for the correctional officers. These officers, as distinguished from the guards and the industrial foremen, increased in number in most prisons, and many of them, recruited in some instances during the depression, had college, even postgraduate, degrees. Some were returning from service with the armed forces, where a few had established contacts with prison officials abroad, developing new interest in, and fresh respect for, the penal programs of other lands. Myrl Alexander, for example, while serving as chief of prisons with the military government, became acquainted with Albert Krebs and others who would assume leadership in prison development in the postwar years. At home the training programs for prison officers were expanded to cover more than security matters; they included instruction in the theory as well as the techniques of prison management, creating a demand for new texts on criminology, as well as penology.[41]

Several scholars were ready and eager to satisfy that demand. Harry Elmer Barnes, whose studies of the history of prisons in Pennsylvania and New Jersey had involved him in key developments, especially in New Jersey, joined forces with Negley K. Teeters of `Temple University in writing *New Horizons in Criminology*, first published in 1943. Teeters also produced two volumes on prisons in other lands which effectively blasted the illusions many prison men in America held of the superiority of their own attainments.[42] Occasional visitors from abroad such as Alexander Paterson, the British prison commissioner, had been restrained in their praise of advances abroad but the appearance of

[40] "Conversations with Correctional Leaders," *American Journal of Correction* 32 (September-October 1970): 38–39, 46–47; Howard B. Gill, "The Future of Prison Employment," *Proceedings* (A.P.A., 1935), pp. 179–185.

[41] "Conversations," *A.J.C.:* 41–42; Walter C. Reckless, "Training of the Correctional Worker," in *Contemporary Correction*, pp. 35–50.

[42] Negley K. Teeters, *World Penal Systems* (Philadelphia, 1944); Negley K. Teeters, *Penology from Panama to Cape Horn* (Philadelphia, 1946).

Max Grunhut's *Penal Reform* placed developments in Europe and America in better perspective, revealing also some special accomplishments, notably in Scandinavia.[43] Other American scholars were writing articles on studies that would eventually appear in book form, and Paul W. Tappan assembled a number of these in a volume on *Contemporary Correction.*[44]

Although few wardens or superintendents were scholars with academic backgrounds, an increasing number were college trained men who accepted minor appointments and advanced in time to administrative posts. Drs. Bixby and Gill were the scholarly exceptions and made their contributions as administrators by applying and demonstrating new penal conceptions. Richard McGee, like Myrl Alexander, was college trained, but although he taught for a time, he made prison administration his profession—so successfully in fact that he won appointments in a highly competitive field to top posts in New York City and, in 1944, in California. Alexander, on the other hand, completed his stint as a college professor after years as an administrator and would return to that field as Bennett's successor in 1964.

Several of these men served as president of the Prison Association, but Edward R. Cass, the long-term secretary, saw the merit of alternating scholars with traditional wardens in that post. James A. Johnston of Alcatraz was not exactly traditional, but he was warden when he served as president in 1941, and wrote a revealing book about his island prison. Joseph W. Sanford, who served as president three years later, was a career man and received credit from Bennett for the transformation of Atlanta penitentiary into a correctional institution. W. Frank Smyth, Jr., warden of Virginia's old penitenitary at Richmond, and John C. Burke, warden of Wisconsin's model prison at Waupun, served as presidents in the last two years of the decade. But the great majority of participants in the successive congresses were neither presidents nor wardens, but doctors, educational directors, clinical examiners, probation or parole supervisors, chaplains and the like. A frequent and always welcome

[43] Max Grunhut, *Penal Reform: A Comparative Study* (1948; reprinted Montclair, N.J., 1972).

[44] Sheldon Glueck, *Crime and Correction: Selected Papers* (Cambridge, Mass., 1952); Paul W. Tappan, ed., *Contemporary Correction* (New York, 1951).

speaker was Maud Ballington Booth, representing the Volunteers of America. Mrs. Blanche LaDu, chairman of the Minnesota Board of Control, was also an eloquent speaker and the first of the only two women to be named president of the Association.[45]

Most of the women in charge of the women's prisons and reformatories were career persons though few of them made a practice of attending the annual congresses. Edna Mahan, who managed the New Jersey Reformatory for Women for many years, was an exception. Her success in developing an honor system and a measure of self-government within the several cottages at the Clinton Farm institution won the admiration of numerous visitors and made her a popular participant at Association committee meetings and programs. Her friendly association with Dr. Miriam Van Waters, at whose institution in Framingham, Massachusetts she had secured some of the training, brought that leading professional to an occasional congress. A report by Elizabeth Munger of Connecticut on the organization of a Committee on Women's Institutions in 1943 failed to produce much participation. A number of women continued to read papers on general penal problems, however, and in 1950 they dominated a session dealing with new experiments with pre-release training. Their papers on this occasion, reporting on an honor cottage at Tehachapi, California, on a release program at the federal reformatory at Alderson, and on a tapering-off process at Framingham, revealed the continued vitality of the leading women's reformatories.[46]

The women superintendents were not the only wardens that skipped the annual congresses on occasion. Despite the increased attendance, a number of leading wardens seldom made an appearance. Possibly the candid criticism of some of their institutions by association leaders, especially in the *Handbook* and the *News Bulletin* of the Osborne Assocation, discouraged attendance by the wardens of the prisons at Columbus, Jackson, and Jefferson City. But Warden Joseph E. Ragen of Joliet, who was generally commended for his firm discipline and was never held responsible

[45] "Conversations," *A.J.C.:* 25–28; James A. Johnston, *Alcatraz Island Prison: And the Men Who Live There* (New York, 1949).

[46] A.P.A., *Proceedings* (1940), pp. 351–356; (1943), pp. 149–150; (1950), pp. 124–137; Osborne Association, *Handbook of American Prisons and Reformatories*, vol. 2, *Pacific Coast States* (New York, 1942), pp. 327–353; Leiby, *Charity*, pp. 251–253, 311–312.

for the unusual and inefficient architectural design of that mammoth penitentiary, was generally too busy to attend. Warden Lewis E. Lawes of Sing Sing, perhaps the most famous warden of the period, did attend as an offical delegate on occasion and served one year as president, but he seldom read a paper or contributed to the discussion. The wartime emergency, however, brought him to the platform to discuss "Correctional Problems in Wartime."[47]

Perhaps the most frequent speaker at the congresses, and on the widest variety of subjects, was Austin H. MacCormick. Back as executive secretary of the Osborne Association and directing its wide-ranging investigations and promotional efforts, he had an interest in all aspects of prison development. In 1944 he appeared at the Atlanta meeting with a model plan for a state penal system designed to provide classification and a diversity of institutions to assure each convict the treatment he required. The next year he presented at the New York meeting a detailed summary of the post-war plans of a score of states gleaned from official reports which displayed a widespread resolve to update and upgrade penal systems.[48]

Governors frequently addressed the annual congresses but none with a more telling message than Governor Earl Warren delivered at the 1947 meeting in California. The governor had taken the lead three years before in revamping the state's penal system. He had brought McGee down from Washington to direct the system and had created an adult, as well as a youth, authority to classify and distribute the convicts, supervise their treatment, and determine their release. He found and gave increased support to several experimental treatment programs, notably that of Kenyon J. Scudder at Chino and the group-counseling programs of Dr. Norman Fenton. These efforts placed California undisputedly in the forefront of American prison developments.[49]

These innovations and accomplishments represented a considerable advance over the uncertainties of the early thirties. The hope of achieving full employment and the discipline it promised had been abandoned; prisons as well as reformatories had endeavored to

[47] Gladys A. Erikson, *Warden Ragen of Joliet* (New York, 1957); A.P.A., *Proceedings* (1942), pp. 20–27.

[48] A.P.A., *Proceedings* (1944), pp. 79–87; (1945), pp. 220–228.

[49] Ibid., (1948), pp. 13–16; Eaton, *Stone Walls*, pp. 60–142.

organize alternative activities. When Professor Clemmer and others analyzed the widespread resistance of inmates as a product of the process of prisonization, alert officials redoubled their efforts to develop techniques of classification to enable them to separate the treatable from the hardcore intransigents, and to concentrate their efforts on rehabilitation. Upgraded programs at Annandale, Chillicothe, Elmira, and several other reformatories, as well as in medium-security prisons such as Norfolk and Lewisburg, were establishing patterns for others to follow.[50] The new architectural designs of Norfolk and Lewisburg were likewise winning adoption elsewhere in medium-security cottage clusters in farm camps in the first case, and in new telephone-pole institutions affording diversified units in the other. The minimum-security federal institution at Seagonville, Texas (which was first to replace the long dining benches with tables for four) and the new federal penitentiary at Terre Haute, Indiana, represented these new designs.[51] The new experiments with group counseling, a creative extension of earlier forms of inmate participation, suggested possibilities for future correctional programing. At the Milwaukee congress in 1949 wardens as well as program directors and scholars displayed an eagerness to consider new correctional devices.[52]

BIBLIOGRAPHIC NOTE

Many articles in the *Proceedings of the American Prison Association* and the *Journal of Criminal Law and Criminology* continue to provide useful analysis and commentary on correctional developments. The *American Journal of Correction (Jail Association Journal* (1939-1940) and *Prison World* (1940-1954)), a monthly, the News Bulletin of the Osborne Association (1930-1941), a bi-monthly, and *Federal Probation* (1937-), a quarterly, contain much material pertinent to this period.

The National Society of Penal Information, combining, in 1932, with the Welfare League Association, to become the Osborne Association, published a series of handbooks of exceptional value of nationwide studies of correctional institutions for adults: *Handbook of American Prisons:*

[50] F. Lovell Bixby, "Reformatories for Men," in *Contemporary Correction*, pp. 323–328.

[51] U.S. Bur. Pris., *Handbook Design*, pp. 74–77, 103–107.

[52] Albert Wagner, "Inmate Participation in Correctional Institutions," *Prison World* 5 (1951): 9–11; A.P.A., *Proceedings* (1949).

Covering the Prisons of the New England and Middle Atlantic States (1925); *Handbook of American Prisons, 1926,* Austin H. MacCormick and Paul W. Garrett, eds. (1926); *Handbook of American Prisons and Reformatories, 1929,* Paul W. Garrett and Austin H. MacCormick, eds. (1929); *Handbook of American Prisons and Reformatories, 1933,* William B. Cox, F. Lovell Bixby, and William T. Root, eds. (1933); *Handbook of American Prisons and Reformatories; West North Central States, 1938,* William B. Cox, F. Lovell Bixby, eds. (1938); and *Handbook of American Prisons and Reformatories: Pacific Coast States, 1942,* Austin H. MacCormick *et al,* eds. (1942).

Four handbooks published by the Osborne Association studied federal and state institutions established for delinquent juveniles: *Handbook of American Institutions for Delinquent Juveniles:* vol. 1, *West North Central States, 1938,* William B. Cox and F. Lovell Bixby, eds. (1938); vol. 2, *Kentucky-Tennessee, 1940,* William B. Cox, Joseph A. Shelly, and George C. Minard, eds. (1940); vol. 3, *Pacific States, 1940,* William B. Cox and Joseph A. Shevy, eds. (1940); vol. 4, *Virginia-North Carolina, 1943,* Austin H. MacCormick *et al,* eds. (1943).

The American Prison Association, *Handbook on Classification in Correctional* Institutions (Washington, D.C., 1947), and U.S. Bureau of Prisons, *Handbook of Correctional Institution Design and Construction* (Washington, D.C., 1949) and the supplement, *Recent Prison Construction, 1950-1960* (Washington, D.C., 1960) serve as sourcebooks for the planning and construction of various types of correctional institutions.

In addition to a number of the volumes mentioned in earlier bibliographic notes, the following are of value to an understanding of the period: James Bennett, *I Chose Prison* (New York, 1970); Donald Clemmer, *The Prison Community* (New York, 1958); Joseph W. Eaton, *Stone Walls Not a Prison Make: The Anatomy of Planned Administrative Change* (Springfield, Ill., 1962); Sheldon Glueck, *Crime and Correction: Selected Papers* (Cambridge, Mass., 1952); Sheldon and Eleanor T. Glueck, *Five Hundred Criminal Careers* (New York, 1930); Alfred Hopkins, *Prisons and Prison Buildings* (New York, 1930); James A. Johnston, *Alcatraz Island Prison: And the Men Who Live There* (New York, 1949); Lloyd W. McCorkle, Albert Elias and F. Lovell Bixby, *The Highfields Story: An Experimental Treatment Project for Youthful Offenders* (New York, 1958); Jacob L. Moreno, *The First Book on Group Psychotherapy,* 3d ed. (n.p., 1957); Paul W. Tappan, ed., *Contemporary Correction* (New York, 1951); Negley K. Teeters, *Penology from Panama to Cape Horn* (Philadelphia, 1946) and *World Penal Systems* (Philadelphia, 1944); H. Ashley Weeks, *Youthful Offenders at Highfields: An Evaluation of the Effects of the Short-Term Treatment of Delinquent Boys* (Ann Arbor, 1958).

13.

TREATMENT FOR CORRECTION: 1950–1968

J. Stanley Sheppard, head of the prison bureau of the Salvation Army and president of the Association in 1950, cited its increased commitment to rehabilitation during the preceeding half century as a major advance. He went on to stress the continuing challenge and urgent need to win public support for that view. Warden Ragen of Joliet voiced the Association's acceptance of that challenge in his address as president a year later.[1] The urgency was already evident and mounting as a succession of convict riots erupted in a dozen prisons in the early fifties. They dramatized the failure of progressive and backward states alike to achieve their announced goals. While some, such as Michigan, retreated, many, responding to the recommendations of investigating commissions, endeavored to fulfill their correctional goals. Some strengthened their classification procedures and developed new experimental treatment programs; others commenced a search for alternatives to imprisonment. A campaign for manpower training for correctional officers had wide effect, but the awakened interest of allied professionals produced a number of disillusioning studies in the mid sixties that revealed unsuspected shortcomings.

Riots and Repercussions in the Fifties

Locked in overcrowded prisons, often two or more in a cell scarcely adequate for one, the convicts needed no outside proof of

[1]American Prison Association, *Proceedings* (1950), pp. 3–9; (1951), pp. 3–8.

their hardships. Yet news of a riot in one institution often served as the catalyst elsewhere. The prisonization process, which had aligned the great majority of inmates against their keepers, had also divided them from one another, making effective collaboration extremely difficult. Only a rumor of an exceptionally brutal incident or a report of revolts elsewhere could arouse a sense of community sufficient to support a riotous outbreak. In Louisiana a succession of brutal floggings ordered by a recently appointed warden provoked fifty convicts to cut the tendons in their heels in order to escape labor assignments in the swamps. Discipline in the camps was harshly maintained, but news of the event leaked out and prompted an investigation, which inaugurated some long-overdue reforms in that state.[2]

It was news of the brutality rather than of the reforms that spread to other prisons, adding to the grievances of convicts everywhere. The outbreak that occurred at Walla Walla in Washington later that year was a result in part of the state's failure to fulfill the promises made by McGee before his departure for California.[3] Similar resentment was building up at the old New Jersey state prison in Trenton where a newly appointed warden was endeavoring to reestablish order after a period of laxity had fostered the growth of inmate gangs. Several disturbing incidents culminated in a planned riot in April 1952 when sixty-odd prisoners captured four guards in the printshop and, holding them as hostages, maintained inmate control of that shop for four days. A demonstration in sympathy erupted at the prison farm in Bordentown, but the reform-minded governor, Commissioner Bates and Director Bixby successfully negotiated a peaceful settlement. Governor Driscoll named Austin MacCormick among others to a committee of inquiry, which proposed some modifications in the parole system but generally endorsed and recommended more adequate support for the programs of Bates and Bixby.[4]

A second major riot erupted at Jackson, Michigan, three weeks after the outbreak at Trenton. The new prison at Jackson, the largest

---

[2] Mark T. Carleton, *Politics and Punishment: The History of the Lousisana State Penal* System (Baton Rouge, 1971), pp. 153–159.

[3] *American Journal of Correction* 24 (November-December 1962): 5–7, 10, 17

[4] James Leiby, *Charity and Correction in New Jersey: A History of State Welfare Institutions* (New Brunswick, 1967), pp. 314–319.

in the country, was likewise overcrowded, and its warden had been content to maintain order with the aid of the leaders of convict gangs that largely dominated the life of the prison. Aroused by reports of revolts elsewhere, an inmate was able to overcome a guard at knife point and released several cellmates. A psychopathic inmate among them asserted leadership and captured control of one cell-block. Gang leaders from other blocks soon joined the revolt and seized twelve guards as hostages. Michigan, like New Jersey, had previously launched a correctional program and had engaged specialists to examine and work with the prisoners. Vernon Fox, as assistant deputy in charge of treatment, had directed an active program and knew the riot leaders; he was able, as a result, to negotiate a settlement that restored control of the prison. But his address announcing that settlement to the inmates, by lauding the good intentions of the insurrectionists, so antagonized the governor and the security officers that the warden rescinded the concessions and requested Fox's resignation.[5]

Several more riots occurred in the next two months in prisons scattered from Concord in the Northeast to a Georgia road camp in the South and Soledad in California. The demands of most of the rioters were for specific reforms—better food, the abolition of the lash and the "hole," more adequate cells and bathing facilities—and although most of the wardens used violent tactics to reestablish authority, many moved to institute reforms as a precaution against further bloodshed.[6] In Louisiana, following a second outbreak at the 18,000-acre Angola penal farm, Governor R. F. Kennon placed Reed Cozart from the federal bureau in charge. Cozart transformed Angola, formerly controlled by armed convict guards and dogs, into a modern prison equipped with a securely built cellhouse, several airy dormitories, and a cluster of factories, all enclosed within a wall.[7]

Concord in Massachusetts became more disciplinary minded following the disturbance there in 1952. However, after a second and more destructive riot at old Charlestown prison in 1955, the state

---

[5] John B. Martin, *Break Down the Walls: American Prisons, Present, Past, and Future* (New York, 1954), pp. 80–106.

[6] Martin, *Break Down*, pp. 211–212; *Prison World* 14 (May-June 1952).

[7] Carleton, *Politics*, pp. 155–165; *Prison World* 16 (March-April 1954): 3–5; *A.J.C.* 22 (November-December 1960): 4–7.

responded more positively. The legislature hastened to create the long-desired state correctional system with a commissioner in charge of eight correctional institutions. Governor C. A. Herter persuaded Russell G. Oswald, the reform-minded director of corrections in Wisconsin, to accept that new post. Oswald pressed forward with the transfer of the men at Charlestown to a new security institution at Walpole and promoted the development of educational and classification programs there and at Norfolk and the other correctional institutions.[8]

An uprising in the seriously overcrowded penitentiary at Columbus, Ohio in 1952 brought some long-overdue reforms to that state. At the request of the division of correction the governor proposed and the legislature passed a bill authorizing the expenditure of $8,500,000. It converted the reformatory at Mansfield into a medium-security prison, to relieve congestion at Columbus, and authorized the construction of a new reformatory at Marion, designed to accommodate young first offenders in diversified units. Although, in contrast with Massachusetts, the old prison in Columbus was retained, each inmate now had a separate cell. The division of correction developed a reception center there, enabling it to select men for transfer to Mansfield, the London prison farm, or to one of the twelve penal camps in the state.[9]

Another destructive riot, which broke out in January 1953 in Western Penitentiary near Pittsburgh and spread to Rockview, prompted the adoption of far-reaching reforms. The state transferred control of its prisons from the unwieldly welfare department to a Bureau of Correction in the justice department and created a Commissioner of Correction to supervise the seven adult institutions, each with its own advisory board. Local boards, designed to assist in placing discharged inmates in the community, had no voice, as in New Jersey, in determining parole. The Bureau developed diagnostic clinics at Cherry Hill and Western into reception centers. It also had the responsibility for assigning men to confinement there, or to the now independently managed Graterford and Rockview prisons, or to Huntingdon, now the center for defective delinquents. Women were sent directly to a correctional

[8] Russell G. Oswald, *Attica: My Story*, (New York, 1972), pp. 155–168; *A.J.C.* 27 (July-August 1965): 16–18.
[9] *Prison World* 15 (March-April 1953).

institution on an 800-acre farm at Muncy, while an industrial school for youths, 15 to 21, housed some 1,300 lads in dormitories without walls on another farm at Camp Hill.[10]

Alarmed by the mounting violence, the American Prison Association created a special committee to study the nature and causes of inmate riots. Richard A. McGee, director of the California Department of Correction which had suffered a riot at its relatively modern prison at Soledad, accepted the chairmanship and submitted a probing report in June 1953. The underlying cause, he declared, was a lack of understanding on the part of the public as well as among the convicts of the rehabilitative functions and purposes of prisons. As a result, prison administrations received inadequate support and had to rely on untrained and poorly paid staffs; moreover the restraints on prison industries created pools of idleness, while limited budgets prevented the employment of professional educators and other treatment personnel. Recurrent campaigns to curb crime prompted long sentences and inhibited early paroles with the result that most states faced steadily mounting convict populations that far exceeded their provisions. Only sufficient support to enable prison administrators to eliminate the major grounds for convict grievances would significantly reduce the number of prison outbreaks, McGee maintained, but such support was hard to find.[11]

Missouri, like many other states, waited until a destructive riot at the prison in Jefferson City in September 1954 forced action. The legislature, as a result, created a department of correction with authority over probation and parole as well as all state penal institutions. Its first director, James D. Carter, created a classification division and a division of prison industries, and hastened to rebuild the burned-out shops at Jefferson City. He developed a reformatory for young men on one of the six farms acquired by the department, removed the women to a separate farm, and designated still another as the site for a medium-security prison for men. An appropriation of ten million dollars helped to speed these develop-

[10]*A.J.C.* 16 (September-October 1954): 7–8, 28–29.
[11]*Prison World* 15 (May-June 1953): 10–11; Richard A. McGee, *Riots and Disturbances in Correctional Institutions* (Washington, D.C., 1953); U.S. Bureau of Prisons, *Recent Prison Construction, 1950–1960* (Washington, D.C., 1960), pp. 3, 9–17.

ments, but the new medium-security prison at Moberly was not opened until 1963.[12]

The Correctional Goal

The prison riots and other disturbances revealed the widespread failure of the reformatory objective. Disturbed by both the indifference and the harsh attitudes of the public and by the hostile response of most convicts, the APA determined in 1954 to proclaim its purposes more effectively. As a first step it voted to change its name to the American Correctional Association and renamed the *Prison World*, its official publication, the *American Journal of Correction*. It encouraged the states to redesignate their prisons as correctional institutions and issued a revised and expanded *Manual of Correctional Standards* that now reached to 425 pages. It suggested that prison officials administer discipline in "adjustment centers," but most convicts continued to describe such centers as "the hole."[13]

Some states had previously announced correctional goals for their prisons, notably Wisconsin and Minnesota. Russell Oswald, who had become director of corrections in Wisconsin in 1950 after two years in charge of its probation and parole services, found its program fairly adequate at the start. He added a maximum-security unit of fifty cells at Waupun prison in order to permit greater freedom of movement for the rest of its population. He assigned each inmate a parole officer who was responsible for learning to know him as well as his family and his probable destination on release. Oswald made the preparation of pre-sentence reports by parole officers mandatory in all criminal cases, as advocated by Sheldon Glueck at The Hague that year, and he utilized some of the forestry camps inherited from his predecessor as pre-release training centers for prospective parolees.[14]

Minnesota had long maintained institutions that adequately housed its convict population, but its support of active correctional programs failed to match that of Wisconsin. A request for 26

---

[12]*A.J.C.* 21 (November-December 1959): 12–20; 26 (July-August 1964): 12–13; U.S. Bur. Pris., *Construction*, pp. 3, 9–17, 38.

[13]A.P.A., *Manual of Correctional Standards* (Washington, D.C., 1954).

[14]Oswald, *Attica*, pp. 135–154; Sheldon Glueck, *Crime and Correction: Selected Papers* (Cambridge, Mass., 1952); pp. 102–110; U.S. Bur. Pris., *Construction*, pp. 53–54.

additional correctional officers in 1961 was cut to eight by the governor and produced funds only for two from the legislature. Nevertheless the department of correction with a sufficient supply of cells and job assignments for all inmates at the prison, the reformatory, and the women's institution, and with educational and work programs at three juvenile institutions and three forest camps, secured funds two years later for the oft-proposed reception, diagnostic and treatment center.[15]

The New England states achieved a significant advance through regional cooperation. Because of the limited size of their populations, the establishment of diversified institutions was discouraged, but an agreement in 1959 to accept transfers from other states provided a wider field for specialization. Rhode Island absorbed the care of state and local adults into one system in 1956 and provided maximum-, medium-, and minimum-security institutions for men, as well as two training schools, one for boys and one for girls. It sent its adult females to Framingham and its defectives to Bridgewater, both situated in Massachusetts. Connecticut concentrated on the provision, of a modern new penal institution at Somers, opened in 1963, to replace the ancient Wethersfield prison.[16]

Several southern and border states achieved tardy reforms in the mid sixties. Maryland opened a new institution at Patuxent in 1955 for serious offenders whose repeated or violent crimes called for special attention. Equipped with a diagnostic center, Patuxent was under the management of psychiatrists who devised a program focusing on small-group therapy comparable to that of progressive asylums. Delaware, prodded by an investigation by the National Council on Crime and Delinquency, reorganized its correctional system in 1964, establishing unified control over its probation, parole, and penal services, and proceeded to erect two modern correctional institutions to house local as well as state commitments.[17] South Carolina moved two years later, after an investigation by Warden Ragen of Illinois (at the request of the governor), and established a reception and classification center from which

[15] A.J.C. 24 (July-August 1962): 22–25; 31 (July-August 1969): 18–19.

[16] A.J.C. 27 (July-August 1965): 30–32, 38–39.

[17] Ronald L. Goldfarb and Linda R. Singer, *After Conviction* (New York, 1973), pp. 98–108; A.J.C. 28 (July-August 1966): 30–34.

convicts were dispatched to appropriate road and farm camps. It commenced construction of a youth correction center and acquired a former junior college for a women's penal institution.[18] A year later Florida, aroused at last by a fire that claimed the lives of 37 convicts chained in a road-camp dormitory built of wood, established a new reception and diagnostic center and developed a vocational training program there with branches extending into a half dozen scattered camps housed in brick buildings. The department hastily closed the camps with wood structures, which had previously comprised most of the 38 work camps. A new maximum-security cellblock at the state prison at Raiford, a new correctional institution for women at Lowell, and a new medium-security institution for young men at Apalachee demonstrated Florida's awakened sense of responsibility.[19]

Texas, with its convict population multiplying at a rate three times that of the state as a whole, soon outgrew the reforms effected at the mid century by O. B. Ellis. He had launched construction of a secure reception center to house 127 newcomers at Shamrock until they could be classified and assigned to one of the thirteen scattered farm units. A new maximum-security cellblock was completed at the Ramsey farm equipped to house 760 hard-core criminals. George J. Beto, who succeeded Ellis, opened a cellblock to house 1,100 young men at the Ferguson farm in 1962, and three years later another maximum-security block for 1,600 prisoners near Huntsville. An investigator described conditions in the "tanks" at the other farms as "pretty decent," but no standards were specified. Apparently the authorities were chiefly interested in increasing production and reducing escapes, both of which were finally achieved in 1965.[20]

Several western states developed classification programs in the late fifties and early sixties. Warden Harry Tinsley engaged professional assistance in the examination and classification of new arrivals at the Colorado state prison in Canon City in 1957 and made a more careful selection of men for assignment to the road camps beyond the walls.[21] Kansas established a reception and diagnostic center at

[18] *A.J.C.* 28 (November-December 1966): 8–19.

[19] *A.J.C.* 21 (July-August 1959): 12–16; 29 (July-August 1967): 18–22; 33 (July-August 1971): 18–23: U.S. Bur. Pris., *Construction*, pp. 26–27.

[20] *Prison World* 14 (January-February 1952): 4–9; *A.J.C.* 25 (July-August 1963): 28–29; 27 (January-February 1965): 24–26; U.S. Bur. Pris., *Construction*, pp. 2, 51–52.

[21] *A.J.C.* 22 (July-August 1960): 10–12; U.S. Bur. Pris., *Construction*, pp. 45–47.

the Lansing prison in 1961, and Washington that year authorized the construction of a classification and training center but gave immediate attention to the placement of over 300 men and 100 youths in forest camps maintained on an honor system. New Mexico opened a new prison in 1956, but its standard of classification, as in Texas, was by residential units for Negroes, Chicanos, and white Americans.[22]

By 1960 most state penal systems had endorsed the concept of classification and had named full- or part-time professionals to their staffs. Many had authorized the creation of reception and diagnostic centers, but when Dr. Chester L. Chiles of the Washington reception unit endeavored that year to collect information concerning their procedures he received a disillusioning response. Of seven diagnostic centers that replied, only one reported that it had an adequate staff and another that it was independent of the control of its host institution. Fourteen of the thirty-six correctional institutions canvassed reported that classification was done by their own staffs. Only two were equipped to supply the treatment recommended by their clinics, but seven were satisfied with the services of their professional counselors.[23]

Much of the classification program may have been a farce, as John B. Martin and most inmate writers maintained, but the professionals were having an influence not always recognized. Their examinations focused attention on the individual convict, rather than on his crime, and often revealed traits that helped to explain his problems. Astute wardens and correctional officers made use of this information, which sometimes helped them cope with and even circumvent the prisonization that generally alienated the inmates. Hardened criminals directed their greatest scorn against the "head shrinkers," but officials charged with selecting men for medium- or minimum-security assignments, or for parole, welcomed reports that offered useful criteria. Several popular penal programs would have been handicapped without their assistance.[24]

[22]*A.J.C.* 24 (March-April 1962): 4–10; 24 (November-December 1962): 5–10, 17; 29 (January-February 1967): 8–11.

[23]*A.J.C.* 22 (January-February 1960): 16, 30; Harry Elmer Barnes and Negley K. Teeters, *New Horizons in Criminology*, 3d ed. (Englewood Cliffs, N.J., 1959), p. 478, report a total of 385 full- and part-time professionals in American prisons in 1954.

[24]*Prison World* 16 (January-February 1954): 4–5, 23–24; *A.J.C.* 26 (January-February 1964): 12–14; 27 (March-April 1965): 10–13.

*   *   *

The road, farm, and forest camps that spread widely through most of the states in these years relied increasingly on the honor of the men assigned to them and on work instructors rather than guards for supervision. Their development not only provided essential relief for overcrowded prisons at a fraction of the cost for new cell-blocks; it also removed inmates from the debilitating atmosphere of largely idle prisons.[25] A survey in 1959 found 94 unwalled and unarmed penal camps in operation under the jurisdiction of 24 states, territories, and the federal government. In several states the work camps offered the most effective rehabilitation programs available. New York, in fact, named several of its camps rehabilitation camps. Massachusetts applied this concept in another direction when it developed halfway-house dormitories in cities as training centers for prospective parolees to assist them in finding jobs and in making adjustments to the community. Many states developed halfway houses, and Michigan extended this system to probation when it established probation camps to assist youthful offenders in developing a social environment to keep them out of prison. Governor Rockefeller approved the development of a nonresident center as a Gifted Offender Treatment Unit for parolees who were ready to take advantage of educational programs and to cooperate in group-centered rehabilitation.[26] The work-release program, first introduced in Wisconsin in the mid teens and widely applied in North and South Carolina in the late fifties and practiced elsewhere in the sixties, was a related and highly practical form of pre-parole training.[27]

No efforts to bridge the gap between prisons and the free community were older or more effective than those of the citizen associations that offered aid and counsel to paroled and discharged convicts. In Philadelphia, always the leader in this field, the Junior

---

[25] *A.J.C.* 23 (January-February 1961): 14–16, 28–29; 23 (July-August 1961): 18–21; American Correctional Association, *Proceedings* (1955), pp. 65–74.

[26] *A.J.C.* 21 (May-June 1959): 2–4; 21 (July-August 1959): 20–34; 24 (January-February 1962): 14–16; 24 (March-April 1962): 30–31; 29 (March-April 1967): 27–29; 29 (May-June 1967): 20–23; 31 (January-February 1969): 6–12.

[27] Sanger B. Powers, "Off-Grounds Activities Present an Opportunity for Correctional Institutions," *Federal Probation* 31 (June 1967): 11–13; President's Commission of Law Enforcement and Administration of Justice, *The Challenge of Crime in a Free Society* (Washington, D.C., 1967), pp. 176–177.

Chamber of Commerce took the initiative in 1952 in persuading the city to create an advisory commission to promote more active citizen participation in the readjustment of parolees to the community. Leon T. Stern who became the first director of that committee was astonished to discover the number and variety of agencies interested in its work. In addition to the still active Philadelphia Prison Society and its committee of volunteers, he found the Volunteers of America, the Salvation Army, the Big Brothers, the Alcoholics Anonymous, and several special local groups all active in that state. The continuing contributions of these and similar groups, including, of course, the Osborne Society in New York, the prisoners' aid societies or Friends Service Committees in many communities, and such special groups as the Northern California Service League in San Francisco, received frequent notice, though none matched the work of similar groups in England and Scandinavia.[28]

American prison officials were becoming more conscious and more appreciative in the fifties than ever before of foreign penal experiments and achievements. Reports of the shorter sentences, the lower rates of recidivism, and the startlingly lower crime rates of northern European countries were hard to brush aside. Sanford Bates reported on the attention and approval given to pre-sentence examinations at the 12th International Penal Congress at The Hague in 1950, the year of its first compulsory adoption in the states by Wisconsin.[29] Dr. Bixby on an extended visit to northern Europe in 1962 reported on the prisons inspected there, many characterized as open institutions. He commented on the short sentences, the generally moderate size of the prisons, the work-training programs, the frequent use of work-release and home-visitation permits, and the early grant of parole, particularly in Sweden. He noted the widespread encouragement of visits by the prisoners families and the provisions for overnight reunions of husbands and wives, as Mississippi alone among the states provided in its "red barns."[30]

[28] Gerald F. Flood, "Citizen Participation in a Community's Penal Problems," *Focus* 33 (January 1954): 1–5, 11; *A.J.C.* 17 (January-February 1955): 3–4; Joseph R. Silver, "Citizen Participation in the Field of Correction," *Proceedings* (A.C.A., 1963), pp. 80–96.

[29] A.P.A., *Proceedings* (1950), pp. 41–51.

[30] *A.J.C.* 24 (May-June 1962): 18–25; 28 (May-June 1966): 30–32; 30 (May-June 1968): 18–19.

*   *   *

Despite some relaxation, the Correctional Industries Association, formed in response to the war emergency, was able in most states to promote production for sale to state and other tax supported institutions. A careful tabulation by the John R. Wald Co., a specialist in the supply of industrial machinery to prisons, disclosed an overall increase in the numbers employed in state-use industries of almost fifty percent during the fifties when the value of their products mounted from $52 to $101 million.[31] Yet the actual numbers thus employed increased only from 13 to 14 percent of the total inmate population, which prompted renewed efforts to develop industrial training programs to relieve the pervasive idleness. Henry J. Noble, warden of the New York City correctional institution, used a teaching machine operated by instructors in the city school system not only to improve the reading ability of many of his short-term inmates, but also to introduce them to mechanical training programs they could follow after their discharge. It was necessary everywhere to break through the inmate's alienation. The director of the Indiana Reformatory achieved an advance when he acquiesced to an inmate's request to instruct other inmates in the operation of an electronic data processing machine he had mastered. Word of the successful experiment brought donations of additional equipment, and in two years he trained 65 fellow inmates in a modern new trade.[32]

Many of the more traditional programs both in academic and industrial instruction continued, but the effect oftentimes was only to break or reduce the monotony of idleness. With declining numbers of foreign-born inmates unable to speak or read English, the old instruction in the three R's lost its usefulness. Efforts to provide high school or more advanced instruction required the engagement of trained instructors, who were not readily available. Correspondence courses and classes taught by volunteer professionals from neighboring institutions solved the need for some eager inmates in scattered prisons and in a few urban jails.[33] By a

[31] John R. Wald Co., Inc., *Correctional Industries: State-Use Sales, 1950–1970* (Huntingdon, Pa., 1971).

[32] *A.J.C.* 24 (November-December 1962): 18–22; 25 (November-December 1963): 10–12; 26 (January-February 1964): 16–18.

[33] *A.J.C.* 27 (January-February 1965): 4–8; 28 (November-December 1966): 21–23.

determined effort, J. Edwin LaVallee, warden of old Auburn prison, made that unlikely institution the chief center in the state in the early 1960s for instruction in 14 practical trades, with lively classes in civic and social subjects that attracted transfers from other adult prisons in the state.[34]

An increasing number of prisons permitted inmates to write, edit, and circulate prison journals. Professor Walter A. Lunden of Iowa State College at Ames offered editorial assistance through the Department of Technical Journalism in 1950 to various inmate editors and by 1952 had received applications from 50 prisons for the *Handbook for Penal Press Editors* which had been prepared in cooperation with other interested officials outside the state. Articles on the penal press appeared in various national journals to spread the movement and a count in 1954 listed 200 prison publications.[35] The output of budding authors at Jackson in Michigan was so great that the state correction commission appointed an Inmate Manuscript Committee to determine which works were worthy of completion for submission to outside readers. The 27 writers enrolled in 1951 increased to 200 five years later when 20 of these were enrolled in a special class in creative writing and many more were studying in their cells.[36]

The need for trained and dedicated instructors was overshadowed by the broader need for trained personnel throughout the prison system. Successive presidents of the A.C.A. stressed this need as did several governors and professors when addressing its congresses. Dr. Peter P. Lejins of the University of Maryland, the second acting professor to become president of the Association, highlighted the need in his address in 1962, and took a major role in planning and reporting the special conference, at Arden House, in 1964, on Manpower and Training for Corrections. Sponsored by the National Council on Crime and Delinquency, the American Correctional Association, and three other national bodies, it debated

---

[34] J. Edwin LaVallee, "Education at Auburn Prison," *A.J.C.* 28 (May-June 1966): 4–9.

[35] Walter A. Lunden and Oliver A. Nelson, "Prison Journalism," *Prison World* 12 (September-October 1950); Walter A. Lunden and William Johnson, "Inmate Publications and the Reader's Digest," *P.W.* 16 (July-August 1954): 25–26; Joseph K. Balogh, Charles Unkovic and Elgie Raymond, "The Penal Press: An Historical Perspective," *A.J.C.* 29 (January-February 1967): 12–14; Russell N. Baird, *The Penal Press* (Evanston, Ill., 1967).

[36] Earnest C. Brooks, "Something New in Prisoner Responsibility," *A.J.C.* 27 (January-February 1965): 14–16.

many aspects of the problem and reached a concensus on several matters, including a proposal for the creation of a Joint Commission on Correctional Manpower and Training. A federal bill adopted and signed by President Johnson the next year provided funds for the first year and launched its work in January 1966.[37]

The federal bureau had taken the lead in developing a nonpolitical and professional staff. James Bennett had continued the policies he helped develop under Bates and introduced several fresh innovations. In an effort to enhance the usefulness of the classification teams, he pressed for the adoption of the indeterminate-sentence act of 1958, which permitted parole after a third of the sentence was completed provided the bureau's staff recommended such action. In the educational field Assistant Director Loveland abandoned the customary reliance on classwork and developed programs that could be assigned individually. Many prisoners were encouraged to complete the high school equivalency curriculum and some to seek credits for work in nearby colleges. Others found employment in the production programs of the Federal Prison Industries, which continued to maintain production in some fifty different industries even after the war contracts were cancelled. The bureau realized a surplus of $5 million on its sales in 1968 and was able to upgrade its vocational programs in the process.[38]

Bennett, who had always had good relations with his chief executives, was able to secure President Johnson's aid in the passage of the Prison Rehabilitation Act of 1965, which authorized the bureau to grant work-release permits and furloughs, and to develop halfway houses for the pre-release training of prospective parolees. Finally, collaborating with a newly appointed assistant, Myrl Alexander, he developed a "cottage life intervention" program at the National Training School for Boys which applied some of the new techniques of group therapy. This was an elaboration of the program launched under the Federal Youth Correction Act of 1950, which had led to the establishment of new institutions for youths at Ashland, Kentucky and Englewood, Colorado. He closed down the maximum-security prison of Alcatraz when the need for it as an answer to gangsterism passed. The opening of community-

[37] A.C.A., *Proceedings* (1955), pp. 190–205; (1963), pp. 11–16; (1964), pp. 13–20; Arden House Conference, *Manpower and Training for Corrections* (New York, 1966).

[38] Robert M. Carter, Daniel Glaser and Leslie T. Wilkins, eds., *Correctional Institutions* (Philadelphia, 1972), pp. 99–102; James V. Bennett, *I Chose Prison* (New York, 1970), pp. 188–189.

treatment centers or halfway houses in six widely scattered metropoles gave federal endorsement to this correctional innovation.[39]

To justify its correctional programs and support its policy of encouraging an early release on parole, the federal bureau with a grant from the Ford Foundation, commissioned Dr. Daniel Glaser of the University of Illinois to make a study of recidivism. Dr. Glaser studied the post-release record of every tenth man released by the federal prisons in 1956. Out of this sampling of over 1,000 cases, the researchers, after checking FBI reports and the record files of each man in 1960 at the prison of his discharge, found a total of 31 percent to have been reimprisoned for new offenses or for parole violations. This rate of recidivism for adult prisoners contrasted with the higher rates, reported by other studies of youthful parolees from reformatories, and of adults in state systems such as New York and California, where the courts made a generous use of probation sentences, but it was supported by studies of adult parolees in Pennsylvania and Wisconsin which also reported recidivism rates of 31 percent.[40]

Treatment in California and Elsewhere

Leadership in the search for treatment and in testing its effectiveness had meanwhile shifted to California. Governor Warren had contributed to that shift as we have seen, by bringing McGee to Sacramento as commissioner in 1944. He had supported the construction of diversified prisons, the recruiting of a professional staff, and the development of an adult authority charged with the classification, correctional assignment, and determination of parole for each inmate. This ambitious program, which applied to adults the provisions earlier made for youthful offenders, prompted the migration to California of many of the most talented professionals. They found support there for innovative treatment programs and for protracted tests of their performance. A number of commissioners, wardens, and correctional professionals elsewhere hastened to launch similar if less massive experiments and helped to make the fifties and early sixties an exciting penological era.

[39] Bennett, *I Chose Prison,* pp. 204–217; *A.J.C.* 25 (January-February 1963): 6–10; 26 (March-April 1964): 4–10.

[40] Daniel Glaser, *The Effectiveness of a Prison and Parole System* (New York, 1964), pp. 15–26.

Governor Warren and Commissioner McGee received support for their penal innovations from many directions. They had borrowed Bixby from the federal bureau to help, as the one experienced member of the first adult authority, in developing its procedures. Bixby had persuaded Norman Fenton, a sociologist at Stanford, to become director of classification and treatment, and Fenton in turn had recruited professionals from neighboring universities to staff a host of treatment programs testing old doctrines and experimenting with new procedures. Innovation proved easier, they found, when attempted in small units. Thus Scudder's success in transforming Chino into a medium-security institution was achieved by dividing its mounting population into several separate cellblock and camp units. By maintaining active programs for each unit within the confines of a chain link fence, Scudder provided a precedent for the more formalized plan for satellite prison facilities at Soledad. The barracks erected at Soledad to house the convicts assigned to build its maximum-security prison, with its 1,500-bed capacity, demonstrated the feasibility of maintaining a separate medium-security adjunct. After completing that major task, the convict work force, still housed in barracks, proceeded to build two permanent structures with 612-bed capacity each. This satellite facility, known as Soledad North, was close enough to share the heating and other maintenance services of the central Soledad prison, but it had two separate yards and inmate facilities that permitted the development of smaller and more specialized prison communities.[41]

California thus not only recaptured some of the advantages of small prisons but also increased the range of differentiation and specialization. McGee and the Adult Authority took full advantage of this diffusion of facilities and increased the number of road and forest camps to eleven. Three well-equipped mobile camps added in the sixties, accommodating from 40 to 80 men each, further extended the services. The correctional department operated twenty additional minimum-security institutions on scattered farms by the end of the decade, as well as three community correctional centers and thirteen major prisons, also called correctional facilities. Indeed, the varied programs applied throughout California's vast system, which housed 26,000 adults in 1968 and supervised another 16,000 on

[41] *A.J.C.* 22 (January-February 1960): 10–12, 29; Kenyon J. Scudder, "The Open Institution," *Annals* 293 (May 1954): 85–87.

parole, more fully justified the correctional title than those of any other state.[42]

Among the programs that early attracted attention to the California system were two actively promoted by Norman Fenton. As director of classification for the Adult Authority he determined to make the period of detention in the reception and diagnostic center a positive experience for its newly convicted charges. In addition to interviews and questionnaires, Fenton devised a variety of maintenance work assignments and industrial laboratory tasks to test the inmate's capacity and challenge his response to correctional programs. He also experimented cautiously with group counseling. When a reorganization of the system placed him under McGee as deputy director in charge of classification and treatment, he launched a group-counseling program for prospective parolees in one cellblock at San Quentin and in another at Folsom. He also liberalized the regulations governing visitors and provided facilities and opportunities for prisoners to reestablish friendly contacts with their families.[43]

But the California leaders were eager to launch still newer programs. McGee cooperated with the Youth Authority in 1959 in establishing an Institute for the Study of Crime and Delinquency financed by a grant from the Ford Foundation. Among its early projects was a survey of correctional techniques in other states and abroad, which took Drs. John Conrad and Clyde Sullivan of the California correctional staffs on a two-year's exploratory junket. They found a wide commitment to the goal of correction but, except for scattered experiments, little progress towards its realization. The most exciting new developments, they reported, were in California, Britain, and Scandinavia, where certain youth programs, community-treatment projects, and the wide reliance on short sentences attracted their interest. They found work programs in Scandinavian, and especially in Russian, prisons that enlisted the

[42] Joseph W. Eaton, *Stone Walls Not a Prison Make: The Anatomy of Planned Administrative Change* (Springfield, Ill., 1962), pp. 82–92; *A.J.C.* 23 (September-October 1961): 4–5, 16–20; 30 (July-August 1968): 18–23, 28–34.

[43] Norman Fenton, *The Prisoner's Family: A Study of Family Counseling in an Adult Correctional System* (Palo Alto, 1959), pp. 6–14ff.; Norman Fenton, "The Prison as a Therapeutic Community," *Federal Probation* 20 (June 1956), pp. 26–29; Eaton, *Stone Walls*, pp. 92–96.

energies of inmates more productively and constructively than was customary in America.[44]

They took a special interest in the treatment program centering around group discussions in a Danish prison at Herstedvester. That special institution, established by Dr. George K. Sturup in 1935 to treat hard-core adults, limited its inmates to 120 at a time in order to facilitate their intensive treatment by a staff of professionals who endeavored to restore their self-respect and self-confidence. After a period of close confinement the inmates moved into an open section where they acquired experience at jobs in the community in preparation for parole. Dr. Sturup had anticipated or paralleled several of the experiments in group therapy in America, but, unlike Highfields, he applied the group approach to hardened adults, and, in contrast to Fenton's group-counseling programs, which occupied but a fraction of the inmate's time, he made it the center of their penal experience.[45] The only comparable project Conrad and Sullivan encountered was one they found at Deuel in California, but they described promising developments in several centers and reported a new spirit of optimism in the profession.[46]

Dr. Elliot Studt, a psychiatrist on the staff of the Deuel Vocational Institution, had secured the backing of McGee and the correctional department for an experimental effort to develop a correctional community in one cellblock of that new medium-security prison. With two professional colleagues she took full charge of the 130 inmate residents of C-Unit and endeavored to combine staff and inmate functions into a mutually participatory experience focusing on the problems and aspirations of the young men involved. The experiment differed from the therapeutic community approach of Sturup in Denmark or of that practiced at Patuxent in Maryland and of some mental hospitals, which treated inmates as patients, for it regarded them as fellow citizens and endeavored to win their cooperation. Much to the surprise of most participants and observers, the plan began to work as the two groups developed a sense of community interest. It enabled the unit, for example, to

[44] John P. Conrad, *Crime and Its Correction: An International Survey of Attitudes and Practices* (Berkeley, 1965).

[45] Georg K. Sturup, *Treating the "Untreatable": Chronic Criminals at Herstedvester* (Baltimore, 1968).

[46] Conrad, *Crime and Its Correction*, pp. 205–212.

escape involvement in an outbreak of racial and ethnic strife that disrupted the rest of the prison. C-Unit maintained a degree of isolation, but its residents had many work and other assignments in the larger prison, and in the second year key changes in the staff, as well as in the inmate population, weakened the community morale. Internal disputes, coupled with mounting outside pressures from the prison's custodial forces, prompted an abandonment of the program at the end of the two-year experiment.[47]

California might abandon one project, but it was pressing ahead on many fronts. Fenton and McGee introduced group counseling throughout the system. At one point in 1956 over 5,000 men were enrolled in such groups, which were generally limited to forty or fifty inmates and met for an hour or so twice a week. These sessions provided a major innovation in the prison routine both for the inmates and for the participating staff members, who included volunteers from the custodial as well as the correctional personnel. Dr. Fenton extended this program at Soledad in the winter of 1957, opening group-counseling sessions to members of a prisoners family. He further expanded that program a year later, with the backing of the Rosenberg Foundation, to provide counseling to the families of prospective parolees.[48] Walter Gordon, chairman of the Adult Authority, promoted the establishment in 1953 of two parolee camps, similar to one opened in Michigan a few months earlier, and assigned selected candidates for parole to these centers for three months of intensive training. And when the opposition to mandatory attendance at discussion groups began to mount, two correctional officers at Soledad secured permission to enroll nineteen inmate volunteers in a therapeutic community experiment, which proved on a second try so successful that several other staff members recruited groups, and the prison switched from mandatory to volunteer group counseling.[49]

Many of the professional workers drawn into these penological experiments were eager to have their programs evaluated, but before reliable tests could be devised and applied, reports of the state's

[47]Elliot Studt, Sheldon L. Messinger and Thomas P. Wilson, *C-Unit: Search for Community in Prison* (New York, 1968).

[48]Fenton, *Prisoner's Family*, pp. 55–66; Eaton, *Stone Walls*, pp. 157–162.

[49]Walter A. Gordon, "An Experiment in Intensive Supervision," *Focus* 33 (March 1954): 33–36; *A.J.C.* 26 (January-February 1964): 4–6.

penal innovations had stirred emulation elsewhere. Minnesota followed California's lead in creating a youth authority, and its governor protested when critics of the difficulties encountered on the west coast, because of the mounting tide of cases there, attacked the youth authority generally, since it worked with considerable success in his state. The warden of the medium-security prison at Haney in British Columbia took members of his staff on a tour of California's correctional institutions in 1961 before launching a number of educational and other inmate services at Haney designed to provide a community-like experience to the inmates there. Dr. Alex J. Cade, a psychologist in charge of the reception and diagnostic center in Michigan, developed a ten-day orientation program of group counseling to introduce new commitments to the correctional programs available to them.[50]

Everywhere the need to form small groups to ward off prisonization by promoting socialization was emphasized. Inmate groups of members of Alcoholics Anonymous, Volunteers of America, and the like were welcomed in most prisons, but when a small group of blacks, members of a recently organized Temple of Islam at the District of Columbia's correctional institution at Lorton, Virginia, requested permission to hold a religious service once a week, officials became alarmed. Even Donald Clemmer, in his new capacity as superintendent, warned of the danger posed by the Black Muslims. New community-participation societies appeared in several states to promote programs for small groups within the prisons and to aid parolees on their return to the community. But the wide penetration of the race issue during the mid sixties focused the attention of penal scholars on new efforts to measure the effectiveness of their programs.[51]

Any evaluative testing of correctional programs requires years of careful observation of the performance of the participants. Most of the California experiments were of too recent origin to check their recidivism ratios in the sixties, but other appraisals of their effectiveness, and that of similar programs elsewhere, were made by scholars endeavoring to formulate correctional theories or to devise

[50] Luther W. Youngdahl, "Give the Youth Corrections Program A Chance," *Federal Probation* 20 (March 1956): 3–8; *A.J.C.* 22 (March-April 1960): 16–27; 24 (January-February 1962): 4–5.

[51] *A.J.C.* 31 (May-June 1969): 16–20; Donald Clemmer and John W. Wilson, "The Muslim in Prison," *Proceedings* (A.C.A., 1960), pp. 147–149, 155.

new treatment techniques. Thus Oscar Grusky, a Los Angeles sociologist who studied the attitudes of the inmates in Camp Davis, observing their participation over several months in group counseling directed towards a preparation for early parole, concluded that they had freed themselves from the traditional inmate hostilities described by Clemmer and his followers. Grusky was more optimistic that cooperation could be developed than Clarence Schrag, who had studied the hostility of inmates to management in the Washington state prison, but he agreed with Donald R. Cressey that the development of social control among prisoners required a rehabilitation of their self-respect and a readiness to grant paroles on terms they could accept.[52]

A few scattered inmate councils were the only survivals of the earlier experiments with self-government. The last of Osborne's Mutual Welfare Leagues had succumbed in the riot at Auburn in December 1929. Several of the more modest efforts to enlist inmate collaboration in the maintenance of institutional discipline had likewise been abandoned. Richard W. Nice, a clinical psychologist at the Bordentown reformatory in New Jersey, studied the work of adjustment committies in several institutions for young men in 1960. Most of them served only to back up the officials, but he found a few that gave the accused inmates a hearing and buttressed morale in the process. The Wardens' Association was firmly opposed to such modifications of their authority, yet at least a half dozen wardens continued to find elective advisory councils of use in the mid sixties, both in the planning of institutional programs and as an aid to communication between the administration and the convict population. No scholars, however, had as yet measured the rehabilitative effect of advisory councils on recidivism.[53]

Several reformatories and other institutions for juveniles were developing new patterns of inmate participation. The informal regimen successfully developed at Highfields in the early fifties had spurred the opening of three additional residential centers for youths in New Jersey and of several similar institutions in New York and Kentucky. Each of these centers limited the number of its residents to a score or two, and endeavored, by intensive group

[52]*A.J.C.* 21 (March-April 1959): 8–9, 20; Richard A. Cloward *et al, Theoretical Studies in Social Organization of the Prison,* (New York, 1960), pp. 20–35.

[53]*A.J.C.* 22 (November-December 1960): 24–26, 30; J. E. Baker, "Inmate Self-Government," in *Correctional Institutions,* pp. 351–355.

counseling and engaging the boys in work programs in neighboring towns, to speed their preparation for an early return to the community. The Ford Foundation, which helped to support several of these projects, also backed Essexfields, a nonresident center, in Newark, New Jersey, which provided daytime programs, similar to those at Highfields, to delinquent boys who returned to their homes at night and on weekends.[54]

Although it was too early to tabulate recidivism rates on most of the experiments for adults, that did not hold for Highfields and other early programs for juveniles. A study by H. E. Freeman and H. A. Weeks of the graduates of that model institution found a lower rate of recidivism there than in a control group from Annandale Farm. A follow up study by Clarence Sherwood and William Walder confirmed the advantage Highfields had over Annandale, but discovered no advantage over a control group selected from probationers. They concluded that the costly treatment at Highfields was not necessarily better. Albert Elias, superintendent at Highfields, responded with a reminder the boys sent to Highfields were believed to be in need of more treatment than could or would be rendered by probation officers.[55]

The debate continued, but popular favor was shifting to alternatives to institutional confinement, especially for youthful delinquents. In California the Youth Authority was attracting criticism because of its inability to give adequate attention to the dozen or so new commitments received every day. Although the capacity of its institutions and camps had increased from 2,500 to 6,400 in fifteen years without catching up with the demand, a slackening occurred in the late sixties as juvenile courts began to grant probation more readily. A state subsidy for intensified probation services, and another promoting compensatory educational programs in urban schools, helped to check the flood of juvenile commitments and signaled a new approach to the delinquency problem.[56]

As the emphasis on community participation programs devel-

[54] Goldfarb and Singer, *After Conviction*, pp. 66–80.

[55] *A.J.C.* 21 (May-June 1959): 8–9, 25; 21 (July-August 1959): 28–31, 34.

[56] Paul W. Tappan, "The Youth Authority Controversy," in *Contemporary Correction*, ed. Paul W. Tappan (New York, 1951), pp. 135–139; *A.J.C.* 30 (July-August 1968): 24–27.

oped, efforts to test them and to use them to test rival theories about crime also appeared. An early experiment at Provo, Utah, demonstrated the possibility of developing peer-group discussions among delinquents on probation in their home neighborhoods where their loyalties could be redirected to community values. This experiment tended to support a theory advanced by Cloward and Ohlin that delinquency was a response to a social condition in which opportunities for conventional achievements were deficient. At Provo juveniles convicted of serious crimes were permitted to avoid incarceration by participating in peer-group efforts to develop acceptable standards of achievement. By demonstrating that peer groups could face problems of delinquency with candor and could promote responsible work habits, the experiment stressed the social character of correction as well as crime. A program in Flint, Michigan, launched in 1958 at the junior high school, which conducted educational and entertainment programs in the local jail and scheduled evening classes for parolees, enlisted the collaboration of other community groups in work-training programs, leading to job placements that produced a sharp drop in delinquency and further corroborated the Cloward-Ohlin theory.[57]

But few even of the theorists could think of dispensing entirely with prisons for adults, and the search for a scientific basis for treatment intensified. Lloyd McCorkle and Richard Korn described several efforts to develop correctional programs as an antidote to prisonization. When McCorkle became warden at Trenton prison he opened its doors to another sociologist, Gresham M. Sykes, who made a probing study of its inmate society as a followup of Clemmer's earlier study in Illinois. Dr. Sykes was especially interested in the reasons for the outbreak of rioting there in 1952, and he highlighted the sharp conflict that developed when a new administration endeavored to displace the control previously acquired by inmate gangs and "merchant" trusties. Several other scholars likewise focused their attention on the riots of the early fifties, among them Maurice Flock and Frank Hartung, who blamed them on the incomplete or inept policies of reformers who removed

---

[57] Lamar T. Empey and Jerome Rabow, "The Provo Experiment in Delinquency Rehabilitation," *Proceedings* (A.C.A., 1960), pp. 304–316; LaMar T. Empey and Maynard L. Erickson, *The Provo Experiment: Evaluating Community Control of Delinquency* (Lexington, Mass., 1972), pp. 1–21, 269–272; *A.J.C.* 32 (March-April 1970): 6–12.

existing convict leaders without bridging the gap thus created between the inmates and their keepers.[58]

Several research institutes and foundations contributed to the study of crime and to the search for effective methods of treatment. The Russell Sage Foundation published a seminal essay by Lloyd E. Ohlin of the University of Chicago in 1956 on "Sociology and the Field of Corrections." Professor Ohlin reviewed several recent studies of the prison community, of the riots that disrupted it, and of the rates of recidivism. He took note of several experimental treatment programs and of efforts to isolate criteria for prognostication. The Social Science Research Council sponsored a series of conference meetings later that year and the next in which Ohlin, Richard A. Cloward, Donald R. Cressey and other professors reported and exchanged views on recent studies in the social organization of prisons. Shortly after the publication of the report of that conference, Professor Cressey received the backing of the Council for a more extensive volume assembling the contributions of ten experts on *The Prison: Studies in Institutional Organization and Change.* They all agreed "with varying degrees of specificity" that criminal behavior is determined by the "social relationships surrounding the actor," but they differed in the extent to which they regarded the prison as a "total institution," the prison community as dominated by progressive or fluctuating processes of prisonization, and the length of the sentence as productive or counter productive of rehabilitation. They however all subscribed to the conclusion of Clarence Schrag, in his search for a theory of correction, that "the typology [or embryo theory he produced] merits further study."[59]

Most of these theoretical reports assembled a considerable amount of empirical evidence from firsthand studies in one or more prisons, and the protracted character of some of their visits provided a new experience for the inmates and officers involved. Richard H. McCleery's study of the problems of transition when a reform administration took over in the Hawaiian prison at Oahu apparent-

[58] Lloyd M. McKorkle and Richard Korn, "Resocialization Within Walls," *Annals* 293 (May 1954): 88–98; Gresham M. Sykes, *The Society of Captives: A Study of a Maximum Security Prison* (Princeton, 1958); Lloyd E. Ohlin, *Sociology and the Field of Corrections* (New York, 1956), pp. 22–26.

[59] Ohlin, *Sociology;* Cloward, *Theoretical Studies;* Donald R. Cressey, ed., *The Prison: Studies in Institutional Organization and Change* (New York, 1961).

ly helped to strengthen its democratic achievements but blocked his return visit there after a political shift restored the old management.[60] A few of the professional scholars received an opportunity to test their theories in administrative posts, notably Clarence Schrag who served for several years as the director of institutions and agencies (including the prisons) in Washington state and Lloyd McCorkle who became warden of New Jersey's Clinton prison. Several professors served on the state parole boards, where their theories concerning the possibility of developing guidelines for prognostication had a bearing. But many endorsed the conclusion expressed by Daniel Glaser, the most persistent advocate of such studies, that most of the efforts to collect data on recidivism and other evidences of correctional performance were faulted by a poverty and inadequacy of theory, for which all the scholars shared a measure of responsibility.[61]

It was no doubt gratifying to some wardens when Donald L. Garrity sought to disprove, or at least question, the popular belief that prisons breed crime. He found evidence of some corrective or at least deterrent value in them, but the gist of the findings in most of these studies called for an intensified search for alternatives to imprisonment. Clear evidence of the greater economy of probation and parole, when contrasted with the cost of housing men in prisons, had helped to speed the adoption of these laws by all states, but judges facing convicted malefactors had continued in many states to mete out long sentences.[62] Even in California, and the few states that gave their parole authorities or classification clinics the power to determine the length of sentences, the desire to avoid premature release held many convicts for prison terms that exceeded any known abroad. Occasionally a parole authority or a governor, prodded by severe congestion in the state institutions, would adopt a more lenient policy. In West Virginia, for example, overcrowding at the Moundsville prison prompted the adoption of a "crash program" that granted numerous paroles in 1961 and relieved

---

[60] Richard H. McCleery, "The Governmental Process and Informal Social Control," in *The Prison*, pp. 149–188.

[61] Cressey, *The Prison*, *pp. x, 309–357*; A.C.A., *Proceedings* (1959), pp. 175–188; Ohlin, *Sociology*, pp. 49–52; *Journal of Research in Crime and Delinquency* 8 (July 1974): 144.

[62] Donald L. Garrity, "The Prison as a Rehabilitation Agency," in *The Prison*, pp. 358–380.

congestion without evident damage to the public. A Supreme Court decision in 1963 ordered the retrial in Florida of 5,000 felons convicted without the assistance of counsel. When the state released 1,252 in order to reduce the burden on its courts even the warden heaved a sigh of relief and reported no repercussions from local sheriffs.[63]

The mounting concern over the continued growth and increasing ramifications of the crime problem had prompted President Johnson to appoint a Commission on Law Enforcement and Administration of Justice. Headed by Nicholas deB. Katzenbach, the commission had collaborated with federal, state, local, and private agencies in making its national survey. The Corrections Task Force was headed by James Vorenberg and engaged the assistance of numerous consultants in the preparation of a comprehensive *Task Force Report: Corrections,* published in 1967. The Task Force was interested not only in the programs and problems of the 400 institutions for adult felons, but also in those for juveniles and misdemeanants, and in probation, parole, and other treatment programs in the community. In fact, the staff concluded, after a comprehensive survey of the entire correctional field, that the most promising developments in corrections in the postwar years were the new community programs that supplied diverse and promising alternatives to imprisonment.[64]

Despite these conclusions the Task Force found a disproportionate expenditure of staff and monetary effort on the least productive correctional activities. With over 67 percent of all offenders in custody on probation or parole, the state and federal authorities devoted only 20 percent of their correctional budgets to the care of these charges. The remaining 80 percent of correctional expenditures and 85 percent of the staff were absorbed in the management and maintenance of the 400 institutions for adults and the 300 institutions for juveniles. The Task Force also found that approximately a fifth of the 120,000 correctional workers employed in institutional and community-centered programs were engaged in activities designed for correctional treatment. The Task Force reported a number of promising experiments in the treatment of

[63] *A.J.C.* 22 (May-June 1960): 12–13; 29 (July-August 1967): 19–21.

[64] President's Commission on Law Enforcement and Administration of Justice, *Task Force Report: Corrections* (Washington, D.C., 1967), pp. 4–6, 38.

misdemeanants and juveniles as well as adult felons; it recorded numerous innovations in the care of probationers and parolees in community-operated centers. But after describing several of these programs with enthusiasm, it was forced to add: "Unfortunately, however, only a few correctional agencies are developing any of them."[65]

Moreover, as the Task Force considered the developments of the previous half century, it was struck by the irony "that trends in modern corrections towards more humane treatment and greater emphasis on rehabilitation and community supervision have increasingly raised issues of fair process and the rights of offenders." In looking to the future it recognized that these issues would have to be faced as well as the challenge to bring local communities more actively into the process of rehabilitating their own deviants. The development of new racial issues further intensified the urgency of these recommendations.[66]

[For Bibliographic Note see end of Chapter 14.]

[65] Ibid., pp. 4–6, 12, 24, 42–43.
[66] Ibid., pp. 12, 111–113; David Matza, *Delinquency and Drift* (New York, 1964).

fifties had brought a new spirit and rising expectations to many blacks in southern cities and created a new restlessness among their convicts. It was in Washington, the national capital, which had repeatedly served as the focus for civil rights demonstrations and where black residents outnumbered the whites more dramatically than in any other metropolis, that the new spirit invaded the ranks of the inmates who crowded the correctional center maintained by the District of Columbia at Lorton, Virginia. When in 1962 its superintendent, fearing the formation of an organized insurrection, attempted to suppress a group of Black Muslims, he provoked the first prison riot charged with racial overtones.[3]

Disenchanted with the chaplains who served or at least worked with the white officers who managed the prisons, many black inmates became followers of Elijah Muhammad, who recognized a group of disciples in San Quentin in the early 1960s. Scattered disciples had appeared in the prisons of New York and other states in the late fifties, and Commissioner Paul McGinnis had assembled at Albany an official list of Muslims in the various state institutions. The success of Warden T. Wade Markley at the federal penitentiary in Terre Haute in "dissipating the Muslim problem" he encountered on his arrival there in 1960, by breaking up their labor detail and distributing the brothers in scattered assignments, attracted praise but failed to dispel the fear with which most prison officials regarded the Muslims. The remarkable success of the Muslim leaders in transforming reckless and dissolute young blacks into disciplined believers won the grudging admiration of James Baldwin among other observers. But that power gave the groups of Black Muslims an ominous character that rivaled the more sinister reputation of the Black Panthers who also made their appearance in many prisons shortly after their formation in 1966 in response to gun battles in the city streets.[4]

Although these groups were small in size, the mounting flood of

[3] Vernon Fox, "Racial Issues in Correction," *American Journal of Correction* 34 (November-December 1972): 12–17.

[4] New York State Special Commission on Attica, *Attica: The Official Report of the New York State Special Commission on Attica*, Robert B. McKay, ed. (New York, 1972), pp. 114–123; Eldridge Cleaver, "On Becoming," in *Prisons, Protest and Politics*, Burton M. Atkins and Henry R. Glick, eds. (Englewood Cliffs, N.J., 1972), pp. 105–111; Daniel Glaser, *The Effectiveness of a Prison and Parole System* (New York, 1964), pp. 152–154.

blacks crowding many prisons in the fifties and sixties supplied a host of potential converts or new recruits. The number of blacks (and other nonwhites) committed annually to adult federal and state prisons had jumped from 17,200 to 28,500, during the fifties. As the use of probation and other diversions increased in the sixties, the number dropped to some 19,000 in 1970, but their proportion of the total commitments increased from 30 to 40 percent over the two decades. Their commitments more than doubled during the fifties in the North Central states and almost quadrupled in several West Coast states. The surge of blacks into these sections boosted their ratios in many cities, but not as sharply as their increase in convictions. Many young blacks in predominantly white states, finding themselves confined in prisons 40 and 60 percent black and under the control of white guards, began to see themselves as political prisoners. The anti-white teachings of the Black Muslims and similar black nationalists found a ready response.[5]

But the Muslims, Panthers, and similar groups did not create the racism, much less the violence that racked American prisons. Despite the relatively small portion of adult criminals sentenced for violent crimes, violence had been an aspect of prison life from the beginning, and if the brutality of disciplinary punishments had been somewhat moderated in most states, as we have observed above, the abandonment of the rigid controls of the silent system had given the inmates greater opportunity to settle personal hostilities with increasing violence.[6] In spite of repeated "shakedowns," during which the guards made systematic searches of each cell and inmate, confiscating knives and other weapons, frequent stabbings and brutal stompings sent hundreds of victims to the prison hospitals and exacted a frightening toll of lives. The toll mounted sharply in many northern prisons as the influx of blacks accentuated the racial strife.

Thus Soledad, hailed in the late forties and fifties as a model prison, suffered a transformation as outbreaks of violence overshad-

[5] U.S. Bureau of Prisons, *National Prison Statistics* (1950), pp. 55; (1960), p. 40; (1970), p. 48; Fox, "Racial Issues," pp. 16–17.

[6] Daniel Glaser, "Politicalization of Prisoners," *A.J.C.* 33 (November-December 1971): 6–9; Don C. Gibbons, "Violence in American Society: The Challenge to Corrections," *A.J.C.* 31 (March-April 1969): 6–11.

owed its experimental programs. By the mid sixties, when Cletus J. Fitzharris became warden, O-wing, the disciplinary unit with 108 dark cells, became the focus of attention, as the number of stabbings and other violent outbreaks mounted. The failure to develop opportunities for employment, after construction of the 2,750-cell prison was completed, aggravated the disciplinary problem, but the influx of blacks and Chicanos injected new sources of friction. A case brought in 1966 by Robert Jordan, a black confined for several months in a "strip cell" in O-wing, protesting the "cruel and unusual punishment" inflicted by such confinement, exposed many wretched conditions. Judge George B. Harris found the conditions revolting and granted Jordan relief from such treatment.[7]

Jordan won some temporary relief, but his fellow blacks had reason to know that the strip cells in O-wing were still in use. After repeated stabbings and several killings, some apparently provoked by guards who released a black troublemaker for exercise with several Chicanos, or vice versa, a second black, W. L. Nolan, brought a suit against the warden charging the administration with fomenting racial strife. That case was terminated when a guard in O-wing shot and killed Nolan and two black companions allegedly in self-defense. That killing prompted the revenge murder a month later of a white guard, the first Soledad officer to be beaten to death. It was not the last, for nineteen men, seven of them guards, lost their lives in a series of violent assaults during the next two years.[8]

Among those drawn into this vicious chain of events was George Jackson, a young black charged along with two companions with the murder of a white guard. Imprisoned for a decade on a minor charge aggravated by numerous disciplinary infractions (resulting in repeated transfers between Soledad and San Quentin), Jackson had become an advocate of black nationalism, an admirer of Eldridge Cleaver, formerly at Soledad, and of Malcolm X. Before his last confinement to O-wing he had taken advantage of the correctional program to organize a Marxist study group and had endeavored to allay the hostilities between the blacks and the

[7]Roger Provost, "Satellite Prisons," *A.J.C.* 22 (January-February 1960): 10–12, 29; Min S. Yee, *The Melancholy History of Soledad Prison: In Which a Utopian Scheme Turns Bedlam* (New York, 1973). pp. 6–10, 13–25; Robert J. Minton, ed., *Inside: Prison American Style* (New York, 1971), pp. 123–132.

[8]Yee, *Soledad* pp. 29–36ff.; Minton, *Inside*, pp. 82–111.

Chicanos. News of the charge of murder against Jackson and his associates prompted the creation of a defense fund to rally support for the Soledad brothers and brought a visit to the prison of several legislators. Identified as the Black Caucus, their investigations proved so disagreeable to the management that Jackson was again transfered to San Quentin to await his trial.[9]

Alienated and embittered, many friends of the Soledad brothers lost faith in California justice. It was in this mood that George Jackson's younger brother, Jonathan, staged a raid on the Marin County Courthouse, kidnapping Judge Harold Haley and several jurors who were trying a case against another black, and demanded the release of the Soledad brothers in exchange for his hostages. In a shoot-out that followed, the judge as well as Jonathan Jackson and two companions lost their lives. The desperate but abortive action repelled some of his brother's liberal supporters, but brought the Black Panther affiliation more clearly into view. Amidst the mounting tension the stage was set, whether by George Jackson and his accomplices or by the San Quentin guards, for his forceful seizure of the adjustment center on August 21, 1971. With the aid of several inmate volunteers he captured a half dozen guards, four of whom they killed before the alarm was sounded, and Jackson was shot down, allegedly in a frantic dash across the yard for freedom.[10]

The death of George Jackson provided a dramatic symbol of penal revolt, but it was only the most widely publicized incident of the mounting resistance that frustrated the correctional objectives of American prisons. A more concerted riot had erupted in Philadelphia on July 4, 1970, in Holmesburg Prison as the frustrated blacks who comprised 90 percent of the inmates attacked their white companions and the guards who sided with them in an outbreak of racial strife.[11] A survey by Willard D. Leeke, director of the department of correction in South Carolina, recorded the outbreak of 39 prison riots in 1969 and 59 in 1970. Most of them involved less than 100 men and were described as spontaneous in origin, protesting against brutal treatment or poor food. But evidence of a concerted plot was reported in 24 cases, several of which were

[9] Yee, *Soledad*, pp. 120–154; Eldridge Cleaver, *Soul on Ice* (New York, 1968), pp. 11–16; Gerald Leinwand *et al,* eds., *Prisons* (New York, 1972), pp. 91–105.

[10] Yee, *Soledad*, pp. 157–174, 202, 225.

[11] A. Leon Higginbotham, Jr., "From the Outside Looking In," *Outside Looking In* (Washington, D.C., 1970), pp. 2–4.

directed towards civil rights issues. The inmates seized hostages in 25 instances, and five men lost their lives in the bloody battles that ensued.[12]

Numerous committees studied these outbreaks, including the National Commission on the Causes and Prevention of Violence. That distinguished body, headed by Milton Eisenhower, made 81 specific recommendations designed to correct some of the more glaring flaws. But one member, Dr. Walter Menninger, reviewing the accomplishments of that and six other investigations in 1971, found that few of their repeated recommendations had been heeded. A more effective form of protest was the prison strike, Burton M. Atkins maintained, citing the successful stoppage at Sing Sing in 1966, when the state legislature was pressured to adopt a less stringent disciplinary penalty. But a 17-day stoppage at Folsom won no concessions, though it publicized the new drive by Willie Holder and others to form a prisoners' union.[13]

Prison officials were reluctant, even under progressive leaders, to respond to moderate forms of protest. Thus at Attica, where the Muslims, Black Panthers, and Young Lords (representing the Puerto Ricans) had submerged their differences after participating in an inmate-led sociology class in the summer of 1971, efforts to stage collaborative but peaceful protests brought transfer for the principal "troublemakers." On receipt of a manifesto listing a series of demands, Russell Oswald, the new commissioner of corrections, busy with plans for widespread reforms, dispatched a brief acknowledgment and a promise to consider the improvements requested. Oswald, however, rejected the recommendations of Superintendent Vincent Mancusi that the five men who had signed the manifesto of the Attica Liberation Faction be transferred to another prison. He also exchanged further letters with the Attica Liberation Faction, which submitted additional grievances, but Oswald delayed his promised visit. When the news of the shooting of George Jackson in San Quentin reached Attica, the inmates marched to breakfast the next morning in complete and eerie

[12] Willard D. Leeke, "Collective Violence in Correctional Institutions," *A.J.C.* 33 (May-June 1971): 12–16; Atkins and Glick, *Prisons,* pp. 101–105.

[13] W. Walter Menninger, "The Violence Commission," *A.J.C.* 33 (May-June 1971): 22–26; Atkins and Glick, *Prisons,* pp. 6–11, 132–139.

silence. Most of them had acquired black armbands and sat in silence without eating in a demonstration of united hostility that frightened the guards also into silence.[14]

Oswald finally made a brief visit to Attica ten days later and gave the inmate committee a hasty hearing, but an emergency call from his sick wife took him back to Albany and his promise of further consideration of inmate demands seemed a put off. That promise was resented even more by the Attica staff, some of whom reacted by bearing down on the disgruntled inmates. When an officer attempted to discipline two inmates engaging in what appeared to be a sparring match during a recreation period on September 8, one of the inmates pushed the guard aside. A crowd gathered and amidst much shouting persuaded the officer and Lieutenant Curtis, who came to his assistance, to retreat. The incident passed, but the guards appeared that evening and forcibly removed the two most obstreperous inmates to the adjustment center. Inmates in Company 5 who witnessed the removal protested noisily, and the resentment increased that night and broke out anew after breakfast when Lieutenant Curtis, who had assured the inmates the day before that nothing would happen, attempted to lead them back to their cells. In the melee that followed in the A-Block corridor the inmates captured several guards, secured their keys to open the gates into the yard, and broke through a defective lock system to gain control of the "Time Square" intersection, which gave them access to most of the other cellblocks.[15]

Within twenty minutes the inmates had captured control of the four main cellblocks, the intersecting corridors and intervening yards, and had seized 40 hostages as a protection against armed attack. Of the total inmate population of 2,243, over three-fifths joined the uprising and 75 percent of those who participated were black or Puerto Rican. The Muslims, though not active in the initial outbreak, soon assumed the lead in securing the safety of the hostages for bargaining purposes. Brother Richard Clark of that faction joined with leaders of the Panthers, the Young Lords, and other outspoken inmates such as L. D. Barkley and Roger Champen, trusted "inmate lawyers," in establishing sufficient order to draft a

[14] N.Y. Comm., *Attica*, pp. 106–140; Russell G. Oswald, *Attica: My Story* (New York, 1972), pp. 194–210.

[15] N.Y. Comm. *Attica*, pp. 140–165; Richard X. Clark, *The Brothers of Attica* (New York, 1973), pp. 3–8, 16–22.

set of demands. The first list of demands called for complete amnesty for all involved, safe transportation to a nonimperialistic country, the reconstruction of Attica by inmates under federal jurisdiction, and the opening of negotiations within "Our Domain" and in the presence of public observers headed by the civil rights attorney, William M. Kunstler, and including the black Assemblyman Arthur O. Eve of Buffalo. When Eve and Professor Herman Schwartz, an attorney for several inmates, arrived and secured permission to enter the yard, preliminary negotiations commenced at three that afternoon.[16]

Comissioner Oswald had arrived and approved the opening of negotiations. At the suggestion of Professor Schwartz the inmates added new and more negotiable demands calling for the provision of food and medical care and the presence of Oswald to negotiate in front of the assembled convicts and under radio and television coverage. Oswald responded by making two visits to the yard that afternoon; the first in the company of Schwartz and Eve, and the second with representatives of the media who recorded and broadcast the session to a startled public. Oswald agreed to assemble a larger committee of observers, to secure a federal injunction protecting the inmates from physical or administrative reprisals, and to return the next morning with his answers to their further demands. He supplied food and medical care that evening and approved the draft of an injunction which Professor Schwartz rushed off to Judge Curtin for his signature. But it was 11:25 rather than 7:00 the next morning when Oswald and five observers, accompanied by a dozen representatives of the media, reentered the yard. The inmates, having discovered that the injunction lacked a seal, suspected a trick and loudly abused Oswald and Schwartz, demanding the presence of the full list of observers before negotiations could continue.[17]

Finally, a group of 24 observers arrived and was admitted under double security searches, first by the officers, and then by the inmates, to the negotiating table in the yard. The unusual procedure was interrupted after a half hour in conference to permit the inmates to complete their list of demands and to enable the observers to reexamine their status with Oswald. William Kunstler, the civil liberties lawyer, arrived during the interval and assumed the lead

[16] N.Y. Comm. *Attica*, pp. 108–113, 116–206; Clark, *Brothers*, pp. 22–72.
[17] N.Y. Comm. *Attica*, pp. 207–232; Clark, *Brothers*, pp. 95–102.

when the observers returned to the yard at 11:30 for a midnight conference. With much speechmaking and a hair-raising interruption when the inmates extinguished the lights in fear of an attack, the conference continued until 5:00 A.M. The observers were now split as the majority accused four members of openly encouraging the inmates' demand for complete amnesty. When negotiations resumed the next day the situation had changed because of the death during the night of one of the guards seriously injured on the first day. As knowledge of that event spread through the prison, the opposing stands of the inmates and the administration on the question of amnesty hardened. Negotiations continued through the weekend, focusing for a time on an appeal to Governor Rockefeller to come to Attica. His refusal and the inmates' insistence on complete amnesty gradually extinguished all hope for a peaceful settlement.[18]

The long period of innovative negotiations was abruptly ended on Monday morning when the assault by the state police commenced at 9:45. Oswald had disregarded many penal administrative principles in his endeavor to reach a peaceful settlement, but the charge of the troopers, supported by prison guards, with an "excessive" use of fire power, exacted a toll of 39 lives and inflicted gunshot wounds on 88 others. The bloody assault during which nine hostages were fatally shot, as well as several of the inmate negotiators, so overshadowed the earlier negotiations that Attica became a symbol of brutal force and suppression. The effort to justify the violence as necessary to prevent the convicts from slashing the throats of all the hostages, as they had threatened to do, boomeranged when the medical examiners who performed the autopsies discovered that, although some suffered severe knife wounds, all nine hostages had died of gunshot wounds. The initial tragedy was further compounded as the infuriated guards wreaked vengence on the surviving inmates.[19] A panel of five observers, named at the governor's request by Judge Harry D. Goldman and including Austin MacCormick, commenced its inspections on Friday the 17th and continued to monitor activities at Attica for a full

---

[18]N.Y. Comm., *Attica*, pp. 233–330; Clark, *Brothers*, pp. 103–219; Oswald, *Attica*, pp. 212–253. See also the detailed and graphic firsthand account by one of the observers, Tom Wicker, *A Time to Die* (New York, 1975), a perceptive and moving book by an associate editor of the *New York Times*.

[19]N.Y. Comm., *Attica*, pp. 332–464.

month. Its early protests against overcrowding in keep-lock cells hastened the transfer of many inmates to other prisons; its call for a complete medical inventory of all prisoners safeguarded against further unrecorded beatings; its insistence on the provision of adequate food and bathing facilities, the replacement of smashed eyeglasses and dentures, and greater access to counsel brought improvements and a progressive return to normal penal procedures.[20]

But normal penal procedures had lost creditability in the Attica holocaust. Convicts in prisons across the land felt a new sense of class consciousness, and to check the trend towards politicalization some guards apparently provoked racial incidents that led to a renewal of the war behind bars. When a dozen stabbings occurred in three months in the four major prisons of California, four in one day at San Quentin, producing several fatalities and culminating in the murder of a corrections officer at Deuel Vocational Institution at Tracy, Director Raymond K. Procunier clamped a "lock down" at San Quentin, Folsom, Soledad and Tracy, suspending all rehabilitation programs, work assignments, and recreational activities for their 9,000 inmates for an indefinite period. This effectively terminated some of the most progressive programs in the land. Meanwhile the unsparing report of the New York State Special Commission on Attica, headed by Robert B. McKay, dean of the New York University Law School, appeared in a 533-page book that stunned thousands of readers but met a frigid official silence.[21]

The department was more concerned to vindicate its actions to Deputy Attorney General Robert E. Fisher and to assist him in prosecuting crimes committed during the riot. Oswald in *Attica: My Story* blotted out the crucial days of hopeful negotiations and concentrated on the collapse of that effort and the tragic events that followed. In contrast, some of his fellow administrators in other states, together with leading sociologists, focused their attention on the proximate causes and inherent character of such uprisings rather than on the means for their suppression.[22] Daniel Glaser blamed riots on a failure of communication and deplored the fact that the

[20] Ibid., pp. 441–470; Oswald, *Attica*, pp. 399–418.

[21] Oswald, *Attica*, pp. 325–326; "Lockdown," *Corrections* 1 (September 1974), pp. 32–34; Atkins and Glick, *Prisons*, pp. 60–76.

[22] Oswald, *Attica*, pp. 210ff, 320–341; N.Y. Comm., *Attica*, pp. 461, 465.

locations of most prisons in isolated rural areas encouraged the employment of guards whose backgrounds prevented them from relating to inmates from urban areas. Maurice H. Sigler, former warden and director of corrections in Nebraska and president of the American Correctional Association in 1972, reviewed the year of riots and declared that new correctional programs would have to be tried. In his capacity as chairman of the Federal Parole Board, he saw the need for a new and more attentive attitude towards the courts, a more hearty welcome to defense lawyers visiting clients, a more open relation with representatives of the media, a more cooperative attitude towards citizen groups interested in the rehabilitation of inmates, and a renewed zeal for improved skills and higher professional standards.[23]

Litigation and Prisoners' Rights

A new concern for the rights of prisoners had been developing since the early sixties. Responding to the civil rights movement in the larger society, several judges, legal scholars and members of the bar, troubled by the disparate character of criminal sentences and of the penal practices that followed, had collaborated in the American Law Institute in devising a model penal code. Correction officers were likewise concerned, and former director Bennett, who had staged a succession of sentencing institutes for federal judges in the late fifties, was pleased to see the practice adopted in several large states. Still another attack on prevailing sentences, by the National Council on Crime and Delinquency, produced a draft of a Model Sentencing Act to assist legislators in adopting more specific guidelines for judges. A number of scholarly criminologists voiced a resurgent concern for principles of criminal justice and advocated a revival of classical concepts of crime and punishment as opposed to either hard or soft determinism. But the chief incentive came from a series of court decisions reviewing the civil rights of convicts and spurring many prisoners to prepare writs and to seek to improve their lot by litigation rather than force.[24]

[23] Glaser, "Politicalization," 6–9; *A.J.C.* 34 (September-October 1972): 8–10, 20–22, 37.

[24] Herbert Wechsler, "Sentencing, Correction, and the Model Penal Code," *University of Pennsylvania Law Review* 109 (February 1961): 465–493; Sol Rubin, *The Law of Criminal Correction* (St. Paul, 1963), pp. 651, 670; James V. Bennett, *I Chose Prison* (New York, 1970), pp. 190–193; Ronald L. Goldfarb and Linda R. Singer, *After Conviction* (New York, 1973), pp. 166–178, 364ff.

*   *   *

Prisoners' grievances had been festering for decades, but it was not until the Supreme Court in the early 1960s relaxed its "hands off" policy that their voices gained a hearing in the courts. Justice Douglas in 1961 cited the Civil Rights Act of 1871 in affirming the duty of the courts to hear claims of citizens against states when their constitutional rights were infringed, and three years later the Warren court recognized such a plea from a state prisoner. And when that court, in *Gideon* v. *Wainwright* (1963), upheld the right of defendants to be provided with attorneys at all stages of their trials, the state of Florida had to release over a thousand improperly convicted men, and prisoners everywhere began to review their trials and seek grounds for redress.[25] "Jailhouse lawyers" multiplied, and their requests for legal reference books, for writing materials, and for opportunities to consult their attorneys or to assist fellow inmates who sought their advice, often strained the patience of prison officials. Some legal authorities favored the trend, however, and Judge Harry Goldman persuaded three law schools in upstate New York to grant academic credits to seniors who assisted jailhouse lawyers in drafting writs. A librarian at one institution reported the development of a new interest in and respect for law among formerly alienated inmates.[26]

Inmates played a vital role in prodding the courts to define the scope of their constitutional rights. Scattered judges hastened to safeguard the freedom of worship, even of Muslims and of a new humanistic sect, the Church of the New Song, organized by white convicts in several prisons. Federal and state courts upheld the right of a prisoner to communicate with his family and friends and under some limitations with the press; they affirmed the equal protection of the laws, which guarded against segregation on grounds of race or religion. The courts moved with less unanimity to assure due process to men in confinement, including written notice and an opportunity to be heard on serious disciplinary matters within prisons and before the parole boards. Under the Eighth Amendment, which prohibits "cruel and unusual punishment," the courts

[25] Goldfarb and Singer, *After Conviction*, pp. 119–180, 368–369. He cites *Monroe* v. *Pope*, 365 U.S. 167 (1961), *Cooper* v. *Pate*, 378 U.S. 546 (1964), *Gideon* v. *Wainwright*, 372 U.S. 355 (1963).

[26] Hazel B. Kerpe, "Writs as a Correctional Aid," *A.J.C.* 29 (November-December 1967): 30–31; Interview with Judge Harry Goldman, 5 January 1975.

declared that "the punishment must not by its severity be degrading to human dignity" nor may it be inflicted in "wholly arbitrary fashion."[27]

Leading judges and legal scholars repeatedly stressed the limited capacity of the courts to determine correctional and other administrative procedures. They urged legislative action, and some rejoiced when Pennsylvania adopted the minimum rules for the treatment of prisoners proposed by the United Nations as a model bill of rights for prisoners. To promote a forthright administration of prisoners' rights, the Department of Correction of South Carolina secured the backing of the Law Enforcement Assistance Administration for a comprehensive compilation of cases and decisions tracing "The Emerging Rights of the Confined."[28]

In a series of somewhat conflicting opinions the Supreme Court in 1972 held the death penalty as enforced in the various states to be in violation of constitutional rights. But many citizens, disturbed by reports of mounting crime in the streets, backed a drive to restore the death penalty, and soon new capital punishment laws won adoption in twenty-nine states. State prisons, which had closed their death rows and refurbished the cells for other uses, had to find new accommodations for men awaiting execution. Legal writs accumulated, delaying action in most cases and focusing attention on a reconsideration of the constitutionality of the death penalty. While the public awaited the final verdict, journalists and professors debated the objectives of punishment and the basic requirements of justice.[29]

Many judges eagerly looked forward to the day when the hands-off doctrine would again be tenable, but they were not abdicating their responsibility to safeguard the constitutional rights of American citizens. Indeed, in 1970, in *Holt* v. *Sarver*, the federal district court found the practices in effect at the Arkansas prison

[27]Donald P. Lay, "Corrections and the Courts," *Resolution* 1 (Fall 1974): 5–11; President's Commission on Law Enforcement and Administration of Justice, *Task Force Report: Corrections* (Washington, D.C., 1967), pp. 84–86; Goldfarb and Singer, *After Conviction*, pp. 403–433. See also *Morrissey* v. *Brewer*, 408 U.S. 471 (1972); *Wolff* v. *McDonnell* 42 U.S.L.W. 3304 (1974); *New York Times* 24 September 1972; 24 January 1973.

[28]Sol Rubin, "Needed: New Legislation in Correction," *Crime and Delinquency* 17 (October 1971): 392–405; *A.J.C.* 34 (September-October 1972): 28; South Carolina Department of Corrections, *The Emerging Rights of the Confined* (Columbia, 1972).

[29]Charles L. Black, Jr., *Capital Punishment* (New York, 1974).

farm at Cummins (16,600 acres), and with few exceptions at Tucker (4,500 acres) as well, so abominable and deficient of acceptable standards that it condemned the state's entire correctional system.[30]

A related series of cases considered the "right to treatment" claimed in some institutions specifically dedicated to rehabilitation but deficient in programing. These cases arose at first in institutions for mentally defective criminals, such as Bridgewater in Massachusetts, and extended to institutions for drug addicts as in New York and California. But the courts dodged claims by normal prisoners for release even when the "program of rehabilitation" mandated by the legislature was not produced.[31] Challenges to transfers and classification assignments were likewise sidestepped by most courts. The possibility that inmates might claim a right not to be rehabilitated had so far only been debated by scholarly observers, some of whom saw it as a forthcoming defense of personal integrity by some alienated delinquents.[32]

Chief Justice Berger, whose court handled more correctional cases than all his predecessors combined, recognized that neither an adequate legislative code nor a fully detailed judicial interpretation would suffice without a conscientious administration. To promote that on the local level he prompted the American Bar Association to create a Commission on Correctional Facilities and Services in 1971 and helped it secure a Ford Foundation grant to develop correctional programs on the local as well as the national level. These included research, education, publications, the establishment of job placement centers, and the recruitment of volunteers as participants in parole programs as well as in the representation of inmate appellants before the courts. The increased knowledge and experience of inmate grievances thus acquired promised further changes.[33]

[30] Lay, "Corrections," p. 7; citing *Holt* v. *Sarver*, 390 F. Supp. 362–367, (E. D. Ark. 1970); Tom Murton and Joe Hyams, *Accomplices to the Crime* (New York, 1969) for an account of the atrocities and corruption in the Arkansas prisons by a professional penologist; Goldfarb and Singer, *After Conviction*, pp. 374–376.

[31] Goldfarb and Singer, *After Conviction*, pp. 395–402; citing *Mason* v. *Superintendent of Bridgewater*, 353 Man. 604, 233 N.E. 2d 908 (1968); *People ex rel. Ceschini* v. *Warden*, 30 APP. Div. 2d 649 (1968); *Wilson* v. *Kelley*, 294 F. Supp. 1005 (N.D. gd. 1968).

[32] S.C. Dept. Corr., *Emerging Rights*, pp. 22–23, 170–180; Massachusetts Correctional Association, *Correctional Research* 22 (November 1972): 25.

[33] American Bar Association, "Commission on Correctional Facilities and Services" (Leaflet, n.d.); *A.J.C.* 33 (July-August 1971): 28–31; 35 (January-February 1973): 20–21, 25.

*   *   *

A grievance that appeared increasingly on every inmate list and at most counseling sessions between inmates and attorneys was a protest against the length and uncertainty of the sentences. Neither the attorneys nor the judges could do much about this widespread complaint, which was most vocal in progressive states, such as California and New York, where the indeterminate gaps in the sentences were most extended. The inmate grievances challenged not only the hasty and often arbitrary conduct of the parole boards, but also the basic principle of the correctional system.[34]

In California, where the Adult Authority represented the extreme application of the reform concept that called for treatment measured to the needs of the criminal, not to the nature of his crime, the protests were most numerous. Careful studies of the results revealed that the median time served by adults had increased from 24 to 30 months between 1960 and 1965 and rose almost to 40 months in 1972. Raymond Brown, chairman of the Adult Authority, blamed it on the tough breed of convicts received as probation screened a larger portion of the lesser offenders out of the stream of commitments. Some critics, however, noted that the social-work viewpoint present on the original board had been displaced by appointments of former police officers who gave security considerations highest priority.[35]

Popular protests were even more outspoken against the Youth Authority and against juvenile courts generally for placing children in institutions indefinitely for minor charges. Paul W. Tappan had condemned the youth-authority principle in the mid fifties and had checked its spread and prompted the American Law Institute, which had drafted the original model, to call for a return of the power to grant probation and short sentences to the courts. The California Youth Authority relieved the pressure on its diversified institutions by developing a Community Treatment Project which diverted seven hundred youngsters into experimental home-treatment programs matched by institutional control groups. The experiment supported the doubts many were expressing as to the social utility of long institutional sentences for youths and spurred the adoption of more

[34]Goldfarb and Singer, *After Conviction,* pp. 162–174, 264–274; Pres. Comm. *Corrections,* pp. 186–188.

[35]Michael S. Serrill, "Profile/California," *Corrections* 1 (September 1974): 8–11.

liberal probation policies and the search for other alternatives.[36]

Critics of the American Law Institute were prodding it to modify its Model Penal Code as well. Sol Rubin, now counsel emeritus of the National Council on Crime and Delinquency and principal author of the leading text in the field, found the objectives of the institute's model code to be inconsistent and the guidelines offered to judges and parole boards vague and indefinite. He much preferred the Model Sentencing Act proposed by an advisory group of judges named by his National Council. But this model, which called for a differentiation of offenders into three categories of "dangerousness" based in part on the pre-sentence probation reports, while it relieved the judge of unlimited discretion in sentencing, and suggested probation for the less dangerous, retained the indeterminate sentence for the great majority of cases. Both models frowned on the imposition of minimum sentences and regarded low maximums (less than five years) as undesirable in most cases, for both codes retained rehabilitation as a major objective. Trial judges, however, continued in most states, when permitted by the statutes, to impose minimums as well as maximums, and to push the two progressively closer together in response to the popular reaction against the mounting crime wave.[37]

Some critics protested the whole correctional approach. An increasing number, following John B. Martin, boldly proposed a wide dissolution and abandonment of prisons and a reliance on fines and other restraints and on a forthright effort to remove the causes of crime. Many legal authorities, similarly impressed by the failings of the correctional system and aware of its inability to predict with any assurance the degree of dangerousness or the probability of recidivism of individual malefactors, were nevertheless responsive to society's desire for security and for retribution when public and private rights were violated. They proposed a return to fixed sentences designed to fit the crime, and they urged judges to measure out sentences according to the public or private

[36] Goldfarb and Singer, *After Conviction*, pp. 172–174, 192–194; Serrill, "California," pp. 4, 43–44, 49–51; Wechsler, "Sentencing," pp. 465–493; Allen F. Breed, "Why Not Justice for Juveniles?," *Resolution* 1 (Fall 1974): 12–18.

[37] Rubin, *Criminal Correction*, pp. 645–670; Wechsler, "Sentencing,"; Goldfarb and Singer, *After Conviction*, pp. 174–205.

injury suffered.[38] Without specifically asserting it, they were calling for an abandonment of deterministic interpretations and a return to classical concepts of crime and punishment.

Some scholars, such as Norval Morris, professor of law at Chicago, reluctantly accepted this basic necessity but refused to abandon the correctional objective or to surrender the reformatory tradition. Instead, as Morris proposed, the search for increased knowledge and for more effective treatment programs should be pressed with redoubled zeal and should be made available on a volunteer basis to offenders, whether confined in institutions, or retained under lesser restraint in the community. But the duration of such treatment programs should never exceed the time limit of the retributive sentence, in Morris' opinion, with which Judge David S. Bazelon, addressing a seminar marking the 150th anniversary of the Yale Law School, agreed.[39]

Legal scholars, concerned with abstract justice, were able to propose such an about-face in penal theory with greater ease than administrators could effect it. But a number of responsible consultants were beginning to ponder the unexpected dilemmas resulting from a combination of rehabilitation with punishment. One of the first groups to consider this question was the Joint Commission on Correctional Manpower and Training. Its members and staff, faced with the task of planning improved training programs, had to define correctional objectives. In the process they discovered a need to remove or at least reduce the sense of injustice among the prisoners and to engender a more cooperative reception of released convicts by the public. These objectives prompted proposals for new attitudes towards probation, parole and the indeterminate sentence. Soon not only the Vera Institute of Justice, established in 1961 in New York to maintain the Manhattan Bail Project and other services, but also the Institute for the Study of Crime and Delinquency in California were considering these problems. Richard McGee, director of the latter and head for many

---

[38]Karl Menninger, *The Crime of Punishment* (New York, 1968); Jessica Mitford, *Kind and Usual Punishment* (New York 1973); American Friends Service Committee, *Struggle For Justice: A Report on Crime and Punishment in America* (New York, 1971).

[39]Norval Morris, "The Future of Imprisonment: Toward a Punitive Philosophy," *University of Michigan Law Review* 72 (1974): 1161–1180; *New York Times* 3 November 1974; David Matza, *Delinquency and Drift* (New York, 1964), pp. 1–27.

years of California's correctional program, finally in 1972 confessed his disillusionment with the indeterminate sentence philosophy of its Adult Authority.[40]

Testing Programs and Seeking Alternatives

A contributory factor in the reassessment of the correctional system and the indeterminate sentence was the mounting skepticism concerning institutional confinement and most treatment programs. Startling increases in reported ratios of recidivism had occurred in the forties and again in the fifties, and Professor Glaser in a painstaking study of over a thousand federal releasees in 1956 and again three years later found that the ratio of failures had climbed from 35 to 49 percent in that brief span. The declining age of the inmate population and the changing character of the crimes helped to account for that sudden jump, but advocates of treatment programs, particularly in the state systems, desired evidence of success to back applications for legislative support and eagerly launched new tests. In spite of many negative findings, improved research techniques encouraged progressive administrators to adopt and test alternative programs in a continuing quest for correctional goals.[41]

California, which had taken the lead in the development of treatment programs in the forties and fifties, assumed the lead also in testing their effectiveness. Possibly the need to justify the large expenditures for correctional purposes had its effect, but so did the presence of a host of social scientists in nearby colleges and their increasing interest in correction. James Robison, from the Research Center in Davis, questioned the value of comparing recidivism ratios of parolees from different institutions where the commitments also differed. Of numerous studies examined only a few followed

[40] Joint Commission on Correctional Manpower and Training, *Perspectives on Correctional Manpower and Training* (Washington, D.C. 1970), pp. 1-7, 59-73; Richard A. McGee, "A New Look at Sentencing," Part I, *Federal Probation* 38 (June 1974): 3-8; and "A New Look at Sentencing," Part II, *Federal Probation* 38 (September 1974): 3-11.

[41] Glaser, *Parole System*, p. 43; R. G. Hood, "Some Research Results and Problems," in *Crime and Justice*, vol. 3, *The Criminal in Confinement*, Leon Radzinowicz and Marvin E. Wolfgang, eds., (New York, 1971), pp. 159-182; Walter C. Bailey, "An Evaluation of One Hundred Reports," ibid., pp. 187-195.

sufficiently rigorous research techniques to give their findings scientific credence, and their evidence for the most part was negative. Leslie T. Wilkins, then at Berkeley, in a more extensive review of penological studies likewise found most of them lacking in precision, both in the definition of recidivism and in the selection of control groups. He noted that while European penologists tended to overstress the *nature* of the individual criminal, Americans overstressed his *nurture* or environment and failed to give his distinctive personality adequate attention. He also deplored the stress on studies of total institutions rather than of treatment programs, which promised greater enlightenment.[42]

The most significant treatment program in the California system was group counseling, and Walter Dunbar, director of the state department of correction, and Robert Harrison, coordinator of the counseling activities, welcomed an offer by Gene Kassebaum, David Ward, and David Wilner to undertake a rigorous test of that program. California Men's Colony—East at San Luis Obispo, which opened in 1961, offered an ideal opportunity for the successful implementation of the counseling program and for the designation of control groups. With elaborate precautions and the full cooperation of superintendent John H. Klinger and his staff, the three scholars developed a research design, trained the counseling and interviewing personnel, and conducted two extended group-counseling programs, one of greater intensity, and carefully recorded the results. To measure the effects of the counseling programs, which commenced in January 1962 (with the exception of C-Block where the control group not subjected to treatment resided), the project continued until December 1963, when the first and the second more intensive program, commenced in September 1962, both came to an end. The collection of data on parolees released from these three groups continued from March 1963 to June 1967, giving at least a three-year followup on all the men involved.[43]

Most of the researchers, as well as the administrators, anticipated a demonstration of effective treatment, but the results proved disap-

---

[42] James Robison and Gerald Smith, "The Effectiveness of Correctional Programs," *Crime and Delinquency* 17 (January 1971): 67–80; Leslie T. Wilkins, *Evaluation of Penal Measures* (New York, 1969), pp. 53–83.

[43] Gene Kassebaum, David Ward and David Wilner, *Prison Treatment and Parole Survival: An Empirical Assessment* (New York, 1971), pp. 57–85.

pointing. The evidence, in fact, was negative since the researchers could find no appreciable difference between the parole records of the intensive and non-intensive counseling groups, or between either of these and the non-treatment control group. Their findings seemed to support the conclusion reached by James Robison that the funding of treatment programs was a waste of money. But while criticizing the rationalization of many treatment coordinators—that more money was needed for more effective programs—Kassebaum and his colleagues recommended more testing of correctional programs to discover which, if any, were effective.[44] Robert Martinson, who had spent a year on the staff of the CMCE project, joined with Douglas Lipton and Judith Wilks for a four-year analysis of 231 American and foreign evaluation studies published from 1945 to 1967 of the treatment of juvenile and adult offenders. The studies were individually annotated, classified into eleven broad categories and evaluated on the basis of the effectiveness of any type of treatment applied to the offender. The analysts looked for changes in recidivism, institutional, vocational and community adjustment, educational achievement, drug and alcohol readdiction, and personality and attitude changes. Only a small number of the studies were found to be free of serious methodological shortcomings. The principal inference that could be drawn from the entire body of research was that no correctional treatment program undertaken to date has had a significant effect on recidivism.[45]

Despite the generally negative findings of most of the evaluative studies, a few did produce suggestive hints to correctional administrators. James O. Standley, a psychiatrist at Huntsville, in his search for variables that would help him to identify men who would be likely to benefit from treatment in one of the medium-security camps in Texas, discovered that inmates with active contacts in the free society were more amenable to correctional programs than isolates or frequent repeaters. John Irwin, who made a study of the careers of 116 California parolees, discovered that while many could be classified under one or another of his seven behavior categories,

---

[44] Ibid., pp. 207–298, 304–324; Charles H. Logan, "Evaluation Research in Crime and Delinquency: A Reappraisal," *J.C.L.C.* 63 (September 1972): 378–387.

[45] Douglas Lipton, Robert M. Martinson and Judith Wilks, *The Effectiveness of Correctional Treatment: A Survey of Treatment Evaluation Studies* (New York, 1975).

many others were ambivalent, and most at one point or another were flexible and ready to respond positively or negatively to new opportunities. He noted, moreover, that in California with its multiplicity of programs and because of the suspense created by the Adult Authority's periodic hearings, the traditional prisonization had been in part superceded by a polarization of inmates, some working for early parole and others alienated and rebellious. Even the latter, most of whom were young, had later and potentially more mature stages, in Irwin's analysis, when they could become dedicated radicals or confirmed criminals. The correctional programs did have an impact, if not the intended effect, but recidivism, in his view, was not the significant gauge.[46]

California staged and tested still another important experiment, which had even greater impact. In 1961, when the Youth Authority's institutions were overflowing with new commitments, Director Allen F. Breed, Dr. Marguerite Q. Warren, supervisor of research, and Dr. Theodore Palmer, the chief researcher, launched a Community Treatment Project to test the relative merits of institutional treatment as opposed to intensive supervision in the community. Two groups, chosen at random from new commitments, were tested and divided into three classes characterized by maturity, toughness, and passivity. One group, designated as the experimentals, was returned to the community under intensive supervision by workers trained for the job. The other, or control group, was held under standard treatment in juvenile institutions for eight or ten months and then released under normal parole supervision. A careful check over a period of eight years revealed that, while the boys among the experimentals who were classified as tough included more failures than that class produced in the control group, in the other two categories those released to the community proved more adjusted than those held in institutions. Dr. Palmer concluded that at least half the youths sent to institutions could, if properly screened, be more successfully treated in the community. Paul Lerman of Rutgers University, who reanalysed the project's findings, judging the application of the three-level classification to be unreliable, disputed Palmer's conclusions. But the state, confident of the merits

---

[46] James O. Standley, "Treatment Oriented Security Screening," *A.J.C.* 31 (March/April 1969): 22–25; John Irwin, *The Felon* (Englewood Cliffs, N.J., 1970).

of community treatment, gave full support through its probation subsidy program to counties that retained delinquent youths and adults as well under intensive supervision in the community. California thus sharply reduced the pressure on its institutions and awaited the completion of a second community-treatment test.[47]

The negative results of many tests of treatment programs prompted some scholars to reassess their basic assumptions. Thus David Matza, on discovering that while youthful delinquents displayed no consistent response to varied correctional experiments, many of them outgrew their delinquency on reaching maturity, developed a theory of *drift* to explain their differing responses. As he saw it, some youths were imbedded in a "subculture of delinquency" which enabled them to negate the sanctions against crime and to develop a sense of injustice when punished for an assertion of their manhood. Instead of outgrowing their delinquency, they drifted, as he put it, into a deeper commitment to crime in a willful encounter with well-meaning but bungling officials. To counter this drift, correctional workers as well as the courts should, he maintained, foster rather than violate the delinquent's sense of justice.

Although the total number of adult commitments to state and federal prisons dropped from a high of 93,500 in 1961 to 87,500 in 1965, the explanation was found in the increased use of probation, for arrests continued to mount. The problems were too pressing to permit a relaxation of effort. In a society whose major companies devoted huge sums to research and development and where defense spent 15 percent of its outlays on research, it did not seem reasonable to ask the correctional system to reduce the less than one percent committed to research. Instead, the federal government, under the Safe Streets Act of 1968, and responding to the recommendations of the Joint Commission on Correctional Manpower and Training, created a Law Enforcement Assistance Administration (LEAA) with authority to fund a variety of correctional as well as enforcement projects, chiefly of an experimental character designed to upgrade

[47] Serrill, "California," pp. 5, 43–44, 49–52; Paul Lerman, "Evaluative Studies of Institutions for Delinquents: Implications for Research and Social Policy," *Social Work* 13 (July 1968): 55–64; see also LaMar T. Empey and Stephen G. Lubeck, *The Silverlake Experiment: Testing Delinquency Theory and Community Intervention* (Chicago, 1971) for an account of still another California effort to test delinquency theory and practice in the juvenile field.

the correctional practices of the states as well as of the Federal Bureau of Prisons.[48]

A major objective of the LEAA program was to explore new directions for criminal justice. In the field of corrections this meant the development of new treatment techniques and more importantly the discovery of alternatives to imprisonment. The President's Commission had emphasized the need for collecting better information on each delinquent at key points in his career, and LEAA backed experiments in pre-trial testing and release without bail, on reclassification at the end of the first year of a sentence, and on work furloughs before parole. An experiment at the National Training School at Morgantown, West Virginia, permitted inmates to select projects and determine the rate of production in order to win points towards an increase of privileges. An even more daring effort to enlist inmate cooperation was the mutual-agreement programing undertaken in Wisconsin, California, and Arizona in 1972. The contracts signed by the inmates with their officers enabled them to determine their own preparation for parole.[49] Renewed emphasis on the work-release furloughs promoted their adoption by all but two states and extended their application to 1.5 percent of all federal and state inmates by 1972. Several attempts to test the results were inconclusive, but the furloughs won increasing acceptance.[50]

Another objective emphasized by President Johnson's Commission, by the Joint Commission on Correctional Manpower and Training, by the Williamsburg Conference on Crime and Correction called by President Nixon in 1971, and by many other investigating committees was the development of community treatment programs. The halfway houses multiplied, some limited to probationers but most serving parolees and other discharged prisoners. Oliver J. Keller, who visited 81 such community

[48]Gordon P. Waldo, "Dilemma of Correctional Research," *A.J.C.* 31 (November-December 1969): 6–8; Law Enforcement Assistance Administration, *Second Annual Report* (Washington, D.C., 1970).

[49]Pres. Comm., *Corrections*, pp. 53–58; Pres. Comm., *The Challenge of Crime in a Free Society* (Washington, D.C., 1967), pp. 159–185; George Mills, "Mutual Agreement Programming," *A.J.C.* 35 (March-April 1973): 17–19, 38; Des Moines Community Correction Project, *Evaluation Report* (1972).

[50]Walter H. Busher, *Ordering Time to Serve Prisoners* (Washington, D.C., 1973); Norman Holt, "Temporary Prison Release: California's Prerelease Furlough Program," *Crime and Delinquency* 17 (October 1971): 414–430; *A.J.C.* 35 (March-April 1973): 36.

treatment centers in 22 states in the late sixties, found many providing useful assistance to youths, to unemployed adults, or to other ex-convicts with special problems. Pennsylvania developed such centers in four of its major cities to house men on work-release assignments as well as on parole. Most of the halfway houses were community projects with some state and federal support; some were wholly self-supporting, such as the Delancey Street Foundation in San Francisco, managed and maintained by its former drug-addict members.[51] Other citizen groups, such as the Bucks County (Pennsylvania) Committee on Rehabilitation and the Norfolk Fellowship Foundation in Massachusetts, developed participatory programs at regional institutions and counseling and job-finding services for parolees. Scores of prisoners' friends societies and ex-convict groups, such as the Seventh-Step and Fortune Society chapters, performed similar services.[52]

Volunteer activity in support of prison reform, prisoners litigation, and discharged convicts mounted sharply in New York following the Attica riots. The Genesee Ecumenical Ministry at Rochester, formed to tackle the problems of the inner city, organized a Judicial Process Commission to study the needed reform of criminal justice and to recommend legislative action. Its director, Virginia Mackey, took the lead in endorsing the efforts of an earlier Prison Action Group, a Prison Assistance Project, Volunteers in Partnership, and among other new groups one called Bridge, which soon established units in Buffalo and elsewhere. Mrs. Mackey also pressed the campaign for reform statewide, and in 1973 organized the New York State Coalition for Criminal Justice to coordinate the activities of a score of local and state prison aid societies and reform groups.[53]

[51] U.S. Attorney General, *First Annual Report on Federal Law Enforcement and Criminal Justice* (Washington, D.C., 1972); Oliver J. Keller, Jr. and Benedict S. Alper, *Halfway Houses: Community-Centered Correction and Treatment* (Lexington, Mass., 1970); Michael S. Serrill, "Delancey Street," *Corrections* 1 (September 1974): 13–28; Brian Lonergan, "Community Treatment Centers," *A.J.C.* 34 (September-October 1972): 34–35.

[52] John D. Case and James F. Henderson, "Correctional Volunteers in Bucks County," *A.J.C.* 35 (January-February 1973): 44–46; Massachusetts Correctional Association, *Correctional Research*, Bulletin 23 (November 1973): 12–15; Goldfarb and Singer, *After Conviction*, pp. 590–610. See also "Correctional Institutions and Agencies," *Proceedings* (A.C.A., 1971), pp. 104–106.

[53] *Am I My Brothers Keeper?*, Handbook, Judicial Process Commission (Rochester, 1974).

Another promising alternative was pretrial diversion launched in New York in 1967 by the Vera Institute of Justice. The Manhattan Court Employment Project it established diverted defendants on felony or misdemeanant charges into a group-therapy program that also provided employment counseling and sometimes jobs. The quick acceptance of that project, which soon handled 2,500 cases annually, spawned a host of similar projects in some thirty jurisdictions including the federal government. And although the early claims of a substantial reduction of recidivism among the diverted participants were seriously questioned by a later and more rigorous test applied by Franklin E. Zimring of the Center for Studies in Criminal Justice at Chicago, he found genuine merit in the "diversion programs, if designed and executed humanely." Of course the chief interests of that research institute were theoretical, but it focused its attention on the search for alternatives to imprisonment. Under the codirection of Professor Norval Morris, it exposed the failures of capital punishment as well as those of long sentences; it also collaborated in efforts to reform the criminal code in Illinois.[54]

One objective of the community treatment centers was to decriminalize many offenses. Too many deviants, both youths and adults, were being converted into hardened criminals by sending them to jail and prison, Lloyd E. Ohlin, among others, declared. Among the alternatives tried out in various states were alcohol- and drug-treatment centers, industrial training institutes, and work-training programs such as one at Rochester designed especially for probationers whose idleness had contributed to their delinquency.[55] A suggestive proposal of the late fifties led to the establishment a few years later of a Restitution House in Minnesota at which criminals and their victims could meet and agree on a settlement that would reimburse the victim for at least some of his losses or injuries and enable the criminal to earn his requital in a practical fashion. Elizabeth Croft estimated that 87 percent of all national crime index

[54] Franklin E. Zimring, "Measuring the Impact of Pretrial Diversion from the Criminal Justice System," *University of Chicago Law Review* 41 (1974): 224–241; Karen Ellsworth, *The Center for Studies in Criminal Justice: 1965-1974* (Chicago, 1974).

[55] Lloyd E. Ohlin, ed., *Prisoners in America: Perspectives on Our Correctional System* (Englewood Cliffs, N.J., 1973), pp. 1–48; Center for Governmental Research, *An Evaluation of the Monroe County Correctional-Rehabilitation Program* (Rochester, 1973).

offenses reported in 1970 were property offenses whose victims would greatly benefit from such an alternative settlement. Following the example of Britain and New Zealand, among others, California, Hawaii, Maryland, Massachusetts and New York passed legislation in the late sixties providing for compensation to victims of crime.[56]

In the frantic search for new treatment programs some traditional activities were somewhat overlooked. Yet real advances were occurring in the educational programs of many prisons as well as reformatories; moreover productive industries, though seldom reaching more than a third of the inmates, were operating in one or more penal institutions in all but two states. The Correctional Industries Association reported an increasing output in several states, forty of which made modest wage payments to the workers, with Illinois paying up to forty cents an hour ranking as the most generous. None, however, rivaled the federal program in extent or productivity. With an average of almost 5,000 inmates employed daily in 1973, the Federal Prison Industries, Inc. paid nearly $4 million in wages out of gross sales of $54 million that produced a net profit, after covering compensation and training costs, of $384,000. The larger gain, in Carlson's opinion, was the purposeful occupation supplied to approximately a fourth of the total population of the federal prisons.[57] Among the states, only North Dakota, Iowa, and South Carolina supplied productive jobs to a comparable fraction of their inmate populations.[58]

The widespread attacks on the correctional system prompted Austin MacCormick to call upon his colleagues to "fight back" by a vigorous assault on their own weakest points. He stressed first the

[56] Elizabeth Croft, "Alternative Methods for Handling Property Offense and Offenders," typescript, 1972; *A.J.C.* 20 (November-December 1958): 20–22; Irving E. Cohen, "The Integration of Restitution in the Probation Services," *J.C.L.C.* 34 (1944): 315–321; "Compensation to Victims of Crimes of Personal Violence: An Examination of the Scope of the Problem, A Symposium," *Minnesota Law Review* 50 (December 1965): 243–254; Goldfarb and Singer, *After Conviction*, pp. 132–142; Stephen Schafer, *Compensation and Restitution to Victims of Crime*, 2d ed. (Montclair, N.J., 1970), pp. 153–157.

[57] Federal Prison Industries, Inc., *Annual Report of the Board of Directors* (1973); Correctional Industries Association, *Directory of State and Federal Industries* (1973–1974).

[58] John R. Wald Co., Inc., *Correctional Industries: State-Use Sales, 1950-1970* (Huntingdon, Pa., 1971); Jude P. West and John R. Stratton, eds., *The Role of Correctional Industries* (Iowa City, [1971]).

need for more adequately trained correctional officers and rejoiced at the increased number of institutes and training programs. He rejoiced also over the improvements effected in the educational programs of numerous correctional institutions as a result of the funds provided by the Manpower Development and Training Act. He urged the replacement of mammoth and archaic prisons by specialized institutions with capacities not to exceed 500 or 600 and with strong community ties. He stressed the need for improved treatment and endorsed the program for self-evaluation developed by Dr. E. Preston Sharp, general secretary of the American Correctional Association.[59]

A major block to most treatment programs had been the hostility and distrust of the inmates for their keepers. Neither the religious and educational reformers nor the social scientists, despite their good intentions, had overcome these obstacles, although each had established some contacts. The sports and recreational programs, several community sponsored arts programs, even the group counseling programs in California, while they achieved some improvements in communication, were often jettisoned by mounting violence, as in California, or by a political shift, as in Hawaii. Some correctional administrators showed ingenuity in devising schemes, as in Florida, to break through the hostility of many young offenders by supplying them with motorbikes and enrolling them in scuba diving courses. But few officials were able to join with Professor Cressey in acknowledging the value of encouraging the transformation of black "gorilla" type prisoners into Black Muslims and other black nationalists rather than into Uncle Toms and similar "right guy" types.[60]

Several efforts to mediate disputes before they reached major proportions produced promising innovations. The successful utilization of ombudsmen to settle penal disputes in Britain and

---

[59]Austin MacCormick, "Fight Back," *A.J.C.* 33 (May-June 1971): 5, 17; U.S. Department of Labor, *An Evaluation of the Training Provided in Correctional Institutions under the Manpower Development and Training Act* (Washington, D.C., 1971); *A.J.C.* 31 (November-December 1969): 24–28; Massachusetts Correctional Association, *Correctional Research*, Bulletin 22 (November 1972): 26–32; E. Preston Sharp, *Study Guide for the Application of the Manual of Correctional Standards* (A.C.A., 1968).

[60]Ronald H. Bailey, "Florida," *Corrections* 1 (September 1974): 65–92; Donald R. Cressey, "Adult Felons in Prison," in *Prisoners in America*, Ohlin, ed., pp. 147–150; *A.J.C.* 32 (May-June 1970): 6–8.

Scandinavia prompted an effort to introduce one in the California system. When that legislative proposal was vetoed by Governor Reagan there, Minnesota became the first to secure a correctional ombudsman, named by the governor.[61] Some states, such as Maryland, created grievance commissions to serve this function, and James V. Bennett was happy in retirement to accept appointment to the Maryland Grievance Commission. Still another approach was that proposed by the Center for Correctional Justice, headed by Linda Singer, a Washington lawyer. It sought to avoid the charge of paternalism sometimes directed at arbitrators appointed by the authorities by offering conciliation by mediators approved by both sides. The proposal required a procedure for chosing representatives for the inmates as well as for the several groups on management's side. After long negotiations the National Center for Dispute Settlement was able to commence negotiations between the inmates at Walpole, Massachusetts, and its officials, and those of the union representing the guards as well as the state commissioner of correction. Although the negotiations failed to reach a final agreement, the process gave sufficient recognition to all concerned to avoid or at least postpone the threatened crisis. In California the Youth Authority secured the assistance of the Institution for Mediation and Conflict Resolution in developing an Independent Review Panel and in conducting training classes to instruct interested inmates and officials in the procedures of mediation. The scheme, first instituted at the Karl Holton School for Boys in Stockton and known as the Holton Experiment, soon attracted imitators elsewhere.[62]

These experiments attacked a basic problem of the correctional system—the affront imprisonment imposed on the self-respect of most inmates. The challenge shouted at Attica, "If we cannot live like men, we will die like men," voiced the resentment of prisoners against the practices of designating them by number, marching them in companies from one compound to another, and disciplining them without a hearing, often with illegal punishments. Although the lockstep, the striped uniform, and other features of the

[61] Timothy L. Fitzharris, *The Desirability of a Correctional Ombudsman* (Berkeley, 1973).

[62] "A Report Concerning the Involvement of the NCDS. . .at Walpole," (January, 1974); George Nicolan, "Grievance Arbitration in a Prison: The Holton Experiment," typescript, 1974.

silent system had disappeared, the mounting racial hostilities and the varied sources of friction engendered by the congregate system had produced outbreaks of violence that created new tensions. The gradual development by some inmates of the self-image of political prisoners represented a radical trend. This trend was aggravated in the sixties as the antiwar movement sent a number of dedicated pacifists to prison. Father Philip Berrigan's activities in several federal prisons added a new intensity to some civil rights issues that the nation, rather than the prisons, would have to solve.[63]

Yet the correctional system could not escape its involvement in the nation's problems. Prisons, however designated, could not shoulder all of society's disciplinary functions, but the states were not ready to dispense with them. A high-level conference on prison reform, sponsored by the Roscoe Pound-American Trial Lawyers Foundation, concluded in June 1972 that nearly half the present jail and prison populations should be handled outside the criminal justice system and that imprisonment should be used only as a last resort with definite, and preferably short, terms for most of the rest.[64] Some alternatives were fortunately at hand, and probation as well as other community treatment projects were playing increasing roles in the correctional system. The civil rights of inmates were receiving increased recognition, even to the extent of checking several aggressive attempts by scholars to use prisoners as guinea pigs to test scientific hypotheses ostensibly for the betterment of their fellows.

The Federal Bureau of Prisons, which under Norman A. Carlson was making a forthright effort to meet its far-reaching responsibilities, had plans for a correctional research center that aroused the fears of many civil rights advocates. Carlson's programs had attracted praise on several counts. His decision to divide the vast system into five regions, and to establish regional offices to integrate the services of the six or seven institutions located in each region, greatly simplified the administration. Since several of the penitentiaries were mammoth in size by modern standards, housing well over a thousand inmates each, Carlson devised a functional-unit system under which the population of each institution was divided into units of 50 to 100 men, with officers attached to each unit and

[63] Ohlin, *Prisoners in America;* Philip Berrigan, *Widen the Prison Gates* (New York, 1973); Fox, "Racial Issues," pp. 12–17.

[64] Chief Justice Earl Warren Conference, *A Program for Prison Reform* (Cambridge, Mass., 1972).

responsible for its activities and services. The successful introduction of this system into the older prisons prompted Carlson to plan for its incorporation in the structure of several new institutions. These included three metropolitan correctional centers, built in San Diego, Chicago, and New York, to house pretrial detention cases and short-term commitments in lofty structures where the floor units supplied a sense of group identity. Carlson heartily endorsed the community treatment program and soon had a network of fourteen centers in nine metropolitan areas. He redoubled the manpower-training efforts of his predecessors by establishing four specialized staff training centers and endeavored to recruit a proportionate number of minority-group trainees.

Yet despite these promising developments, Carlson could not tolerate complacency. His computer disclosed that 56 percent of the inmates of all federal institutions in 1973 had previous convictions and that some 27 percent had at least three previous convictions. How to turn some of these habitual recidivists about was the question he hoped the research-oriented Federal Center for Correctional Research to open at Butner, North Carolina, in early 1976 would help to answer. But the widespread outcry against "behavior modification" programs, as some of the experimental uses of drugs and other devices at the California Medical Facility at Vacaville were described, prompted Carlson and Dr. Martin Groder, a psychiatrist and warden-designate in charge of development, to deny any such plans. At hearings before a subcommittee of the House Judiciary Committee, the program was defined as more limited in its research techniques and open only to prisoners eager to take advantage of its treatment. Groder resigned as a result of what he considered an overemphasis on such "Skinner-type" behavior modification in the programs and Donald A. Deppe, a former University of Maryland professor who had been educational director of the Bureau of Prisons since 1973, succeeded him as director.[65]

Civil rights had their limits, too, and in the opinion of several courts the constitutional protection against unusual punishments did not abridge the state's authority to impose indeterminate

[65] Norman A. Carlson, "Trends in Criminal Justice (Typescript of speech given at Springfield, Mo., 5 November 1974); "New Prison Stirs Experiment Fears," *Washington Post,* 17 December 1973 and 1 December 1974; *New York Times,* 30 September 1975, p. 34; Mitford, *Kind and Usual Punishment,* pp. 124–125, 187–188.

sentences or to supervise released men on parole. A citizens' committee in New York, headed by Ramsey Clark, strongly urged the abandonment of parole but concluded with a plea that meanwhile parolees should have the right to see their records and present witnesses when threatened with a revocation of parole. That right was slowly winning favor, as courts in New York and elsewhere moved to require parole boards to give reasons for the postponement of parole. Alert correctional officials were endeavoring to meet other grievances by recruiting minority representatives for their staffs and by increasing the opportunities for inmates to receive visits from their families or attorneys. As with earlier gestures of good intentions, the commissioners and wardens who adopted these more humane regulations hoped to engender a sense of responsibility along with that of self-respect.[66]

The Institute of Corrections of the American Foundation engaged William G. Nagel in 1972 to make a survey of American prisons for the LEAA. That agency was seeking advice on the use of funds granted by the federal government for construction of state and local prisons. Accompanied by an architect and a psychologist, Nagel visited over a hundred correctional institutions in 26 states— prisons, reformatories, jails, and community correctional centers. So appalled were they by the oppressive effect of the regimes they observed that, instead of proposing specific reforms, they recommended a moratorium on all new construction until satisfactory replacements could be devised. Other investigators and consultants were proposing similar restraints.[67]

Whether because of these admonitions or because of a sudden reversal in the upward climb of penal populations in the early sixties, the wide construction of new correctional institutions slowed sharply in the mid sixties. Only three of the 150 new institutions built by federal, state, and local authorities during the next half dozen years had facilities for as many as 1,000 inmates, and only five others accommodated 500; the great majority were

[66] Citizen's Inquiry on Parole and Criminal Justice, *Report on New York Parole*, typescript, 1974; *A.J.C.* 29 (May-June 1967): 10–12, 14–18; 35 (March-April 1973): 40–43; *Washington Post* 17 December 1973; *Matter of Cummings* v. *Regan*, 45 Appellate Division, *Reports*, 2d Series: 222–226.

[67] William G. Nagel, *The New Red Barn: A Critical Look at the Modern American Prison* (New York, 1973); Carter, Glaser and Wilkins, *Correctional Institutions*, pp. 123–127, 212–231, 428–432.

community correction centers designed to serve 30 or 40 men or women each. Seven additional states established reception and diagnostic centers equipped to handle 300 or so new commitments, and a dozen opened two or more new youth centers able to house 50 or 100 lads. The trend at long last was definitely towards the small institution. But the attack on mammoth prisons had only halted their growth, and 35 of the 56 prisons and reformitories equipped to handle over 1,000 were still overcrowded in 1970. Nine of the 19 over 2,000 were among the overcrowded, although the two largest, Jackson in Michigan and Statesville in Illinois, were now somewhat under occupied. Their elimination, as frequently proposed, would be a herculean task.[68]

Uncertain Future Prospects

An historian's responsibility ceases with the completion of his · record of the past, but it is impossible to conclude this study of the history of American prisons without observing some striking changes in their prospects. The current disillusionment is by no means the first to have beset the architects and managers of American prisons. When, a century and a half ago, the first congregate prisons in Philadelphia and New York, designed to dispense with the brutal corporal and capital punishments of earlier years, engendered vicious and riotous practices, reformers appeared who replaced them with more substantial penitentiaries equipped to house hundreds of prisoners in separate cells and to prepare them for a return to the community by employing them in strict silence, or, in Pennsylvania, in complete solitude in their cells. When again the procedures failed to produce the expected penitence among the prisoners, including many immigrants and sons of immigrants, a new group of reformers adapted educational techniques to instruct the inmates in American ways; they also devised indeterminate sentences to induce especially the youths and first offenders to cooperate in reformatory programs to hasten their release under newly developed parole supervision.

Unfortunately, these well-intended projects were not developing in a vacuum, but in a turbulent society where both organized labor

[68]"Correctional Institutions and Agencies," *Proceedings* (A.C.A., 1971), pp. 104–106.

and industrialists were becoming increasingly aroused by the competition of cheap prison-made goods. Hostile labor laws progressively shut down the contract and state-account industries, even the industrial training schools of the reformatories, transforming their populations, as well as that of most prisons, into great pools of idleness. Educational and recreational programs and, in a number of prisons, state-use industries, absorbed part of the time of many inmates, but disorder mounted. Psychiatrists and psychologists undertook to classify and separate the defectives and the more vicious malcontents from the more tractable majority. This procedure gave new hope to prison managers and presented a challenge to educators and social scientists to develop treatment programs for the rehabilitation of the great mass of convicts in the prisons, now renamed correctional institutions.

But again, the euphoria that marked the development of the treatment programs disappeared in the face of climactic changes in the social environment. A sudden rise in the number of blacks committed to the prisons, following the waves of their migration from the rural South to the cities of the entire nation, created outbreaks of racial strife, which disrupted recreational as well as treatment programs and brought a revival of disciplinary measures that in turn stirred demands for prisoners' rights. Efforts to enforce discipline by prolonging the sentences focused the attack of civil rights advocates on the indeterminate sentence and parole systems—the keystones of the earlier reformatory movement. And when it became apparent that the group counseling sessions—the high point in the correctional institution's treatment program—had facilitated the recruitment of members for the Symbionese Liberation foray in California as well as for scattered Black Muslim temples and for Father Berrigan's fellowship of radical pacifists, many wardens began to take a more critical look at the correctional programs.

Scholars, too, had taken a second look at these programs and had tabulated their slight or nonexistent effect on the rates of recidivism. And when judges and legal scholars began to question the justice of combining retributive punishments with reformatory sentences, correctional administrators reassessed their responsibilities. Some renewed the search for alternatives to imprisonment; others redoubled their efforts to win the voluntary participation of offenders in community-centered programs looking towards their readjustment to full citizenship. But, again, these developments were occurring in a society plagued by outbreaks of violence in civic, social and economic fields. The spreading use of drugs and society's impulsive efforts to suppress them; the relaxed almost libertarian social standards and the public's indignant reaction to scattered excesses; the unprecedented degree of mobility, both geographic and social, available to all, and the recklessness with which some abused their opportunities—these and other trends produced an upsurge of crimes of passion, greed and corruption, in high as well as low places, that threatened to exhaust the capacity of state and national authorities for conciliatory action.

Yet the country's long hard experience with the tragedies of prisonization and with the failures, or at least the limitations, of corrections could not be brushed aside and forgotten. Proposals for the decriminalization of deviant behavior patterns not injurious to others, and for the development of restitution procedures as a means of enabling malefactors to win a respected place in the community by reimbursing their victims demonstrated the continued ingenuity of American society. Certainly, if experience demonstrated the need for more than a resurgence of good intentions, it also proved the folly of inaction and irresponsibility. The quest for order with justice demanded more, not less, dedication and participation.

Yet the country's long hard experience with the tragedies of prisonization and with the failures, or at least the limitations, of corrections cannot be brushed aside and forgotten. Have the correctional programs been failures in themselves, or disappointing because they were inadequately supported and irresolutely carried through? Have the recipients of indeterminate sentences been convinced that they could help to secure their early release, and do the parole granting authorities give them adequate hearings and clearly explain their decisions? No investigation has submitted an affirmative answer to these questions, and many have cited numerous deficiencies in both administration and support. One review of diagnostic clinics found only two that considered themselves adequately staffed. Is the enforced idleness of 50% to 80% of the inmates of most prisons a constructive preparation for their return to society? And do the parole services find places and jobs in which their charges have a chance to make good? Such efforts would require larger appropriations, more resolute and understanding staffs, and a readiness of communities everywhere to maintain halfway houses and to accept discharged convicts as fellow citizens. It's a large order that only a society committed to corrections could fulfill. Yet proposals for the decriminalization of deviant behavior patterns not injurious to others, and for the development of restitution procedures as a means of enabling malefactors to win a respected place in the community by reimbursing their victims demonstrate the continued ingenuity of the American society. Certainly, if experience has demonstrated the need for more than a resurgence of good intentions, it has also proved the folly of inaction and irresponsibility. The quest for order with justice demands more, not less, dedication and participation.

BIBLIOGRAPHIC NOTE

The reports of a number of special state and federal commissions have exceptional documentary value in these decades. These include, among others, the Advisory Commission on Inter-Governmental Relations, especially its *Report on State and Local Relations in the Criminal Justice System* (Washington, D.C., 1971); Arden House Conference, *Manpower and Training for Corrections* (New York, 1966); New York State Special Commission on Attica, *Attica: The Official Report of the New York State Special Commission on Attica,* Robert B. McKay, ed. (New York, 1972); New York State Select Committee on Correctional Institutions and Programs, *Reports,* 4 vols. (Albany, 1972); President's Commission on Law Enforcement and Administration of Justice, *The Challenge of Crime in a Free Society* (Washington, D.C., 1967); the Commission's *Task Force Report: Corrections* (Washington, D.C., 1967); and the Joint Commission on Correctional Manpower and Training, *Perspectives on Correctional Manpower and Training* (Washington, D.C., 1970).

The annual *Proceedings of the American Prison Association* (1955 on, the American Correctional Association) and the monthly issues of its *American Journal of Correction* (*Prison World,* 1940-1950) provide a continuing commentary and analysis of correctional developments throughout the country.

Federal Probation (1937-) and *Journal of Criminal Law and Criminology* (1909-) contain many useful articles. Several journals of more recent origin are of interest: *Correctional Research: Bulletin* published by the United Prison Association of Massachusetts; *Corrections Magazine* published by the Correctional Information Service, Inc.; *Resolution of Correctional Problems and Issues* published by the South Carolina Department of

Corrections; and *Crime and Delinquency* published by the National Council on Crime and Delinquency.

A number of penological and criminological texts and readers are of special value. Among them are: Burton M. Atkins and Henry R. Glick, eds., *Prisons, Protest and Politics* (Englewood Cliffs, N.J., 1972); Harry Elmer Barnes and Negley K. Teeters, *New Horizons in Criminology*, 3d ed. (Englewood Cliffs, N.J., 1959) (the 1st ed. is also of value—see Bibliographic Note to Chapter 1); Robert M. Carter, Daniel Glaser, and Leslie T. Wilkins, eds., *Correctional Institutions* (Philadelphia, 1972); Richard A. Cloward *et al, Theoretical Studies in Social Organization of the Prison* (New York, 1960); Donald R. Cressey, ed., *The Prison: Studies in Institutional Organization and Change* (New York, 1961); Don C. Gibbons, *Delinquent Behavior* (Englewood Cliffs, N.J., 1970); ibid., *Society, Crime and Criminal Careers: An Introduction to Criminology*, 2d ed. (Englewood Cliffs, N.J., 1973); Lawrence Hazelrigg, ed., *Prison Within Society: A Reader in Penology* (New York, 1969); Lloyd E. Ohlin, ed., *Prisoners in America: Perspectives on Our Correctional System* (Englewood Cliffs, N.J., 1973); ibid., *Sociology and the Field of Corrections* (New York, 1956); Edwin H. Sutherland and Donald R. Cressey, *Criminology*, 9th ed. (Philadelphia, 1974); Paul W. Tappan, ed., *Contemporary Correction* (New York, 1951); ibid., *Crime, Justice and Correction* (New York, 1960).

Biographical accounts of prison officials in this period include: James V. Bennett, *I Chose Prison* (New York, 1970); Gladys A. Erickson, *Warden Ragen of Joliet* (New York, 1957); Lewis E. Lawes, *Life and Death in Sing Sing (New York, 1928)*; Tom Murton and Joe Hyams, *Accomplices to the Crime* (New York, 1969); Russell G. Oswald, *Attica: My Story* (New York, 1972); Frank Tannenbaum, *Osborne of Sing Sing* (Chapel Hill, 1933). Tom Wicker, *A Time to Die* (New York, 1975) is an account by one of the observers of the negotiations in the Attica confrontation and has a unique inside quality.

Of special value are a number of accounts and compilations of inmate views: Lester D. Johnson, *The Devil's Front Porch* (Lawrence, Kansas, 1970) and Robert J. Minton, ed., *Inside: Prison American Style* (New York, 1971) are representative examples. John Irwin, *The Felon* (Englewood Cliffs, N.J., 1970) is a study of criminal careers.

Scholarly studies of a theoretical quality include: Sol Chaneles, *The Open Prison: Saving Their Lives and Our Money* (New York, 1973); Donald Clemmer, *The Prison Community* (New York, 1940); LaMar T. Empey and Maynard L. Erickson, *The Provo Experiment: Evaluating Community Control of Delinquency* (Lexington, Mass., 1972); Don C. Gibbons, *Changing the Lawbreaker: The Treatment of Delinquents and Criminals* (Englewood Cliffs, N.J., 1965); Sheldon Glueck, *Crime and Correction: Selected Papers* (Cambridge, Mass., 1952); William Healy and Augusta F.

Bronner, *New Light on Delinquency and Its Treatment*, (New Haven, 1936); David Matza, *Delinquency and Drift* (New York, 1964); Jacob L. Moreno, *The First Book on Group Psychotherapy*, 3d ed. (n.p., 1957); Gresham M. Sykes, *The Society of Captives: A Study of a Maximum Security Prison* (Princeton, 1958).

Descriptive and historic volumes on prisons in America and abroad include: Russell N. Baird, *The Penal Press* (Evanston, Ill., 1967); John P. Conrad, *Crime and Its Correction: An International Survey of Attitudes and Practices* (Berkeley, 1965); Joseph W. Eaton, *Stone Walls Not a Prison Make: The Anatomy of Planned Administrative Change* (Springfield, Ill., 1962); Alfred Hopkins, *Prisons and Prison Buildings* (New York, 1930); James A. Johnston, *Alcatraz Island Prison: And the Men Who Live There* (New York, 1949); Norman Johnston, *The Human Cage: A Brief History of Prison Architecture* (New York, 1973); James Leiby, *Charity and Correction in New Jersey: A History of State Welfare Institutions* (New Brunswick, 1967); Austin H. MacCormick, *The Education of Adult Prisoners* (New York, 1931); John B. Martin, *Break Down the Walls: American Prisons, Present, Past and Future* (New York, 1954); Ernest E. Means, *Prison Industries and Rehabilitation Programs* (Tallahassee, 1959); Negley K. Teeters, *World Penal Systems* (Philadelphia, 1944); Jude P. West and John R. Stratton, eds., *The Role of Correctional Industries* (Iowa City [1971]); Min S. Yee, *The Melancholy History of Soledad Prison: In Which A Utopian Scheme Turns Bedlam* (New York, 1973).

Studies of special research projects and experiments include: LaMar T. Empey and Stephen G. Lubeck, *The Silverlake Experiment: Testing Delinquency Theory and Community Intervention* (Chicago, 1971); Norman Fenton, *The Prisoner's Family: A Study of Family Counseling in an Adult Correctional System* (Palo Alto, 1959); Timothy L. Fitzharris, *The Desirability of a Correctional Ombudsman* (Berkeley, 1973); Daniel Glaser, *The Effectiveness of a Prison and Penal System* (New York, 1964); Gene Kassebaum, David Ward and David Wilner, *Prison Treatment and Parole Survival: An Empirical Assessment* (New York, 1971); Oliver J. Keller, Jr. and Benedict S. Alper, *Halfway Houses: Community-Centered Correction and Treatment* (Lexington, Mass., 1970); Douglas Lipton, Robert M. Martinson and Judith Wilks, *The Effectiveness of Correctional Treatment: A Survey of Treatment Evaluation Studies* (New York, 1975); Lloyd W. McCorkle, Albert Elias and F. Lovell Bixby, *The Highfields Story: An Experimental Treatment Project for Youthful Offenders* (New York, 1958); Elliot Studt, Sheldon L. Messinger and Thomas P. Wilson, *C-Unit: Search for Community in Prison* (New York, 1968); Georg K. Sturup, *Treating the "Untreatable": Chronic Criminals at Herstedvester* (Baltimore, 1968); Leslie T. Wilkins, *Evaluation of Penal Measures* (New York, 1969).

A number of scholarly studies of criminal law and its application to correctional practice include: Ronald L. Goldfarb and Linda R. Singer, *After Conviction* (New York, 1973); Charles Goodell, *Political Prisoners in America* (New York, 1973); Norval Morris, *The Future of Imprisonment* (Chicago, 1974); Harvey S. Perlman and Thomas B. Allington, eds., *The Tasks of Penology: A Symposium on Prisons and Correctional Law* (Lincoln, Neb., 1969); Sol Rubin, *The Law of Criminal Correction*; (St. Paul, 1963; 2d ed, 1973); Stephen Schafer, *Compensation and Restitution to Victims of Crime*, 2d ed. (Montclair, N.J., 1970); South Carolina Department of Correction, *The Emerging Rights of the Confined* (Columbus, 1973); James Q. Wilson, *Thinking About Crime* (New York, 1975).

Sharply critical appraisals of penal and correctional shortcomings include: American Friends Service Committee, *Struggle for Justice: A Report on Crime and Punishment in America* (New York, 1971); Karl Menninger, *The Crime of Punishment* (New York, 1968); Jessica Mitford, *Kind and Usual Punishment* (New York, 1973); William G. Nagle, *The New Red Barn: A Critical Look at the Modern American Prison* (New York, 1973); Giles Playfair, *The Punitive Obsession: An Unvarnished History of the English Prison System* (London, 1971); Margaret Wilson, *The Crime of Punishment* (New York, 1931).

Useful as a source of basic information is the *Directory of Juvenile and Adult Correctional Departments, Institutions, Agencies and Paroling Authorities, United States and Canada,* published annually by the American Correctional Association.

APPENDICES

AMERICAN CORRECTIONAL ASSOCIATION
SCHEDULE OF CONGRESSES, 1870–1976

The association was known as the National Prison Association from 1870 to 1907, as the American Prison Association from 1908 to 1954, and as the American Correctional Association thereafter. The Proceedings of each congress were published in a separate volume, except for the combined publications of the 1884 and 1885 congresses and the Indianapolis and New Orleans meetings of 1898/99. No congresses were held in the years not listed.

YEAR	PLACE	PRESIDENT	SECRETARY
1870	Cincinnati, Ohio	Rutherford B. Hayes (Ohio)	Enoch Cobb Wines (N.Y.)
1873	Baltimore, Md.	Horatio Seymour (N.Y.)	Enoch Cobb Wines (N.Y.)
1874	St. Louis, Mo.	Horatio Seymour (N.Y.)	Enoch Cobb Wines (N.Y.)
1876	New York, N.Y.	*Horatio Seymour (N.Y.)	Enoch Cobb Wines (N.Y.)
1883	Saratoga Springs, N.Y.	Rutherford B. Hayes (Ohio)	William M. F. Round (N.Y.)
1884	Saratoga Springs, N.Y.	Rutherford B. Hayes (Ohio)	William M. F. Round (N.Y.)
1885	Detroit, Mich.	Rutherford B. Hayes (Ohio)	William M. F. Round (N.Y.)
1886	Atlanta, Ga.	Rutherford B. Hayes (Ohio)	William M. F. Round (N.Y.)
1887	Toronto, Ont.	Rutherford B. Hayes (Ohio)	Frederick Howard Wines (Ill.)
1888	Boston, Mass.	Rutherford B. Hayes (Ohio)	Frederick Howard Wines (Ill.)
1889	Nashville, Tenn.	Rutherford B. Hayes (Ohio)	Frederick Howard Wines (Ill.)
1890	Cincinnati, Ohio	Rutherford B. Hayes (Ohio)	Frederick Howard Wines (Ill.)
1891	Pittsburgh, Pa.	Rutherford B. Hayes (Ohio)	John L. Milligan (Pa.)
1892	Baltimore, Md.	Rutherford B. Hayes (Ohio)	John L. Milligan (Pa.)
1893	Chicago, Ill.	Roeliff Brinkeroff (Ohio)	John L. Milligan (Pa.)
1894	St. Paul, Minn.	Roeliff Brinkeroff (Ohio)	John L. Milligan (Pa.)
1895	Denver, Col.	Roeliff Brinkeroff (Ohio)	John L. Milligan (Pa.)
1896	Milwaukee, Wis.	Roeliff Brinkeroff (Ohio)	John L. Milligan (Pa.)

*Richard Vaux (Pa.) presided due to illness of Horatio Seymour.

YEAR	PLACE	PRESIDENT	SECRETARY
1897	Austin, Tex.	Roeliff Brinkeroff (Ohio)	John L. Milligan (Pa.)
1898	Indianapolis, Ind.	Zebulon R. Brockway (N.Y.)	John L. Milligan (Pa.)
1899	New Orleans, La.	Robert W. McClaughry (Ill.)	John L. Milligan (Pa.)
1899	Hartford, Conn.	Robert W. McClaughry (Ill.)	John L. Milligan (Pa.)
1900	Cleveland, Ohio	Edward S. Wright (Pa.)	John L. Milligan (Pa.)
1901	Kansas City, Mo.	Joseph F. Scott (Mass.)	John L. Milligan (Pa.)
1902	Philadelphia, Pa.	Charles R. Henderson (Ill.)	John L. Milligan (Pa.)
1903	Louisville, Ky.	Henry Wolfer (Minn.)	John L. Milligan (Pa.)
1904	Quincy, Ill.	†Charlton T. Lewis (N.Y.)	John L. Milligan (Pa.)
1905	Lincoln, Neb.	Albert Garvin (Conn.)	John L. Milligan (Pa.)
1906	Albany, N.Y.	Cornelius V. Collins (N.Y.)	Amos W. Butler (Ind.)
1907	Chicago, Ill.	E. J. Murphy (Ill.)	Amos W. Butler (Ind.)
1908	Richmond, Va.	John L. Milligan (Pa.)	Amos W. Butler (Ind.)
1909	Seattle, Wash.	J. T. Gilmour (Ont.)	Joseph P. Byers (N.J.)
1910	Washington, D.C.	Amos W. Butler (Ind.)	Joseph P. Byers (N.J.)
1911	Omaha, Neb.	T. B. Patton (Pa.)	Joseph P. Byers (N.J.)
1912	Baltimore, Md.	Frederick G. Pettigrove (Mass.)	Joseph P. Byers (N.J.)
1913	Indianapolis, Ind.	James A. Leonard (Ohio)	Joseph P. Byers (N.J.)
1914	St. Paul, Minn.	Samuel G. Smith (Minn.)	Joseph P. Byers (N.J.)
1915	Oakland, Cal.	Joseph P. Byers (N.J.)	George L. Sehon (Ky.)
1916	Buffalo, N.Y.	Arthur Pratt (Utah)	Joseph P. Byers (Pa.)
1917	New Orleans, La.	David C. Peyton (Ind.)	Joseph P. Byers (Pa.)
1919	New York, N.Y.	B. M. Spurr (W.Va.)	Joseph P. Byers (Pa.)
1920	Columbus, Ohio	George W. Wickersham (N.Y.)	Joseph P. Byers (Ky.)
1921	Jacksonville, Fla.	C. B. Adams (Ill.)	Orlando F. Lewis (N.Y.)
1922	Detroit, Mich.	Hastings H. Hart (N.Y.)	Edward R. Cass (N.Y.)
1923	Boston, Mass.	Lewis E. Lawes (N.Y.)	Edward R. Cass (N.Y.)
1924	Salt Lake City, Utah	Charles H. Johnson (N.Y.)	Edward R. Cass (N.Y.)
1925	Jackson, Miss.	Frank Moore (N.J.)	Edward R. Cass (N.Y.)
1926	Pittsburgh, Pa.	Sanford Bates (Mass.)	Edward R. Cass (N.Y.)
1927	Tacoma, Wash.	William F. Penn (Pa.)	Edward R. Cass (N.Y.)
1928	Kansas City, Mo.	Edward R. Cass (N.Y.)	Howard C. Hill (Md.)
1929	Toronto, Ont.	George C. Erskine (Conn.)	Edward R. Cass (N.Y.)
1930	Louisville, Ky.	Carl J. Swendsen (Minn.)	Edward R. Cass (N.Y.)
1931	Baltimore, Md.	Leon C. Faulkner (N.Y.)	Edward R. Cass (N.Y.)
1932	Indianapolis, Ind.	Oscar Lee (Wis.)	Edward R. Cass (N.Y.)
1933	Atlantic City, N.J.	Walter N. Thayer, Jr. (N.Y.)	Edward R. Cass (N.Y.)
1934	Houston, Tex.	Calvin Derrick (N.J.)	Edward R. Cass (N.Y.)
1935	Atlanta, Ga.	Stanley P. Ashe (Pa.)	Edward R. Cass (N.Y.)
1936	Chicago, Ill.	Blanche L. LaDu (Ill.)	Edward R. Cass (N.Y.)
1937	Philadelphia, Pa.	William J. Ellis (N.J.)	Edward R. Cass (N.Y.)
1938	St. Paul, Minn.	Rice M. Youell (Va.)	Edward R. Cass (N.Y.)
1939	New York, N.Y.	Austin H. MacCormick (N.Y.)	Edward R. Cass (N.Y.)
1940	Cincinnati, Ohio	James V. Bennett (D.C.)	Edward R. Cass (N.Y.)
1941	San Francisco, Cal.	James A. Johnston (Cal.)	Edward R. Cass (N.Y.)
1942	Asheville, N.C.	G. Howland Shaw (D.C.)	Edward R. Cass (N.Y.)
1943	New York, N.Y.	Richard A. McGee (Wash.)	Edward R. Cass (N.Y.)
1944	New York, N.Y.	Joseph W. Sanford (Ga.)	Edward R. Cass (N.Y.)

†Frederick Howard Wines (N.J.) presided due to death of Charlton T. Lewis.

YEAR	PLACE	PRESIDENT	SECRETARY
1945	New York, N.Y.	Garrett Heyns (Mich.)	Edward R. Cass (N.Y.)
1946	Detroit, Mich.	Sam A. Lewisohn (N.Y.)	Edward R. Cass (N.Y.)
1947	Long Beach, Cal.	Harold E. Donnell (Md.)	Edward R. Cass (N.Y.)
1948	Boston, Mass.	W. Frank Smyth, Jr. (Va.)	Edward R. Cass (N.Y.)
1949	Milwaukee, Wis.	John C. Burke (Wis.)	Edward R. Cass (N.Y.)
1950	St. Louis, Mo.	J. Stanley Sheppard (N.Y.)	Edward R. Cass (N.Y.)
1951	Biloxi, Mass.	Joseph E. Ragen (Ill.)	Edward R. Cass (N.Y.)
1952	Atlantic City, N.J.	James W. Curran (Md.)	Edward R. Cass (N.Y.)
1953	Toronto, Ont.	Ralph B. Gibson (Ont.)	Edward R. Cass (N.Y.)
1954	Philadelphia, Pa.	Walter M. Wallack (N.Y.)	Edward R. Cass (N.Y.)
1955	Des Moines, Iowa	Kenyon J. Scudder (Cal.)	Edward R. Cass (N.Y.)
1956	Los Angeles, Cal.	Myrl E. Alexander (D.C.)	Edward R. Cass (N.Y.)
1957	Chicago, Ill.	E. Preston Sharp (Pa.)	Edward R. Cass (N.Y.)
1958	Detroit, Mich.	Roberts J. Wright (N.Y.)	Edward R. Cass (N.Y.)
1959	Miami Beach, Fla.	O. B. Ellis (Tex.)	Edward R. Cass (N.Y.)
1960	Denver, Col.	Gervase Brinkman (Ill.)	Edward R. Cass (N.Y.)
1961	Columbus, Ohio	Sanger B. Powers (Wis.)	Edward R. Cass (N.Y.)
1962	Philadelphia, Pa.	Arthur T. Prasse (Pa.)	Edward R. Cass (N.Y.)
1963	Portland, Ore.	Peter P. Lejins (Md.)	John M. Wilson (D.C.)
1964	Kansas City, Mo.	Harry C. Tinsley (Col.)	John M. Wilson (D.C.)
1965	Boston, Mass.	Donald Clemmer (D.C.)	E. Preston Sharp (D.C.)
1966	Baltimore, Md.	Harold V. Langlois (R.I.)	E. Preston Sharp (D.C.)
1967	Miami Beach, Fla.	Walter Dunbar (D.C.)	E. Preston Sharp (D.C.)
1968	San Francisco, Cal.	Parker L. Hancock (N.H.)	E. Preston Sharp (Md.)
1969	Minneapolis, Minn.	Ellis C. MacDougall (Conn.)	E. Preston Sharp (Md.)
1970	Cincinnati, Ohio	George Beto (Tex.)	E. Preston Sharp (Md.)
1971	Miami Beach, Fla.	Louis L. Wainwright (Fla.)	E. Preston Sharp (Md.)
1972	Pittsburgh, Pa.	Maurice H. Sigler (D.C.)	E. Preston Sharp (Md.)
1973	Seattle, Wash.	Martha E. Wheeler (Ohio)	E. Preston Sharp (Md.)
1974	Houston, Tex.	Joseph S. Coughlin (Ill.)	Anthony P. Travisono (Md.)
1975	Louisville, Ky.	John W. Braithwaite (Ont.)	Anthony P. Travisono (Md.)
1976	Denver, Col.	Oliver J. Keller (Fla.)	Anthony P. Travisono (Md.)

APPENDIX II

INTERNATIONAL PENITENTIARY CONGRESSES

The first three congresses listed below were informally organized meetings of which scant record survives. At the trend-setting 1872 International Congress on the Prevention and Repression of Crime, an International Penitentiary Commission was formed, under whose auspices the succeeding congresses were held through 1950. The functions of the International Penal and Penitentiary Commission (as it was renamed in 1930) were transferred in 1950 to the United Nations, which starting in 1955 has convened quinquennial Congresses on the Prevention of Crime and Treatment of the Offender.*

YEAR	LOCATION	YEAR	LOCATION
1846	Frankfort-on-Main	1910	Washington
1847	Brussels	1925	London
1857	Frankfort-on-Main	1930	Prague
1872	London	1935	Berlin
1878	Stockholm	1950	The Hague
1885	Rome	1955	Geneva
1890	St. Petersburg	1960	London
1895	Paris	1965	Stockholm
1900	Brussels	1970	Kyoto
1905	Budapest	1975	Geneva

PRESIDENTS OF THE INTERNATIONAL PENITENTIARY COMMISSION

TERM	PRESIDENT	NATIONALITY
1872–1878	Enoch Cobb Wines	United States
1878–1880	G. F. Almquist	Sweden
1880–1885	Martini Beltrani-Scalia	Italy
1885–1890	Mikhail N. Gálkine-Wraskoy	Russia
1890–1893	Louis Herbette	France
1893–1895	Ferdinand Duflos	France
1895–1900	F. C. De Latour	Belgium
1900–1905	Jules Rickl De Bellye	Hungary
1905–1909	Samuel J. Barrows	United States
1909–1910	Charles R. Henderson	United States
1910–1925	Hugh Evelyn Ruggles-Brise	England
1925–1928	Emerich Polák	Czechoslovakia
1928–1930	August Miricka	Czechoslovakia
1930–1935	Erwin Bumke	Germany
1935–1943	Giovanni Novelli	Italy
1946–1955	Sanford Bates	United States

*For additional details of the congresses, see Benedict S. Alper and Jerry F. Boren, *Crime: International Agenda* (Lexington, Mass., 1972) and Negley K. Teeters, *Deliberations of the International Penal and Penitentiary Congresses* (Philadelphia, 1949).

INDEX

Abbott, Edith, mentioned, 273

adjustment center, new name for disciplinary wing, 327

adjustment committees, work of, studied, 342

Adler, Dr. Herman, study of, 271, 272

Adult Authority, in California, 312, 336–38, 340, 364, 367, 370

Alabama: prison at Wetumpka, 47, 202; imprisonment for debt in, 51; lease system in, 202–03, 209; prison industry in, 253, 288; prison opened at Kilby, 288; jails of, 287–88

Alcatraz, federal prison, 317

Alcoholics Anonymous, activities of in prison, 332, 341

Alexander, Myrl, in federal system, 316, 317, 335

Allen, Edmund, as warden, 282

Altgeld, Governor John P., prison policies of, 125, 157, 162, 175

American Correctional Association: new name for American Prison Association, 327; *Manual of Correctional Standards* by, 327; programs of, 334, 360, 376, Appendix I; *see also* American Prison Association; National Prison Association

American Federation of Labor: anticontract policy of, 128, 251; *see also* labor unions; prison industries

American Institute of Criminal Law and Criminology: organization of, 269; *Journal* of, 269; supports mental research, 275

American Journal of Correction, new name for *Prison World,* 327

American Law Institute, proposals of, 313, 360, 364, 365

American Prison Association: increased size of, 235, 275; interest of in European reforms, 237; western visits of, 243; functions of, 269, 299, 309, 322; *Handbook on Classification* of, 314; study of riots by, 326; name of changed, 327; *see also* American Correctional Association; National Prison Association

Anderson, Dr. Victor V., clinic of, serves court, 270

anticontract movement, *see* labor unions

architecture: in early penal models, 5, 8, 9, 10, 11, 12; Panopticon pattern, 11, 17, 282–83; Auburn cellblock model, 12–13, 16–17, 283; Cherry Hill design, 18–19; Baltimore pattern, 45–46, 61; federal innovations in, 302–03, 308, 320; future design prospects, 380; *see also* Auburn system; Cherry Hill penitentiary

Arizona: territorial prison in, 232; lease system in, 232; road camps in, 254; mutual agreement project in, 372

393